The New

1991 Savvy Shoppers' Survey

**Everything from Pearls to Plumbers,
Rated for Quality, Style, Service and Value.**

Published by:
Custom Databanks, Inc.
Germantown, MD 20874-3313

To moms, and especially to Mary, our best researcher

The New York Edge
Copyright © 1996 by
Susan B. Dollinger and Jane R. Lockshin

Published by Custom Databanks, Inc.
13925 Esworthy Road, Germantown, MD 20874-3313

ISBN 1-889782-50-5

First printing

Cover Design: Solutions, Inc.

10 9 8 7 6 5 4 3 2 1
First Edition

The information in this book has been compiled by surveying and
summarizing the shopping experiences of individuals believed to be
reliable. In some cases, the opinions and shopping experience of a single
individual has been used. Because of the possibility of error by its
sources, neither Custom Databanks, Inc. nor the Authors warrant the
accuracy, currency, or completeness of the information or accept
responsibility for any errors, omissions, or adverse consequences
resulting from the use of or reliance on such information. No
endorsement, rating, or qualification of any store or service
establishment is implied by its inclusion in this book. The ratings and
survey responses reflect the judgment and comments of the individuals
surveyed.

The New York Edge

Contents

Introduction ix
  The Ratings.. x
  Neighborhoods xi

Clothing & accessories
  Clothing... 1
  Clothing-casual.. 7
  Clothing-children.. 15
  Clothing-men 21
  Clothing-casual-men 27
  Clothing-women... 27
  Clothing-casual-women...................................... 38
  Accessories... 43
  Bridal, wedding & formal 45
  Buttons, beads & trims 49
  Costumes 51
  Custom... 52
  Department stores... 56
  Eyeglasses 59
  Fabric 60
  Furriers 63
  Hats... 65
  Jewelry & watches 66
  Jewelry & watches-costume................................ 77
  Jewelry & watches-supply................................... 78
  Leathers.. 79
  Maternity 87
  Shirts & blouses.. 88
  Shoes, socks & stockings 90
  Special size 107

Sweaters 108
Thrift shops...109
Underwear & lingerie 112
Uniforms...116
Vintage 116
Western wear 120

Cosmetics, bath & beauty **121**
Cosmetics, etc...121
Haircuts & hairstylists 128
Personal care 131
Pharmacies...132

Food & beverages **134**
Appetizers 134
Bakery 137
Beverages 149
Bread...149
Candy, fruit & nuts..152
Cheese..156
Coffees, teas & spices..159
English 163
Fish & meat 164
General stores 172
Gifts 173
Health food..173
Indian...175
Italian...175
Oriental..178
Produce 180
Superstores 181
Takeout...185
Wines & liquors..190

Furniture & furnishings 194

Accessories.....................194
American 206
Antiques 206
Appliances 209
Art & artifacts 211
Art deco/art nouveau.........213
Auction houses 215
Beds & bedding..............216
Chairs & tables 217
Children.........................217
China, crystal & silver......218
Contemporary.................231
Cookware & cutlery..........236
Country..........................238
Electronics, etc. 239
Empire & Biedermeier.......246
English 247
European.........................250
Fabric 252
Fans 253
Fireplace.........................253
Garden & wicker..............254
Hardware & fixtures 257
Kitchen 264
Light fixtures...................267
Linens 270
Medieval & Renaissance 273
Office 274
Oriental..........................274
Quilts & quilting 277
Rentals 278
Rugs & carpets................279
Superstores......................282
Timepieces......................283
Window treatments 284

Home & home office 287

Art supplies 287
Film services 288
Flags 289
Marketing services 289
Printers 290
Rentals 290
Stationery 290
Supplies 293

Home renovation 295

Air conditioning 295
Architects 295
Cabinetry/carpenters 296
Electrician 296
Electronics 296
Expediter 297
Flooring 297
Garden 297
General contractors 298
Marble & granite 299
Paint, plaster & tiles 300
Plumbing & heating 300
Project manager 301
Stained glass 301

Leisure hours & parties **302**

Balloons 302
Books & magazines 302
CDs, tapes & records 321
Caterers 325
Classes & activities 328
Coins & stamps 336
Coordinators 336
Entertainment 338
Florists 338
Gyms 341
Hunting 347
Locations 347
Museum shops 353
Music 356
Musical instruments 357
Personal trainers 358
Photographs & video 359
Rentals 360
Riding 360
Sailing 361
Service help 361
Skating 361
Tennis 362
Theater 363
Tobacco 364
Toys, games & hobbies 364

Personal & repair services

.... 372

Car 372
China, crystal & silver..372
Closet design...373
Decorators...373
Electronics, etc. 374
Exterminator...375
Jewelry & watches 375
Light fixtures..376
Limo rentals 376
Locksmiths 377
Luggage & handbags..377
Metals 379
Miscellaneous 379
Movers 381
Ovens..382
Personal shoppers..382
Rugs & carpets 383
Sewing machines 383
Shoe repair...384
Sofa 385
Tailors 385
Upholsterers...386

Pet services & supplies

.... 387
Adoption 387
Boarding..387
Grooming & supplies...388
Transportation..388
Veterinarians 389
Walking 390

Sporting goods 391
  Bicycles 391
  Billiards 392
  Camping 393
  Dance 393
  Darts 394
  Diving 394
  Exercise 395
  Fencing 395
  Fishing 396
  Golf 397
  Guns 398
  Hunting 398
  Marine 398
  Riding 399
  Running 399
  Skating 399
  Skiing 400
  Soccer 400
  Sports-general 401
  Swimming 402
  Tennis 403
  Windsurfing 403

Travel & vacation 404
  Discount 404

The Sharpest Edge—the top picks 407

  Discounters 407
  Deluxe 411

  Quality 5 5 5 5 5 414

  Quality 4 4 4 4 419

Style **5 5 5 5 5** 424

Style **4 4 4 4** 428

Service **5 5 5 5 5** 433

Service **4 4 4 4** 437

Value **5 5 5 5 5** 439

Value **4 4 4 4** 442

Index **447**

Talk to us **464**
1998 Survey Request 464
Order form 465

The New York Edge

Introduction

Every savvy New Yorker has secret sources for the best quality, value and service. By surveying scores of New York's smartest shoppers and then checking on their recommendations, *The New York Edge* brings you the best shopping information available.

The New York Edge covers the shopping experience from "Best Bargains" to "Price Is No Object." It brings you news of stores and services for everyone from infants to the elderly and for men, women and children.

The New York Edge contains up-to-date intelligence on more than 1,900 stores and services. In describing each, we first define its *Edge* —why it made our list. We then describe what the establishment has to offer. And our survey ranks two-thirds for quality, style, service and value. Most of the stores and services we list are terrific. Some, unfortunately, are coasting along on reputations they no longer deserve. We feel it's important that you know that, too, which is why you'll find some pans among our picks.

As two busy New York career women, we work hard to combine demanding jobs and quality family life. We know that living well takes time and money, scarce resources for most of us. *The New York Edge* highlights our best tips garnered from years of shopping, but it's much more than our opinions alone. The strength of this book is the collective shopping intelligence of some of New York's most sophisticated shoppers. Scores of extremely knowledgeable New Yorkers let us know which stores and services they use and what they think about them. Our survey participants provide great tips on best buys which we pass on to you. Where to haggle and how to do it. Which high-end Madison Avenue furniture stores offer discounts. Who knocks off Armani. Who discounts Hickey-Freeman. We quote our panel's views and ratings in this book.

Talk to us

The participation of New York shoppers makes *The New York Edge* special among shopping guides. We welcome your comments, recommendations and requests and invite you to participate in next year's survey. Send a stamped (2 ounces) self-addressed business size envelope to *The New York Edge*, % Custom Databanks, Inc., 13925 Esworthy Road, Germantown, MD 20874, marked "Attention: Survey Department." To help you, a survey request form is included at the end of this book. Please invite your friends to request a survey.

In appreciation for your response,
you will receive a free copy of next year's survey.

The ratings

A broad spectrum of New York shoppers, primarily professional associates and friends of the authors, were surveyed for their opinions and ratings. Each store and service was rated in terms of quality, style, service and value. Ratings are scaled as follows:

The ratings: **5** excellent **4** very good **3** good **2** fair **1** so-so

These ratings are subjective. In the case of value in particular, the ratings are relative and related to expected service and quality. A deluxe store and a discounter may both receive high ratings for value, given the shoppers' expectations for each type of store. With regard to deluxe, your initial response may be: How can such a high-priced store provide good value? These ratings reflect the quality and service provided by deluxe stores, so price becomes secondary when judging value.

Those judging the stores and services in this book are primarily women, ranging in age from 20 to 70 years old. The typical panel member is a 40-year-old vice president of a New York corporation who lives in Manhattan. She shops frequently for clothes, furniture and services.

Information

The New York Edge is arranged by category (and by subcategory) in alphabetical order from "Clothing & accessories" to "Travel & vacation." The table of contents lists these categories and subcategories. In addition, useful lists are included at the back of the book. There you can find listings of discounters and deluxe stores as well as those stores that received the top ratings (5 "excellent" and 4 "very good") for quality, style, service and value. In addition, there's a complete index at the back of the book.

Hours are included for each store. For multistore chains, hours are listed for individual stores only if their hours differ. Most stores accept credit and charge cards and deliver or send by UPS or FedEx. Stores that do not accept credit cards or do not send are noted. Subcategories and neighborhoods are listed for each store. A list of neighborhoods and a map of Manhattan follows.

Sue Dollinger   Jane Lockshin

August 26, 1996

About the authors

Sue Dollinger and Jane Lockshin are New York career women with a major sideline in shopping. Sue is a vice-president of a major international bank and a former president of the Financial Women's Assocation of New York. Jane is president of Custom Databanks, Inc., and a member of the New York YWCA's Academy of Women Achievers. Both are married parents with hard-won survival skills in getting the best out of New York in the least amount of time and for the least amount of money.

MANHATTAN NEIGHBORHOODS

1. LOWER MANHATTEN

2. SOHO / TRIBECA

3. LOWER EAST SIDE
   CHINATOWN

4. GREENWICH VILLAGE

5. FLATIRON
   EAST VILLAGE

6. CHELSEA

7. GRAMERCY PARK
   MURRAY HILL

8. MIDTOWN WEST

9. MIDTOWN EAST

10. UPPER EAST SIDE

11. UPPER WEST SIDE

12. UPPER UPPER EAST SIDE

13. UPPER UPPER WEST SIDE

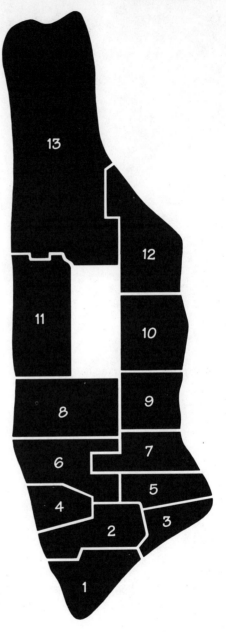

Clothing & accessories

Aquascutum of London

680 5th Avenue
near 54th Street
New York, NY 10019
212-975-0250
Monday-Wednesday Friday Saturday 10-6
Thursday 10-7 Sunday noon-5.

Clothing
Midtown West

4	3	4	4
quality	style	service	value

The Edge: English plaid look. Famous for their raincoats. Not as pricey as Burberrys. Sales, at the end of January and after July 4th, reduce prices dramatically.

Burberry Limited

9 East 57th Street
between Madison and 5th Avenues
New York, NY 10022
212-371-5010
Monday-Wednesday Friday Saturday 9:30-6
Thursday 9:30-7 Sunday noon-5.

Clothing
Midtown East

5	5	5	4
quality	style	service	value

The Edge: Classic British clothing. Traditional English clothing (blouses, slacks, suits, sweaters and topcoats) including of course, their signature trench coat with their famous plaid lining. Deluxe.

"You can find the same merchandise much cheaper at Woodbury Commons even when compared to the sales at 57th Street."

Burlington Coat Factory

45 Park Place
between Church Street and West Broadway
New York, NY 10007
212-571-2630
Weekdays 8-7 Saturday 10-6 Sunday 11-5.

Clothing
Lower Manhattan

3	3	3	4
quality	style	service	value

The Edge: Good discounts on moderately priced coats. Five floors of casual to dress clothing for men, women and children (children for outerwear only). Brands are the more inexpensive lines discounted 25%-30%.

"Good for coats, OK for clothes. Great discounts on brand names."

Charivari

18 West 57th Street
between 5th and 6th Avenues
New York, NY 10019
212-333-4040

Clothing
Midtown West

4	5	4	2
quality	style	service	value

Monday-Wednesday 10-7 Thursday 10-8
Saturday 10-6:30 Sunday 12:30-6.

The Edge: Always original. Prides itself on being always the first, or among the first, to discover new designers. Cutting-edge clothing sold in three separate stores including avant-garde Japanese designs. Merchandise for both men and women. Deluxe.

"Very 'in'"

1001 Madison Avenue	**Upper East Side**
near 78th Street/10021	
212-650-0078	
Weekdays 10-8 Saturday 10-6:30 Sunday 12:30-6.	

257 Columbus Avenue	**Upper West Side**
near 72nd Street/10023	
212-789-7272	
Weekdays 10-8 Saturday 10-6:30 Sunday 12:30-6.	

Christian Dior
703 5th Avenue
at 55th Street
New York, NY 10022
212-223-4646
Monday-Saturday 10-6.

Clothing
Midtown East

5	4	5	4
quality	style	service	value

The Edge: The full Dior line. Three floors carrying the full Dior range, including his less expensive lines, plus fragrances and cosmetics. Deluxe.

Comme des Garçons
116 Wooster Street
between Prince and Spring Streets
New York, NY 10012
212-219-0660
Monday-Saturday 11-7 Sunday noon-6:30.

Clothing
SoHo/TriBeCa

The Edge: High-fashion Japanese designs. Men's and women's cutting-edge, high-quality expensive clothing priced from $15 for socks to $6,000 for evening gowns. Deluxe.

Daffy's Fifth Avenue
111 5th Avenue
near 18th Street
New York, NY 10003
212-529-4477
Monday-Saturday 10-9 Sunday 11-6.

Clothing
Flatiron/East Village

3	3	2	4
quality	style	service	value

The Edge: Best for inexpensive children's clothing. Crammed full of fashion-forward, inexpensive sportswear, shoes and accessories for the entire family. Wonderful children's things. No delivery. 30% off.

"Once in a while it's good." "Good for kids' clothing."

335 Madison Avenue
near 44th Street/10017
212-557-4422
Weekdays 8-8 Saturday 10-6 Sunday noon-6.

Midtown East

135 East 57th Street
near Lexington Avenue/10022
212-376-4477. Fax 212-376-4478
Weekdays 10-8 Saturday 10-6 Sunday noon-6.

Midtown East

Davide Cenci

801 Madison Avenue
near 67th Street
New York, NY 10021
212-628-5910. Fax 212-439-1650
Monday-Wednesday Friday Saturday 10:30-6:30
Thursday 10:30- 7:30.

Clothing
Upper East Side

5	5	5	4
quality	style	service	value

The Edge: Expensive, classic Italian styling. Offers classic Italian menswear from casual to formal. Luxurious Italian fabrics and styling. Sells A. Testoni footwear. Both made-to-measure and hand-finished suits. Off-the-rack suits from $750 and made-to-measure from $1,900. Only trousers for women.

"Sensational clothing."

Dollar Bill's

99 East 42nd Street
between Lexington and Park Avenues
New York, NY 10017
212-867-0212
Weekdays 8-7 Saturday 10-6.

Clothing
Midtown East

4	4	3	4
quality	style	service	value

The Edge: Armani for men, always discounted. Close-outs from top Italian designers. Primarily sportswear, including sports jackets, dress shirts, ties and sun glasses. When you walk, in resist the temptation to walk out as the windows and initial impact often look flashy and cheap. However, you always seem to find Armani (for men) sport shirts, often Missoni sweaters and Zegna. Upstairs for women (at times Armani, Versache and other top Italian designers), great handbags, coats, sweaters, slacks and skirts. 33% off.

"Look twice—there's much to find." "Deals! Deals! Deals!" "Better for men." "Merchandise is still pricey."

Enz's

48 West 8th Street
near 6th Avenue
New York, NY 10003
212-475-0997
Daily noon-8.

Clothing
Flatiron/East Village

The Edge: Fashion-forward even for the downtown crowd. Clothing and boots from London. The current look—rubber clothing, bustiers and body piercing! No delivery.

Filene's Basement

620 Avenue of the Americas
between 18th and 19th Streets
New York, NY 10011
212-869-5756
Monday-Saturday 10-9 Sunday 11-6.

Clothing
Chelsea

3	3	2	4
quality	style	service	value

The Edge: Well-known discounter. Lower-end discount clothing for the entire family. No delivery. 30%-35% off.

"Not the same as the original in Boston."

2222 Broadway
near 79th Street/10024
212-873-8000

Upper West Side

Giorgio Armani

760 Madison Avenue
near 65th Street
New York, NY 10021
212-988-9191
Monday-Wednesday Friday Saturday 10-6 Thursday 10-7.

Clothing
Upper East Side

5	5	3	4
quality	style	service	value

The Edge: It's Armani. Elegant, easy, unconstructed clothing in wonderful rich fabrics with a conservative but up-to-date look. Find suits to evening wear. These are clothes you can wear anywhere, from the office to the Academy Awards! Deluxe.

House of Nubian

35 West 8th Street
near 5th Avenue
New York, NY 10011
212-475-7553. Fax 212-505-5157
Monday-Thursday noon-9 Friday-Saturday noon-11 Sunday 1-8.

Clothing
Chelsea

The Edge: African clothing items. A variety of African bags, clothing, hats, incense, jewelry and oils. In addition, hand-carved African figures, most under $75. Prices ranging from 50¢ to $1,000.

Issey Miyake

992 Madison Avenue
near 77th Street
New York, NY 10021
212-439-7822
Weekdays 10-6 Saturday 11-6.

Clothing
Upper East Side

The Edge: Miyake's signature detailing. Features jackets, shirts, slacks and coats. Very expensive. Women's pants from $185 to $300. Jackets from $800 to $1,800, with some to $3,000. Deluxe.

Klein's of Monticello

105 Orchard Street

Clothing
Lower East Side/Chinatown

near Delancey Street
New York, NY 10002
212-966-1453
Monday-Saturday 10-5.

quality style service value

The Edge: The Barney's look discounted on the Lower East Side. High-fashion, European clothing, including many Barney's labels, discounted. Features pants and skirt suits, silk shirts and accessories, including those fabulous designer silver (thousand-dollar) buckled belts, hats, scarves and jewelry. Small but excellent selection. Clothing tends to be in muted colors with lots of black and brown. Virtually all items are for women. For men, cashmere sports jackets only. 25% off.

"Wonderful things." "High-quality sportswear." "Basic good style and tailoring."

Laura Ashley

398 Columbus Avenue
near 79th Street
New York, NY 10024
212-496-5110
Monday-Wednesday Saturday 11-7 Thursday Friday 11-8.

Clothing
Upper West Side

The Edge: That sweet English country look—best for youngsters. Lots of florals. Best for children's clothing for boys and girls age six months to 12 years. Their home furnishings are English Country and well priced.

Matsuda

156 5th Avenue
between 20th and 21st Streets
New York, NY 10010
212-645-5151
Weekdays 11-7 Saturday 11-6:30 Sunday noon-5.

Clothing
Gramercy Pk/Murray Hill

quality style service value

The Edge: Top Japanese designer. Elegant sportswear in unconstructed easy styles and wonderful fabrics. Celebrity clientele.

Polo/Ralph Lauren

867 Madison Avenue
near 70th Street
New York, NY 10021
212-606-2100. Fax 212-606-2132
Monday-Wednesday Friday Saturday 10-6 Thursday 10-8.

Clothing
Upper East Side

quality style service value

The Edge: The Connecticut preppy look in Manhattan! Traditional preppy look in a full line of clothing and shoes for boys from age 4, men and women. Also antique jewelry and housewares. Best feature is the shop itself, which is in the beautifully restored Rhinelander mansion. Very expensive.

SYMS

42 Trinity Place
near Rector Street
New York, NY 10007

Clothing
Lower Manhattan

quality style service value

212-797-1199
Monday-Wednesday 9-6:30 Thursday Friday 9-8
Saturday 10-6:30 Sunday noon-5:30.

The Edge: Designer discount clothing for men and women. Prices reduced depending upon how long item remains unsold. The New York store has the best quality items. Can be hit or miss. Some upscale merchandise at times among more low-end clothing. No delivery. 33% off.

"Great if you go often and hunt." "Great men's suits." "Well below retail for some designers."

Saint Laurie Ltd.

897 Broadway
near 16th Street
New York, NY 10003
212-473-0100
Weekdays 10-6:30 Saturday 9:30-6:30 Sunday noon-5.

Clothing
Flatiron/East Village

quality	style	service	value
4	3	4	3

The Edge: Traditional men's and women's suits. Suits, sport jackets and slacks made in house. For women a petite and tall department with sizes from 2 to 18. Made-to-measure available with delivery in four weeks. Swatch club for mail order.

"Men's and women's suits of styles gone by."

Yohji Yamamoto

103 Grand Street
near Mercer Street
New York, NY 10013
212-966-9066
Monday-Saturday 11-7.

Clothing
SoHo/TriBeCa

The Edge: Yamamoto's own tailored and minimalist line. Deep, dark colors. Very expensive. Deluxe.

Zara

750 Lexington Avenue
near 59th Street
New York, NY 10022
212-935-2853
Weekdays 10-8 Saturday 10-7 Sunday noon-6.

Clothing
Midtown East

The Edge: For the young hip crowd. Trendy medium-priced clothing from Spain. Blazers from $100.

Zitomer

969 Madison Avenue
between 75th and 76th Streets
New York, NY 10021
212-737-2037. Fax 212-650-0513
Weekdays 9-8 Saturday 9-7 Sunday 10-6.

Clothing
Upper East Side

quality	style	service	value
4	4	4	3

The Edge: An upscale general store featuring pharmaceuticals, cosmetics and children's clothing. Neighborhood shop with a full-line drugstore and cosmetics center on the first floor, and on the second, British and French designer children's clothing, lingerie and toys.

A/X Armani Exchange

568 Broadway
near Prince Street
New York, NY 10012
212-431-6000. Fax 212-431-4669
Weekdays 10-8 Saturday 11-6 Sunday noon-7.

Clothing-casual
SoHo/TriBeCa

4	5	4	3
quality	style	service	value

The Edge: It's Armani. Lower-priced casual Armani items including jeans and sport shirts. An upscale the Gap. Jeans ($48 to $68), sport shirts and sweaters.

Abercrombie & Fitch

725 5th Avenue
near 56th Street
New York, NY 10022
212-832-1001. Fax 212-832-1001
Monday-Saturday 10-6.

Clothing-casual
Midtown East

3	3	4	3
quality	style	service	value

The Edge: Rugged outdoor clothing. Same name, new management since the 1980s. Focus is on quality sports clothing, including rugged outdoor clothing. Sells only its own label.

199 Water Street
near South Street Seaport/10038
212-809-9000. Fax 212-809-9003
Monday-Saturday 10-7 Sunday 11-6. Summer Monday-Saturday 10-9 Sunday 11-9.

Lower Manhattan

Banana Republic

89 5th Avenue
near 16th Street
New York, NY 10003
212-366-4630
Monday-Thursday 10-8 Friday-Saturday 10-7
Sunday noon-6.

Clothing-casual
Flatiron/East Village

4	4	4	3
quality	style	service	value

The Edge: Classic casual clothing that's meant to be worn. Colors tend to be muted (khaki, gray, brown and olive). You'll find slacks, bush jackets, Oxford cloth shirts, fleece-lined suits and accessories (canvas and leather belts, canvas duffels and shoulder bags).

205 Bleecker Street
near 6th Avenue/10012
212-473-9570
Monday-Thursday 10-9 Friday-Saturday 10-10 Sunday noon-7.

SoHo/TriBeCa

1131 3rd Avenue
near 67th Street/10021
212-288-4279
Monday-Thursday 10-8 Friday-Saturday 10-7 Sunday noon-6.

Upper East Side

130 East 59th Street   **Midtown East**
near Lexington Avenue/10022
212-751-5570
Monday-Thursday 10-9 Friday-Saturday 10-7 Sunday noon-6.

215 Columbus Avenue   **Upper West Side**
near 71st Street/10023
212-873-9048
Monday-Thursday 10-8 Friday-Saturday 10-7 Sunday noon-6.

2376 Broadway   **Upper West Side**
near 88th Street/10024
212-874-3500
Monday-Thursday 10-9 Friday-Saturday 10-7 Sunday noon-6.

1136 Madison Avenue   **Upper East Side**
near 85th Street/10028
212-570-2465
Monday-Thursday 10-9 Friday-Saturday 10-7 Sunday noon-6.

Benetton

Clothing-casual
Flatiron/East Village

749 Broadway
near 8th Avenue
New York, NY 10003
212-533-0230
Monday-Saturday 10-7 Sunday noon-5.

3	5	3	3
quality	style	service	value

The Edge: Like the Gap, sometimes snappier. Some years, it's good. Some less so. This looks like a good year! You'll find sneakers, pants and accessories. Moderate prices.

597 5th Avenue   **Midtown East**
near 48th Street/10017
212-223-4444

666 5th Avenue   **Midtown West**
near 53rd Street/10019
212-399-9860

805 3rd Avenue   **Upper East Side**
near 62nd Street/10021
212-752-5283

14 East 60th Street   **Midtown East**
near 5th Avenue/10022
212-355-3444

542 5th Avenue   **Midtown West**
near 45th Street/10036
212-398-1209

586 5th Avenue   **Midtown West**
near 47th Street/10036

212-688-2055

Cockpit
595 Broadway
near Prince Street
New York, NY 10012
212-925-5455
Monday-Saturday 11-7 Sunday 12:30-6.

Clothing-casual
SoHo/TriBeCa

3	4	3	3
quality	style	service	value

The Edge: Clothing related to aviation. Great jackets related to flying—bomber, flight, leather and unisex jackets plus other aviation-related items.

"The novelty—good fun."

Eisner Brothers
75 Essex Street
between Delancey and Broome Streets
New York, NY 10002
212-475-6868. Fax 212-756-824
Monday-Thursday 8:30-6:30 Friday 8:30-3 Sunday 8:30-4:30.

Clothing-casual
Lower East Side/Chinatown

The Edge: Source for NBA, NHL and collegiate team items. Sells wholesale licensed team merchandise. Find caps, sweatshirts, team jackets and more. Sizes toddlers through adult extra-large. Inexpensive. No credit cards.

Emporio Armani
110 5th Avenue
at 16th Street
New York, NY 10011
212-727-3240
Monday-Saturday 11-7 Sunday 1-6.

Clothing-casual
Chelsea

4	4	4	3
quality	style	service	value

The Edge: It's Armani. Sportswear less (but still) expensive than Giorgio Armani's main line. Casual sweaters, jeans, slacks, soft tailored dresses and Emporio shoes.

Gap
60 West 34th Street
near Broadway
New York, NY 10001
212-643-8960
Monday-Saturday 9-9 Sunday 11-8.

Clothing-casual
Midtown West

4	5	4	5
quality	style	service	value

The Edge: Basic inexpensive casual clothing. Basically T-shirts, flannels, sweatshirts, sweaters and jeans. The basics are priced right and the jeans are great!! The rest doesn't seem to last, but then it isn't priced to last. Everyone shops here from preteens to adults and it's certainly a must for the college crowd.

"Consistent, dependable."

750 Broadway   Flatiron/East Village

near 8th Street/10003
212-674-1877
Monday-Saturday 10-9 Sunday noon-8.

113 East 23rd Street   **Gramercy Pk/Murray Hill**
near Lexington Avenue/10010
212-533-6670
Weekdays 9:30-8 Saturday 10-7 Sunday noon-5.

91-97 7th Avenue   **Chelsea**
between 16th and 17th Streets/10011
212-989-1110
Monday-Saturday 10-8 Sunday noon-7.

122 5th Avenue   **Chelsea**
near 17th Street/10011
212-989-0550
Monday-Friday 10-9 Saturday 10-8 Sunday noon-7.

345 Avenue of the Americas   **Greenwich Village**
near West 4th Street/10014
212-727-2210
Monday-Saturday 10-9 Sunday noon-8.

445 5th Avenue   **Gramercy Pk/Murray Hill**
near 39th Street/10016
212-532-8633
Weekdays 9-7:30 Saturday 10-7 Sunday noon-5.

549 3rd Avenue   **Gramercy Pk/Murray Hill**
near 36th Street/10016
212-213-6007
Monday-Saturday 10-8 Sunday 11-6.

757 3rd Avenue   **Midtown East**
near 47th Street/10017
212-223-5140
Weekdays 9-7:30 Saturday 10-7 Sunday noon-5.

657-659 3rd Avenue   **Midtown East**
near 42nd Street/10017
212-697-3590
Weekdays 9-7:30 Saturday 10-7 Sunday noon-5.

250 West 57th Street   **Midtown West**
near Broadway/10019
212-315-2250
Weekdays 10-8 Saturday 10-7 Sunday 11-6.

1131 3rd Avenue   **Upper East Side**
near 66th Street/10021
212-472-5559
Monday-Saturday 10-9 Sunday 11-8.

1066 Lexington Avenue   **Upper East Side**
near 75th Street/10021
212-879-9144
Monday-Saturday 10-7:30 Sunday 11-6.

1131-1149 3rd Avenue   **Upper East Side**
near 66th Street/10021
212-472-4555
Weekdays 10-8 Saturday 10-7 Sunday 11-7.

734 Lexington Avenue   **Midtown East**
near 59th Street/10022
212-751-1543
Weekdays 9:30-9 Saturday 9:30-8 Sunday 11-7.

900 3rd Avenue   **Midtown East**
near 54th Street/10022
212-754-2290
Weekdays 8-7:30 Saturday 10-6 Sunday noon-5.

527 Madison Avenue   **Midtown East**
near 54th Street/10022
212-688-1260
Monday-Saturday 9:30-8 Sunday 11-5.

2101 Broadway   **Upper West Side**
near 73rd Street/10023
212-787-6698
Monday-Saturday 10-9 Sunday 11-8.

335 Columbus Avenue   **Upper West Side**
near 76th Street/10023
212-873-9272
Monday-Saturday 10-9 Sunday 10-8.

1988 Broadway   **Upper West Side**
near 65th Street/10023
212-721-5304
Weekdays 9-7:30 Saturday 10-7 Sunday noon-5.

2373 Broadway   **Upper West Side**
near 86th Street/10024
212-873-1244
Monday-Saturday 9-10 Sunday 11-8.

535 Columbus Avenue   **Upper West Side**
near 86th Street/10024
212-874-8377
Weekdays 10-9 Saturday 10-8 Sunday noon-7.

2559 Broadway   **Upper West Side**

near 96th Street/10025
212-864-3600
Monday-Saturday 10-9 Sunday noon-7.

1164 Madison Avenue   **Upper East Side**
near 86th Street/10028
212-517-5763
Weekdays 10-8 Saturday 10-7 Sunday noon-6.

1511 3rd Avenue   **Upper East Side**
near 85th Street/10028
212-794-5781
Monday-Saturday 10-9 Sunday 11-7.

1466 Broadway   **Midtown West**
near 42nd Street/10036
212-768-2987
Weekdays 9-7:30 Saturday 10-7:30 Sunday 11-5.

1212 Avenue of the Americas   **Midtown West**
near 48th Street/10036
212-730-1087
Weekdays 9-7:30 Saturday 10-7 Sunday noon-5.

89 South Street, 2nd Floor   **Lower Manhattan**
South Street Seaport, Pier 17/10038
212-374-1051
Monday-Saturday 10-9 Sunday 11-8.

157 World Trade Center   **Lower Manhattan**
near Cortlandt Street/10048
212-432-7086
Monday-Saturday 7:30-7:30 Sunday noon-5.

Henry Lehr   **Clothing-casual**
772 Madison Avenue   **Upper East Side**
near 66th Street
New York, NY 10021
212-535-1021. Fax 212-535-8360
Monday-Wednesday Friday 10-6 Thursday 10-7 Saturday 10-6 Sunday noon-5.

The Edge: Upscale European country-western sportswear look. Find great prewashed jeans from Blue System, Replay and Rivet with a great fit for $100 in sizes 2 to 14. Sportswear from $59 to $500 with slacks from $200.

J. Crew   **Clothing-casual**
203 Front Street   **Lower Manhattan**
South Street Seaport
New York, NY 10038
212-385-3500. Fax 212-233-0963
Monday-Saturday 10-9 Sunday 11-7.
January-April: Monday-Saturday 10-7 Sunday 11-6.

4	4	4	4
quality	style	service	value

The Edge: Wonderful classic sportswear that appeals to all ages. Styling and colors are excellent. Good fabrics including cottons, silks, wools and cashmeres. Find shoes, jeans, shorts, shirts, skirts, pants, plus accessories. Women's sizes mostly 2 to 12, some 14s. Men's suit sizes from 38 to 46. Great sales. For the college crowd to seniors, you can't go wrong.

"Good basic stuff worthy of *Vogue*." "Great styles."

J. McLaughlin
1343 3rd Avenue
near 77th Street
New York, NY 10021
212-879-9565. Fax 212-650-1078
Weekdays 11-8 Saturday 11-6 Sunday noon-6.

Clothing-casual
Upper East Side

4	4	4	4
quality	style	service	value

The Edge: Somewhat updated Talbots' look. Good-quality, well-cut, conservative sportswear. The definition of preppy. Quality fabrics. Moderately high prices.

"Good quality."

Old Navy Clothing Company
610 Avenue of the Americas
near 18th Street
New York, NY 10011
212-645-0663
Monday-Saturday 9:30-9 Sunday 11-8.

Clothing-casual
Chelsea

The Edge: Less expensive Gap-style casual clothing. This subsidiary of the Gap offers a less expensive Gap-type clothing. Basically T-shirts, flannels, sweatshirts, sweaters and jeans.

Peter Elliot
1070 Madison Avenue
near 81st Street
New York, NY 10028
212-570-2300
Weekdays 10:30-7 Saturday 10-30-6 Sunday 1-5.

Clothing-casual
Upper East Side

5	5	5	4
quality	style	service	value

The Edge: Beloved by all—classic men's and women's sportswear. The basics attractive and well fitting, conservative styling.

"Steady." "Lots of help for the shopping impaired."

Urban Outfitters
374 Avenue of the Americas
near Waverly Place
New York, NY 10011
212-677-9350
Monday-Saturday 10-10 Sunday noon-8.

Clothing-casual
Chelsea

The Edge: Weekend work clothing. Good fabrics and durable. The Gap look at higher prices. No delivery.

127 East 59th Street   **Midtown East**
between Park and Lexington Avenues/10022
212-688-1200
Monday-Saturday 10-9 Sunday noon-7.

628 Broadway   **SoHo/TriBeCa**
between Houston and Bleecker Streets/10012
212-475-0009
Monday-Saturday 10-10 Sunday noon-8.

Weiss & Mahoney
142 5th Avenue
near 19th Street
New York, NY 10011
212-675-1915. Fax 212-633-3873
Weekdays 9-7 Saturday 10-6:30 Sunday 11-5.

Clothing-casual
Chelsea

The Edge: A New York City army-navy surplus store. Some used items, but mostly new. Priced from $5.

Wings
155 East 23rd Street
between Lexington and 3rd Avenues
New York, NY 10010
212-460-8963
Monday-Saturday 9-9 Sunday 10-8.

Clothing-casual
Gramercy Pk/Murray Hill

4	4	3	5
quality	style	service	value

The Edge: Basic weekend clothing, jeans and sweats, at good prices. Features brand-name jeans like Jordache, Levis and Wrangler, plus sweats and sneakers from Reebok, Nike and New Balance. Oshkosh jeans for kids from $30 to $50. All sizes. No delivery.

666 Broadway   **SoHo/TriBeCa**
near Bleecker Street/10021
212-254-9002
Daily 9-9.

270 West 38th Street   **Midtown West**
near 8th Avenue/10018
212-768-4220
Daily 8:30-8.

2824 Broadway/10025   **Upper West Side**
near 110th Street
212-666-8330
Monday-Saturday 9-9 Sunday 10-8.

1523 3rd Avenue   **Upper East Side**
near 86th Street/10028
212-628-6214

Monday-Saturday 9-9 Sunday 10-8.

210 East 86th Street   **Upper East Side**
between 2nd and 3rd Avenues/10028
212-879-2575
Monday-Saturday 9-9 Sunday 10-8.

Ben's Up and Up
1335 3rd Avenue
near 75th Street
New York, NY 10021
212-744-2520
Daily 10-6 Saturday 11-6.

Clothing-children
Upper East Side

The Edge: You need it, they have it in children's clothing. Bright, colorful, casual separates, pretty party dresses, blazers and wool pants. Quality clothing for all occasions. Good, basic clothing befitting its East Side clientele, but not a grandma's shop. For newborns to 12 years.

Ben's for Kids
1380 3rd Avenue
near 79th Street
New York, NY 10021
212-794-2330
Monday-Wednesday Friday 10-5 Thursday 10-8 Saturday 11- 5.

Clothing-children
Upper East Side

4	4	4	4
quality	style	service	value

The Edge: Reliable neighborhood children's store. Meets all baby's needs from toys to clothes to furniture and accessories (no disposables). Practical, more moderate focus. Prices: $10 to $60. Sizes from newborn to 4 years old.

"Very good selection of children's equipment."

Bonpoint
1269 Madison Avenue
near 90th Street
New York, NY 10128
212-722-7720
Monday-Saturday 10-6.

Clothing-children
Upper East Side

3	3	2	2
quality	style	service	value

The Edge: Exclusive French-designed children's clothing. French children's clothing (newborn to size 16). Good fabrics and quality workmanship. Everything from the basics to party dresses. Inspired children's antique style furniture. A grandma's favorite resource. Deluxe.

"The sales people think they're still in France."

Chocolate Soup
946 Madison Avenue
near 75th Street
New York, NY 10021
212-861-2210
Monday-Saturday 10-6.

Clothing-children
Upper East Side

5	5	4	3
quality	style	service	value

The Edge: Fun, colorful, creative children's clothing. Doesn't ever seem to change. You'll find cotton T-shirts and leggings (wide range of colors), Oshkosh overalls, hand-painted with whimsical, colorful storybook themes, knit sweaters, Hawaiian shirts, fun jewelry, small toys and the old reliable Danish school bag that's unbelievably durable. Newborn to preteen sizes. A small, quality selection.

Citykids

37 West 20th Street, Suite 604
near 5th Avenue
New York, NY 10011
212-620-0906. Fax 212-620-0120
Monday-Saturday 9:30-5.

Clothing-children
Chelsea

The Edge: Great children's play clothes. Functional durable children's play clothes and shoes (sneakers and sturdy play shoes). Find name designers plus Citykids' own line. Styles are playful and whimsical. Sizes newborn to 10 years. Also educational books.

Coco & Z

222 Columbus Avenue
near 70th Street
New York, NY 10023
212-721-0415
Monday-Saturday 11-7 Sunday noon-5.

Clothing-children
Upper West Side

The Edge: Absolutely adorable and affordable children's clothing. Wonderful children's clothing in sizes infant to 8 from small California manufacturers (Malina, Tess et Cie, Baby Armadillo and Cow and Lizzard) and some European designers. Casual, perky clothing, often with animal and flower designs and almost always with unusual and pretty patterns. However, they also have lots of black clothing, even for infants. Will make up gift baskets and maintains a baby registry.

"New to the neighborhood, a must-see."

Dinosaur Hill

302 East 9th Street
near 2nd Avenue
New York, NY 10003
212-473-5850
Daily 11-7.

Clothing-children
Flatiron/East Village

The Edge: An international collection of children's toys and clothing. Hand-painted, embroidered and hand-knit clothing and toys from around the world for children from 6 months to 6 years old.

Exclusive Oilily Store

870 Madison Avenue
near 70th Street
New York, NY 10021
212-628-0100. Fax 212-570-4618
Monday-Wednesday Friday Saturday 10-6
Thursday 10-7 Sunday noon-5.

Clothing-children
Upper East Side

3	4	4	3
quality	style	service	value

The Edge: Adorable expensive kids clothing. Fashions for children and mom from the Dutch company Oilily. Styles are comfortable, pants are rolled, tops are oversized, dresses are long and coats lined to span the season. The kids' clothing is very cute, but expensive with sweatshirts for infants at $53 and denims for toddlers at $95. Their women's clothing is an acquired taste. Deluxe.

Gap Kids and Baby Gap

60 West 34th Street, upper level
near Broadway
New York, NY 10001
212-643-8995
Weekdays 9-9 Saturday 10-9 Sunday 11-8.

Clothing-children
Midtown West

3	4	4	5
quality	style	service	value

The Edge: Basic, good-looking kids and infants clothing. Find jeans, plaid flannel shirts, sweaters, T-shirts, shoes, caps, jackets and Gap-style infants' clothing. Children's sizes from newborn to 13 years. Prices are moderate, with jeans from $19.50 to $30.

"Hot stuff."

354 Avenue of the Americas
near West 4th Street/10011
212-777-2420
Monday-Saturday 10-9 Sunday noon-8.

Chelsea

657 3rd Avenue
near 42nd Street/10017
212-697-9007
Weekdays 9-7:30 Saturday 10-7 Sunday noon-5.

Midtown East

1037 Lexington Avenue
near 75th Street/10021
212-988-4460
Monday-Saturday 10-7:30 Sunday 11-6.

Upper East Side

545 Madison Avenue
near 55th Street/10022
212-980-2570
Weekdays 9:30-8 Saturday 9:30-7 Sunday noon-5.

Midtown East

2373 Broadway
near 86th Street/10024
212-873-2044
Monday-Saturday 10-9 Sunday 11-8.

Upper West Side

1535 3rd Avenue
at 87th Street/10028
212-423-0444
Monday-Saturday 9-9 Sunday 11-8.

Upper East Side

1212 Avenue of the Americas
near 48th Street/10036

Midtown West

212-764-0285
Weekdays 9-7:30 Saturday 10-7 Sunday noon-5.

1466 Broadway   **Midtown West**
near 42nd Street/10036
212-302-1266
Weekdays 9-7:30 Saturday 10-7:30 Sunday 11-5.

89 South Street, 1st level   **Lower Manhattan**
South Street Seaport, Pier 17/10038
212-786-1707
Monday-Saturday 10-9 Sunday 11-8.

250 West 57th Street   **Midtown West**
near Broadway/10019
212-956-3140
Weekdays 9:30-8 Saturday 10-7 Sunday 11-6.

Greenstone & Cie   **Clothing-children**
442 Columbus Avenue   **Upper West Side**
near 81st Street
New York, NY 10024

4	4	4	4
quality	style	service	value

212-580-4322
Monday-Saturday 10:30-7 Sunday noon-6.

The Edge: Beautiful high-end European children's clothing. Features unique, imported
European children's clothing and sturdy American lines. Sizes from 3 months to 12 years. A full
range of styles from play to school to party.

Jacadi   **Clothing-children**
1281 Madison Avenue   **Upper East Side**
near 91st Street
New York, NY 10128

5	5	3	3
quality	style	service	value

212-369-1616
Monday-Wednesday Friday Saturday 10-6
Thursday 10-7 Sunday noon-5.

The Edge: Fabulous French fashions for children. Full range of French clothing from infant to
age 12. Deluxe.

"Go at sale times—prices are less obscene."

Kidding Around   **Clothing-children**
60 West 15th Street   **Chelsea**
near 6th Avenue
New York, NY 10011
212-645-6337. Fax 212-645-6372
Weekdays 10-7 Saturday 11-7 Sunday 11-6.

The Edge: Well-chosen clothes and toys. Wonderful selection of children's clothing and toys.
Great party wrappings.

Kids "R" Us

1293 Broadway
near 34th Street
New York, NY 10001
212-643-0714
Monday Friday 9-9 Tuesday Wednesday Saturday 9-8
Thursday 9-9:30 Sunday 11-7.

Clothing-children
Midtown West

quality	style	service	value
3	2	2	4

The Edge: Inexpensive basics from infants' to girls' and boys' sizes. Features Carters, Jet Set and Oshkosh, etc. The atmosphere is chaotic. No delivery. Discounter.

Kids Are Magic

2287 Broadway
near 82nd Street
New York, NY 10024
212-875-9240. Fax 212-875-0742
Monday-Wednesday 10-8 Thursday-Saturday 10-9 Sunday noon-7:30.

Clothing-children
Upper West Side

The Edge: Inexpensive hip children's clothing. Features Baby Dior, French Toast, Sahara Club and more. Sahara Club is the big seller. Cheap jeans from $12.97, dresses and sweaters from $15.97, coats from $60. No shoes. Sizes from infants to girls' size 14 and boys' size 20. No delivery. Discounter.

La Layette et Plus

170 East 61st Street
between Lexington and 3rd Avenues
New York, NY 10021
212-688-7072
Monday-Saturday 11-6.

Clothing-children
Upper East Side

quality	style	service	value
5	5	5	3

The Edge: Attention, Grandma: top-of-the-line clothing for newborns. Simply fabulous elegant children's clothing. Top of the line from practical to dress for all occasions. Gorgeous, gorgeous items. Linens and furnishings equally grand. Deluxe.

Little Folks

123 East 23rd Street
near Park Avenue
New York, NY 10010
212-982-9669. Fax 212-228-7889
Monday-Thursday 9:30-7 Friday 9-5 Sunday noon-5.

Clothing-children
Gramercy Pk/Murray Hill

The Edge: Uptown service at downtown prices in an almost midtown location. The basics to party items for infant to girls' and boys' size 14. Features Aprica, Levis, Maclaren, Oshkosh, Perego and more. Moderately priced snowsuits at $45 to $88. Down jackets $75 to $120. Girls' dress coats $80 to $100. Periodic sales (past-season items) reduce prices to 40% off. Also furniture, strollers, cribs and car seats.

M. Kreinen Sales
301 Grand Street
near Allen Street
New York, NY 10002
212-925-0239
Sunday-Thursday 9-5 Friday 9-3.

Clothing-children
Lower East Side/Chinatown

quality   style   service   value

The Edge: Good prices for sturdy children's clothing. Children's clothing by Carters, Oshkosh, Quiltex and Trinfett. Find pants, jackets (including down), sweaters and more. Priced from $10 to $50. No credit cards. 20% off.

Magic Windows
1186 Madison Avenue
between 86th and 87th Streets
New York, NY 10028
212-289-0028. Fax 212-289-7794
Monday-Saturday 10-6 Sunday noon-5.

Clothing-children
Upper East Side

quality   style   service   value

The Edge: One-stop shopping for children's clothing from all the best designers. Classic traditional clothing from Florence Eiseman, Vive La Fête and Sylvia Whyte. Sizes from infant to junior size 9. Find clothing for all occasions from infants' receiving blankets, monogrammed and plain sweaters (at $52 to $86), dresses (including wonderful party dresses into the $100s), blazers ($80 to $120) and coats ($60 to $250). Shoes for infants to toddlers. Fills that tough preteen niche when you're seeking something special.

Space Kiddets
46 East 21st Street
near Broadway
New York, NY 10010
212-420-9878
Monday Tuesday Friday 10:30-6 Wednesday
Thursday 10:30-7 Saturday 11:30-5:30.

Clothing-children
Gramercy Pk/Murray Hill

quality   style   service   value

The Edge: Fun, funky children's clothing. Small selection, but adorable clothing for newborns to age 10 years. Styles range from classic to funky.

"Love it."

Wicker Garden's Baby/Children
1327 Madison Avenue
between 93rd and 94th Streets
New York, NY 10128
212-410-7001
Monday-Saturday 10-6.

Clothing-children
Upper East Side

quality   style   service   value

The Edge: Exceptionally priced and styled clothing and hand-painted wicker furniture. Wonderful collection of children's clothing, shoes, linens and furniture. Clothing from layettes to practical school clothing, play clothes and party dresses. Infant furniture on the second floor includes iron and wood cribs, some with canopies. Also bureaus and armoires hand-painted with pastoral scenes. Also antique quilts and linens to adorn the cribs. Deluxe.

"Grandma heaven, if price is irrelevant." "Expensive, but good."

Aldo Ferrari, Inc.

321 5th Avenue
near 32nd Street
New York, NY 10016
212-685-5131. Fax 212-683-5060
Monday-Saturday 10-6.

Clothing-men
Gramercy Pk/Murray Hill

The Edge: Inexpensive. Their own label European-style clothing (suits, shirts, raincoats, jackets, cashmere sweaters and accessories). Low prices, from $20 for men's shirts. Recommended to us, but not known. Let us know what you think.

Alfred Dunhill of London

420 Park Avenue
near 57th Street
New York, NY 10022
212-888-4000. Fax 212-980-2959
Weekdays 9:30-6:30 Saturday 9:30-6.

Clothing-men
Midtown East

5	4	4	3
quality	style	service	value

The Edge: High-quality luxurious menswear. Offers three levels of suits, shirts, ties and shoes: off the peg, special order and custom tailored. Fine fabrics and good tailoring. Custom tailoring means the garment is sewn entirely by hand. Accessories include attaché cases, luggage and Dunhill lighters. A well-known, top source for very expensive menswear. Deluxe.

Bijan

699 5th Avenue
near 55th Street
New York, NY 10022
212-788-7500. Fax 212-207-8124
By appointment.

Clothing-men
Midtown East

5	5	5	3
quality	style	service	value

The Edge: Exclusivity. European styling for dress and casual clothing. For those who want to shop by appointment only (or chance the doorman not letting you in). Entry is easier from the St. Regis Hotel lobby. Prices are extreme. Service and quality make the place. Deluxe.

Brooks Brothers

346 Madison Avenue
near 45th Street
New York, NY 10017
212-682-8800
Monday-Wednesday Friday 8:30-6:30
Thursday 8:30-7:30 Saturday 9-6:30 Sunday noon-5.

Clothing-men
Midtown East

4	3	5	3
quality	style	service	value

The Edge: Memories of childhood shopping trips. They have it all for boys to men from underwear to tuxedos! Conservative, well-tailored clothing unchanging year after year. Find three-button blazers and suits. A small women's department with ultra-preppy men's clothing cut for women.

One Liberty Plaza
near Broadway /10006
212-267-2400
Weekdays 8-6 Saturday 10-5.

Lower Manhattan

Eisenberg and Eisenberg

85 5th Avenue, 6th Floor
near 16th Street
New York, NY 10003
212-627-1290. Fax 212-627-1293
Monday-Wednesday Friday 9-6 Thursday 9-7 Saturday 9-5 Sunday 10-4.

Clothing-men
Flatiron/East Village

The Edge: Inexpensive men's formal wear. Since 1898 has offered a full range of men's clothing from casual to tuxedos at discount. Tuxedos priced from $190 to $550 for sale and $75 to $115 for rental. Mostly their own label.

Ermenegildo Zegna

743 5th Avenue
near 57th Street
New York, NY 10022
212-428-4488
Weekdays 10-7 Saturday 10-6.

Clothing-men
Midtown East

5 5 5 3
quality style service value

The Edge: Best styling, best quality Italian men's clothing. You can't get more top-of-the-line than this. Prices are high—$975 to $1,800 for rack suits. See the entry for Gilcrest—they say their suits are made in the same factory as Zegnas. Deluxe.

"This look and quality doesn't come cheap."

Euromoda Ltd.

56 Orchard Street
south of Grand Street
New York, NY 10002
212-219-3972. Fax 212-219-3973
Monday-Wednesday Friday Sunday 10-6
Thursday 10-9:30.

Clothing-men
Lower East Side/Chinatown

4 4 4 4
quality style service value

The Edge: Beautiful top-line suits featuring fine Italian fabrics at $695. Tailoring included. A top choice for high-quality, fine, well-tailored suits 40% off.

Fenwick Clothes

85 5th Avenue
near 16th Street
New York, NY 10003
212-243-1100
Weekdays 9-5:45 Saturday 9-4 Sunday 10-4.

Clothing-men
Flatiron/East Village

The Edge: Men's suit discounter. A small selection of quality conservative men's suits priced mostly $400-$500. Find women's coats in the fall.

G&G International

62 Orchard Street
between Grand and Hester Streets
New York, NY 10002
212-431-4530
Sunday-Wednesday 9-6 Thursday 9-8 Friday 9-3.

Clothing-men
Lower East Side/Chinatown

The Edge: Moderately priced men's lines at discount prices. Designer clothing (mostly Italian) including Canali, Principe, San Remo, Zegna and some American designers (Geoffrey Beene, Ralph Lauren) at up to 40% off retail.

Gianni Versace

816 Madison Avenue
near 68th Street
New York, NY 10021
212-744-5572. Fax 212-734-8394
Monday-Saturday 10:30-6:30.

Clothing-men
Upper East Side

4	5	4	3
quality	style	service	value

The Edge: Au courant high-fashion men's clothing. Features casual to business wear. Very expensive rack suits: $1,700 to $3,000. Custom shirts: $230 to $700. Their fabrics are luxurious. Suits in sizes 36 to 50. Hottest sellers are leather jackets (to size 58) priced from $3,200 to $6,000. Cutting-edge and very expensive. Deluxe.

Gilcrest Clothes Company

900 Broadway, 3rd Floor
near 20th Street
New York, NY 10003
212-254-8933. Fax 212-475-3541
Weekdays 7:30-5:30 Saturday 8:30-5 Sunday 9:30-4:30.

Clothing-men
Flatiron/East Village

4	4	4	3
quality	style	service	value

The Edge: Good discounts on classic men's business suits. Features a full line of business clothing. Suits from $249 to $500, with most from $400 to $500. Hottest look is European, primarily Italian-styled suits. Also offers shirts, ties and coats. No charge for alternations. They claim they sell designer suits at the lowest prices in town. Their most exciting claim is that one of their suit lines is made at the same factory as Zegna suits. Wide range of sizes (to 54 long).

"Recommended."

Gorsart

9 Murray Street
between Broadway and Church Street
New York, NY 10007
212-962-0024. Fax 212-349-4427
Monday-Wednesday Friday 9-6
Thursday 9-7 Saturday 9-5:30.

Clothing-men
Lower Manhattan

4	4	5	4
quality	style	service	value

The Edge: Conservative men's suits. They describe their hottest store item as "gray stripe or navy" and that says it all! Suits from $295 to $750. Sizes to 50 long. Also shirts and shoes. Discounter.

Harry Rothman's

200 Park Avenue South
near 17th Street
New York, NY 10003
212-777-7400. Fax 212-979-2216
Monday-Wednesday Friday 10-7 Thursday 10-8
Saturday 9:30-6 Sunday noon-5.

Clothing-men
Flatiron/East Village

3	3	3	4
quality	style	service	value

The Edge: More moderately priced men's clothing. Carries Canali, Hickey Freeman, Joseph Abboud and Perry Ellis. Find suits, coats, shirts, ties, shoes, socks and sweaters. 20% off.

Irving Baron Clothes

343 Grand Street
between Essex and Ludlow Streets
New York, NY 10002
212-475-1718
Monday-Wednesday 9:30-6 Thursday 9:30-7 Friday-Sunday 9-5.

Clothing-men
Lower East Side/Chinatown

The Edge: Moderately priced men's lines. Features Countess Mara, Le Baron, Louis Roth and more. Suits $285 to $1,100. Shirts $30+. Hottest items they feature are in the sportswear category. Discounter.

J. Press

17 East 44th Street
between 5th and Madison Avenues
New York, NY 10017
212-687-7642. Fax 800-765-7737
Monday-Saturday 9-6.

Clothing-men
Midtown East

5	3	4	4
quality	style	service	value

The Edge: The Connecticut look. Full range of clothing from shorts to tuxedos. Fabrics and styling are traditional. Sizes to 52. Suits from $500 to $800. Jackets from $300. In summer, sports clothing, slacks and shorts come in bright colors with patterned/madras fabrics.

Jekyll and Hyde Ltd

93 Greene Street
between Prince and Spring Streets
New York, NY 10012
212-966-8503. Fax 212-941-0135
Monday-Wednesday 11:30-7 Thursday 11:30-7:30 Friday- Saturday noon- 7:30.

Clothing-men
SoHo/TriBeCa

The Edge: Forward, contemporary-looking clothing. English and Italian men's clothing from sportswear to dress (no shoes). Their current best sellers are five-button suits from $725. Suits to size 46.

L.S. Men's Clothing

19 West 44th Street
between 5th and 6th Avenues
New York, NY 10036
212-575-0933
Monday-Thursday 9-7 Friday 9-4:30 Sunday 9-5.

Clothing-men
Midtown West

4	2	4	5
quality	style	service	value

The Edge: Discounted brand-name suits, some Hickey Freeman and Perry Ellis. Brand names and custom tailored. Custom made suits from Italian and English fabrics take four weeks for delivery. 50% off.

"Great hidden nook for suits."

Moe Ginsburg
162 5th Avenue
near 21st Street
New York, NY 10010
212-242-3482
Monday-Wednesday Friday 9:30-7 Thursday 9:30-8
weekends 9:30-6.

Clothing-men
Gramercy Pk/Murray Hill

quality style service value

The Edge: Five showroom floors running the gamut from shoes to formal wear. Offers some named designers along, for the most part, with their own brand. Primarily moderately priced lines. Full range of sizes including a Big and Tall Department. 35% off.

"New York's best discount store—high quality and great price."

Napoleon
725 5th Avenue
Trump Tower at 57th Street
New York, NY 10019
212-759-1110
Monday-Saturday 10-6.

Clothing-men
Midtown West

quality style service value

The Edge: One of the top men's boutiques, featuring expensive Italian sportswear. Lots of Ermenegildo Zegna, among others. Good service. Deluxe.

New Republic Clothiers
93 Spring Street
near Broadway
New York, NY 10012
212-219-3005. Fax 212-219-3049
Monday-Saturday noon-7 Sunday noon-6.

Clothing-men
SoHo/TriBeCa

The Edge: An elegant retro look. Designs new clothing with the classic elegance of 1940s styling. Features a full range of clothing—sportswear and business. Small selection of good traditional English-made shoes.

Paul Smith
108 5th Avenue
near 16th Street
New York, NY 10011
212-627-9770. Fax 212-627-9773
Monday-Saturday 11-7 Sunday noon-6.

Clothing-men
Chelsea

quality style service value

The Edge: Fine menwear. Traditional clothing with a twist (unusual fabrics, patterns or colors). Prices are high, matching the quality.

"He, He style." "Too Brooks Brothers-y for women."

Paul Stuart
Madison Avenue
at 45th Street
New York, NY 10017
212-682-0320. Fax 212-983-2742
Monday-Wednesday Friday 8-6:30 Thursday 8-7
Saturday 9-6 Sunday noon-5.

Clothing-men
Midtown East

quality style service value

The Edge: Conservative, but more up-to-date than Brooks. Meets all the needs of the Wall Street man from casual to work to formal. Good fabrics, good looks, good quality.

"Casual wear is sort of the J. Crew look but much more expensive."

Today's Man
625 Avenue of the Americas
between 18th and 19th Streets
New York, NY 10011
212-924-0200
Monday-Saturday 9:30-9:30 Sunday 10-6.

Clothing-men
Chelsea

3	3	3	3

quality style service value

The Edge: Offers a full block of moderately priced, own label clothing. Featured as a discounter. Much of the stock is their own label with some designer clothing, mostly from Hugo Boss, Perry Ellis and Pierre Cardin. No delivery. 10% off.

"OK for casual stuff."

Trend Clothiers
40 East 41st Street
between Madison and Park Avenues
New York, NY 10017
212-889-4686
Weekdays 11-7.

Clothing-men
Midtown East

The Edge: Moderately priced traditional American and European men's suits. Specializes in French and Italian designer suits and its own line of American cut suits. Also overcoats, shirts, ties and shoes. Tailoring on premises. No delivery.

W. Weber and Company
22 West 21st Street
near 5th Avenue
New York, NY 10010
212-255-6630
Sunday-Friday 11-6 Saturday 11-5.

Clothing-men
Gramercy Pk/Murray Hill

The Edge: Men's clothing only. Manufactures traditional men's suits.

Pan Am Sportswear and Menswear

50 Orchard Street
between Grand and Hester Streets
New York, NY 10002
212-925-7032. Fax 212-219-8742
Sunday-Wednesday 9-6 Thursday 9-8 Friday 9-4.

Clothing-casual-men
Lower East Side/Chinatown

quality style service value

The Edge: Good discounts on basic suits. Designer suits, including Hugo Boss, Perry Ellis and Ralph Lauren, with raincoats from Christian Dior. 50% off.

"Great hidden nook for suits."

Tobaldi Huomo

83 Rivington Street
near Orchard Street
New York, NY 10002
212-260-4330
Sunday-Thursday 9:30-6 Friday 9:30- one hour before sunset.

Clothing-casual-men
Lower East Side/Chinatown

quality style service value

The Edge: Very cutting-edge high-style Italian menswear. Features very flashy designer suits and sportswear. Discounter.

Aaron's

627 5th Avenue
near 17th Street
Brooklyn, NY 11215
718-768-5400. Fax 718-965-2462
Monday-Wednesday Friday-Saturday 9:30-6
Thursday 9:30-9.

Clothing-women
Brooklyn

quality style service value

The Edge: Good values on top fashions, when you hit it right. Hit or miss, but occasionally great buys on stylish clothing. Best for more moderately priced clothing. Misses and petite sizes 4 to 16. Car service from Manhattan. 30% off.

Ann Taylor

645 Madison Avenue
near 60th Street
New York, NY 10022
212-832-2010
Weekdays 10-8 Saturday 10-7 Sunday noon-6.

Clothing-women
Midtown East

quality style service value

The Edge: Classic, young, professional look. Same price range as Talbots, but better looking sportswear and young career clothing, shoes and accessories. Great sales. Misses sizes 4 to 12, some 14s.

901 Avenue of the Americas
Manhattan Mall/10001
212-564-3992

Midtown West

575 5th Avenue   **Midtown East**
near 47th Street/10017
212-922-3621

1320 3rd Avenue   **Upper East Side**
near 75th Street/10021
212-861-3392

805 3rd Avenue   **Midtown East**
near 50th Street/10022
212-308-5333

2015-17 Broadway   **Upper West Side**
near 69th Street/10023
212-873-7344

2380 Broadway   **Upper West Side**
near 87th Street/10024
212-721-3130

1055 Madison Avenue   **Upper East Side**
near 80th Street/10028
212-988-8930

4 Fulton Street   **Lower Manhattan**
South Street Seaport/10038
212-480-4100

225 Liberty Street   **Lower Manhattan**
World Financial Center/10281
212-945-1991

Atelier 45
347 Madison Avenue
near 45th Street
New York, NY 10017
212-687-6877
Weekdays 10-7:30 Saturday 11-6.

Clothing-women
Midtown East

4	4	3	3
quality	style	service	value

The Edge: Basic clothing for the professional women. Features Kenar, Tahari and Vertigo. Prices from $60 to $300. 15% off.

Atelier 86
144 East 86th Street
near Lexington Avenue
New York, NY 10028
212-427-2211
Weekdays 10:30-7 Saturday 11-6 Sunday noon-6:30.

Clothing-women
Upper East Side

4	4	3	4
quality	style	service	value

The Edge: Basic clothing for the professional women. Features Kenar, Tahari and Vertigo. Prices from $60 to $300. 15% off.

Bagutta Boutique

402 West Broadway
between Spring and Broome Streets
New York, NY 10012
212-925-5216. Fax 212-925-5262
Weekdays 11-7 Saturday 11-7:30 Sunday noon-6:30.

Clothing-women
SoHo/TriBeCa

The Edge: High-fashion upscale European look. Wonderful top European-designed clothing. Shirts $200 to $1,200. Smaller sizes. Deluxe.

Betsey Johnson

130 Thompson Street
near Houston Street
New York, NY 10012
212-420-0169
Monday-Saturday noon-7 Sunday 1-6.

Clothing-women
SoHo/TriBeCa

3	4	3	3
quality	style	service	value

The Edge: Fashion-forward clothing for the high school and/or club crowd. Avant garde without being totally way out. Moderately priced from $20 to $200.

"Fun for teenagers." "Very quirky clothing."

251 East 60th Street
near 2nd Avenue/10021
212-319-7699
Monday-Saturday noon-7 Sunday 1-6.

Upper East Side

248 Columbus Avenue
near 71st Street/10023
212-362-3364
Monday-Saturday 11-7 Sunday noon-7.

Upper West Side

Bolton's

90 Broad Street
near Stone Street
New York, NY 10004
212-785-0513
Monday-Saturday 10-7 Sunday noon-5.

Clothing-women
Lower Manhattan

3	3	3	4
quality	style	service	value

The Edge: Easily accessible, good for inexpensive wardrobe "fillers". Sportswear a specialty, but also stocks dresses and coats. OK source for the basics. Carries moderately priced lines, e.g., skirts priced from $19.99 and up (to $79). Misses sizes to size 14 with some 16s. No delivery. 25% off.

"Great for 'basics'. Have to shop these stores frequently."

53 West 23rd Street
near 6th Avenue/10010
212-924-6860
Monday-Saturday 10-7 Sunday noon-5.

Gramercy Pk/Murray Hill

4 East 34th Street   **Gramercy Pk/Murray Hill**
near 5th Avenue/10016
212-684-3750

685 3rd Avenue   **Midtown East**
near 44th Street/10017
212-682-5661
Monday-Saturday 10-7 Sunday noon-5.

27 West 57th Street   **Midtown West**
near 6th Avenue/10019
212-935-4431. Fax 212-751-376

110 West 51st Street   **Midtown West**
near 6th Avenue/10020
212-245-5227

477 Madison Avenue   **Midtown East**
near 51st Street/10022
212-355-5860

225 East 57th Street   **Midtown East**
near 3rd Avenue/10022
212-755-2527

2251 Broadway   **Upper West Side**
near 82nd Street/10024
212-873-8545

1180 Madison Avenue   **Upper East Side**
near 86th Street/10028
212-722-4419

Chanel Boutique
5 East 57th Street
between 5th and Madison Avenues
New York, NY 10022
212-355-5050. Fax 212-355-2305
Weekdays 10-6:30 Saturday 10-6 Sunday noon-5.

Clothing-women
Midtown East

quality	style	service	value
5	5	5	3

The Edge: It's Chanel. Everything Chanel from ready-to-wear, accessories, jewelry, fragrances and cosmetics. Suits priced in the thousands of dollars. Deluxe.

Country Road
411 West Broadway
near Spring Street
New York, NY 10012
212-343-9544
Monday-Saturday 11-7 Sunday noon-6.

Clothing-women
SoHo/TriBeCa

quality	style	service	value
4	4	3	3

The Edge: The movie *Out of Africa* look. Casual chic contemporary sportswear by this Australian sportswear company. Some career looks. Materials are good quality and colors tend to be muted.

"Stylish."

335 Madison Avenue   **Midtown East**
near 43rd Street/10017
212-949-7380. Fax 212-687-6459
Monday-Wednesday Friday 9:30-7 Thursday 9:30-8 Saturday 10-6 Sunday noon-5.

199 Water Street   **Lower Manhattan**
near John Street/10038
212-248-0810
Monday 10-7 Tuesday-Friday 8:30-7 Saturday 10-7 Sunday 11-6.

Dana Buchman

65 East 57th Street
near Park Avenue
New York, NY 10022
212-319-3257
Weekdays 10-7 Saturday 10-6 Sunday noon-5.

Clothing-women
Midtown East

4	5	4	4
quality	style	service	value

The Edge: Elegant tailored, yet feminine, clothing for the executive woman. Classic elegant suits and shirts in fine fabrics. Feminine yet appropriately conservative. Mix 'n' match sizes to fit well and easily. Popular among our respondents.

"Good selection in petites." "Excellent size availability, free alterations."

Emanuel Ungaro

792 Madison Avenue
near 67th Street
New York, NY 10021
212-249-4090. Fax 212-675-28
Monday-Wednesday Friday Saturday 9:30-6:30
Thursday 9:30-7:30.

Clothing-women
Upper East Side

5	5	5	3
quality	style	service	value

The Edge: It's Ungaro's entire couture collection. The couture line is sexy, made from rich fabrics and put together in unusual combinations. Offers day to evening wear. Day dresses priced at about $1,800. Also offers Parallel and Solo Donna high-end lines designed by Emanuel. Deluxe.

"Gorgeous and extremely expensive."

Episode Sportswear

601 Madison Avenue
near 57th Street
New York, NY 10022
212-355-3589
Weekdays 10-7 Saturday 10-6 Sunday noon-5.

Clothing-women
Midtown East

4	4	4	3
quality	style	service	value

The Edge: Chic styled work clothing. Well-styled sportswear and suits made from natural fibers. Colors and styles tend to be muted. Check out their VIP program. Buy $1,000+ in any two-month period. Then enjoy a 10% discount forever (regardless of purchase amount) and an extra 5% on your birthday! The VIP program applies to any of their stores.

"Nice elegant casual." "A New York chic professional look."

805 3rd Avenue   Midtown East
near 49th Street/10022
212-754-2442. Fax 212-754-2449

Escada Boutique

Clothing-women
7 East 57th Street   Midtown East
between 5th and Madison Avenues
New York, NY 10022

5	5	5	3
quality	style	service	value

212-755-2200

`Monday-Wednesday Friday Saturday 10-6 Thursday 10-7.

The Edge: The full Escada line. Full line from ready-to-wear to couture is sold here. Extremely expensive chic, if not flashy, sports line. Priced from $400 for slacks and $1,400 for jackets. Catalogs are available to clients spending $10,000 plus. Deluxe.

"My secret source for Escada is Giselle on the Lower East Side. Escada is kept on the top floor behind closed doors, so ask. Also if you can stand the trip, First Choice in Wayne N.J. and Woodbury Commons have Escada at discount."

Fashion Plaza

Clothing-women
77 Orchard Street   Lower East Side/Chinatown
near Broome Street
New York, NY 10002
212-966-3510
Sunday-Thursday 9:30-6 Friday 9:30-3.

The Edge: Louis Feraud and Grossman discounted.

Fishkin Knitwear

Clothing-women
314 Grand Street   Lower East Side
near Allen Street
New York, NY 10002-4591

4	3	3	4
quality	style	service	value

212-226-6538. Fax 212-226-6544
Monday-Thursday 10-5 Friday 10-4 Sunday 9-4:30.

The Edge: Mid-price range clothing carried at discount. Full range of women's discount clothing (sportswear, sweaters, shoes, silk shirts, dresses). Coats sold in the fall. Sometimes carries Dana Buchman, DKNY, Liz Claiborne and Eileen Fisher. Sizes 2 to 18, petites to 3X. 30% off.

"Very good for sweaters and shirts." "Not always the lowest prices; department stores are getting competitive."

Forman's

Clothing-women
82 Orchard Street   Lower East Side/Chinatown

near Delancey Street
New York, NY 10002
212-228-2500. Fax 212-529-1458
Sunday-Wednesday 9-6 Thursday 9-8 Friday 9-2.

quality style service value
4   3   3   4

The Edge: Moderately priced designer sportswear at discount. Designers include Evan Picone, Jones of New York, Gianni and Kasper at 20% to 30% off retail prices. Petites to size 24 sold in four locations.

59 John Street   **Lower Manhattan**
near William Street/10038
212-791-4100
Monday-Wednesday 7:30-6:30 Thursday-Friday 7:30-3:30 Sunday 11:30-5:30.

Fowad
                                                  Clothing-women
2554 Broadway   **Upper West Side**
near 96th Street
New York, NY 10025
212-222-8000. Fax 212-322-2888
Monday-Saturday 9:30-7:30 Sunday 11-5.

The Edge: Large clothing store selling inexpensive off-price lines. Features Jones of New York and similar designers at low prices. Full range of inexpensive clothing items. Discounter.

Giselle Sportswear, Inc.
                                                  Clothing-women
143 Orchard Street   **Lower East Side/Chinatown**
near Delancey Street
New York, NY 10002
212-673-1900
Sunday-Thursday 9-6 Friday 9-4.   quality style service value
                                                  5   5   3   4

The Edge: If you negotiate well, a fabulous source for discounted (30% off) designer clothing. Three floors filled with discounted (20% offered) middle- to top-priced designer sportswear, including Escada (top floor—you need to ask for it), Emanuel and Laurel. If you buy several things which add up, bargain hard with the man behind the counter downstairs. You could lower the price even more (we've seen a woman achieve 40%). Sundays are too crowded for effective bargaining. Their official policy is not to take charge-and-send orders, but if you're a big spender, they'll send you the Basler and Mondi catalogs (described as their own) and will send your purchases via UPS anywhere in the U.S. without charge.

"Quality stuff. Huge sales at end of the season." "The reason I go downtown."

Givenchy Boutique
                                                  Clothing-women
954 Madison Avenue   **Upper East Side**
near 75th Street
New York, NY 10021
212-772-1040. Fax 212-288-7186   quality style service value
Monday-Saturday 10-6.   5   5   5   3

The Edge: It's Givenchy. Elegant ready-to-wear in sizes 4 to 16. Evening gowns are Givenchy's specialty. Special orders are possible. Very expensive, dresses $1,800 to $3,000. Deluxe.

If Boutique

Clothing-women
SoHo/TriBeCa

474 West Broadway
between Houston and Prince Streets
New York, NY 10012
212-533-8660. Fax 212-473-7290
Monday-Saturday noon-7:30 Sunday noon-7.

The Edge: Cutting-edge young European designer look. Features Vivien Westwood and Colonna. Also shoes and accessories. It's expensive: jackets priced from $500 to $1,500, bags from $200 to $600 and skirts/pants from $200 to $800. Carries sizes 4 to 8 with some 10s. One-of-a-kind look, very elegant and great service.

Jaeger

Clothing-women
Upper East Side

818 Madison Avenue
near 69th Street
New York, NY 10021
212-628-3350. Fax 212-579-9530
Monday-Saturday 10-6.

5	3	5	4
quality	style	service	value

The Edge: Classic clothing made for the Queen, not Princess Di. Classic suits and sportswear from an English institution known for its mainstream timeless clothing. It's the Talbots' look, updated somewhat and featuring much better fabrics.

Joseph

Clothing-women
Upper East Side

804 Madison Avenue
near 68th Street
New York, NY 10021
212-570-0077. Fax 212-570-0487
Monday-Wednesday Friday Saturday 10-6:30 Thursday 10-7.

The Edge: Cutting-edge young look. In-house designer features flare pants this year, but who knows what next year will bring. Prices for pants from $275, dresses from $200 to $400 and skirts from $110 to $150 in misses sizes 2 to 12.

Kenar

Clothing-women
Lower East Side/Chinatown

96 Orchard Street
near Houston Street
New York, NY 10002
212-254-8899. Fax 212-677-8750
Monday-Saturday 9:30-5 Sunday 9:30-5:30.

3	3	3	4
quality	style	service	value

The Edge: The Kenar line at 20% off. Further discounts possible if you negotiate and it isn't Sunday when the store is crowded.

Lea's Designer Fashion

Clothing-women
Lower East Side/Chinatown

119 Orchard Street
near Delancey Street
New York, NY 10002
212-677-2043. Fax 212-677-7637
Weekdays 9:30-5 Sunday 9-5.

5	5	4	4
quality	style	service	value

The Edge: Discounts high-end top designers. Features an especially large collection of Louis Feraud, Kenzo and other top designers. Suits from $250 to $1,000, skirts from $50 and pants from $60. 30% off.

"My favorite designer is here and nowhere else."

Limited

691 Madison Avenue
near 62nd Street
New York, NY 10021
212-838-8787
Monday-Saturday 10-8 Sunday noon-6.

Clothing-women
Upper East Side

2	4	3	3
quality	style	service	value

The Edge: The high school set loves their clothes. Young fun clothing, great sportswear and a contemporary look at moderate prices.

Linda Dresner

484 Park Avenue
near 58th Street
New York, NY 10022
212-308-3177. Fax 212-755-6737
Monday-Saturday 10-6. Closed Saturday in summer.

Clothing-women
Midtown East

5	5	4	4
quality	style	service	value

The Edge: Very hip, selective expensive clothing. Features Europeans like Jil Sander, Prada, Jean Muir and more in misses sizes 6 to 12, with shoes in sizes 7 to 9. Prices are high: pants $600+, shoes $300+ and suits $1,500+. Find jewelry, bags and accessories that complement their line. Their top item is a leather shoulder bag with sterling-silver charms for $2,790.

"Fabulous."

Max Mara

813 Madison Avenue
near 68th Street
New York, NY 10021
212-879-6100. Fax 212-879-2135
Monday-Wednesday Friday Saturday 10-6 Thursday 10-7.

Clothing-women
Upper East Side

3	3	3	3
quality	style	service	value

The Edge: Italian women's clothing—conservative to very stylish, depending on the line. Various lines and price points for coats, suits ($400 to $900), skirts, pants, shoes and evening wear. Dresses are cut well in fine fabrics. Misses sizes from 4 to 12, with limited 2s and 14s. Publishes MM magazines twice a year featuring their fashions and living trends.

Miriam Rigler

14 West 55th Street
near 5th Avenue
New York, NY 10019
212-581-5519
Monday-Saturday 10-6.

Clothing-women
Midtown West

4	4	5	4
quality	style	service	value

The Edge: Miriam can put together what's right for you. Features moderately discounted women's sportswear, day dresses, knits, suits and evening wear from less well-known moderately expensive European designers as well as their own designs. Caters to tourists and working women. Best for their conservative office and "mother of the bride" clothing.

"Don't let the windows deter you from going in."

Nicole Miller

780 Madison Avenue
near 66th Street
New York, NY 10021
212-288-9779. Fax 212-517-3485
Monday-Saturday 10-7.

Clothing-women
Upper East Side

4	4	4	3
quality	style	service	value

The Edge: Excellent little black dresses for evening. Favored by young career women. Complete line of sportswear, day dresses and evening wear. Moderate prices, excellent styling.

109

115 St. Marks Place
near 3rd Avenue
New York, NY 10009
212-475-8072
Daily noon-8.

Clothing-women
Flatiron/East Village

The Edge: Reasonably priced, sexy dresses for the young. Mostly petite sizes up to 10 misses. Designers include Sab, Annae and Onyx. Also bags, hats, jewelry and scarves. Dresses about $100 and higher, depending on the fabric.

S&W

165 West 26th Street
near 7th Avenue
New York, NY 10001
212-675-7883
Monday-Wednesday 10-6:30 Thursday 10-8
Friday 10-3 Sunday 10-6.

Clothing-women
Midtown West

4	3	3	4
quality	style	service	value

The Edge: Discounted designer clothing, shoes and accessories. Designer clothing including sportswear, dresses, evening wear, coats, suits and accessories. You can usually get more off the price if you push, possibly to 40%.

"Great bags and shoes, must go often—depends on the shipment." "OK." "Negotiate or overpay!"

Saint Laurent Rive Gauche

855 Madison Avenue
near 70th Street
New York, NY 10021
212-988-3821
Monday-Saturday 10-6.

Clothing-women
Upper East Side

5	5	5	3
quality	style	service	value

The Edge: The Paris legend! Timeless, well-cut clothing from pants to gowns. Well-cut styles, excellent tailoring and wonderful fabrics at extremely high prices. Deluxe.

"My 15-year-old jackets and suits still look new and in style."

Shulie's

175 Orchard Street
near Houston Street
New York, NY 10002
212-473-2480
Sunday-Friday 9:30-5:30.

Clothing-women
Lower East Side/Chinatown

4	4	3	4
quality	style	service	value

The Edge: Tahari's line at 20% off. For women from sportswear to dresses. The complete line is there or can be gotten. Also classic but spunky moderately priced shoes in an adjacent shop, accessible from the store. Prices are posed at 20% off, but negotiate for additional savings.

"Don't forget to negotiate."

St. John Boutique

665 5th Avenue
near 52nd Street
New York, NY 10022
212-755-5252
Monday-Wednesday Friday Saturday 10-6 Thursday 10-7.

Clothing-women
Midtown East

5	5	5	4
quality	style	service	value

The Edge: Knits that travel well and look good. The Nancy Regan White House look beloved by the Executive Crowd, especially those who travel on business. Elegant lady-like knit suits, always available in navy, white and black plus the current year's colors, with silk shirts and accessories to complement the outfit. Their more contemporary line is Griffith and Grey, featuring woven knit patterns. Misses sizes 2 to 14, some 16s. Free alternations. Expensive, with suits in the $700 to $1,200 range. Deluxe.

Sue's Discount Better Dresses

638 Lexington Avenue
near 54th Street
New York, NY 10022
212-752-5574. Fax 212-752-5574
Weekdays 9:30-6:30 Sunday 11-5.

Clothing-women
Midtown East

4	4	3	4
quality	style	service	value

The Edge: Moderately priced basic business clothing. Manufacturers close-outs of labels like Grossman and Nippon. Primarily dresses and suits. No delivery. 25% off.

Tahari

225 Liberty Street
near Vessey Street
New York, NY 10281
212-535-1515
Weekdays 10-7 Saturday 11-6 Sunday noon-5.

Clothing-women
Lower Manhattan

4	4	3	3
quality	style	service	value

The Edge: Tailored suits designed to take the busy executive from the office to evening. Graceful silk, rayon and gabardine dresses, nicely cut slacks and ultra-feminine silk blouses. The designer factory outlet store in Ridgefield, N.J. (201-943-9470), is a treasure and staffed by Sue and Mae, truly special ladies.

"Love their styles." "Nice look, especially on sale." "Great work clothes."

Talbots

1251-1255 3rd Avenue
near 72nd Street
New York, NY 10021
212-988-8585
Weekdays 10-8 Saturday 10-7 Sunday noon-6.

Clothing-women
Upper East Side

4	3	4	4
quality	style	service	value

The Edge: Ultra-conservative, casual to business clothing. Known for the Connecticut look, featuring tailored slacks, skirts, suits, evening wear and shoes. Full range of styles and if not in the store, call the toll-free number (800-882-5268) for quick delivery. Sizes from petite to misses 20. See the twice-yearly sale when prices get really low.

"If you're into the Darien look." "Very good value"

525 Madison Avenue
near 54th Street/10022
212-838-8811. Fax 212-752-7090
Weekdays 10-7 Saturday 10-6 Sunday noon-5.

Midtown East

2289-2291 Broadway
at 82nd Street/10024
212-875-8753
Weekdays 10-9 Saturday 10-8 Sunday noon-6.

Upper West Side

Valentino

825 Madison Avenue
between 68th and 69th Streets
New York, NY 10021
212-772-6969
Monday-Saturday 10-6.

Clothing-women
Upper East Side

5	5	5	3
quality	style	service	value

The Edge: Classic sexy Italian clothing. A favorite of all our all-time favorite stylish ladies—Audrey Hepburn, Jacqueline Onassis and Sophia Loren. Broad range of prices, depending on the line, from Couture to Miss V and Studio V. Deluxe.

Agnes B.

116 Prince Street
near Greene Street
New York, NY 10012
212-925-4649. Fax 212-517-5784
Monday-Saturday 11-7 Sunday noon-6.

Clothing-casual-women
SoHo/TriBeCa

4	5	4	3
quality	style	service	value

The Edge: Conservative, but zippy, French-styled sports clothes. Well-made, well-cut French clothing for men, women and children at this location. For women: find wonderful leggings, slacks, T-shirts, sweaters and accessories. The look is 'Audrey Hepburn' in smaller sizes. For men: find suits (priced about $615) to size 48.

1063 Madison Avenue
near 81st Street/10028
212-570-9333. Fax 212-517-5784

Upper East Side

Ann Crabtree
1310 Madison Avenue
near 93rd Street
New York, NY 10128
212-996-6499. Fax 212-996-5641
Weekdays 10-6:30 Saturday 10-6.

Clothing-casual-women
Upper East Side

quality style service value
5   4   5   3

The Edge: Sportswear for the ladies who lunch. Mostly elegant European and Calvin Klein sportswear. The look is New York chic. Full retail. Misses sizes 4 to 12.

Eileen Fisher Boutique
314 East 9th Street
near 1st Avenue
New York, NY 10003
212-529-5715
Monday-Saturday noon-8 Sunday noon-7.

Clothing-casual-women
Flatiron/East Village

quality style service value
4   4   4   3

The Edge: Comfortable clothing. Features unstructured cuts, loose, casual clothing in pastel colors made from natural fabrics. Moderately priced, easy care, pull-on clothing.

"Clothes are comfortable, fit well and look good."

103 5th Avenue
near 17th Street/10003
212-924-4777. Fax 212-741-3732
Monday-Saturday 11-8 Sunday noon-6.

Flatiron/East Village

1039 Madison Avenue
near 79th Street/10021
212-879-7799
Monday-Saturday 10-7 Sunday noon-5.

Upper East Side

521 Madison Avenue
near 53rd Street/10022
212-759-9888. Fax 212-750-6063
Monday-Saturday 10-7 Sunday noon-6.

Midtown East

341 Columbus Avenue
near 76th Street/10024
212-362-3000
Monday-Saturday 10-7 Sunday noon-6.

Upper West Side

Express
7 West 34th Street
between 5th and 6th Avenues
New York, NY 10001
212-629-6838

Clothing-casual-women
Midtown West

Weekdays 10-8 Saturday 10-7 Sunday noon-6.

The Edge: Inexpensive teenager heaven featuring good-looking clothing. Beloved by the high school set. Mostly casual, comfortable and colorful clothing. You'll find sweaters, slacks, gauzy skirts and dresses. Watch for promotions, when prices get even lower.

901 Avenue of the Americas   **Midtown West**
near 33rd Street/10019
212-971-3280
Monday-Saturday 10-8 Sunday 11-7.

667 Madison Avenue   **Upper East Side**
near 60th Street/10021
212-754-2721
Monday-Wednesday Friday Saturday 10-7 Thursday 10-8 Sunday noon-6.

321 Columbus Avenue   **Upper West Side**
near 75th Street/10023
212-580-5833
Monday-Saturday 11-8 Sunday 11-7.

Harriet Love

Clothing-casual-women
SoHo/TriBeCa

126 Prince Street
between Wooster and Greene Streets
New York, NY 10012
212-966-2280
Tuesday-Sunday 11:30-7.

3	3	3	3
quality	style	service	value

The Edge: Young fun clothing. Moderately priced jewelry and casual young clothing. No longer that wonderful vintage source.

Labels for Less

Clothing-casual-women
Flatiron/East Village

204 Park Avenue South
near 17th Street
New York, NY 10003
212-529-7440
Weekdays 10-7 Saturday 10-6 Sunday noon-5.

3	3	3	3
quality	style	service	value

The Edge: Conservative, less expensive suits and sportswear. Fabrics of choice appear to be polyesters rather than silks, wools or cottons. Find pants and skirts at $40+, suits averaging $99 and handbags at $39. No delivery. 20% off.

"Occasional good buys." "Good for fillers."

95 Wall Street   **Lower Manhattan**
near Water Street/10005
212-514-9388
Weekdays 10-7:30 Saturday 10-6 Sunday noon-5.

286 1st Avenue   **Flatiron/East Village**
near 16th Street/10009
212-674-6223

Weekdays 10-7:30 Saturday 10-6 Sunday noon-5.

130 East 34th Street   **Gramercy Pk/Murray Hill**
near Lexington Avenue/10016
212-689-3455
Weekdays 10-7:30 Saturday 10-6 Sunday noon-5.

639 3rd Avenue   **Midtown East**
near 42nd Street/10017
212-682-3330
Weekdays 10-7:30 Saturday 10-6 Sunday noon-6.

345 Madison Avenue   **Midtown East**
near 45th Street/10017
212-697-6659
Weekdays 9:30-8 Saturday 10-6 Sunday 11-5.

1345 Avenue of the Americas   **Midtown West**
near 57th Street/10019
212-956-2450
Weekdays 10-7:30 Saturday 10-6 Sunday noon-5.

1430 2nd Avenue   **Upper East Side**
near 75th Street/10021
212-249-4080
Weekdays 10-7:30 Saturday 10-6 Sunday noon-5.

1302 1st Avenue   **Upper East Side**
near 68th Street/10021
212-249-4800
Weekdays 10-7:30 Saturday 10-6 Sunday noon-5.

800 3rd Avenue   **Midtown East**
near 50th Street/10022
212-752-2443
Weekdays 9:30-6:30 Saturday 10-6 Sunday noon-5.

551 Madison Avenue   **Midtown East**
near 55th Street/10022
212-888-8390
Weekdays 9:30-7:30 Saturday 10-6 Sunday noon-5.

181 Amsterdam Avenue   **Upper West Side**
near 68th Street/10023
212-787-0850
Weekdays 10-7:30 Saturday 10-6 Sunday noon-5.

1124 Avenue of the Americas   **Midtown West**
near 44th Street/10036
212-302-7808
Weekdays 10-7:30 Saturday 10-6 Sunday noon-5.

130 West 48th Street
near 6th Avenue/10036
212-997-1032
Weekdays 9-6 Saturday 10-6.

Midtown West

175 East 96th Street
near 3rd Avenue/10128
212-987-3637
Weekdays 10-7:30 Saturday 10-7 Sunday noon-5.

Upper East Side

Lee Anderson
23 East 67th Street
near Madison Avenue
New York, NY 10021
212-772-2463
Monday-Saturday 11-6.

Clothing-casual-women
Upper East Side

5	5	5	4
quality	style	service	value

The Edge: Pret-à-porter and custom clothing in classic styles with a European twist. Mostly skirts, shirts, pants and peacoats. Prices are high with $275 skirts, $325 pants and $195+ shirts and all from their in-house designer. Wonderful peacoat jacket in great colors. Deluxe.

Omo Norma Kamali
11 West 56th Street
west of 5th Avenue
New York, NY 10019
212-957-9797
Monday-Saturday 10-6.

Clothing-casual-women
Midtown West

The Edge: Kamali designs. The full line, covering jewelry, bathing suits, swimwear, shoes, lingerie, suits and wedding gowns.

Patricia Field
10 East 8th Street
near 5th Avenue
New York, NY 10003
212-254-1699. Fax 212-529-0834
Monday-Saturday noon-8 Sunday noon-6.

Clothing-casual-women
Flatiron/East Village

3	5	4	4
quality	style	service	value

The Edge: Trend-setting clothing. Fun items for the club crowd. This year's hot items—a yellow patent-leather skirt at $125. Now featuring designer Kitty Boots, Living Doll and Deborah Maruit. Never the same items.

Putumayo
147 Spring Street
near West Broadway
New York, NY 10012
212-966-4458
Monday-Saturday 11-7 Sunday noon-6.

Clothing-casual-women
SoHo/TriBeCa

3	3	3	4
quality	style	service	value

The Edge: Moderately priced upbeat South American casual clothing. Beloved by the high school set. Clothes and accessories from South America and India. Patterned sun dresses and wrap skirts and comfortable loose-styled clothing. Year-round bulky cotton sweaters. Woven sashes, South American jewelry, straw hats, bags and more.

Rodier

575 5th Avenue
near 47th Street
New York, NY 10017
212-599-2495
Monday-Saturday 10-6.

Clothing-casual-women
Midtown East

quality	style	service	value
3	3	3	3

The Edge: The French version of Jaeger. Lots of coordinated knits, slacks, shirts and accessories. Conservative styling. Sales are seasonal and excellent.

610 5th Avenue
near 50th Street (Rockefeller Center)/10020
212-489-9427
Monday-Wednesday Friday Saturday 10-6:30 Thursday 10-8 Sunday noon-6.

Midtown West

1310 3rd Avenue
near 75th Street/10021
212-439-0104
Monday Tuesday Saturday 10-6 Wednesday Thursday 10-7 Sunday noon-5.

Upper East Side

Gallery of Wearable Art

34 East 67th Street
between Madison and Park Avenues
New York, NY 10021
212-425-5379
Tuesday-Saturday 10-6.

Accessories
Upper East Side

quality	style	service	value
4	4	4	-

The Edge: Entrance-making clothing. Unusual, one-of-a-kind, eye-catching clothing (evening and day dresses and jackets). Sizes 6 to 18 but can custom make to other sizes.

"Fun and funky." "Everything is special."

Julie Artisan's Gallery

687 Madison Avenue
near 62nd Street
New York, NY 10021
212-688-2345
Monday-Saturday 11-6.
Closed Saturday July and August.

Accessories
Upper East Side

quality	style	service	value
5	5	4	5

The Edge: One-of-a-kind traffic-stopping clothing and jewelry. Clothing and jewelry designed by American Artists. Cutting-edge jewelry including Vintage Bakelite bracelets from $90 to $650.

"Fun looking!" "Great place." "Wonderful gifts but expensive."

New York Exchange for Women's Work

1095 3rd Avenue
near 64th Street
New York, NY 10021
212-753-2330
Monday-Saturday 10-6.

Accessories
Upper East Side

4	3	4	4
quality	style	service	value

The Edge: Unique hand-crafted gift items. Find knit toys, lingerie, children's clothing, painted furniture and gift items. Best known for dresses, sweaters and knits for babies. With the Elder Craftsmen now closed, many of their craftspeople are selling here. If you love nostalgia, you'll love the New York Exchange.

"Engaging unique." "Good for gifts." "Some wonderful finds."

New York Firefighter's Friend

263 Lafayette Street
near Prince Street
New York, NY 10012
212-226-3142. Fax 212-226-3164
Monday-Saturday 10-6.

Accessories
SoHo/TriBeCa

The Edge: Everything related to fires and the fire department. Find caps, T-shirts, sweatpants and shorts with the FDNY insignia plus men's steel-toed rubber boots and children's boots. There's the *Big Red Book of Fire Trucks*, vintage fire hose nozzles for collectors, Dalmatians and fire fighters pictured on everything.

Only Hearts

386 Columbus Avenue
near 78th Street
New York, NY 10024
212-724-5608. Fax 212-685-0853
Monday-Saturday 11-8 Sunday noon-7.

Accessories
Upper West Side

The Edge: The name says it all. Lingerie and giftware with a heart motif.

Vision of Tibet

167 Thompson Street
between Houston and Bleecker Streets
New York, NY 10012
212-995-9276
Daily 11-7.

Accessories
SoHo/TriBeCa

The Edge: Go there for silver cuff bracelets. Clothing, jewelry and accessories from Nepal and Tibet.

Whittall & Son

485 7th Avenue, Room 1411
near 36th Street
New York, NY 10018
212-594-2626. Fax 212-268-2862
Weekdays 10-5:45.

Accessories
Midtown West

The Edge: Traditionally styled women's hats and sportswear below wholesale for all holidays and occasions. No delivery.

A.T. Harris
11 East 44th Street
near 5th Avenue
New York, NY 10017
212-682-6325. Fax 212-682-6148
Monday-Wednesday Friday 9-5:45 Thursday 9-6:45 Saturday 10-3:45 and by appointment.

Bridal, wedding & formal
Midtown East

The Edge: Quality formal rentals, including cutaways and tails. Rents and sells a full range of conservatively styled formal wear (cutaways, tails and tuxedos) including accessories, shirts, Chesterfield topcoats, shoes (for sale only), studs, cufflinks and kid or suede gloves. Tuxedos are worsted wool. Rentals from $125 plus tax include everything but shoes.

Arnold Scassi
681 5th Avenue
near 54th Street
New York, NY 10022
212-755-5105
Weekdays by appointment.

Bridal, wedding & formal
Midtown East

quality style service value

The Edge: Lean, sensual evening gowns. American couturier known for his custom evening wear. Priced from $10,000 to $20,000. Customers only by recommendation, but it can't hurt to call, since this is the '90s and customers are at a premium. Ask for Steve. No credit cards. No delivery. Deluxe.

Baldwin Formals
52 West 56th Street
between 5th and 6th Avenues
New York, NY 10019
212-245-8190. Fax 212-956-5831
Monday-Friday 8:30-7 Saturday 10-4.

Bridal, wedding & formal
Midtown West

The Edge: Rents formal wear. Rents and sells formal wear, including gowns, suits, overcoats, top hats and shoes (for sale only). Rentals $85 to $145.

Betsy
744 Madison Avenue
near 64th Street
New York, NY 10021
212-734-6494. Fax 212-734-6991
Weekdays 10-6.

Bridal, wedding & formal
Upper East Side

quality style service value

The Edge: Gorgeous designer evening gowns. European-styled evening gowns and coats. Simple, but high style. From $1,500 to $10,000. Deluxe.

"Can be very snooty."

Cinderella Flower & Feather Company

Bridal, wedding & formal
Midtown West

60 West 38th Street
between 5th and 6th Avenues
New York, NY 10018
212-840-0644. Fax 212-398-6458
Weekdays 9-5:15 Saturday 9-4:15.

The Edge: Affordable Chanel-like camellias. The place for silk flowers, veils, feathers, sequins, pearls and rhinestones. Full range of bridal supplies, including headpieces to be used as the base for spectacular hairpieces. Will make custom headpieces and flowers from your own fabric. Discounter.

Diane Wagner

Bridal, wedding & formal
Upper East Side

90th Street
near Lexington Avenue
New York, NY 10128
212-663-1079
By appointment.

The Edge: Sensational one-of-a-kind bridal headpieces. Designs unique bridal headpieces, floral bouquets and accessories which are shown in *Modern Bride* and sold at Kleinfeld and Bergdorf's. Beautiful work. Prices average $250 to $350. No credit cards. No delivery. Deluxe.

Gene London's Studio

Bridal, wedding & formal
Chelsea

22 West 19th Street
between 5th and 6th Avenues
New York, NY 10011
212-929-3349
Tuesday-Saturday noon-7.

The Edge: Their month-long December sale. The styling is movie and theater dramatic. In December there's usually a month-long sale of clothing which has been acquired for and loaned to movie sets. Best for formal and bridal clothing. No delivery.

Jack and Company Formal Wear

Bridal, wedding & formal
Upper East Side

128 East 86th Street
near Park Avenue
New York, NY 10028
212-722-4609
Weekdays 10-7 (during July and August Monday Wednesday Friday 10-6) Saturday 10-4.

The Edge: Formal wear—less expensive rentals and sales. In business since 1925, they sell and rent formal wear. Rentals from $99 to $136, and if you buy you can apply the fee to the purchase price. Tuxes sell for $169 to $500. They stock a full range of sizes in middle-of-the-line tuxes in fabrics that are often blends.

Just Once Ltd.

Bridal, wedding & formal
Midtown West

292 5th Avenue, 3rd Floor
between 30th and 31st Streets
New York, NY 10001

212-465-0960. Fax 212-714-3510
Weekdays 11-6:30 Saturday 11-3 by appointment only.

The Edge: Rents quality bridal, formal gowns and headpieces. Great designer clothing to buy at $500 to $3,500 or to rent at $400 to $800. Rent headpieces from $75. Sizes from petite 2 to misses 14.

Kleinfeld and Son

8202 5th Avenue and 8209 3rd Avenue
Brooklyn, NY 11209
718-238-1500
Tuesday Thursday 11-9
Wednesday Friday Saturday 11-6 (by appointment).

Bridal, wedding & formal
Brooklyn

| 5 | 5 | 4 | 4 |
| quality | style | service | value |

The Edge: Virtually no one gets married without a pilgrimage to Kleinfeld. It has it all for the bride, her mom and her attendants. It's always a scene, packed with brides from every state. Dressing rooms are full with staff grabbing dresses and sometimes brides checking out other brides and their choices. However, it's one of the most complete sources for bridal wear and accessories in New York, perhaps the U.S. If you've seen a dress somewhere, it's likely they have it! Good prices, lower than most elsewhere. Thousands of dresses are in stock with every major supplier represented. Prices from moderate to high end. Mom has a separate store. Appointments are required. Their vans leave from the Parker Meridien at 10am and noon weekdays and 9am and 1pm Saturday (cost $10 per person, reservations required).

"Often long waits for service."

La Sposa Veils

252 West 40th Street
near 8th Avenue
New York, NY 10018
212-354-4729. Fax 212-944-9142
Weekdays 9-6 Saturday 9-5.

Bridal, wedding & formal
Midtown West

The Edge: Fantasy wedding party dresses for those young attendants. Offers their own custom veils ($125 to $1,000), fabrics, junior bridal dresses ($300 to $500) and gowns from their Just Once line. Featured in *Brides* magazine. Discounter.

Nancy Wedding Center, Inc.

118 Bowery
near Grand Street
New York, NY 10013
212-966-6686. Fax 212-219-3640
Daily 9-7.

Bridal, wedding & formal
SoHo/TriBeCa

| 4 | 3 | 3 | 4 |
| quality | style | service | value |

The Edge: Traditional Chinese wedding gowns. The source of the wedding gowns in the movie *The Wedding Banquet.* Features ornate Western wedding dresses for the bride and bridal party. Best for elaborate fancy Chinese traditional red wedding dresses. A glittery clothing emporium—fun just to visit.

One of a Kind Bride

89 5th Avenue, Suite 902
near 16th Street
New York, NY 10012
212-645-7123
By appointment.

Bridal, wedding & formal
SoHo/TriBeCa

quality style service value

The Edge: Put your own wedding look together. Tailored, sophisticated dresses. Create your own look by choosing various style alternatives, skirts, sleeves, necklines and trims. Quality dresses. Priced from $1,850 to $3,000.

Paul's Veil and Net

42 West 38th Street
between 5th and 6th Avenues
New York, NY 10018
212-391-3822. Fax 212-575-5141
Weekdays 8:30-4 Saturday 8:30-2.

Bridal, wedding & formal
Midtown West

quality style service value

The Edge: Great source of bridal veils and crowns, accessories and supplies. Priced from $50 to $500. Accessories include garters, money bags, pillows and the like. Flower accessories sold separately. No credit cards. No delivery.

"Anything you want, they'll do."

RK Bridal

2276 Broadway
near 82nd Street
New York, NY 10024
212-362-9512. Fax 212-823-7045
Monday-Wednesday Friday 10-6 Thursday 10:30-7 Saturday 10-4:30.

Bridal, wedding & formal
Upper West Side

The Edge: Seventh Avenue wedding gown source. Wedding gowns from $200 (is it possible?) to $2,000. They'll ship anywhere. Call to see what they're featuring and if they can get what you want.

Sander Witlin

27 East 61st Street
near Madison Avenue
New York, NY 10021
212-421-0869
Weekdays 10-6.

Bridal, wedding & formal
Upper East Side

quality style service value

The Edge: Custom made gala gowns. Makes gowns and day suits, but best known for its evening wear. Priced from $2,000 to $4,500. Deluxe.

Sheru Enterprises

49 West 38th Street
between 5th and 6th Avenues
New York, NY 10018
212-730-0766. Fax 212-840-2368
Weekdays 9:30-6 Saturday 10-5.

Bridal, wedding & formal
Midtown West

The Edge: Craft store featuring beads and trimmings at wholesale prices. In addition to artificial flowers, bases for hair clips and shoe clips, beads, buttons, cords, ribbons and more. Minimum telephone order is $35. Do ask for their catalog, although not everything they sell is in it.

Ted's Fine Clothing

83 Orchard Street
near Broome Street
New York, NY 10002
212-966-2029
Sunday-Friday 10-6.

Bridal, wedding & formal
Lower East Side/Chinatown

The Edge: Discounted tuxedos. Sells only tuxedos. Features Dior and San Remo as well as Nicole Miller accessories. From $300 to $600.

Vera Wang Bridal House Ltd.

991 Madison Avenue
near 77th Street
New York, NY 10021
212-628-3400
Monday-Saturday 9-6 by appointment.
No appointment needed at the Thursday open house 6-8. Deluxe.

Bridal, wedding & formal
Upper East Side

quality style service value

The Edge: Gorgeous and expensive bridal gowns. Gowns are priced from $3,000 to $7,000. Appointments necessary except on Thursday evenings when the salon hosts an open house for viewing gowns.

A. Feibush

30 Allen Street
near Canal Street
New York, NY 10002
212-226-3964
Weekdays 9-5 Sunday 9-4. Closed Sunday June-August.

Buttons, beads & trims
Lower East Side/Chinatown

The Edge: Custom zippers as needed. Zippers: all styles, colors, metals, teeth and shapes, plus matching threads. No delivery. Discounter.

A.A. Feather Company

16 West 36th Street, 8th Floor
between 5th and 6th Avenues
New York, NY 10018
212-695-9470. Fax 212-695-9471
Monday-Thursday 9-5 Friday 9-3.

Buttons, beads & trims
Midtown West

The Edge: An affordable source for Chanel-like flowers. Since 1915, fine quality feathers (all sorts), feather boas and silk flowers. The feathers are good for quilts, hats, etc. No credit cards. Discounter.

Bead Store

132 Spring Street
near Wooster Street
New York, NY 10012
212-941-6450. Fax 212-941-8082
Daily 11-7.

Buttons, beads & trims
SoHo/TriBeCa

The Edge: Large selection of beads from everywhere. The shop sells beads, jewelry-making basics, leather and silk cording. Provides workshops and classes for a fun and useful craft. Prices mostly from 10¢ to $2 per bead.

1065 Lexington Avenue
near 75th Street/10021
212-628-4383. Fax 212-941-8082
Monday-Wednesday 11-6 Thursday-Friday 11-7 Saturday 10-6.

Upper East Side

Gampel Supply

11 West 37th Street
near 5th Avenue
New York, NY 10018
212-398-9222. Fax 212-840-7810
Weekdays 8:30-4.

Buttons, beads & trims
Midtown West

The Edge: Craft jewelry and tools. Everything (tools included) to make fine and costume jewelry and related crafts. Beads and pearls sold below retail price. Wide range of sizes, colors and shapes.

Gordon Button Company

222 West 38th Street
between 7th and 8th Avenues
New York, NY 10018
212-921-1684
Weekdays 9:30-5:30.

Buttons, beads & trims
Midtown West

The Edge: High-fashion quality buttons at Seventh Avenue prices. Large button wholesaler since 1925. Offers styles featured in the current season's designer clothing. You won't find Tender Buttons' wonderful antique collection of buttons, but you'll find everything else at great prices. No credit cards. No delivery. Discounter.

M&J Trimming

1008 Avenue of the Americas
near 37th Street
New York, NY 10018
212-391-6200. Fax 212-764-5854
Weekdays 9-6 Saturday 10-5.

Buttons, beads & trims
Midtown West

The Edge: Loved for their selection of fabric trimmings, tassels and buttons. Great source for dressmaking accessories. Find buttons, flowers, feathers, tassels, threads, trims and more. Hundreds of items on display. Mail order requires a $50 minimum. Discounter.

"Great selection." Great tassels and trims." "Good buttons."

So-Good

28 West 38th Street
between 5th and 6th Avenues
New York, NY 10018
212-398-0236. Fax 212-764-1325
Weekdays 9-5.

Buttons, beads & trims
Midtown West

quality style service value

The Edge: The wholesale source for wondrous ribbons and trimmings. A store filled with beautiful patterned ribbons, roses (very small button size) and trimmings. The sign says $10 minimum order, and we've never been tempted to buy less. Ribbon prices range from 25¢ to $5 a yard. No credit cards. Discounter.

Tender Buttons

143 East 62nd Street
between Lexington and 3rd Avenues
New York, NY 10021
212-758-7004
Weekdays 11-6 Saturday 11-5:30.

Buttons, beads & trims
Upper East Side

| 5 | 5 | 4 | 4 |
quality style service value

The Edge: Universally loved, everyone's favorite button source. A small store chock full of great, top-quality (new and antique) button treasures and cufflinks. A terrific way to update an old outfit, repair a cleaner's mistakes and provide oomph for clothing. From moderate prices into the hundreds and thousands of dollars for antique cufflinks. No credit cards. No delivery.

"One-of-a kind." "Expensive, but it's still fabulous." "Unique, wonderful resource."

Abracadabra

10 Christoper Street
near 6th Avenue
New York, NY 10014
212-627-5745. Fax 212-627-5876
Monday-Saturday 11-7 Sunday noon-5.

Costumes
Greenwich Village

The Edge: Great costume rentals. One of the largest selections of costumes in the city. Also makeup, masks, props, wigs and supplies for magicians.

Allan Uniform Rental Service

121 East 24th Street
between Lexington and Park Avenues
New York, NY 10010
212-529-4655. Fax 212-505-7781
Monday-Friday 9-5.

Costumes
Gramercy Pk/Murray Hill

The Edge: Costume rentals. Period, animal and masquerade costumes for rent in adult sizes.

Gordon Novelty Company

933 Broadway
between 21st and 22nd Streets
New York, NY 10010
212-254-8616
Weekdays 9-4:30.

Costumes
Gramercy Pk/Murray Hill

The Edge: Wonderful costumes. 65-year-old company that features a vast selection of costumes and accessories. Mostly adult sizes. Some shoes, primarily clown and monster feet. Seasonal themes and decorations. Costumes priced at $35 and up. No credit cards. No delivery.

"It's a great way to make the fun start early."

Alan Flusser at Saks

611 5th Avenue
near 49th Street, in Saks
New York, NY 10022
212-888-7100. Fax 212-940-4699
Monday-Wednesday Friday Saturday 10-6:30
Thursday 10-8.

Custom
Midtown East

4	5	4	4
quality	style	service	value

The Edge: Glamorous suits. Designed Michael Douglas' suits in the movie *Wall Street*. Upscale, investment banker look. Their custom line is now sold at Saks on its 6th floor. Suits from $1,600. Deluxe.

Alexander Kabbaz

903 Madison Avenue
between 72nd and 73rd Streets
New York, NY 10021
212-861-7700
Weekdays 7-7 Saturday 10-6.

Custom
Upper East Side

The Edge: Exceptionally fine custom-made shirts and suits. Wide range of fabrics and good tailoring. Very expensive, with shirts from $350 and suits from $2,850. Deluxe.

Arthur Gluck

37 West 57th Street
between 5th and 6th Avenues
New York, NY 10019
212-755-8165
Saturday-Thursday 9-5 Friday 9-2.

Custom
Midtown West

The Edge: Top-quality custom men's shirts. Wide choice of fine fabrics. Shirts are $200 each with a minimum order of six. Orders take two months. No credit cards. No delivery. Deluxe.

Ascot Chang

7 West 57th Street
between 5th and 6th Avenues
New York, NY 10019
212-759-3333. Fax 212-644-5071

Custom
Midtown West

5	4	4	4
quality	style	service	value

Monday-Saturday 9:30-6.

The Edge: Fine custom shirts and suits. Hong Kong shirt maker offers ready-made and custom shirts and Italian made-to-measure suits. 2,000 fabrics and 12 different collar styles to choose from. Also silk pajamas, dressing gowns and accessories. Very expensive. Deluxe.

"I wait for their Hong Kong visits."

Brioni

55 East 52nd Street	**Custom**
between Park and Madison Avenues	**Midtown East**
New York, NY 10022	
212-355-1940. Fax 212-754-2056	
Monday-Saturday 9-6.	

The Edge: Impeccable tailoring. Traditionally styled custom suits. Extensive selection of all the best fabrics (cashmeres, silks and wools) to choose from. Priced from $2,700. Deluxe.

Cheo Tailors

30 East 60th Street	**Custom**
between Madison and Park Avenues	**Midtown East**
New York, NY 10022	
212-980-9838	
Weekdays 10-6 Saturday 11-3 by appointment.	

The Edge: Quality London-trained tailor. Exquisite custom suits made exclusively from European wools. Suits take two to three months to make. No delivery. Deluxe.

Chris-Arto Custom Shirt Company

39 West 32nd Street, 6th Floor	**Custom**
between 5th Avenue and Broadway	**Midtown West**
New York, NY 10001	
212-563-4455. Fax 212-563-4457	
Weekdays 7:30-4:30.	

The Edge: Luxurious custom shirts. Shirts are well fitted and made from a choice of hundreds of quality fabrics. Multiple fittings. A minimum of five shirts required for the first order. Prices are $165 to $175 per shirt. Also custom-made pajamas. Telephone orders for established customers only. No credit cards. No delivery. Deluxe.

Gilberto Designs

142 West 36th Street, 8th Floor	**Custom**
between 7th Avenue and Broadway	**Midtown West**
New York, NY 10018	
212-698-4925. Fax 212-563-0524	
Weekdays 9-4 Saturday 9:30-3. Closed Saturday in July and August.	

The Edge: Knockoffs for men. Custom suits, jackets, tuxes and overcoats. Can knock off any jacket. They manufacture their own line in fine Italian and English fabrics with suits priced from

$800 to $2,500, shirts from $75 (minimum order 4) and ties from $60. All work is done on site. Allow three weeks for a suit.

H. Herzfeld

507 Madison Avenue
near 52nd Street
New York, NY 10022
212-753-6756
Weekdays 9-6 Saturday 9-5:30.

Custom
Midtown East

The Edge: Fine custom shirts. Conservative English- styled clothes. Known for their shirts, sweaters and ties, but suits and slacks also.

House of Maurizio

18 East 53rd Street
between Madison and 5th Avenues
New York, NY 10022
212-759-3230
Weekdays 8:30-5 by appointment.

Custom
Midtown East

The Edge: One of the top-of-the-line custom tailors. For 34 years, exquisite custom suits starting at $3,000, as well as blazers and coats. Thousands of fabrics from England and Italy. Custom shirts from $195 and custom ties from $75. Suits take four to five weeks. No credit cards. Deluxe.

Ilana Designs

150 East 69th Street
between Lexington and 3rd Avenues
New York, NY 10021
212-570-9420
By appointment—leave message on machine anytime.

Custom
Upper East Side

The Edge: Copies of the great designs. Located in the Imperial House (ask the doorman). Does alterations and makes custom suits and dresses to order. Can copy top European and American designers (Armani, Lacroix, Tiel). Will work on any fabrics. Excluding fabric, women's jackets priced from $650, skirts from $250 and suits from $900. No credit cards. No delivery.

Leonard Logsdail

510 Madison Avenue, Suite 200
near 53rd Street
New York, NY 10022
212-752-5030. Fax 212-752-4928
Weekdays 9-5.

Custom
Midtown East

The Edge: Quality English wool custom suits at $2,200+. Great tailoring. Allow eight weeks for an order. No credit cards. Deluxe.

Mandana

1175 Lexington Avenue
near 80th Street
New York, NY 10028

Custom
Upper East Side

4	4	4	3
quality	style	service	value

212-988-0800
Weekdays 9-6 Saturday 9-4.

The Edge: Good copies of top designer clothing. Offers alterations and copies of top designer clothing such as Valentino evening dresses and Armani suits. Workmanship looks good. Allow two weeks to complete a suit. Very expensive, suits from $1,200. No delivery. Deluxe.

Mr. Ned
85 5th Avenue
near 16th Street
New York, NY 10011
212-924-5042. Fax 212-654-1250
Weekdays 8-6 Saturday 8-4.

Custom
Chelsea

4 | 4 | 4 | 4
quality style service value

The Edge: Semi-custom suits priced well. Features suits from $525 to $750 in a wide range of fabrics including wools and cashmere from all the top European houses.

"Fabrics are great, good style, but tailoring can be uneven."

One-of-a-Kind
767 Lexington Avenue
near 60th Street
New York, NY 10021
212-371-4842
Weekdays 9-5.

Custom
Upper East Side

The Edge: Elegant designer clothing copied well. Since 1971, originals and copies of designer lines, Armani and Chanel especially. Suits from $1,000, depending on fabric. Featured in *New York Magazine* in 1991 as one of the best. House calls for $75 per hour. No credit cards. No delivery. Deluxe.

Uma Reddy Ltd.
30 West 57th Street, Room 6E
between 5th and 6th Avenues
New York, NY 10019
212-757-7240
Weekdays 9:30-5:30 by appointment only.

Custom
Midtown West

The Edge: Another top tailor. Mostly English wool and Italian silk suits with extra fabric kept on hand for alterations. Suits take four to six weeks. Priced from $2,600. Also custom ties ($75+) and shirts ($165+). Prices depend on materials. No credit cards. Deluxe.

William Fioravanti
45 West 57th Street
between 5th and 6th Avenues
New York, NY 10019
212-355-1540
Weekdays 9-5 by appointment.

Custom
Midtown West

The Edge: Quality custom, all hand-worked, suits and coats. Uses only fabrics imported from England and Italy. They're so booked up that new customers need a referral for an appointment. Suits take 10 to 12 weeks. Very expensive. No credit cards. No delivery. Deluxe.

Winston-Tailors

Custom
Midtown East

11 East 44th Street
between Madison and 5th Avenues
New York, NY 10017
212-687-0850
Weekdays 9-5:30 Saturday 10-3. Closed Saturday June-August.

The Edge: The Chip II line. Conservative made-to-measure two- and three-button American-style suits, sports jackets and coats. Custom tailoring for women. Fabrics most often are imported English wools. Private label manufacturer at the same address and telephone number as Chip II. Suits average $875, priced from $750 to $1,200. New to us—let us know what you think.

Barney's New York

Department stores
Chelsea

106 7th Avenue
near 17th Street
New York, NY 10011
212-593-7800
Monday-Thursday 10-9 Friday 10-8 Saturday 10-7
Sunday noon-6.

5	5	4	3
quality	style	service	value

The Edge: The best of everything, priced accordingly. Go to Bergdorf's and Barney's for large selection and some of the best cutting-edge looks in the city. A large selection of top designer and designed-for-Barney's clothing from casual to formal wear. Styles from traditional to the cutting-edge they're known for. Chelsea Passage has items for the home. Jewelry from costume to real. The focus in the downtown store is on men; uptown both men and women. How will their recent bankruptcy impact this fashion-forward top retailer? Deluxe.

"In Barney's Private Label, ask for Robin. Best clothes for the dollar." "Love this place, but size for larger persons can be a problem." "Best values are found at the warehouse sale. Best for men." "Dazzling home accessories, great jewelry."

660 Madison Avenue
at 61st Street/ 10021
212-826-8900
Monday-Friday 10-8 Saturday 10-7 Sunday noon-6.

Upper East Side

Two World Financial Center
at 225 Liberty Street/100281
212-945-1600
Monday-Friday 9-7 Saturday 11-5 Sunday noon-5.

Lower Manhattan

Bergdorf Goodman

Department stores
Midtown West

754 5th Avenue
between 57th and 58th Streets
New York, NY 10019
212-753-7300
Monday-Wednesday Friday Saturday 10-6 Thursday 10-8.

5	5	4	4
quality	style	service	value

The Edge: Designer fashion for women. Features a full range of women's designer fashion from conservative to more high fashion. Top prices, but check the sales—they're fantastic. All the great names have boutiques in the store. Wonderful accessories, including costume and quality day jewelry. Home accessories are wonderful and include an outlet of Kentshire for a traditional English look. Less cutting-edge than Barney's. Real clothes for real ladies. Coming soon—Susan Ciminelli's spa. Deluxe.

"Sales can be unbelievable."

Bergdorf Goodman Men's Store

754 5th Avenue
between 57th and 58th Streets
New York, NY 10019
212-753-7300
Monday-Wednesday Friday Saturday 10-6 Thursday 10-8.

Department stores
Midtown West

| 5 | 5 | 5 | 3 |
quality style service value

The Edge: Wide range of quality designer fashions for men. 45,000 square-foot store and getting bigger. Features a full range of men's designer fashion from conservative to more high fashion. Top prices, but check the sales. Find a combination of traditional and high-fashion menswear. All the great names. To Boot is their shoe concession. Deluxe.

"Sales can be unbelievable." "Who would have thought that men would fight over buys?"

Bloomingdale's

1000 3rd Avenue
near 59th Street
New York, NY 10022
212-705-2000
Weekdays 10-8:30 Saturday 10-7 Sunday 11-7.

Department stores
Midtown East

| 4 | 4 | 4 | 4 |
quality style service value

The Edge: It has it all. What Bloomies has is range—from clothing to furniture and virtually anything in between. Especially good for young designers. Seems to be coming back!

"My favorite—you can find anything. Particularly good for moms who shop with their teenage daughters."

Century 21

22 Cortlandt Street
between Broadway and Church Street
New York, NY 10007
212-227-9092. Fax 212-374-1123
Monday-Wednesday 7:45-7 Thursday 7:45-8:30
Friday 7:45-8 Saturday 10-7.

Department stores
Lower Manhattan

| 4 | 4 | 2 | 4 |
quality style service value

The Edge: Replaces the old Alexanders in its best days. Full-range discount department store for the entire family. Features clothing with a contemporary look as well as small appliances, shoes and cosmetics. Range from the basics to top European designs with focus on moderately priced items. Best for children's clothing and shoes. No try-ons. Many irregulars, so pay attention to your purchase. No delivery. 40% off.

"Annoying atmosphere, but great deals." "Be careful—sometimes a find, must go often." "Not the place it was when it was a hole in the wall." "Men's department more outstanding than the women's."

Henri Bendel

712 5th Avenue
near 56th Street
New York, NY 10019
212-247-1100. Fax 212-397-8519
Monday-Wednesday Friday Saturday 10-7
Thursday 10-8 Sunday noon-6.

Department stores
Midtown West

quality	style	service	value
4	4	3	3

The Edge: Not the old Bendel's but still good. Not the Bendel's we loved that had cutting-edge, understated chic. This small store is a full women's department store featuring cosmetics, hair accessories, leggings, casual to evening clothing by new designers and top-flight known talent. The Young Creators shop is where you'll find some cutting-edge new talent while Bendel's Fancy has established designers. The tableware shop still has lovely modern things you remember. Visit the Salon de Thè to rest after shopping with a tea or cappuccino.

Lord & Taylor

424 5th Avenue
near 39th Street
New York, NY 10018
212-391-3344. Fax 212-391-3494
Monday-Tuesday 10-7 Wednesday-Friday 10-8:30
Saturday 9-7 Sunday 11-6.

Department stores
Midtown West

quality	style	service	value
4	4	4	5

The Edge: Focus on classic American clothing, particularly good for dresses. Features some of the top designers, including Anne Klein, Calvin Klein, Oscar de La Renta and Ralph Lauren. Has menswear and a well-stocked children's department. Classic, not necessarily cutting-edge and less expensive than Bergdorf's, Barney's and Henri Bendel. Particularly well-stocked swimsuit department in season.

"The only store I trust to find exactly what I need. Sometimes they have great sales with coupons in the paper—excellent."

Macy's

Broadway at Herald Square
at 34th Street
New York, NY 10001
212-695-4400
Monday Thursday Friday 10-8:30 Tuesday Wednesday
Saturday 10-7 Sunday 11-6.

Department stores
Midtown West

quality	style	service	value
4	4	3	5

The Edge: Huge department store with broad selection. Everything for everyone plus a full range of housewares with kitchenware, appliances and tableware particularly strong. One of the best sources for a wide range of teenagers' clothing. Mid-price focus.

"Whenever Bloomies failed my teen daughter, Macy's came through—especially for shoes and boots."

Saks Fifth Avenue

611 5th Avenue
between 49th and 50th Streets
New York, NY 10022
212-753-4000. Fax 914-337-5900
Monday-Wednesday Friday Saturday 10-6:30 Thursday 10-8 Sunday noon-6.

Department stores
Midtown East

quality style service value

The Edge: Terrific New York chic—the place to shop now. Somewhat more affordable than Barney's and Bergdorf's and featuring a very good New York style. Has it all for children, women and men—from cosmetics and jewels and day wear to formal wear. Good designs and wide style range tending to a more tailored look. With wonderful sales really early in the season. Check the Saks First program, which offers discounts when you reach prearranged (high) spending levels.

"A great place."

Takashimaya

693 5th Avenue
near 54th Street
New York, NY 10022
212-350-0100. Fax 212-350-0192
Monday-Wednesday Friday Saturday 10-6 Thursday 10-8.

Department stores
Midtown East

quality style service value

The Edge: Marvelous taste. American flagship store of this 162-year-old Japanese company. First two floors feature an art gallery and flowers. On the third and fourth floors find Japanese items including stationery, clothing, furniture and accessories. They have wonderful things with simple lines, top fabrics and quality. The top floor looks like a duty-free shop, selling high-end European goods to Japanese tourists. There's a Japanese cafe and tea salon downstairs. Deluxe.

"What an oasis—like a vacation."

Gruen Optika

599 Lexington Avenue
near 52nd Street
New York, NY 10022
212-688-3580. Fax 212-628-2794
Weekdays 9:30-7 Saturday 10-6 Sunday noon-6.
Closed Saturday July and August.

Eyeglasses
Midtown East

quality style service value

The Edge: High-fashion designer glasses. Chic but conservative styling. Selection includes Armani, Donna Karan and Gaultier. Priced from $100 to $1,000+.

740 Madison Avenue
near 64th Street/10021
212-988-5832
Weekdays 9:30-7 Saturday 10-6 Sunday noon-5. Closed Sunday July and August.

Upper East Side

1076 3rd Avenue
near 63rd Street/10021
212-751-6177
Weekdays 9:30-7 Saturday 10-6 Sunday noon-5. Closed Sunday July and August.

Upper East Side

2382 Broadway   **Upper West Side**
near 87th Street/10024
212-724-0850
Weekdays 9:30-7 Saturday 10-6 Sunday noon-5. Closed Sunday July and August.

1255 Lexington Avenue   **Upper East Side**
near 82nd Street/10028
212-628-2493
Weekdays 9:30-7 Saturday 10-6 Sunday noon-5. Closed Sunday July and August.

A&N Fabrics

Fabric
Midtown West

268 West 39th Street
between 7th and 8th Avenues
New York, NY 10018
212-719-1773
Weekdays 9-5:45 Saturday 9-5.

The Edge: Clothing and decorating fabrics discounted about 15%. Features more moderate lines, but has a wide selection of fabric types and colors. Offers decorating services and will make drapes, tablecloths, bedclothes, etc.

Art Max Fabrics

Fabric
Midtown West

250 West 40th Street
near 8th Avenue
New York, NY 10018
212-398-0755. Fax 212-768-3927
Weekdays 8:45-5:45 Saturday 9-5.

5 5 5 5
quality style service value

The Edge: Couture fabrics. Every couture fabric you can imagine from men's suiting to women's dress needs, including beaded and jeweled chiffons, brocades, cut velvets, metallics and silks. A large selection of fabrics for weddings (including laces, satins, Swiss embroideries and taffetas, along with dozens of netting and tulles for veils). Priced from $5 to $150 per yard. Volunteered 10% off to our researcher (without any prompting), so price appears negotiable. Discounter.

B&J Fabrics

Fabric
Midtown West

263 West 40th Street
between 7th and 8th Avenues
New York, NY 10018
212-354-8150. Fax 212-764-3355
Weekdays 8-5:45 Saturday 9-4:45.

5 5 4 5
quality style service value

The Edge: Three floors of fine, mostly European ladies' fashion fabrics. Three floors of European silks, brocades and natural fibers. Mostly dressy fabrics. Bargain fabrics are on the third floor. Priced from $200 to $300 per yard. Discounter.

Beckenstein's Men's Fabrics

Fabric
Lower East Side/Chinatown

121 Orchard Street
near Delancey Street
New York, NY 10002
212-475-6666. Fax 212-473-1718

4 4 4 4
quality style service value

Sunday-Friday 9-5:30.

The Edge: You can't find a more complete source for men's suit fabric. Find higher fashion, better lines, quality fabrics at a small discount. Discounter.

Felsen Fabrics
264 West 40th Street
between 7th and 8th Avenues
New York, NY 10018
212-398-9010. Fax 212-840-2268
Weekdays 8:30-5:45 Saturday 9-4:45.

Fabric
Midtown West

The Edge: Bridal fabrics. Primarily fabrics for bridal wear. Will send swatches and they accept telephone and fax orders. Discounter.

Kordol Fabrics
194 Orchard Street
near Houston Street
New York, NY 10002
212-254-8319. Fax 212-254-8333
Sunday-Friday 8-5.

Fabric
Lower East Side/Chinatown

The Edge: Wide selection of suit fabrics for men and women. Good prices on linens, silks and cottons. Discounter.

Paron Fabrics
206 West 40th Street
near 7th Avenue
New York, NY 10018
212-768-3266. Fax 212-768-3260
Monday-Saturday 9-5.

Fabric
Midtown West

quality style service value

The Edge: Designer fabrics. The main store on 57th Street sells a good variety of linens, wools, imported silk and other clothing fabrics. The clearance center on the second floor of 57th Street sells fabrics at 50% off. Paron West on West 40th Street specializes in designer and big-name fabrics.

"The place to go for fabric hounds. 50% discount only on selected fabrics."

56 West 57th Street
near 6th Avenue/10019
212-247-6451

Midtown West

Poli Fabrics
227 West 40th Street
between 7th and 8th Avenues
New York, NY 10018
212-245-7589. Fax 212-768-7118
Weekdays 8:30-5:45 Saturday 9-4:45.

Fabric
Midtown West

5 5 5 5

quality style service value

The Edge: European and American designer fabrics. They say they sell high-fashion fabrics at close to wholesale prices. Discounter.

Rosen & Chadick

246 West 40th Street
between 7th and 8th Avenues
New York, NY 10018
212-869-0136. Fax 212-730-5865
Weekdays 8-5:45 Saturday 9-5.

Fabric
Midtown West

The Edge: Designer evening and bridal fabrics. Specializes in European silks, beaded lace plus a wide range of quality designer fabrics. Moderate to very expensive. They'll discount their prices further for large bulk orders.

Saint Remy

818 Lexington Avenue
near 62nd Street
New York, NY 10021
212-486-2018. Fax 212-759-8240
Weekdays 10-7 Saturday 10:30-6.

Fabric
Upper East Side

4	4	4	-
quality	style	service	value

The Edge: Fabrics and porcelain from Provence. Expect to find tiny floral potpourri, printed cottons, sachets, scented drawer liners, wreaths and wonderful hand-painted French country pottery.

"Like a trip to Provence."

Weller Fabrics, Inc.

24 West 57th Street
between 5th and 6th Avenues
New York, NY 10019
212-247-3790. Fax 212-247-8147
Weekdays 9-6:30 Saturday 9-6.

Fabric
Midtown West

The Edge: Upscale European fabrics. An excellent source for ladies' designer fabrics. Full price and fine quality.

William N. Ginsburg Company

242 West 38th Street
between 7th and 8th Avenues
New York, NY 10018
212-244-4539
Weekdays 9-5.

Fabric
Midtown West

The Edge: Custom trims. A minimum of 36 yards is required for retail orders. Features unusual tassels, braids, fringes, gimps and rope trims. Owner will create custom braids, cords and ropes to match a fabric. Discounter.

Alixandre

150 West 30th Street, 13th Floor
near 7th Avenue
New York, NY 10001
212-736-5550
By appointment weekdays 9-5 Saturday 9-2.

Furriers
Midtown West

quality style service value

The Edge: Fabulous classic furs designed by Oscar de la Renta, Valentino and Yeohlee. Top-quality furs from the softest shearlings to sable. Styling is divine. Check their furs, which are often featured in the Sunday *Times* magazine section and written up in *W*. Appointments are required—ask for Brad or Larry Schulman, sons of the Senior Schulmans, Edwin and Stanley. Line is sold at Bergdorf and Neiman Marcus, among other places. Discounter. Deluxe.

"Listen to Edwin—his recommendations on coloring and styling are always right." "Good for the money."

Ben Kahn Salon

150 West 30th Street, 18th Floor
near 7th Avenue
New York, NY 10001
212-279-0633
By appointment weekdays 9-5 Saturday 9-2.

Furriers
Midtown West

quality style service value

The Edge: Gorgeous furs. Designers include Nicolas Petrou and Michael Lund, Byron Lars. Find Ben Kahn at Neiman Marcus. Top-quality furs from shearling to sable. Priced from $2,000 to $40,000. Discounter. Deluxe.

"Very expensive, gorgeous furs."

Birger Christensen

150 West 30th Street
near 7th Avenue
New York, NY 10001
212-947-7910
By appointment.

Furriers
Midtown West

The Edge: Another Seventh Avenue fur source. Danish and Swedish furrier. B. Christensen is their exclusive designer. Stores and remodels furs. Will take trade-ins. No credit cards. Discounter. Deluxe.

Christie Bros.

333 7th Avenue, 11th Floor
near 28th Street
New York, NY 10001
212-736-6944
Weekdays 9-5. Also by appointment.

Furriers
Midtown West

quality style service value

The Edge: Traditional styling, quality furs. Features mostly classic but also contemporary styled furs from minks to sables. Discounter. Deluxe.

Goldin Feldman

345 7th Avenue
near 29th Street
New York, NY 10001
212-594-4415
Weekdays 9-5 Saturday 9-1.

Furriers
Midtown West

5	5	5	4
quality	style	service	value

The Edge: Fine furs. Since 1909. Classic designs. Features a full range of furs from wild mink, Canadian fisher, Russian sable and much more. Buy off-the-rack or order a custom-made fur. Discounter. Deluxe.

"Best value." "Chic styling."

Michael Forrest

345 7th Avenue
near 29th Street
New York, NY 10001
212-564-4726
Weekdays 9-5.

Furriers
Midtown West

4	4	4	5
quality	style	service	value

The Edge: Seventh Avenue furrier. Another choice for wholesale furs. Anne Klein had been the designer, but not now. Now features their own in-house designers. Discounter. Deluxe.

Mohl Furs

345 7th Avenue
near 29th Street
New York, NY 10001
212-736-7676. Fax 212-629-4832
By appointment weekdays 9-5.

Furriers
Midtown West

The Edge: Arnold Scaasi-designed furs. Full line of furs: mink, sable and others. Discounter. Deluxe.

Ritz Thrift Shop

107 West 57th Street
near 6th Avenue
New York, NY 10019
212-265-4559
Monday-Saturday 9-6. Closed Saturday in July.

Furriers
Midtown West

The Edge: Selling used furs for over 50 years. Full range of furs, including shearlings, mink, sable, fox and beaver. However, the stock can show its real age and look used and dated.

Trendsetters

150 West 30th Street, 11th Floor
near 7th Avenue
New York, NY 10001
212-244-0773
Weekdays 9:30-5 Saturday 10-2.

Furriers
Midtown West

The Edge: Clearance center for designer fur selections. Name changed from New York Fur Manufacturers Clearance Center. Carries excess stock, when available, from all the designers. It's new to us and not known to our survey respondents, but included because "opportunity" could present itself for a top name fur at a great price. Let us know. No delivery. Discounter.

Georgia Hughes Designs
45 East 89th Street
entrance on Madison Avenue
New York, NY 10128
212-996-5183
By appointment.

Hats
Upper East Side

The Edge: Truly unique fashion-forward hats. Features one-of-a-kind handmade and silk lined hats. Hats from $200 to $265; fur-lined or trimmed hats from $200 to $700. Annual sale in January.

Lola Ehrlich Millinery
2 East 17th Street
near 5th Avenue
New York, NY 10003
212-366-5708
Monday-Saturday 11-7.

Hats
Flatiron/East Village

quality style service value

The Edge: Dazzling hats. One-of-a-kind creations in a variety of colors, shapes and textures. Expensive. Deluxe.

Manny's Millinery Supply Company
26 West 38th Street
near 5th Avenue
New York, NY 10018
212-840-2235. Fax 212-944-0178
Weekdays 9-5:30 Saturday 9-3:30.

Hats
Midtown West

quality style service value

The Edge: The source in the "hat district" for millinery supplies and finished hats. Carries millinery supplies, including decorations like silk flowers, beads and feathers, as well as finished hats. Hats are very reasonable—add oomph by adding the various decorations they sell. The silk flowers are also a wonderful add-on to suits. Discounter.

"No. 1 in New York!!"

Vander Linde Designs
111 East 56th Street, 2nd Floor
in the Lombardy Hotel
New York, NY 10022
212-758-1686. Fax 212-758-1686
Weekdays 10-5 Saturday by appointment.

Hats
Midtown East

The Edge: Matched hat and suit ensembles in quality fabrics. For 45 years. Custom-made hats for all seasons. Hats stand alone or as part of a suit ensemble. No credit cards. Deluxe.

Worth & Worth

331 Madison Avenue
near 43rd Street
New York, NY 10017
212-867-6058. Fax 212-867-5693
Weekdays 9-6 Saturday 10-5.

Hats
Midtown East

5	5	5	4
quality	style	service	value

The Edge: Well-stocked men's hat store. Oldest hat shop in New York. Features a wide selection of fur, felt and straw fedoras, cowboy hats and caps, as well as ties, leather gloves and belts. You'll find their own line of hats plus the Stetson and Christys of London brands.

"Nice hattery. Women should shop here—their men's hats look great on women."

A La Vieille Russie

781 5th Avenue
near 59th Street
New York, NY 10022
212-752-1727
Weekdays 10-6 weekends 11-4.

Jewelry & watches
Midtown East

5	4	5	3
quality	style	service	value

The Edge: Breathtaking jewels. Museum-quality furniture. Features fabulous objets d'art, including those by Peter Carl Fabergé, 18th- and 19th-century European jewelry, silver snuff boxes, etc. On the second floor museum quality 18th-century French and Russian furniture, paintings, porcelains and candelabra. Deluxe.

"Wish I could shop here more." "Expensive, but great stuff."

Aaron Faber Gallery

666 5th Avenue
near 53rd Street
New York, NY 10019
212-586-8411. Fax 212-582-0205
Monday-Wednesday Friday 10-6 Thursday 10-7 Saturday 11- 6.

Jewelry & watches
Midtown West

4	4	3	2
quality	style	service	value

The Edge: Interesting and different jewelry, particularly their vintage watches. Find estate and art deco jewelry along with collectible watches and sterling-silver contemporary items.

"Prices are high but their reputation is good." "Beautiful antique watches and jewelry but extra-high prices."

Asprey Limited

725 5th Avenue
Trump Tower at 56th Street
New York, NY 10022
212-688-1811. Fax 212-826-3746
Monday-Saturday 10-5:30
Closed Saturday July and August.

Jewelry & watches
Midtown East

5	4	5	3
quality	style	service	value

The Edge: On the Queen's list of "Palace" sources. New York outpost of a British institution. Features home accessories, antique and modern silver pieces and clocks, antique jewels and fabulous South Sea pearl necklaces. A good source for gift items. On the lower levels, luggage and brief cases. Deluxe.

Balogh Jewelers
798 Madison Avenue
near 67th Street
New York, NY 10021
212-517-9440
Monday-Saturday 10-6. Closed Saturday July and August.

Jewelry & watches
Upper East Side

quality style service value
3   3   4   3

The Edge: Fabulous baubles. Since 1910. Unique, expensive jewels from $1,000 to $1 million+. Most jewelry includes precious stones (diamonds, rubies, etc.) and has a contemporary look. Some estate jewelry. Deluxe.

Boris Le Beau Jewelers
721 Madison Avenue
near 63rd Street
New York, NY 10021
212-752-4186
Monday-Friday 10-5:30 Saturday noon-5.

Jewelry & watches
Upper East Side

quality style service value
3   2   3   2

The Edge: Modern styling. Expensive 18-karat jewelry most of which features semiprecious and precious stones. Lots with large South Sea pearls. Prices from $200 and up, mostly in the thousands of dollars.

Buccellati
46 East 57th Street
near 5th Avenue
New York, NY 10022
212-308-5533
Monday-Saturday 10-6.
Closed Saturday June-August.

Jewelry & watches
Midtown East

quality style service value
5   5   5   4

The Edge: Simply gorgeous Florentine styling. Buccellati's golden weave designs are treasures. Some jewelry includes precious stones—emeralds, rubies, sapphires. For the home, antique and new Florentine silver, including hand-hammered sterling-silver candlesticks, trays, tureens and tea and coffee services. Also silver plate centerpieces and flatware. Deluxe.

"Truly beautiful."

Bulgari
730 5th Avenue
near 57th Street
New York, NY 10019
212-315-9000. Fax 212-758-9789
Monday-Saturday 10-6:30.

Jewelry & watches
Midtown West

quality style service value
5   5   5   4

The Edge: Statement baubles. Large-scale jewels in unusual color and stone combinations. Cufflinks for men of semiprecious stones in the shape of animals. Also table-top items. Great presents. Deluxe.

"Pricey."

Camilla Dietz Bergeron
New York, NY 10021
212-794-9100 Fax 212-794-7012
Weekdays 9-5 by appointment.

Jewelry & watches
Upper East Side

| 5 | 5 | 5 | 4 |

quality style service value

The Edge: Perfect taste, exquisite selection and good prices. There's life after Wall Street. Camilla, a principal with Furman, Selz, Dietz, etc., left Wall Street, turning her avocation into a profession. Camilla and partner Gus Davis offer antique and estate jewelry from rings to tiaras (at times). Day and evening jewelry, gold, pearls and stones Wide price range: many earrings for less than $1,000 with other jewelry over $1,000 and evening jewelry higher. Featured in *Vogue* for her antique cufflinks and often in *W*. Call for an invitation to see the collection. No credit cards. Deluxe.

"Wonderful jewelry and wonderful taste!"

Carlos Colonna
400 Madison Avenue, Suite 706
near 47th Street
New York, NY 10017
212-838-7980
Weekdays 9-6.

Jewelry & watches
Midtown East

The Edge: Engraving silver jewelry. Designer and engraver of silver and gold jewelry. No credit cards.

Cartier
653 5th Avenue
near 52nd Street
New York, NY 10022
212-753-0111
Monday-Saturday 10-5:30
Closed Saturday July and August.

Jewelry & watches
Midtown East

| 5 | 5 | 5 | 4 |

quality style service value

The Edge: Those little red boxes. Les Must de Cartier has made the place more democratic. While there are still unique gems, much of the store is more affordable. On the first floor you'll find diamonds and other precious stones and gold combinations in unique settings, plus the famous Tank watch. On the second floor, find gift items, briefcases, sterling-silver tableware, scarves, handbags and leather goods and, of course, classic stationery and invitations.

"That red box really makes the gift!!" "Really a wonderful source for wedding gifts, if you're paying full retail."

725 5th Avenue
Trump Tower at 56th Street/10022
212-308-0840

Midtown East

Chopard
725 Madison Avenue

Jewelry & watches
Upper East Side

between 63rd and 64th Streets
New York, NY 10021
212-247-3300. Fax 212-247-7445
Monday-Saturday 10-5:30.

The Edge: Another fine jewelry store. Outpost of a Vienna store, featuring watches and jewelry.

Christopher Walling

608 5th Avenue
near 50th Street
New York, NY 10020
212-581-7700
By appointment weekdays 10-5.

Jewelry & watches
Midtown West

quality style service value

The Edge: Breathtaking one-of-a-kind jewels. Very expensive jewelry. Large settings featuring gold and precious stones (diamonds, diamond-cut pink sapphires and rubies) priced from $900 to many thousands of dollars, but mostly in the low to mid double digits. For example a beautiful pair of statement earrings in South Sea pearls and precious stones at $42,000. Walling loves working with large South Sea pearls. Ask for Allan to get in. Deluxe.

"You either love it or think the styling is too glitzy." "Very expensive."

David Webb

445 Park Avenue
near 57th Street
New York, NY 10022
212-421-3030
Weekdays 10-5:30 Saturday 10-5.

Jewelry & watches
Midtown East

5 5 5 4
quality style service value

The Edge: Statement jewels to be shown off. Favors large-scale jewelry and semiprecious stones often in unusual combinations. Opulent and expensive. Deluxe.

Demner

740 Madison Avenue
near 64th Street
New York, NY 10021
212-794-3786. Fax 212-794-3923
Monday-Saturday 10:45-5:30. Closed Saturday in August.

Jewelry & watches
Upper East Side

5 5 4 3
quality style service value

The Edge: Elegant jewels. Favors contemporary evening jewelry, some of which is made for them in Italy. An elegant collection of diamond necklaces and other jewels with large precious and semiprecious stones. Also some day jewelry. Deluxe.

"Great stuff! Expensive." "Can negotiate price."

Dyckman's

73 West 47th Street
between 5th and 6th Avenues
New York, NY 10036
212-819-0355

Jewelry & watches
Midtown West

4 2 3 5
quality style service value

Monday-Thursday 9-5 Friday 9-2.

The Edge: Been selling diamonds forever—reliable and honest. Open since 1928, a reliable source for diamonds and some precious stones. Typical 47th Street styling, but they'll copy anyone's design or setting (be specific). Prices roughly 40% off retail.

Edith Weber & Company

994 Madison Avenue
between 77th and 78th Streets
New York, NY 10021
212-570-9668
Monday-Saturday 11-4:30.

Jewelry & watches
Upper East Side

3	3	3	2
quality	style	service	value

The Edge: Diverse offerings of antique and estate jewelry. Offers antique jewelry from the 17th to 19th centuries. Favors semiprecious and precious stones.

Ellagem

580 5th Avenue, Room 210
near 47th Street
New York, NY 10036
212-398-0101. Fax 212-302-0153
Weekdays 10-5 by appointment through Ella.

Jewelry & watches
Midtown West

5	5	5	4
quality	style	service	value

The Edge: One-of-a-kind breathtaking jewels. Incredibly beautiful and expensive evening jewelry designed by Ella Gafter and her daughter Talila. Pieces most often include diamonds, precious stones (emeralds, rubies, sapphires) and pearls. No credit cards. Deluxe.

"Really worth a look."

Fortunoff

681 5th Avenue
near 54th Street
New York, NY 10022
212-758-6660
Monday Thursday 10-7
Tuesday Wednesday Friday Saturday 10-6.

Jewelry & watches
Midtown East

4	4	4	4
quality	style	service	value

The Edge: 47th Street style uptown, but not 47th Street's low, low prices. Find 14- and 18-karat gold and sterling-silver jewelry in mostly standard designs. Selection is large, including some antiques. Fortunoff has good prices on its contemporary flatware patterns in sterling, stainless and gold and silver plate. Jewelry appears to be full retail.

"One-stop shopping." "Commercial." "Good value in flatware."

Fred Leighton

773 Madison Avenue
near 66th Street
New York, NY 10021
212-288-1872
Monday-Saturday 10-6.
Closed Saturday July and August.

Jewelry & watches
Upper East Side

4	5	4	3
quality	style	service	value

The Edge: One-of-a-kind fabulous antique jewels. Originally a small Greenwich Village clothing store selling only black and white clothing. Re-created into a jewelry store specializing in really fabulous antique jewels. Offers diamonds (including colored diamonds), the highest quality pearls and wonderful chokers and tiaras for those who need them. Top-quality designs by all the greats. Very expensive. Deluxe.

"Breathtaking jewels."

George Paul Jewelers

Jewelry & watches
Midtown East

51 East 58th Street
between Park and Madison Avenues
New York, NY 10022
212-838-7660
Weekdays 11-5:30 Saturday 11-4.

The Edge: Good source for watch bands. Buys and sells estate jewelry. Jewelry is pleasant. Best as a source for watch bands.

Globemark Enterprises, Inc.

Jewelry & watches
Midtown West

230 5th Avenue, Room 1803
between 26th and 27th Streets
New York, NY 10001
212-725-3488. Fax 212-481-3964
Weekdays 10-6.

The Edge: Periodic watch sales. No credit cards. No delivery. Discounter.

H. Stern

Jewelry & watches
Midtown East

645 5th Avenue
near 51st Street
New York, NY 10022
212-688-0300. Fax 212-888-5137
Monday-Saturday 10-5:30.

4	3	4	3
quality	style	service	value

The Edge: Quality precious stones. Brazilian company featuring three-tone gold jewelry and sterling-silver pieces for day wear. Specialty is diamonds, rubies, emeralds and sapphires crafted in contemporary settings. Second-floor gallery is filled with home gift items. Deluxe.

Harry Winston

Jewelry & watches
Midtown West

718 5th Avenue
near 56th Street
New York, NY 10019
212-245-2000
Weekdays 10-5:30 Saturday 10:30-5.

5	5	5	4
quality	style	service	value

The Edge: Investment-quality jewels. Features large superb quality stones in classic settings. You'll find gold and diamond jewelry from $5,000 up to diamond solitaires in the millions. Deluxe.

Ilias Lalaounis

733 Madison Avenue
near 64th Street
New York, NY 10021
212-739-9400
Monday-Saturday 10-5:30.
Closed Saturday July and August.

Jewelry & watches
Upper East Side

4	**4**	**4**	**3**
quality	style	service	value

The Edge: Jewelry designs in ancient Greek styles. Large-scale heavy gold jewelry, hand-finished in Athens and mostly in 18- to 22-karat gold. Deluxe.

"Still the best."

J. Mavec & Company Ltd

19 East 74th Street
between 5th and Madison Avenues
New York, NY 10021
212-517-7665. Fax 212-517-4826
Weekdays 10-5:30 Saturday by appointment.

Jewelry & watches
Upper East Side

5	**3**	**4**	**2**
quality	style	service	value

The Edge: Lovely Georgian antique jewelry. Features antique jewelry (Georgian) through 20th century and glass objects. A special collection.

Josie Atplace

1050 2nd Avenue, Gallery 50F
near 56th Street
New York, NY 10022
212-838-6841. Fax 212-355-4403
Monday-Saturday 11-6.

Jewelry & watches
Midtown East

The Edge: Nice jewelry from the turn of the century to the 1950s. Mostly diamonds and precious stones set in gold. Features smaller pieces. Lovely people. No pressure.

La Valencia

899 Madison Avenue
near 72nd Street
New York, NY 10021
212-472-9600. Fax 212-472-9522
Monday-Saturday 10-6.

Jewelry & watches
Upper East Side

The Edge: Fine Italian 18-karat jewelry. Some plain gold, others with semiprecious stones and/or diamonds. Expensive, with prices from the hundreds to the thousands of dollars. Simple gold knot earrings were $500, about as basic as you get here.

Lawrence W. Ford

608 5th Avenue
near 49th Street
New York, NY 10020
212-581-4600. Fax 212-581-2820
Monday-Thursday 10-3:30.

Jewelry & watches
Midtown West

The Edge: Beautiful antique pieces. Primarily wholesale. Expect to see beautiful expensive antique pieces and wonderful treasures. No credit cards. Discounter.

Leekan Designs, Inc.
93 Mercer Street
near Spring Street
New York, NY 10012
212-226-7226. Fax 212-226-3419
Sunday-Friday 11-6 Saturday 11-7.

Jewelry & watches
SoHo/TriBeCa

The Edge: Hundreds of types of antique and new beads. Unique bead collection including bone, brass, copper, crystal, glass, horn, quartz, semiprecious stones and silver.

Manfredi
737 Madison Avenue
near 64th Street
New York, NY 10021
212-734-8710. Fax 212-734-4741
Weekdays 10-5:30 Saturday 11-5.
Closed Saturday July and August.

Jewelry & watches
Upper East Side

quality style service value

The Edge: Contemporary precious and semiprecious stones set into 18-karat gold. Jewels plus crystal, silver and wood table-top items.

Marina B
809 Madison Avenue
near 68th Street
New York, NY 10021
212-288-9708. Fax 212-744-6532
Monday-Saturday 10-5:30.
Closed Saturday July and August.

Jewelry & watches
Upper East Side

quality style service value

The Edge: Extravagant gems set in 18-karat-gold modern settings. One-of-a-kind precious stones.

Maurice Badler
578 5th Avenue
near 47th Street
New York, NY 10036
212-575-9632
Monday-Saturday 10-5.

Jewelry & watches
Midtown West

quality style service value

The Edge: Fortunoff styling at exceptionally good prices. Sells retail, wholesale and mail order in the heart of the jewelry district. Basic day jewelry, some copies of designer jewels, with evening glitter an option. Prices are 47th Street prices, about 50% of retail. To obtain a $3 catalog, write Badler Catalog, 578 Fifth Avenue, Department F, New York, NY 10036.

"Bring them the Tiffany's catalog and they'll copy any design you want. Trustworthy and honest."

Mikimoto

730 5th Avenue
near 57th Street
New York, NY 10019
212-644-1800. Fax 212-307-1807
Monday-Saturday 10-5:30.

Jewelry & watches
Midtown West

quality style service value

The Edge: Pearls only sold at this branch of the famous Tokyo store. Full range of good-quality pearls—all sizes, styles and colors.

"Used to be great."

Paul Seiden Jeweler

52 West 47th Street
between 5th and 6th Avenues
New York, NY 10036
212-869-5147. Fax 212-768-0862
Weekdays 10-5.

Jewelry & watches
Midtown West

The Edge: Among the best on 47th Street copying Bulgari. Excellent styling. Copies Tiffany, Van Cleef and Bulgari at 47th Street prices. Discounter.

Reinstein/Ross

122 Prince Street
near Greene Street
New York, NY 10012
212-226-4513
Monday-Saturday 11:30-6:30 Sunday noon-6.

Jewelry & watches
SoHo/TriBeCa

quality style service value

The Edge: Contemporary styled 22-karat-gold jewelry. 22-karat-gold jewelry set with unusual semiprecious and precious stones and some freshwater pearls. Beautiful styling. Somehow reminiscent of Greek jewelry, but modern.

"Very progressive modern styles, expensive."

29 East 73rd Street
near Madison Avenue/10021
212-772-1901. Fax 212-861-3376
Monday-Saturday 11-6:30.

Upper East Side

Robert Lee Morris

400 West Broadway
near Spring Street
New York, NY 10012
212-431-9405. Fax 212-219-9027
Weekdays 11-6 Saturday 11-7 Sunday noon-6.

Jewelry & watches
SoHo/TriBeCa

quality style service value

The Edge: Mostly jewelry—very creative styling. Mostly jewelry, some belts, bags, scarves and other artistic inspirations. Silver jewelry or metals dipped in gold. Very creative, priced from $500 to $1,000. Sold at Bergdorf's also.

"Elegant."

Saity Jewelry

425 5th Avenue
near 38th Street
New York, NY 10018
212-223-8125. Fax 212-223-2763
Monday-Saturday 10-6.

Jewelry & watches
Midtown West

quality style service value

The Edge: Native American jewelry. They feature a large quality collection of Native American jewelry priced from $200, including rings, bracelets and necklaces. Also offers modern jewelry from Nepal, Tibet, Africa and Europe.

Sally Hawkins Gallery

448 West Broadway
near Prince Street
New York, NY 10012
212-477-5699
Daily 11-7.

Jewelry & watches
SoHo/TriBeCa

The Edge: Modern, moderately priced jewelry. Sterling-silver and gold, some with semiprecious stones and crystals, at very moderate prices from $30 to $1,000.

Seaman Schepps

485 Park Avenue
near 58th Street
New York, NY 10022
212-753-9520. Fax 212-753-9541
Weekdays 10:30-6:30 Saturday 11-5.

Jewelry & watches
Midtown East

quality style service value

The Edge: Jewelry with enameling and stones in this well-known look. Prices tend to be high—$1,000 and up.

Stephen P. Kahan Ltd.

25 East 61st Street
near Madison Avenue
New York, NY 10021
212-750-3456. Fax 212-750-3459
Weekdays 10:30-5:30 Saturday 11-5.
Closed Saturday July and August.

Jewelry & watches
Upper East Side

quality style service value

The Edge: Elegant jewelry to be shown. Features contemporary and antique jewelry from the grand designers, including early David Webb. Favors large precious stones set in statement pieces. Mostly (95%) wholesale, but he'll let you up.

Swatch

500 5th Avenue
near 42nd Street
New York, NY 10036
212-730-7530. Fax 212-840-6254
Weekdays 9-6 Saturday 10-6 Sunday 10-5.

Jewelry & watches
Midtown West

The Edge: The full Swatch watch line. The well-known Swatch line priced from $40 to $100.

89 South Street   **Lower Manhattan**
Pier 17, South Street Seaport/10038
212-571-6400. Fax 212-732-3110
Monday-Saturday 10-7 Sunday 10-6:30.

Tiffany & Company

727 5th Avenue
near 57th Street
New York, NY 10022
212-755-8000. Fax 212-675-4046
Monday-Wednesday Friday Saturday 10-6 Thursday 10-7.

Jewelry & watches
Midtown East

quality	style	service	value
5	5	5	4

The Edge: Everyone loves their signature blue box and white ribbon bows. They're best for their own label and surprisingly inexpensive wedding presents. Jewelry surrounds you on the first floor. Designers include Elsa Peretti, Paloma Picasso and Schlumberger. Their watch selection is among the largest in the city. Go to the second floor for clocks, silver (flatware, jewelry, table-top items), knickknacks, leather accessories, scarves and stationery. The accessories, handbags and briefcases, are classic and up-to-date chic. Our favorite is the third floor, wedding present heaven and surprisingly inexpensive. Their own and top-name china and glass table items range from reasonably priced to high end. Corporate accounts get a small discount. Deluxe.

"I always go to Tiffany's for baby gifts." "I buy my wife's birthday presents there—attractive gold jewelry from $300 to $500 and their blue box and white ribbon makes a statement!"

Tourneau and Gorevic Collection at Tourneau

635 Madison Avenue
near 59th Street
New York, NY 10022
212-832-9000
Monday-Wednesday Friday Saturday 10-6
Thursday 10-7.

Jewelry & watches
Midtown East

quality	style	service	value
4	4	4	3

The Edge: Large selection of watches from all major companies. Will trade in your old watch for a credit toward a new one. Its prices are list, not discounted, but they offer a good selection. Repairs. Shares space with the Gorevic Collection at the 635 Madison Avenue store.

"Their repair department always does a good job." "Vintage timepiece collection."

200 West 34th Street   **Midtown West**
near 7th Avenue/10001
212-563-6880
Weekdays 9-7 Saturday 10-6 Sunday noon-5.

488 Madison Avenuez   **Midtown East**
between 51st and 52nd Streets/10022
212-758-6346

500 Madison Avenue   **Midtown East**
near 52nd Street/10022

212-750-6098
Tuesday Wednesday Friday Saturday 10-6 Monday Thursday 10-6:30.

Van Cleef & Arpels

744 5th Avenue
near 57th Street
New York, NY 10019
212-644-9500
Monday-Friday 10-5:30 Saturday 10-5.

Jewelry & watches
Midtown West

quality style service value

The Edge: Serious gems. Two Van Cleefs—one in Bergdorf's off on the side of the main floor and the serious statement gems next door in the main salon. Things at Bergdorf's tend to be more daytime and less expensive. Deluxe.

Gale Grant Ltd.

485 Madison Avenue
near 52nd Street
New York, NY 10022
212-752-3142
Monday-Saturday 10-6.

Jewelry & watches-costume
Midtown East

quality style service value

The Edge: Great costume jewelry. Good imitations of all the top designers for all occasions from office to evening. Huge selection with colors to accent all your outfits.

"Excellent style and quality for the price."

Ilene Chazanof

New York, NY 10003
212-254-5564
Monday-Saturday by appointment.

Jewelry & watches-costume
Flatiron/East Village

quality style service value

The Edge: Ilene herself is the edge. Ask and she'll give you straight advice on quality, present appropriateness and value. You must call ahead since Ilene insists on knowing who is coming to her fourth-floor loft store. It's crammed full of vintage handbags (many lizards), a full range of jewelry (costume to real) and household accessories (crystal, platters and silver picture frames). Fine jewelry, including cufflinks, pins, bracelets and earrings are in glass display cases. Lots of sterling-silver from top lines like Georg Jensen and much, much more. Reasonable prices.

Jaded

1048 Madison Avenue
near 80th Street
New York, NY 10021
212-288-6631
Monday-Saturday 10:30-6:30 Sunday noon-5.

Jewelry & watches-costume
Upper East Side

quality style service value

The Edge: Costume jewelry that looks as real as it gets. Mostly day jewels, with some costume jewelry for evening wear.

"Can't tell if it's real or not."

Joia

1151 2nd Avenue
near 60th Street
New York, NY 10021
212-754-9017
Weekdays 11-7 Saturday 11-6.

Jewelry & watches-costume
Upper East Side

The Edge: 1930s costume jewelry. Offers both period costume jewelry (some with stones) and Native American Southwest silver and turquoise jewelry. Best are 1930s to 1940s glittering costume jewelry. Much priced in the hundreds.

Linda Morgan Antiques

152 East 70th Street
near Lexington Avenue
New York, NY 10021
212-628-4330
Tuesday-Friday 10:30-6 Saturday 11-5.

Jewelry & watches-costume
Upper East Side

The Edge: Victorian accessories. French costume jewelry from the 1920s and 1930s. English Victorian jewelry. Some crocodile and lizard handbags. No delivery.

Ro Star, Inc.

27 West 47th Street, Suite 11, Plaza Arcade
between 5th and 6th Avenues
New York, NY 10036
212-221-3144. Fax 212-575-2378
Weekdays 9:30-4:30.

Jewelry & watches-costume
Midtown West

quality style service value

The Edge: Top-quality CZs (Cubic Ziconia)—can't tell they're not real. The TV show *20/20* took a Ro Star stone and a $50,000 Harry Winston diamond to 47th Street where apparently half the dealers picked the Ro Star CZ. Already set pieces include pierced earrings set in 14-karat gold, rings and pendants. Also unset CZs in a range of shapes and sizes. A 1-karat pair of pierced earrings was priced at $36. The store can be hard to find. Go midway down the Plaza Arcade on the right-and side, going from 47th to 48th Street. No credit cards. No delivery. Discounter.

"A real find!"

Jewelry Display of New York

32 West 47th Street
near 6th Avenue
New York, NY 10036
212-768-3623. Fax 212-575-1198
Weekdays 9-5.

Jewelry & watches-supply
Midtown West

quality style service value

The Edge: Best source in the jewelry district for upscale jewelry gift boxes at great prices. Go straight downstairs for wonderful gift boxes. Features cotton-filled (white, gold, silver) Japanese-style patterned-paper-wrapped ring-size boxes, Cartier- styled red boxes, Florentine leathers with gold trim lines, velvets (in pink, gray and black) and jewelry traveling rolls, paper

wrap, bows and bags. If you make jewelry, see their jewelry tools. They charge
United Parcel. Discounter.

Platt Box Company, Inc.
66 West 47th Street
near 6th Avenue
New York, NY 10036
212-869-9140. Fax 212-869-6647
Weekdays 9:30-5.

Jewelry & watc........ ...,
Midtown West

4	3	2	5
quality	style	service	value

The Edge: Jewelry boxes and displays. Go to the back far right off the main floor. They'll imprint a label on boxes for a sizable order. Boxes range from under $1 to several dollars for those Cartier/Harry Winston–style red boxes with velvet interiors. No credit cards. Discounter.

Altman Luggage
135 Orchard Street
near Delancey Street
New York, NY 10002
212-254-7275. Fax 212-254-7663
Sunday-Friday 9-6.

Leathers
Lower East Side/Chinatown

4	4	3	4
quality	style	service	value

The Edge: Wide selection and good prices. Discounts all major luggage brands (Boyt, Samsonite, Travelpro), pens and briefcases. Prices in a spot check appeared to be discounted 20%.

"Watch yourself! All prices negotiable."

Ananias
901 Avenue of the Americas
near 33rd Street
New York, NY 10001
212-947-0323
Sunday-Wednesday Friday 11-8 Thursday 11-9 Saturday 11-10.

Leathers
Midtown West

The Edge: Leather for college. Handmade leather products made in Greece. Large selection of small leather items: purses to school bags, briefcases and sandals. School bags priced from $50 to $169. Remember the end-of-summer sale.

Arivel Fashions
150 Orchard Street
near Rivington Street
New York, NY 10002
212-673-8992. Fax 212-673-8992
Daily 10:30-6.

Leathers
Lower East Side/Chinatown

The Edge: Basic moderately priced leather items. All types of leathers from gloves to coats, as well as fur and felt hats. Discounts to 40% advertised by the shop. Recommended to us, but not known here. Let us know what you think. Discounter.

Barbara Shaum

60 East 4th Street
near Broadway
New York, NY 10003
212-254-4250. Fax 212-254-4250
Wednesday-Friday 1-8 Saturday 1-6.

Leathers
Flatiron/East Village

The Edge: Custom-designed sandals with an upscale look. Shaum designs a full range of leather items which have been featured in *Gentlemen's Quarterly* and *Mirabella*. Custom sandals are her specialty. Priced from $100 to $400.

Bettinger's Luggage Shop

80 Rivington Street
between Orchard and Allen Streets
New York, NY 10002
212-674-9411. Fax 212-475-1750
Sunday-Friday 9:30-6.

Leathers
Lower East Side/Chinatown

quality	style	service	value
4	4	4	5

The Edge: Among the best luggage prices in the city. 81-year-old shop. Carries top-line luggage and briefcases, including Andiamo, Boyt, Lucas, Travelpro and more. In our spot check, cheaper than anyone else on luggage. Bargaining is standard. Does repairs. 35% to 40% off.

"Least expensive source on the Lower East. A riot! Like shopping on the streets of Europe." "Can negotiate."

Bottega Veneta

635 Madison Avenue
near 59th Street
New York, NY 10022
212-371-5511
Monday-Friday 10-6 Saturday 11-6.

Leathers
Midtown East

quality	style	service	value
4	5	5	3

The Edge: An Italian landmark. Expensive soft Italian leather items in great colors, including handbags, accessories (gloves and wallets), shoes, briefcases and luggage. Widely copied, especially their woven leathers. Deluxe.

"Beautiful purses."

Coach Store

342 Madison Avenue
near 44th Street
New York, NY 10017
212-599-4777
Monday-Wednesday Friday 8:30-7 Thursday 8:30-8
Saturday noon-6 Sunday noon-5.

Leathers
Midtown East

quality	style	service	value
5	3	5	4

The Edge: Durable, simple classic accessories. Features durable soft leathers. Find belts, briefcases, diaries, handbags, luggage, wallets and small accessories. Their discount stores sell Coach at 20% off, the closest in Amagansett on Long Island or Woodbury Commons in Central Valley, N.Y.

710 Madison Avenue **Upper East Side**
near 63rd Street/10021
212-599-4777
Monday-Wednesday Friday Saturday 10-6 Thursday 10-7 Sunday noon-5.
Closed Sunday in June.

595 Madison Avenue **Midtown East**
near 57th Street/10022
212-754-0041
Monday-Wednesday Friday 10-7 Thursday 10-8 Saturday 10-6 Sunday noon-5.

725 5th Avenue, 3rd Floor **Midtown East**
at 57th Street/10022
212-355-2427
Monday-Saturday 10-6.

193 Front Street **Lower Manhattan**
near John Street/10038
212-947-1727
Monday-Saturday 10-9 Sunday 11-8.

5 World Trade Center, Concourse Level **Lower Manhattan**
near Vesey Street/10048
212-488-0080
Weekdays 7:30-7:30 Saturday noon-5:30.

Crouch & Fitzgerald

400 Madison Avenue
near 46th Street
New York, NY 10017
212-755-5888. Fax 212-832-6461
Monday-Saturday 9-6.

Leathers
Midtown East

4	4	5	4
quality	style	service	value

The Edge: $69 per bag at their August sale. Since 1939. Classic styled handbags in leathers and exotic skins. Carries all the best known manufacturers plus their own private-label designs in fine-quality leathers. Also wallets, belts and other small leather goods. The luggage department is upstairs.

Eclectiques

483 Broome Street
near Wooster Street
New York, NY 10013
212-966-0650
Wednesday-Sunday 12:30-5:30.

Leathers
SoHo/TriBeCa

The Edge: Designer vintage trunks, bags and steamers. Store focuses on designer 18th-century to 1920s lines. Moderate prices.

Fendi

720 5th Avenue
near 56th Street
New York, NY 10019
212-767-0100. Fax 212-767-0548
Monday-Saturday 10-6.

Leathers
Midtown West

quality style service value

The Edge: Classic Italian styling. Find leather shoes, bags, briefcases, wallets and suitcases. Deluxe.

"When they started adding their initials, the chic dropped." "Pricey."

Ferragamo

725 5th Avenue
near 56th Street
New York, NY 10022
212-759-7990. Fax 212-980-4171
Monday-Wednesday Friday Saturday 10-6 Thursday 10-7.

Leathers
Midtown East

quality style service value

The Edge: Quiet elegant styling. Known most for their traditional shoes (casual to formal) with styles for women and men. But don't forget the clothes and accessories. Gorgeous sportswear made in soft sensuous wools and silks. Great tailoring and detail. Deluxe.

Fine and Klein

119 Orchard Street
near Delancey Street
New York, NY 10002
212-674-6720
Sunday-Friday 9-5.

Leathers
Lower East Side/Chinatown

quality style service value

The Edge: Large selection of discounted name-brand and knock-off pocketbooks. Good-quality pocketbooks in a wide price range from $100 up. Accepts phone orders, if you know what you want. 30% off.

"Good 'knock-offs' of expensive bags."

Furla

705 Madison Avenue
near 63rd Street
New York, NY 10021
212-755-8986
Monday-Wednesday Friday 10-6 Thursday 10-6:30
Saturday 10-6.

Leathers
Upper East Side

quality style service value

The Edge: Good colors and up-to-date styling. Good-looking Italian handbags in the moderate to upper price range. Deluxe.

"Pretty."

Ghurka

41 East 57th Street
between Madison and Park Avenues
New York, NY 10022
212-826-8300. Fax 212-826-8303
Monday-Wednesday Friday Saturday 10-6 Thursday 10-7.

Leathers
Midtown East

5	5	4	4
quality	style	service	value

The Edge: Expensive, but wears forever. Handbags in a range of sizes and styles—canvas and leather, artist portfolios and picnic baskets. Quality leather products that last.

Goldpfeil

777 Madison Avenue
near 66th Street
New York, NY 10021
212-472-4500. Fax 212-472-4650
Monday-Saturday 10-6.

Leathers
Upper East Side

5	4	5	3
quality	style	service	value

The Edge: Stunning handbags with wonderful hardware. Super-expensive handbags with innovative, very noticeable hardware. Also jewelry boxes, and small leather accessories. Offers classic styles in strong colors. Deluxe.

"Wish I could afford one (let alone more)."

Gucci

683 5th Avenue
near 54th Street
New York, NY 10022
212-826-2600. Fax 212-230-0894
Monday-Wednesday Friday Saturday 9:30-6
Thursday 9:30-7.

Leathers
Midtown East

4	4	5	3
quality	style	service	value

The Edge: Go straight to the top floor where items are often on sale, including those fabulous wool scarves. Find boots, briefcases, key cases, luggage, purses, shoes and wallets in wonderful colors and beautiful leather textures. Also silk scarves and clothing, including shirts, suits, sweaters and trousers. Deluxe.

Hermès

11 East 57th Street
between 5th and Madison Avenues
New York, NY 10022
212-751-3181. Fax 212-751-8143
Monday-Wednesday Friday Saturday 10-6 Thursday 10-8.

Leathers
Midtown East

5	5	5	3
quality	style	service	value

The Edge: Top-quality leathers that last a lifetime. Expensive, luxurious leathers in wonderful shades. From small leather items to the Kelly bag as well as shoes, luggage and saddles plus clothing (including silk scarves, gloves, trousers, riding clothes) and home needs (china and bar tools). Check out the sales which last only a few days (summer is one), when buys are fabulous, but are as crowded as the subway at rush hour. Deluxe.

Il Bisonte

72 Thompson Street
near Spring Street
New York, NY 10012
212-966-8773
Sunday Monday noon-6 Tuesday-Saturday noon-6:30.

Leathers
SoHo/TriBeCa

5	4	5	4
quality	style	service	value

The Edge: Italian leather goods stamped with bison logo. Bags are soft, simply styled and come in natural colors. Prices moderate to high.

J.S. Suarez

450 Park Avenue
between 55th and 56th Streets
New York, NY 10022
212-753-3758
Weekdays 10-6 Saturday 10-5.

Leathers
Midtown East

4	4	4	4
quality	style	service	value

The Edge: Among the best sources for bags. They discount name-brand bags 30% to 50% and sell copies of the top labels, including Bottega Veneta, Chanel, Hermès and Mark Cross. Same look and high quality, but without the signature, hardware and label. Beloved by all.

"The best source for bags." "I love this store and its owners." "Great place."

Jobson's Luggage

666 Lexington Avenue
between 55th and 56th Streets
New York, NY 10022
212-355-6846. Fax 212-753-3295
Monday-Saturday 9-6 Sunday 11-5.

Leathers
Midtown East

4	4	2	4
quality	style	service	value

The Edge: if you're hard-hitting at bargaining, among the best prices in the city. Large selection of discounted luggage, attaché cases and small leather goods. Brands include Andiamo, Halliburton, American Tourister, Lark, Travelpro and Boyt. Free monogramming, free repair and delivery. They carry Mont Blanc and Shaeffer pens. Pluses are a convenient midtown location and large selection of high-quality luggage. Negatives are that you really have to push to get the best price. Items are marked at list, but substantial discounts are possible if you're prepared to follow these rules: (1) assume the listed prices are full retail; (2) think substantial discount; (3) move negotiations to a manger, but the manager may be hard to identify; (4) be prepared to walk out (that's part of the negotiating strategy); but (5) buy on the spot if they come within striking distance of your price. Same rules and description apply to Lexington Luggage. Management told our researchers that pricing is almost wholesale, "10% above cost!" Free initials/monograms.

"Some places are fun to hondle, but here I always feel I've overpaid."

La Bagagerie

727 Madison Avenue
near 64th Street
New York, NY 10021
212-758-6570
Monday-Saturday 10-6:30.

Leathers
Upper East Side

5	5	4	3
quality	style	service	value

The Edge: High-quality/high-fashion handbags. Features bags plus classic briefcases and luggage in great colors! Moderate to expensive.

Lancel

690 Madison Avenue
near 62nd Street
New York, NY 10021
212-753-6918
Monday-Saturday 10-6.

Leathers
Upper East Side

The Edge: Classic French handbags in bold colors. A full range of leather items in bold colors and exotic skins.

Leather 99

976 Avenue of the Americas
near 36th Street
New York, NY 10018
212-563-1828
Weekdays 9:30-7 Saturday 11-6 Sunday 11-5.

Leathers
Midtown West

The Edge: Leather jackets for the high school set. Store says they're the cheapest source for leather jackets in town. Leathers are from Pakistan and Korea. Jackets priced at $50 to $300 and coats at $150 to $200. Discounter.

Leather Facts

262 West 38th Street
between 7th and 8th Avenues
New York, NY 10018
212-382-2788. Fax 212-730-2486
Weekdays 9:30-6 Saturday by appointment.

Leathers
Midtown West

The Edge: Custom-made dresses, skirts, pants, jackets and coats. Dresses from $150 to $700, pants $80 to $300. Leather coats are the biggest seller at $150. Leathers in a wide variety of colors. Clothing can be custom-made. No credit cards.

Leather Outlet

327 Avenue of the Americas
near 3rd Street
New York, NY 10014
212-229-1500. Fax 212-229-1981
Monday-Thursday 11-9 Friday Saturday 11-11 Sunday 1-8.

Leathers
Greenwich Village

The Edge: Hip leather jackets for the college set. They sell only jackets, which are priced from $100 to $250. A hot seller is a hip-length jacket for men. Discounter.

Lederer de Paris, Inc.

613 Madison Avenue
near 58th Street
New York, NY 10022
212-355-5515. Fax 212-838-1378

Leathers
Midtown East

quality style service value

Weekdays 9:30-6 Saturday 10-6.

The Edge: Copies the top fashion houses like Chanel and Hermès. Known for a full range of quality leather items plus canvas hunting bags, garment bags, shooting and riding jackets and Wellington boots. Much less expensive than the originals.

Lexington Luggage

793 Lexington Avenue
near 61st Street
New York, NY 10021
212-223-0698. Fax 212-795-5238
Monday-Saturday 9-6 Sunday 11-5.

Leathers
Upper East Side

quality	style	service	value
4	4	2	4

The Edge: If you're hard-hitting at bargaining, among the best prices in the city. Large selection (250 brands) of discounted luggage, attaché cases and small leather goods. Pluses are a convenient midtown location and large selection of high-quality luggage. Negatives are that you really have to push to get the best price. Items are marked at list, but substantial discounts are possible if you're prepared to follow these rules: (1) assume listed prices are full retail; (2) think large discount; (3) move negotiations to a manger, but the manager may be hard to identify; (4) be prepared to walk out (that's part of the negotiating strategy); but (5) buy on the spot if they come within striking distance of your price. Same rules apply to Jobson's Luggage. 30% off.

"Aggressive salespeople; prices bargainable."

Louis Vuitton

51 East 57th Street
near Madison Avenue
New York, NY 10022
212-371-6111. Fax 212-759-5591
Weekdays 10:30-6 Saturday 10-5:30.

Leathers
Midtown East

quality	style	service	value
4	4	5	3

The Edge: Their famous logo. Known for their signature handbags made of laminated vinyl on Egyptian cotton canvas and adorned with their logo. Find train cases, steamer trunks, golf bags, kitty carriers, wig boxes and attaché cases. Their line is expanding now to more traditional styles in strong colors. Deluxe.

Luggage Plus

92 Orchard Street
near Delancey Street
New York, NY 10002
212-673-0274
Sunday-Thursday 10-5:30 Friday 10-2.

Leathers
Lower East Side/Chinatown

The Edge: Moderately priced luggage discounted. Find luggage, backpacks and briefcases. Discounter.

Mark Cross

645 5th Avenue
near 51st Street
New York, NY 10022
212-421-3000. Fax 212-421-3006
Monday-Wednesday Friday Saturday 10-6

Leathers
Midtown East

quality	style	service	value
5	5	5	4

Thursday 10-7 Sunday noon-5.

The Edge: Fine leather items. Terrific leather desk accessories. A full li...
from small accessories to briefcases, handbags, luggage and leather desk access...
and leathers, including calfskin, lizard, alligator and crocodile. Deluxe.

"My favorite for wonderful gifts for my husband."

North Beach Leather

Leathers
Upper East Side

772 Madison Avenue
near 66th Street
New York, NY 10021
212-772-0707. Fax 212-772-8468
Monday-Wednesday Friday 10-6:30 Thursday 10-7
Saturday 10-6 Sunday noon-5.

quality	style	service	value
4	4	4	3

The Edge: Hot-looking leather outfits. While the emphasis is on jackets, coats and outerwear,
they feature some dresses (sexiest is a cutout sun dress in red, among other colors), skirts and slacks
with matching jackets. Favors pastel colors for spring and hot reds and dark colors for fall/winter.
Dresses from $195 to $1,150 with jackets from $550 to $700. Deluxe.

Prada

Leathers
Midtown East

45 East 57th Street
between Madison and Park Avenues
New York, NY 10022
212-308-2332. Fax 212-980-1278
Monday-Saturday 10-6.

quality	style	service	value
4	4	4	3

The Edge: Fashion-forward, yet conservative, bags and shoes. Highest-quality leathers,
including exotic skins and embossed leather. Full range of leather items from shoes to beautiful
handbags, briefcases and accessories. Casual clothing in exceptional fabrics. Simply gorgeous.
Deluxe.

Tuscany & Company

Leathers
Midtown West

12 West 57th Street
west of 5th Avenue
New York, NY 10019
212-362-1258. Fax 212-307-0418
Weekdays 9-5.

quality	style	service	value
5	5	3	5

The Edge: A treasured source for top Italian leathers and shearlings. A distributor to top
department and the finest Madison Avenue stores and boutiques of fine Italian leather and
shearling jackets and coats. Mostly women's, some men's. Half of retail prices. Great selection. Ask
for Antonio Di Capua. No credit cards. No delivery.

Motherhood Maternity

Maternity
Chelsea

641 20th Street
near 6th Avenue
New York, NY 10011

quality	style	service	value
3	4	4	4

12-741-3488. Fax 212-741-2855
Daily 10-7.

The Edge: Maternity career clothing. Career suits in silks and wools as well as casual, lingerie and underwear. Designers include their own plus Rand, Japanese Weekend and St. Simone. Prices are moderate to high.

Veronique
1321 Madison Avenue
near 93rd Street
New York, NY 10128
212-831-7800
Monday-Wednesday Friday Saturday 10-6
Thursday 10-7.

Maternity
Upper East Side

5	5	5	4
quality	style	service	value

The Edge: High fashion maternity wear. European maternity chain featuring clothing from designer Véronique Delachaux. Full range of clothing, from casual and office to evening. Very upscale and lovely!

Addison on Madison
698 Madison Avenue
near 62nd Street
New York, NY 10021
212-308-2660. Fax 212-750-4444
Monday-Saturday 10:30-6:30.

Shirts & blouses
Upper East Side

4	4	4	3
quality	style	service	value

The Edge: Breadth of selection and great sales. Sells only business shirts and shirt accessories (silk ties, cufflinks and pocket squares). High-quality fabrics used exclusively. European styling combined with an American fit. Prices are good, given the quality.

"Great $19 silk ties." "Great sales."

Custom Shop
115 Broadway
near Pine Street
New York, NY 10013
212-267-8535
Weekdays 8:30-5:30.

Shirts & blouses
SoHo/TriBeCa

2	2	2	2
quality	style	service	value

The Edge: Inexpensive dress shirts. Wide selection of fabrics—cotton and cotton blends. Allow six weeks for delivery. Minimum order is four shirts.

338 Madison Avenue
near 44th Street/10017
212-867-3650
Monday-Saturday 9-6.

Midtown East

618 5th Avenue
near 49th Street/10020
212-245-2499
Monday-Wednesday Friday Saturday 9-6 Thursday 9-8.

Midtown West

18 East 50th Street, 10th Floor
between 5th and Madison Avenues/10022
212-223-3600
Monday-Saturday 9-6.

Midtown East

555 Lexington Avenue
near 50th Street/10022
212-759-7480
Monday-Saturday 9-6.

Midtown East

Penn Garden Shirts
63 Orchard Street
near Grand Street
New York, NY 10002
212-431-8464
Sunday-Wednesday Friday 9-6 Thursday 9-8.

Shirts & blouses
Lower East Side/Chinatown

The Edge: Designer shirts and menswear discounted. Features Valentino, among others. Men's shirts, socks and sweaters discounted. Known for neckwear.

Shirt Store
51 East 44th Street
between Vanderbilt and Madison Avenues
New York, NY 10017
212-557-8040. Fax 212-557-1628
Weekdays 8-6:30 Saturday 10-5.

Shirts & blouses
Midtown East

5	4	5	4
quality	style	service	value

The Edge: Ready-to-wear and custom-made pure cotton shirts. Shirts sold direct from the manufacturer for $37 to $85 for ready-to-wear and $85 to $250 for custom-made. Swatches and pictures are available for mail order. Monogramming and alterations also available. Semiannual sales (January and June). 10% corporate discount program for companies of 100 employees or more. Full line of accessories.

"Great selection and value!" "Very homey and personal."

Victory, the Shirt Experts
125 Maiden Lane
between Pearl and Water Streets
New York, NY 10038
212-480-1366
Daily 8:30-6.

Shirts & blouses
Lower Manhattan

4	5	5	4
quality	style	service	value

The Edge: Quality moderately priced shirts. Manufactures and sells cotton two-ply broadcloth to Sea Island broadcloth in ready-to-wear and made-to-measure shirts. Will taper, shorten sleeves and monogram shirts. Prices from $45 to $95 for Sea Island cotton. Sells ties, cufflinks and belts. Discounter.

Anbar Shoes

60 Reade Street
1 block north of Chambers Street
New York, NY 10007
212-964-4017
Weekdays 9-6:30 Saturday 11-6.

Shoes, socks & stockings
Lower Manhattan

The Edge: Discounts moderately priced shoes. 20,000 pairs of shoes sold on two floors. Priced from $21 to $70. No delivery.

Andrea Carrano Boutique

850 Madison Avenue
near 70th Street
New York, NY 10021
212-570-1443
Monday-Saturday 10-7 Sunday noon-6.

Shoes, socks & stockings
Upper East Side

quality style service value

The Edge: Great classic flats in wonderful colors. Classic to trendy Italian shoes made from glove-soft leathers and fine suedes. Features the baby-styled, sophisticated flats like Jackie O used to wear.

Bally of Switzerland

628 Madison Avenue
near 59th Street
New York, NY 10021
212-751-9082
Weekdays 10-6:30 Saturday 9:30-6.

Shoes, socks & stockings
Upper East Side

quality style service value

The Edge: Classic quality shoes for women and men. Classic, traditional, well-made shoes in glove-soft leathers. Fans call the styles understated and timeless. The 45th Street store carries shoes for men only. The 59th Street store carries women's shoes also.

347 Madison Avenue
near 45th Street/10022
212-986-0872. Fax 212-682-4937
Weekdays 9:30-6:30 Saturday 10-6.

Midtown East

Belgian Shoes

60 East 56th Street
near Park Avenue
New York, NY 10022
212-755-7372. Fax 212-755-7627
Weekdays 9:30-4:15.

Shoes, socks & stockings
Midtown East

quality style service value

The Edge: Perfect for the country club set, casual loafers. Handmade, soft leathers, solid and two-tone casual loafers made in Belgium in 50 color combinations. Priced from $200.

"Ask for Basil." "Very comfortable."

Benedetti Custom Shoes

225 West 34th Street
between 7th and 8th Avenues
New York, NY 10001
212-594-6033
Weekdays 9-7 Saturday 10-6.

Shoes, socks & stockings
Midtown West

quality style service value

The Edge: Discounts men's shoes. All major brands, including Bass, Timberland, Bally, Johnson and Murphy. Some women's shoes, Easy Spirit, Reebok and Rockport. Sizes 5 to 15EEE.

530 7th Avenue
near 38th Street/10018
212-719-5075. Fax 212-629-8665

Midtown West

Botticelli

666 5th Avenue
near 53rd Street
New York, NY 10019
212-582-2984
Monday-Wednesday Friday 10-7:30 Thursday 10-8
Saturday 10-7 Sunday 11-6.

Shoes, socks & stockings
Midtown West

quality style service value

The Edge: Italian leather staples from the classic to the trendy. Men's store filled with classic Italian footwear, socks, ties and leather jackets. Footwear includes office, formal and casual styles. Shoes are hand-stitched. Priced from $125.

"Intimidating."

Broadway Sneakers

430 Broadway
between Canal and Howard Streets
New York, NY 10013
212-334-9488
Daily 9-7.

Shoes, socks & stockings
SoHo/TriBeCa

quality style service value

The Edge: Unbelievable choice of sneaker labels. 67 sneaker labels, but largest selection is in Nike and Reebok. Also hiking shoes and in-line skates. Running gear from socks to windbreakers at a modest discount. No delivery.

"No-return policy."

323 Canal Street
near Broadway/10013
212-966-1125

Lower East Side

25 West 45th Street
between 5th and 6th Avenues/10036
212-944-9844

Midtown West

Bruno Magli

677 5th Avenue
near 53rd Street
New York, NY 10022
212-752-7900. Fax 212-826-8671
Monday-Wednesday Friday 10-6:30 Thursday 10-7 Saturday 10-6 Sunday noon-5.

Shoes, socks & stockings
Midtown East

The Edge: An Italian institution. Casual to dressy shoes made of soft Italian leathers in basic colors with good feminine styling. Priced from $150 to $1,000.

Church English Shoes

428 Madison Avenue
near 49th Street
New York, NY 10017
212-755-4313. Fax 212-750-0985
Monday-Friday 9-6 Saturday 9-5:30.

Shoes, socks & stockings
Midtown East

| 4 | 4 | 4 | 3 |
| quality | style | service | value |

The Edge: Hand-crafted conservatively styled English shoes. Unchanging styles that can take an English gentleman from casual to dress occasions. Quality leathers. Large stock of widths and sizes from AAA to EEE and 6 to 13.

"I sometimes wonder if they bring in different merchandise for their sales."

Cipriano Shoes

148 Orchard Street
between Stanton and Rivington Streets
New York, NY 10002
212-477-5858. Fax 212-674-5037
Daily 7:30-6.

Shoes, socks & stockings
Lower East Side/Chinatown

| 4 | 4 | 1 | 3 |
| quality | style | service | value |

The Edge: Discounts on work boots. Small shop that carries mostly men's shoes and some women's, including New Balance, Nike, Timberland and more. Prices are 10% to 15% off retail and most sales are work boots. Like most discounters, don't come here for the service.

"Service is nonexistent."

Cole-Haan

620 5th Avenue
near 50th Street
New York, NY 10020
212-765-9747
Monday Thursday 9:30-8
Monday-Wednesday Friday Saturday 10-7 Sunday noon-6.

Shoes, socks & stockings
Midtown West

| 4 | 5 | 4 | 4 |
| quality | style | service | value |

The Edge: Conservative, nicely styled shoes and boots. Classic shoes for men, women and children in casual to dress styles. Also belts, handbags, luggage and umbrellas.

667 Madison Avenue
near 60th Street/10021
212-421-8440

Upper East Side

Diego Della Valle

41 East 57th Street
between Madison and Park Avenues
New York, NY 10022
212-644-5945. Fax 212-644-0379
Monday-Saturday 10-6.

Shoes, socks & stockings
Midtown East

quality style service value

The Edge: Updated classic shoes, an expensive 9 West look. Find Diego's own line plus name-brand shoes like Calvin Klein and J.P. Tod in casual to dressy styles. Children's shoes (priced from $70 to $110) to adult sizes.

"Cool loafers but expensive."

East Side Kids

1298 Madison Avenue
near 92nd Street
New York, NY 10128
212-360-5000. Fax 212-360-5001
Weekdays 9:30-6 Saturday 9-6.

Clothing-children
Upper East Side

quality style service value

The Edge: A fun place to take your children to buy shoes. Full stock of infants' to teenagers' basic to party shoes and boots. In summer, stocks sandals and camp shoes. Large range of designer shoes in sizes from 2 to adult 10. Priced from $24 (Keds) to $195.

"It's a pleasure to buy here. Love the popcorn machine and the grandstand for sitting!"

Eric Shoes

1333 3rd Avenue
near 76th Street
New York, NY 10021
212-288-8250
Monday-Wednesday Friday 11-7 Thursday 11-8
Saturday 10-6 Sunday 1-6.

Shoes, socks & stockings
Upper East Side

quality style service value

The Edge: Great style. Sells current designs from all the top designers, including Robert Clergerie, Miss Maud, Fratelli Rosseti, plus their own label. Expensive.

"Great shoes, high prices."

1021 2nd Avenue
near 54th Street/10022
212-223-0378
Monday-Wednesday Friday 11-7 Thursday 11-8 Saturday 10-6 Sunday 1-6.

Midtown East

1222 Madison Avenue
near 88th Street/10128
212-289-5762
Monday-Wednesday Friday 11-7 Thursday 11-8 Saturday 10:30-6:30 Sunday 1-6.

Upper East Side

Fogal

680 Madison Avenue
between 61st and 62nd Streets
New York, NY 10021
212-759-9782
Monday-Wednesday Friday Saturday 10-6:30
Thursday 10-8.

Shoes, socks & stockings
Upper East Side

5	5	4	3
quality	style	service	value

The Edge: Great hosiery. Hosiery for men and women in hundreds of hues, designs and patterns. Prices are high (from $17.50), but the hose is long-lasting. Wide range of fabrics from cottons and wools to wonderful cashmere-silk blends.

"High quality and very expensive."

French Sole

985 Lexington Avenue
near 72nd Street
New York, NY 10021
212-737-2859
Weekdays 10-7 Saturday 11-6.

Shoes, socks & stockings
Upper East Side

5	5	5	4
quality	style	service	value

The Edge: Chanel-inspired ballet slippers. Slippers by Hirica come in 122 solid and/or two-color patterns. Made from French glove leather with adjustable drawstring bows and street soles. Shoes priced at $45 to $50 for flats and $60 to $75 for quilted styles. Also Italian sneakers and winter boots priced from $45 to $250 for boots.

"Adorable."

Friedman Hosiery

326 Grand Street
near Orchard Street
New York, NY 10002
212-674-3292. Fax 212-941-6787
Sunday-Thursday 9-6 Friday 9-3.

Shoes, socks & stockings
Lower East Side/Chinatown

The Edge: Hose and underwear for the whole family, discounted. Find BVD, Berkshire, CK, Christian Dior, Dufold, Hanes and Jockey as well as high-end European hose as sold on Madison Avenue. All sizes from infant to adult.

"Something for everyone."

Gelman Custom

404 East 73rd Street
near 1st Avenue
New York, NY 10021
212-249-3659
Weekdays 7-7 Saturday 7-5 by appointment.

Shoes, socks & stockings
Upper East Side

The Edge: Custom shoes and boots. Adjusts shoes and boots for comfort and to alleviate foot problems. Priced at $450+ for size 10 pumps. Takes three weeks to complete. Deluxe.

Giordano's Shoes

1150 2nd Avenue
near 60th Street
New York, NY 10021
212-688-7195. Fax 212-688-7199
Weekdays 11-7 Saturday 11-6.

Shoes, socks & stockings
Upper East Side

The Edge: Stylish shoes in small sizes. More moderate labels, including Evan Picone, Liz Claiborne and Via Spiga. Small sizes to size 6 only.

Giraudon Shoes

339 West Broadway
near Grand Street
New York, NY 10013
212-334-9867. Fax 212-219-1800
Monday-Saturday 11:30-7:30 Sunday 1-6.

Shoes, socks & stockings
SoHo/TriBeCa

The Edge: Avant garde casual (thick rubber shoes) to dressy. Look is chunky downtown styling. Average price $150 for men's and $130 for women's shoes. Cutting-edge styling.

Great Feet

1241 Lexington Avenue
near 84th Street
New York, NY 10028
212-249-0551
Monday-Wednesday Saturday 9:30-5:30
Thursday Friday 9:30-7:30 Sunday noon-4:30.

Shoes, socks & stockings
Upper East Side

5 4 4 4
quality style service value

The Edge: An enormous stock of stylish children's shoes. From casual to dress pumps in a full range of styles and sizes. Go at off-times to avoid the crowds. Good at fitting your child.

"The only place to buy children's shoes." "Keep it secret—it's already too crowded."

Harry's Shoes

2299 Broadway
near 83rd Street
New York, NY 10024
212-874-2035. Fax 212-874-7617
Monday Thursday-Saturday 10-6:45
Tuesday-Wednesday 10:30- 6:45 Sunday noon-5:30.

Shoes, socks & stockings
Upper West Side

4 4 4 4
quality style service value

The Edge: Family shoe store that has everything. One-stop shopping for family shoe basics that include casual and dressy shoes, sneakers and boots. Labels include Easy Spirit, Sebago, Dexter and Rockport.

"Comfort oriented." "A wonderland of shoes."

Helene Arpels, Inc.

Shoes, socks & stockings
Midtown East

470 Park Avenue
between 57th and 58th Streets
New York, NY 10022
212-755-1623. Fax 212-832-0094
Monday-Saturday 10-6. Closed Saturday July and August.

5	4	3	3
quality	style	service	value

The Edge: Elegant styling for the ladies who lunch. Handmade shoes in soft leathers. From elegant low heels to sexy satin and leather pumps, some with skinny high heels. Favored by the "crowd"—Nancy Reagan, Brooke Astor and friends. Some handmade sweaters and dresses are made exclusively for the store. No returns. Very expensive, shoes priced from the hundreds to thousands of dollars per pair. Deluxe.

"Can't find prettier shoes in the city"

J.M. Weston

Shoes, socks & stockings
Midtown East

42 East 57th Street
near Madison and Park Avenue
New York, NY 10022
212-308-5655. Fax 212-308-2710
Monday-Saturday 10-6. Saturday 10-5 June-August.

The Edge: For over 100 years, classic handmade luxury footwear. Priced from $600. Parisian shoe company with branches in New York. Wide range of sizes and widths. Some classic women's shoes. They keep a record of each customer's size for phone orders. Deluxe.

Jandreani

Shoes, socks & stockings
Midtown East

220 East 60th Street
between 2nd and 3rd Avenues
New York, NY 10022
212-753-4666. Fax 212-755-7291
Monday-Saturday 10:30-8 Sunday noon-6.

The Edge: Young-looking glove-soft Italian shoes. Features casual to dress shoes plus accessories (belts, socks and ties). Shoes priced from $95 to $180.

Joan & David

Shoes, socks & stockings
Chelsea

104 5th Avenue
near 15th Street
New York, NY 10011
212-627-1780. Fax 212-627-4497
Monday-Saturday 11-7.

3	3	3	3
quality	style	service	value

The Edge: Conservative, moderately priced, good-looking shoes. Initially sold at Ann Taylor. Their own label shoes, boots, belts, bags and some clothing. Conservative moderately priced shoes. Features a limited range of men's shoes.

816 Madison Avenue
near 68th Street/10021
212-772-3970. Fax 212-772-3541
Monday-Saturday 10-6.

Upper East Side

200 Vesey Street
near West Street/10281
212-945-2735. Fax 212-233-4164
Weekdays 10-7 weekends noon-5.

Lower Manhattan

John Fluevog
104 Prince Street
near Greene Street
New York, NY 10012
800-381-3538. Fax 800-381-3338
Monday-Saturday 11-7 Sunday noon-6.

Shoes, socks & stockings
SoHo/TriBeCa

The Edge: Outrageous women's and men's shoes. Shoe styles are extreme, but seem to appeal to high schoolers.

Kenneth Cole
353 Columbus Avenue
between 76th and 77th Streets
New York, NY 10024
212-873-2061. Fax 212-875-0265
Monday-Saturday 11-7:30 Sunday noon-7.

Shoes, socks & stockings
Upper West Side

3	3	3	3
quality	style	service	value

The Edge: Trendy and classic styles. Classic shoes.

Lace Up Shoe Shop
110 Orchard Street
near Delancey Street
New York, NY 10002
212-475-8040. Fax 212-979-6377
Sunday-Friday 9-5:30 Saturday 11-4.

Shoes, socks & stockings
Lower East Side/Chinatown

4	3	3	4
quality	style	service	value

The Edge: Moderately priced shoes at discount. Features more moderately priced designer shoes. Will special order shoes if you know the style. Some better designer lines show up occasionally. Call 800-475-8040 for a catalog or to order by phone. 25% off.

Leach-Kale
1261 Broadway, Suite 815-816
near 31st Street
New York, NY 10001
212-683-0571
Weekdays 7:30-4:30 by appointment.

Shoes, socks & stockings
Midtown West

The Edge: Custom shoes. A place to go for custom shoes. Prices start at $700, with the Second pair for $500. They pay attention to foot problems. No credit cards. Deluxe.

Leggiadro
700 Madison Avenue
near 62nd Street
New York, NY 10021
212-753-5050

Shoes, socks & stockings
Upper East Side

Monday-Saturday 10:30-6.

The Edge: Hundreds of stocking options. Broad selection of imported pantyhose, stockings, knee-highs and leggings.

Lismore Hosiery

334 Grand Street
between Ludlow and Orchard Streets
New York, NY 10002
212-674-3440. Fax 212-674-3974
Sunday-Friday 10:30-5:30.

Shoes, socks & stockings
Lower East Side/Chinatown

quality style service value

The Edge: Inexpensive hose. Sells their own line plus Berkshire, Calvin Klein, Dior and Hanes socks, tights and pantyhose. Priced from $1 to $24. Discounter.

Little Eric Shoes

1331 3rd Avenue
near 76th Street
New York, NY 10021
212-288-8987. Fax 212-288-4197
Monday-Friday 10-6 Saturday 10-7 Sunday noon-6.

Shoes, socks & stockings
Upper East Side

quality style service value

The Edge: The first to feature Italian designer shoes for children. A full range of shoes, including sneakers, school shoes, dress shoes and boots. Some women's shoes.

"Has everything for little feet."

1118 Madison Avenue
near 83rd Street/10028
212-717-1513

Upper East Side

Louis Chock

74 Orchard Street
near Grand Street
New York, NY 10001
212-473-1929
Sunday-Thursday 9-5 Friday 9-1.

Shoes, socks & stockings
Lower East Side/Chinatown

quality style service value

The Edge: Good Lower East Side source for discounted hosiery for the entire family. All the better brand-name (but not the very top of the line) hosiery (Berkshire, Calvin Klein, Hanes), underwear and sleep wear discounted. 25% off.

"Good for hosiery."

M. Stever Hosiery Company

31 West 32nd Street
near 5th Avenue
New York, NY 10001
212-563-0052. Fax 212-268-7549
Daily 7:45-5:20.

Shoes, socks & stockings
Midtown West

The Edge: Lingerie discounted. The basics—hose, lingerie and active wear at discount prices. For men, socks only. Sells both retail and wholesale. Discounter.

Manolo Blahnik

15 West 55th Street
between 5th and 6th Avenues
New York, NY 10019
212-582-3007. Fax 212-582-5778
Weekdays 10:30-6 Saturday 11-5:30.

Shoes, socks & stockings
Midtown West

5	5	3	1
quality	style	service	value

The Edge: Cutting-edge Italian made shoes. Offers wonderful daytime styles and fabulous evening shoes, including bridal shoes. Expensive. Deluxe.

Maraolo

1321 3rd Avenue
near 76th Street
New York, NY 10021
212-535-6225. Fax 212-717-1336
Monday-Wednesday Friday Saturday 10-7
Thursday 10-8 Sunday noon-6.

Shoes, socks & stockings
Upper East Side

4	4	4	3
quality	style	service	value

The Edge: Well known for good conservative Italian women's shoes from casual to business styles. Highly rated by those over 40! Also features Armani, DKNY and Donna Karan shoes, bags and belts. Some men's shoes also.

"Great find." "Great sales."

835 Madison Avenue   **Upper East Side**
near 69th Street/10021
212-628-5080
Monday-Wednesday Friday Saturday 10-6:30 Thursday 10-7 Sunday noon-6.

782 Lexington Avenue   **Upper East Side**
near 61st Street/10021
212-832-8182. Fax 212-980-2542
Monday-Wednesday Friday Saturday 10-7 Thursday 10-8 Sunday noon-5.

551 Madison Avenue   **Midtown East**
near 57th Street/10022
212-308-8793. Fax 212-223-0045
Monday-Wednesday Friday Saturday 10-7 Thursday 9:30-7 Sunday noon-5.

131 West 72nd Street   **Upper West Side**
near Columbus Avenue/10023
212-787-6550. Fax 212-787-1735
Monday-Wednesday Friday Saturday 10-7 Thursday 10-8 Sunday noon-5.

Medici Shoes

163 5th Avenue
near 22nd Street
New York, NY 10010

Shoes, socks & stockings
Gramercy Pk/Murray Hill

4	4	3	3
quality	style	service	value

212-260-4253. Fax 212-677-0823
Weekdays 10-8 Sunday 11:30-7:30.

The Edge: European clothing, shoes and accessories. Moderate prices. Classic, stylish shoes. Discounter.

"Wide selection, aggressive salespeople."

Nana

138 Prince Street
near West Broadway
New York, NY 10012
212-274-0749. Fax 212-941-7910
Monday-Saturday 11-7 Sunday noon-6.

**Shoes, socks & stockings
SoHo/TriBeCa**

The Edge: Moderately priced trendy young clothes and lots and lots of shoes. Downtown, trendy clothing, backpacks, candles, hair dye and their own shoe line. Uptown, mostly shoes, their own and Doc Martens.

Nine West

757 3rd Avenue
near 47th Street
New York, NY 10017
212-371-4597
Weekdays 10-7:30 Saturday 10-7 Sunday noon-5.

**Shoes, socks & stockings
Midtown East**

3	4	3	4
quality	style	service	value

The Edge: At last—moderately priced, high-style, classic shoes. A full range of good looking-flats, heels and boots—staples to higher fashion. Priced from $50 to $150.

1195 3rd Avenue
near 69th Street/10021
212-472-8750
Weekdays 10-8 Saturday 10-7 Sunday noon-5.

Upper East Side

711 Madison Avenue
near 63rd Street/10021
212-752-8030
Weekdays 10-8 Saturday 10-7 Sunday noon-5.

Upper East Side

750 Lexington Avenue
near 59th Street/10022
212-486-8094
Weekdays 10-8 Saturday 10-7 Sunday noon-5.

Midtown East

2305 Broadway
near 83rd Street/10024
212-799-7610
Weekdays 10-8 Saturday 10-9 Sunday noon-7.

Upper West Side

313 World Trade Center
concourse level/10048
212-488-7665

Lower Manhattan

Weekdays 7:30-8 Saturday 10-6.

99X
84 East 10th Street
between 3rd and 4th Avenues
New York, NY 10003
212-460-8599. Fax 201-795-1320
Monday-Saturday noon-8 Sunday noon-7.

Shoes, socks & stockings
Flatiron/East Village

The Edge: For the punk and high school set: sturdy, funky shoes and clothing. Features Dr. Marten, Getta Grips and John Fluevog shoes. Sneakers by Puma, Fred Perry, etc. Fresh "Jive" clothing with a casual, trendy look.

Peter Fox Shoes
105 Thompson Street
near Spring Street
New York, NY 10012
212-431-6359
Monday-Saturday 11-7.

Shoes, socks & stockings
SoHo/TriBeCa

quality style service value

The Edge: Fun stylish shoes. Whimsical women's shoes, boots and slippers. Known for their evening and bridal shoes. Bridal shoes at their SoHo location only.

"Has great selection in larger sizes."

806 Madison Avenue
near 67th Street/10021
212-744-8340. Fax 212-744-8368
Monday-Saturday 10-6.

Upper East Side

Plus 9
11 East 57th Street, 3rd Floor
between Madison and 5th Avenues
New York, NY 10022
212-593-3030
Monday-Saturday 10:30-6.

Shoes, socks & stockings
Midtown East

quality style service value

The Edge: Quality women's classic pumps and flats in sizes 9 and over. Features styles and designers you'd find at Bergdorf's shoe saloon, including Bruno Magli, Cole-Haan, Pancaldi, Stuart Weitzman, Via Spiga and others. Priced from $110 to $250. Great looks.

"The only place in NYC to buy high-quality shoes in big sizes. Good selection, very expensive, but worth it."

Richie's Discount Children's Shoes
183 Avenue B
near 14th Street
New York, NY 10009
212-228-5442
Daily 10-5.

Shoes, socks & stockings
Flatiron/East Village

The Edge: Alphabet City's recommended place for children's shoes. For 80 years a family business! We're not wild about Alphabet City, but this place delivers the latest shoes at 15% to 25% off list. Labels include Babybotte, Jonathan Bennett, Jumping Jacks, Keds, Shoe B'Doo, Stride Rite and European brands. Infant to teenage sizes and styles. No delivery. Discounter.

Robert Clergerie

41 East 60th Street
between Park and Madison Avenues
New York, NY 10022
212-207-8600. Fax 212-593-2741
Weekdays 10-6 Saturday 11-6.

Shoes, socks & stockings
Midtown East

quality style service value
5 5 4 4

The Edge: Shoes that define "with it" chic. Cutting-edge French shoes for those who "dress". Deluxe.

Sacco Shoes

94 7th Avenue
near 16th Street
New York, NY 10011
212-675-5180
Weekdays 11-8 Saturday 11-7 Sunday noon-7.

Shoes, socks & stockings
Chelsea

The Edge: Discounted Italian classics. Mostly Italian classic pumps and flats at moderate prices. Discounter.

111 Thompson Street
near Prince Street/10021
212-925-8010. Fax 212-243-2450
Weekdays 11-8 Saturday 11-7 Sunday noon-7.

SoHo/TriBeCa

40 West 57th Street
near 7th Avenue/10019
212-586-7176
Weekdays 11-8 Saturday 11-7 Sunday noon-7.

Midtown West

1024 3rd Avenue
near 70th Street/10021
212-759-2868
Weekdays 11-8 Saturday 11-7 Sunday noon-6.

Upper East Side

324 Columbus Avenue
near 75th Street/10023
212-799-5229
Weekdays 11-8 Saturday 11-7 Sunday noon-7.

Upper West Side

2355 Broadway
near 86th Street/10024
212-874-8362
Weekdays 11-8 Saturday 11-7 Sunday noon-7.

Upper West Side

Schmooz

317 Grand Street
near Allen Street
New York, NY 10002
212-925-6363. Fax 212-925-6399
Sunday-Friday 9:15-5:30.

Shoes, socks & stockings
Lower East Side/Chinatown

4	4	3	4
quality	style	service	value

The Edge: High-fashion shoes and accessories discounted. Discounts top Italian designer shoes as well as Cole-Haan, Nicole Miller and Cosci of Italy. Belts and accessories are also featured. 30% off.

Shoe City

133 Nassau Street
near City Hall
New York, NY 10038
212-732-3889
Weekdays 8-6 Saturday 10-4.

Shoes, socks & stockings
Lower Manhattan

The Edge: Discounts basic sneakers and shoes, including Timberland.

Shoofly

465 Amsterdam Avenue
between 82nd and 83rd Streets
New York, NY 10024
212-580-4390. Fax 212-580-4390
Monday-Saturday 11-7 Sunday noon-6.

Shoes, socks & stockings
Upper West Side

The Edge: Classic to funky shoe and hat shop for infants and young women. Features European shoes, bow ties, gloves, hair accessories, hats, shoes and suspenders at reasonable prices. Priced from $50.

Sole of Italy

125 Orchard Street
near Delancey Street
New York, NY 10002
212-674-2662. Fax 212-533-4220
Sunday-Friday 9:30-6.

Shoes, socks & stockings
Lower East Side/Chinatown

The Edge: Moderately priced Italian lines discounted. Shoes in sizes 4½ to 11 from lots of unknown designers. Styling tends to be trendier. Priced from $50.

Stapleton Shoe Company

68 Trinity Place
near Rector Street
New York, NY 10007
212-964-6329. Fax 212-608-2838
Weekdays 8-6.

Shoes, socks & stockings
Lower Manhattan

The Edge: Discounts basic moderately priced men's shoes. Bass-Weejun, Florsheim, Rockport and the like.

Statesman Shoes

Shoes, socks & stockings
Midtown East

6 East 46th Street
between 5th and Madison Avenues
New York, NY 10017
212-867-0450. Fax 212-867-0451
Weekdays 8-6:30.

The Edge: Discounts basic moderately priced shoes. Mostly men's, but some women's shoes. Features Bostonian, Easy Spirit, Florsheim, Keds, Rockport and the like. Sizes 5 to 15 A to EEE.

Stephane Kelian

Shoes, socks & stockings
SoHo/TriBeCa

quality style service value

120 Wooster Street
near Prince Street
New York, NY 10012
212-925-3077. Fax 212-925-3145
Monday-Saturday 11-7 Sunday noon-6.

The Edge: High-style designer shoes for women (and some for men). Features Gaultier, Montana, and Kelian's own line. Prices average $350 a pair. Deluxe.

717 Madison Avenue
near 62nd Street/10021
212-980-1919. Fax 212-921-9094
Monday-Friday 10-6 Saturday 11- 6.

Upper East Side

Susan Bennis / Warren Edwards

Shoes, socks & stockings
Midtown West

quality style service value

22 West 57th Street
between 5th and 6th Avenues
New York, NY 10019
212-755-4197. Fax 212-582-2342
Monday-Saturday 10-7 Sunday noon-6.

The Edge: As expensive as it gets for shoes. Stylish, sexy shoes ranging from loafers to evening in beautiful colors and materials. This store defines "expensive." Deluxe.

Tall Size Shoes

Shoes, socks & stockings
Midtown West

quality style service value

3 West 35th Street
near 5th Avenue
New York, NY 10001
212-736-2060. Fax 212-594-7088
Monday-Wednesday Saturday 9:30-6 Thursday Friday 9:30-7.

The Edge: Moderately priced women's shoes for widths other than medium. Features shoes sizes 5 to 14, in narrow to wide widths. Stocks designers like Amalfi, Evan Picone and Via Spiga. Priced from $40 to $225.

"No choice—sometimes I must buy there." "Great if you need widths other than medium!"

To Boot

256 Columbus Avenue
near 76th Street
New York, NY 10023
212-724-8249
Monday-Saturday noon-8 Sunday 1-6.

Shoes, socks & stockings
Upper West Side

quality style service value

The Edge: Stylish men's shoes. Carries a wide selection of casual to dressy top designer shoes. Also at Bergdorf's. No delivery.

"They have a wonderful selection, but you pay for it."

Tootsi Plohound

137 5th Avenue
between 20th and 21st Streets
New York, NY 10010
212-460-8650
Monday-Friday 11:30-7:30 Saturday 11-8
Sunday noon-7.

Shoes, socks & stockings
Gramercy Pk/Murray Hill

quality style service value

The Edge: Young offbeat shoes. Cutting-edge shoes that tend to be clunky. Favorites are men's classics but for women.

413 West Broadway
near 21st Street/10012
212-925-8931
Monday-Friday 11:30-7:30 Saturday 11-7 Sunday noon-6.

SoHo/TriBeCa

Trevi Shoes

141 Orchard Street
near Delancey Street
New York, NY 10002
212-505-0293. Fax 212-979-7817
Daily 10-6.

Shoes, socks & stockings
Lower East Side/Chinatown

The Edge: Moderately priced shoes for the entire family. Moderately priced shoes from $50 to $150. Children's party and adult shoes. Their own label is featured. No delivery. Discounter.

Vamps

1421 2nd Avenue
near 74th Street
New York, NY 10021
212-744-0227
Monday-Saturday 10-7 Sunday noon-6.

Shoes, socks & stockings
Upper East Side

quality style service value

The Edge: Moderately priced stylish shoes. Features casual to bridal shoes from Anne Klein, DKNY, Via Spigal and Aerosole. Dyes bridal party shoes within 24 hours. Price range $39 to $150. No delivery.

"Good value, average selection."

Vanessa Noel

12 West 57th Street, Suite 901
between 5th and 6th Avenues
New York, NY 10019
212-737-0115. Fax 212-333-7637
Weekdays 10-6 Saturday 11-5:30 by appointment.

Shoes, socks & stockings
Midtown West

quality style service value

The Edge: Glamour dress shoes, sometimes trendy. Evening and wedding designs, including traditional pumps with silk hearts hiding the toes to trendy white silk cowboy boots. Glamorous dress shoes priced from $350 to $425. Sizes 4 to 12. Deluxe.

Walter Steiger

739 Madison Avenue
between 64th and 65th Streets
New York, NY 10021
212-570-1212
Monday-Saturday 10-6.

Shoes, socks & stockings
Upper East Side

quality style service value

The Edge: Trendy gorgeous French shoes and, believe it or not, stunning golf shoes. Sexy, high-heeled designer evening shoes, casual shoes and absolutely stunning two-tone golf shoes. Makes you want to go to the course! Very expensive, priced from $245 to $295. Some shoes custom made—they're much more expensive and take six to eight weeks for delivery. Deluxe.

"Simply divine, completes a look."

417 Park Avenue
near 55th Street/10022
212-826-7171
Weekdays 9:30-6 Saturday 10-5.

Midtown East

Yaska Shoes

875 3rd Avenue
near 52nd Street
New York, NY 10022
212-371-3633
Weekdays 10-7 Saturday 11-6.

Shoes, socks & stockings
Midtown East

quality style service value

The Edge: Great sales on cutting-edge young shoes and classic work shoes with oomph. Wonderful European-style shoes from classic pumps and flats to more trendy styles. Designers include Gritti, Visconto and Pensato. Expensive at $95 to $450 with most $150 to $200, but the twice-yearly sales are great, particularly after the second markdown. For those seeking conservative, look past the very hip styles, since there's much to find. Sizes 6 to 12 with an extensive stock of larger sizes.

"Great, great, great."

1088 Madison Avenue
near 82nd Street/10028
212-734-0818
Monday-Saturday 10-6.

Upper East Side

Ashanti

872 Lexington Avenue
between 65th and 66th Streets
New York, NY 10023
212-535-0740
Monday-Wednesday Friday Saturday 10-6 Thursday 10-8.

Special sizes
Upper West Side

The Edge: Good clothing for the larger women. Clothing and accessories for the larger woman. Much of the clothing is Ashanti's own design. Off-the-rack clothing to size 28, custom clothing in larger sizes. Down the block from Forgotten Woman (another larger size store).

Chelsea Atelier

128 West 23rd Street
between 6th and 7th Avenues
New York, NY 10011
212-255-8803
Monday-Saturday noon-7 Sunday noon-5.

Special sizes
Chelsea

4	4	5	3
quality	style	service	value

The Edge: Nice clothing in hard-to-find sizes. Designs and makes clothing in one size fits all plus misses sizes 6 to 20. Stock is mostly 12 to 16s. Made in natural fabrics including cotton, crêpe de chine, raw silk, rayon, and wool. Carries the Flax line by Angel Heart. Priced from $59 to $300.

Forgotten Woman

60 West 49th Street
between 5th and 6th Avenues
New York, NY 10020
212-247-8888
Monday-Wednesday Friday Saturday l0-6
Thursday 10-7:30 Sunday noon-5.

Special sizes
Midtown West

5	5	5	3
quality	style	service	value

The Edge: Favored source for larger sized clothing. Two locations. Full range of quality clothing for women sizes 14 to 24. From casual clothing to formal wear with everything in between. Name designers like Ellen Tracy as well as some designers exclusive to them. Moderate to expensive, with coats from $100 to $2,500. The Lexington Avenue shop is down the street from Ashanti.

"Expensive, but worth it." "Helpful salespeople."

888 Lexington Avenue
near 66th Street/10021
212-535-8848. Fax 212-861-2483

Upper East Side

Rochester Big & Tall

1301 Avenue of the Americas
near 52nd Street
New York, NY 10019
212-247-7500. Fax 212-247-7245
Weekdays 9:30-6:30 Saturday 9:30-6.

Special sizes
Midtown West

5	5	4	5
quality	style	service	value

The Edge: Enormous selection of hard-to-find large sizes. Stock includes suits, shoes, shirts and more from Canali, Docker, Gant, Hickey Freeman, Levi, Oxxford, Zegna and others. Sizes from 48 regular to 60 extra-long.

"Wide variety for wide men."

Berk of Burlington Arcade London

781 Madison Avenue
near 66th Street
New York, NY 10021
212-570-0285. Fax 212-570-1019
Monday-Saturday 10-6.

Sweaters
Upper East Side

5	5	5	4
quality	style	service	value

The Edge: Top classic cashmeres. To six-ply cashmere items in a wide range of colors. Priced from $199 to $900. Capes and wonderful velvet slippers in deep autumn colors (slippers $185 to $200). Deluxe.

Best of Scotland

581 5th Avenue
between 47 and 48th Streets
New York, NY 10017
212-644-0415. Fax 212-644-6278
Monday-Saturday 10-5.

Sweaters
Midtown East

4	4	4	4
quality	style	service	value

The Edge: Beautiful sweaters somewhat less expensive than the top known spots. Sweaters, cashmere capes and stoles are priced from $160 to $325. Hundreds of colors. 30% off.

Cashmere-Cashmere

840 Madison Avenue
between 69th and 70th Streets
New York, NY 10021
212-988-5252. Fax 212-439-0638
Weekdays 10-6 Saturday noon-6 Sunday noon-5.

Sweaters
Upper East Side

4	4	3	3
quality	style	service	value

The Edge: Quality and colors. Classic to high fashion (to 10-ply) cashmere clothing and accessories in a range of excellent colors. Find blankets, dresses, robes, socks, sweat suits and sweaters. Prices start at $195. Great size range. Guests at the Four Seasons Hotel get a 10% discount. Deluxe.

Granny-Made

381 Amsterdam Avenue
near 78th Street
New York, NY 10024
212-496-1222. Fax 212-496-5362
Weekdays 11-7 Saturday 10-6 Sunday noon-5.

Sweaters
Upper West Side

5	4	4	-
quality	style	service	value

The Edge: Grandma-designed but machine-executed sweaters. Sweaters for children through adult sizes. A full range of knit items from ski caps to suits and dresses. Sweaters only for men.

"Wonderful treasures, including baby gifts."

Manrico Cashmere

804 Madison Avenue
near 68th Street
New York, NY 10021
212-794-4200. Fax 212-794-8515
Monday-Saturday 10-6.

Sweaters
Upper East Side

The Edge: Quality cashmere sweaters. 2- to 10-ply cashmere sweaters from Inner Mongolia with Italian design and detailing. Priced from $285 to $1,000. Gorgeous.

Missoni

836 Madison Avenue
near 69th Street
New York, NY 10021
212-517-9339. Fax 212-439-6037
Monday-Saturday 10-6.

Sweaters
Upper East Side

4	4	5	3
quality	style	service	value

The Edge: Bright one-of-a-kind wool-weave garments. Best known for sweaters. They also offers coats, dresses, jackets, scarves, socks and ties that never seem to change. Misses sizes 6 to 14 and men's sizes 48 to 56. Deluxe.

N. Peal

118 East 57th Street
between Park and Lexington Avenues
New York, NY 10022
212-826-3350. Fax 212-826-3057
Monday-Saturday 10-6. Closed Saturday July and August.

Sweaters
Midtown East

5	4	4	4
quality	style	service	value

The Edge: Scottish cashmere knitwear. Wonderful cable sweaters, running suits, his and hers cashmere robes. Priced from $300 to $1,500. Deluxe.

TSE Cashmere

827 Madison Avenue
at 69th Street
New York, NY 10021
212-472-7790. Fax 212-472-7485
Monday-Wednesday Friday Saturday 10-6 Thursday 10-7.

Sweaters
Upper East Side

5	5	4	4
quality	style	service	value

The Edge: Luxurious cashmeres. Classic cashmere turtlenecks, cardigans and polos, sportswear, coats and natural-tone robes and blankets. TSE has an outlet at Woodbury Commons where you'll find their wonderful things discounted. Deluxe.

Allan & Suzi

416 Amsterdam Avenue
near 80th Street
New York, NY 10024
212-724-7445
Monday-Saturday noon-7 Sunday 1-6.

Thrift shops
Upper West Side

5	5	3	4
quality	style	service	value

The Edge: Dramatic evening wear. Both new and barely worn top-designer evening wear. You never know which designer you'll find. Mixes new gowns with clothing from the 1930s to 1950s. Allan and Suzi are very friendly and helpful. Also shoes (platforms), boas, jewelry and wigs and ladies' shoes in extra-large sizes. Priced from $10 to $10,000! Outrageous clothing a specialty.

"Very dramatic funky items." "A favorite for drag queens!"

Cancer Care Thrift Shop

1480 3rd Avenue
between 83rd and 84th Streets
New York, NY 10028
212-879-9868
Monday Tuesday Friday 11-6 Wednesday Thursday 11-7
Saturday 10-4:30 Sunday 12:30-5.

Thrift shops
Upper East Side

3	3	4	5
quality	style	service	value

The Edge: Designer evening dresses—sometimes. Mostly clothing with some furniture. When in the neighborhood check out the costume jewelry, vintage lingerie and designer evening dresses. On occasion wonderful finds, like Chanel costume jewelry and designer items. A good place to donate clothing. For larger donations, items can be scheduled for pickup. No delivery.

"Give good receipts for donations." "Fabulous designer evening dresses—must go often—sometimes nothing."

Encore

1132 Madison Avenue
near 84th Street
New York, NY 10028
212-879-2850
Monday-Wednesday Friday 10:30-6:30
Thursday 10:30-7:30 Saturday 10:30-6 Sunday noon-6.

Thrift shops
Upper East Side

4	4	3	4
quality	style	service	value

The Edge: Barely used designer clothing. Sells barely used clothes from top American and European designers. Clothes for day and for those splashy evening events. Some men's clothing. No credit cards. No delivery. Discounter.

"Hit or miss."

Good-Byes

230 East 78th Street
between 2nd and 3rd Avenues
New York, NY 10021
212-794-2301
Weekdays 11:30-6 Saturday 10:30-5.

Thrift shops
Upper East Side

5	5	3	5
quality	style	service	value

The Edge: High-quality secondhand clothing, accessories and toys for children from infant through age 14. Everything is cleaned and in great condition and looks like new. They'll take consigned clothes with the shop getting 50% of the sales dollars. Priced from $10 to $100. No credit cards. No delivery.

INA

101 Thompson Street
between Houston and Spring Streets
New York, NY 10012
212-941-4757
Daily noon-7.

Thrift shops
SoHo/TriBeCa

quality style service value

The Edge: Consignment shop for avant-garde cutting-edge designers. Carries top European and Japanese designers like Alaida, Comme des Garçons, Gaultier and Matsuda. A truly special source for day to evening wear. Merchandise comes from fashion insiders—magazine shoots, samples, walkers, etc., so in very good condition. No delivery.

"Seems expensive for used, but the designers are tops."

Irvington Institute Thrift Shop

1534 2nd Avenue
near 80th Street
New York, NY 10021
212-879-4555
Monday Tuesday Friday Saturday 10-6
Thursday 10-8 Sunday noon-5.

Thrift shops
Upper East Side

quality style service value

The Edge: A great place for your own donations. Mostly very basic clothing, not in perfect condition, and some furniture. Find costume jewelry, vintage clothing and accessories. A good source for furniture for that first post-college apartment. Irvington House is perhaps the best place to donate used items. They'll give you a set appointment for pickup and they provide good valuations to be used for tax deductions.

Memorial Sloan-Kettering Thrift Store

1440 3rd Avenue
near 81st Street
New York, NY 10028
212-535-1250. Fax 212-737-9746
Monday-Wednesday Friday 10-5:30 Thursday 10-7
Saturday 10-5. July and August Thursday 10-8.

Thrift shops
Upper East Side

quality style service value

The Edge: Vintage clothing and accessories at times. Good place for donations. Offers mostly clothing and accessories with some furniture and housewares. Vintage clothing and accessories can be good and this is an excellent place to donate used clothing and household items for favorable tax deductions. They'll pick up if the donation is furniture or a large amount of clothing. No delivery.

Michael's Resale Dress Shop

1041 Madison Avenue
near 79th Street
New York, NY 10021
212-737-7273. Fax 212-737-7211
Monday-Wednesday Friday Saturday 9:30-6
Thursday 9:30-8.

Thrift shops
Upper East Side

quality style service value

The Edge: Slightly used designer clothing. Find designer day to evening clothes. You never know what they get. Favors top designers and stocks wedding gowns. Priced from $40 to $900. No delivery.

"Best clothes are sizes 4 and 6."

Spence-Chapin Thrift Shop

1430 3rd Avenue
between 81st and 82nd Streets
New York, NY 10028
212-737-8448. Fax 212-794-2384
Monday-Wednesday Friday 10-7 Thursday 10-8
Saturday 10-5 Sunday noon-5.

Thrift shops
Upper East Side

quality	style	service	value
4	4	3	5

The Edge: Vintage lingerie and accessories, which at times are great. Two floors, including a separate designer area upstairs. Vintage lingerie and linens are favorites. Accessories (handbags, jewelry and hats) are sometimes great. Proceeds benefit Spence-Chapin Adoption Resource Center. Good donations. Will pick up furniture. No delivery.

A.W. Kaufman

73 Orchard Street
between Broome and Grand Streets
New York, NY 10002
212-226-1629. Fax 212-226-1787
Monday-Thursday 10:30-5 Friday 10:30-2 Sunday 10-5.

Underwear & lingerie
Lower East Side/Chinatown

quality	style	service	value
5	4	4	5

The Edge: Could be the best-stocked top-quality designer lingerie shop in the city—plus it's discounted. Crammed with quality lingerie, lounge wear, underwear, gowns and robes at about 20% off. Features European (France, Switzerland and Belgium) lingerie. Virtually impossible to see what they have since the store is stocked so tightly and is often crowded. Labels include Calida, Christian Dior, David Brown, Hanro, Lejaby, Pluto and more. Phone orders are routine.

"If I can't find what I want uptown, I come here. I should start here—they have it all!!"

AM/PM

109 Thompson Street
between Prince and Spring Streets
New York, NY 10012
212-219-0343
Daily noon-7.

Underwear & lingerie
SoHo/TriBeCa

The Edge: Outrageous lingerie, including bustiers if you're so inclined. Lingerie from the demure (Hanro) to the outrageous. A little of everything. No delivery.

Brief Essentials

1407 Broadway
between 38th and 39th Streets
New York, NY 10018
212-921-8344
Weekdays 8:30-5:30.

Underwear & lingerie
Midtown West

The Edge: The basics in moderately priced lingerie and exercise wear. Discounter.

Chas. Weiss Fashions

331 Grand Street
near Orchard Street
New York, NY 10002
212-966-1143
Sunday-Thursday 10:30-4:30 Friday 10:30-2:30.

Underwear & lingerie
Lower East Side/Chinatown

3	2	2	4
quality	style	service	value

The Edge: Basic underwear discounted. Mostly a bra and panty store. Basic functional inexpensive items including jogging suits, nightgowns and Danskins. Telephone orders make it convenient.

Enelra

48½ East 7th Street
near 5th Avenue
New York, NY 10003
212-473-2454. Fax 212-874-6328
Sunday-Wednesday noon-8:30 Thursday Friday noon-9:30.

Underwear & lingerie
Flatiron/East Village

The Edge: Sexy lingerie. Runs the gamut from practical to sexy (her specialty) lingerie (teddies, slips and nightgowns) to funky, including jeweled bustiers, to vinyl bondage wear (if you find that funky). Lingerie from $5 to $250.

Grand Lingerie

330 Grand Street
between Orchard and Ludlow Streets
New York, NY 10002
212-473-0969
Sunday-Friday 10-5.

Underwear & lingerie
Lower East Side/Chinatown

The Edge: 25% off on brand-name underwear. Features Lollipop, Maidenform, Vanity Fair and many other brands, but no Calvin Klein. No credit cards. No delivery.

Howron Sportswear

295 Grand Street
near Allen Street
New York, NY 10002
212-226-4307. Fax 212-226-4307
Sunday-Friday 9-5:30.

Underwear & lingerie
Lower East Side/Chinatown

The Edge: The basics discounted. While they feature men's sportswear (Countess Mara, Pierre Cardin and Sansabelt), they're a better source for men's and women's underwear (Bali, Olga, Vanity Fair and Warner) and hosiery (Berkshire, CK, Givenchy, Hanes and Round the Clock). Wide range of sizes.

Joovay

436 West Broadway
near Prince Street
New York, NY 10012

Underwear & lingerie
SoHo/TriBeCa

5	5	5	4
quality	style	service	value

212-431-6386
Daily noon-7.

The Edge: Feminine delicate lingerie. Features delicate colors, fine fabrics and feminine trims. Stocks top lines like Christian Dior, Hanro, La Perla and Pluto. Prices for bras from $22 to $147 and panties from $9 to $95.

"Wonderful things."

La Lingerie
Underwear & lingerie
Upper East Side

792 Madison Avenue
near 67th Street
New York, NY 10021
212-517-4700. Fax 212-628-7528
Friday-Wednesday 9:30-6:30 Thursday 9:30-7:30.

The Edge: One of the city's most glamorous lingerie stores. Lingerie made from the finest fabrics, featuring sexy but refined styling. Prices are stratospheric.

Lauren Bogen Loungerie
Underwear & lingerie
Upper East Side

1042 Lexington Avenue
between 74th and 75th Streets
New York, NY 10021
212-570-9529. Fax 212-570-9534
Monday-Wednesday Friday Saturday 10-6:30 Thursday 10-7.

The Edge: Lingerie for all occasions. Wonderful lingerie from the practical to the feminine soft and sexy. Lovely gifts.

Mendel Weiss
Underwear & lingerie
Lower East Side/Chinatown

quality	style	service	value
3	3	3	4

91 Orchard Street
near Broome Street
New York, NY 10002
212-925-6815
Sunday-Thursday 9:30-4 Friday 9:30-3.

The Edge: T-Shirts in all colors. T-shirts from Action Tee and Fruit of the Loom and bras from Bali, Carnival and Maiden Form. Very inexpensive. Discounter.

Montenapoleone
Underwear & lingerie
Upper East Side

quality	style	service	value
5	5	4	3

789 Madison Avenue
near 66th Street
New York, NY 10021
212-535-2660. Fax 212-535-8967
Monday-Saturday 10-6.

The Edge: Exquisite, high- high-end lingerie. Sexy lingerie in fabulous silks with lace detailing. Colors tend to be muted but some more statement colors are available. Go upstairs for equally fabulous Italian swimwear. Deluxe.

Peress

739 Madison Avenue
near 64th Street
New York, NY 10021
212-861-6336
Monday-Saturday 10-6.

Underwear & lingerie
Upper East Side

quality style service value

The Edge: Lovely intimate apparel. High-end lingerie from all the top moderate to very expensive lines. Bras $13 to $150. Check the sales in January and August.

Roberta

1252 Madison Avenue
near 90th Street
New York, NY 10128
212-860-8366. Fax 212-860-8366
Monday-Saturday 10-6.

Underwear & lingerie
Upper East Side

quality style service value

The Edge: Well-stocked neighborhood lingerie shop. Everything you'd want in a lingerie store from basic to sexy styles. Extras include swimsuits and nursing bras. They offer top lines and attention to fit. Prices on bras $18 to $125.

"Good local lingerie shop."

Round-the-Clock Pantyhose by Mail

800-926-4022. Fax 717-840-5855
Weekdays 8-5 EST.

Underwear & lingerie
Mail/phone

The Edge: Carries Round-the-Clock and Givenchy hosiery discounted.

Samantha Jones

1074 3rd Avenue
near 63rd Street
New York, NY 10021
212-308-6680. Fax 212-308-6680
Weekdays 10-7 Saturday 10-6 Sunday 1-6.

Underwear & lingerie
Upper East Side

quality style service value

The Edge: Sexy lingerie. Lingerie and accessories, including silk scarves and fragrances. Features La Perla, Lise Charmel, Samantha Jones and other lines.

Schachner Fashions

95 Delancey Street
between Orchard and Ludlow Streets
New York, NY 10002
212-677-0700
Daily 9-5:30 Sunday 9-6.

Underwear & lingerie
Lower East Side/Chinatown

quality style service value

The Edge: Value for the lingerie basics. Features robes, sleep wear, underwear and lounge wear discounted. Brands carried include Vanity Fair, Exquisite Form, Barbizon, Maidenform, Carnival, Warner's, Bali and others.

Sue Ekahn/New York

212-929-4432
By appointment.

Underwear & lingerie
Mail/phone

The Edge: Focus is on custom lingerie and home wear. Her specialty is custom bridal trousseaus and gifts for bridal attendants. She used to be Diana Vreeland's personal shopper. Creative and flexible, she'll make it or find it for you.

Victoria's Secret

691 Madison Avenue
near 62nd Street
New York, NY 10021
212-838-9266
Monday-Saturday 10-8 Sunday noon-6.

Underwear & lingerie
Upper East Side

3	4	3	4
quality	style	service	value

The Edge: Nice-looking inexpensive lingerie. Owned by The Limited and in malls all over the U.S. The shop is devoted to attractive lingerie in a wide price range. Both sexy and functional items. No delivery.

Other locations
34 East 57th Street
between Park and Madison Avenues/10022
212-758-5592
Monday-Wednesday Friday 10-7 Thursday 10-8 Saturday 10- 6 Sunday noon-5.

Midtown East

Dornan

653 11th Avenue
between 47th and 48th Streets
New York, NY 10036
212-247-0937. Fax 212-956-7672
Monday-Wednesday Friday 8:30-4 Thursday 8:30-6.

Uniforms
Midtown West

The Edge: One-stop shopping for uniforms. Uniforms for chauffeurs, butlers, maids and cooks and, if you're on your coop/condo board, uniforms for doormen, handymen, superintendents and the like. They'll customize and distribute uniforms worldwide.

Ideal Department Store

1814-1816 Flatbush Avenue
Brooklyn, NY 11210
718-252-5090. Fax 718-692-0492
Monday-Saturday 10-5:45.

Uniforms
Brooklyn

The Edge: Boy and Girl Scout uniforms in children's sizes with some for adults.

Academy Clothes

1703 Broadway
near 54th Street
New York, NY 10019
212-765-1440
Weekdays 10-6:30 Saturday 10-5.

Vintage
Midtown West

The Edge: Dramatic, inexpensive clothing for college men. Vintage clothing in good condition. Menswear is largest selection. You never know what they have, but expect to find it all, from casual to formal. Favors period pieces. No delivery.

Alice Underground

380 Columbus Avenue
near 78th Street
New York, NY 10024
212-724-6682
Sunday-Friday 11-7 Saturday 11-8.

Vintage
Upper West Side

quality	style	service	value
3	4	3	5

The Edge: Vintage Heaven!! Casual to formal period clothing from the 1930s to the 1970s. Strong on the 1950s and 1960s. Vintage jeans and antique linens too. Find $1 scarves and $200 leather jackets. Great beaded sweaters.

"Don't send a kid to college without stopping here." "Fun vintage clothing." "Lots to look through to find the winners!"

Andy's Chee-Pee's

691 Broadway
between West 3rd and West 4th Streets
New York, NY 10012
212-420-5980. Fax 212-254-3610
Monday-Saturday 11-9 Sunday noon-5.

Vintage
SoHo/TriBeCa

quality	style	service	value
4	5	4	5

The Edge: Fun used stuff, mostly for the younger set. Vintage clothing primarily for women, with some for men. Day dresses to wedding gowns and formal wear. Period pieces from the 1920s, but most from the 1950s and 1960s. Used Levis are a specialty ($30 a pair). Most of the merchandise is well worn. A large selection of suede and leather jackets from $35 to $150. Collector's items are priced at $600. No delivery.

"A better selection for non-average sizes." "Vintage clothing bargains—why buy a new tux?"

Antique Boutique

712 Broadway
near Washington Place
New York, NY 10003
212-460-8830. Fax 212-598-9024
Monday-Thursday 11-9 Friday Saturday 11-10
Sunday noon-8.

Vintage
Flatiron/East Village

quality	style	service	value
4	4	2	3

The Edge: Vintage clothing in good condition. Another favorite source for the younger set. You'll never know what you'll find: sequined sweaters, bathing suits, jeans, wedding dresses and more. Shop here to dress for the club scene.

Cheap Jack's Vintage Clothing

841 Broadway
near 13th Street
New York, NY 10003

Vintage
Flatiron/East Village

quality	style	service	value
2	3	2	3

212-777-9564
Monday-Saturday 11-8 Sunday noon-7.

The Edge: Huge selection of vintage treasures. You'll never know what to expect, from evening dresses, leather and wool coats, military clothing, tweed jackets, suits, shirts, tuxedos and slacks of all kinds. Largest selection for men. Beaded sweaters and wool skirts for women. Levis jeans priced from $5 to $2,000 (collector's items), with most $35 to $65. More expensive than many other vintage stores. No delivery.

"A scream."

Dorothy's Closet

335 Bleecker Street
near Christopher Street
New York, NY 10014
212-206-6414
Daily noon-7.

Vintage
Greenwich Village

The Edge: Carefully selected vintage clothing. Small shop with limited, but excellent, vintage clothing from the 1930s to 1960s for men and women. Expect the always-useful little black cocktail dress, luxurious lingerie, fitted women's jackets, vests and great accessories. Good selection of vintage Levis from $15. All in good condition. No delivery.

Jana Starr Antiques

236 East 80th Street
near 3rd Avenue
New York, NY 10021
212-861-8256
Monday-Saturday 11-6 or by appointment.

Vintage
Upper East Side

5	5	5	4
quality	style	service	value

The Edge: Jana Star and former partner, Jean Hoffman are among the best sources for exquisite Victorian wedding gowns. Picture-perfect Victorian white and Irish-lace bridal dresses from 1890 to the 1950s. Favors gowns from 1890 to 1930. Wedding dresses are priced from $700 up, with most averaging $1,000 to $1,200 but some much more. Some 1930s evenings gowns and shoes, veils and jewelry to match. Also christening gowns. Jana Starr has been featured in *Vogue* and *Martha Stewart*. Provides props to photographers and stylists.

"A very special place. Don't miss this."

Jean Hoffman

207 East 66th Street
near 3rd Avenue
New York, NY 10021
212-535-6930
Monday-Saturday noon-6 or by appointment.

Vintage
Upper East Side

5	5	5	4
quality	style	service	value

The Edge: Hoffman and former partner, Jana Starr, are among the best sources for exquisite Victorian wedding gowns. Quality vintage items from 1890 to 1950 in perfect condition. Features absolutely beautiful vintage Victorian wedding gowns plus a limited selection of other period clothing and accessories.

"Worth a look just to escape back to more elegant times." "Simply delightful, exciting clothes to wear to so many places."

Legacy
109 Thompson Street
near Spring Street
New York, NY 10012
212-966-4827
Daily noon-7.

Vintage
SoHo/TriBeCa

The Edge: Another vintage source plus some new designs inspired by old styles. Great for beading, sequins and Victorian white dresses.

Love Saves the Day
119 2nd Avenue
near 7th Street
New York, NY 10003
212-228-3802
Sunday-Thursday noon-9 Friday Saturday noon-11.

Vintage
Flatiron/East Village

The Edge: 1950s and 1960s kitsch items. Clothing and TV sitcom collectibles from the 1950s and 1960s. Tremendous selection of period collectibles. Collectible toys from *Star Wars* to Barbie.

Nicolina of New York
247 West 46th Street
between 6th and 7th Avenues
New York, NY 10036
212-302-6426. Fax 212-302-6426
Monday-Saturday 10-10 Sunday 10-8.

Vintage
Midtown West

The Edge: Best known for new clothes in old styles by local artists. Features accessories and unique ready-to-wear with styling from the early 1920s to the 1940s. Very few men's items (cufflinks, ties, shirts, vests). Loose and flowing women's clothing.

Reminiscence
74 5th Avenue
near 13th Street
New York, NY 10011
212-243-2292. Fax 212-807-0321
Monday-Saturday 11-8 Sunday noon-7.

Vintage
Chelsea

3	4	3	4
quality	style	service	value

The Edge: Retro 1950s and 1960s clothing, some jewelry and accessories. Favored by our younger respondents. Funky items. Ever changing.

"Style is used. Fun to shop."

Screaming Mimi's
382 Lafayette Street
near Great Jones Street
New York, NY 10003

Vintage
Flatiron/East Village

212-677-6464. Fax 212-677-6464
Weekdays 11-8 Saturday noon-8 Sunday noon-6.

The Edge: Fashion-forward store. Vintage clothing and new "hot" designers—Dollhouse, Living Doll, Girlie, NYC and Blackheat. Vintage styles from the 1950s to the 1970s in clothing, accessories and gloves. Whatever they have is fashion forward!

Trash and Vauderville

Vintage
Flatiron/East Village

4 St. Mark's Place
between 2nd and 3rd Avenues
New York, NY 10003
212-982-3590
Monday-Thursday noon-8 Friday 11:30-8 Saturday 11:30-9 Sunday 1-7:30.

The Edge: Funky, hot young styles. Clothing, accessories and footwear for the very young. Styles from leather bras and g-strings to statement East Village–style prom wear! Some new clothing from Europe. No delivery.

Billy Martin's Western Wear

Western wear
Upper East Side

812 Madison Avenue
near 68th Street
New York, NY 10021
212-861-3100. Fax 212-861-2205
Weekdays 10-7 Saturday 10-6 Sunday noon-5.

5	4	3	2
quality	style	service	value

The Edge: The source for top western gear. The city's best-known spot for top-quality and high priced western gear. Features boots, shirts, riding pants, western hats, parkas, jackets and accessories. Wonderful sterling jewelry. Boots mostly priced from $350 to $695 for lizard; their most expensive boot costs $5,000!

"Western wear with an attitude." "Great but pricey."

Whiskey Dust

Western wear
Greenwich Village

526 Hudson Street
between West 10th and Charles Streets
New York, NY 10014
212-691-5576
Monday-Saturday 12:30-7 Sunday 1-6.

The Edge: Vintage western gear for sale or rent. Rentals at 30% of the retail price for a three-day period. An affordable alternative to buying for those western theme parties. Rentals cater to the film industry. No delivey.

The ratings: **5** excellent **4** very good **3** good **2** fair **1** so-so

Cosmetics, bath & beauty

Alcone Warehouse
5-49 49th Avenue
Long Island City, NY 11101
718-361-8373. Fax 718-729-8296
Weekdays 9-4:30.

Cosmetics, etc.
Queens

The Edge: Professional theater makeup for all via mail order. The Alcone warehouse provides makeup, makeup cases, brushes and supplies through its mail-order service. Originally targeted to professional theater personnel, now for all.

Aveda Lifestyle Store
140 5th Avenue
near 19th Street
New York, NY 10011
212-645-4797
Weekdays 10-7 Saturday noon-7 Sunday noon-6.

Cosmetics, etc.
Chelsea

quality style service value

The Edge: Reputed as the source for aroma therapy and products. Find biodegradable products made from flowers and plants for your hair and body, scented candles, fabric and household cleaners. Also haircuts, facials, body massages and makeup at $65 for a haircut, shampoo and blow dry, $45 (for a half hour) to $95 (for 1½ hours) for a massage and facials from $45 to $90. Home appointments are possible (but are not common and need arranging) by calling the West Broadway store. No delivery.

456 West Broadway
between Prince and Houston Streets/10012
212-473-0280
Monday-Saturday 11-8 Sunday noon-6.

SoHo/TriBeCa

233 Spring Street
between 6th Avenue and Varick Street/10013
212-807-1492
Weekdays 10-7 Saturday 10-6 Sunday noon-6.

SoHo/TriBeCa

509 Madison Avenue
near 53rd Street/10022
212-832-2416. Fax 212-832-2551
Weekdays 10-7 Saturday noon-6 Sunday noon-5.

Midtown East

Body Shop
901 Avenue of the Americas
near 33rd Street
New York, NY 10001
212-268-7424
Weekdays 9-7 Saturday 11-7 Sunday 11-5.

Cosmetics, etc.
Midtown West

4 3 3 4
quality style service value

The Edge: Environmentally safe lotions and soaps. Known for their custom-made baskets filled with your choice of fragrant soaps and lotions. Offers free makeovers, no purchase required. 10% discount available with the Transmedia card.

747 Broadway near 8th Avenue/10003 212-979-2944	**Flatiron/East Village**
135 5th Avenue near 20th Street/10010 212-254-0145	**Gramercy Pk/Murray Hill**
1270 Avenue of the Americas near 52nd Street/10020 212-397-3007	**Midtown West**
773 Lexington Avenue near 61st Street/10021 212-755-7851	**Upper East Side**
485 Madison Avenue near 52nd Street/10022 212-832-0812	**Midtown East**
2159 Broadway near 77th Street/10023 212-721-2947	**Upper West Side**
World Trade Center Concourse #340 Building 5/10048 212-488-7595	**Lower Manhattan**

Boyd's Chemist

655 Madison Avenue
near 60th Street
New York, NY 10021
212-838-6558. Fax 212-832-0972
Weekdays 8:30-7:30 Saturday 9:30-7 Sunday noon-6.

Cosmetics, etc.
Upper East Side

quality	style	service	value
4	4	4	3

The Edge: Superb makeovers and excellent products. Excellent makeup instruction (including instructional diagrams) with their own and/or name-brand products. You name the beauty need and they have it. Also brushes, soaps, jewelry, hair accessories and more. Prescriptions service. High-end prices.

"Great advice."

Caswell-Massey Company Ltd.

518 Lexington Avenue
near 48th Street
New York, NY 10017
212-755-2254. Fax 212-888-4915

Cosmetics, etc.
Midtown East

quality	style	service	value
5	3	4	3

Weekdays 9-7 Saturday 10-6.

The Edge: Old-fashioned shop, selling soaps, colognes, lotions and powders. Large selection of herbal, glycerine, coconut oil, oatmeal, buttermilk treatments and gift packages.

Cosmetic Show

919 3rd Avenue
at 56th Street
New York, NY 10022
212-750-8418
Weekdays 8-7 Saturday 10-5 Sunday 11-5.

Cosmetics, etc.
Midtown East

| 3 | 3 | 3 | 5 |
| quality | style | service | value |

The Edge: Overstocks or older styles from all the major cosmetic houses deeply discounted. Worth the time to browse for cosmetics and perfumes from all the major houses deeply discounted. Lots of gift packages (like those inducements you get at cosmetic counters). Not necessarily the latest colors or scents, but virtually everything you use, if you're at all flexible. Also boxed candies and cookies. Yes, it's in the office building (side entrance) slightly off 3rd Avenue on 56th Street. No delivery.

Cosmetic World and Gift Center

393 5th Avenue, 2nd Floor
between 36th and 37th Streets
New York, NY 10016
212-213-4047
Monday-Friday 10-6. Closed Saturday, but open December Saturdays 10-6.

Cosmetics, etc.
Gramercy Pk/Murray Hill

The Edge: Cosmetics showroom open to the public. Like the duty-free shops at airports. An eclectic mix of cosmetics, men's and women's fragrances, handbags, jewelry and ties at discounts that range from 15% to 50% (50% on discontinued items). They stock major brands and have a multilingual staff. Telephone and mail orders are possible.

Cosmetics Plus

170 Broadway
near Maiden Lane
New York, NY 10003
212-843-6656
Weekdays 9-7 Saturday 11-7 Sunday 11-5.

Cosmetics, etc.
SoHo/TriBeCa

| 5 | 4 | 4 | 4 |
| quality | style | service | value |

The Edge: Cosmetics from the top companies at 10% to 20% off list. Find Borghese, Lancôme, Elizabeth Arden and many others. Virtually all brands of cosmetics, hair treatments, perfumes as well as accessories, hair bands, hosiery, costume jewelry, nonprescription drugs and fragrances for men.

275 7th Avenue
near 26th Street/10001
212-924-3493
Weekdays 8-7:30 Saturday 10-6.

Midtown West

605 3rd Avenue
near 40th Street/10016
212-986-1407. Fax 212-843-2626

Gramercy Pk/Murray Hill

Weekdays 8:30-7:30 Saturday 10-6.

1320 Avenue of the Americas   **Midtown West**
at 55th Street/10019
212-247-0444
Weekdays 9-9 Saturday 10-8 Sunday 11-7.

171 West 57th Street   **Midtown West**
between 6th and 7th Avenues/10019
212-399-9783. Fax 212-843-2626
Weekdays 9-9 Saturday 10-8 Sunday 11-8.

666 5th Avenue   **Midtown West**
near 53rd Street/10019
212-757-2895
Weekdays 8-7 Saturday 10-6 Sunday 11-6.

1601 Broadway   **Midtown West**
near 48th Street/10019
212-757-3122
Weekdays 9-8 weekends 10-8.

1201 3rd Avenue   **Upper East Side**
near 70th Street/10021
212-628-5600
Weekdays 9:30-8 Saturday 10-7 Sunday 11-7.

1388 3rd Avenue   **Upper East Side**
near 79th Street/10021
212-772-3633
Weekdays 10-8 Saturday 10-8 Sunday 11-7.

875 3rd Avenue   **Midtown East**
at 53rd Street/10022
212-319-2120
Weekdays 9-6.

515 Madison Avenue   **Midtown East**
near 53rd Street/10022
212-644-1911
Weekdays 8-7:30 Saturday 10-7 Sunday 11-6.

500 Lexington Avenue   **Midtown East**
between 47th and 48th Streets/10017
212-832-5460
Weekdays 8-7 Saturday 10-6.

2151 Broadway   **Upper West Side**
near 76th Street/10023
212-595-7727
Weekdays 9-7 Saturday 11-7 Sunday 11-5.

1920 Broadway   **Upper West Side**

near 65th Street/10023
212-875-8604
Monday-Wednesday 10-8:30 Thursday Friday 10-9 weekends 11-8.

516 5th Avenue   **Midtown West**
near 43rd Street/10036
212-221-6560. Fax 212-768-4553
Weekdays 8-7:30 Saturday 10-6 Sunday noon-5.

Crabtree and Evelyn   Cosmetics, etc.
620 5th Avenue   **Midtown West**
near 49th Street
New York, NY 10020
212-581-5022. Fax 212-262-7079
Monday-Saturday 10-6 Sunday 11-5.

quality style service value

The Edge: Custom gift baskets filled with your special picks. Baskets include sachets, baby products, shampoos and conditioners, soaps, gels, hangers, brushes, potpourri and candles. All natural ingredients and no animal testing. They offer many fragrances as well as cookies and jams.

520 Madison Avenue   **Midtown East**
between 53rd and 54th Streets/10022
212-758-6919. Fax 212-758-7847
Monday-Saturday 10-6.

World Trade Center   **Lower Manhattan**
at Fulton Street/10048
212-432-7134
Weekdays 7:30-7 Saturday noon-5.

1310 Madison Avenue   **Upper East Side**
near 93rd Street/10128
212-289-3923. Fax 212-289-3923
Monday-Saturday 10-6.

Floris   Cosmetics, etc.
703 Madison Avenue   **Upper East Side**
near 62nd Street
New York, NY 10021
212-935-9100. Fax 212-888-2001
Monday-Wednesday Friday Saturday 10-6 Thursday 10-7.

The Edge: Old-fashioned Victorian English shop offering wonderful floral fragrances. New York branch of an English shop offering floral scented fragrances, soaps, room sprays, sachets and dusting powders

Jay's Perfume Bar   Cosmetics, etc.
14 East 17th Street   **Flatiron/East Village**
near 5th Avenue
New York, NY 10003
212-243-7743. Fax 212-620-0198

Weekdays 9-6 Saturday 9-4:30 Sunday 10-4.

The Edge: Discounts perfume 20%. In spot checks, Jay's appears slightly cheaper than other sources, but like many discounters, they do not have a complete selection of brands and fragrances. Find perfume copies as well.

Jean Laporte L'Artisan Parfumeur
870 Madison Avenue
near 71st Street
New York, NY 10021
212-517-8665. Fax 212-517-7131
Monday-Saturday 10-6.

Cosmetics, etc.
Upper East Side

The Edge: Only natural fragrances for the home or body.

MAC Cosmetics
14 Christopher Street
near 6th Avenue
New York, NY 10014
212-243-4150. Fax 212-243-4168
Monday-Saturday noon-7 Sunday 1-6.

Cosmetics, etc.
Greenwich Village

5	5	4	4
quality	style	service	value

The Edge: The not-so-secret source where models get done and buy supplies. Their own line of cosmetics—light, easy to apply and less expensive than other top lines. Good colors and selections.

"Makeup applications are terrific."

Perfumania
1585 Broadway
near 48th Street
New York, NY 10036
212-541-8047
Monday-Saturday 9-9 Sunday 11-7.

Cosmetics, etc.
Midtown West

The Edge: Perfume discounted 20% to 75% off retail. Sells perfume at 20% off for newer fragrances to 40% to 75% off retail for older lines. They carry American and European brands and offer discounts on gift sets. Call first to check prices and stock, since like most discounters, they don't have everything.

One Penn Plaza
lower level across from LIRR/10001
212-268-0049
Weekdays 7:30-8 Saturday 7:30-7:30 Sunday 10-6.

Midtown West

20 West 34th Street
near 5th Avenue/10001
212-736-0414
Weekdays 9-8 Saturday 10-7 Sunday 11-7.

Midtown West

755 Broadway
at 8th Street/10003

Flatiron/East Village

212-979-7674
Monday-Saturday 10-9 Sunday noon-7.

782 Lexington Avenue   **Upper East Side**
near 60th Street/10021
212-750-2810
Monday-Saturday 9-8 Sunday 11-6.

2321 Broadway   **Upper West Side**
near 84th Street/10024
212-595-8778
Monday-Saturday 10-9.

Revlon Employee Store

Cosmetics, etc.
767 5th Avenue   **Midtown East**
near 58th Street
New York, NY 10022

4	3	2	5
quality	style	service	value

Monday-Friday 10-4.

The Edge: Employee prices. In the basement (past the Vidal Sassoon salon) is the Revlon company store. Follow the signs—the shop is off the main corridor behind closed but unlocked doors. It's a wonderful source for a wide range of Revlon products, especially the more moderate lines at close to 50% off. While officially a company store only, they're flexible and ask no questions.

Ricky's

Cosmetics, etc.
501 2nd Avenue   **Gramercy Pk/Murray Hill**
near 28th Street
New York, NY 10016
212-679-5435. Fax 212-679-0704
Daily 8-11

The Edge: Discounts top-brand cosmetics. Find Nexxus, Paul Michell and Sebastian hair products, Cover Girl, Lancôme and Revlon makeup as well as CK1 and Coal Water perfume. Offers a pharmacy as well. Wouldn't quote prices over the phone. No delivery.

718 Broadway   **Flatiron/East Village**
at Washington Place/10003
212-979-5232. Fax 212-979-8257

44 East 8th Street   **Flatiron/East Village**
near Greene Street/10003
212-254-5247. Fax 212-254-6523

180 3rd Avenue   **Flatiron/East Village**
near 17th Street/10003
212-228-4485. Fax 212-260-0969

466 Avenue of the Americas   **Chelsea**
at 11th Street/10011
212-924-3401. Fax 212-924-3404

590 Broadway
near Houston Street/10012
212-226-5552. Fax 212-226-5595

SoHo/TriBeCa

585 2nd Avenue
near 32nd Street/10016
212-685-5518. Fax 212-685-5202

Gramercy Pk/Murray Hill

608 Columbus Avenue
near 89th Street/10024
212-769-1050

Upper West Side

2200 Broadway
near 78th Street/10024
212-579-6959

Upper West Side

1675 3rd Avenue
near 94th Street/10128
212-348-7400. Fax 212-348-4286

Upper East Side

Astor Place Hair Stylists
2 Astor Place
near Broadway
New York, NY 10003
212-475-9854
Monday-Saturday 8-8 Sunday 9-6.

Haircuts & hairstylists
Flatiron/East Village

quality style service value

The Edge: Good haircuts for $12. Is it ever not crowded? Haircuts and men's shaves. Everyone goes, from staid bankers to orange-haired in-line skaters. No appointments taken.

"Fabulous—see Dominick!"

Brunellier Salon
692 Madison Avenue
near 62nd Street
New York, NY 10021
212-758-7779
Monday-Wednesday Friday Saturday 9-5 Thursday 9-6:30.

Haircuts & hairstylists
Upper East Side

quality style service value

The Edge: Specializes in hair-conditioning treatments. All agree service is first-rate. No credit cards.

Bumble and Bumble
146 East 56th Street
between 3rd and Lexington Avenues
New York, NY 10022
212-521-6500
Monday 8:30-6:30 Tuesday-Friday 8:30-7:30
Saturday 9-5.

Haircuts & hairstylists
Midtown East

quality style service value

The Edge: If you're 35 and under and want great looks, this is the place. Widely known. A good resource for hair styling, makeup lessons and applications.

Garren

712 5th Avenue
at Henri Bendel
New York, NY 10019
212-841-9400
Monday-Wednesday Friday Saturday 10-7 Thursday 10-8.

Haircuts & hairstylists
Midtown West

The Edge: Another one of the top salons. Fashionable salon at Henri Bendel's featuring Garren as the top stylist. Cozy—just six chairs. Clients have included Linda Evangelists and Lucie de la Falaise. Other services include hair treatments, manicures and pedicures. Priced $100 to $300 (for Garren) for a haircut only.

Jacques Dessange

505 Park Avenue
near 59th Street
New York, NY 10022
212-308-1400
Monday-Saturday 8:30-6:30.

Haircuts & hairstylists
Midtown East

3	5	3	3
quality	style	service	value

The Edge: A chic place to look chic. A chain of 500 salons around the world, but only one is in New York. Top stylists are Jerome and Bruno.

Julius Caruso Salon

27 62nd Street
near Madison Avenue
New York, NY 10021
212-759-7574. Fax 212-486-0975
Monday-Saturday 9-5.

Haircuts & hairstylists
Upper East Side

4	4	5	4
quality	style	service	value

The Edge: See Nathan, a genius with color. Recommended by one of our most stylish respondents.

Kenneth's Salon

301 Park Avenue
near 50th Street in the Waldorf Astoria
New York, NY 10022
212-752-1800. Fax 212-838-7357
Monday-Tuesday Thursday-Saturday 9-6
Wednesday 9-8.

Haircuts & hairstylists
Midtown East

5	5	5	3
quality	style	service	value

The Edge: The Dean of the stylists. This is not where the models go now. The clientele is an older, more established crowd. There's a separate men's styling area. Was First Lady's Jacqueline Kennedy's White House stylist. She later used Joseph at Thomas Morrisey Salon. Noted for chic service aimed at the ladies who lunch crowd. Reliable and expensive.

"I'm a regular, I love the place."

La Coupe

694 Madison Avenue
near 63rd Street
New York, NY 10021
212-371-9230. Fax 212-421-1358
Monday Tuesday Friday Saturday 8:30-5
Wednesday Thursday 8:30-8.

Haircuts & hairstylists
Upper East Side

quality   style   service   value

The Edge: A no-frills salon catering to busy professional women. Moderately priced haircuts ($30 to $85). Also manicures, pedicures and waxing. Hair-care products are available for sale. Will mail products. Carrie is a top stylist there.

Louis Guy D

41 East 57th Street
near Madison Avenue
New York, NY 10022
212-753-6078. Fax 212-644-5761
Monday-Saturday 9-6.

Haircuts & hairstylists
Midtown East

The Edge: Hair salon specializing in longer hair. Only hair care—cuts and coloring. Best for longer hair. Sells their own hair-care products. Highlights from $100 to $200, depending on length. Haircut from $70 to $75. No credit cards.

Louis Licari Color Group

797 Madison Avenue
near 67th Street
New York, NY 10021
212-517-8084. Fax 212-861-9436
Monday Tuesday Thursday Friday 7:30-6
Wednesday Saturday 8:30-4.

Haircuts & hairstylists
Upper East Side

quality   style   service   value

The Edge: Full-service salon with early hours for working women. Full-service salon specializing in hair color. Supposed to be where Ivana Trump and Anna Wintour get their hair colored. Did styles and color for many movies including *The Age of Innocence*. Top colorist is Louis.

"Louis makes the place."

Minardi Minardi Salon

29 East 61st Street
between Park and Madison Avenues
New York, NY 10021
212-308-1711. Fax 212-753-6831
Tuesday 8-6 Wednesday 9-9 Thursday 11-9
Friday 9-7 Saturday 9-6.

Haircuts & hairstylists
Upper East Side

quality   style   service   value

The Edge: Hair styling and color treatments. Haircuts $75 to $150. Coloring $65 and up. Highlights $165.

Orbibe

691 5th Avenue, at Elizabeth Arden
near 54th Street
New York, NY 10022
212-319-3910: Fax 212-319-3918
Monday-Saturday 9-5.

Haircuts & hairstylists
Midtown East

quality style service value

The Edge: Elizabeth Arden's full-service salon. Tends to attract an older crowd. A good source for gifts from a manicure to a full day of beauty. Offers coloring, facials, hair styling, hair treatments, makeup and massages. Orbibe is the top hair stylist. He works with top European designers, including Dolce, Gabbana, Karl Lagerfeld and Versace.

Salvatore Macri

520 Madison Avenue
between 53rd and 54th Streets
New York, NY 10022
212-355-0031
Weekdays 9:30-5:30.

Haircuts & hairstylists
Midtown East

quality style service value

The Edge: An unusually good men's stylist. It's rare to find an up-to-date barber, who keeps to his appointments and provides (if asked) well-suited recommendations. Shop is off the lobby in the Continental Illinois building. Crowd is conservative investment banker/ law firm–oriented, although he can do more casual styling.

"I'm hooked on Sal."

Thomas Morrisey Salon

787 Madison Avenue
between 66th and 67th Streets
New York, NY 10021
212-772-1111
Monday-Saturday 9-5:30.

Haircuts & hairstylists
Upper East Side

quality style service value

The Edge: Top talent, as low key and nice as you can get. How many salons get front-page second-section write-ups in the *New York Times* when the team bolted from Kenneth's? See Morrisey for color, Joseph for cutting and styling. Clients include Caroline Kennedy Schlossberg, introduced to the salon by her mother, who used to be a regular. No credit cards.

"Not only is Joseph talented but he couldn't be nicer. Even though he never, and I mean never seems to run late, he squeezed my daughter in for her high school prom—but how could he not when she ran over to show him her dress? He's a treasure."

Lori Klein

212-996-9390
By appointment.

Personal care
Mail/phone

quality style service value

The Edge: Marvelous looks. Lori, a former model, does makeovers and gives makeup lessons. She couldn't give you a better look. Does Barbara Walters before her shows. Great at weddings. She helps make it happen.

"Couldn't be a nicer person, offering practical advice and instruction, matching her recommendations to your style." "A real find."

Mario Badescu

320 East 52nd Street
near 1st Avenue
New York, NY 10022
212-758-1065. Fax 212-838-2568

Personal care
Midtown East

5	4	5	4
quality	style	service	value

Monday Tuesday Friday 10-4 Wednesday Thursday 11-7 Saturday 9-3:30.

The Edge: Top facials and services. 25 years' experience. Facials by hand only. Creates all the products they use in the salon's lab.

"Excellent! Own products are excellent. Same services as Georgette Klinger but less expensive and less pretentious."

Miriam Vasicka

897 Park Avenue
between 78th and 79th Streets
New York, NY 10021
212-734-1017
Flexible hours 8-6 by appointment.

Personal care
Upper East Side

5	5	5	5
quality	style	service	value

The Edge: Highly recommended electrolysis. Recommended by one of our more stylish respondents as her personal resource.

Kaufman Pharmacy

557 Lexington Avenue
near 50th Street
New York, NY 10022
212-755-2266. Fax 212-980-1988
Daily 24 hours.

Pharmacies
Midtown East

3	3	5	2
quality	style	service	value

The Edge: The prescription department is open 24 hours a day, 365 days a year. A full-service, old-fashioned pharmacy including a soda fountain, bath treasures, cigarettes, cosmetics, traveling needs and a prescription department that's always open. A New York necessity for emergencies. Expensive.

Love Discount

2030 Broadway
near 69th Street
New York, NY 10023
212-877-4141. Fax 212-724-7439
Sunday-Thursday 7-12:30 Friday 7-2 Saturday 8-2.

Pharmacies
Upper West Side

The Edge: Open really really late for your prescription needs. Full prescription service. Also sundries. No delivery. Discounter.

Prescriptions Limited

Pharmacies
Upper East Side

1151 Madison Avenue
near 86th Street.
New York, NY 10028
212-628-3210. Fax 212-535-3189
Weekdays 9-7 Saturday 10-4.

The Edge: Good prices for vitamins and dietary supplements.

Union Square Drugs

Pharmacies
Flatiron/East Village

859 Broadway
between 17th and 18th Streets
New York, NY 10003
212-242-2725. Fax 212-242-2208
Weekdays 7:30-7 Saturday 9-4.

The Edge: Good prices on prescription drugs and a notary on premises.

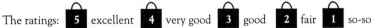

The ratings: **5** excellent **4** very good **3** good **2** fair **1** so-so

Food & beverages

Aaron Streit, Inc.
150 Rivington Street
between Suffolk and Clinton Streets
New York, NY 10002
212-475-7000
Monday-Thursday Sunday 8:30-4:30.

Appetizers
Lower East Side/Chinatown

4	4	4	5
quality	style	service	value

The Edge: Passover nostalgia. Fresh-baked matzoth. Varieties include regular, whole-wheat, onion and low-sodium. Also matzoth meal and farfel and bags of matzoth broken in production. No credit cards. No delivery.

Barney Greengrass
541 Amsterdam Avenue
near 87th Street
New York, NY 10024
212-724-4707
Tuesday-Sunday 8:30-6.

Appetizers
Upper West Side

4	3	4	3
quality	style	service	value

The Edge: Consistently good and appetizing, best for breakfast. Despite the crowds and lines (go before 10am or expect to wait) and atmosphere (none), you can't beat a Barney Greengrass breakfast of lox n' eggs, sturgeon and other smoked fish. Bagels of course accompany all. Clients allegedly include Calvin Klein and David Geffen. No credit cards.

"Terrific nova, marvelous decor (if you're into nostalgia)."

Caviarteria
502 Park Avenue
near 59th Street
New York, NY 10022
212-759-7410. Fax 212-750-0358
Monday-Saturday 9-8 Sunday 11-4.

Appetizers
Midtown East

3	∘3	3	3
quality	style	service	value

The Edge: For those still living in the '80s, caviar. They've moved to a new location, redesigned their space (very upscale) and added a champagne bar for blinis and caviar. Unchanged is that they sell good-quality caviar and foie gras at good prices. The least expensive caviars they sell are American sturgeon and red caviar. For home use, they sell "broken egg" caviar which brings the price down to almost affordable. Much of their business is mail order, call 800-4-CAVIAR. Deluxe.

D'Artagnan, Inc.
399 St. Paul Avenue
Jersey City, NJ 07306
201-792-0748. Fax 201-792-6113
Weekdays 9-6.

Appetizers
New Jersey

5	5	5	4
quality	style	service	value

The Edge: For special occasions and special presents. Gift and special Christmas baskets filled with luxury foods, including prunes soaked in Armagnac, top-notch foie gras, pheasant terrine en herbette with fennel, duck galantine with apricots and foie gras, wild hare terrine with cherries, venison terrine and cassoulet. For the health-conscious, baskets filled with free-range poultry, rabbit, wild boar from Texas, American buffalo, venison from New Zealand, free-range lamb from Australia, organic imported veal and exotic meats like alligator tail and turtle meat. If that's not enough, whole suckling pigs and more! Delivers via overnight air anywhere and by messenger to New York. For telephone orders call 800-327-8246. Very expensive.

Fine & Schapiro

138 West 72nd Street
between Broadway and Columbus Avenue
New York, NY 10023
212-877-2874. Fax 212-799-4145
Daily 10-11.

Appetizers
Upper West Side

The Edge: A neighborhood institution offering kosher deli items. Basic dinners for at-home consumption include roast chicken, chicken in a pot, stuffed cabbage and other standards. Of course the complete line of cold cuts.

"Tasty!"

Guss Pickles

35 Essex Street
near Hester Street
New York, NY 10002
212-254-4477
Sunday-Thursday 9:30-6 Friday 9:30-3.

Appetizers
Lower East Side/Chinatown

The Edge: A Lower East Side landmark. Inspired the movie *Crossing Delancey Street*. Features pickles, pickled tomatoes, sauerkraut, sweetkraut and superb grated horseradish. Mail order available. No credit cards. Discounter.

Homarus, Inc.

76 Kisco Avenue
Mt. Kisco, NY 10549
914-666-8992. Fax 914-666-8734
October 1-April 1 Saturday 10-3
retail shop and mail order.

Appetizers
Westchester

The Edge: Wholesale smoked fish. Sells wholesale to all the fine hotels, restaurants and shops (Zabar's and Stew Leonard's included). Offers freshly smoked (on premises) fish including eel, scotch salmon and trout. Also baked salmon, jumbo shrimp and sturgeon. Our favorite is a dill-wrapped gravlax. All natural high-quality products. Mail order from October through early April only. Great prices. Discounter.

Hors d'Oeuvres Unlimited

4209 Dell Avenue
North Bergen, NJ 07047

Appetizers
New Jersey

201-865-4545. Fax 201-861-1175
Weekdays 7-3.

The Edge: Inexpensive adequate hors d'oeuvres. They sell to restaurants, caterers and hotels such as the Holiday Inn chain. Large selection including asparagus rollups, clams casino, chicken sate, mushroom caps with nine fillings, shrimp toast, spinach phyllo, water chestnut wrapped in bacon and lots more. Delivers daily to New York for a $25 delivery charge. Call 800-648-3787 for phone orders.

Murray's Sturgeon Shop

2429 Broadway
between 89th and 90th Streets
New York, NY 10024
212-724-2650
Sunday-Friday 8-7 Saturday 8-8.

Appetizers
Upper West Side

quality	style	service	value
5	4	5	4

The Edge: Absolutely outstanding smoked salmon. The prices may be the highest in the city for smoked fish, but some say no one has better tasting smoked salmon. In addition to smoked salmon, find caviar, egg salad, mushroom salad, sturgeon, whipped tuna salad, and of course, assorted terrific cream cheeses and bagels (from Columbia Hot Bagels). They prepare and send platters. Clients are reputed to include Norman Lear, Barbra Streisand and Robert Duvall.

"The best."

Petrossian

182 West 58th Street
near 7th Avenue
New York, NY 10019
212-245-2217. Fax 212-315-0508
Weekdays 10-10 Saturday 10-8 Sunday 10-6.

Appetizers
Midtown West

quality	style	service	value
4	4	5	3

The Edge: First-rate luxuries priced accordingly. First rate luxury items including caviar, French chocolates, foie gras, Scottish salmon and selected packaged goods are sold in the "boutique" of this fashionable restaurant. Very creative gift baskets are a specialty and can include champagne and vodka (purchased through their link to selected liquor stores). Prices are sky high. Deluxe.

"As expected, given the prices, very helpful, pleasant staff."

Russ & Daughters

179 East Houston Street
between Allen and Orchard Streets
New York, NY 10002
212-475-4880. Fax 212-475-0345
Monday-Wednesday 9-6 Thursday-Saturday 10-7.

Appetizers
Lower East Side/Chinatown

quality	style	service	value
5	-	5	5

The Edge: A Lower East Side institution. Very good smoked fish and herring from around the world plus the accouterments (cream cheese and bagels). The cream cheese and farmer cheese are very good. Also caviar, pickles, dried fruits, nuts and candies. Prices are higher than other Lower East Side outlets, but much lower than the uptown favorites. The quality is consistently good and the selection is broader than elsewhere downtown.

Sable's

1489 2nd Avenue
between 77th and 78th Streets
New York, NY 10021
212-249-6177
Monday-Friday 8-8 Saturday 8-7:30 Sunday 8-5.

Appetizers
Upper East Side

4	2	3	4
quality	style	service	value

The Edge: Used to be the team at Zabar's appetizer department. Ran Zabar's appetizer department for 11 years. Appetizers is what Sables sells—chopped liver, cream cheese, salmon, smoked fish etc. Platters and catering available. Delivers in the neighborhood.

Schacht Appetizing & Deli

99 2nd Avenue
near 5th Street
New York, NY 10003
212-420-8219
Daily 8-midnight.

Appetizers
Flatiron/East Village

4	4	4	4
quality	style	service	value

The Edge: Less expensive Nova. Find the standards: Nova, smoked fish and bagels. No delivery.

"No longer tops."

Yonah Schimmel's Knishes Bakery

137 East Houston Street
between 1st and 2nd Avenues
New York, NY 10002
212-477-2858
Daily 8-6.

Appetizers
Lower East Side/Chinatown

3	3	3	3
quality	style	service	value

The Edge: Knishes like grandma's. A New York institution. Sells only knishes of all kinds, including potato, kasha, fruit and cheese and more. Will make cocktail size knishes and franks in the blanket. No credit cards.

Baked Ideas

450 Broadway
near Grand Street
New York, NY 10013
212-925-9097. Fax 212-925-9097
Monday-Saturday 10-6 by appointment.

Bakery
SoHo/TriBeCa

The Edge: Delicious and pretty, a winning combination. Custom-designed cakes and holiday-oriented, icing-covered cookies (no one does them better) carried in the best food shops. Cookies can be used as party favors or place cards with guest names at $6 to $10 each. Works exclusively with buttercream frostings. Cakes start at $100. No credit cards.

Bakery Soutine

104 West 70th Street
near Columbus Avenue
New York, NY 10023

Bakery
Upper West Side

5	3	5	5
quality	style	service	value

212-496-1450
Weekdays 8-7 Saturday 9-5 Sunday 9-3.

The Edge: Wonderful creative pastries. Specialties include chocolate cake (seven inch at $19) and miniatures ($1 each), including tiny fudge cakes, chocolate raspberry mousse cakes, honeybourbon cakes and crème brûlée. No credit cards.

Bijoux Doux

304 Mulberry Street
near Houston Street
New York, NY 10012
212-226-0948. Fax 212-226-0948
By appointment.

Bakery
SoHo/TriBeCa

The Edge: Classically inspired wedding and special-occasion cakes. Ornate graceful cakes, for example, a wonderful model of a baroque Prague church for a wedding (it was the couple's favorite building). Everything is custom made and requires consultation to ensure you get what you want. Their French-style cakes are wonderful and creative and taste great! No credit cards. No delivery.

Black Hound

149 1st Avenue
between 9th and 10th Streets
New York, NY 10003
212-979-9505
Weekdays noon-8 Saturday noon-7. Sunday noon-6
Closed Saturday during July. Closed August.

Bakery
Flatiron/East Village

5	5	5	4
quality	style	service	value

The Edge: Just wonderful cakes and cookies—gifts worthy of any occasion. They think of themselves as the Neiman Marcus of bakers. Their flourless chocolate cake, made with cocoa, chocolate, very little sugar and lots of eggs, is rich. Cookies are exceptional, very buttery and their chocolate truffles are among the best in the city. Deliveries within Manhattan for large orders. For mail orders call 800-344-4417.

"Great packaging! Great gifts!"

Bonte Patisserie

1316 3rd Avenue
between 75th and 76th Streets
New York, NY 10021
212-535-2360
Monday-Saturday 9-6:30.

Bakery
Upper East Side

5	4	4	4
quality	style	service	value

The Edge: The best French bakery in the city and the nicest shop owners. The owner/baker came to New York to bake for Lutèce until he opened his shop in 1974. Everything is outstanding. Find fruit tarts (blueberry, plum, raspberry and tart tatin), mousse cakes, a triangle cake (sponge cake, with meringue, almonds and liquor), brioches, macaroons, petit fours (miniatures and large), Grand Marnier and mocha cakes. The tarts appear to be held together just by the fruit alone, which is always of superb quality. Wonderful wedding cakes, which feature a vial of fresh flowers in the center. Decorations on other cakes are made from spun sugar. For the holidays, Bouche Noël. No credit cards. No delivery.

"Did Julie Nixon's White House wedding cake." "If you're a known client and there at closing, you come home with bags and bags of pastry, since nothing stays overnight."

Cafe Lalo
201 West 83rd Street
near Broadway
New York, NY 10024
212-496-6031
Weekdays 9-2am Weekends 9-4am.

Bakery
Upper West Side

The Edge: Classic Viennese bakery. Takeout plus table service for coffee and desserts. Large selection and variety of cake, cheesecakes and pies. No delivery.

Caffè Roma
385 Broome Street
between Mulberry and Mott Streets
New York, NY 10013
212-226-8413
Daily 8-midnight.

Bakery
SoHo/TriBeCa

3	3	3	4
quality	style	service	value

The Edge: Classic southern Italian pastry, at good prices. Caffè Roma is a lower keyed less expensive Ferrara's. Decor is casual, old-fashioned soda-shop-style table and chairs. A great place to stop for cappuccino and espresso with typical southern Italian pastry, biscotti, cannolis and Italian cheesecake. Wonderful Italian rum cake which can be decorated for special occasions. An inexpensive alternative to uptown party cakes. No credit cards. No delivery.

"Good . . . and cheap."

Ceci-Cela
55 Spring Street
near Mulberry Street
New York, NY 10012
212-274-9179
Daily 7-7.

Bakery
SoHo/TriBeCa

The Edge: Finally a good French-style pastry shop near Mulberry Street. Features French pastries, plain and stuffed croissants, tarts and rich cakes. No credit cards.

Cheryl Kleinman Cakes
448 Atlantic Avenue
Brooklyn, NY
718-237-2271. Fax 718-237-2271
Monday-Saturday 9-5 by appointment.

Bakery
Brooklyn

The Edge: Known for whimsical, highly personal custom cakes. Kleinman's personalized cakes take every shape from Fabergè eggs to porcelain jewelry boxes to the New York Yanks winning the pennant. Very creative, and perhaps more importantly, good-tasting cakes. No credit cards.

Chez Laurence
245 Madison Avenue
near 38th Street
New York, NY 10016
212-683-0284. Fax 212-683-0298
Weekdays 7-10 Saturday 8-10.

Bakery
Gramercy Pk/Murray Hill

The Edge: Standard French pastry fare. Features brioches, pains au chocolats, croissants and standard French pastries.

City Bakery
22 East 17th Street
between 5th Avenue and Broadway
New York, NY 10003
212-366-1414. Fax 212-645-0810
Monday-Saturday 7:30-6.

Bakery
Flatiron/East Village

The Edge: Best known for their fresh fruit tarts. The fruit tarts are wonderful, as are the chocolate and crème brûlée tarts. Our favorite fruit tarts in season are blueberry, pear and plum. Offers a limited seasonal luncheon menu and catering.

Colette Cakes
327 West 11th Street
between Greenwich and Washington Streets
New York, NY 10014
212-366-6530. Fax 212-807-7473
By appointment.

Bakery
Greenwich Village

The Edge: High styled delicious custom-made cakes. Their specialty is whimsical, classic and lavish cakes to order, beginning at $8 per person. They did "Madonna goes Platinum" for a *New York* magazine contest. Very creative, good, tasty, rich moist cakes. No credit cards.

Cupcake Cafe
522 9th Avenue
near 39th Street
New York, NY 10018
212-465-1530. Fax 212-465-1069
Weekdays 7-7:30 Saturday 8-6 Sunday 9-5.

Bakery
Midtown West

3	3	4	4
quality	style	service	value

The Edge: Cakes, and of course cupcakes, that are as beautiful as they are tasty. The artist-owner creates highly styled floral cakes that are good, rich and butter creamy. All the standard flavors plus Bohemian (maple-walnut) with icings to match or mix. Also wonderful coffee cake, crumb pies, doughnuts and excellent pies. Expensive, priced from $30 to $35 for an 8-inch cake without decoration. No credit cards. No delivery.

"If you like butter cream, this is the place."

De Robertis Pastry
176 1st Avenue
between 10th and 11th Streets
New York, NY 10009

Bakery
Flatiron/East Village

4	5	4	5
quality	style	service	value

212-674-7137
Tuesday-Thursday 9-11 Friday Saturday 9-midnight.

The Edge: A good neighborhood choice. Features good to usually very good Sicilian pastries. When available, the fig tarts are exceptional. The chocolate-covered, traditional cannollis are great! No credit cards.

Ecce Panis

Bakery
Upper East Side

1120 3rd Avenue
between 65th and 66th Streets
New York, NY 10021
212-535-2099. Fax 212-535-2388
Weekdays 8-8 weekends 8-6.

5 | 4 | 4 | 3
quality style service value

The Edge: Could be the city's top bread source. Standard breads plus exotics, including chocolate (Friday through Sunday only), raisin-pecan-sourdough rye, focaccia-type loaves with onion and sun-dried tomatoes and walnut bread. Their breads are served at the Sign of the Dove and Contrapunto, among other restaurants. They offer excellent biscotti (including pistachio-almond, chocolate-macadamia nut, bourbon-pecan and chocolate-hazelnut) and cookies, including wonderful chocolate chip. Traditional Italian pan forte (fruit and nut Christmas cake) from Sienna in season. No delivery.

"Wish they were cheaper." "Great bread."

Eileen's Special Cheesecake

Bakery
SoHo/TriBeCa

17 Cleveland Place
between Lafayette and Spring Streets
New York, NY 10012
212-966-5585
Daily 9-6.

The Edge: More than a dozen types of cheesecake. The cheesecake is light but rich with a graham cracker crust. Flavors include fruit and chocolate. Also pies, including a Granny Smith apple pie which is quite good. No credit cards.

Erotic Baker

Bakery
Mail/phone

212-362-7557
Tuesday-Friday 10-6.

4 | 4 | 4 | 4
quality style service value

The Edge: Cake toppings only—you ask for it, they'll do it! Sculpture out of marzipan designed as the name suggests. $35 for an 8-inch marzipan topping.

Ferrara's

Bakery
SoHo/TriBeCa

195 Grand Street
near Mulberry Street
New York, NY 10013
212-226-6150. Fax 212-226-0667
Daily 8-midnight.

2 | 3 | 3 | 2
quality style service value

The Edge: Standard Sicilian pastry shop. A Little Italy landmark for 104 years, featuring Italian pastries, light lunches, cappuccino and espresso. The style is glitzy (catering hall feel) with a few decent pastries.

"Many homemade items."

Food Attitude

127 East 60th Street
between Lexington and Park Avenues
New York, NY 10022
212-980-1818. Fax 212-980-2447
Weekdays 7-7 Saturday 8-5 Sunday 9-4.

Bakery
Midtown East

The Edge: Good source for baked items and light lunches. Features brioches, croissants, desserts, quiche, salads and soups. A wonderful pear tatin in season. Delivery only very locally 3rd to 5th Avenues and 53rd to 67th Streets.

Friend of a Farmer

77 Irving Place
between 18th and 19th Streets
New York, NY 10003
212-477-2188. Fax 212-529-9178
Tuesday-Saturday 8-10 Sunday 9:30-3:30.

Bakery
Flatiron/East Village

4	4	4	4
quality	style	service	value

The Edge: Simple all-American food. Offers wholesome food (a meat-and-mashed potato place). Desserts are especially good, particularly their fruit pies like cherry and apple. Also delicious cinnamon raisin, white and rye bread. A restaurant/takeout combo.

Gail Watson Custom Cakes

335 West 38th Street
between 8th and 9th Avenues
New York, NY 10018
212-967-9167. Fax 212-967-3856
By appointment Monday-Wednesday 9-6:30.

Bakery
Midtown West

The Edge: Serious chocolate cakes here. Watson does custom cakes (non-chocolate too). Favors artful tiered wedding cakes. Minimum with delivery is $100 for a cake that serves 25. Prices (depending on the detailing) run $4.25 per person to $10 for molded flowers. No credit cards.

Gertel's

53 Hester Street
between Essex and Ludlow Streets
New York, NY 10002
212-982-3250. Fax 212-677-2870
Sunday-Thursday 6:30-5:30 Friday 6:30-3.

Bakery
Lower East Side/Chinatown

4	3	3	3
quality	style	service	value

The Edge: Strictly kosher traditional food. Babkas, cakes, chocolate rolls and strudels. Thursdays potato kugel. Breads include challah, cornbread, pumpernickel and sour rye. Holiday cakes. A few tables for coffee and cake.

Glendale Bake Shop

1290 Lexington Avenue
near 87th Street
New York, NY 10128
212-410-5959. Fax 212-410-5373
Weekdays 6-8 Saturday 7-7 Sunday 7-5.

Bakery
Upper East Side

2	2	2	3
quality	style	service	value

The Edge: Standard fare—save the calories. Baked goods from cheesecake to chocolate layer cakes. Rye bread and pretzel rolls. A deli and gift department offering baskets, piñatas and cookie jars. Prices aren't that great, given the quality.

Grossinger's Uptown

570 Columbus Avenue
near 88th Street
New York, NY 10024
212-874-6996. Fax 212-362-8627
Monday-Thursday 7:30-7 Friday 7:30-sundown
Sunday 7:30-5.

Bakery
Upper West Side

4	3	3	5
quality	style	service	value

The Edge: A good kosher bakery. Best known for their cheese and ice cream (especially praline ice cream) cakes. Also challah, six-grain bread and strudels. The prices are good. No credit cards.

Houghtaling Mousse Pie Ltd

389 Broome Street
near Mulberry Street
New York, NY 10013
212-226-3724. Fax 212-226-3724
Monday-Thursday 9-6 Friday-Saturday noon-9.

Bakery
SoHo/TriBeCa

The Edge: Rich dense desserts. Their specialty is chocolate truffle cake, intensely rich. Ten varieties of mousse pies and six kinds of mousse cakes are featured. A decorated cake is available for special occasions. Mail order. Deliveries with two days' notice only on Wednesdays. No credit cards.

Hungarian Viennese Pastry, Inc.

314 East 78th Street
between 1st and 2nd Avenues
New York, NY 10021
212-988-0052
Tuesday-Saturday 8-6 Sunday Monday 9-4.

Bakery
Upper East Side

The Edge: Local Hungarian pastry shop. Specialties are Rigo cake (chocolate-mousse cake), Linzer tortes, Sachertorte and seven-layer mocha cake. In season, a chocolate-chestnut cake is exceptional. Also babkas, danish and strudels. Specialty cakes require two-day advance notice. Reasonable prices. No credit cards. No delivery.

Little Pie Company

424 West 43rd Street
between 9th and 10th Avenues
New York, NY 10036

Bakery
Midtown West

5	4	3	4
quality	style	service	value

212-736-4780. Fax 212-695-3750
Weekdays 8-8 Saturday 10-6 Sunday noon-6.

The Edge: The best American-style pies! Wonderful fresh fruit pies and other specialties that change with the season. Also cakes and muffins. A Martha Stewart source.

Margaret Braun Cakes

Bakery
Mail/phone

212-929-1582. Fax 212-929-1582
By appointment.

The Edge: Braun, a former artist, expresses herself in her cakes. Fabulous sweet-tasting cakes featuring lifelike sugar portraits which could include reproductions of photos, magazine covers and the like. In a *New York* magazine contest she did a lifelike stage bill of Kathleen Battle returning to the Met. Priced from $250. No credit cards.

Marnie Carmichael/Noonie's Traditional Southern

45 Carmine Street, Suite 5A
near Bedford Street
New York, NY 10014
212-691-0673
By appointment.

Bakery
Greenwich Village

The Edge: Delicious, beautifully presented sweet-looking and -tasting gifts. Customized, creatively styled southern round pound cakes displayed in fancy hat boxes with a nosegay of fresh flowers packed in the middle. These customized cakes can be all her imagination and your pocketbook will allow! Cakes from $60 to $250 and up. These cakes are apparently a favorite gift item of Conde Nast, Gitanos jeans and Mike Ovitz, formerly of Creative Artists Agency. Ovitz traditionally sent her cakes to his Creative Artists Agency clients celebrating their Oscar wins!

Marquet Patisserie

15 East 12th Street
near 5th Avenue
New York, NY 10003
212-229-9313
Monday-Saturday 7:30-8.

Bakery
Flatiron/East Village

The Edge: Sophisticated French desserts. Known for her elegant marquise cake rimmed with ladyfingers and filled with chocolate mousse and topped with decorative chocolate. Also petit fours iced in pastel colors. Inexpensive. No credit cards. No delivery.

Moishe's Homemade Kosher Bakery

181 East Houston Street
near Orchard Street
New York, NY 10002
212-475-9624
Sunday-Thursday 7-6 Friday 7-4.

Bakery
Lower East Side/Chinatown

The Edge: Traditional Jewish bakery. Inexpensive, mostly standard fare, including Jewish rye, pumpernickel, challah on Thursday and Friday and very good cornbread, babka (chocolate or topped with nuts and cinnamon), rugalach and a superb (for kosher) chocolate cake. Delivers anywhere in Manhattan once daily for orders placed before 9am. No credit cards.

Once Upon a Tart

135 Sullivan Street
near Houston Street
New York, NY 10012
212-387-8869. Fax 212-387-8869
Monday-Saturday 9-8 Sunday 9-6.

Bakery
SoHo/TriBeCa

The Edge: Expensive catering service for mostly corporate clients. Catering items are primarily salads, soups and sandwiches served in baskets and platters. Desserts are best of all, including poached-pear tart tatin and other fruit tarts (whatever is in season). Individual fruit tarts are $3 to $3.75. They have tables for eating in. No credit cards. No delivery.

Patisserie Claude

187 West 4th Street
between 6th and 7th Avenues
New York, NY 10014
212-255-5911
Daily 8-8.

Bakery
Greenwich Village

The Edge: Good French pastry. Features a full range of French bakery items. First-rate fruit tarts. The croissants and brioches are good. Moderate prices.

Patisserie Lanciani

414 West 14th Street
near 9th Avenue
New York, NY 10014
212-989-1213
Daily 8-8.

Bakery
Greenwich Village

5	4	4	5
quality	style	service	value

The Edge: A pleasant cafe plus a good French bakery. Good country French bread and pastries. Expect to wait in line for the few tables on Friday and Saturday nights. Owner Lanciani was the pastry chef at the Plaza Hotel and later at the Palace. Specialties are wonderful tarts, including French nut tarts, tarte tatin, lemon tarts as well as a signature white-chocolate-mousse cake. Of course croissants, brioches and the rest. Wonderful special-occasion cakes. Special orders require at least three days' notice. Will accommodate customer preferences on special orders. No credit cards.

"Love the lemon tarts! A fun place to hang out—nice, casual, quiet location."

Patisserie Les Friandises

972 Lexington Avenue
near 70th Street
New York, NY 10021
212-988-1616. Fax 212-249-6078
Monday-Saturday 9-7 Sunday 10-5. Closed Sunday July and August.

Bakery
Upper East Side

The Edge: Good French tarts. Specialty tarte tatin sold in 6-, 8- and 10-inch sizes for $10.50, $21 and $38 respectively. Also sticky buns and lemon tarts.

Poseidon Bakery

629 9th Avenue
near 44th Street
New York, NY 10036
212-757-6173
Tuesday-Saturday 9-7 Sunday 10-4.

Bakery
Midtown West

The Edge: Traditional Greek desserts and dinner items. Since 1925 has offered dinner pies, including meat and cheese, spinach and feta, spinach, potatoes and cabbage and onion plus party-size appetizers. Standard desserts to accompany dinner. Find both fresh, handmade and machine-made phyllo dough. They'll ship nationwide. Prices are reasonable. No credit cards. No delivery.

Ron Ben Israel

130 West 25th Street
between 6th and 7th Avenues
New York, NY 10001
212-627-2418
By appointment.

Bakery
Midtown West

The Edge: Custom-designed, special-occasion cakes. Sugar flowers are his specialty. Cakes are light, moist and on the sweet side with a minimum price of $250. Cakes should be ordered six months in advance. No credit cards.

Rosie's Creations

212-362-6069
By appointment.

Bakery
Mail/phone

The Edge: Edible cake toppers that can be kept for years as mementos. Ricki Arno's husband nicknamed her Rosie—hence Rosie's Creations is her name for this unique business which uses her talents as an artist, confectioner and baker. She will make your wedding topper to resemble you and your groom, complete with faces, clothing, furniture and hobbies. She is not cheap—toppers start at $2,000 plus the cost of the cake. Allow two to three months' notice. Requires 50% deposit.

Royale Pastry Shop

237 West 72nd Street
between Broadway and West End Avenue
New York, NY 10023
212-874-5642
Monday-Thursday 6-8 Friday 6-3:30 Sunday 7-midnight.

Bakery
Upper West Side

3	2	4	4
quality	style	service	value

The Edge: Standard kosher bakery with tasty matzoth. Features French and Danish pastries and breads, including Jewish rye, corn rye, challah, and whole-wheat. The rugelach and babka are particularly good.

"Particularly tasty Passover matzoth, but the Passover cakes were so-so."

Sant Ambroeus Ltd.

1000 Madison Avenue
between 77th and 78th Streets
New York, NY 10021
212-570-2211. Fax 212-570-2874

Bakery
Upper East Side

3	4	4	4
quality	style	service	value

Monday-Saturday 9:30-10:30 Sunday 10:30-6.

The Edge: Desserts are good, but it's beauty over taste. This is a bakery in front of a branch of a Milanese restaurant which serves mostly light pasta meals. You'll find eclairs, cream puffs, cupcakes dotted with candied fruit, rich cakes made with chestnut purée, chocolate, orange liqueur and whipped cream at the bakery. The cakes are gorgeous, among the prettiest in the city, but don't taste as good as they look. Very expensive, plus there's a delivery charge.

Sylvia Weinstock Cakes

273 Church Street
between Franklin and White Streets
New York, NY 10013
212-925-6698
Weekdays 8-6:30 by appointment.

Bakery
SoHo/TriBeCa

quality style service value
  5   5   4   4

The Edge: A top choice for absolutely beautiful floral bouquet specialty cakes. One of the first of the creative custom cake designers. Best known for her elegant English garden floral bouquet cakes, but fun and imaginative designs are possible, including a Keds sneaker accurate down to the side label. Go down and taste the various cake and icing combinations to ensure your cake is perfect in design and captures your sweet-tooth fantasies. Very expensive. No credit cards. Deluxe.

"Gorgeous, gorgeous, gorgeous in taste and looks." "Make sure you taste the cake beforehand. I didn't (the Weinstocks didn't suggest it) and was disappointed in the taste, although I loved the look."

Taylor's

523 Hudson Street
between West 10th and Charles Streets
New York, NY 10014
212-645-8200
Weekdays 6-9 weekends 7-9.

Bakery
Greenwich Village

The Edge: Baked items are best. Breakfast specialties include muffins for start-the-day meetings. Dinner entrees include chicken pot pies, vegetable lasagna and three-cheese pasta. Best are the baked goods, which include a chocolate soufflé cake studded with walnuts, praline cookies and iced cinnamon buns. No credit cards.

Trois Jean

154 East 79th Street
between Lexington and 3rd Avenues
New York, NY 10021
212-988-4858
Weekdays noon-6:30 weekends 10-9.

Bakery
Upper East Side

quality style service value
  5   5   3   4

The Edge: Very good traditional French fare. Takeout dishes include salads, cassoulet and other traditional items. They're most famous for desserts, which include tarts, mousse and crème brûlée plus their chocolate pyramid, a birthday must. No delivery.

Umanoff & Parsons

467 Greenwich Street
near Watts Street
New York, NY 10013
212-219-2240
Weekdays 8:30-5:30.

Bakery
SoHo/TriBeCa

The Edge: Wholesale bakery which sells retail. Features apple brown Betty, turtle cheesecake (with pecans, chocolate and caramel), orange bundt cake and three kinds of quiche (broccoli and cheddar, spinach and mushroom and Lorraine). No credit cards. No delivery.

Veniero's Pasticceria

342 East 11th Street
near 1st Avenue
New York, NY 10003
212-674-7264. Fax 212-228-1002
Daily 8-midnight.

Bakery
Flatiron/East Village

4	5	5	4
quality	style	service	value

The Edge: Good Sicilian pastry at very reasonable prices. Excellent biscotti, candies, crisp ricotta cheesecakes and rum cakes. Best of all small (petit four size) Italian pastries which are great for dessert parties. Delivery service is a real bonus. Prices are very reasonable.

"NYC's best Italian confectioner."

William Greenberg Jr. Desserts

518 3rd Avenue
between 34th and 35th Streets
New York, NY 10016
212-686-3344. Fax 212-213-2487
Weekdays 9:30-6:30 Saturday 9-5.

Bakery
Gramercy Pk/Murray Hill

5	3	4	3
quality	style	service	value

The Edge: Old-fashioned American-style desserts. Best known for their dense, rich, bitter-chocolate-frosted chocolate cake, strawberry shortcake, brownies and honey buns. Once a year in late summer, the brownies go on sale for 10% off. The decorated cakes are works of art and priced to match. He did the enormous cake for President Clinton's recent 50th New York City birthday-party fund-raiser. Very expensive. No delivery.

"I love his pies at Thanksgiving."

2187 Broadway
between 77th and 78th Streets/10024
212-580-7300. Fax 212-580-4458
Weekdays 7:30-7 Saturday 9-5 Sunday 9-4:30.

Upper West Side

1100 Madison Avenue
between 82nd and 83rd Streets/10028
212-744-0304. Fax 212-731-0413
Weekdays 9:30-6:30 Saturday 9-6. Sunday 10-4:30.

Upper East Side

B&E

511 West 23rd Street
near 10th Avenue
New York, NY 10011
212-243-6812. Fax 212-243-7035
Monday-Thursday 9-6:30 Friday Saturday 9-7.

Beverages
Chelsea

The Edge: Substantial discounts on all standard brands of soda and beer.

Cork & Bottle

1158 1st Avenue
near 63rd Street
New York, NY 10021
212-838-5300. Fax 212-751-4268
Monday-Thursday 9-10 Friday Saturday 9-11.

Beverages
Upper East Side

5	.	4	4
quality	style	service	value

The Edge: Good selection of wines. Cork & Bottle merged with Jim McMullen Wine & Liquor which was owned by restaurateur Jim McMullen who is beloved by the Upper East Side senior set. Prices are OK for a local Upper East Side shop.

"Family favorite for selection and value." "Nice selections."

Milkman

P.O. Box 794
Midtown Post Office
New York, NY 10018
212-279-6455. Fax 212-594-7262
Weekdays 7-3.

Beverages
Mail/phone

.4	.	4	4
quality	style	service	value

The Edge: Excellent-quality milk delivered at a reasonable price. Milk, juice and bottled water delivered to your door—daily, weekly or on request.

A. Zito and Son's Bakery

259 Bleecker Street
between 6th and 7th Avenues
New York, NY 10014
212-929-6139
Weekdays 6-6 Saturday 6-6:30 Sunday 6-2.

Bread
Greenwich Village

4	3	3	4
quality	style	service	value

The Edge: Some say the best Sicilian bread in the city. Italian whole-wheat, semolina and white breads plus bread made with prosciutto and provolone. All handmade and baked in brick ovens. No credit cards.

"Great crusty whole-wheat breads."

Bagelry

1324 Lexington Avenue
between 88th and 89th Streets
New York, NY 10128
212-996-0567
Weekdays 7-7 Saturday 7-6 Sunday 7-5.

Bread
Upper East Side

The Edge: Good bagels in a city known for bagels. Uses salt instead of sugar. Also find bialys and high-quality smoked fish from Maine's Duck Trap River Farms, including smoked trout, salmon and peppered salmon. Free delivery in the neighborhood or mail order by phone to 800-43-BAGEL. No credit cards.

Bagels on the Square

7 Carmine Street
near 7th Avenue
New York, NY 10014
212-691-3041
Daily 24 hours.

Bread
Greenwich Village

The Edge: A good source for bagels and the fixings. They make 18 varieties of old-fashioned, hand-formed bagels as well as 20 different kinds of cream cheeses to match. Mail order available.

Columbia Hot Bagels

2836 Broadway
Corner 110th Street
New York, NY 10025
212-222-3200. Fax 212-222-3200
Daily 24 hours.

Bread
Upper West Side

5	4	4	3
quality	style	service	value

The Edge: Some of the best of the New York bagels. A wide selection of bagels. These are the bagels sold at Murray's and Zabar's, among other places. No credit cards. No delivery.

"Best bagel in the city."

D&G Bakery

45 Spring Street
between Mott and Mulberry Streets
New York, NY 10012
212-226-6688
Daily 8-2.

Bread
SoHo/TriBeCa

4	4	2	4
quality	style	service	value

The Edge: Among the best bread in the city. Handmade, crusty, flavorful Sicilian bread, baked in a 100-year-old coal-fired brick oven. Breads includes white, whole-wheat, prosciutto and provolone. D&G supplies bread to Balducci's, Jefferson Market, Fairway, East Village Cheese, among others. Good prices. No credit cards. No delivery.

Ess-A-Bagel

359 1st Avenue
near 21st Street
New York, NY 10010
212-260-2252

Bread
Gramercy Pk/Murray Hill

5	3	3	5
quality	style	service	value

Monday-Saturday 6:30-10 Sunday 6:30-5.

The Edge: Another great bagel source. The standard bagel assortment. With the bagels—fish, cream cheese and vegetarian spreads. Will Fed Ex bagels anywhere.

"Great place for lunch."

831 3rd Avenue   **Midtown East**
near 51st Street/10022
212-980-1010

H&H Bagels
2239 Broadway   **Bread**
near 80th Street   **Upper West Side**
New York, NY 10024

4	4	4	4
quality	style	service	value

212-595-8000. Fax 212-764-7391
Daily 24 hours.

The Edge: Among the top contenders for the best bagels in NYC. Baked fresh daily with new batches every few hours. Prices are among the highest in the city. Deliveries on orders of 10 dozen or more. Mail order available (call 800-NYBAGEL). They ship worldwide. Those who love it, love it, but others find the bagels too heavy.

"The best bagels in NYC. No question!" "Huge NY bagels."

1551 2nd Avenue   **Upper East Side**
near 80th Street/10028
212-734-7441. Fax 212-535-6791

Kossar's Bialystoker Kuchen Bakery
367 Grand Street   **Bread**
between Essex and Norfolk Streets   **Lower East Side/Chinatown**
New York, NY 10002

5	3	2	5
quality	style	service	value

212-473-4810. Fax 212-473-4810
Daily 24 hours.

The Edge: Best bialys and onion boards in the city. Also bagels and onion rolls. Four items, that's it! No credit cards. No delivery.

Orwasher's Bakery
308 East 78th Street   **Bread**
near 2nd Avenue   **Upper East Side**
New York, NY 10021

4	3	3	3
quality	style	service	value

212-288-6569
Monday-Saturday 7-7.

The Edge: 36 types of bread and rolls sold to many top New York restaurants. Bread varieties made by hand, including challah, cinnamon raisin, Irish soda bread, onion boards, raisin pumpernickel and rye. Special-order breads the day before by 3pm. Their bread sells fast, so reserve or go early if you want to ensure a particular item. Also a small selection of standard imported cheeses. Very reasonable. No credit cards. No delivery.

Pick a Bagel

1475 2nd Avenue
near 77th Street
New York, NY 10021
212-717-4668
Daily 6-midnight.

Bread
Upper East Side

4	4	4	4
quality	style	service	value

The Edge: A standard bagel cafe selling good bagels and adequate accouterments. No credit cards. No delivery.

Vesuvio Bakery

160 Prince Street
near West Broadway
New York, NY 10012
212-925-8248
Monday-Saturday 7-7.

Bread
SoHo/TriBeCa

4	4	3	4
quality	style	service	value

The Edge: Excellent, handmade Italian bread. No credit cards. No delivery.

Bazzini Importers

339 Greenwich Street
near Jay Street
New York, NY 10013
212-334-1280. Fax 212-924-5840
Weekdays 8-7 Saturday 9:30-6.

Candy, fruit & nuts
SoHo/TriBeCa

The Edge: The nuts are what's special. This is a wholesale operation open for retail sales. They supply Dean & DeLuca and many of the best gourmet shops with nuts and dried fruits. Best are butter toffee peanuts, fresh-roasted cashews and nut crunches. Also find candy and imported packaged cookies, coffee, condiments, gift baskets and good baked goods. Deliveries for very large orders only. Good prices always, but even better prices if you buy more than five pounds. Discounter.

Economy Candy Corp.

108 Rivington Street
between Essex and Ludlow Streets
New York, NY 10002
212-254-1531. Fax 212-254-2606
Weekdays 8:30-6 Saturday 10-5.

Candy, fruit & nuts
Lower East Side/Chinatown

The Edge: Prices are about half those uptown. Find hundreds of kinds of chocolates (including baking varieties), dried fruits, nuts and penny candies. The wide-ranging candy selection includes Baby Ruths, Baci, fresh halvah cut to order, chocolates of every conceivable kind and boxed gift candies, as well as sugar-free varieties. Pick N' Mix gift baskets from $25. Prices are excellent, wholesale (for very large orders) or retail at near-wholesale prices. Mail-order catalog available.

Elk Candy Company and Marzipan

240 East 86th Street
between 2nd and 3rd Avenues

Candy, fruit & nuts
Upper East Side

New York, NY 10028
212-650-1177
Monday-Saturday 9-6:45 Sunday 10-5:45.

The Edge: Marzipan and, at Christmas, classic gingerbread houses. Marzipan in wonderful animal shapes and styles (fruits and artifacts), Florentines, wonderful jellybeans at Easter and gingerbread houses at Christmas. Good dark chocolate, including semisweet break-up chocolate for baking.

Fifth Avenue Chocolatiere

Candy, fruit & nuts
Midtown East

510 Madison Avenue
near 53rd Street
New York, NY 10022
212-935-5454
Monday-Saturday 9-6.

The Edge: The style of the old Kron Chocolatiere. Chocolates come packaged in attractive wooden crates. Specialties include fresh and dried fruits dipped in semisweet chocolate, fresh truffles and bittersweet or milk chocolate molded into telephones, champagne bottles, records, tennis racquets, golf balls and women's legs. Will make a chocolate version of anything you want with two weeks' notice. Charges for deliveries in Manhattan. Mail order elsewhere.

Godiva Chocolatier

Candy, fruit & nuts
Midtown West

30 Rockefeller Plaza
near 50th Street
New York, NY 10020
212-765-4336
Weekdays 9-6.

The Edge: Department store sweets—the Bergdorf's of its kind. Sweets in gold boxes sold prepackaged or purchased loose. Mostly chocolates filled with cream fillings and some with nuts.

"Too bad the cafes are gone."

701 5th Avenue
between 54th and 55th Streets10022
212-593-2848. Fax 212-906-0140
Monday-Saturday 10-7 Sunday 11-6.

Midtown East

200 Park Avenue
at 45th Street/10166
212-697-9128. Fax 212-697-9150
Weekdays 8-7.

Midtown East

30 Rockefeller Plaza
near 50th Street/10020
212-765-4336
Weekdays 9-6.

Midtown West

245 Columbus Avenue
between 71st and 72nd Streets/10023

Upper West Side

212-787-5804
Monday-Saturday 10-9 Sunday noon-8.

33 Maiden Lane   **Lower Manhattan**
near Nassau Street/10038
212-809-8990. Fax 212-809-8991
Weekdays 9-6.

225 Liberty Street   **Lower Manhattan**
World Financial Center, Winter Garden/10281
212-945-2174. Fax 212-945-2174
Weekdays 10-7 Saturday 11-6 Sunday noon-5.

560 Lexington Avenue   **Midtown East**
near 50th Street/10022
212-980-9810. Fax 212-223-4633
Monday-Saturday 9-7 Sunday 11-6.

Kadouri & Son, Inc.

Candy, fruit & nuts
51 Hester Street   **Lower East Side/Chinatown**
near Essex Street
New York, NY 10002
212-677-5441. Fax 718-381-8103
Sunday-Thursday 8-6 Friday 8-3.

The Edge: Low, low prices. Shop looks rundown, but they sell nuts, dried fruit, coffees, beans
and herbs and spices at close to wholesale prices.

La Maison du Chocolat

Candy, fruit & nuts
25 East 73rd Street   **Upper East Side**
between 5th and Madison Avenues
New York, NY 10021

5 5 5 5

212-744-7117. Fax 212-744-7141
Weekdays 10-6:30 Saturday 10-6.   quality style service value

The Edge: Exceptional Parisian chocolates, the best in New York. This shop is an affiliate of a
Parisian chocolate store on Rue du Faubourg Saint-Honoré. Very rich, fabulous chocolate, 27+
combinations. Specialties include fruit pâtés, rich and buttery chocolate truffles, arribas
(bittersweet wafers filled with a thin layer of chocolate ganache), valencia (fresh orange peel and
orange liquor), rochers (hazelnut and almond praline covered in dark or light chocolate) and
chocolate-covered chestnuts in season. The chocolate truffles are bittersweet, extremely fresh and
should be eaten immediately, everything else within two weeks! Very very expensive, but you only
live once!

"Heaven."

Li-Lac Chocolates

Candy, fruit & nuts
120 Christoper Street   **Greenwich Village**
between Bleecker and Hudson Streets
New York, NY 10014

212-242-7374. Fax 212-366-5874   quality style service value
Monday-Saturday 10-8 Sunday noon-6. Memorial-Labor Day: Tuesday-Sunday 10-8.

The Edge: New York landmark moldings in chocolate. A Greenwich Village tradition since 1923. Chocolates, made by hand daily in small batches using fresh ingredients. No preservatives. Specialties include turtles, butter crunch, French cream rolls and their Taste of New York collection—hand-molded solid-chocolate replicas of the Empire State Building and the Statue of Liberty. Messenger service delivers chocolates in Manhattan (you pay their charge), mail order elsewhere.

"Old-fashioned, small and nice."

Mondel Chocolates

2913 Broadway
near 114th Street
New York, NY 10025
212-864-2111
Weekdays 11-7 Sunday noon-5. Closed Sunday July and August.

Candy, fruit & nuts
Upper West Side

The Edge: Chocolate happiness for Columbia students. Since 1943 has offered candy corn, chocolate-covered ginger and fruit, chocolate cups (filled with espresso, mint or kirsch), hand-dipped apricots, hard candies, jellybeans, lollipops and very good turtles. Find chocolates molded as alligators, cowboys, guitars, mice, pigs, Rolls-Royces, tennis racquets, Volkswagens and holiday gift packages. No delivery.

Neuchâtel Chocolates

60 Wall Street
near William Street
New York, NY 10005
212-480-3766
Weekdays 10-6.

Candy, fruit & nuts
Lower Manhattan

quality style service value

The Edge: Unique flavored truffles. Very fresh rich truffles. Intensely flavorful chocolates are packaged in constantly changing gift packages for all occasions, including Bar Mitvahs, weddings and birthdays. Unique chocolate gift packages are a specialty. Expensive.

2 West 59th Street
in the Plaza Hotel/10019
212-751-7742. Fax 212-391-5835
Weekdays 9-10 Saturday 10-10 Sunday 10-7.

Midtown West

Perugina

520 Madison Avenue
between 53rd and 54th Streets
New York, NY 10022
212-688-2490. Fax 212-750-9225
Weekdays 10-6 Saturday 11-5.

Candy, fruit & nuts
Midtown East

quality style service value

The Edge: Everyone knows their chocolates, or at least Baci. The shop features the familiar Baci, butter creams, pralines, gianduia, hard candies, chocolate ore liete and lazzaroni cookies in attractive gift boxes and pretty porcelain bowls. Moderately expensive.

Plumbridge

P.O. Box 219
Bradford, CT 06404
212-744-6640
Weekdays 9-5 plus special holiday hours.

Candy, fruit & nuts
Mail/phone

4	4	4	3
quality	style	service	value

The Edge: Gourmet gifts, now exclusively mail order. For more than a century a source for gourmet gifts, including candies and nuts (the standards plus pecans coated with brown sugar and cinnamon), glazed apricots, stuffed dates, mint chocolates and more. Lovely packaging in boxes and china. Very expensive.

Sweet Life

63 Hester Street
near Ludlow Street
New York, NY 10002
212-598-0092. Fax 212-598-0092
Sunday-Friday 9-6.

Candy, fruit & nuts
Lower East Side/Chinatown

The Edge: An old-fashioned candy store. Features candy, chocolates, coffees, dried fruit, fruit slices, jams, nuts, 10 kinds of halvah and teas. Gift baskets with stuffed animals and mugs, to enhance the present, are available. Good prices. Discounter.

Wolsk's Confections

81 Ludlow Street
near Delancey Street
New York, NY 10002
212-475-7946. Fax 212-672-2233
Sunday-Thursday 9-5 Friday 9-3.

Candy, fruit & nuts
Lower East Side/Chinatown

The Edge: Old-fashioned, hand-dipped chocolates. Chocolates, 50 varieties of nuts fresh roasted at the store and 30 kinds of dried fruit. Extensive gift basket options. Discounter.

9th Avenue Cheese Market

525 9th Avenue
between 39th and 40th Streets
New York, NY 10018
212-564-7127. Fax 212-757-8265
Monday-Saturday 8-7.

Cheese
Midtown West

5	4	4	4
quality	style	service	value

The Edge: Hundreds of cheeses, best are Greek and Middle Eastern. Broad selection of traditional cheeses from all over, although Greek products are emphasized. They have 15 kinds of feta cheese alone. Also find breads, caviars, coffees, dried fruits, jams, olives, Russian sausages and more. Low prices.

Alleva Dairy

188 Grand Street
near Elizabeth Street
New York, NY 10013
212-226-7990. Fax 800-425-5382
Monday-Saturday 8:30-6 Sunday 8:30-3.

Cheese
SoHo/TriBeCa

The Edge: The oldest Italian cheese store in the city. All the Italian cheese greats: ricotta and mozzarella (plain, smoked and rolled around prosciutto), Mascarpone and Gorgonzola torta with basil. Plus fresh and dried pasta, with sauces to complement. Mail order available. Discounter.

Ben's Cheese Shop

181 East Houston Street
near Orchard Street
New York, NY 10002
212-254-8290
Monday-Thursday 8:30-5:30 Friday 7:30-3:30
Sunday 7:30-6.

Cheese
Lower East Side/Chinatown

3	3	3	5
quality	style	service	value

The Edge: The place for variety and quality in cream cheese and farmer cheese. This is the Lower East Side, so don't expect service and do expect Sunday crowds. Here the farmer cheese comes in multiple flavors, including nut and raisin, blueberry, strawberry and pineapple. Cream cheese in multiple flavors, including garlic, herb, scallion and vegetable. The cheese is sold as well at Fairway, at close to Ben's prices. Unbelievably fresh. Inexpensive. No credit cards. Discounter.

East Village Cheese Shop

40 3rd Avenue
near 10th Street
New York, NY 10003
212-477-2601
Weekdays 9-6:30 weekends 9-5:30.

Cheese
Flatiron/East Village

3	3	4	5
quality	style	service	value

The Edge: Limited selection of foods, but good quality at East Village prices. A fine but limited selection of basic imported cheese, good breads and other items, including coffee, cold cuts and olive oil. The prices are good but the help can be rude. No credit cards. No delivery. Discounter.

Harry Wils & Company

182 Duane Street
between Greenwich and Hudson Streets
New York, NY 10013
212-431-9731. Fax 212-431-3620
Weekdays 9-5.

Cheese
SoHo/TriBeCa

The Edge: Supplies butter and eggs to better restaurants and gourmet shops. Will deliver for $150+ orders if you have an account. Reasonable prices and top quality. No credit cards.

Ideal Cheese Shop

1205 2nd Avenue
between 63rd and 64th Streets
New York, NY 10021
212-688-7579
Weekdays 9-6:30 Saturday 9-6.

Cheese
Upper East Side

5	3	5	5
quality	style	service	value

The Edge: For many, this is New York's only cheese shop. Hundreds of domestic and imported cheeses, in perfect condition, are available in this very small shop. Some rare cheeses are here only. Additional specialties include pâtés, smoked salmon, French saucisson, specialty meats, olives, cheese straws and La Semeuse coffee (served at Lutèce). Price list available for mail order. Expensive.

"They Fed Ex to other cities."

Joe's Dairy

Cheese
SoHo/TriBeCa

156 Sullivan Street
near Houston Street
New York, NY 10012
212-677-8780
Tuesday-Saturday 9-6:30.

The Edge: Among the best mozzarella in the city. Smoked and plain mozzarella made daily and on weekends smoked and pepper-cured prosciutto balls. Also find bocconcini (small marinated mozzarella balls with garlic and red pepper). No credit cards. No delivery.

LaMarca Cheese Shop

Cheese
Gramercy Pk/Murray Hill

161 East 22nd Street
near 3rd Avenue
New York, NY 10010
212-673-7920. Fax 212-982-1482
Weekdays 10-6:45 Saturday 10:30-5:30.

The Edge: Top quality, reasonable prices for Italian cheese, bread and pasta. Offers fresh mozzarella made daily, plus a wide range of pastas and fresh soups. Terrific breads. Some from Marie's in Hoboken. Reasonable prices. Delivery during the week from 6pm to 10pm. No credit cards.

Murray's Cheese Shop

Cheese
Greenwich Village

257 Bleecker Street
near Cornelia Street
New York, NY 10014
212-243-3289. Fax 212-243-5001
Monday-Saturday 8-8 Sunday 9-6.

4	4	4	4
quality	style	service	value

The Edge: Very high-quality cheeses at reasonable, often discounted, prices. Large selection of moderately priced excellent cheeses, limited variety of fresh pastas, sauces, breads, pâtés, sliced meats and a whole line of gourmet groceries. Check the weekly specials for their best prices. No credit cards.

Russo & Son Dairy Products

Cheese
Flatiron/East Village

344 East 11th Street
between 1st and 2nd Avenues
New York, NY 10003
212-254-7452
Monday-Saturday 9-7 Sunday 11-3.

The Edge: Quality classic Italian products. A small store that makes fresh mozzarella several times daily, smoked mozzarella, mozzarella with prosciutto and salami. Also pastas, cheeses, sliced meats and breads. Inexpensive. No delivery. Discounter.

Sal's Gourmet & Cheese Shop

169 1st Avenue
between 10th and 11th Streets
New York, NY 10003
212-529-7903
Monday-Saturday 9-8 Sunday 9-4.

Cheese
Flatiron/East Village

The Edge: Good basic Italian products. Italian cheeses, breads, fresh and dried pastas, homemade sauces and regular and smoked mozzarella made daily. Discounter.

Adriana's Caravan

409 Vanderbilt Street
Brooklyn, NY 11218
800-316-0820. Fax 718-436-8565
Daily 9-8.

Coffees, teas & spices
Mail/phone

The Edge: Wide range of condiments and seasonings. It's virtually impossible to need something they don't have. While the selection is good and sometimes they're the only source, prices are high. You'll find spices and packaged and dried ingredients from all over the world. Mail, phone and fax order only.

Angelica's Traditional Herbs and Spices

147 1st Avenue
near 9th Street
New York, NY 10003
212-529-4335
Monday-Saturday 10-7:45 Sunday 11-6:45.

Coffees, teas & spices
Flatiron/East Village

| 5 | 4 | 5 | 3 |
| quality | style | service | value |

The Edge: One of the best herb and spice shops in the city. Features thousands of Western and Chinese herbs. Also organic foodstuff, including organically grown grains (10 different types of rice) and 50 types of teas and dried fruits. No credit cards. No delivery.

Aphrodisia

264 Bleecker Street
near 10th Avenue
New York, NY 10014
212-989-6440. Fax 212-989-8027
Monday-Saturday 11-7 Sunday noon-5.

Coffees, teas & spices
Greenwich Village

| 5 | 4 | 5 | 4 |
| quality | style | service | value |

The Edge: The oldest herb and spice store in the city. Features more than 1,000 different herbs and spices. Half the store is devoted to cooking and the other half to medicinal herbs.

Coffee Grinder

348 East 66th Street
between 1st and 2nd Avenues
New York, NY 10021
212-737-3490. Fax 212-249-7768
Weekdays 9:30-7 Saturday 9:30-6.

Coffees, teas & spices
Upper East Side

The Edge: Best known for its custom-blended coffees and teas. Also features coffee makers and coffee gift baskets, plus salad dressings and marmalades.

Empire Coffee and Tea

592 9th Avenue
between 42nd and 43rd Streets
New York, NY 10036
212-586-1717
Weekdays 8-7 Saturday 9:30-6:30 Sunday 11-5. Closed summer Sundays.

Coffees, teas & spices
Midtown West

5	4	4	4
quality	style	service	value

The Edge: Selection. 90 kinds of coffee and 75 varieties of loose teas from every imaginable region. Prices are reasonable if not dirt cheap, but 9th Avenue in the 40s is not our favorite shopping area.

Hot Stuff Spicy Food, Inc.

P.O. Box 2210
Stuyvesant Station
New York, NY 10009
800-926-8468. Fax 718-218-9310
Daily 24 hours.

Coffees, teas & spices
Mail/phone

The Edge: Hot sauces and spices only. Here "mild is a four-letter word!" Find products from around the world, including fresh chili from Hatch, N.M. (America's chili capital), in season. Find New Mexican chilies, chili pepper wreaths, Indian and West Indian and Indonesian sauces and spices. Gift items include hot sauces of the world, assorted peppers, and cookbooks to tell you what to do with the sauces. Now mail order only, but we're not sure how they do it since either the line is busy or you get voice mail!

M. Rohrs

1692 2nd Avenue
between 87th and 88th Streets
New York, NY 10128
212-427-8319
Monday-Saturday 9-7.

Coffees, teas & spices
Upper East Side

The Edge: Excellent coffees, before the current coffee craze. Since 1896. Features over 30 kinds of coffees and more than 19 kinds of loose tea, as well as candies, honeys and accessories, including coffee pots, filters, tea pots and strainers. Coffee and teas are sold in antique red-and-gold coffee tins. They're fighting the trend with "no coffee bar now envisioned." Prices are very good, and made even better by the high quality.

McNulty's Tea and Coffee

109 Christopher Street
between Bleecker and Hudson Streets
New York, NY 10014
212-242-5351
Monday-Saturday 10-9 Sunday 1-7.

Coffees, teas & spices
Greenwich Village

5	5	5	5
quality	style	service	value

The Edge: Broad selection of teas and coffees. More than 75 varieties of coffees and 25 varieties of teas, from the standard to the rare. Good prices. Call 800-356-5200 for phone orders. Delivery by UPS.

Open Pantry
184 2nd Avenue
near 11th Street
New York, NY 10003
212-677-2640
Daily 7:30-11.

Coffees, teas & spices
Flatiron/East Village

The Edge: Another good choice for coffees and teas. Full range of coffee and teas. Check out their weekly specials. Inexpensive.

Oren's Daily Roast
31 Waverly Place
near University Place
New York, NY 10003
212-420-5958
Monday-Thursday 7-8 Friday 7-7 Saturday 10-6.

Coffees, teas & spices
Flatiron/East Village

quality style service value

The Edge: Good prices and a wide selection of coffees. Coffee is roasted daily and brought to the shop's six locations. More than 50 kinds of coffees from all over the world, including flavored coffees. Expensive, with prices per pound starting at $7.99 and going to $35.99 for Jamaica Blue Mountain.

434 3rd Avenue
near 31st Street/10016
212-779-1241
Weekdays 7-8 Saturday 9-6 Sunday 10-6.

Gramercy Pk/Murray Hill

1144 Lexington Avenue
between 79th and 80th Streets/10021
212-472-6830
Weekdays 7:30-8 Saturday 10-6 Sunday 11-6.

Upper East Side

33 East 58th Street
between Madison and Park Avenues/10022
212-838-3345
Weekdays 7-7 Saturday 10-6.

Midtown East

985 Lexington Avenue
near 71st Street/10021
212-717-3907
Weekdays 7-7 Saturday 10-6 Sunday 10-5.

Upper East Side

1574 1st Avenue
between 81st and 82nd Streets/10028
212-737-2690
Weekdays 7-6 Saturday 9-6 Sunday 10-5.

Upper East Side

Porto Rico Importing Company
40½ St. Marks
near 1st Avenue
New York, NY 10009

Coffees, teas & spices
Flatiron/East Village

212-533-1982. Fax 212-533-1982
Monday-Saturday 8-8 Sunday 12-7.

The Edge: Top quality, great value and enormous variety of coffees and teas. Huge selection of coffees and loose teas. Carries flavored coffees, spices, chocolates and condiments. You'll find a full line of coffee and tea makers. Inexpensive. Discounter.

201 Bleecker Street   **SoHo/TriBeCa**
near 6th Avenue/10012
212-477-5421. Fax 212-979-2303
Monday-Saturday 9-9 Sunday noon-7.

Sensuous Bean

Coffees, teas & spices
Upper West Side

66 West 70th Street
near Columbus Avenue
New York, NY 10023
212-724-7725. Fax 718-238-5512
Monday Thursday Friday 10-9 Tuesday Wednesday 10-7
Saturday 9:30-7 Sunday 11-6.

5	5	4	5
quality	style	service	value

The Edge: Really large selection of coffees and teas. All you'll find is coffee, tea and coffee and tea makers. Features 72 kinds of coffee and 28 kinds of tea. The shop will blend coffees and teas to suit. This is a good source for La Semeuse. Prices are reasonable and quality good.

Starbucks Coffee Company

Coffees, teas & spices
Flatiron/East Village

141 2nd Avenue
at 9th Street
New York, NY 10003
212-780-0024
Sunday-Thursday 6:30-midnight Friday-Saturday 6:30-2.

4	4	5	3
quality	style	service	value

The Edge: If you don't mind paying $2 for a large cup of coffee, it's delicious. The Seattle coffee company with a conscience (read their first annual report for amusement) and a name synonymous with coffee. Find good freshly brewed coffee in three sizes and prices and with European names. Espresso, cappuccino, latte and standard brewed coffee offered, among others. Also muffins, bagels and scones. No delivery.

585 2nd Avenue   **Gramercy Pk/Murray Hill**
at 32nd Street/10016
212-684-1299
Monday-Thursday 6:30-10 Friday 6:30-11 Saturday 7:30-11 Sunday 7:30-10.

1117 Lexington Avenue   **Upper East Side**
at 78th Street/10021
212-517-8476
Weekdays 6-9:30 Saturday 7-10 Sunday 7-8.

1128 3rd Avenue   **Upper East Side**
at 66th Street/10021
212-472-6535
Sunday-Wednesday 6-10 Friday Saturday 6-11.

1290 3rd Avenue
at 74th Street/10021
212-772-6903
Sunday-Thursday 6:30-10 Friday Saturday 7-11.

Upper East Side

1445 1st Avenue
at 75th Street/10021
212-472-7784
Weekdays 6-10:30 weekends 7-11:30.

Upper East Side

400 East 54th Street
at 1st Avenue/10022
212-688-8951
Monday-Thursday 6:30-10 Friday Saturday 6:30-11 Sunday 7-11.

Midtown East

2379 Broadway
at 87th Street/10024
212-875-8470
Daily 6-1.

Upper West Side

1559 2nd Avenue
at 81st Street/10028
212-472-7972
Weekdays 6:30-11 Saturday 6:30-midnight Sunday 7-11.

Upper East Side

Ten Ren Tea Company
75 Mott Street
near Canal Street
New York, NY 10013
212-349-2286. Fax 212-349-2180
Daily 10-8.

Coffees, teas & spices
SoHo/TriBeCa

quality	style	service	value
4	4	3	4

The Edge: Asian remedies—teas for taste and medicinal herbs. A full range of Asian teas and some lovely simple tea sets. Teas are grown for them at their own plantations in Taiwan. The shop holds a traditional tea service daily at an ornate mahogany table in the center of the store. You can try the tea you're considering buying. Also a large selection of herbal medicines. No delivery.

Myers of Keswick
634 Hudson Street
near Jane Street
New York, NY 10014
212-691-4194. Fax 212-691-7423
Weekdays 10-7 Saturday 10-6 Sunday noon-5.

English
Greenwich Village

The Edge: A bit of Britain in the city. Features British food products, including steak-and-kidney pie, Stilton, kippers, homemade sausage, baked hams, beans, teas, jams and fruit sodas. No delivery.

Akron

1424 3rd Avenue
near 80th Street
New York, NY 10028
212-744-1551. Fax 212-744-3591
Weekdays 8-6:30 weekends 8-5. Closed weekends July and August.

Fish & meat
Upper East Side

quality	style	service	value
4	3	4	4

The Edge: Excellent top-of-the-line meats. Prime meats for over 30 years with high prices, but excellent quality and service. Used more for phone and delivery service rather than for walk-in service. After all, why bother to make the trip, given the consistency of their quality?

"Good meat."

Albert's

836 Lexington Avenue
near 63rd Street
New York, NY 10021
212-751-3169
Weekdays 8-7 Saturday 8-6:30 Sunday noon-5.

Fish & meat
Upper East Side

quality	style	service	value
4	4	4	3

The Edge: Custom-cut butcher shop known for game and suckling pigs. Also good-quality regular meats. Mostly a telephone and delivery business. Quality, as is price, is high.

Baldwin Fish Market

1584 1st Avenue
between 82nd and 83rd Streets
New York, NY 10028
212-288-9032
Monday-Saturday 8-7:30.

Fish & meat
Upper East Side

The Edge: Good, reliable neighborhood fish market. The selection is limited but it's always very fresh and includes fish, some shellfish and well-kept fresh lobsters. Usually the standards—lobster, salmon, sole, swordfish and tuna. Delivers within a 20-block radius. No credit cards.

Catalano's

431 East 91st Street
near 1st Avenue in Vinegar Factory
New York, NY 10128
212-628-9608. Fax 212-369-5700
Daily 8-8.

Fish & meat
Upper East Side

The Edge: A reliable neighborhood source for fish. They accept personal checks. Expensive. No credit cards.

Central Fish Company

527 9th Avenue
near 39th Street
New York, NY 10018
212-279-2317. Fax 212-967-1049
Monday-Saturday 8-6:15 Sunday 8-5:30.

Fish & meat
Midtown West

quality	style	service	value
4	3	3	5

The Edge: Affordable lobsters. They specialize in seafood—fresh Maine lobster, Brazilian lobster tails shipped flash frozen, Florida shrimp, frozen Gulf shrimp plus the regulars like salmon and tuna. Come for the prices, not the service. No delivery. Discounter.

Citarella

2135 Broadway
near 75th Street
New York, NY 10023
212-874-0383. Fax 212-595-3738
Monday-Saturday 8-9 Sunday 9-7.

Fish & meat
Upper West Side

5	5	4	4
quality	style	service	value

The Edge: Almost universal agreement that this is one of the best fish stores in the city. Fish is always fresh and well maintained. Now in addition to fish, they offer meats and prepared foods, including homemade sausage, pasta, sauces, custardy rice pudding and rotisserie chicken. Best for fish, fowl and meats. Prices are very high, but the quality is consistently good. They cater also. Call 874-0383 for fish and 873-0909 for meats.

"A great fish market (and now meats too)."

East Village Meat Market

139 2nd Avenue
between St. Mark's Place and 9th Street
New York, NY 10003
212-228-5590
Monday-Saturday 8-6.

Fish & meat
Flatiron/East Village

The Edge: A Polish/Ukrainian meat store featuring great kielbasa. Specialty items include double-smoked kielbasa (Polish sausage) and Polish and Lithuanian breads. No credit cards. No delivery.

Empire Purveyors

901 1st Avenue
between 50th and 51st Streets
New York, NY 10022
212-755-7757
Weekdays 7-5 Saturday 10-5.

Fish & meat
Midtown East

The Edge: A wholesale meat operation. Delivers in the neighborhood only. While they say they're a wholesale meat operation selling meat at prices about 30% off retail, they wouldn't quote prices over the phone. Sells beef, veal, pork, chicken and duck. No credit cards.

F. Rozzo & Sons

159 9th Avenue
between 19th and 20th Streets
New York, NY 10011
212-242-6100
Weekdays 4am-3:30pm.

Fish & meat
Chelsea

The Edge: Wholesale seafood operation, sometimes open to the public. Occasional sales when this seafood-only place is officially open to the public. Buy here anytime for 100 pounds of seafood, plus or minus. Great lobster prices in those quantities.

Faicco's

260 Bleecker Street
between 6th and 7th Avenues
New York, NY 10014
212-243-1974
Tuesday-Thursday 8-6 Friday 8-7 Sunday 9-2.

Fish & meat
Greenwich Village

5	4	4	5
quality	style	service	value

The Edge: The place for first-rate Italian sausages. Known most for their pork products, pork roasts, pork chops and sausages. Their Italian sweet and hot sausages are among the best in the city. Their provolone cheese and parsley sausage is a specialty. Offers, as well, a full range of meats and Italian prepared foods. No credit cards. No delivery.

Florence Meat Market

5 Jones Street
near West 4th Street
New York, NY 10014
212-242-6531
Monday 8:30-1 Tuesday-Friday 9-6:30 Saturday 9-6.

Fish & meat
Greenwich Village

5	4	5	5
quality	style	service	value

The Edge: Quality meat market, less expensive than uptown. Full-line butcher priding themselves on very old-fashioned service. No longer any prepared foods. No credit cards.

Giovanni Esposito & Sons Meat Shop

500 9th Avenue
between 37th and 38th Streets
New York, NY 10018
212-279-3298
Monday-Saturday 8-7:30.

Fish & meat
Midtown West

The Edge: Another good Italian butcher. Old-fashioned old-time store offering a full line of meat products, including wonderful Italian sausages. Good quality and good prices. Phone orders. Delivers throughout the city with a $50 minimum order. Payment by cash or personal check. Order the evening before or early in the morning as the truck leaves before 10am.

H. Oppenheimer Company

2606 Broadway
between 98th and 99th Streets
New York, NY 10025
212-662-0246
Monday-Saturday 8-7.

Fish & meat
Upper West Side

5	5	5	5
quality	style	service	value

The Edge: Excellent meats and German cold cuts. Full range of meats and game. 42 years in business. 50% of their business is telephone and they deliver on the East Side for orders put in before 2pm. Specials are posted at the shop. House charge accounts. No credit cards.

Hoi Sing Seafood

17-19 Catherine Street

Fish & meat
Lower Manhattan

between East Broadway and Henry Street
New York, NY 10038
212-964-9694
Daily 8:30-7.

The Edge: Less expensive fish. No English spoken. Beautiful, much less expensive fish than uptown. You need to get used to shopping in Chinatown, however, as they don't feature uptown cleanliness. Prices are about half of uptown. No credit cards.

Jefferson Market

450 Avenue of the Americas
near 10th Street
New York, NY 10011
212-533-3377. Fax 212-533-6095
Monday-Saturday 8-9 Sunday 9-8.

Fish & meat
Chelsea

5	4	5	4
quality	style	service	value

The Edge: One of the best meat markets in the city. Top meats and fish. Also salads and prepared foods. The prepared shrimp is as good as it gets in New York, tasting like the cocktail shrimp featured at 21. Fifteen cuts of steak alone. Catering available. Prices are high, matching the quality.

Joe's Ninth Avenue Meat Market

533 9th Avenue
near 40th Street
New York, NY 10018
212-947-8090. Fax 914-946-9116
Monday-Saturday 8-6:30.

Fish & meat
Midtown West

The Edge: Reasonable prices and specials on all basic meats. No credit cards.

Jordan Lobster Dock

315 Harkness Avenue
between Bell Parkway and Knapp Street
Brooklyn, NY 11235
800-404-2529. Fax 718-934-6325
Daily 9-6:30.

Fish & meat
Mail/phone

The Edge: Lobster at low prices, shipped anywhere. Prices are great. They'll ship live lobsters anywhere in the United States with packaging and Fed Ex shipping extra.

Kurowycky Meat Products

124 1st Avenue
near 7th Street
New York, NY 10009
212-477-0344
Monday-Saturday 8-6. Closed Monday July and August.

Fish & meat
Flatiron/East Village

The Edge: The best kielbasa! Come here for the homemade kielbasa plus a full line of the standard meats. Wonderful Russian breads. Prices are very low. No credit cards. No delivery.

Leonard's Market

1241 3rd Avenue
near 71st Street
New York, NY 10021
212-744-2600
Weekdays 8-7 Saturday 8-6.

Fish & meat
Upper East Side

4	3	3	4
quality	style	service	value

The Edge: Top-quality meats for over 80 years. Has now broadened the offerings to include a good selection of fresh fish and seafood. Some takeout, including Manhattan clam chowder. Very expensive, among the highest prices in town.

Les Halles

411 Park Avenue South
between 28th and 29th Streets
New York, NY 10016
212-679-4111. Fax 212-725-1747
Daily noon-midnight.

Fish & meat
Gramercy Pk/Murray Hill

The Edge: French-styled meats. The butcher is French trained and cuts meat "French style." Specialties include pork stuffed with prunes and hangar steak. Requires minimum order for delivery.

Lien Phat Seafood & Meat

225 Grand Street
east of the Bowery
New York, NY 10013
212-941-6363
Daily 9-7.

Fish & meat
SoHo/TriBeCa

The Edge: Quality fish at Chinatown prices. The *New York Times* describes this and its neighbor (Tan My My) as the best fish (Lien Phat) and produce (Tan My My) stores in the area. Excellent quality fish always kept well iced. Great selection and good prices, although not the lowest in the area. The range of fish is wide—five types of snapper, three different groupers, blue fish, mackerel, pickerel, razor clams, tuna and much much more. Prices are less than half of uptown. Why items are kept iced? This is not uptown—iced often means on ice outdoors. No credit cards. No delivery.

Lobel's Prime Meats

1096 Madison Avenue
between 82nd and 83rd Streets
New York, NY 10028
212-737-1372. Fax 212-650-1934
Monday-Saturday 9-6. Closed Saturday July and August.

Fish & meat
Upper East Side

5	5	5	4
quality	style	service	value

The Edge: To some this is the top butcher in New York. Caters to the "carriage crowd and working women," featuring a full line of gourmet meats, game and exotic products (alligator and ostrich on special order with one-week notice). The steaks are buttery and chickens are from a breeder who reputedly feeds the chicken to Lobel's specifications. They offer house charges. 90% of their business is telephone and their toll-free number for out-of-town callers is 800-556-2357.

"Wonderful steaks."

Lobster Place

418 West 15th Street
between 9th and 10th Avenues
New York, NY 10011
212-255-5672
Monday-Saturday 5am-2pm.

Fish & meat
Chelsea

The Edge: Fresh, fresh seafood favored by New York's finest restaurants. The place for fresh Maine lobster and other seafood, including shrimp, crab, clams, oysters and mussels. Reputed to supply Le Cirque, La Côte Basque and the Four Seasons with seafood. Mainly wholesale but will sell retail with a minimum size order (for example, five pounds of shrimp, eight pounds of salmon, wholesale-size orders). Prices discounted about 30%. A great resource. No credit cards. No delivery.

Nevada Meat Market

2012 Broadway
between 68th and 69th Streets
New York, NY 10023
212-362-0443
Monday-Saturday 8-6.

Fish & meat
Upper West Side

The Edge: Top top butcher. Nevada features all the expected prime meats and a range of specialty items from liverwurst to osso buco. High-quality; attentive service with matching prices. Delivers all over Manhattan. Surprisingly they charge $2 for deliveries. No credit cards.

Ocean Sea Food

19-21 Henry Street
near Catherine Street
New York, NY 10002
212-227-3067. Fax 212-731-0848
Daily 9-7.

Fish & meat
Lower East Side/Chinatown

The Edge: Another Chinatown favorite for fresh seafood. From lobsters to turtles to shrimp, this is the place. Limited English and typical Chinatown service—curt and efficient. Cash and carry only. Inexpensive. No credit cards.

Ottomanelli Brothers

1549 York Avenue
between 82nd and 83rd Streets
New York, NY 10028
212-772-7900. Fax 212-772-8436
Weekdays 7-6:30 Saturday 7-6.

Fish & meat
Upper East Side

4	4	4	4
quality	style	service	value

The Edge: Old-fashioned full-service Italian butcher shop. Good quality for all the standards, plus game, fresh sausage, rolled roasts, osso buco and other dinner items. Not-bad southern Italian specialties, including baked ziti, lasagna, chicken parmigiana and pasta sauces as well as basic fresh Italian breads.

Ottomanelli's Meat Market

285 Bleecker Street
off 7th Avenue
New York, NY 10014
212-675-4217. Fax 212-620-7286
Weekdays 8-6:30 Saturday 7-6.

Fish & meat
Greenwich Village

quality style service value

The Edge: Old-fashioned, full-service Italian butcher shop. Not related to the uptown Ottomanelli Brothers. Full-line quality butcher featuring the standards plus specialty items like chicken sausage, veal roast and, in season, fresh game and venison. No credit cards.

Park East Kosher Butcher

1163 Madison Avenue
near 86th Street
New York, NY 10028
212-737-9800. Fax 212-737-6027
Monday-Wednesday 6:30-6:30 Thursday 6:30-8 Friday 6:30-3.

Fish & meat
Upper East Side

The Edge: Top-quality kosher butcher. All the regular meats plus cooked chickens, barbecued turkey or duck and some prepared foods (breast of veal, chopped liver and more). Good service. Will deliver anywhere in the tri-state area for free except for the $10 service charge to the Hamptons. Very expensive. This store is the Upper East Side source for kosher meat.

Pisacane Midtown Corp.

940 1st Avenue
between 51st and 52nd Streets
New York, NY 10022
212-355-1850
Weekdays 7:30-6 Saturday 9-5.

Fish & meat
Midtown East

quality style service value

The Edge: Excellent fish market. The shop stocks a wide variety of the freshest fish, including tanks of live Dungeness crabs, brook trout, lobsters and live soft-shell crabs in season. Also find smoked salmon, cooked lobster, shrimp and crabmeat. The prepared foods are very good, especially if kept simple. No credit cards.

Premier Veal

555 West Street
near West 12th Street
New York, NY 10014
212-243-3170. Fax 212-633-2744
Monday-Friday 4am-1pm.

Fish & meat
Greenwich Village

The Edge: Wholesale veal products. Top quality and excellent prices. Wholesale only, but will take retail orders depending on their mood. Very reasonable. No credit cards. Discounter.

Prime Access

P.O. Box 8187
White Plains, NY 10602
800-314-2875
Daily 24 hours.

Fish & meat
Mail/phone

The Edge: Meats served at top NYC restaurants. Unlike at most mail-order butchers, steaks are shipped fresh and need to be frozen or used within five days. The prime dry-aged steaks are flavorful and well marbled with the outside fat trimmed so closely that they don't flare when grilled. Apparently these are the steaks used at Chanterelle, among other four-star restaurants. Recently added veal and lamb to their line. Very, very, expensive, well over $20 per pound for steak and lamb. Overnight and weekend shipping extra.

Rosedale Fish & Oyster Market

1129 Lexington Avenue
between 78th and 79th Streets
New York, NY 10021
212-861-4323. Fax 718-463-4196
Monday-Saturday 8-6.

Fish & meat
Upper East Side

4	-	5	4
quality	style	service	value

The Edge: Top, top quality fresh fish. The Neuman family has owned Rosedale since 1906. The store is noted for superb service. Pricey but very good fish, including all the standards and whatever is fresh on Mr. Neuman's daily trip to the Fulton Fish Market. They can and will get any fish you want. Takeout includes lobster salad, fresh tuna salad, clam chowder and poached salmon, with appropriate sauces. Clams, oysters and salmon are routinely cooked or shucked to order. If you stick with simple fresh fish, the takeout is fine. Daily specials are posted in the window. Mr. Neuman will take customers on his daily trip to the Fulton Fish Market for an interesting 4am experience. House charges are available.

Salumeria Biellese

376-378 8th Avenue
near 29th Street
New York, NY 10001
212-736-7376. Fax 212-736-7376
Weekdays 7-6 Saturday 9-6.

Fish & meat
Midtown West

4	4	4	3
quality	style	service	value

The Edge: The homemade sausage served at top Italian and French restaurants. Since 1925. You'll find 40 kinds of homemade sausages, including all the standards plus sausage boudin blanc with truffles, sausage boudin noir and sausage from rabbit, venison and more. Reputed to be the sausage served at Le Cirque, among others. Also homemade prosciutto, salamis and fresh hams. Now has a restaurant, Birichino (moderately priced northern Italian at 260 West 29th Street). The shop has added a catering and takeout service, including dinner dishes made with chicken and veal. Mail order is available if the order is large enough. No credit cards.

Schaller & Weber

1654 2nd Avenue
between 85th and 86th Streets
New York, NY 10028
212-879-3047. Fax 212-879-9260
Monday-Saturday 9-6.

Fish & meat
Upper East Side

3	3	4	3
quality	style	service	value

The Edge: Yorkville neighborhood butcher. The shop features all the standard meats plus 100 varieties of German deli meats and sausages. Unusual meats include smoked goose breast and suckling pig.

"Not what it was."

Schatzie's Prime Meats
1200 Madison Avenue
between 87th and 88th Streets
New York, NY 10028
212-410-1555
Monday-Saturday 8-6.

Fish & meat
Upper East Side

The Edge: Prime meats at very good prices. Quality prime meats plus every kind of fresh game from mallard duck to venison (in season). Catering service available (no setups). The shop will prepare dishes and foods to order. For Thanksgiving they will, with several weeks' notice, prepare the entire dinner, including fresh-killed turkey, cranberry sauce, sweet potatoes, gravy, vegetables, pastas (lasagna, etc.) and pies for dessert. Advance notice is key during the holidays. Reasonable prices.

Sea Breeze Fishmarket
541 9th Avenue
near 40th Street
New York, NY 10018
212-563-7537
Monday 7:30-6 Tuesday-Friday 7:30-6:30 Saturday 7:30-5:30.

Fish & meat
Midtown West

The Edge: Reasonably priced quality fish. Expect to find the standards plus live lobsters which are stored in saltwater tanks. Priced about half of what you'd pay uptown. No delivery. Discounter.

Vin Hin Company
129 Mott Street
close to Canal Street
New York, NY 10013
212-431-5297
Daily 8-8.

Fish & meat
SoHo/TriBeCa

The Edge: Cheap, cheap fish. Little English is spoken here. Fish can be great or OK—what is always spectacular is the prices. No credit cards. No delivery. Discounter.

National Wholesale Liquidators
632 Broadway
between Houston and Bleecker Streets
New York, NY 10012
212-979-2400
Monday-Saturday 9:3-8 Sunday 11-7.

General stores
SoHo/TriBeCa

3	3	3	5
quality	style	service	value

The Edge: Close-outs of basic household and food supplies. Two packed floors holding everything from furniture to hairspray and everything in between. Find furniture, furnishings, food, household supplies and personal hygiene products. Ever-changing inventory (dependent on close-outs) in this store with a Woolworth/K Mart atmosphere. No delivery. Discounter.

Ralph's Discount City
93-95 Chambers Street
near Broadway
New York, NY 10007

General stores
Lower Manhattan

212-267-5567
Weekdays 7:30-7 Saturday 8:45-5 Sunday 10-5.

The Edge: If you're lucky and have the time. Features cheap products from close-outs or overstocking, including health and beauty products, food, housewares, candy and soda. Now in a new bigger store. No delivery. Discounter.

E.A.T. Gifts

1062 Madison Avenue
near 80th Street
New York, NY 10028
212-861-2544. Fax 212-628-1625
Monday-Saturday 10-6 Sunday noon-5.

Gifts
Upper East Side

3	4	4	4
quality	style	service	value

The Edge: Always welcome comfort gifts. Stuffed animals, party favors and basic jams and herbs available in attractive gift baskets. Very, very expensive.

Fraser-Morris

1264 3rd Avenue
between 72nd and 73rd Streets
New York, NY 10021
212-288-2727. Fax 212-288-8795
Monday-Saturday 8:30-7 Sunday 10-5.

Gifts
Upper East Side

4	3	3	3
quality	style	service	value

The Edge: Standard, mail-order gift packages their specialty. Features imported specialty items, package items, OK cheeses, chocolates and biscuits. Fruit baskets feature the standard pile of fruit, cellophane wrapped and shipped.

Manhattan Fruitier

105 East 29th Street
between Park and Lexington Avenues
New York, NY 10016
212-686-0404. Fax 212-686-0479
Weekdays 9-5.

Gifts
Gramercy Pk/Murray Hill

5	5	5	4
quality	style	service	value

The Edge: Glorious, gorgeous healthy gifts. Expensive but beautiful fruit baskets which look like "edible Dutch still lifes." Included in the baskets are the freshest fruits plus biscotti graced with fresh flowers. Baskets could include chocolate, dried fruit, Australian crystallized ginger, or dried pear. Gift baskets from $50 to $200. Delivery in the New York area (within 50 miles) or by Federal Express elsewhere. Staff is accommodating and efficient. They even keep track of what you sent, when and to whom, to avoid repeats. They couldn't be nicer to work with.

"The classiest fruit baskets." But one respondent warned "out-of-state Fed Ex box arrived with overripe fruit."

Bell Bates Company

107 West Broadway
near Reade Street
New York, NY 10013

Health food
SoHo/TriBeCa

212-267-4300. Fax 212-267-4362
Monday-Wednesday 9:30-6 Thursday Friday 9:30-6:30 Saturday 11-5.

The Edge: Gourmet health-food store. They feature organic items, including foods, herbs, spices and vitamins. A monthly flyer features special bargains. No delivery.

Commodities
117 Hudson Street
near North Moore Street
New York, NY 10013
212-334-8330. Fax 212-343-9602
Daily 10-8.

Health food
SoHo/TriBeCa

The Edge: Well-stocked health-food supermarket. Find dairy, frozen foods, grains, package foods, pasta and produce. No delivery.

Good Health
324 East 86th Street
between 1st and 2nd Avenues
New York, NY 10028
212-439-9682
Monday-Thursday 11:30-10 Friday Saturday 11:30-11 Sunday 11-10.

Health food
Upper East Side

The Edge: Standard health-store fare. Health store items and restaurant. Features food, personal products and vitamins. Some good prices on selected items.

Health Nuts
835 2nd Avenue
near 45th Street
New York, NY 10017
212-490-2979. Fax 212-490-2983
Weekdays 8:30-8 Saturday 10-7.

Health food
Midtown East

The Edge: Healthy items only. Find dietary supplements, organic items, personal-care products and books and pamphlets on health issues.

Healthy Pleasures
93 University Place
near 11th Street
New York, NY 10003
212-353-3663. Fax 212-353-3224
Weekdays 8-10 weekends 9-9.

Health food
Flatiron/East Village

4	3	3	4
quality	style	service	value

The Edge: Health-food supermarket and salad bar. Items include organic milk and free-range roasted chickens. Limited delivery between 23rd and Houston Streets and between 3rd and 6th Avenues.

Herban Kitchen
290 Hudson Street
between Dominick and Spring Streets
New York, NY 10013

Health food
SoHo/TriBeCa

212-627-2257. Fax 212-627-2513
Monday-Saturday 11-10 Sunday 11-5.

The Edge: Health-food items, as you'd expect. Open for breakfast and lunch, seven days a week. Eat at the establishment or take out food, including Caesar salad with grilled chicken, grilled vegetable sandwich and vegetarian grain burgers. Organic ingredients only. They cater and deliver to the Village, SoHo and TriBeCa only.

Nature Food Centres

28 West 57th Street
west of 5th Avenue
New York, NY 10019
212-757-1539
Weekdays 8-8 Saturday 10-7 Sunday 10-6.

Health food
Midtown West

3	3	3	3
quality	style	service	value

The Edge: Franchise operation, 27 stores in Manhattan alone. Each store is separate, but the formula is the same: packaged, frozen and dried food, personal care and vitamin products. Frequent two-for-one sales on Nature Food brands bring prices down substantially on selected items.

"Boring but serviceable."

Foods of India

121 Lexington Avenue
near 28th Street
New York, NY 10016
212-683-4419. Fax 212-251-0946
Monday-Saturday 10-8 Sunday 11-6.

Indian
Gramercy Pk/Murray Hill

The Edge: The full range of Indian cooking ingredients. Wholesaler which stocks a full range from beans and flours to spices for Indian cooking. Good prices. Discounter.

Kalustyan Orient Export Trading

123 Lexington Avenue
between 28th and 29th Streets
New York, NY 10016
212-685-3451. Fax 212-683-8458
Monday-Saturday 10-8 Sunday and holidays 11-7.

Indian
Gramercy Pk/Murray Hill

The Edge: Features Indian and Middle Eastern spices and cooking ingredients. Offers cheeses, dried lemons, exotic vegetables, four kinds of homemade mango chutney, Middle Eastern sweets, delicious mango ice cream, fresh California dates in season, grains, olives, roasted almonds, more than 20 kinds of rice and sun-dried mulberries. Some Middle Eastern prepared foods. Same-day delivery available depending on destination. Inexpensive.

Bianca Pasta

22-24 Carmine Street
near Bleecker Street
New York, NY 10014

Italian
Greenwich Village

212-242-4871
Monday-Saturday 8-7.

The Edge: The takeout department of Restaurant Tutta Pasta. Large selection of filled pasta plus ready-made pasta sauces. Inexpensive. No credit cards. Discounter.

Bruno the King of Ravioli

249 8th Avenue
near 21st Street
New York, NY 10011
212-627-0767
Weekdays 9-9 weekends 10-8.

Italian
Chelsea

5	3	4	4
quality	style	service	value

The Edge: All sorts of homemade pasta. Homemade gnocchi, lasagna (sold frozen), pasta, ravioli, tortellini and homemade sauces made in the factory behind the 45th Street store. Delivers with a $50 minimum. Frozen or not, the lasagna is great. Discounter.

"Excellent pasta and sauces." "Great service."

2204 Broadway
between 78th and 79th Streets/10024
212-580-8150
Weekdays 10-8 Saturday 9-7 Sunday 11-7.

Upper West Side

653 9th Avenue
between 45th and 46th Streets/10036
212-246-8456. Fax 212-582-2776
Monday-Saturday 8-6:30 Sunday 9-6.

Midtown West

DiPalo's Fine Food, Inc.

206 Grand Street
corner of Mott and Grand Streets
New York, NY 10013
212-226-1033
Monday-Saturday 9-6:30 Sunday 9-3.

Italian
SoHo/TriBeCa

5	3	4	5
quality	style	service	value

The Edge: A neighborhood Italian spot for 70 years. Find good pastas, canned tomatoes, breads, olive oils, cheeses (fresh mozzarella, ricotta, Parmesan and Gorgonzola), sausages and of course biscotti in this small storefront. Best prices in Little Italy. Will send UPS with two-day delivery. Service is wonderful and best during the week when the store is less crowded. No credit cards. Discounter.

"Lovely owners. Without my asking they offered a 10% discount for a large order."

Italian Food Center

186 Grand Street
near Mulberry Street
New York, NY 10013
212-925-2954
Daily 8-7.

Italian
SoHo/TriBeCa

The Edge: Good prices on Italian products. Good assortment of Italian necessities from olive oil to pasta to sauces and meats and breads. Discounter.

Manganaro's Food and Restaurant

488 9th Avenue
near 37th Street
New York, NY 10018
212-563-5331. Fax 212-239-8388
Weekdays 8-7 Saturday 9-7.

Italian
Midtown West

4	4	4	4
quality	style	service	value

The Edge: Good basic Sicilian specialties and pastry. An Italian food store best known for its cheeses, Italian breads, canned tomatoes from San Marzano, dried and fresh pasta, olive oils and fresh chestnuts at Christmas. Salads and sandwiches can be taken out or eaten at the shop with espresso. Does the six-foot sandwich, but focus is on takeout and grocery items. Same-day delivery in Manhattan only.

"Let's describe their service as efficient—it beats brusque."

Patrician Foods

58-66 57th Street
near Grand Avenue
Maspeth, NY 11378
718-417-4650. Fax 718-417-4838
Weekdays 10-4 Saturday 9-3.

Italian
Queens

The Edge: Sells Italian specialty foods at wholesale. The source used by Italian restaurants and food shops for cheese, oils, pastas, vinegars and more. Quality items at good prices. Recommended to us, but not known. Let us know what you thing. No credit cards.

Piemonte Ravioli Company

190 Grand Street
between Mott and Mulberry Streets
New York, NY 10013
212-226-0475. Fax 212-226-0476
Tuesday-Saturday 8-6 Sunday 8-4.

Italian
SoHo/TriBeCa

5	-	4	5
quality	style	service	value

The Edge: Perhaps the city's best pasta source: high-quality, enormous variety and good prices. More than 25 varieties of pasta and assorted sauces made fresh daily. Favorites include cannelloni and their lobster, pumpkin and porchini ravioli. Deliveries throughout Manhattan on large orders. For smaller orders, delivery by Fed Ex or UPS is possible, but they're concerned about spoilage in warm weather. Excellent prices, about half of uptown. Crowded on weekends. No credit cards. No delivery. Discounter.

"Truly delicious and cheap."

Raffetto's

144 West Houston Street
between Sullivan and MacDougal Streets
New York, NY 10012

Italian
SoHo/TriBeCa

4	4	4	4
quality	style	service	value

212-777-1261
Tuesday-Saturday 8-6.

The Edge: Good broad selection of pasta and sauces. Since 1906 has featured more than 50 kinds of fresh and dried pastas and sauces to complement the pastas. Cheese and spinach ravioli, pumpkin ravioli, garlic parsley fettuccine are among the specialties. Pasta sheets can be cut to your specification. Also breads, bread sticks, cheese, canned olive oil, imported Italian tomatoes, spices and other basic Italian products. Inexpensive. No credit cards. No delivery. Discounter.

"Once there was the one and only."

Ravioli Store   Italian
75 Sullivan Street   SoHo/TriBeCa
between Spring and Broome Streets
New York, NY 10012
212-925-1737. Fax 212-925-4807
Weekdays 10-7 Saturday 11-5 Sunday noon-5.

The Edge: Exotic pastas. The shop (owned by Geraldine Ferraro's son, John) features fresh pasta and ravioli, from the basic to the innovative, including tomato ravioli with five cheese filling, tomato-basil pasta with walnut pesto and lobster-mousse-filled ravioli. Dean & DeLuca carries Ravioli Store products. Very expensive, from $7 to $12 per pound.

Chinese American Trading Company   Oriental
91 Mulberry Street   SoHo/TriBeCa
near Canal Street
New York, NY 10013
212-267-5224
Daily 9-8.

The Edge: Good prices and quality for Oriental food. Features a wide variety of imported Oriental foodstuffs. Inexpensive. No credit cards. No delivery. Discounter.

Fung Wong Bakery   Oriental
30 Mott Street   SoHo/TriBeCa
near Chatham Square
New York, NY 10013
212-267-4037
Daily 8-9.

The Edge: Fortune cookie source. No English spoken here. Fortune cookies and almond cookies plus traditional Chinese pastry. No credit cards. No delivery. Discounter.

Han Arum   Oriental
25 West 32nd Street   Midtown West
between 5th and 6th Avenues
New York, NY 10001
212-695-3283. Fax 212-947-6566
Daily 9-9.

The Edge: Largest Korean supermarket in Manhattan. Little, if any, English spoken. All the standard Korean items plus a salad bar featuring 20 Korean dishes, as well as Korean baked goods and cookies. No delivery. Discounter.

Kam Kuo Food

7 Mott Street
near Lombard Street
New York, NY 10013
212-233-5387. Fax 212-349-3097
Daily 9-9.

Oriental
SoHo/TriBeCa

quality style service value

The Edge: A full-scale Oriental supermarket in the heart of Chinatown. Downstairs find canned and frozen products, condiments, fresh noodles and dumplings in refrigerator cases, grains, meats, oils, rice, teas, won tons and won ton wrappers. Upstairs find chopsticks, cooking utensils, plates, pottery, serving bowls and tea sets. While aisles are labeled in English and Chinese, English is not spoken in the shop. Prices are extremely low, a fraction of uptown. Mail order is available with very large orders. Discounter.

Kam Man Food Products

200 Canal Street
near Mulberry Street
New York, NY 10013
212-571-0330. Fax 212-966-9085
Daily 9-9.

Oriental
SoHo/TriBeCa

quality style service value

The Edge: One of the largest Asian supermarkets. They have everything from fresh fish to meats (including excellent barbecued pork and roasted duck) to Chinese mushrooms, desserts and teas to housewares and exotic Chinese remedies. The store features Chinese, Japanese, Vietnamese, Philippine, Thai and Singapore products. Prices are great. Discounter.

"Problem is the non-English-speaking help."

Katagiri and Company

224 East 59th Street
between 2nd and 3rd Avenues
New York, NY 10022
212-755-3566. Fax 212-752-4197
Monday-Saturday 10-7 Sunday 11-6.

Oriental
Midtown East

quality style service value

The Edge: The city's oldest Japanese food store. A very small gourmet supermarket stocked full with Japanese fresh foods, including sushi ingredients, vegetables (seaweeds too), rice and exquisitely fresh fish. Also cooking utensils. Expensive.

"Not bad for midtown."

Lung Fong Chinese Bakery

41 Mott Street
near Biddle Street
New York, NY 10013
212-233-7447

Oriental
SoHo/TriBeCa

Daily 8-8.

The Edge: Chinese pastry. Chinese fortune and almond cookies plus standard Chinese pastries. No credit cards. No delivery.

Tan My My

249 Grand Street
near Chrystie Street
New York, NY 10002
212-966-7878
Daily 9-8:30.

Oriental
Lower East Side/Chinatown

5	-	2	5
quality	style	service	value

The Edge: Perhaps the best Chinatown source for fresh fish and vegetables. Prices are amazingly low, but, better still, the quality is as good as it gets anywhere in the city. The fish look as if they're still swimming and the fruits and vegetables look as though they've jumped from the ground to the store. Like most Chinatown places—no service, no deliveries and no English. No credit cards. No delivery.

Annie's

1204 Lexington Avenue
near 82nd Street
New York, NY 10028
212-861-4957
Monday-Saturday 7:30-7:30.

Produce
Upper East Side

The Edge: Quality conventional fruits, vegetables and dairy products. Takes personal checks. Expensive. No credit cards.

Aux Délices des Bois

4 Leonard Street
between Hudson Street and West Broadway
New York, NY 10013
212-334-1230
Monday-Thursday 10-7 Friday 10-6.

Produce
SoHo/TriBeCa

The Edge: The best for mushrooms and truffles, in season. Features fresh and a limited selection of dried mushrooms. Good but not the lowest prices. No credit cards.

Likitsakos

1174 Lexington Avenue
between 80th and 81st Streets
New York, NY 10021
212-535-4300. Fax 212-423-0357
Weekdays 8-9 Weekends 8-8.

Produce
Upper East Side

5	5	4	5
quality	style	service	value

The Edge: Could be the freshest produce on the Upper East Side. Excellent selection of fresh, fresh produce. This store has taken the Upper East Side by storm. It's one of the top sources for just about any kind of produce, plus gourmet items from charcuterie and cheese to Greek and pasta-based prepared foods and staples (breads, coffees, oils, vinegar and more).

Nature's Gifts

1297 Lexington Avenue
between 87th and 88th Streets
New York, NY 10128
212-289-6283. Fax 212-534-2524
Weekdays 8-9 weekends 8-8.

Produce
Upper East Side

quality	style	service	value
4	1	3	3

The Edge: Good prices on good produce. Items just outside the store are where the really good values are. Mostly sells fresh fruits and vegetables. Also butter, juice, milk, pastas, couscous, dressings, Eli's Breads and Ciao Bella gelati. The takeout counter features fruit, Greek, health and pasta salads. Delivery within a 10-block radius.

Paradise Market

1081 Lexington Avenue
corner 76th Street
New York, NY 10028
212-570-1190. Fax 212-570-1192
Weekdays 7-7 Saturday 7-6.

Produce
Upper East Side

quality	style	service	value
4	4	3	3

The Edge: Impeccable produce. Always favorably reviewed by the *New York Times* and *New York* magazine. Carries fresh and unusual produce, including wild mushrooms, fresh herbs and all the standard produce, but selected for its quality. Extremely expensive. Payment by cash or check only.

1100 Madison Avenue
near 83rd Street/10028
212-737-0049
Weekdays 8-7 Saturday 8-6.

Upper East Side

Agata & Valentina

1505 1st Avenue
near 79th Street
New York, NY 10021
212-452-0690. Fax 212-452-0694
Monday-Saturday 9-9:30 Sunday 8-9.

Superstores
Upper East Side

quality	style	service	value
5	5	5	4

The Edge: Quality takeout. Another Balducci's-style gourmet shop, emphasizing Italian ingredients. You'll find bakery items, breads, candies, caviar, gourmet dishes, cheeses, extra-virgin olive oil, fresh vegetables, gelati, meats and smoked fish. Good desserts, better breads and good Sicilian-style prepared foods. Surprisingly, prices on some fruits and vegetables were in the supermarket range.

"One-stop shopping for great meals." "Great look and atmosphere."

Balducci's

424 Avenue of the Americas
between 9th and 10th Streets
New York, NY 10011
212-673-2600. Fax 212-995-5065
Daily 7-8:30.

Superstores
Chelsea

quality	style	service	value
5	4	4	3

The Edge: Impeccable source for everything. You'll find breads, cheeses, fresh pastas and sauces, meats, produce, salads, smoked fish and a full range of baked goods, candy, coffee/tea, condiments, dried fruits and nuts, oils, packaged items, prepared foods and vinegars. In fish they carry the standards plus specialties. Prepared foods are good, the simpler the better though. Well known for quality gift and picnic baskets. The shop is always crowded and the isles are narrow. Surprisingly, for such high-end quality, prices are not bad. Delivers anywhere in the five boroughs. Mail order also.

"Great mail order." "One of the 'grand-daddies' of the rich and famous foods." "Expensive, but quality."

Broadway Farm
2339 Broadway
near 85th Street
New York, NY 10024
212-787-8585. Fax 212-787-4076
Daily 24 hours.

Superstores
Upper West Side

3	1	3	3
quality	style	service	value

The Edge: Grocery store styled after Fairway. Like Fairway it features quality inexpensive food items, coffee, cheeses, fruits and vegetables, smoked fish, specialty beers and unusual imported items. Delivers from Central Park West to Riverside Drive between 70th and 93rd Streets.

Butterfield Market
1114 Lexington Avenue
near 78th Street
New York, NY 10021
212-288-7800
Weekdays 7:30-8 Saturday 7:30-5:30.

Superstores
Upper East Side

4	3	4	4
quality	style	service	value

The Edge: Service. Service is excellent with special attention to every customer. They carry a full range of high-quality food items from basic to gourmet. Very expensive.

Dean & Deluca
560 Broadway
corner Prince Street
New York, NY 10012
212-431-1691
Monday-Saturday 8-8 Sunday 9-7.

Superstores
SoHo/TriBeCa

5	5	4	3
quality	style	service	value

The Edge: Only the best of everything lands here. If it's a food or related item, chances are it's here. Find breads, candy, cheeses, coffees, dairy, desserts, the freshest of fish, fruits, prime meats, oils, pasta, prepared foods, vegetables and vinegars. The foods displayed are picture perfect. D&D is, as expected, the best source for new, out-of-the-ordinary products. Prices are high, but what is always surprising, is that not-as-good competitors are often even higher. The place could be called Tiffany—it has that quality. Joining the food are top-of-the-line, first-class kitchenware, including copper, earthenware, porcelain, stainless-steel pots, including pâté crocks, steamers and stock pots. Also baking equipment, cutlery, kitchen utensils and gadgets, table linen and the best of the new cookbooks. Deluxe.

"The finest store/market in New York City—tops all others." "Beautifully displayed exotica." "Pricey."

Fairway Market

2127 Broadway
near 74th Street
New York, NY 10023
212-595-1888. Fax 212-595-9843
Daily 7-midnight.

Superstores
Upper West Side

quality style service value

The Edge: The best prices and the best-quality produce and cheeses, if you can stand the crowds. Features a wide selection of produce, coffees, deli, breads, pastas and sauces, packaged cookies, olives, cakes and only so-so prepared foods. Will put picnic baskets together in only 15 minutes—just call ahead. Catering service for platters of smoked fish, fresh fruit, cookies, sliced meats, pâté and cheese and vegetables. The space is so narrow and crowded, you can hardly get around the store. The checkout lines are long, but move fast. Prices are even lower at their new 35,000-square-foot Harlem store located at 133rd Street and 12th Avenue. No credit cards. No delivery. 30% off.

"One of the best, if not *the* best produce market in New York City." "Best market in the city." "A nightmare to move around in."

2328 12th Avenue
near 133rd Street/10027
212-234-3883

Upper Upper West Side

Gourmet Garage

453 Broome Street
near Mercer Street
New York, NY 10013
212-941-5850. Fax 212-343-1601
Daily 8-8.

Superstores
SoHo/TriBeCa

quality style service value

The Edge: Gourmet food items at better prices. The original of this new trend for gourmet foods at good prices. Features greens, meat, dairy, prepared foods, coffees and juices. Quality is high. Features good products from top distributors. No delivery.

"Worth the trip to Broome Street." "Pricey."

Grace's Marketplace

1237 3rd Avenue
near 71st Street
New York, NY 10021
212-737-0600. Fax 212-535-7431
Monday-Saturday 7-8:30 Sunday 8-7.

Superstores
Upper East Side

quality style service value

The Edge: Good selection and quality. Inspired by Balducci's. Great selection of candy, condiments, baked goods, breads, cheeses, coffees, dairy, deli meats, dried fruits, nuts, pasta/sauces, smoked fish, fruits and vegetables. Can be expensive, for example, a platter of sandwiches (mozzarella and sun-dried tomatoes essentially) for $160.

"Expensive, but worth it."

International Groceries and Meat Market

529 9th Avenue
between 39th and 40th Streets
New York, NY 10018
212-279-5514
Monday-Saturday 8-6.

Superstores
Midtown West

The Edge: Excellent prices, good quality. Near the Port Authority, they specialize in food products from around the world. Expect to find it all, from flours and dried pastas to condiments and meat, fish and cheeses. Greek products are a specialty. Local deliveries only. No credit cards.

Nader International Foods

1 East 28th Street
near 5th Avenue
New York, NY 10016
212-686-5793
Weekdays 9-7 Saturday 10-6 Sunday noon-5.

Superstores
Gramercy Pk/Murray Hill

The Edge: Specializes in Middle Eastern food products. Find cooking ingredients, including bulgur wheat, lentils, spices, imported pistachio nuts, several kinds of halvah, dried fruits and candies. Very good prices. No credit cards.

Ninth Avenue International Foods

543 9th Avenue
near 40th Street
New York, NY 10018
212-279-1000
Monday-Saturday 8:30-7.

Superstores
Midtown West

The Edge: Great Middle Eastern products. Features good prices on coffees (40 kinds), spices, chocolates, caviar spreads, European cheeses, grains (in bulk bags) and more. Great prices—for example, all coffees are sold at $4.99 a pound. It's a cash-and-carry place. Discounter.

Sahadi Importing Company, Inc.

187-189 Atlantic Avenue
near Court Street
Brooklyn, NY 11201
718-624-4550. Fax 718-643-4415
Weekdays 9-7 Saturday 8:30-7.

Superstores
Brooklyn

4	3	4	5
quality	style	service	value

The Edge: Wonderful prices on Middle Eastern delights. An old-fashioned turn-of-the-century style store featuring Middle Eastern specialties. Really low prices and everyone is friendly and helpful. You'll find breads, candies, canned goods, cheeses, dried fruits, fresh coffee beans, frozen foods, jams, nuts, pastas, prepared foods, rice and spices. Phone orders and delivery are possible through Sultan's Delight. Discounter.

Sultan's Delight

P.O. Box 090302
Brooklyn, NY 11209
718-745-2121. Fax 718-745-2563
Daily 24 hours.

Superstores
Mail/phone

4	3	4	5
quality	style	service	value

The Edge: Ships for Sahadi Importing. Brooklyn prices on more than 250 Middle Eastern specialty items, including herbs, spices, nuts, dried beans, dried fruits, teas, rice, barley, flours, pastas, canned goods and coffee. Sultan's Delight ships Sahadi Importing products worldwide. They'll send you a catalog, if you provide a legal-size self-addressed and stamped return envelope. Discounter.

Todaro Brothers
555 2nd Avenue
between 30th and 31st Streets
New York, NY 10016
212-532-0633. Fax 212-689-1679
Monday-Saturday 7:30-9 Sunday 8-8.

Superstores
Gramercy Pk/Murray Hill

quality	style	service	value
4	4	4	5

The Edge: A much less expensive Balducci's. A large Italian market featuring appetizers, baked goods, bread, cheeses, coffee, dairy, Italian cold cuts, meat, pasta, poultry, prepared foods, sandwiches, sauces, smoked fish and tea. Moderate prices on most items.

Zabar's Appetizers & Caterers
2245 Broadway
between 80th and 81st Streets
New York, NY 10024
212-787-2000. Fax 212-580-4477
Weekdays 8-7:30 Saturday 8-8 Sunday 9-6.

Superstores
Upper West Side

quality	style	service	value
5	3	4	4

The Edge: Legendary for selection and price. The best of Zabar's includes its appetizer department, the annual New Year caviar price war, breads, candy, cheese, dried fruits, great coffee cakes, nuts, rugelach, sticky buns, pasta and their coffees and teas. Not up to par are the prepared foods. Delivery and phone orders are available for large orders. Catering and picnic baskets are also available. Upstairs find an unbelievable range of kitchen cookware at some of the best prices in the metro area. 25% off.

Barocca Alimentari
297 Church Street
between Walker and White Streets
New York, NY 10013
212-431-0065. Fax 212-274-1618
Weekdays 7:30-6.

Takeout
SoHo/TriBeCa

quality	style	service	value
2	3	3	3

The Edge: Takeout from Restaurant Barocca. This takeout shop adjacent to the Restaurant Barocca features Italian dishes. Deliveries from Houston to Chambers Street.

"Not what it was."

Benny's Burritos To Go
93 Avenue A
near 8th Street
New York, NY 10009
212-254-2054

Takeout
Flatiron/East Village

quality	style	service	value
4	3	3	4

Daily 11-midnight.

The Edge: What New Yorkers expect of standard Mexican food. 12-inch-long party-size burritos, guacamole, enchiladas, tacos and chili. Inexpensive. No credit cards.

112 Greenwich Avenue   **Chelsea**
between Jane and West 13th Streets/10011
212-633-9210

Between the Bread

145 West 55th Street   **Takeout**
between 6th and 7th Avenues   **Midtown West**
New York, NY 10019
212-581-1189. Fax 212-262-2359

4	3	4	3
quality	style	service	value

Weekdays 7:30-2:30.

The Edge: Either you love it or you think the prices are unconscionable. At breakfast, find a wide variety of fresh-fruit muffins, which seem to have a similar taste after a while, but the coffee is good and rich. At lunch, the standard salads, pasta, tuna and steak. Very expensive. "Recently a simple lunch for two of canned tuna salad, ice teas, fresh fruit and cookies came to over $60!"

141 East 56th Street   **Midtown East**
between Lexington and 3rd Avenues/10022
212-888-0449. Fax 212-262-2359
Weekdays 8:00-2:30.

Canard and Company

1292 Madison Avenue   **Takeout**
near 92nd Street   **Upper East Side**
New York, NY 10128
212-722-1046. Fax 212-360-1756
Weekdays 7-9 weekends 7-7:30.

The Edge: Catering and mail order. Gift baskets available. Santa Fe–style dishes, designer sandwiches and excellent pies, coffee cakes, chocolate-chip cookies made for the shop by Kathleen's. Catering is a specialty. For gifts, find custom gift baskets, fine candies, jams and jellies. Also Beluga and Ossetra caviar and smoked salmon.

Corrado Kitchen

1375 Avenue of the Americas   **Takeout**
between 55th and 56th Streets   **Midtown West**
New York, NY 10019
212-333-7696

4	3	3	3
quality	style	service	value

Daily 8-10.

The Edge: Quality Italian takeout. Food market and catering shop affiliated with the restaurant next door. You'll find breads, cheeses, produce and high-end packaged groceries, including olive oils and pasta. Good takeout includes baked butternut squash, linguine with porcini mushrooms and penne pasta with eggplant.

David's Chicken

1323 3rd Avenue
corner 76th Street
New York, NY 10021
212-628-2700
Weekdays 9-8:30 weekends 9-7:30.

Takeout
Upper East Side

quality	style	service	value
4	3	3	4

The Edge: The Williams of the East Side. Rotisserie chickens, duck, turkey, capon and rock Cornish hen, all moist and piping hot. Accompanying the chicken is egg barley, kasha varnishkes, mushrooms, string beans and other cold salads. Also chicken soup with your choice of noodles or matzoth balls. The soup can be salty.

"The food is good for what it is. The chickens taste great."

E.A.T.

1064 Madison Avenue
between 80th and 81st Streets
New York, NY 10028
212-772-0022. Fax 212-628-1625
Daily 7-10.

Takeout
Upper East Side

quality	style	service	value
5	4	4	2

The Edge: Great food, but those prices and attitude! Owned by Eli Zabar, Inc. Excellent sandwiches, salads, made-to-order appetizers, wonderful desserts and catering. Prices are sky-high, and even with these prices they charge for delivery.

"Worth a peek to watch what people will pay!" "Overpriced, touristy."

El Pollo

1746 1st Avenue
between 90th and 91st Streets
New York, NY 10128
212-996-7810
Weekdays 11:30-11 weekends 12:30-11.

Takeout
Upper East Side

quality	style	service	value
4	2	4	5

The Edge: Good cheap meals. Grilled roasted chicken served with a good sauce, crispy french fries or even better papa-rellenas (ground meat, fried potato and raisins) and salads.

"Good value."

Fisher & Levy

875 3rd Avenue
near 53rd Street, concourse level
New York, NY 10022
212-832-3880. Fax 212-832-3409
Weekdays 7:30-5:30.

Takeout
Midtown East

The Edge: Specialty office catering. They'll do big functions to individual sandwich orders. Breakfast to dinner. Also assortments of sandwiches (the shrimp is delicious) and salads.

Good & Plenty To Go

410 West 43rd Street
between 9th and 10th Avenues
New York, NY 10036
212-268-4385. Fax 212-564-2722
Weekdays 8:30-8 Saturday 10-6 Sunday 8-6.

Takeout
Midtown West

The Edge: A Word of Mouth offshoot with good comfort food to take out. Owned by one of the original owners of Word of Mouth. Good high-quality food includes rare sliced steak, divine cornbread, meatloaf and, for nostalgia, macaroni and cheese. Desserts taste like you imagine grandma's did. Prices are high.

Hale & Hearty

849 Lexington Avenue
between 64th and 65th Streets
New York, NY 10021
212-517-7600
Monday-Thursday 8:30-7 Friday 8:30-6 Saturday 10-5:30.

Takeout
Upper East Side

3	3	3	3
quality	style	service	value

The Edge: Healthy, well-prepared, but not exceptional, food. Menu favors soups, salads and sandwiches for the office lunch crowd. Delivery available within a 10-block radius.

International Poultry Company

983 1st Avenue
near 54th Street
New York, NY 10022
212-750-1100. Fax 212-750-5319
Weekdays 10-9 weekends 10-8.

Takeout
Midtown East

4	4	4	4
quality	style	service	value

The Edge: A reasonable takeout alternative. Barbecued, grilled chicken served with salsa and soups, including chicken soup. Offers picnic baskets and catering.

1133 Madison Avenue
between 84th and 85th Streets/10028
212-879-3600
Weekdays 10-9 weekends 9-8.

Upper East Side

Lorenzo & Maria's Kitchen

1418 3rd Avenue
between 80th and 81st Streets
New York, NY 10028
212-794-1080. Fax 212-628-0964
Monday-Saturday 9-8.

Takeout
Upper East Side

4	4	4	4
quality	style	service	value

The Edge: Expensive takeout, but very good, if you know what to order. Top items include marinated shrimp with fresh dill, rare and tender leg of lamb, flaky salmon, crunchy French string beans, mashed potatoes, roast potatoes and desserts, including crème caramel and rice pudding. Caters to telephone orders and delivers all over the city. The takeout menu changes daily, but much of the top choices mentioned above appears to be offered daily. Their catering is flexible, with the kitchen accommodating a wide range of preferences.

"Don't order their ravioli—it tastes like Chef Boyardi and is expensive to boot!"

Pranzo Fine Foods

1500 2nd Avenue
near 78th Street
New York, NY 10021
212-439-7777
Weekdays 7-10 weekends 8-9.

Takeout
Upper East Side

The Edge: Takeout favoring standard American and Italian favorites. For breakfast, more American than Italian, including assorted muffins and smoked-salmon platters. For evening, hors d'oeuvres include smoked-salmon triangles, assorted mini quiches, mini shrimp and crab cakes and goat cheese bruschetta. Dinner specialties include salads, pastas and grilled items representing various regional Italian specialties. Keep it simple and it's OK.

Remi To Go

145 West 53rd Street, in the aetrium
between 6th and 7th Avenues
New York, NY 10019
212-581-7115. Fax 212-581-7182
Weekdays 7-7.

Takeout
Midtown West

The Edge: Very good Italian takeout. Affiliated with the Restaurant Remi. Features business luncheon fare mostly, pasta salads, sandwiches and some hot entrees. Full coffee bar and gourmet groceries. There're a few tables in the atrium to eat at. Caters to the business crowd for lunch and breakfast meetings. Local deliveries.

William Poll

1051 Lexington Avenue
between 74th and 75th Streets
New York, NY 10021
212-288-0501. Fax 212-288-2844
Monday-Saturday 9-6:30.

Takeout
Upper East Side

4	4	4	3
quality	style	service	value

The Edge: Some good things but out of sight expensive. Best items are the frozen hors d'oeuvres (phyllo dough stuffed with spinach and cheese, meatballs, etc.) Known for their caviar, dips and smoked salmon. Will make up sandwiches, which are small and expensive. At Christmas they offer handmade gingerbread houses, which incorporate music boxes and Christmas lights, for $150+.

Williams Bar-B-Que

2350 Broadway
between 85th and 86th Streets
New York, NY 10024
212-877-5384
Daily 8-8.

Takeout
Upper West Side

5	3	3	5
quality	style	service	value

The Edge: Traditional Friday-night Jewish dinners. Chicken and all the fixings, including chicken soup with egg barley, mushrooms and noodles, chopped liver, kasha varnishkes, potato pancakes and more. Plus capons, duck, fried chicken and turkey. No credit cards.

"Top drawer! Try the barley."

Word of Mouth

Takeout
Upper East Side

1012 Lexington Avenue
between 73rd and 74th Streets
New York, NY 10021
212-734-9483. Fax 212-737-1637
Weekdays 10-7 Saturday 10-6 Sunday 11:30-5:30.

quality	style	service	value
4	4	4	4

The Edge: Good basic takeout. One of the first gourmet takeout stores. Specialties include meatloaf, sliced steak, lamb stew, salads, rice pudding, brownies, pecan bars and peanut cup bars. Catering and picnic baskets available. Delivery for a fee.

67 Wine & Spirits Merchants

Wines & liquors
Upper West Side

179 Columbus Avenue
between 67th and 68th Streets
New York, NY 10023
212-724-6767. Fax 212-580-6893
Monday-Thursday 9-9 Friday Saturday 9-10.

quality	style	service	value
4	-	4	4

The Edge: First-rate selection of French and California wines. A large selection California, French, Australian and Italian wines and champagnes. Good, but not rock-bottom, prices.

"Local star with good selection." "Good selection for a small store."

Acker Merrall and Condit

Wines & liquors
Upper West Side

160 West 72nd Street
near Broadway
New York, NY 10023
212-787-1700. Fax 212-799-1984
Monday-Saturday 9-10.

quality	style	service	value
4	-	3	3

The Edge: Strong selection of German and Alsatian wines. They're strongest in Californian, German and Alsatian wines but feature a good selection of Australian, French and Italian wines. Carries wine-related gift items, including corkscrews, baskets, books and glassware. Delivers all over the NY area and by UPS anywhere else.

"Excellent selection, but can be a bit pricey." "Great wedding/engagement gift packages."

Astor Place Wines & Spirits

Wines & liquors
Flatiron/East Village

12 Astor Place
corner of Lafayette Street
New York, NY 10003
212-674-7500. Fax 212-673-1218
Monday-Saturday 9-9.

quality	style	service	value
4	-	4	4

The Edge: Huge inventory of wines from around the world. The shop has a huge inventory and following. They're particularly strong on South American wines and champagnes and offer a large selection of moderately priced wines.

Burgundy Wine Company Limited

323 West 11th Street
between Greenwich and Washington Streets
New York, NY 10014
212-691-9092. Fax 212-691-9244
Tuesday-Saturday 10-7.

Wines & liquors
Greenwich Village

The Edge: Great selection of—what else—burgundies. Find a very good, large selection of top Burgundy and Rhone wines often from smaller vineyards. An ever-changing inventory. Expensive.

Crossroads Wine & Liquor

55 West 14th Street
between 5th and 6th Avenues
New York, NY 10011
212-924-3060. Fax 212-633-2863
Monday-Saturday 9-9.

Wines & liquors
Chelsea

4	.	4	4
quality	style	service	value

The Edge: Good selection. A cluttered store featuring a large selection of wines with good coverage of Australian, Californian, French, Italian, and Oregonian wines plus port. Large selection of champagnes. 10% off.

"If I had to choose three liquor stores in New York, Crossroads would be one." "Good prices."

Fairfax Liquor

211 East 66th Street
near 3rd Avenue
New York, NY 10021
212-734-6871
Monday-Saturday 10-8.

Wines & liquors
Upper East Side

The Edge: Good basic selection of wines. Service was disappointing. They refused to quote prices to our researchers to confirm their claim of having among the best prices in the city

First Avenue Wines & Spirits

383 1st Avenue
between 22nd and 23rd Streets
New York, NY 10010
212-673-3600. Fax 212-673-1198
Monday-Saturday 9-8:30.

Wines & liquors
Gramercy Pk/Murray Hill

The Edge: German wines. A large broad selection of wines.

Garnet Wine & Liquor

929 Lexington Avenue
between 68th and 69th Streets
New York, NY 10021
212-772-3211. Fax 212-517-4029
Monday-Saturday 9-9.

Wines & liquors
Upper East Side

3	.	3	5
quality	style	service	value

The Edge: Excellent prices and huge selection. Features quality wines, liqueurs, ports and standard drinks. A noteworthy selection of wines from California, Australia, France and Italy. The place is often crowded. Weekly specials are advertised in their flyers and in the Wednesday *New York Times*. The help is uneven. But if you know what you want, call—they'll most likely have it, and will deliver it within hours. Discounter.

Gotham Liquors

2519 Broadway
near 94th Street
New York, NY 10025
212-876-4120. Fax 212-866-2472
Monday-Saturday 9-9.

Wines & liquors
Upper West Side

5	-	4	5
quality	style	service	value

The Edge: Excellent prices and service. The owners have a good knowledge of wines and offer a limited but quality selection. Watch for their advertised specials in the *New York Times*. Mail order is available for out of the area. Discounter.

"Best wine values with good selection."

K&D Liquors

1366 Madison Avenue
between 95th and 96th Streets
New York, NY 10128
212-289-1818. Fax 212-996-4954
Monday-Saturday 9-9:30.

Wines & liquors
Upper East Side

The Edge: Good coverage of less expensive (under $10) wines. Good broad selection. Features less expensive wines (under $10) from Chile, Greece and Australia. Wouldn't quote prices on the phone but advertises in the *New York Times* Wednesdays. Mail order.

Morrell & Company

535 Madison Avenue
between 54th and 55th Streets
New York, NY 10022
212-688-9370. Fax 212-223-1846
Weekdays 9-6:45 Saturday 9:30-6:30.

Wines & liquors
Midtown East

4	-	4	3
quality	style	service	value

The Edge: Best for special gifts from their huge inventory of vintage wines. Offers often unique labels and vintages. The liquor store feels like a library. Excellent selection and service, but you pay for it. Offers wine appreciation seminars periodically.

"Top-notch spirits at top-notch prices."

Park Avenue Liquors

292 Madison Avenue
between 40th and 41st Streets
New York, NY 10017
212-685-2442. Fax 212-689-6247
Weekdays 8-7 Saturday 8-5.

Wines & liquors
Midtown East

3	-	3	2
quality	style	service	value

The Edge: Good selections. Features a large range of hard-to-find wines from less well known Italian and California vineyards and a good selection of champagnes. Expensive.

Quality House

2 Park Avenue
between 32nd and 33rd Streets
New York, NY 10016
212-532-2944
Weekdays 9-6:30 Saturday 9-4.
Closed Saturday during July and August.

Wines & liquors
Gramercy Pk/Murray Hill

5 . 5 4
quality style service value

The Edge: Good selections, particularly of French wines and champagnes. Helpful staff. Prices are average to high, reflecting the level of service. No credit cards. No delivery.

Rosenthal Wine Merchant

1200 Lexington Avenue
between 81st and 82nd Streets
New York, NY 10028
212-249-6650. Fax 212-744-3354
Weekdays 9:30-7 Saturday 9:30-6.

Wines & liquors
Upper East Side

The Edge: Unique, one-of-a-kind wines. The specialty is small outstanding unknown vineyards. Most of the selection is French. No large brand names. Very expensive. No credit cards. No delivery.

Sherry-Lehmann Wine & Spirits Merchants

679 Madison Avenue
near 61st Street
New York, NY 10021
212-838-7500. Fax 212-593-4584
Monday-Saturday 9-6:45.

Wines & liquors
Upper East Side

4 . 4 4
quality style service value

The Edge: A New York institution, offering a broad selection of wines. Great wines sold at OK prices, which on special become actually good prices. Their selection of Californian, French and Italian wines and champagnes, ports and other after-dinner drinks is outstanding. The catalog is excellent, very extensive and features some of their best prices. The store stocks plenty of inexpensive wines under $10. Free delivery in New York State for orders over $75.

"New York City top-end liquor store." "Always good selection and knowledgeable." "Superb selection."

Warehouse Wines & Spirits

735 Broadway
between Waverly Place and 8th Streets
New York, NY 10003
212-982-7770. Fax 212-982-7791
Monday-Thursday 9-9 Friday Saturday 9-10.

Wines & liquors
Flatiron/East Village

5 . 3 5
quality style service value

The Edge: A large selection of premium liquor and wines. OK Prices.

Furniture & furnishings

Accscentiques

1418 2nd Avenue
near 74th Street
New York, NY 10021
212-288-3289. Fax 212-288-3289
Wednesday-Friday 11-7 Saturday 11-6 Sunday noon-5
Tuesday by appointment.

Accessories
Upper East Side

3	4	4	4
quality	style	service	value

The Edge: An eclectic mix best for decorative accents. Features sachets and dried flowers, decorative and other items, some small (pillows, picture frames) and some more significant (bed and window) treatments. Also sofas and beds.

"Great for gifts."

Adrien Linford

1320 Madison Avenue
near 93rd Street
New York, NY 10128
212-289-4427. Fax 212-628-1322
Daily 11-7.

Accessories
Upper East Side

5	5	5	3
quality	style	service	value

The Edge: Unique garden furniture and accessories. A good source for beautiful garden furniture and accessories (gift items and tableware) crafted by artisans.

"Not a bargain."

Alphabet's

115 Avenue A
near St. Marks Place
New York, NY 10009
212-475-7250. Fax 212-477-2813
Daily noon-8.

Accessories
Flatiron/East Village

5	5	3	3
quality	style	service	value

The Edge: Unique adult games. Befitting Alphabet City, features adult toys, T-shirts and eclectic personal decorative gifts.

Amy Perlin Antiques

1020 Lexington Avenue
between 72nd and 73rd Streets
New York, NY 10021
212-744-4923. Fax 212-717-5326
Weekdays 11-5.

Accessories
Upper East Side

5	5	5	4
quality	style	service	value

The Edge: Eclectic shop with 18th-century accessories and furniture. Decorator discounts to 25% are possible. No credit cards.

"Interesting point of view, not common."

Aris Mixon & Company

381 Amsterdam Avenue
near 79th Street
New York, NY 10024
212-724-6904
Weekdays noon-7 Saturday 11-6 Sunday 1-5:30.

Accessories
Upper West Side

4	5	5	4
quality	style	service	value

The Edge: Intriguing giftware. Contemporary giftware from the basics (stemware and barware) to ceramics, picture frames, vases to selected Japanese antique dolls and more. Great Christmas ornaments from all over the world displayed starting in early October. No delivery.

"Worth visiting regularly for new items."

Bob Pryor Antiques

1023 Lexington Avenue
near 73rd Street
New York, NY 10021
212-688-1516
Monday-Saturday 10:30-5:30.
Closed Saturday July and August.

Accessories
Upper East Side

4	5	5	4
quality	style	service	value

The Edge: One-of-a-kind gift items. For over 22 years, unique one-of-a-kind gift items. Find unusual carved wooden walking sticks, corkscrews, fire tools, picture frames, snuffboxes and more.

Candle Shop

118 Christoper Street
between Bleecker and Hudson Streets
New York, NY 10014
212-989-0148
Monday-Thursday noon-8 Friday Saturday noon-9 Sunday 1-7.

Accessories
Greenwich Village

The Edge: Candles in all sizes, shapes and hues. Hundreds of candles in a broad range of styles (paperweights, seasonals, conventional dinner) and candle holders made in an assortment of materials and styles. Also incense and oil lamps. No delivery.

Clear Plastics

45 Lispenard Street
between Church Street and Broadway
New York, NY 10013
212-925-6782. Fax 212-925-8261
Weekdays 9:30-6 Saturday 10-5.

Accessories
SoHo/TriBeCa

The Edge: Plastic designs to order. Cuts plastic for shelves or dividers in any length and width. Sells plastic storage boxes.

Coca-Cola Fifth Avenue

711 5th Avenue
near 55th Street
New York, NY 10022

Accessories
Midtown East

3	3	3	2
quality	style	service	value

212-418-9260
Monday-Saturday 10-8 Sunday noon-6.

The Edge: The Coke logo on everything. Over 600 items featuring Coca-Cola's logo and memorabilia ranging from postcards to a vintage Coke vending machine.

Common Ground, Inc.

Accessories
Greenwich Village

19 Greenwich Avenue
near Christopher Street
New York, NY 10014
212-989-4178. Fax 212-989-0573
Monday Tuesday Thursday Friday 11:30-7 Wednesday Saturday 10-7 Sunday noon-7.

The Edge: Authentic Native American crafts. Features Native American, Mexican and South American crafts and jewelry. Expect to find quality Navaho and other Native American rugs dating from the 1880s to the 1930s, with some contemporary Indian rugs. Priced from $1,500 to $20,000.

Craft Caravan

Accessories
SoHo/TriBeCa

63 Greene Street
near Spring Street
New York, NY 10012
212-431-6669
Tuesday-Friday 10-6 weekends 11-6.

3	3	3	3
quality	style	service	value

The Edge: Traditional African crafts. In business 30 years, featuring traditional African handicrafts mainly from East and West Africa, priced from $1 to $5,000.

Distant Origin

Accessories
SoHo/TriBeCa

153 Mercer Street
between Prince and Houston Streets
New York, NY 10012
212-941-0024. Fax 212-941-8502
Monday-Wednesday Friday Saturday 11:30-6:30 Thursday 11:30-7.

The Edge: Eclectic furniture and accessories. From antique to modern, Mexico to Italy. Complementing the furniture, find accessories from all over the world, including silk lamps from Italy.

Dragon Gate Import and Export Company

Accessories
Gramercy Pk/Murray Hill

1115 Broadway
near 25th Street
New York, NY 10010
212-691-8600
Daily 10-6.

The Edge: Higher end furniture imported from China. Some furnishings and antiques.

Felissimo

10 West 56th Street
between 5th and 6th Avenues
New York, NY 10019
212-247-5656
Monday-Wednesday Friday Saturday 10-6
Thursday 10-8.

Accessories
Midtown West

quality	style	service	value
5	5	4	2

The Edge: Unusual Oriental-feeling gifts. A less expensive Takashimaya. An entire town house selling accessories, bed and bath products, gifts, some clothing for men and women, table-top items, and unusual furniture. Top-floor tea room. Japanese owned and influenced. A catalog for the Christmas/New Year holidays only, call 800-708-7690.

"Great gifts!" "My favorite retreat." "Very unique."

Flights of Fancy

1502 1st Avenue
near 78th Street
New York, NY 10021
212-772-1302
Monday Tuesday Thursday Friday noon-7 Wednesday noon-8 Saturday 10-6
Sunday noon-6.

Accessories
Upper East Side

The Edge: Gifts from a bygone era. Special gift items, including reproduction jewelry, candles, Victorian and art deco jewelry and decorative items, pottery and more. Wonderful Christmas ornaments. Prices range from under $10 to several thousand dollars. Watch for the annual summer sale, which reduces everything 15%.

41

41 Wooster Street
near Broome Street
New York, NY 10013
212-343-0935. Fax 212-343-0847
Weekdays 10-6 Saturday 11-6.

Accessories
SoHo/TriBeCa

The Edge: Favorite shop for top decorators. Decorative arts, pottery and costume jewelry. No credit cards.

Framed on Madison

740 Madison Avenue
between 64th and 65th Streets
New York, NY 10021
212-734-4680. Fax 212-988-0128
Monday-Wednesday Friday Saturday 10-6
Thursday 10-7 Sunday noon-5.

Accessories
Upper East Side

quality	style	service	value
5	5	5	3

The Edge: Beautiful picture frames. Specializes in high-end picture frames in all shapes, sizes and materials. A large, quality selection with mostly wood and some silver and silver-plate frames. Priced from $18 to $1,500.

Gargoyles Ltd. of Philadelphia

138 West 25th Street
between 6th and 7th Avenues
New York, NY 10001
212-255-0135. Fax 212-242-3923
Weekdays 9:30-5 weekends by appointment.

Accessories
Midtown West

quality	style	service	value
4	5	5	-

The Edge: An eclectic collection of potentially decorative items. New York showroom of an established Philadelphia company featuring vintage suitcases, equestrian equipment (helmets and trophies), general sporting goods, nautical items, trunks and much, much more.

"Unusual pieces." "Would never go—reminds me of my family, the Adams family."

Gifted Ones

150 West 10th Street
between Greenwich Street and Waverly Place
New York, NY 10014
212-627-4050. Fax 212-627-4053 _
Monday-Saturday noon-7.

Accessories
Greenwich Village

The Edge: Customized gift baskets. Imaginative baskets for all occasions filled with gourmet food, bath treats, spirits and you name the treasure. Customized to meet your gift needs.

Goldust Memories

38 Gramercy Park
near 3rd Avenue
New York, NY 10010
212-677-2590
Weekdays 11-7 Saturday 11-6 Sunday noon-5.

Accessories
Gramercy Pk/Murray Hill

The Edge: Antiques and reproductions cast from the original molds. Features English and American furniture, jewelry and paintings from Victorian times to the 1930s. Some reproductions.

H.M. Luther

61 East 11th Street
between Broadway and University Place
New York, NY 10003
212-505-1485. Fax 212-505-0401
Weekdays 9-5.

Accessories
Flatiron/East Village

quality	style	service	value
5	5	5	2

The Edge: Favorite of top decorators. Unique accessories. No credit cards.

Hammock World

66 East 7th Street
between 1st and 2nd Avenues
New York, NY 10003
212-673-1910
Monday-Saturday 2-10.

Accessories
Flatiron/East Village

The Edge: Special Mexican things. Mexican pottery, clothing and toys priced from $5 to $250.

Hoshoni

309 East 9th Street
between 1st and 2nd Avenues
New York, NY 10003
212-674-3120
Tuesday-Saturday noon-8 Sunday noon-6.

Accessories
Flatiron/East Village

The Edge: Santa Fe in New York. Features exclusively New Mexican artisans creating furniture, accessories and jewelry. Favors handmade custom-designed products, some exclusive to the store.

Hubert Des Forges

1193 Lexington Avenue
near 81st Street
New York, NY 10028
212-744-1857
Monday-Thursday 10-6 Friday Saturday 10-5.

Accessories
Upper East Side

quality style service value

The Edge: An eclectic shop crammed full of odd antique accessories. Items from the 18th-century through the 1940s. Features small furniture items and home decorations, cookie jars, framed prints, platters and porcelain.

John Rosselli International

523 East 73rd Street
near York Avenue
New York, NY 10021
212-772-2137. Fax 212-535-2989
Weekdays 10-5.

Accessories
Upper East Side

quality style service value

The Edge: Decorative accessories from the 17th-century to the present. Unique accessories, some antique, some reproduction. Prices to $20,000. Accessories featured at John Rosselli Antiques on 72nd Street. Supposed to be "to the trade only", but this is the '90s so visit anyway. No credit cards. No delivery.

255 East 72nd Street
near 2nd Avenue/10021
New York, NY 10021
212-737-2252. Fax 212-535-2989
Weekdays 9:30-6.

Upper East Side

La Boutique Fantasque

620 5th Avenue
Rockefeller Promenade at 49th Street
New York, NY 10020
212-332-1830
Daily 10-6.

Accessories
Midtown West

The Edge: One of the few Russian folk art stores in the city. Features hand-painted matroska (nesting dolls), lacquered boxes and Fabergé style eggs. The matroska dolls come in every size and feature presidents and Russian leaders.

Linda Horn Antiques

1015 Madison Avenue
near 78th Street
New York, NY 10021
212-772-1122. Fax 212-288-0449
Monday-Saturday 10-6. Closed Saturday July and August.

Accessories
Upper East Side

3	5	2	2
quality	style	service	value

The Edge: Very ornate English and European 19th-century antiques. Features an eclectic collection of small furniture, accessories, including crystal pitchers and decanters (many with sterling-silver stoppers), picture frames and walking sticks. The focus is whimsical ornate styles many in bamboo, lacquer, marble and papier-mâché. Deluxe.

"10 for style."

London Connection Design

123 East 33rd Street
near Lexington Avenue
New York, NY 10016
212-779-4418. Fax 212-779-4419
Weekdays 9-5.

Accessories
Gramercy Pk/Murray Hill

The Edge: Handmade pillows. Most pillows covered in French tapestries or English and American needlepoints. Also some contemporary custom-designed pillows.

Mabel's

849 Madison Avenue
near 71st Street
New York, NY 10021
212-734-3263. Fax 212-734-7914
Monday-Saturday 10-6 Sunday noon-5.

Accessories
Upper East Side

4	3	4	3
quality	style	service	value

The Edge: Animal-inspired objects. For animal lovers—silver and gold animal jewelry, home furnishings and hand-hooked rugs. Jewelry includes our favorite—simple leather-banded sports watches with a painted face of your favorite pet. Furnishings include animal foot rests, hand-hooked rugs, kitty doorstops, papier-mâché animals and puppy cushions. Special-order items include hand-painted items featuring your favorite pet.

Man-Tiques Ltd.

1050 2nd Avenue
between 55th and 56th Streets
New York, NY 10022
212-759-1805
Monday-Saturday 11-5:30.

Accessories
Midtown East

4	4	4	5
quality	style	service	value

The Edge: Unique antique gift items for hard-to-please men. Selection includes canes, German beer steins, porcelain shaving mugs, scientific instruments, walking sticks and more. The canes seemed particularly nice.

"The shop looks faded, but some unique men's objects."

Marco Polo

1135 Madison Avenue
between 84th and 85th Streets
New York, NY 10028
212-734-3775. Fax 212-249-3245
Weekdays 10:30-5:30 Saturday noon-4:30.

Accessories
Upper East Side

The Edge: English antique gift items. Find items expected in a proper Victorian home, including cut crystal, letter openers, magnifying glasses, pens and inkwells, sterling-silver picture frames, sterling-silver capped boudoir jars and more.

Matt McGhee

22 Christoper Street
near Waverly Place
New York, NY 10014
212-741-3138. Fax 212-741-3139
Tuesday-Saturday noon-7. December noon-9.

Accessories
Greenwich Village

The Edge: Wonderful traditional Christmas ornaments. At Christmas stocks old-fashioned tree ornaments and stocking stuffers, including carved wooden figures of angels, nativity scenes and more. Also hand-painted Limoge porcelain boxes and unique pewter figures. No delivery.

Mediterranean Shop

780 Madison Avenue
near 66th Street
New York, NY 10021
212-879-3120
Monday-Saturday 10-5:30.

Accessories
Upper East Side

5	5	4	3
quality	style	service	value

The Edge: Reproductions of antique French and Italian faïence. Specialty papers and ceramics. Designs range from their 12th-century Palio collection to the Moustiers and Rouen patterns of the late 18th-century.

"Fun—good registry place." "Unique."

Pierre Deux

870 Madison Avenue
near 71st Street
New York, NY 10021
212-570-9343
Monday-Saturday 10-6. Closed Saturday July and August.

Accessories
Upper East Side

The Edge: French country wares—fabrics and home furnishings. Features fabrics from all the regions of France, including Souleiado hand-screened fabrics in traditional Provençal patterns. Also a wide range of home furnishings such as napkins, pewter, place mats and tablecloths in addition to flatware and faïence by Moustiers. 18th- and 19th-century handcrafted French country furniture and antiques, mostly from Provence. Deluxe.

Pillowry

132 East 61st Street
between Park and Lexington Avenues
New York, NY 10021
212-308-1630
Weekdays 11:30-5:30 Saturday by appointment.

Accessories
Upper East Side

The Edge: Pillows of all sorts. Old and one-of-a-kind pillows made from tapestries, rugs and textiles dating from the 16th-century to modern times. Most things are 19th-century. Priced from $25 to $3,200.

Piston's

1050 2nd Avenue
near 57th Street
New York, NY 10022
212-753-8322
Weekdays 10:30-4 Saturday by appointment.

Accessories
Midtown East

quality	style	service	value
5	5	5	5

The Edge: Rare 17th- to 19th-century decorative brass, copper and pewter accessories. Accessories include candlesticks, copper kettles, pewter plates, curtain tiebacks, cornices and more. No credit cards. No delivery.

Plexi-Craft

514 West 24th Street
between 10th and 11th Avenues
New York, NY 10011
212-924-3244
Weekdays 9-5.

Accessories
Chelsea

The Edge: Customized Plexiglass shelving, tables and stands. Custom- and ready-made plastic furnishings. Discounter.

Pondicherri

454 Columbus Avenue
near 82nd Street
New York, NY 10024
212-875-1609. Fax 212-875-1679
Monday-Saturday 11-7 Sunday noon-6.

Accessories
Upper West Side

The Edge: Pottery from Indonesia and Africa. Pottery, plus fabrics made into decorative household items, including bed linens and tableware. Very large selection. Pillows from $9.50 to $80.

Portico Home

379 West Broadway
near Spring Street
New York, NY 10012
212-941-7800. Fax 212-925-4279
Monday-Saturday 11-7 Sunday noon-6:30.

Accessories
SoHo/TriBeCa

quality	style	service	value
4	4	4	4

The Edge: Clean country styling in furniture and bed and bath accessories. Special-order Shaker adaptation furniture priced from $500 to $5,000. Accessories include candles, candlesticks, linens, natural bath products and potpourri.

"Cool stuff, country chic." "Very cool, but pricey." "Beautiful things."

René, Inc.
1184 Madison Avenue
near 86th Street
New York, NY 10128
212-860-7669. Fax 212-360-1976
Monday-Saturday 10-6.

Accessories
Upper East Side

The Edge: Antique accessories. Shifting their focus from beautiful antique linens to accessories. The mood remains English Victorian with gift items appropriate to an English manor house—silver picture frames, pillows, crystal and more. No delivery.

Rita Ford Music Boxes
19 East 65th Street
near Madison Avenue
New York, NY 10021
212-535-6717. Fax 212-772-0992
Monday-Saturday 9-5.

Accessories
Upper East Side

5	5	5	4
quality	style	service	value

The Edge: Wonderful music boxes and carousels. Features contemporary music boxes and carousels. Contemporary carousels are handmade by artists. Music boxes from inexpensive to unbelievably expensive. Unique Christmas tree music boxes are designed for the shop. Pricing into the mega-thousands. Repairs music boxes as well.

Russian Arts
451 Avenue of the Americas
near 11th Street
New York, NY 10011
212-242-5946
Tuesday-Saturday noon-8 Sunday noon-7.

Accessories
Chelsea

The Edge: Soviet memorabilia. Expect military uniforms, Russian dolls and decorative items. Priced from $1 to $2,000.

Serendipity
225 East 60th Street
between 2nd and 3rd Avenues
New York, NY 10022
212-838-3531
Monday-Thursday 11:30-12:30 Friday 11:30-1
Saturday 11-2 Sunday 11:30- midnight.

Accessories
Midtown East

4	4	3	3
quality	style	service	value

The Edge: Every child's (and the child is everyone) favorite restaurant. Known for frozen hot chocolate, foot-long hot dogs and ice cream sundaes. The front of the store is a gift boutique featuring an eclectic selection of hand-painted T-shirts, vests, coffee mugs and more.

Slatkin & Company

Accessories
Upper East Side

131 East 70th Street
near Lexington Avenue
New York, NY 10021
212-794-1661. Fax 212-794-4249
Monday-Saturday 10-6. Closed Saturday July and August.

4	5	5	4
quality	style	service	value

The Edge: Well-chosen traditional accessories. Small furniture items. Best known for accessories, including candles, hand-painted porcelains, picture frames and table linens.

"See the owners: Harry, Howard or Laura."

Primavera Gallery

Accessories
Upper East Side

808 Madison Avenue
near 68th Street
New York, NY 10021
212-288-1569. Fax 212-288-2102
Monday-Saturday 11-6. Closed Saturday July and August.

5	5	4	4
quality	style	service	value

The Edge: Glorious 20th-century art and jewelry. Features furniture, jewelry and decorative items. Wonderful art deco furniture from top designers. Also decorative items such as glass by Lalique and Jean Luce. Art deco and art nouveau jewelry, including designs by Boucheron, Cartier, David Webb, Lalique, Van Cleef & Arpels and Tiffany. High-end.

"Fabulous taste!"

Terracotta

Accessories
Greenwich Village

259 West 4th Street
between Perry and Charles Streets
New York, NY 10014
212-243-1952
Tuesday-Saturday noon-7 Sunday noon-6.

The Edge: An artisan gift store. Features home and personal accessories. For home: candles, gifts, picture frames, pretty pillows and more. For you: wonderful hats, jewelry and ties. Priced from $5 to $300.

Things Japanese

Accessories
Midtown East

127 East 60th Street
between Lexington and Park Avenues
New York, NY 10022
212-371-4661
Monday Wednesday-Saturday 11-5 Thursday 11-6.

5	3	5	5
quality	style	service	value

The Edge: Japanese decorative items. Features dolls, ivory carvings, lacquerware, pottery and wood block prints. Some vintage kimonos.

"Outstanding, terrific!"

Tim McKoy Gallery
318 Bleecker Street
near Christopher Street
New York, NY 10014
212-242-3456. Fax 212-675-3029
Tuesday-Sunday noon-7.

Accessories
Greenwich Village

The Edge: Specializes in antique dolls. Dolls range in price from $750 to $5,000. No delivery.

U.S.E.D.
17 Perry Street
near 7th Avenue
New York, NY 10014
212-627-0730
Daily 12:30-8.

Accessories
Greenwich Village

The Edge: Eclectic knickknacks. He buys what he likes—much of which is used (hence the name) decorative items, including boxes, glassware and games. No delivery.

Urban Archaeology
285 Lafayette Street
between Prince and Houston Streets
New York, NY 10012
212-431-6969. Fax 212-941-1918
Monday-Thursday 8-6 Friday 8-5 Saturday 10-4.
Closed Saturday July and August.

Accessories
SoHo/TriBeCa

4	4	4	3
quality	style	service	value

The Edge: You never know what they've found. Truly unique urban treasures. An eclectic mix of treasures gathered from buildings, homes and offices with no rhyme or reason for their salvage. Find antique and reproduction garden furniture, bathroom fixtures, bookcases, columns, lighting, mantels, mirrors, old paneled doors and more. Wide price range.

"Pretty cool." "Very interesting point of view."

William Wayne & Company
850 Lexington Avenue
at 64th Street
New York, NY 10021
212-288-9243. Fax 212-288-8915
Daily 10:30-6:30.

Accessories
Upper East Side

4	5	5	3
quality	style	service	value

The Edge: Treasures from the turn-of-the-century. Find small furniture and accessories, including desk lamps, bamboo magazine racks, sconces and more. Old-world styling. Christmas ornaments are lovely.

Zona
97 Greene Street
between Spring and Prince Streets
New York, NY 10012
212-925-6750. Fax 212-941-1792

Accessories
SoHo/TriBeCa

5	5	4	3
quality	style	service	value

Monday Tuesday Wednesday Friday Saturday 11-6:30
Thursday 11:30-7 Sunday noon-6.

The Edge: Beautiful unique accessories. Handmade, mostly sterling-silver, jewelry, plus home accessories, including small furniture, candles, pottery, soaps and more.

"Beautiful things if high priced." Good faux marble fruit." "Expensive."

Barton-Sharpe Ltd.

66 Crosby Street
below Spring Street
New York, NY 10012
212-925-9562. Fax 212-925-9687
Monday-Saturday 10-6 Sunday noon-5.

American
SoHo/TriBeCa

5	5	3	5
quality	style	service	value

The Edge: Exact reproductions of English and Shaker-inspired American furniture. Find wonderful fabrics along with the furniture reproductions.

Peter Roberts Antiques

134 Spring Street
near Greene Street
New York, NY 10012
212-226-4777. Fax 212-431-6417
Monday-Saturday 11-7 Sunday noon-6.

American
SoHo/TriBeCa

5	5	5	4
quality	style	service	value

The Edge: Signed pieces of American Arts and Crafts and Mission furniture. Full range of furniture. Accessories include copper, lighting and pottery as well as reproduction Gustav Stickley rugs and runners. No credit cards.

A Repeat Performance

156 1st Avenue
near 10th Street
New York, NY 10009
212-529-0832
Monday-Saturday 10-8 Sunday 2-8.

Antiques
Flatiron/East Village

3	3	4	4
quality	style	service	value

The Edge: Eclectic collection of period furniture and household accessories. Period odds and ends favoring the witty. Complementing the furniture, expect some clothing and costume jewelry to decorative items and period shades. Cozy and cluttered.

Ann Morris Antiques

239 East 60th Street
near 2nd Avenue
New York, NY 10022
212-755-3308
Weekdays 9-6.

Antiques
Midtown East

5	5	5	4
quality	style	service	value

The Edge: Mostly English country furniture. Allegedly to the trade only. Mostly English country furniture with some furniture from Scotland and France. Favorite of top decorators. 25% decorator discount. No credit cards.

Annex Antiques Fair and Flea Market

Avenue of the Americas
at 26th Street
New York, NY 10001
212-243-5343
Weekends year round sunrise to sunset.

Antiques
Midtown West

quality style service value

The Edge: Ever-changing eclectic treasures. Come early and bring a flashlight. Collectibles range from costume and estate jewelry to furniture and home and personal accessories. Make sure to bargain hard. $1 admission. No credit cards. No delivery.

Arkitektura

96 Greene Street
near Spring Street
New York, NY 10013
212-334-5570. Fax 212-334-8028
Weekdays 10:30-5:30.

Antiques
SoHo/TriBeCa

quality style service value

The Edge: Licensed replicas of 1930s to 1990s furniture. Loft-size showroom featuring a large array of contemporary (1930s to 1990s) furniture priced from $1,000 to $40,000. They manufacture their own lighting ($350 to $650).

Depression Modern

150 Sullivan Street
near Houston Street
New York, NY 10012
212-982-5699
Wednesday-Sunday noon-7. Closed Saturday in August.

Antiques
SoHo/TriBeCa

quality style service value

The Edge: Furniture from the Depression period. Find quality furniture, lamps, rugs and decorative accessories. The garden features vintage summer furniture. No credit cards.

George N. Antiques

67 East 11th Street
between Broadway and University Place
New York, NY 10003
212-505-5599. Fax 212-353-3051
Weekdays 10:30-5:30.

Antiques
Flatiron/East Village

The Edge: Fine period furniture and chandeliers. Mostly to the trade, but some retail. Primarily 19th and 20th century with some 18th-century pieces. Favors French and English, with some American, continental and Italian furniture.

Graham Arader

29 East 72nd Street
near Madison Avenue
New York, NY 10021
212-628-3668. Fax 212-879-8741
Monday-Saturday 10-6.

Antiques
Upper East Side

quality style service value

The Edge: Rare prints of birds and botanicals.

Hyde Park Antiques

Antiques
Flatiron/East Village

836 Broadway
near 13th Street
New York, NY 10003
212-477-0033. Fax 212-477-1781

5	5	5	3
quality	style	service	value

Weekdays 9-5 Saturday 10-2:30. Closed Saturday July and August.

The Edge: **A vast inventory of fine 18th-century English furniture.** Two floors of furniture and accessories (paintings, mirrors and English and Chinese porcelains). Items priced from $1,000 to $500,000. No credit cards.

James Hepner Antiques

Antiques
Upper East Side

130 East 82nd Street
between Park and Lexington Avenues
New York, NY 10028
212-737-4470. Fax 212-737-4782
Monday-Friday 11-5. Other hours call for appointment.

The Edge: **Quality 17th- to 19th-century antiques.** Often unique pieces. Great taste. No credit cards.

James II Galleries

Antiques
Midtown East

11 East 57th Street, 4th Floor
between 5th and Madison Avenues
New York, NY 10022
212-355-7040. Fax 212-593-0341

5	5	5	4
quality	style	service	value

Weekdays 10-5:30 Saturday 10:30-5.
Closed Saturday July and August.

The Edge: **Exquisite antique table items.** Find Victorian china, furniture, glass, jewelry, pottery and silver. The history for each piece is outlined. China includes all the famous top English brands. Floral patterns are favored. Stocked items include full dinner sets, plus children's tea sets, dessert sets, silver serving pieces, pitchers, trays in all sizes, Victorian silver-plates and mother-of-pearl–handled fish forks and knives. Deluxe.

"Beautiful collection, expensive." "Lovely things, knowledgeable."

Lee Calicchio Ltd.

Antiques
Upper East Side

134 East 70th Street
near Lexington Avenue
New York, NY 10021
212-717-4417. Fax 212-717-5755

5	4	4	3
quality	style	service	value

Weekdays 11-5. Saturday by appointment.
Closed Friday in August.

The Edge: **Quality 18th- and 19th-century French and continental furniture.** Furniture, plus accessories, including crystal pieces, lamps and objets d'art. 15% off to decorators.

Portantina

895 Madison Avenue
near 72nd Street
New York, NY 10021
212-422-0636
Monday-Saturday 10:30-6.

Antiques
Upper East Side

quality	style	service	value
4	5	4	3

The Edge: Small Italian objets d'art from the 17th- and 18th centuries. Wonderful Venetian treasures.

"Exquisite—very expensive."

Secondhand Rose

270 Lafayette Street
near Prince Street
New York, NY 10012
212-431-7673
Weekdays 10-6 weekends noon-5.

Antiques
SoHo/TriBeCa

The Edge: More used than antique furniture and knickknacks. Features furniture from the 1920s to the 1950s like you found at grandma's.

William Lipton Ltd.

27 East 61st Street
between Park and Madison Avenues
New York, NY 10021
212-751-8131. Fax 212-751-8133
Weekdays 10-6 Saturday noon-5. Summer Saturdays by appointment.

Antiques
Upper East Side

The Edge: Unique objets d'art.

ABC Trading Company

31 Canal Street
between Essex and Ludlow Streets
New York, NY 10002
212-228-5080. Fax 212-529-5579
Sunday-Friday 10-6.

Appliances
Lower East Side/Chinatown

quality	style	service	value
3	-	3	4

The Edge: Appliances geared for the export market. Features small and large appliances (refrigerators, air conditioners, televisions) converted for the export market. Wouldn't quote prices over the phone. 25% off.

Bernie's Discount Center

821 Avenue of the Americas
between 28th and 29th Streets
New York, NY 10001
212-564-8582. Fax 212-564-3894
Weekdays 9-5:30 Saturday 11-4. Closed Saturday July and August.

Appliances
Midtown West

quality	style	service	value
4	-	4	4

The Edge: Discounts appliances. Since 1948. Sells a full range of small to large appliances.

Bloom and Krup

202-206 1st Avenue
near 12th Street
New York, NY 10009
212-673-2760. Fax 212-539-9787
Monday-Saturday 9-6 Sunday 11-4.

Appliances
Flatiron/East Village

quality style service value

The Edge: Service over price. Since 1928. Principally appliances and plumbing fixtures. Good service and installation with prices about 10% to 20% higher than the discounters.

"Excellent—never have to go there, just call and order."

Dembitzer Brothers

5 Essex Street
near Canal Street
New York, NY 10002
212-254-1310
Monday-Thursday 10-4:30 Friday 10-2 Sunday 10-4:30.

Appliances
Lower East Side/Chinatown

The Edge: Appliances for export. Features discounted appliances, especially those geared for overseas shipment. Staff speaks six languages. Won't quote prices over the phone.

Electrical Appliances Rental Sales Company

40 West 29th Street
between 6th Avenue and Broadway
New York, NY 10001
212-686-8884. Fax 212-686-8885
Weekdays 8:30-5:30.

Appliances
Midtown West

The Edge: Wide range of appliances. Sells a wide range of appliances from fans and heaters to refrigerators. Rents TVs and VCRs. VCRs from $30 per day.

Home Sales Enterprises

212-513-1513
Weekdays 9-5 Saturday 9-1.

Appliances
Mail/phone

5 . 5 5

quality style service value

The Edge: Discount buying service for appliances. Often really low prices and a wide range of product. Call up with model numbers and schedule delivery, sometimes for the next day. Requires payment by certified check or cash, but price includes delivery. No credit cards. Discounter.

LVT Price Quote Hotline

P.O. Box 444
Commack, NY 11725
800-582-8884. Fax 516-234-8808
Monday-Saturday 9-6.

Appliances
Mail/phone

The Edge: Appliances by phone, efficient and among the lowest prices. Instant prices by phone on a wide range of small and large appliances, air conditioners and electronic equipment and more. Virtually all the top brands. Order by calling with the manufacturer and model number of the item you want. Delivers to New York, New Jersey, Connecticut and Pennsylvania. Among the lowest prices we found in our spot check on price, plus they had most of the items we were checking. Very polite and efficient. No credit cards. Discounter.

Peninsula Buying

212-838-1010
Weekdays 9-5 Saturday 9-11.

Appliances
Mail/phone

The Edge: Appliance buying services offering low prices. They say they sell 5% above wholesale and were among the best prices surveyed in our spot survey. However, ordering required patience since they can be slow to answer and provide prices. A more limited selection than others we checked.

Price Watchers

718-470-1620
Weekdays 9-6 Saturday 9-5.

Appliances
Mail/phone

5	-	5	5
quality	style	service	value

The Edge: Great prices on electronics and appliances. Discount buying service for TVs, video equipment and large appliances. Phone with model number and compare prices. Payment via cash, money order, or certified check. When we spot-tested prices, they were among the lowest quoted to our research team.

Altar Egos

110 West Houston Street
near Sullivan Street
New York, NY 10012
212-677-9588
Tuesday-Sunday 1-8.

Art & artifacts
SoHo/TriBeCa

The Edge: Exclusively religious objects. Find candles, holy water, incense and jewelry from every religion from East to West.

Gallery of Graphic Arts

1601 York Avenue
near 85th Street
New York, NY 10028
212-988-4731
Monday-Saturday 11-6:30.

Art & artifacts
Upper East Side

4	4	4	4
quality	style	service	value

The Edge: Graphic art from around the globe. Find graphic art priced from $50 to $4,000. Specializes in problem framing.

James Lowe Autographs

Art & artifacts
Midtown East

30 East 60th Street, Suite 304
between Madison and Park Avenues
New York, NY 10022
212-759-0775. Fax 212-759-2503
Weekdays 9:30-4:30 Saturday by appointment.

The Edge: Signed memorabilia from the makers and shakers. Celebrated signatures from autographed photos, documents and letters from the Revolution on. Covers all areas of history, literature, music and more. Civil War a specialty. No credit cards.

Kraushaar Galleries, Inc.

Art & artifacts
Midtown West

724 5th Avenue
near 56th Street
New York, NY 10019
212-307-5730
Tuesday-Friday 9:30-5:30 Saturday 10-5.

The Edge: 20th-century artists. Specializes in Maine artists from 1900 to 1950. Expensive, with prices into the hundreds of thousands.

Lost City Arts

Art & artifacts
SoHo/TriBeCa

275 Lafayette Street
near Prince Street
New York, NY 10012
212-941-8025. Fax 212-219-2570
Weekdays 10-6 weekends noon-6.

The Edge: Whimsical Americana decorative items. Features furniture and decorations from the 1930s (mostly) to the 1950s, as well as architectural ornamentation. Memorabilia from beloved places and images. Favors pop American decorative items. Priced from $2 to $20,000.

Poster America

Art & artifacts
Chelsea

138 West 18th Street
near 6th Avenue
New York, NY 10011
212-206-0499. Fax 212-727-2495
Tuesday Wednesday Friday Saturday 11-6 Thursday 11-7 Sunday noon-5.
Closed Sunday June-August.

The Edge: Collectible posters from 1910 to 1965. Posters, graphic designs and original advertising art. Priced from $400 to $2,000.

Rosenberg & Stiebel, Inc.

Art & artifacts
Midtown East

32 East 57th Street, 5th and 6th Floors
between Madison and Park Avenues
New York, NY 10022
212-753-4368. Fax 212-935-5736
Weekdays 10-5 or by appointment.

5	5	5	5
quality	style	service	value

The Edge: Fabulous collection of old-master paintings and drawings. A top art gallery featuring exceptional quality old master works. Some porcelains, sculpture and more contemporary works. No credit cards. Deluxe.

"Very expensive." "Very knowledgeable art dealers."

Untitled/Fine Art in Printing

159 Prince Street
near West Broadway
New York, NY 10012
212-982-2088. Fax 212-925-9533
Monday-Saturday 10-10 Sunday 11-7.

Art & artifacts
SoHo/TriBeCa

The Edge: Unique books and postcards. Favors beautiful reproduction postcards which make wonderful note cards and invitations. No delivery.

Works Gallery

1250 Madison Avenue
near 90th Street
New York, NY 10128
212-996-0300. Fax 212-996-0300
Monday-Thursday 10-7 Friday Saturday 10-6
Sunday noon-5.

Art & artifacts
Upper East Side

quality style service value

The Edge: For those who like crafts. Quality craft items. Favors crystal and ceramics, but also fine jewelry and watches.

Alice's Antiques

72 Greene Street
near Spring Street
New York, NY 10012
212-874-3400. Fax 212-334-3273
Daily 11:30-7.

Art deco/art nouveau
SoHo/TriBeCa

quality style service value

The Edge: Best known for their antique American iron beds. Iron beds are available in a range of sizes from single to king. Decorator discount possible to (we believe) 20%.

Barry of Chelsea Antiques

154 9th Avenue
between 19th and 20th Streets
New York, NY 10011
212-242-2666
Tuesday-Saturday noon-6 Sunday noon-7.

Art deco/art nouveau
Chelsea

quality style service value

The Edge: Great art deco lighting. Good selection of antique, especially art deco lighting, including antique hanging lamps. Restores vintage lamps. Prefers dealing with decorators.

Delorenzo

958 Madison Avenue
near 75th Street
New York, NY 10021
212-249-7575
Monday-Saturday 10-6.

Art deco/art nouveau
Upper East Side

quality   style   service   value

The Edge: Collector of art deco furniture and accessories turned dealer. Delorenzo features French art deco furniture from top designers. Also rugs and lighting fixtures, including torchères, table and floor lamps. They sell furniture as art. Deluxe.

"The highest of the high-end deco pieces and prices."

Joia Interiors, Inc.

149 East 60th Street
between Lexington and 3rd Avenues
New York, NY 10022
212-759-1224. Fax 212-226-3956
Monday-Thursday 10-6 Friday call for hours.

Art deco/art nouveau
Midtown East

quality   style   service   value

The Edge: Good source for vintage art deco furniture and accessories. The real thing, plus well-executed reproductions. Full range of furniture. Accessories include Lalique designs and paintings.

Macklowe Gallery & Modernism

667 Madison Avenue
near 60th Street
New York, NY 10021
212-644-6400. Fax 212-755-6143
Weekdays 10:30-6 Saturday 10:30-5:30.
Closed Saturday July and August.

Art deco/art nouveau
Upper East Side

quality   style   service   value

The Edge: Large collection of art nouveau furniture and jewelry. Features furniture and accessories from late Victorian period to 1950s. Decorative items, including wonderful Tiffany lamps. Jewelry includes designs from Cartier, Fouquet, Van Cleef and others. Incredible furnishings.

Maison Gerard

36 East 10th Street
near Broadway
New York, NY 10003
212-674-7611. Fax 212-475-6314
Weekdays 11-6 Saturday by appointment.

Art deco/art nouveau
Flatiron/East Village

quality   style   service   value

The Edge: 90% of the shop is filled with top French art deco furniture. Furniture, accessories, objets d'art and jewelry.

Minna Rosenblatt

844 Madison Avenue
near 69th Street
New York, NY 10021

Art deco/art nouveau
Upper East Side

212-288-0257
Monday-Saturday 10-5:30.

The Edge: Small-scale art nouveau and art deco objects. Find Tiffany lamps and vases and Steuben perfume bottles. Featured artists include Daum, Galle and more. No credit cards.

Oldies, Goldies & Moldies

1609 2nd Avenue
near 83rd Street
New York, NY 10028
212-737-3935
Tuesday-Friday noon-7 Saturday 11-6 Sunday 11-5.
Closed Sunday July and August.

Art deco/art nouveau
Upper East Side

The Edge: More used than antique, but functional, furniture and accessories. Prices are reasonable. Furniture and accessories are largely pieces from the Victorian era to the early 1950s with the owners' preference being art deco and art moderne. Most pieces are small. Also large selection of lighting and accessories.

Christie's

502 Park Avenue
near 59th Street
New York, NY 10022
212-546-1000
Weekdays 9:30-5:30 Saturday 10-5 Sunday 1-5.

Auction houses
Midtown East

The Edge: The December jewelry and spring art sales. Features a wide range of collectibles, including furniture, historical letters and documents, jewelry, paintings and silver. Spring and fall art courses are available (call 546-1092 for details). Auctions and showing times are posted in Friday's *New York Times*.

Christie's East

219 East 67th Street
near 2nd Avenue
New York, NY 10021
212-606-0400. Fax 212-737-6076
Weekdays 9-5 Saturday 10-5 Sunday 1-5.

Auction houses
Upper East Side

The Edge: Less serious collectibles. Less expensive collectibles, including decorative arts, drawings, furniture, rugs and stamps.

Sotheby's

1334 York Avenue
near 72nd Street
New York, NY 10021
212-606-7000
Monday-Friday 9-6 Saturday 9-5.

Auction houses
Upper East Side

3 3 4 4
quality style service value

The Edge: The spring art sales. Noted auction house featuring a wide range of items from those lesser priced at the arcade to high-end paintings, jewelry and silver. Auction details and showing times listed in the Friday *New York Times*. Their two to three day short course for collectors costs $300 to $500.

William Doyle Galleries

175 East 87th Street
between 3rd and Lexington Avenues
New York, NY 10128
212-427-2730. Fax 212-369-0892
Daily 8-5 for pickup. Call for auction dates and times.

Auction houses
Upper East Side

3	3	3	4
quality	style	service	value

The Edge: Auction house with unique estate sales sometimes. Right after the big two international houses, Sotheby's and Christie's, is William Doyle. The owners' New York social connections sometimes generate unique estate sales merchandise. 30 auctions per year. Mostly jewelry, furniture and silver. Favors 17th- and 18th-century estate furniture. The gallery features a tag sale area for items that didn't get sold at auction or are less expensive. Check for the 7pm Monday lectures on current sales.

Charles P. Rogers Brass Bed Company

899 1st Avenue
between 50th and 51st Streets
New York, NY 10022
212-594-8777
Weekdays 11-7 Saturday 10-6 Sunday noon-5.

Beds & bedding
Midtown East

3	3	4	3
quality	style	service	value

The Edge: Over 50 brass bed models. Shows over 50 bed models in four-posters, contemporary and hand-painted styles Replicas of original designs and old-time beds. All sizes available in stock or by special order. Worldwide delivery available.

Dial-A-Mattress

31-10 48th Avenue
near Van Dam Street
Long Island City, NY 11101
718-472-1200
Daily 24 hours.

Beds & bedding
Mail/phone

4	3	4	4
quality	style	service	value

The Edge: Beloved by all—the place to call for mattresses. Widely used by our respondents. Same day you phone your order they deliver and assemble (provided it's in stock). Good prices. 20% off.

"I would never have believed it—call up, order, it's here on time and discounted." "Fast service, good prices, courteous."

Town Bedding

205 8th Avenue
near 21st Street
New York, NY 10011
212-243-0426. Fax 212-243-1197
Monday-Wednesday Friday Saturday 9-6 Thursday 9-8 Sunday 11-6.

Beds & bedding
Chelsea

The Edge: Charges and delivers major-brand bedding anywhere in the metropolitan area. They claim good prices on major brands. But they wouldn't quote prices over the phone.

Chairs and Stools, Etc.

222 Bowery
between Prince and Spring Streets
New York, NY 10012
212-925-9191
Weekdays 9-5 Saturday 10-3.

Chairs & tables
SoHo/TriBeCa

The Edge: Chairs and stools, tables, table-tops and bases. Wholesale and retail orders. Wide variety of mostly basic styles. Discounter.

Albee's

715 Amsterdam Avenue
near 95th Street
New York, NY 10025
212-662-5740. Fax 212-316-4140
Monday-Saturday 9-5:30.

Children
Upper West Side

4	4	3	4
quality	style	service	value

The Edge: A large stock of the basics for baby's room. A full range of moderately priced baby carriages, furniture and accessories, including car seats.

"Everyone talks about making a pilgrimage."

Art 'n Tapisserie

1242 Madison Avenue
near 89th Street
New York, NY 10128
212-722-3222. Fax 212-722-3222
Monday-Friday 10:30-6:30 Saturday 10-6 Sunday 12-5.

Children
Upper East Side

5	4	4	4
quality	style	service	value

The Edge: Children's toys and decorative items which can be personalized. The shop is filled with wonderful painted toys, artist easels and room accessories designed to be personalized. Employs a resident artist who can personalize items within three days.

Bellini

1305 2nd Avenue
near 68th Street
New York, NY 10021
212-517-9233
Monday-Wednesday Friday 10-6 Thursday 10-8
Saturday 10- 5:30 Sunday noon-5.

Children
Upper East Side

5	5	3	3
quality	style	service	value

The Edge: Unique, sophisticated baby furniture and accessories befitting the New York baby! Contemporary and European-made cribs which are color coordinated with bedding and furniture for a pulled-together designer look. Furniture converts to junior beds and changing tables transform to dressers. Colors are sophisticated and there're matching decorative accessories as well as carriages, high chairs and strollers.

Henry Olko, Inc.

Children
Upper East Side

21 East 73rd Street
east of 5th Avenue
New York, NY 10021
212-249-5096. Fax 212-249-5097
By appointment.

The Edge: Painted custom cabinets for your child's room. Custom cabinets painted to look like English countryside scenes, Parisian streets or medieval castles. Great fun for children's rooms. Priced from $960.

Ages Past Antiques

China, crystal & silver
Upper East Side

450 East 78th Street
near 1st Avenue
New York, NY 10021
212-628-0725
Monday-Saturday 11-5 but it's a good idea to call ahead.

The Edge: British memorabilia. A small shop featuring 19th-century English pottery and porcelain, including platters, figurines, cups and saucers and commemorative items. A source for royalty commemorative memorabilia.

Alice Kwartler

China, crystal & silver
Midtown East

5 5 5 3
quality style service value

125 East 57th Street
between Park and Lexington Avenues
New York, NY 10022
212-752-3590. Fax 212-752-4715
Monday-Saturday 11-6.

The Edge: Where Edith Wharton would shop for gifts. Find turn-of-the-century (and later) silver, crystal, decorative items and some antique cufflinks. Wonderful Tiffany pieces, including an enormous selection of tea sets, picture frames, candlesticks, vases and trays. Great gifts. Engraving available. Very expensive—for example, silver frames from $400 to $800. Deluxe.

"First rate gifts for all occasions."

Avventura Glassware Gifts

China, crystal & silver
Upper West Side

5 5 4 3
quality style service value

463 Amsterdam Avenue
near 83rd Street
New York, NY 10024
212-769-2510. Fax 212-769-2511
Weekdays 10:30-7 Sunday 11-6.

The Edge: Simply superb contemporary Italian items. Features Murano glass and Italian ceramic work, including dishes, flatware, serving pieces and tables. Some jewelry. Bridal registry.

"Wonderful inventory, much available only here."

Baccarat, Inc.
625 Madison Avenue
near 58th Street
New York, NY 10022
212-826-4100. Fax 212-826-5043
Monday-Saturday 10-6.

China, crystal & silver
Midtown East

5	5	5	3
quality	style	service	value

The Edge: You know it. Fabulous and expensive crystal. While they specialize in crystal, you'll find Limoge china and silver by Christofle and Puiforcat. Full retail. Deluxe.

Bardith Ltd.
901 Madison Avenue
near 72nd Street
New York, NY 10021
212-737-3775. Fax 212-650-9388
Monday-Saturday 11-5:30.

China, crystal & silver
Upper East Side

5	5	5	4
quality	style	service	value

The Edge: Quality antique English porcelain (18th-century on) and papier-mâché trays. Complete china sets and accessories from all the name houses. Wonderful trays and tray tables. Decorator discounts. No credit cards. Deluxe.

31 East 72nd Street
between Madison and Park Avenues/10021
212-737-8660. Fax 212-650-9388
Monday-Friday 11-5:30.

Upper East Side

Bernardaud Limoges
499 Park Avenue
near 59th Street
New York, NY 10021
212-737-7775. Fax 212-794-9730
Monday-Saturday 10-6.

China, crystal & silver
Upper East Side

5	5	4	3
quality	style	service	value

The Edge: The full line of Bernardaud at full price. Features Bernardaud Limoge and crystal (Saint Louis, Baum, Baccarat, Lalique). Deluxe.

"Great designs, very expensive." "Beautiful things—great staff—not cheap."

Block China Warehouse Store
57 Brighton Avenue
near Ocean Avenue
Long Branch, NJ 07740
908-222-1144
Monday-Saturday 10-5 Sunday 11-4.

China, crystal & silver
Mail/phone

4	-	3	5
quality	style	service	value

The Edge: The outlet for Block china and Atlantis crystal. Phone orders welcomed. Discount depends on the popularity of the design. For discontinued or older brands, discount can range to 70%.

Cardel

621 Madison Avenue
near 58th Street
New York, NY 10022
212-753-8690. Fax 212-826-6685
Monday-Saturday 10-6.

China, crystal & silver
Midtown East

5 3 2 2
quality style service value

The Edge: Hundreds of crystal and silver platters. China from all the great houses, plus traditional housewarming and wedding presents.

"Pricey."

Ceramica

59 Thompson Street
between Spring and Broom Streets
New York, NY 10012
212-941-1307. Fax 212-941-1308
Monday-Saturday 11:30-7 Sunday 11:30-6.

China, crystal & silver
SoHo/TriBeCa

5 5 5 4
quality style service value

The Edge: Absolutely fabulous Italian tableware. Best known for its large selection of Majolica (Italian) tableware, featuring rich bold colors in traditional 15th-century and contemporary motifs. Complete dinner sets and platters and bowls always available.

"Unique designs." "Wonderful useful gifts."

Ceramica Gift Gallery

1009 Avenue of the Americas
between 37th and 38th Streets
New York, NY 10018
212-354-9216
Weekdays 9:30-6 Sunday noon-5.

China, crystal & silver
Midtown West

The Edge: Discount prices on top-brand china, crystal and silver. Bridal registry giftware at discount prices. Carries all the expected and even the hard-to-find at discount. Brands like Georg Jensen and Royal Copenhagen at very good prices.

Christofle

680 Madison Avenue
near 62nd Street
New York, NY 10021
212-308-9390. Fax 212-644-7487
Weekdays 10-6 Saturday 10-5:30.

China, crystal & silver
Upper East Side

5 5 5 4
quality style service value

The Edge: The Christofle line at full retail. Features their own brand of flatware (stainless to sterling), plus crystal by Baccarat and St. Louis, china by Haviland and Ceralene and their own elegant table linens. Also sterling-silver, gold and silver and silver-plate bowls, ice buckets, pitchers, sugar bowls and creamers, tea services and trays. Bridal registry. Deluxe.

Daum Boutique

694 Madison Avenue
near 62nd Street
New York, NY 10021
212-355-2060. Fax 212-355-2074
Monday-Saturday 10-6.

China, crystal & silver
Upper East Side

The Edge: Only Daum crystal, including decorative and limited-edition items.

Eastern Silver Company

54 Canal Street, 2nd Floor
near Orchard Street
New York, NY 10002
212-226-5708. Fax 212-966-2754
Sunday-Thursday 9:30-5 Friday 9:30-1.

China, crystal & silver
Lower East Side/Chinatown

The Edge: Table-top items at discount prices. Specializes in table-top gift items such as candlesticks, decanters, vases and the like in crystal, pewter and silver.

Eastside Gifts & Dinnerware

351 Grand Street
between Essex and Ludlow Streets
New York, NY 10002
212-982-7200. Fax 212-529-8260
Weekdays 10-6 Sunday 10-5.

China, crystal & silver
Lower East Side/Chinatown

quality style service value

The Edge: China, crystal and silver discounter. Moving soon—call for their new location—the phone number will not change. Discounts all major brands of crystal and china, including Bernardaud, Limoge, Mikasa, Oneida, Royal Doulton, Wedgwood, Baccarat and Lenox. Bridal registry and corporate gifts. Very good prices particularly in china, often the lowest in the city. The current shop is cluttered and dusty. The high ratings reflect wonderful telephone service. Call and order. If it's not in stock, they'll get it for you.

Fishs Eddy

889 Broadway
near 19th Street
New York, NY 10003
212-420-9020. Fax 212-353-1454
Monday-Saturday 10-9 Sunday 11-7.

China, crystal & silver
Flatiron/East Village

quality style service value

The Edge: Functional chinaware. Functional china, glassware and food-related accessories. Seconds or overruns from restaurants and hotels sold by the piece or in sets. Their own patterns now, as well. 25% off.

"Fun stuff." "Fun shopping experience!" "Good source for funky dinnerware."

2176 Broadway
near 77th Street/10024
212-873-8819

Upper West Side

Gem Antiques

China, crystal & silver
Upper East Side

1088 Madison Avenue
near 82nd Street
New York, NY 10028
212-535-7399. Fax 212-249-7267
Monday-Saturday 10:30-5:30.

The Edge: Antique and modern European and American porcelains and paper weights. Find Coichy, Baccarat, Gouda, Grueby, Moorcroft, Newcomb, Ohr, Pilkington, Rookwood and Saint Louis. Features unique pieces. Priced from $100 to $15,000. Deluxe.

Guild Antiques

China, crystal & silver
Upper East Side

1095 Madison Avenue
near 82nd Street
New York, NY 10028
212-472-0830. Fax 212-472-0830
Monday-Saturday 10-5.

4	5	5	5
quality	style	service	value

The Edge: Simply first-rate 18th- and 19th-century English china and Chinese export porcelains. Full sets of dishes and serving pieces. Also small-scale 18th- and early 19th-century English furniture.

Hoffman Gampetro Antiques

China, crystal & silver
Midtown East

1050 2nd Avenue, Gallery 37
between 55th and 56th Streets
New York, NY 10022
212-755-1120
Monday-Saturday 10:30-5:30.

5	5	5	4
quality	style	service	value

The Edge: Wonderful collection of Arts and Crafts Movement silver. English ceramics and etched glass complement the silver.

Hoya Crystal Gallery

China, crystal & silver
Upper East Side

689 Madison Avenue
near 62nd Street
New York, NY 10021
212-223-6335. Fax 212-223-6371
Monday-Saturday 10-6. Closed Saturday July and August.

5	4	4	4
quality	style	service	value

The Edge: Top crystal designed by Japanese artists. Simple to elaborate designs. You'll find wonderful decorative accessories, including art pieces, candlesticks, decanters and vases. Top items. The Japanese Steuben. Deluxe.

"I love their Snow Lake bowl. The larger size makes a terrific, unusual wedding present."

Jamar
1714 Sheepshead Bay Road
Brooklyn, NY 11235
718-615-2222. Fax 718-615-2224
Tuesday-Saturday 11-5:45.

China, crystal & silver
Brooklyn

quality	style	service	value
3	3	3	4

The Edge: Discount china, crystal and silver. They claim they match or beat any advertised price on silver, crystal, china and gift items. Tends to feature the more widely available, moderately priced items.

James Robinson
480 Park Avenue
near 58th Street
New York, NY 10022
212-752-6166
Weekdays 10-5 Saturday 10:30-4:30.
Closed Saturday July and August.

China, crystal & silver
Midtown East

quality	style	service	value
5	5	5	4

The Edge: Wonderful 17th- to 19th-century fine English tableware and jewelry. Some old English porcelain. Best known for their Georgian cut-glass stemware, bowls and centerpieces and estate jewelry priced from $500 to $250,000, 17th- to 19th-century English hallmark silver and hand-forged sterling-silver flatware antique reproductions in 18 classic patterns. Silver tends to have simple classic lines. Flatware is sometimes discounted 25%. Find portable canvas silver chests, practical gift items. Deluxe.

"The essence of style." "Glorious jewelry!"

Jean's Silversmiths
16 West 45th Street
near 5th Avenue
New York, NY 10036
212-575-0723. Fax 212-921-0991
Monday-Thursday 9-4:30 Friday 9-3:30.

China, crystal & silver
Midtown West

quality	style	service	value
5	3	4	4

The Edge: Discontinued silver and china patterns. Sells discontinued and current flatware and china patterns and some antique silver, gold and diamond jewelry. Carries almost 1,000 silver patterns. Wonderful table accessories, including candlesticks and trays in every size. New silver flatware is discounted. Also polishes silver (for about $4 per piece) via a commercial polish process, which takes out all nicks and scratches, or butler's satin, which is gentler on the silver. A reputable dealer in vintage silver. Will deliver jewelry the day you buy it, but not silver, which requires polishing. 10% off.

"Often find discontinued patterns." "The place!" "The best for used silver."

L.S. Collection
469 Broadway
south of Houston Street
New York, NY 10012
212-673-4575
Monday-Saturday 11:30-7 Sunday noon-6.

China, crystal & silver
SoHo/TriBeCa

quality	style	service	value
4	4	4	3

The Edge: Unique modern gifts. L.S. (Lazy Susan) has brought their giftware collection (china, glasses, hand-blown crystal, sterling, etc.) from Japan to the U.S. Many items in the $500 price category. Elegant tableware.

"Very modern, stylish." "Unique things." "Nice for gifts." "Expensive."

La Terrine

1024 Lexington Avenue
near 73rd Street
New York, NY 10021
212-988-3366
Monday-Saturday 10:30-6.

China, crystal & silver
Upper East Side

quality style service value

The Edge: Hand-painted, mostly Portuguese and Italian, ceramics. Practical and attractive ceramics, including coffee mugs, covered butter dishes, large pasta bowls, pitchers and platters. Complete dinner services can be special ordered. Cloth place mats and napkins from Provence and India and simply wonderful paper napkins. The mugs range from $15 to $20; platters and large pasta bowls up to the $100 area.

"Good, but not as unique as it once was."

Lalique

680 Madison Avenue
near 61st Street
New York, NY 10021
212-355-6550. Fax 212-752-0203
Weekdays 10-6 Saturday 10-5:30.

China, crystal & silver
Upper East Side

quality style service value

The Edge: Wonderful art deco glass. Art deco Lalique pieces from stemware to gift items, including crystal vases and clocks. Catalog costs $10. Deluxe.

Lanac Sales

73 Canal Street
near Allen Street
New York, NY 10002
212-925-6422. Fax 212-925-8175
Monday-Thursday 9-6 Friday 9-2 Sunday 10-5.

China, crystal & silver
Lower East Side/Chinatown

quality style service value

The Edge: Prices are among the best in the city. Discount prices on chinaware, cut glass, silverware, flatware and gifts. Stocks or is able to get virtually all major brands. Was able to quote on everything in our spot check price comparison from Georg Jensen silver to Royal Copenhagen and Bernardaud china. Individually they matched or beat their competitors on virtually every item in our sample. Bridal registry available. Most items in stock with immediate shipment.

"Inexpensive." "Best prices."

Leo Kaplan Ltd.

967 Madison Avenue
near 75th Street
New York, NY 10021
212-249-6766. Fax 212-861-2674

China, crystal & silver
Upper East Side

quality style service value

Monday-Saturday 10-5:30. Closed Saturday in summer.

The Edge: Beautiful items for the collector. 18th-century English porcelain and stemware, including all the top period designers. Wonderful paperweights and art nouveau glass from Baccarat, Daum, Galle and Webb. Very expensive. Deluxe.

Locaters, Inc.
2217 Cottontail Lane
Little Rock, AR 72202
800-367-9690. Fax 501-372-4006
Weekdays 9-5 Central Time.

China, crystal & silver
Mail/phone

The Edge: Replaces irreplaceable stemware and china. Mail-order business finding discontinued china and stemware from the major brands. Stocks a huge selection of patterns.

Malvina L. Solomon
1122 Madison Avenue
near 83rd Street
New York, NY 10028
212-535-5200
Weekdays 11-5:30 Saturday 11-5.

China, crystal & silver
Upper East Side

quality	style	service	value
4	3	3	3

The Edge: Vintage jewelry and American art pottery. Vintage jewelry, including wonderful Bakelite items. American art pottery from Fulper, Rookwood, Ohr and others.

Michael C. Fina
580 5th Avenue
near 47th Street
New York, NY 10036
212-869-5050. Fax 212-575-4621
Monday-Wednesday Friday 9:30-6 Thursday 9:30-7
Saturday 10:30-6.

China, crystal & silver
Midtown West

quality	style	service	value
4	4	4	4

The Edge: Well-known discounter of giftware. Over 5,000 patterns. Offers discounts on all major brands of china, cookware, crystal, giftware, jewelry, sterling and more. 15% off.

Nat Schwartz
549 Broadway
between 25th and 26th Streets
Bayonne, NJ 07002
800-526-1440. Fax 201-437-4903
Monday-Wednesday Friday 9:30-6 Thursday 9:30-8 Saturday 10-5.

China, crystal & silver
Mail/phone

The Edge: Small discounts on all major lines of silver, crystal and china. Features all the top lines.

Nathan Horowicz
1050 2nd Avenue
near 55th Street
New York, NY 10022

China, crystal & silver
Midtown East

quality	style	service	value
5	4	3	4

212-755-6320. Fax 212-755-6438
Monday-Thursday 10:30-6 Friday 10:30-sunset.

The Edge: Estate silver. Large selection of more ordinary to better-quality silver items from silverware and serving pieces to tea and coffee sets to bowls, trays and more.

Niels Bamberger

1070 Madison Avenue
near 80th Street
New York, NY 10028
212-737-7118. Fax 212-434-2497
Weekdays 9-5:30.

China, crystal & silver
Upper East Side

4	4	4	4
quality	style	service	value

The Edge: Vintage Scandinavian china. Find vintage and new pieces of Scandinavian china, sterling-silver tableware accessories and porcelains. Stocks wonderful Royal Copenhagen china patterns. Deluxe.

Orrefors

58 East 57th Street
near Park Avenue
New York, NY 10022
212-752-1095. Fax 212-752-3705
Weekdays 10-6 Saturday 10:30-5:30.

China, crystal & silver
Midtown East

3	3	4	3
quality	style	service	value

The Edge: Scandinavian glassware. Large selection, full retail prices.

Pottery Barn

100 7th Avenue
near 16th Street
New York, NY 10011
212-633-8405
Monday-Friday 10-8 Saturday 10-7 Sunday noon-6.

China, crystal & silver
Chelsea

4	4	4	4
quality	style	service	value

The Edge: Lower-end basic housewares. For housewares (no delivery on these items) and furniture (sold through their catalog). The furniture—full-size chairs, sofas, tables and queen-size beds—is delivered. Best known, however, for their basic china, candlesticks, coffee mugs, platters and wine glasses. Their sister chain Williams-Sonoma is more upscale and features cooking equipment and cookbooks for "true cooks" as well as good-looking china, glasses and general tableware.

"I like their catalog—easy to order and you know what you'll get."

600 Broadway
near Houston Street/10012
212-505-6377. Fax 212-219-2420
Monday-Saturday 10-8 Sunday noon-7.

SoHo/TriBeCa

51 Greenwich Avenue
near 6th Avenue/10014
212-807-6321
Monday-Saturday 11-8 Sunday noon-6.

Greenwich Village

1451 2nd Avenue   **Upper East Side**
near 76th Street/10021
212-988-4228
Monday-Friday 10-8 Saturday 11-7 Sunday noon-5.

117 East 59th Street   **Midtown East**
between Park and Lexington Avenues/10022
212-753-5424
Monday-Wednesday Friday Saturday 10-7 Thursday 10-8 Sunday noon-6.

2109 Broadway   **Upper West Side**
near 73rd Street/10023
212-595-5573
Monday-Friday 10-8 Saturday 10-7 Sunday noon-6.

1292 Lexington Avenue   **Upper East Side**
near 87th Street/10128
212-289-2477
Monday-Saturday 10-8 Sunday noon-5.

Replacement Ltd.

China, crystal & silver

1089 Knox Road   **Mail/phone**
(P.O. Box 26029)
Greensboro, NC 27420
910-697-3000. Fax 910-697-3100
Daily 8-10.

The Edge: A top source for discontinued hard-to-find flatware, china and crystal patterns.
Handles discontinued flatware, china, crystal and collectibles (56,000 patterns, three million
pieces). Features hard-to-find patterns from all the top labels and manufacturers no longer in
business. They say they're the largest replacement company in the world. If you're in North
Carolina, go see their showroom.

Royal Copenhagen Porcelain/Georg Jensen

683 Madison Avenue   **China, crystal & silver**
near 61st Street   **Upper East Side**
New York, NY 10021
212-759-6457. Fax 212-355-1529
Monday-Saturday 10-6.

The Edge: The full-price retail outlet for Scandinavian tablewares. The shop features a large
selection of Royal Copenhagen and seemingly all the Georg Jensen silver patterns. Also more
moderate lines, including Orrefors and Kosta Boda crystal and Dansk wood pieces. The Georg
Jensen collection includes the full range of flatware, plus sterling table-top items. Deluxe.

S. Wyler, Inc.

941 Lexington Avenue   **China, crystal & silver**
near 69th Street   **Upper East Side**
New York, NY 10021
212-879-9848. Fax 212-879-9848
Monday-Saturday 9:30-5:45.

quality	style	service	value
4	4	4	3

Closed Saturday July and August.

The Edge: From the practical to the sublime antique English silver and porcelain. The shop is crammed full of one-of-a-kind 18th- and 19th-century English silver and porcelain. Some silver reproductions. Excellent quality and style. A large inventory of flatware, picture frames, serving pieces and tea sets. Priced from $100 to the six figures.

"Great silver!"

S.J. Shrubsole
104 East 57th Street
between Lexington and Park Avenues
New York, NY 10022
212-753-8920. Fax 212-754-5192
Weekdays 9:30-5:30 Saturday 10-5.
Closed Saturday July and August.

China, crystal & silver
Midtown East

quality style service value

The Edge: Features rare high-quality antique silver and period jewelry. A small collection of treasures, some dating from the late 1700s but most from the 19th-century. Silver bowls, flatware, picture frames, serving pieces, tea sets, etc. Also wonderful unique period jewelry. You can expect to find work from renowned silversmiths like Paul Revere. Deluxe.

Scully & Scully
504 Park Avenue
near 59th Street
New York, NY 10022
212-755-2590. Fax 212-486-1430
Monday-Saturday 9-6.

China, crystal & silver
Midtown East

quality style service value

The Edge: Great for basic English country–house style gift items. The store features china, glassware, desk sets, those hard-to-find wooden salad bowls with pewter (not silver) bases, brass fire tools, enameled boxes, English print place mats, globes and more. China patterns include Ceraline, Crown Derby, Herend and Wedgwood. 18th-century reproduction English and American-made furniture, including classic Queen Anne and Chippendale chairs scaled to children's sizes.

"Great place mats!" Good place for gifts." "Old standby expanded recently." "High prices."

Simon Pearce
120 Wooster Street
near Spring Street
New York, NY 10013
212-334-2393
Monday-Saturday 11-7 Sunday noon-6.

China, crystal & silver
SoHo/TriBeCa

quality style service value

The Edge: Primarily handmade modern but, somehow, traditionally styled glass tableware. Vases to glasses. Some pottery. Not expensive. Simple but elegant styling. All handmade in their workshop in Quechee, Vermont.

500 Park Avenue
near 59th Street/10022
212-421-8801. Fax 212-421-8802
Monday-Saturday 10-6.

Midtown East

Solanee, Inc.

866 Lexington Avenue
near 65th Street
New York, NY 10021
212-439-6109. Fax 212-288-3065
Weekdays 10-6 Saturday 11-6.

China, crystal & silver
Upper East Side

The Edge: Traditional French pottery and glassware. Features or can get virtually all patterns of Segries and hand-painted pottery from Moustiers, France. Also stocks glassware from Brittany. Can order complete Segries dinner sets. Their catalog costs $20.

Steuben Glass

715 5th Avenue
near 56th Street
New York, NY 10022
212-752-1441
Monday-Wednesday Friday Saturday 10-6 Thursday 10-8.

China, crystal & silver
Midtown East

5	5	5	4
quality	style	service	value

The Edge: Top-quality American-designed glass. Find all sorts of glass items, stemware, tableware accessories (vases, bowls, candlesticks) and palm-sized animals. Steuben glass is a standard White House gift to heads of state. Corporate discounts. Call 800-424-4240 for phone orders. Deluxe.

Stupell Ltd.

29 East 22nd Street
near Broadway
New York, NY 10010
212-260-3100. Fax 212-260-3100
Monday-Saturday 10-6.

China, crystal & silver
Gramercy Pk/Murray Hill

The Edge: All major china and crystal patterns. Wonderful selection of traditional to modern table settings, including Venetian glassware, silver and stainless flatware and linens. Gift items, including picture frames and porcelains.

Susan P. Meisel Decorative Arts

133 Prince Street
near Greene Street
New York, NY 10012
212-254-0137
Tuesday-Saturday 10-6. Closed in July and August.

China, crystal & silver
SoHo/TriBeCa

The Edge: Eclectic collection of home accessories. The shop features decorative kitchen items from the 1920s, including art deco pottery, bowls, teapots, plus silver jewelry (Mexican and Jensen pieces). Priced from $5 to $100,000.

Tudor Rose Antiques

28 East 10th Street
between University Place and Broadway
New York, NY 10003

China, crystal & silver
Flatiron/East Village

2	3	5	3
quality	style	service	value

212-677-5239. Fax 212-677-5239
Monday-Friday 10:30-6 Saturday 10-5.

The Edge: Victorian knickknacks. Victorian crystal and sterling gift items, including candlesticks, crystal, flatware, frames and bowls. Offers a bridal registry and corporate gifts program.

Villeroy & Boch

974 Madison Avenue
near 76th Street
New York, NY 10021
212-535-2500. Fax 212-535-8536
Monday-Saturday 10-6.

China, crystal & silver
Upper East Side

quality style service value

The Edge: Their entire line of china, plus silver flatware and crystal. Look here to see their entire line. But don't forget the Villery & Boch outlet shops which offer good-quality seconds that are virtually indistinguishable from their first-quality merchandise. Prices at their 24 outlet stores are discounted 40%, with frequent special sales reducing prices to 55% off. Call with phone orders to the city's closest one in Norwalk, Connecticut, 203-831- 2821.

Waterford/Wedgwood

713 Madison Avenue
near 63rd Street
New York, NY 10021
212-759-0500. Fax 212-486-6570
Monday-Friday 10-6 Saturday 10-5. August Saturday 11-5.

China, crystal & silver
Upper East Side

quality style service value

The Edge: Full selection of Waterford/Wedgwood. Very expensive traditional china, glassware, lamps and linens. Store is on two levels with higher-priced items upstairs.

Williams-Sonoma Outlet

231 10th Avenue
between 23rd and 24th Streets
New York, NY 10011
212-206-8118
Weekdays 11-6 weekends 10-5.

China, crystal & silver
Chelsea

quality style service value

The Edge: Three floors of discontinued, returned and close-out merchandise from Williams-Sonoma, Pottery Barn, Hold Everything and Gardener's Eden. A creaky, dingy warehouse space with a staircase that serves as the only access to the various floors. The main level features china, glass and cookware. The second floor has decorative items for the house. Good prices (25% to 50% off retail) but very uneven stock featured in an out-of-the-way location. No delivery.

"You never know, you may find something good."

Williams-Sonoma, Inc.

110 7th Avenue
near 17th Street
New York, NY 10011
212-633-2203
Weekdays 10-8 Saturday 10-7 Sunday noon-6.

China, crystal & silver
Chelsea

quality style service value

The Edge: High-styled, well-priced kitchen accessories and cooking items. Nicely styled, basic pottery and china, bowls, platters, pitchers, teapots and specialty food items. A wide range. Bridal registry with a nationwide listing. Everyone seems to register for wedding gifts here. Features cooking equipment and cookbooks from around the world for "true cooks" as well as general tableware. Delivers by UPS. Phone and fax orders 24 hours daily. Call 800-541-2223 to order.

1309 2nd Avenue   **Upper East Side**
near 69th Street/10021
212-288-8408
Weekdays 10-8 Saturday 10-6 Sunday noon-5.

20 East 60th Street   **Midtown East**
between Madison and Park Avenues/10022
212-980-5155. Fax 212-753-8170
Weekdays 10-7 Saturday 10-6 Sunday noon-5.

1175 Madison Avenue   **Upper East Side**
near 86th Street/10028
212-289-6832
Weekdays 10-7 Saturday 10-6 Sunday noon-5.

Wolfman Gold & Good Company

China, crystal & silver
SoHo/TriBeCa

116 Greene Street
between Prince and Spring Streets
New York, NY 10012
212-431-1888. Fax 212-226-4955
Monday-Wednesday Friday Saturday 11-6
Thursday 11-7 Sunday noon-5.

quality style service value

The Edge: Simple, elegant, mostly white dishes. Features simple, but elegant, and mostly white dishes and serving pieces from France and England. Glassware ranges from the practical to the more formal. Find antique silver, crystal decanters, some silver-plate serving pieces and English-style linens. Sometimes wonderful wicker butler trays. Understated country elegance is their styling.

Yellow Door

China, crystal & silver
Brooklyn

1308 Avenue M
near East 13th Street
Brooklyn, NY 11230
718-998-7382. Fax 718-998-6465
Weekdays 10-5:45 Sunday 11-5.

quality style service value

The Edge: High-end giftware discounted. China, giftware, jewelry and tableware from all the top names, including Alessi, Baccarat, Lalique, Villeroy & Boch. Discounts from 20% to 30% off retail.

"Good value." "Slow in providing quotes."

Archetype Gallery

Contemporary
SoHo/TriBeCa

115 Mercer Street

near Prince Street
New York, NY 10012
212-334-0100. Fax 212-226-7880
Wednesday-Friday 10-6 weekends noon-6.

quality style service value
4   4   4   5

The Edge: Cutting-edge furniture and accessories. Features a large and diverse selection of contemporary furniture and accessories (door knobs, glassware, jewelry, lighting and textiles) made by artists. Priced from $9 to $5,000, with occasional items to $20,000.

Carlyle Custom Convertibles Ltd.

Contemporary
Upper East Side

1375 3rd Avenue
between 78th and 79th Streets
New York, NY 10021
212-570-2236
Weekdays 10-7 Saturday 10-6 Sunday noon-5.

quality style service value
4   4   4   3

The Edge: Finally, beautiful convertible sofas. Top-quality convertible sofas, beautifully crafted and covered with fine fabrics along with matching chairs and ottomans. Wonderful trims. Discontinued items and samples (not always on the floor) are often discounted, bringing them into a more reasonable price range. Ask about sale items. Photographs of these items and fabric samples are usually available. Deluxe.

120 West 18th Street
between 6th and 7th Avenues/10011
212-675-3212

Chelsea

1056 3rd Avenue
between 62nd and 63rd Streets/10021
212-838-1525. Fax 212-458-752

Upper East Side

Classic Sofa

Contemporary
Gramercy Pk/Murray Hill

5 West 22nd Street
between 5th and 6th Avenues
New York, NY 10010
212-620-0485
Monday Wednesday Friday Saturday 10-6 Tuesday Thursday 10-8 Sunday noon-5.

The Edge: Quality traditional furniture deliverable within two weeks. Custom chairs and sofas, handmade to your specifications in their own workroom. Down-filled and delivered within two weeks. Very, very expensive, but good quality. Deluxe.

Door Store

Contemporary
Chelsea

123 West 17th Street
between 6th and 7th Avenues
New York, NY 10011
212-627-1515. Fax 212-627-1518
Monday-Wednesday Friday Saturday 10-6 Thursday 10-8
Sunday noon-5.

quality style service value
2   3   3   2

The Edge: Come here for furniture price, not longevity. Inexpensive functional country pine furniture with immediate delivery.

1 Park Avenue
near 33rd Street/10016
212-679-9700
Monday-Wednesday Friday Saturday 10-6 Thursday 10-8 Sunday noon-5.

Gramercy Pl

1201 3rd Avenue
near 70th Street/10021
212-772-1110
Monday-Wednesday Saturday 10-6 Thursday 10-8 Friday 10-7 Sunday noon-5.

Upper East Side

599 Lexington Avenue
near 53rd Street/10022
212-832-7500. Fax 212-755-4995
Monday-Wednesday Friday Saturday 10-6 Thursday 10-8 Sunday noon-5.

Midtown East

Driade/Modern Age
102 Wooster Street
between Spring and Prince Streets
New York, NY 10012
212-966-0669. Fax 212-966-4167
Tuesday-Friday 11-7 weekends noon-6.

Contemporary
SoHo/TriBeCa

5	5	3	3
quality	style	service	value

The Edge: Modern designs by leading architects and designers. Features two floors of modern furniture and home accessories, priced from $50 to $50,000. Important contemporary furniture as seen in the Museum of Modern Art.

"Unique modern designs."

Foremost Furniture Showrooms
8 West 30th Street
between 5th Avenue and Broadway
New York, NY 10001
212-889-6347
Monday-Wednesday Friday 10-6 Thursday 10-7
Saturday 10-5 Sunday 11-5.

Contemporary
Midtown West

2	2	3	3
quality	style	service	value

The Edge: Discounts brand-name furniture. Discounts on Henredon, Stanley and Century. 48,000 square feet of display space on four floors, laid out by floor and room plans.

Jensen-Lewis
89 7th Avenue
near 15th Street
New York, NY 10011
212-929-4880
Monday-Wednesday Friday Saturday 10-7
Thursday 10-8 Sunday noon-5.

Contemporary
Chelsea

3	4	3	3
quality	style	service	value

The Edge: Basic apartment furnishings and housewares. Furnishings and lighting for every room in a range of styles from Shaker to contemporary. Offers bunk beds, durable porch and patio furniture, housewares, kitchen accessories and small bureaus.

.oll

105 Wooster Street
near Prince Street
New York, NY 10012
212-343-4000. Fax 212-343-4170
Weekdays 10-6 weekends noon-5.

Contemporary
SoHo/TriBeCa

quality	style	service	value
4	4	4	4

The Edge: Classic and contemporary furniture designs. Formerly available only through decorators, now retail also.

Maurice Villency

200 Madison Avenue
near 35th Street
New York, NY 10016
212-725-4840. Fax 212-779-2461
Tuesday Wednesday Friday Saturday 10-6
Monday Thursday 10-9 Sunday noon-5.

Contemporary
Gramercy Pk/Murray Hill

quality	style	service	value
3	3	4	3

The Edge: Best known for their contemporary leather sofas and chairs. Features a large showroom filled with a wide range of modern furniture, including leather sofas and chairs, lacquer furniture and wall units. Prices: $1,800 to $6,000. Catalog $10.

"Good follow-through maintenance on leather sales."

North Carolina Furniture Showrooms

12 West 21st Street, 2nd Floor
near 5th Avenue
New York, NY 10010
212-260-5050. Fax 212-267-8670
Monday Wednesday Friday Saturday 10-6
Thursday 10-8 Sunday noon-5.

Contemporary
Gramercy Pk/Murray Hill

quality	style	service	value
4	4	3	4

The Edge: Furniture direct from the manufacturer. Offers furniture and bedding from hundreds of top furniture houses, including Hekman, Henredon, Hickory, Stanley and more. Features styles ranging from 18th-century reproductions to contemporary furnishings. Discounts range from 40% to 45% off the suggested retail price. Credit cards for deposits only. You shop primarily by catalog.

Nuovo Melodrom

60 Greene Street
between Spring and Broome Streets
New York, NY 10012
212-219-0013. Fax 212-431-3931
Weekdays 9-6:30 weekends noon-6.

Contemporary
SoHo/TriBeCa

The Edge: Designer contemporary furniture exclusively. Represents almost a dozen contemporary furniture designers, including Anonimo, Barocco, Bistrot, Bucciarelli (sold exclusively here) Haus Killer/Hoffmann, Jean Michel Frank, Mies van der Rohe, Noguchi, Palio, Piuma, and more. The classics are generally in stock with a standard chrome frame and black leather upholstery. Lead time for special orders is six to eight weeks. 50 different canvas colors available on upholstered items. Priced from $1,000 to $5,000.

Palazzeti

Contemporary
Midtown East

515 Madison Avenue
near 53rd Street
New York, NY 10022
212-832-1199. Fax 212-832-1385
Weekdays 10-6 Saturday 11-5 Sunday noon-5.

quality	style	service	value
3	4	3	3

The Edge: Reproductions of the classics in 20th-century furniture. Sells licensed copies of top modern designers' furniture styles, including Eames, Breuer, Le Corbusier, Mies van der Rohe and more at to-the-trade prices.

"Average-quality copies of 20th-century classics."

Scott Jordan Furniture

Contemporary
SoHo/TriBeCa

137 Varick Street
near Spring Street
New York, NY 10013
212-620-4682
Monday-Wednesday Friday Saturday 11-6
Thursday 11-8 Sunday noon-5.

quality	style	service	value
4	4	4	4

The Edge: Traditional, quality crafted furniture. Quality traditionally styled furniture made in solid hardwoods.

"The antiques of tomorrow."

SEE Ltd.

Contemporary
Gramercy Pk/Murray Hill

920 Broadway
near 21st Street
New York, NY 10010
212-228-3600
Monday-Saturday 10-7 Sunday noon-6.

quality	style	service	value
3	4	4	2

The Edge: SEE equals Spatial Environmental Elements—need we say more. Avant-garde furniture sold direct. 70 different designers featured. Priced from $1,000 to $10,000.

Shabby Chic

Contemporary
SoHo/TriBeCa

93 Greene Street
near Prince Street
New York, NY 10012
212-274-9842. Fax 212-274-9845
Daily 10-7.

quality	style	service	value
1	1	4	3

The Edge: Expensive overstuffed furniture. Furniture with the old English country look. Faded, classical slipcovered furniture, throw pillows, linens and period accessories. Pieces are made in cream and white, slipcovered in your choice of fabric. Very expensive (couches $4,000 to 7,000 slipcovered).

Winslow Furniture

Contemporary
SoHo/TriBeCa

464 Broome Street
near Mercer Street
New York, NY 10013
212-219-9244. Fax 212-219-9332
Monday-Saturday 11-5 Sunday 1-5.

The Edge: Reasonably priced custom-made furniture. Winslow manufactures his adaptation of Mission to modern furniture. Priced from $500 to $5,000.

Workbench

Contemporary
SoHo/TriBeCa

quality	style	service	value
3	3	4	3

176 Avenue of the Americas
between Prince and Spring Streets
New York, NY 10013
212-675-7775
Monday-Wednesday Friday 9-7 Thursday 9-8
Saturday 9-6 Sunday noon-6.

The Edge: Price is the driver for these simply styled pieces. A large selection of Shaker-style basics from trundle beds and desks to storage units and toy chests in a variety of finishes. Their inexpensive lower-end furniture is scaled to apartment living.

"Excellent value for standard teak and rosewood furniture." "Good quality, delivery on time."

470 Park Avenue South
near 32nd Street/10016
212-481-5454

Gramercy Pk/Murray Hill

2091 Broadway
near 72nd Street/10023
212-724-3670

Upper West Side

336 East 86th Street
between 1st and 2nd Avenues10028
212-794-4418

Upper East Side

Bridge Kitchenware

Cookware & cutlery
Midtown East

quality	style	service	value
5	4	3	4

214 East 52nd Street
between 2nd and 3rd Avenues
New York, NY 10022
212-688-4220
Weekdays 9-5:30 Saturday 10-4:30.

The Edge: Exceptionally well-stocked cooking store for serious cooks. Since 1945, professional cooking equipment, china and serving accessories. Everything you could possibly need. Few stores carry as many specialty cookware items. Much of the wares hang overhead or are piled in open containers. A virtual warehouse of cooking supplies. Full retail prices.

"Not discount but very complete." "We love this place—essential."

Broadway Panhandler

477 Broome Street
near Wooster Street
New York, NY 10013
212-966-3434. Fax 212-266-9017
Weekdays 10:30-7 Saturday 11-7 Sunday noon-6.
Closed Sunday July and August.

Cookware & cutlery
SoHo/TriBeCa

quality	style	service	value
4	4	4	4

The Edge: Best for bakeware. Good neighborhood source (SoHo and East Village) for top-quality kitchenware pots and pans from basic to gourmet quality. Baking and pastry equipment are the store's chief attraction. 20% off.

"A bit pricey, not a lot of service, great selection." "Not as good as years ago; never go in—use the catalog."

Daroma Restaurant Equipment Corp.

196 & 231 Bowery
near Prince Street
New York, NY 10002
212-226-6774. Fax 212-979-1335
Weekdays 9-5 Saturday 9-3:30.

Cookware & cutlery
Lower East Side/Chinatown

quality	style	service	value
5	1	1	5

The Edge: Unbelievable prices. Sells restaurant supplies and equipment, including professional refrigerators and stoves. Large selection. As with most discounters, come here for the prices, not the service.

E. Rossi

191 Grand Street
near Mulberry Street
New York, NY 10013
212-226-9254. Fax 212-925-0545
Weekdays 10-6 Saturday 10-7 Sunday 10-5.

Cookware & cutlery
SoHo/TriBeCa

The Edge: A wholesale source for Italian cooking needs. Mostly wholesale but can buy hand-cranked pasta makers, ravioli plates, rolling pins and boards, cappuccino makers, coffee pots, heavy crockery bowls for serving and making pasta and general gadgets needed for Italian kitchens. Discounter.

Hung Chong Import

14 Bowery
between Pell and Doyers Streets
New York, NY 10013
212-349-1463. Fax 212-385-0806
Daily 9-7.

Cookware & cutlery
SoHo/TriBeCa

The Edge: Good source for Chinese cooking instruments at lower prices than uptown. Features kitchenware and some hardware. Family to restaurant size equipment. Prices are 50% below uptown. Supplies many Chinese restaurants. Not much English spoken. No credit cards. Discounter.

Lamalle Kitchenware

Cookware & cutlery
Gramercy Pk/Murray Hill

36 West 25th Street, 6th Floor
between 5th Avenue and Broadway
New York, NY 10010
212-242-0750. Fax 212-645-2996
Weekdays 8:30-5:30 Saturday 10-4:30. Closed Saturday June-August.

The Edge: The shop for serious kitchen professionals. In operation since 1927, now owned by Fisher & Levy's owner, Lamalles caters to chefs seeking quality oven and bakeware, assorted specialty tools, cutlery and more.

Matas Restaurant Supply

Cookware & cutlery
SoHo/TriBeCa

210 Bowery
between Prince and Spring Streets
New York, NY 10012
212-966-2251. Fax 212-966-0791
Weekdays 8-5 Saturday 10-4.

The Edge: The basics in cookware, more for restaurants. 30,000 items, including dishes, glassware and pots. Known for basic restaurant supplies. Discounter.

New Cathay Hardware Corporation

Cookware & cutlery
SoHo/TriBeCa

49 Mott Street
near Bayard Street
New York, NY 10013
212-962-6648. Fax 212-962-6648
Daily 10-7.

The Edge: One of the largest sources for Chinese cooking items. Meets all Chinese cooking needs. Much cheaper than uptown! Items priced from $5 to the low hundreds. Stocks one of the largest selection of Oriental cookware in the city. Discounter.

Cobweb

Country
SoHo/TriBeCa

5	5	5	5
quality	style	service	value

116 West Houston Street
between Thomas and Sullivan Streets
New York, NY 10012
212-505-1558
Weekdays noon-7 Saturday noon-5.
Closed Saturday July and August.

The Edge: Antique Spanish and Central and South American furniture. Two-story shop filled with a mix of antique Spanish and Central and South American rustic and formal furniture, plus accessories. Accessories include antique tiles, chandeliers, earthenware water jugs, hand-painted ceramic plates, iron washstands, terra-cotta bowls and wood plant stands.

Le Fanion

Country
Greenwich Village

4	4	4	3
quality	style	service	value

299 West 4th Street
near Bank Street
New York, NY 10014
212-463-8760. Fax 212-633-8340

Monday-Friday 11-7 Saturday noon-6.

The Edge: Antique furniture and decorative items from the south of France. Features 18th- and 19th-century country French furniture, plus decorative items (including contemporary handmade pottery) painted in Provence.

Martell Antiques

53 East 10th Street
near Broadway
New York, NY 10003
212-777-4360
Weekdays 10-5:30 Saturday 11-5.
Closed Saturday in August.

Country
Flatiron/East Village

3 3 5 4
quality style service value

The Edge: Dedicated to antique formal French country furniture. Mostly 18th- and early 19th-century formal French country furniture. Priced from $5,000 to $15,000. No credit cards.

Adorama Camera

42 West 18th Street
between 5th and 6th Avenues
New York, NY 10011
212-675-6789. Fax 212-463-7223
Monday-Thursday 9-6:30 Friday 9-1:30 Sunday 9:30-5:30.

Electronics, etc.
Chelsea

The Edge: Wide range of camera equipment. Mail order for amateurs and professionals featuring basic cameras to dark room equipment. Everything for photography at good prices. See their 14+-page ads in most photography publications. Very large inventory.

B&H Photo & Electronics

119 West 17th Street
between 6th and 7th Avenues
New York, NY 10011
212-807-7474. Fax 212-242-1400
Monday Tuesday 9-6 Wednesday Thursday 9-7:15
Friday 9-2 Sunday 10-4:45.

Electronics, etc.
Chelsea

4 - 3 4
quality style service value

The Edge: The source for high-end video equipment. Features professional photo, video and imaging equipment. Very good prices on cameras, lenses and supplies. More than 200 styles of top-brand cameras. Monthly flyer features specials. Also large catalog. Ships worldwide.

"The best source for high-end video equipment—must know what you want." "Good selection, knowledgeable staff."

Canal Hi-Fi

319 Canal Street
near Broome Street
New York, NY 10013
212-925-6575. Fax 212-925-6607
Daily 10-6.

Electronics, etc.
SoHo/TriBeCa

The Edge: Discounts on quality audio components. Find professional sound equipment, speakers and compact disc players from Pioneer and Sony, among others. No delivery. Discounter.

Computers

7 Great Jones Street
near Broadway
New York, NY 10012
212-254-9000
Weekdays 10-6 Saturday 11-6.

Electronics, etc.
SoHo/TriBeCa

The Edge: Software and computers for sale or rent. In business since 1978. Sells hardware, software and accessories for computers and desktop-publishing systems. Also magazines and books. You can rent and use the equipment at the store. Discounter.

Crocodile Computers

240 West 73rd Street
between Broadway and West End Avenue
New York, NY 10023
212-769-3400. Fax 212-724-3501
Weekdays 10-7 Saturday 11-5.

Electronics, etc.
Upper West Side

2	-	4	4
quality	style	service	value

The Edge: Sells refurbished and new computers. Brands include Macs and IBMs and compatibles, all with store warranty. No credit cards. Discounter.

47th Street Photo

115 West 45th Street
between 6th Avenue and Broadway
New York, NY 10036
212-398-1530
Monday-Thursday 8:30-8 Friday 9-2 Sunday 10-5.

Electronics, etc.
Midtown West

4	-	2	4
quality	style	service	value

The Edge: Full range of electronic and photographic equipment. Three floors of electronic equipment, including cameras, photographic equipment, fax machines, phones, video items, CD and cassette players, sunglasses, watches and more. Like most discounters, come here for price, not service. Not the place it was. 25% off.

"Prices aren't competitive anymore and service is fair to middling." "Generally rude, tough. You need to know what you're looking for."

Foto Electric Supply Company

31 Essex Street
near Grand Street
New York, NY 10002
212-673-5222
Sunday-Thursday 9-6 Friday 9-3.

Electronics, etc.
Lower East Side/Chinatown

The Edge: Discounts small appliances, cameras, sunglasses and watches. Like the items found in most duty-free shops.

Harvey Electronics

2 West 45th Street
near 5th Avenue
New York, NY 10036
212-575-5000. Fax 212-944-9083
Weekdays 9:30-6 Saturday 10-6.

Electronics, etc.
Midtown West

5	-	4	4
quality	style	service	value

The Edge: The place for state-of-the-art home theaters. Offers top-of-the-line audio and video equipment, plus a design and installation division. Very expensive.

Hi Fi Electronics

152 Delancey Street
at Clinton Street
New York, NY 10002
212-260-7222. Fax 212-274-3520
Daily 10-7:30.

Electronics, etc.
Lower East Side/Chinatown

The Edge: New and refurbished equipment by Fisher, Pioneer, Sony, etc. Refurbished equipment carries a three-month warranty.

J&R Music World

23 Park Row
near Broadway
New York, NY 10038
212-238-9000. Fax 212-238-9191
Monday-Saturday 9-6:30 Sunday 11-6.

Electronics, etc.
Lower Manhattan

4	-	3	4
quality	style	service	value

The Edge: A great source for computers, cameras and the like. Stocks a huge inventory of cameras, CD players, computers, radios, stereos, tapes, telephones, televisions, microwaves and watches. Authorized dealers for Apple, AST, Canon, Hewlett-Packard, NEC, Toshiba and more. Order by fax or phone. 20% off.

"J&R more interested in computers now." "Excellent place for discount items." "Big selection, good values."

Ken Hansen Imaging

920 Broadway, 3rd Floor
between 20th and 21st Streets
New York, NY 10010
212-777-5900. Fax 212-473-0690
Weekdays 9:30-5.

Electronics, etc.
Gramercy Pk/Murray Hill

5	-	5	5
quality	style	service	value

The Edge: Rents top-quality lighting and electronic imaging equipment. Sells and rents top-quality equipment from Contax, Hasselblad, Rollei, Nikon and more. Features a large selection of lighting and electronic imaging equipment, including cameras, digital points, scanners and work stations. Offers excellent service. Digital studio and equipment-rental program at full-day rental rates. Seven-day weekly rentals are available at four times the daily rate. Provides training.

Manhattan Electronics Corporation

17 West 45th Street
near 5th Avenue
New York, NY 10036
212-354-6462. Fax 212-354-4476
Weekdays 9-5:30 Saturday 9:30-3:30.

Electronics, etc.
Midtown West

The Edge: Exclusively computer equipment and parts. New equipment only. Discounter.

Micro U.S.A. Computer Depot

55 Avenue of the Americas
near Canal Street
New York, NY 10013
212-941-0270.
Weekdays 10-6 Saturday 11-5.

Electronics, etc.
SoHo/TriBeCa

The Edge: Computers and software at good prices. Sells custom-made IBM-compatible computers, accessories, software and supplies at good prices. No delivery. Discounter.

Olden Camera

1265 Broadway
near 31st Street
New York, NY 10001
212-725-1234. Fax 212-725-1325
Weekdays 9-7 weekends 10-5.

Electronics, etc.
Midtown West

quality	style	service	value
3	-	3	3

The Edge: Discounts on new and used camera equipment. Sells new and used cameras, cellular phones, computers, faxes and video equipment at discounted prices.

Phone Boutique

828 Lexington Avenue
near 63rd Street
New York, NY 10021
212-319-9650. Fax 212-319-5277
Monday-Saturday 10-6:30.

Electronics, etc.
Upper East Side

quality	style	service	value
3	-	2	3

The Edge: Buys, sells and repairs vintage telephones. Vintage telephones range from 1920s candlesticks in black metal and brass to more current 1950s styles. Phones can be updated with push-buttons. Repairs start at $45. Also sells answering machines, fax machines and telephone-related accessories. Rents cellular phones and beepers.

Sharper Image

4 West 57th Street
between 5th and 6th Avenues
New York, NY 10019
212-265-2550
Monday-Friday 10-7 Saturday 10-6 Sunday noon-5.

Electronics, etc.
Midtown West

quality	style	service	value
4	4	4	3

The Edge: Executive toys and comforts. Wonderful catalog featuring binoculars, desk accessories, fitness equipment, globes, high-end stereo equipment, massage chairs, power fish tanks and telescopes.

900 Madison Avenue
near 73rd Street/10021
212-794-4974
Monday-Saturday 10-6 Sunday noon-5.

Upper East Side

Pier 17, South Street Seaport
between South and Fulton Streets/10038
212-693-0477. Fax 212-693-0489
September-April: Monday-Saturday 10-9 Sunday 11-8.
May-September: Monday-Saturday 10-7 Sunday 11-6.

Lower Manhattan

Software Etc.

1282 Broadway
near 33rd Street
New York, NY 10001
212-967-9070
Weekdays 10-7 Saturday 10-6 Sunday 11-6.

Electronics, etc.
Midtown West

4	-	3	4
quality	style	service	value

The Edge: The staff is very knowledgeable about computers. Computer accessories, books and
software sold at good prices.

101 5th Avenue
between 17th and 18th Streets/10003
212-727-3280. Fax 212-645-0624
Weekdays 9:30-8 Saturday 10-6 Sunday 11-6.

Flatiron/East Village

743 Broadway
near Astor Place/10003
212-979-7678
Monday-Thursday 10-9 Friday Saturday 10-10 Sunday noon-7.

Flatiron/East Village

595 5th Avenue
near 48th Street/10017
212-752-7305
Weekdays 9:30-7 Saturday 10-8 Sunday 11-6.

Midtown East

666 5th Avenue
near 52nd Street/10019
212-315-4744
Weekdays 8:30-7 Saturday 9:30-6:30 Sunday noon-6.

Midtown West

162 East 53rd Street
near 3rd Avenue/10022
212-753-7780
Weekdays 8:30-6 Saturday 11-5.

Midtown East

2300 Broadway
near 83rd Street/10024
212-362-3460. Fax 212-645-0624
Monday-Thursday 10-9 Friday Saturday 10-10 Sunday 11-7.

Upper West Side

128 East 86th Street   **Upper East Side**
near Lexington Avenue/10028
212-423-1844
Monday-Saturday 10-8 Sunday 11-7.

1120 Avenue of the Americas   **Midtown West**
near 44th Street/10036
212-921-7855
Weekdays 9:30-7 Saturday 11-6 Sunday noon-6.

150 Broadway   **Lower Manhattan**
near Maiden Lane/10038
212-233-5913
Weekdays 10-6 Saturday 10-4:30.

Sound City

Electronics, etc.
Midtown West

58 West 45th Street
between 5th and 6th Avenues
New York, NY 10036
212-575-0210. Fax 212-944-7907
Weekdays 9-7 Saturday 9-6.

The Edge: Discounts all major brands of stereo, video, photo and home electronics.

Spectra Research Group

Electronics, etc.
Upper East Side

762 Madison Avenue
between 65th and 66th Streets
New York, NY 10021
212-744-2255. Fax 212-628-7069
Monday-Saturday 10-6.

The Edge: State-of-the-art audio-visual and surveillance equipment. Surveillance equipment and general consumer electronic goods. Discounts possible depending on the amount you buy.

Stereo Exchange

Electronics, etc.
SoHo/TriBeCa

627 Broadway
near Houston Street
New York, NY 10012
212-505-1111. Fax 212-995-5524
Weekdays 11-7:30 Saturday 10:30-7 Sunday noon-7.

3	-	4	4
quality	style	service	value

The Edge: Repairs and sells used high-end stereos. Features top-end stereos and components for stereos, video and audio systems. Refurbished items carry a 30-day warranty. Discounter.

Vicmarr Stereo and TV

Electronics, etc.
Lower East Side/Chinatown

88 Delancey Street
near Orchard Street
New York, NY 10002
212-505-0380. Fax 212-614-9846
Sunday-Thursday 9-7 Friday 9-2.

The Edge: Full line electronics shop. Offers a large selection of basic electronic products, including answering machines, camcorders, car audio systems, microwave ovens, stereos, telephones, etc. Good prices. Discounter.

Waves

Electronics, etc.
Flatiron/East Village

32 East 13th Street
between University Place and 5th Avenue
New York, NY 10003
212-989-9284. Fax 201-461-7121
Tuesday-Friday noon-6 Saturday noon-5.

The Edge: Vintage electronics. Sells old radios, record players and telephones. Also repairs radios.

Willoughby's Camera Store

Electronics, etc.
Midtown West

136 West 32nd Street
between 6th and 7th Avenues
New York, NY 10001
212-564-1600. Fax 212-564-1608
Weekdays 8:30-9 weekends 10-7.

The Edge: Good selection of computers, cameras and electronics.

Wiz

Electronics, etc.
Midtown West

871 Avenue of the Americas
at 31st Street
New York, NY 10001
212-876-4400
Monday-Saturday 10-8 Sunday 11-7.

4	.	3	4

quality style service value

The Edge: Chain of audio/video discount stores. Discounts TVs, CDs, computers, fax machines, automatic cameras, etc. They say they'll meet any price. They're like most discounters, so don't go there for the service. 20% off.

726 Broadway
near Astor Place/10003
212-677-4111
Monday-Saturday 10-10 Sunday 10-7.

Flatiron/East Village

337 5th Avenue
near 33rd Street/10016
212-447-0100
Daily 10-7.

Gramercy Pk/Murray Hill

212 East 57th Street
between 2nd and 3rd Avenues/10022
212-754-1600
Daily 10-9.

Midtown East

2577 Broadway
at 97th Street/10025

Upper West Side

212-663-8000
Monday-Saturday 10-10 Sunday 10-7.

1536 3rd Avenue   **Upper East Side**
at 86th Street/10028
212-876-4400
Monday-Saturday 10-8 Sunday 11-7.

12 West 45th Street   **Midtown West**
between 5th and 6th Avenues/10036
212-302-2000
Monday-Friday 9-8 Saturday Sunday 10-7.

49 West 45th Street   **Midtown West**
between 5th and 6th Avenues/10036
212-302-6944
Monday-Friday 9-8 Saturday Sunday 10-7.

Barry Friedman Ltd.

Empire & Biedermeier
Upper East Side

32 East 67th Street, 3rd Floor
near Madison Avenue
New York, NY 10021
212-794-8950. Fax 212-794-8889
Monday-Saturday 11-6.

The Edge: Features Vienna Secession furniture, paintings and accessories. With Vienna Secessionist pieces, also Italian modern pieces from the 1920s and 1930s. Periodic special exhibitions with a catalog produced for the show. No credit cards. No delivery.

Eileen Lane Antiques

Empire & Biedermeier
SoHo/TriBeCa

150 Thompson Street
near Houston Street
New York, NY 10012
212-475-2988. Fax 212-673-8669
Daily 11-7.

The Edge: Large selection of Biedermeier and Empire furniture. Two-story furniture and accessory warehouse. Its specialty is Biedermeier and Empire furniture matched with accessories, including art deco pieces, vintage chandeliers and more. Manufactures a line of Biedermeier reproductions. Chandelier prices: $1,350 to $7,200.

Niall Smith

Empire & Biedermeier
SoHo/TriBeCa

96 Grand Street
between Greene and Mercer Streets
New York, NY 10013
212-941-7354
Monday-Saturday noon-6. Closed Saturday July and August.

The Edge: Neoclassic early 19th-century European furniture and accessories. Wonderful for Biedermeier. No credit cards. No delivery.

344 Bleecker Street
between West 10th and Christopher Streets/10014
212-255-0660
Tuesday-Friday 1-7 Saturday 1-6.

Ritter Antik
35 East 10th Street
near University Place
New York, NY 10003
212-673-2213
Weekdays 10-5:30 Saturday noon-5.

Empire & Biedermeier
Flatiron/East Village

3	2	4	3
quality	style	service	value

The Edge: Expensive Biedermeier furniture. No credit cards.

Victor Antiques Ltd.
223 East 60th Street
between 2nd and 3rd Avenues
New York, NY 10022
212-752-4100. Fax 212-752-2747
Weekdays 10-6 Saturday 11-5.

Empire & Biedermeier
Midtown East

3	5	5	3
quality	style	service	value

The Edge: Loft-size store featuring continental furniture. Favors 19th-century European, Russian and Scandinavian furniture. Favors Biedermeier furniture with prices from $4,000.

Agostino Antiques Ltd.
808 Broadway
near 11th Street
New York, NY 10003
212-533-3355. Fax 212-477-4128
Weekdays 9-5.

English
Flatiron/East Village

4	4	5	3
quality	style	service	value

The Edge: Large selection of 18th- and 19th-century English furniture. Used to be to the trade only, but now takes retail clients. Features two floors of primarily 18th- and 19th-century English furniture and accessories, plus some French and continental pieces. Priced from $1,000 to many hundreds of thousands. High quality. Decorator discount possible to 20%. No credit cards.

Charlotte Moss & Company
1027 Lexington Avenue
near 73rd Street
New York, NY 10021
212-772-3320. Fax 212-794-8764
Monday-Thursday 10-5:30 Friday 10-5 Saturday 11-5.
Closed Saturday July and August.

English
Upper East Side

5	5	4	3
quality	style	service	value

The Edge: A great resource for that English country look. Expect to find furniture and accessories befitting a cozy creative environment, accessories and gift items, china, chintz-covered hat boxes, drapery ties and satin tassel pulls, luggage racks, needlepoint panels, screens, tapestry cushions and trays. Some antiques, more reproductions. Custom-made slipper chairs from $1,200. Even their own fragrance candle called Jugmia.

Eagles Antiques

1097 Madison Avenue
near 83rd Street
New York, NY 10028
212-772-3266
Weekdays 9:30-5:30 Saturday 10-5:30.

English
Upper East Side

quality	style	service	value
4	4	4	4

The Edge: Quality period English formal furniture. Specializes in formal 18th- and 19th-century English period furniture, including some unique Georgian pieces priced from $9,000 to $50,000, 17th- to 19th-century Aubusson pillows priced from $1,000 to $5,000, 16th- to 19th-century antique accessories, including porcelain lamps and candlesticks. No credit cards. Deluxe.

"Expensive."

Florian Papp

962 Madison Avenue
near 76th Street
New York, NY 10021
212-288-6770
Weekdays 9-5:30 Saturday 10-5.

English
Upper East Side

quality	style	service	value
5	5	5	2

The Edge: Museum-quality, formal 17th- to 19th-century English furniture. Third-generation family business. Three floors of furniture and accessories priced from $2,000 to $300,000. Deluxe. No credit cards.

Kentshire Galleries

37 East 12th Street
near University Place
New York, NY 10003
212-673-6644. Fax 212-979-0923
Weekdays 9-5 Saturday 10:30-3.
Closed Saturday May-October.

English
Flatiron/East Village

quality	style	service	value
5	5	5	3

The Edge: A large selection of very expensive English antique furniture and furnishings. Ever-changing stock on seven floors, but staples include fine English china, Majolica plates, crystal decanters and desk accessories. An excellent selection of furniture from Queen Anne through William IV. They maintain a small gift annex at Bergdorf's. Deluxe.

Lynn Hollyn

520 Madison Avenue
between 53rd and 54th Streets
New York, NY 10022
212-319-0520. Fax 212-223-3791
Monday-Wednesday Friday Saturday 10:30-6
Thursday 10:30-8.

English
Midtown East

quality	style	service	value
5	5	4	4

The Edge: Splendid English country look. Good home-decorating resource. The showroom features quality reproduction furniture with an elegant Edwardian English country look.

"Unusual, beautiful home furnishings."

Malcolm Franklin, Inc.

762 Madison Avenue
between 65th and 66th Streets
New York, NY 10021
212-288-9054. Fax 212-288-0560
Weekdays 10-5:30 Saturday 10-4. Closed Saturday June-August.

English
Upper East Side

The Edge: Rare Queen Anne furniture. Features 17th- to early 19th-century English furniture, plus wonderful porcelain and brass accessories. Priced from $2,000 to $40,000. No credit cards. Deluxe.

Philip Colleck of London Ltd.

830 Broadway
near 12th Street
New York, NY 10003
212-505-2500
Weekdays 10-5:30 or by appointment.

English
Flatiron/East Village

5	5	5	4
quality	style	service	value

The Edge: Museum-quality 18th-century formal English furniture. Features Adam, Chippendale and Queen Anne furniture. Full range of furniture, plus decorative accessories, including museum-quality gilded mirrors. No credit cards. Deluxe.

Stair & Company

942 Madison Avenue
near 74th Street
New York, NY 10021
212-517-4400. Fax 212-737-4751
Weekdays 9:30-5:30 Saturday 11-4.
Closed Saturday July and August.

English
Upper East Side

4	5	4	3
quality	style	service	value

The Edge: Quality 18th- and early 19th-century English furniture. Since 1812. Two floors of furniture and accessories. Mostly furniture but also accessories, including carpets, chandeliers, Chinese export porcelains, lacquerware, mirrors, paintings and screens. Furniture prices range from $5,000 to $250,000. No credit cards. No delivery. Deluxe.

"Like being in England—gracious."

Trevor Potts Reproductions

1065 Lexington Avenue
between 75th and 76th Streets
New York, NY 10021
212-570-5573
Weekdays 9:30-5 by appointment. Saturdays after Labor Day by appointment.

English
Upper East Side

The Edge: Filled with reproductions of English Regency painted and gilded furniture. High-style quality reproductions of antique English furniture. No credit cards.

European
Midtown East

5 5 3 3
quality style service value

...reet
...en Madison and Park Avenues
New York, NY 10022
212-758-2297
Monday-Saturday 10-5:30. Closed Saturday July and August.

The Edge: Five floors of fine 18th-century French furniture and accessories. Wonderful antique furnishings, including clocks and porcelains. Deluxe.

Didier Aaron, Inc.

32 East 67th Street
between Park and Madison Avenues
New York, NY 10021
212-988-5248. Fax 212-737-3513
Weekdays 9:30-6 Saturday by appointment.

European
Upper East Side

5 5 5 4
quality style service value

The Edge: Impeccable 18th- and 19th-century French Furniture. While mostly French 18th- and 19th-century furniture, some non French-antiques (Anglo-Indian, English, Irish, Italian, Russian and others) also. Features exceptional pieces. Some old master and 19th-century paintings. No credit cards. Deluxe.

Frederick P. Victoria and Son, Inc.

154 East 55th Street
between 3rd and Lexington Avenues
New York, NY 10022
212-755-2549. Fax 212-888-7199
Weekdays 9-5.

European
Midtown East

The Edge: Collector-quality 19th-century French furniture. Fine selection of 18th-century French clocks, important crystal chandeliers and works of art from around the globe. A favorite shop of top decorators. Prices from $5,000 to $350,000. No credit cards. Deluxe.

French & Company, Inc.

17 East 65th Street
between 5th and Madison Avenues
New York, NY 10021
212-535-3330. Fax 212-772-1756
By appointment.

European
Upper East Side

The Edge: Museum-quality 18th-century French and English furniture. A small, select collection of high-quality antique furniture. Plus some old master paintings. Caters to museums seeking important furniture. No credit cards. Deluxe.

Grange Furniture

200 Lexington Avenue
near 32nd Street
New York, NY 10016
212-685-9057. Fax 212-213-5132
Weekdays 9-6.

European
Gramercy Pk/Murray Hill

3 4 5 4
quality style service value

The Edge: Quality expensive reproductions of French period furniture. Features a full range of quality reproductions of period French furniture, including 18th-century French Provençal, 19th-century Louis XVI, Louis Philippe and Directoire. Also wicker, painted furniture and garden furnishings and more. Choice of wood and painted finishes. Very attractive styling. Delivery, if in stock, takes two to three weeks, or 12 weeks if ordered from France.

John Rosselli Antiques

255 East 72nd Street
near 2nd Avenue
New York, NY 10021
212-737-2252. Fax 212-535-2989
Weekdays 9:30-6.

European
Upper East Side

quality	style	service	value
3	5	5	3

The Edge: Antiques, reproductions and modern decorative pieces. Three floors of decorative pieces: antiques from the 17th-century on, reproductions and modern furnishings. Prices to $20,000. No credit cards.

Le Cadet de Gascogne

1015 Lexington Avenue
near 73rd Street
New York, NY 10021
212-744-5925. Fax 212-744-5925
Weekdays 10-6. Summer Tuesday-Thursday 10-6 or by appointment.

European
Upper East Side

The Edge: Quality French antique furniture from Louis XIV on. Many signed pieces. Also accessories, including paintings and objets d'art. No credit cards.

Newel Art Galleries, Inc.

425 East 53rd Street
near 1st Avenue
New York, NY 10022
212-758-1970. Fax 212-371-0166
Weekdays 9-5.

European
Midtown East

quality	style	service	value
4	5	5	4

The Edge: Vast selection of antique furniture. Six full floors of antiques, ranging from Renaissance through art deco. Lots of English period furniture, including wicker and bamboo. Lovely garden furniture. Also a large selection of 18th- and 19th-century fireplace accessories. Wonderful decorative items. Newel favors the unique. One of the largest antique sources in the city. No credit cards.

Oak-Smith & Jones

1510 2nd Avenue
near 79th Street
New York, NY 10021
212-327-3462. Fax 212-327-3434
Monday-Saturday 10-9 Sunday 11-8.

European
Upper East Side

quality	style	service	value
3	4	4	3

The Edge: Good prices for collectible (aka "used") furniture and accessories. Eclectic collection of furniture, including armoires converted to entertainment centers, upholstered furniture, tables and chairs. Priced from $10 to $7,000.

"Interesting pieces at good prices." "New antiques." "Well selected."

Reymer-Jourdan Antiques

European
Flatiron/East Village

43 East 10th Street
near Broadway
New York, NY 10003
212-674-4470. Fax 212-228-9471
Weekdays 10-5:30 Saturday noon-5.
Closed Saturday June-August.

5	5	5	3
quality	style	service	value

The Edge: Excellent-quality continental and French 19th-century furniture. Favors Biedermeier, Directoire and Empire. Priced from $500 (for accessories) to $500,000. No credit cards. Deluxe.

Harry Zarin Company

Fabric
Lower East Side/Chinatown

72 Allen Street
near Grand Street
New York, NY 10002
212-925-6112. Fax 212-925-6589
Daily 9-5:30.

4	3	4	4
quality	style	service	value

The Edge: Vast selections of decorator fabrics. A huge inventory, 50,000 pieces of fabrics in stock, discounted 10% to 25% off retail. Don't forget to bargain to lower prices even further. Best for drapery and upholstery fabrics. Prices mostly from $3 to $35 per yard.

"Some good things."

Hyman Hendler and Sons

Fabric
Midtown West

67 West 38th Street
between 5th and 6th Avenues
New York, NY 10018
212-840-8393. Fax 212-704-4237
Weekdays 9-5:15 Saturday 10-3.

5	5	4	5
quality	style	service	value

The Edge: Fabulous quality and variety of color and patterns. Beautiful French and Swiss ribbons and tassels. No credit cards. Discounter.

Intercoastal Textiles

Fabric
SoHo/TriBeCa

480 Broadway
near Broome Street
New York, NY 10013
212-925-9235. Fax 212-925-2783
Monday-Thursday 9-6 Friday 9-5.
Closed July 1-14. October-December Sunday 10-4.

4	4	5	4
quality	style	service	value

The Edge: Close-outs on quality, top decorator upholstery fabrics. They'll recommend a source to make slipcovers. Large inventory. Unbelievable selections. Discounter.

Island Fabric Warehouse

Fabric
SoHo/TriBeCa

406 Broadway
near Canal Street
New York, NY 10013
212-431-9510
Monday-Wednesday Friday 9-6 Thursday 9-7:30 weekends 10- 5.

The Edge: Three floors of fabrics for clothing, upholstery and drapes. Fabrics from $1 to $45 per yard. A wide range from wedding to drapery fabrics. Hundreds of fabrics including chiffon, silk, satin and wool. Remnants and odd pieces at incredible prices. No delivery. Discounter.

Silk Surplus

Fabric
Midtown East

235 East 58th Street
near 3rd Avenue
New York, NY 10022
212-753-6511. Fax 212-980-2057
Monday-Friday 10-6 Saturday 10-5:30.

4	3	4	4
quality	style	service	value

The Edge: Outlet for Scalamandre close-outs. Source for Scalamandre fine fabrics, trimmings and wallpaper. Periodic sales in the fall, usually in late October. Priced from $9 to $78 per yard. 50% off.

Tinsel Trading Company

Fabric
Midtown West

47 West 38th Street
between 5th and 6th Avenues
New York, NY 10018
212-730-1030. Fax 212-768-8823
Weekdays 10-5 Saturday 11-3. Closed Saturday July and August.

The Edge: Wonderful trims from the 1920s. Features (in every conceivable space) elaborate antique tassels and trims used for tiebacks, elaborate silk tiebacks, braids, cords, fringes and more. Tassels made of gold and silver metallic threads.

Modern Supply Company

Fans
Lower Manhattan

19 Murray Street
between Broadway and Church Street
New York, NY 10007
212-267-0100. Fax 212-267-0100
Weekdays 10-5 Saturday noon-5.

5	-	3	5
quality	style	service	value

The Edge: All kinds of fans, with and without lights.

Danny Allessandro Ltd./Edwin Jackson, Inc.

146 East 57th Street
near Lexington Avenue
New York, NY 10022
212-421-1928. Fax 212-759-3819
September-March weekdays 10-6

Fireplace
Midtown East

5	5	4	4
quality	style	service	value

April-September weekdays 10-5 Saturday noon-4.

The Edge: Incredible selection of 17th-century and 18th-century fireplace mantels. Since 1979, six floors of fireplace mantels and equipment with mantels in a wide range of styles, including art deco, contemporary, early American and 18th-century Louis XV. Also antique andirons, screens and tools. A large selection of reproduction mantels and equipment. Custom orders are available. Prices range from $3,800 to $100,000. Deluxe.

William H. Jackson

210 East 58th Street
between 2nd and 3rd Avenues
New York, NY 10022
212-753-9400. Fax 212-753-7872
Weekdays 9:30-5.

Fireplace
Midtown East

5	4	5	3
quality	style	service	value

The Edge: Intricate and interesting fireplace equipment. Equipment includes fireplace mantels, andirons, screens and fire sets. Specializes in antiques, but also sells reproduction equipment.

Antique Cache

1050 2nd Avenue
near 55th Street
New York, NY 10022
212-752-0838
Weekdays 10:30-5:30.

Garden & wicker
Midtown East

The Edge: Antique bamboo and lacquer furniture. Gallery 64 at the Manhattan Art and Antiques Center. Known for their antique English bamboo and lacquer furniture and accessories. Accessories include desk sets, letter openers, pens and inkwells and boxes.

April Cornell

487 Columbus Avenue
between 83rd and 84th Streets
New York, NY 10024
212-799-4342. Fax 212-873-4401
Monday-Saturday 10-8 Sunday 11-7.

Garden & wicker
Upper West Side

3	3	3	3
quality	style	service	value

The Edge: Indian wicker furniture and fabrics. Store features Indian furniture and a large selection of Indian fabrics made into bedspreads and duvets. Also fabrics sold as piece goods. Prices for fine fabric bedding range from $500 to $1,200.

Claycraft

101 West 28th Street
between 6th and 7th Avenues
New York, NY 10001
212-242-2903. Fax 212-989-0844
Weekdays 8-4.

Garden & wicker
Midtown West

The Edge: Large selection of planters, garden ornaments and pottery.

Deutsch Wicker Furniture
31 East 32nd Street
between Madison and Park Avenues
New York, NY 10016
212-683-8746
Weekdays 9-5:30 Saturday 10:30-3:30.

Garden & wicker
Gramercy Pk/Murray Hill

quality style service value

The Edge: Unbelievable selection of wicker furniture. For 30 years has featured wicker furniture. A huge inventory, over 6,000 pieces with styles from Victorian to contemporary, imported from Hong Kong, Indonesia, Italy and the Philippines.

Farm & Garden Nursery
2 Avenue of the Americas
near White Street
New York, NY 10013
212-431-3577. Fax 212-431-4162
Tuesday-Sunday 9-6 Spring Mondays 9-6.

Garden & wicker
SoHo/TriBeCa

The Edge: Suburban nursery in the city. Fully stocked with shrubs, plants, soil, gardening gloves, equipment, etc. Features both indoor and outdoor plants.

Gazebo
114 East 57th Street
between Park and Lexington Avenues
New York, NY 10022
212-832-7077
Monday-Saturday 10-7 Sunday noon-6.

Garden & wicker
Midtown East

quality style service value

The Edge: Pricey but gorgeous quilts and wicker furniture. Features fine antique and reproduction white and natural wicker furniture and accessories. A large collection of handmade patchwork quilts complement the furniture. Most are new, but made from traditional quilting patterns. The small selection of antique quilts is first-rate. Gift items include floral painted china, girls' smocked dresses, pastel rag rugs and more. Dazzling handmade Christmas ornaments during the season.

"Spanking clean, nice displays."

Horticultural Society of New York
128 West 58th Street
between 6th and 7th Avenues
New York, NY 10019
212-757-0915. Fax 212-246-1207
Weekdays 10-6.

Garden & wicker
Midtown West

quality style service value

The Edge: A small greenhouse in the city. Greenhouse is filled with plants, bulbs and books that are for sale. Frequent classes and lectures. Undertakes community projects for the city. Sponsors the New York Flower Show. Their huge library is open to the public.

"Plants at low prices."

Irreplaceable Artifacts

14 2nd Avenue
at Houston Street
New York, NY 10003
212-777-2900. Fax 212-780-0642
Weekdays 10-6 weekends 11-5.

Garden & wicker
Flatiron/East Village

quality style service value

The Edge: Huge selection of one-of-a-kind accessories salvaged from old buildings. You'll likely find antique bathroom fixtures, antique cast-iron garden benches, chairs, doors, fountains, gates, hardware in brass, copper and crystal, stained glass windows, mantels and urns. Also sells new aluminum chairs made from the original Victorian molds. No credit cards.

Lexington Gardens

1011 Lexington Avenue
near 72nd Street
New York, NY 10021
212-861-4390. Fax 212-988-0943
Monday-Friday 10-6 Saturday 11-5.

Garden & wicker
Upper East Side

quality style service value

The Edge: Fabulous dried arrangements. Antique and new garden furniture and accessories, plus English-style dried flower arrangements and garden books. At Christmas, outstanding hand-decorated angels and miniature Christmas trees. In addition, find mundane gardening equipment, including hoes, rakes, gloves, clippers and watering cans

New York Botanical Garden's Shop

200 Southern Boulevard
near 200th Street
Bronx, NY 10458
718-817-8723. Fax 718-817-8734
Tuesday-Sunday: fall and winter 10-4
spring 10-5 summer 11-5

Garden & wicker
Bronx

quality style service value

The Edge: Call the Bronx for great gardening advice. The shop in Manhattan is now regrettably closed while they look for a new location. We list it to remind you that you can call the New York Botanical Garden for their wonderful plant information service (718-817-8681) which offers advice on any problem, including how to save annuals.

"Got great, detailed advice on how to winter the potted geraniums at my weekend house." "Very helpful and polite."

Pimlico Way

1028 Lexington Avenue
near 73rd Street
New York, NY 10021
212-439-7855
Monday-Saturday 10-5. Closed Saturday in summer.

Garden & wicker
Upper East Side

quality style service value

The Edge: A large selection of faux bamboo furniture. Small-scale Victorian antique furniture and accessories, including fire tools. A large selection of faux bamboo furniture. Accessories include trays, brass candlesticks, vases and picture frames (silver and shells).

Treillage Ltd.
418 East 75th Street
between 1st and York Avenues
New York, NY 10021
212-535-2288
Monday-Saturday 10-5. Closed Saturday July and August.

Garden & wicker
Upper East Side

quality style service value

The Edge: Stocked with unique antique garden furniture and objects. Features antique and reproduction Victorian garden furniture. Also the basics: very attractive terra-cotta pots as well as birdhouses, gardening aprons, gloves, plant markers, pottery, tools and watering cans. Unusual pieces. Expensive.

Wicker Garden
1318 Madison Avenue
between 93rd and 94th Streets
New York, NY 10128
212-410-7000. Fax 212-410-6609
Monday-Saturday 10-6.

Garden & wicker
Upper East Side

quality style service value

The Edge: Broad selection of very beautiful wicker furniture. Incredibly expensive, antique white and natural wicker furniture in perfect condition. Wicker chairs from $300 to $5,000. A large selection of linens upstairs, some antique and others that look antique. Deluxe.

"Expensive."

A.F. Supply Corporation
22 West 21st Street
between 5th and 6th Avenues
New York, NY 10010
212-243-5400. Fax 212-243-2403
Weekdays 8-5 and by appointment.

Hardware & fixtures
Gramercy Pk/Murray Hill

quality style service value

The Edge: Luxury bathroom fixtures. Full line of luxury bathroom fixtures and hardware. Line ranges from toilets to saunas and spas. Over 100 American and Japanese lines. Decorator discount possible to 30%.

American Steel Window Service
108 West 17th Street
between 6th and 7th Avenues
New York, NY 10011
212-242-8131. Fax 212-924-8536
Weekdays 7:30-4:30.

Hardware & fixtures
Chelsea

The Edge: Vintage window hardware to order. Bring in a piece of hardware and they'll either match it from their large stock of vintage pieces, supply a reproduction or make a new piece. No credit cards.

Brookstone Company

18 Fulton Street
South Street Seaport
New York, NY 10038
212-344-8108
Monday-Saturday 10-7 Sunday noon-6.

Hardware & fixtures
Lower Manhattan

quality style service value

The Edge: Unique fun gadgetry gifts. Here necessities include items from foot massagers to garden hoses, hammocks and more.

"Terrific, fun store." "Interesting products." "Fun to browse—good values"

Country Floors

15 East 16th Street
near 5th Avenue and Union Square
New York, NY 10003
212-627-8300. Fax 212-627-7742
Monday-Wednesday Friday 9-6 Thursday 9-8 Saturday 9-5.
Closed Saturday July and August.

Hardware & fixtures
Flatiron/East Village

quality style service value

The Edge: Designer ceramic tiles. Features a full range of designer patterns from plain to richly patterned and from every tile-producing country. Wonderful selection.

"High-priced, but my only source for what I purchased." "Stunning store."

Eigen Plumbing Supply

236 West 17th Street
between 7th and 8th Avenues
New York, NY 10011
212-255-1200. Fax 212-691-9882
Weekdays 6:30-4:30.

Hardware & fixtures
Chelsea

The Edge: Where your super probably shops! A full range of plumbing supplies. Although professionals buy at Eigen, their staff can help you with your bathroom and kitchen problems. Eigen has the full American Standard showroom on-site. Telephone orders for customers who purchase with credit cards only.

Garrett Wade

161 Avenue of the Americas
near Spring Street
New York, NY 10013
212-807-1155. Fax 800-566-9525
Weekdays 9-5:30 Saturday 10-3.

Hardware & fixtures
SoHo/TriBeCa

The Edge: Tools and hardware that can't be found anywhere else. Tools and hardware from around the world. Helpful staff. The catalog is over 200 pages! Catalog describes in detail the piece's function and advantages. Tools priced from $20 to $2,500 (for table saws).

George Taylor Specialties Company

100 Hudson Street
near Franklin Street
New York, NY 10013
212-226-5369. Fax 212-274-9487
Monday-Wednesday 7:30-5 Thursday 7:30-7 Friday 7:30-4.

Hardware & fixtures
SoHo/TriBeCa

The Edge: Stocks over 50,000 pieces of obsolete plumbing replacement parts or will make one to order. Specialties are antique hardware and bathroom fixtures and accessories in traditional styles. If none in stock is suitable they'll manufacture a comparable part in their machine shop. If you can't get it here, it's unlikely you'll find it elsewhere. Decorator discounts to 25%.

Hammacher Schlemmer

147 East 57th Street
between Lexington and 3rd Avenues
New York, NY 10022
212-421-9000. Fax 212-644-3875
Monday-Saturday 10-6.

Hardware & fixtures
Midtown East

5	4	4	3
quality	style	service	value

The Edge: Strange gadgets galore. Since 1848. Offers a hard-to-categorize range. Includes all-in-one beach chair and carry cart, exercise equipment, luggage, miniature TV golf game, saunas and much, much more.

"Fun, but no longer unique." "A favorite place and a great catalog too."

Hastings

230 Park Avenue South
near 19th Street
New York, NY 10003
212-674-9700. Fax 212-673-8083
Weekdays 9:30-5:30 Saturday 10-5.

Hardware & fixtures
Flatiron/East Village

4	4	4	4
quality	style	service	value

The Edge: High-style sleek kitchen and bathroom appliances and fixtures. Italian modern lines favored. Shop features ceramic tiles, mosaics, stones, shower/tub enclosures and accessories. Designers are available to redo bathrooms and kitchens. Discounter.

Hold Everything

1311 2nd Avenue
near 69th Street
New York, NY 10021
212-535-9446
Weekdays 10-8 Saturday 10-7 Sunday noon-6.

Hardware & fixtures
Upper East Side

3	3	3	3
quality	style	service	value

The Edge: Specializes in space savers. Another division of Pottery Barn and Williams-Sonoma. Space savers include containers, shelving and other gadgets for the home.

Howard Kaplan Bath Shop
827 Broadway
near 12th Street
New York, NY 10003
212-674-1000. Fax 212-228-7204
Weekdays 9-6.

Hardware & fixtures
Flatiron/East Village

3 3 4 3
quality style service value

The Edge: Antiques and reproductions of 18th- to 20th-century French and English bathroom furnishings. From necessities like bathtubs and sinks to accessories such as soap dishes and hardware. Sinks to $30,000!

"No other shop has what they have."

Ideal Tile of Manhattan
405 East 51st Street
near 1st Avenue
New York, NY 10022
212-759-2339. Fax 212-826-0391
Weekdays 9-5 Saturday 10-5.

Hardware & fixtures
Midtown East

4 4 3 4
quality style service value

The Edge: Specializes in kitchen and bathroom tiles and counter tops. They feature ceramic, porcelain, marble, granite and terra-cotta tiles from Italy, Spain and Portugal. Two designers on staff. Hand-painted pottery, platters and vases. Not related to the West Side store.

"Excellent materials."

Ideal Tile of Manhattan West
2048 Broadway
near 70th Street
New York, NY 10023
212-799-3600
Monday-Wednesday Friday 10-5:30
Thursday 10-7 Saturday 10-5.

Hardware & fixtures
Upper West Side

4 4 3 4
quality style service value

The Edge: Tiles for your kitchen and bathroom. Find a wide variety of tiles, marble and granite from Italy, Portugal, Spain and other places.

Janovic Plaza
215 7th Avenue
near 23rd Street
New York, NY 10011
212-645-5454
Weekdays 7:30-6:30 Saturday 9-6 Sunday 11-5.

Hardware & fixtures
Chelsea

4 4 4 4
quality style service value

The Edge: Everything in moderately priced paper and paint. Find an enormous range of paints, wallpaper and window treatments. Knowledgeable and helpful staff. Custom paint colors of course.

161 Avenue of the Americas
near Mulberry Street/10013
212-627-1100. Fax 212-924-7641
Weekdays 7:30-6:30 Saturday 9-6 Sunday 11-5.

SoHo/TriBeCa

771 9th Avenue
near 52nd Street/10019
212-245-3241
Weekdays 7:30-6:30 Saturday 8-5:45.

Midtown West

1150 3rd Avenue
near 67th Street/10021
212-772-1400. Fax 212-249-0608
Weekdays 7:30-6:30 Saturday 8-5:45 Sunday 11-5.

Upper East Side

159 West 72nd Street
near Broadway/10023
212-595-2500. Fax 212-724-7846
Monday-Wednesday Friday 7:30-6:30 Thursday 7:30-8 Saturday 9-6 Sunday 11-5.

Upper West Side

Kraft Hardware

306 East 61st Street
between 1st and 2nd Avenues
New York, NY 10021
212-838-2214. Fax 212-449-254
Weekdays 9-5.

Hardware & fixtures
Upper East Side

5	4	3	4
quality	style	service	value

The Edge: Mostly hardware basics. At 12,000 square feet, the city's largest hardware store. You'll find the basics: nails and screws, hand and power tools, plumbing and electrical supplies, paints and brushes, decorative hardware, small appliances and cleaning supplies. Also some upscale shower enclosures, sinks, toilets and tubs. The majority of their customers are contractors and building maintenance staff and they seem to prefer professionals rather than the less experienced customer.

Nemo Tiles Company

48 East 21st Street
near Park Avenue South
New York, NY 10010
212-505-0009. Fax 212-777-9053
Weekdays 9:30-5:45 Saturday 11-4:45.

Hardware & fixtures
Gramercy Pk/Murray Hill

The Edge: Vast tile selection. Showroom carries domestic and imported ceramic and marble tiles. Features top designers of hand-painted tiles from all over the world. Fixtures, hardware and bathroom accessories in fine materials and styles complement the tiles.

P.E. Guerin

23 Jane Street
near Greenwich Street
New York, NY 10014
212-243-5270
By appointment. Closed first two weeks in July.

Hardware & fixtures
Greenwich Village

5	5	3	4
quality	style	service	value

The Edge: Handmade decorative hardware. Stocks handmade decorative hardware/fixtures in brass and bronze. Will copy or reproduce hardware. Priced from $9 per piece to tens of thousands of dollars. Reproduction jobs can be small. No credit cards.

"Expensive but worth it."

Pintchik
278 3rd Avenue
near 22nd Street
New York, NY 10010
212-982-6600. Fax 212-598-9046
Weekdays 8:30-6:50 Saturday 9-5:50 Sunday 11-6.

Hardware & fixtures
Gramercy Pk/Murray Hill

The Edge: A home-decorating center. Full range of paints and wallpapers. Also mirrors and thousands of appliances.

Putname Rolling Ladder Company
32 Howard Street
near Broadway
New York, NY 10013
212-226-5147. Fax 212-941-1836
Weekdays 8-4:30.

Hardware & fixtures
SoHo/TriBeCa

The Edge: Ladders in all shapes and sizes. Since 1905 they have been known for their custom-made ladders, including rolling library ladders (favored in grand old homes), in any hardwood finish. They also manufacture extension ladders, library carts, step stools and steel ladders for industry, window cleaning and home use. No credit cards.

Quarry Tile Marble and Granite, Inc.
128 East 32nd Street
between Park and Lexington Avenues
New York, NY 10016
212-679-2559. Fax 212-889-1364
Weekdays 9-5 Saturday 10-3. Closed Saturday July and August.

Hardware & fixtures
Gramercy Pk/Murray Hill

The Edge: High-end kitchen and bathroom tiles and marbles from around the world. Find wallpaper, accessories and fixtures to go with the marble and tile line. Also granite, limestone and slate. Priced from $4 to $45 per square foot.

Sepco Industries
491 Wortman Avenue
near Linden Boulevard
Brooklyn, NY 11208
718-257-2800. Fax 718-257-2144
Weekdays 9-5.

Hardware & fixtures
Brooklyn

The Edge: Wholesale fine hardware and bath accessories. Supplier of bath and kitchen faucets, fine hardware and bath accessories. Modern but somewhat ornate styling. Lots of gilded options. Up to 50% off retail.

Sherle Wagner International
60 East 57th Street
near Madison Avenue
New York, NY 10022
212-758-3300. Fax 212-207-8010

Hardware & fixtures
Midtown East

3	4	3	3
quality	style	service	value

Weekdays 9:15-5.

The Edge: Bathroom fixtures made in semiprecious materials with suitable hardware. Top-of-the-line bathroom fixtures offered in semiprecious stones with hand-painted porcelain bowls and crystal, marble and gold-plated hardware. Fixtures in every possible material. Even the toilet bowls are decorated. Simple pedestal sinks without fixtures start at $4,000. No credit cards. Deluxe.

Simon's Hardware

421 3rd Avenue
near 29th Street
New York, NY 10016
212-532-9220. Fax 212-725-3609
Monday-Wednesday Friday 8-5:30
Thursday 8-7 Saturday 10-6.

Hardware & fixtures
Gramercy Pk/Murray Hill

4	4	3	4
quality	style	service	value

The Edge: Everyday hardware as well as custom-made decorative fixtures. Styles range from antique brass reproductions to modern chrome and stainless steel. Offers a 20% discount to decorators.

"Madhouse, but great." Unique assortment of handles and knobs." "Great fun, especially the clearance area."

Solar Antique Tiles

971 1st Avenue
near 54th Street
New York, NY 10022
212-755-2403. Fax 212-980-2649
By appointment.

Hardware & fixtures
Midtown East

The Edge: Unique antique tiles from the 14th-century. Tiles from the 14th-century to the 1920s. Original antique tiles and a reproduction line. Wide range of patterns from Dutch to Turkish. From $16 to $100 per tile. No credit cards.

Terra Verde Trading Company

120 Wooster Street
near Prince Street
New York, NY 10012
212-925-4533. Fax 212-925-4540
Monday-Saturday 11-7 Sunday noon-6.

Hardware & fixtures
SoHo/TriBeCa

4	4	4	4
quality	style	service	value

The Edge: An ecological department store. Restricted to environmentally sound home and office products. Items sold include cleaning supplies and energy-saving appliances.

Tiles - A Refined Selection

42 West 15th Street
between 5th and 6th Avenues
New York, NY 10011
212-255-4450. Fax 212-727-3851
Monday-Wednesday Friday 9:30-6 Thursday 9:30-8 Saturday 10-5.

Hardware & fixtures
Chelsea

Closed Saturday June- August.

The Edge: Large range of tiles. Quality glass tiles, granite, handmade tiles, limestone, marble, molded tiles, mosaics and slate. High-end tiles favored by decorators but available to all. Prices $3 per square foot and up. Catalog for $20. No credit cards.

Waterworks

237 East 58th Street
between 2nd and 3rd Avenues
New York, NY 10022
212-371-9266. Fax 212-371-9263
Weekdays 9-5:30.

Hardware & fixtures
Midtown East

5	5	3	3
quality	style	service	value

The Edge: English designer bathroom and kitchen fixtures and tiles. Specializes in traditional bathroom and kitchen fixtures, designer ceramic tiles, granite and marble. Showroom has full line on display. Architects and designers are major customers, but available to the public. Also branches in Connecticut—Danbury, Greenwich, Westport.

Cobblestones

314 East 9th Street
between 1st and 2nd Avenues
New York, NY 10003
212-673-5372
Tuesday-Saturday noon-7 Sunday noon-5.

Kitchen
Flatiron/East Village

The Edge: Unique vintage collectibles. Vintage handbags, glassware and kitchenware, plus linens (napkins, tablecloths and 1930s and 1940s printed fruit and flower kitchen towels). No delivery.

Kitschen

380 Bleecker Street
near Christopher Street
New York, NY 10014
212-727-0430. Fax 212-627-0730
Daily 1-8.

Kitchen
Greenwich Village

The Edge: Wonderful old-fashioned kitchen wares. From linens to cupboards, plus the basics. No delivery.

Lechter's

901 Avenue of the Americas
near 33rd Street
New York, NY 10001
212-268-7303
Monday-Saturday 10-8 Sunday 11-6.

Kitchen
Midtown West

3	3	3	4
quality	style	service	value

The Edge: Low-end basic housewares. Basic source for moderately priced (not discounted) kitchenware.

"Basic household gadgets." "Low-end versions of housewares." "Trendy items."

55 East 8th Street
near Mercer Street/10003
212-505-0576
Monday-Wednesday 9:30-9 Thursday-Saturday 9:30-10 Sunday 10:30-7:30.

Flatiron/East Village

536 Broadway
near Spring Street/10012
212-274-0890
Monday-Saturday 9:30-8:30 Sunday 11-7.

SoHo/TriBeCa

401 Avenue of the Americas
near 8th Street/10014
212-741-0016
Monday-Wednesday 9-8:30 Thursday-Saturday 10-10 Sunday 11-6:30.

Greenwich Village

475 5th Avenue
near 41st Street/10017
212-889-4754
Weekdays 8-8 Saturday 9-7 Sunday 11-6.

Midtown East

250 West 57th Street
near Broadway/10019
212-956-7290
Weekdays 8-8 Saturday 10-8 Sunday 11-7.

Midtown West

1198 3rd Avenue
near 69th Street/10021
212-744-1427
Weekdays 8-8 Saturday 8:30-8 Sunday 11-6.

Upper East Side

2141 Broadway
near 75th Street/10023
212-580-1610
Weekdays 9-9 Saturday 9-9:30 Sunday 11-7.

Upper West Side

2503 Broadway
near 93rd Street/10025
212-864-5464
Monday-Thursday 10-9 Friday Saturday 10-9:30 Sunday 11-6.

Upper West Side

2875 Broadway
between 111th and 112th Streets/10025
212-864-5591
Monday-Saturday 10-9 Sunday 11-7.

Upper West Side

1504 3rd Avenue
near 85th Street/10028
212-988-3730
Monday-Saturday 10-9 Sunday 11-7.

Upper East Side

Five World Trade Center
near Liberty Street (inside mall) /10048

Lower Manhattan

212-432-0844
Weekdays 7-8 Saturday 10-6 Sunday 11-5.

10 West 34th Street   **Midtown West**
between 5th and 6th Avenues/10118
212-564-3226
Weekdays 8-9 Saturday 9-9 Sunday 11-6.

60 East 42nd Street   **Midtown West**
near Madison Avenue/10165
212-682-8476
Weekdays 8-8 Saturday 9-5 Sunday 11-5.

Lee Sam Kitchen & Bath   **Kitchen**
124 7th Avenue   **Chelsea**
near 18th Street
New York, NY 10011
212-243-6482. Fax 212-243-6482
Monday-Wednesday Friday 9:30-6 Thursday 9:30-8 Saturday noon-5.

The Edge: One-stop shopping for kitchen and bathroom fixtures. All major brands of
bathroom and kitchen hardware and fixtures. Lots of in-stock cabinets. Very large selection.

Pantry & Hearth   **Kitchen**
121 East 35th Street   **Gramercy Pk/Murray Hill**
near Lexington Avenue
New York, NY 10016
212-889-0026. Fax 212-545-0758
By appointment.

The Edge: Unique early American hearth and home accessories and furniture. Features early
American furniture and related hearth and home accessories, including folk art and kitchen
implements. Mostly 18th and 19th-century, with some rare Pilgrim period pieces. No credit cards.

Platypus   **Kitchen**
126 Spring Street   **SoHo/TriBeCa**
near Greene Street
New York, NY 10013
212-219-3919
Monday-Saturday 11-6 Sunday noon-6.

quality style service value

The Edge: Eclectic household items. Hard to describe the themes—home accessories,
kitchenware, some furniture, plus chocolates and coffees. Kitchenware (china, cutlery, glassware
and equipment) from around the world. The tableware, mostly from Italy and France, has a chunky
country feel.

"Great stuff at high prices." "Great coffee!"

Two World Financial Center   **Lower Manhattan**
225 Liberty Street/100281
212-786-0577
Weekdays 10-7 Saturday 11-6 Sunday noon-5.

Grand Brass

221 Grand Street
near Chatham Square
New York, NY 10013
212-226-2567. Fax 212-226-2573
Tuesday Wednesday Friday Saturday 8-5 Thursday 8-8.

Light fixtures
SoHo/TriBeCa

4 · 3 4
quality style service value

The Edge: Parts to be found nowhere else. A good source for lamp replacement parts from chandelier crystals to glass globes. Stocks hundreds of parts and fixtures. Where the contractors go.

"Take a number, join the crowd. A unique resource."

Jerrystyle

380 Lafayette Street, Suite 204
near 4th Street
New York, NY 10003
212-353-9480. Fax 212-353-5006
Tuesday-Friday 11-6 Saturday 11-5.

Light fixtures
Flatiron/East Village

3 4 3 3
quality style service value

The Edge: All forms of lighting. Unique designs favoring period styles from the 1930s to contemporary lighting fixtures. All the lighting is made by hand and requires six weeks for delivery. From $300 to $3,000.

Just Bulbs

936 Broadway
near 22nd Street
New York, NY 10010
212-228-7820. Fax 212-529-3307
Monday-Wednesday Friday 9-6 Thursday 9-7
Saturday 10-6 Sunday noon-5.

Light fixtures
Gramercy Pk/Murray Hill

5 4 4 3
quality style service value

The Edge: Any and every kind of light bulbs under the sun. The source for electric lights (American and European voltage) in dozens of hues. Priced from $5 to $30.

"Helpful—huge selection." "Excellent and knowledgeable regarding unusual light bulbs."

Lee's Studio

1755 Broadway
near 56th Street
New York, NY 10019
212-247-0110. Fax 212-247-0507
Weekdays 9-7 Saturday 9:30-6:30 Sunday noon-5:30.

Light fixtures
Midtown West

4 4 4 3
quality style service value

The Edge: Wonderful contemporary designer lighting. Track and recessed lighting, halogen lamps, outdoor landscape fixtures, plus floor, table and desk lamps and sconces. Reproductions of art deco and retro classics. Installation and repair services. Priced from $100 to thousands of dollars. Catalog $7.

"Gorgeous modern lamps. East Side store is cramped." "Great selection."

1069 3rd Avenue

Upper East Side

near 63rd Street/10021
212-371-1122. Fax 212-826-1493
Weekdays 10-6:30 Saturday 9:30-6:30 Sunday noon-5:30.

Let There Be Neon City, Inc.

Light fixtures

38 White Street
near Church Street
New York, NY 10013
212-226-4883. Fax 212-431-6731
Weekdays 8:30-5:30.

SoHo/TriBeCa

5	4	5	4
quality	style	service	value

The Edge: Custom neon lighting and signs. Allow two weeks to design and produce neon lighting.

Lightforms

Light fixtures

168 8th Avenue
near 18th Street
New York, NY 10011
212-255-4664. Fax 212-627-7678
Weekdays 11-7 Saturday 10-6
Sunday noon-5 (1-5 in summer).

Chelsea

4	3	3	3
quality	style	service	value

The Edge: American and European lighting designs. Many styles, including overhead track lighting, traditional table lamps, floor lamps and sconces. Prices on lamps range mostly from $59 to $300, but can go to the thousands of dollars.

"Good neighborhood resource."

509 Amsterdam Avenue

Upper West Side

near 85th Street/10024
212-875-0407. Fax 212-627-7678

Lighting By Gregory

Light fixtures

158 and 160 Bowery
near Delancey Street
New York, NY 10012
212-226-1276. Fax 212-226-2705
Daily 9-5:30.

SoHo/TriBeCa

4	2	3	4
quality	style	service	value

The Edge: Large selection of traditional and contemporary lighting. Two stores. Number 158 specializes in traditional lighting styles and number 160 mixes traditional with contemporary. They carry a large selection of well-known brands and will order any brand for you (even if they don't carry it) at close to wholesale prices. Priced from $10 to $3,000. 20% off.

"Commercial stock."

Lighting Plus

Light fixtures

676 Broadway
near Great Jones Street
New York, NY 10012

SoHo/TriBeCa

212-979-2000. Fax 212-979-2032
Monday-Saturday 10-7 Sunday 11-7.

The Edge: Best for repairs. Sells anything connected with electricity. Will repair lighting fixtures if they have the materials. No delivery.

Marvin Alexander

315 East 62nd Street
near 2nd Avenue
New York, NY 10021
212-838-2320. Fax 212-759-0173
Weekdays 9-5.

Light fixtures
Upper East Side

5	5	5	3
quality	style	service	value

The Edge: Breathtaking unique antique lighting treatments. Features distinctive 18th- to early 20th-century one-of-a-kind lighting fixtures. Chandeliers and sconces priced from $600 to $60,000. No credit cards. Deluxe.

Nestle

151 East 57th Street
near 3rd Avenue
New York, NY 10022
212-755-0515
Weekdays 9-5.

Light fixtures
Midtown East

5	5	5	4
quality	style	service	value

The Edge: Simply fabulous 18th- and 19th-century French crystal chandeliers and candelabra. Mostly high-end elaborate French crystal chandeliers and candelabra. Lots of very large, statement, exceptional, breathtaking museum-quality pieces. Deluxe.

"Absolutely spectacular."

Price Glover

59 East 79th Street, 3rd Floor
near Madison Avenue
New York, NY 10021
212-772-1740. Fax 212-772-1962
Weekdays 10-5.

Light fixtures
Upper East Side

5	5	5	4
quality	style	service	value

The Edge: Antique and reproduction 18th- and 19th-century lighting devices. Lighting includes sconces (from $500), chandeliers ($4,000 to $6,500) and lanterns ($1,000 to $2,500). Also hurricane shades. No credit cards.

Rosetta Electric Company

21 West 46th Street
between 5th and 6th Avenues
New York, NY 10036
212-719-4381. Fax 212-719-5257
Weekdays 9-6 Saturday 9-5.

Light fixtures
Midtown West

4	2	4	3
quality	style	service	value

The Edge: Good discounts on top-name lighting fixtures. Brands include Kovacs, Lightolier and Stiffel. Special orders are taken; delivery service is available. To facilitate installations, a small inventory of electrical supplies. Priced from $2 to $5,000. 10% off.

"Appreciate their downtown location." "Terrific values." Good for hard-to-find parts."

Tudor Electrical Supply

222 East 46 Street
between 2nd and 3rd Avenues
New York, NY 10017
212-867-7550. Fax 212-867-7569
Monday-Thursday 8:30-5 Friday 8:30-4:30.

Light fixtures
Midtown East

5	3	4	5
quality	style	service	value

The Edge: Broad range of discounted electrical supplies. Features a wide variety of light bulbs, lighting fixtures and electrical supplies.

Uplift, Inc.

506 Hudson Street
between Christopher and West 10th Streets
New York, NY 10014
212-929-3632. Fax 212-929-3632
Daily noon-8.

Light fixtures
Greenwich Village

The Edge: Unique art deco period lighting fixtures. Features a large collection of lighting fixtures from the 1930s, art deco and Victorian era. Originals and reproductions all in working order. Will restore lighting fixtures and/or sell lamp parts. Priced from $39 to $2,400.

Ad Hoc Softwares

410 West Broadway
near Spring Street
New York, NY 10012
212-925-2652. Fax 212-941-6910
Monday-Saturday 11-7 Sunday 11:30-6.

Linens
SoHo/TriBeCa

5	5	4	4
quality	style	service	value

The Edge: Household items with a high-tech style softened by traditional linens. Shop carries at-home wear, bath accessories, housewares, metal furniture and table-top items (china and linens). Wonderful taste. Higher-end items.

E. Braun & Company

717 Madison Avenue
near 63rd Street
New York, NY 10021
212-838-0650. Fax 212-832-5640
Monday-Saturday 10-6.
Closed Saturday July and August.

Linens
Upper East Side

5	5	4	4
quality	style	service	value

The Edge: Exquisite Irish bed and table linens. Most are embroidered and lace trimmed in pastels or whites. Wonderful baby things from layettes to hand-embroidered and smocked clothing and hand-knit sweaters. Unique custom linens priced from $500 to $1,000.

"Provided practical suggestions to give me the look I wanted, more reasonably than I would have done it."

Frette

799 Madison Avenue
near 67rd Street
New York, NY 10021
212-988-5221. Fax 212-988-5257
Weekdays 10-6 Saturday 10-6.

Linens
Upper East Side

| 5 | 5 | 2 | 3 |
| quality | style | service | value |

The Edge: Fine Italian linens and lingerie. Expensive (but not as expensive as the French linens at Porthault) linens priced from $800 to $2,000 for sets. Also luxurious lingerie. Deluxe.

"Good value on mid-priced to expensive linens."

Harris Levy

278 Grand Street
near Eldridge Street
New York, NY 10002
212-226-3102. Fax 212-334-9360
Sunday-Thursday 9-5 Friday 9-3:30.

Linens
Lower East Side/Chinatown

| 4 | 3 | 2 | 4 |
| quality | style | service | value |

The Edge: Quality bed, bath and table linens and accessories discounted. Features basic to more expensive items. Can charge and send anywhere. Will monogram. 20% off.

"Prices equivalent to Bloomingdale's sales."

J. Schachter

5 Cook Street
near Graham Avenue
Brooklyn, NY 11206
718-384-2732. Fax 718-384-7634
Monday-Thursday 9-5 Friday and Sunday by appointment.

Linens
Brooklyn

The Edge: Will custom-make or adjust ready-made linens. Recently moved to Williamsburg, Brooklyn, after generations on the Lower East Side. Adjustments include adding appliqués, embroidery lace and monogramming. Will restuff, mend and sew cushions to look like new. Works in cotton, lambs wool and polyester. Can make quilts in all sizes and in 20 different patterns. Discounter.

Laura Fisher/Antique Quilts & Americana

1050 2nd Avenue
near 55th Street
New York, NY 10022
212-838-2596. Fax 212-355-4403
Monday-Saturday 11-6 or by appointment.

Linens
Midtown East

| 5 | 5 | 3 | 4 |
| quality | style | service | value |

The Edge: Gorgeous early American quilts. Find antique quilts, hand-knit bedspreads, hooked rugs, European bedspreads, woolen coverlets and more. Coverings and rugs are available in a wide range of colors, patterns and sizes. Most items from early 1800s to the 1940s. Prices into the thousands of dollars.

"Excellent collection."

Laytner's Linen and Home Center

2270 Broadway
near 81st Street
New York, NY 10024
212-724-0180. Fax 212-769-0620
Weekdays 10-7:30 Saturday 10-6:30 Sunday noon-6.

Linens
Upper West Side

quality	style	service	value
4	5	3	4

The Edge: A large selection of home furnishings in stock or available from catalogs. A wide selection of designer bed, bath and table linens. A smaller Bed, Bath and Beyond. Top brands at retail, not discounted prices.

"Beautiful inventory." "Attentive sales staff."

237 East 86th Street
between 2nd and 3rd Avenues/10028
212-996-4439

Upper East Side

Leron

750 Madison Avenue
near 65th Street
New York, NY 10021
212-753-6700. Fax 212-249-3610
Weekdays 10-6 Saturday 10-5.
Closed Saturday July and August.

Linens
Upper East Side

quality	style	service	value
5	4	4	4

The Edge: Hand-sewn, custom-made linens and lace lingerie. Linens and lingerie, often embroidered. Can order custom-designed linens and towels to match a fabric pattern in your home. Table linens can be made in any size and shape with hand lacework or other trims. Children's terry robes appliquéed with story-book characters.

"Lovely old world style." "Excellent linens."

Porthault

18 East 69th Street
near Madison Avenue
New York, NY 10021
212-688-1660. Fax 212-772-8450
Monday-Friday 10-5:30 Saturday 11-6.

Linens
Upper East Side

quality	style	service	value
4	4	4	4

The Edge: High high-end luxurious French linens. Features table and bed linens in over 600 ready-made and custom designs in scores of colors and weaves. Signature prints in printed terry towels, decorative accessories, including trays, table linens, wastebaskets, tissue-box covers, drawer liners and room sprays. A set of standard queen-size sheets and two pillow cases are priced from $1,860 (printed patterns) to $3,000 (for embroidered sets), so go in January for the half-price sale! Also smocked dresses, rompers, shirts and hooded terrycloth robes for children. Deluxe.

"Beautiful, expensive!" Overpriced, but unusually fine quality." "What cost, but what quality."

Pratesi

829 Madison Avenue
near 69th Street
New York, NY 10021
212-288-2315. Fax 212-628-4038
Monday-Saturday 10-6.

Linens
Upper East Side

5	5	4	3
quality	style	service	value

The Edge: Italian top-of-the-line beautiful linens. Crafted from the finest fabrics in classic styles. Twice yearly sales. A standard set of queen-size sheets and two pillow cases priced from $1,080 to several thousand dollars. Deluxe.

"Expensive but worth the price." "So Italian, so superior."

Schweitzer Linens

1132 Madison Avenue
near 84th Street
New York, NY 10028
212-249-8361. Fax 212-737-6328
Monday-Saturday 10-6.

Linens
Upper East Side

5	4	4	4
quality	style	service	value

The Edge: Neighborhood shop offering standard linens. Quality standard name brands in bed, bath and table linens, including Palace Royale and Wamsutta at a modest discount. Also items from Italy, France, Ireland and Portugal made exclusively for the store. Towels can be made up in just about any color combination. Monogramming available. No delivery.

Trouvaille Francaise

New York, NY
212-737-6015
By appointment.

Linens
Upper East Side

The Edge: Imported European bed linens. This tiny shop is on the top floor of the owner's brownstone. She gives out the address when you get an appointment. Features unique wedding gifts, mostly elegant antique bed linens and new bed linens imported from France and England. Also Victorian white adult and children's clothing. No credit cards. No delivery.

Blumka

101 East 81st Street
near Lexington Avenue
New York, NY 10028
212-734-3222. Fax 212-249-1087
By appointment.

Medieval & Renaissance
Upper East Side

4	4	4	4
quality	style	service	value

The Edge: Medieval focus. Medieval art and sculpture alongside the 15th- to early 17th-century furniture. Mostly walnut wood tables, medieval and Renaissance tapestries, Venetian glass goblets and more. No credit cards.

"Unusual."

L'Antiquaire & the Connoisseur

36 East 73rd Street
between Madison and Park Avenues
New York, NY 10021
212-517-9176. Fax 212-988-5674
Weekdays 9-5:30.

Medieval & Renaissance
Upper East Side

quality style service value

The Edge: Museum-quality medieval and Renaissance furnishings. French, Italian and Spanish furniture, paintings and decorative accessories, including tapestries from medieval to 18th-century. Wonderful Victorian painted pieces and old master paintings. Same-day delivery depends on the customer. No credit cards. Deluxe.

"Lovely collection."

Office Furniture Heaven

22 West 19th Street
near 5th Avenue
New York, NY 10011
212-989-8600. Fax 212-727-8028
Weekdays 9-6 Saturday 9-2.

Office
Chelsea

The Edge: Used office furniture and close-outs of office furniture from top companies. Features more contemporary pieces.

Art Asia

1086 Madison Avenue
near 82nd Street
New York, NY 10028
212-249-7250
Monday-Saturday 10:30-6:30 Sunday noon-6.

Oriental
Upper East Side

4 4 4 4
quality style service value

The Edge: Small shop featuring moderately priced Asian antiques. A source for lacquerware boxes and bowls, paintings, porcelains, silk kimonos, Tanzu chests as well as contemporary Asian jewelry. Items priced from $36 to $250+ for jewelry, $2,000+ for paintings and $5,000+ for statues.

"An interesting array." "Wait for 50% off sales."

Asian House

120 West 56th Street
near Avenue of the Americas
New York, NY 10019
212-581-2294
Tuesday-Saturday 11-6 Sunday noon-5.

Oriental
Midtown West

The Edge: Asian decorative items. Since 1961, new and old porcelains, planters, vases, lamps, furniture and screens from China, Japan and Korea. Deluxe.

Chinese Porcelain Company

475 Park Avenue

Oriental
Midtown East

near 58th Street
New York, NY 10022
212-838-7744. Fax 212-838-4922
Weekdays 10-6 Saturday 11-5.
Closed Saturday July and August.

quality style service value

The Edge: Museum-quality Chinese antiques. Offers a wide range of early to 19th-century Chinese treasures, including carpets, ceramics, furniture and jade and ivory carving, lacquer, table screens and more. Deluxe.

"Fabulous items, a must-see!"

E&J Frankel Ltd.

Oriental
Upper East Side

1040 Madison Avenue
near 79th Street
New York, NY 10021
212-879-5733. Fax 212-879-1998
Monday-Saturday 10-5:30.

quality style service value

The Edge: Quality Chinese and Japanese antiques. Asian, mostly Chinese and Japanese, antiques. Edith, of E. Frankel, chaired the Department of Far Eastern Studies at the New School. Collection includes antique accessories, furniture, jewelry and paintings. Special exhibition (with catalog) annually. Jewelry from $300 to several thousand dollars and furniture easily into the thousands of dollars. Deluxe.

Flying Cranes Antiques Ltd.

Oriental
Midtown East

1050 2nd Avenue
near 55th Street
New York, NY 10022
212-223-4600. Fax 212-223-4601
Monday-Saturday 10:30-6. Closed weekends July-August.

quality style service value

The Edge: Wonderful 18th- and 19th-century Japanese artifacts. Galleries 55 and 56 at the Manhattan Art & Antiques Center. An extensive collection of quality antiques from the 18th and 19th centuries. Mostly Japanese porcelains, ivories, cloisonné and swords. Some ornate and beautiful Japanese silver.

Truly unusual beautiful pieces."

J.J. Lally & Company Oriental Art

Oriental
Midtown East

41 East 57th Street, 14th Floor
between Madison and Park Avenues
New York, NY 10022
212-371-3380. Fax 212-593-4699
Weekdays 9-5 Saturday 10-4.

The Edge: A small museum-quality collection of Chinese artifacts. Lally, formerly head of Sotheby's Chinese Art Department, specializes in early Chinese sculpture from the 5th millennium B.C. through the Song period. Some later works. Costly at $1,000 to $1 million, but items are museum quality. No credit cards. Deluxe.

Koreana Art and Antiques

Oriental
Upper East Side

963 Madison Avenue
near 75th Street
New York, NY 10021
212-249-0400. Fax 212-249-0400
Monday-Saturday 10-6.

The Edge: Korean antiques from the 18th and 19th-centuries. Since 1978, has offered antique Korean furniture and ceramics at prices from $1,000 to $20,000. No reproductions. Some pieces as early as the 13th and 14th centuries, but most from the 18th to 19th century.

Krishna Gallery of Asian Arts, Inc.

Oriental
Midtown East

153 East 57th Street
near Lexington Avenue
New York, NY 10022
212-249-1677. Fax 212-759-5812
Monday-Saturday 11-6.

The Edge: Antiques and furniture from Tibet, Nepal and India. Furniture, plus bronze and terra-cotta sculptures, Tanka (Tibetan paintings), Indian miniatures, and jewelry. Pieces from the 2nd-century B.C. to 18th-century works. Prices run $100 to $15,000.

Naga Antiques Ltd.

Oriental
Upper East Side

145 East 61st Street
near Lexington Avenue
New York, NY 10021
212-593-2788. Fax 212-308-2451
Weekdays 10-5. Closes Friday at 3 in July and August.

4	5	5	3
quality	style	service	value

The Edge: Top-of-the-line 17th- to 19th-century Japanese antiques. A large selection of art, antique furniture, fine lacquerware, rare hand-painted screens, early ceramics, dolls and unusual baskets. No credit cards.

"A beautiful shop. I wish I could afford to shop there."

Oriental Porcelain and Furniture Outlet

Oriental
SoHo/TriBeCa

255 Canal Street
near Lafayette Street
New York, NY 10013
212-941-5632. Fax 212-925-4033
Daily 10-7.

The Edge: Traditional Chinese furnishings. Expect decorative items, furniture and planters. Discounter.

Orientations Gallery Ltd.

Oriental
Upper East Side

802 Madison Avenue
between 67th and 68th Streets
New York, NY 10021
212-772-7705. Fax 212-772-9661
Monday-Saturday 11-6.

The Edge: 18th- and 19th-century Japanese decorative arts. High-quality collectibles.

Ralph M. Chait Galleries

12 East 56th Street
between Madison and 5th Avenues
New York, NY 10022
212-758-0937. Fax 212-319-0471
Monday-Saturday 10-5:30. Closed Saturday June-August.

Oriental
Midtown East

5 5 5 5
quality style service value

The Edge: Museum-quality Chinese works of art. One of the top sources for early Chinese antiques, including bronze sculpture, crystal, export silver, jade, porcelains, pottery and paintings. Priced from $1,000 to millions! Decorator discounts given "if they have a relationship with the decorator." Deluxe.

"Excellent Chinese antiques—museum quality."

Regal Collection

5 West 56th Street
near 5th Avenue
New York, NY 10019
212-582-7696. Fax 212-582-1657
Monday-Saturday 9:30-5:30. Closed Saturday July and August.

Oriental
Midtown West

The Edge: Eclectic knickknacks. 19th-century Chinese (mostly) decorative items, including antique porcelains, carved snuff bottles, rock crystal bowls and more. Priced from $100 to $100,000.

Weisbrod Chinese Art

36 East 57th Street, 3rd Floor
near Madison Avenue
New York, NY 10022
212-319-1335. Fax 212-319-1327
Weekdays 9:30-5.

Oriental
Midtown East

5 4 4 3
quality style service value

The Edge: Museum-quality classic Chinese antiques. Moved from the Carlyle Hotel to East 57th Street. Features museum-quality Oriental antiques, including jade, ancient Chinese bronzes, blue and white Chinese pottery and Han dynasty porcelains. Some of our favorite pieces include Tang dynasty unglazed pottery, 6th-century limestone reliefs and more. No credit cards. Deluxe.

America Hurrah

766 Madison Avenue, 3rd Floor
near 66 Street
New York, NY 10021
212-535-1930. Fax 212-249-9718
Tuesday-Saturday 11-6. Closed Saturday June July and August.

Quilts & quilting
Upper East Side

The Edge: Museum-quality American antique quilts. While most quilts are priced from $750 to $2,500, with some quilts $2,500 to $25,000, they're best known for their museum-quality collectible quilts at $100,000+. Lots of collectibles from the 1920s to 1940s. Also baskets, decoys, folk paintings, hooked rugs, painted furniture and weather vanes. Cleans and restores antique rugs. Deluxe.

"Couldn't be nicer people to deal with."

Susan Parrish

Quilts & quilting
Greenwich Village

390 Bleecker Street
near Perry Street
New York, NY 10014
212-645-5020
Tuesday-Saturday noon-6 or by appointment.

The Edge: Large selection of beautiful antique American quilts. This shop with its country ambience features antique Americana at affordable prices. Features American folk paintings from before 1850, antique folk art and toys. Quilts from $200 to $35,000, with the majority priced from $500 to $3,000. No delivery.

Woodard & Greenstein

Quilts & quilting
Upper East Side

5	4	4	3
quality	style	service	value

506 East 74th Street
near York Avenue
New York, NY 10021
212-794-9404. Fax 212-734-9665
Weekdays 10:30-6 Saturday 11-6.
Saturday 11-5 July and August.

The Edge: Renowned collection of early 19th-century American quilts. Hundreds of antique and museum-quality quilts. Also painted and unpainted Shaker-style furniture and antique garden furnishings from England, France and the United States. Deluxe.

"The Woodards couldn't have been nicer" (a rare comment from our researchers).

AFR (the Furniture Rental People)

Rentals
Midtown East

711 3rd Avenue
between 44th and 45th Streets
New York, NY 10017
212-867-2800. Fax 212-573-6869
Monday-Saturday 9-6.

The Edge: Home and office furniture rentals. Provides accessories, electronics and furnishings for home or office. Classic to modern styles with a three-month minimum rental. Delivery within 48 hours.

Churchill-Winchester Furniture Rentals

6 East 32nd Street
between 5th and Madison Avenues
New York, NY 10016
212-686-0444
Monday-Thursday 9-6 Friday 9-4 Sunday 11-5.

Rentals
Gramercy Pk/Murray Hill

The Edge: Rentals of traditional to contemporary furniture. Rents all household items, including furniture, housewares and appliances. Free professional decorating advice available.

International Furniture Rentals

Rentals
Midtown East

345 Park Avenue
near 51st Street
New York, NY 10022
212-421-0340. Fax 212-421-0624
Monday-Thursday 9-6 Friday 9-5:30 Saturday 10-2.

The Edge: One of the largest furniture-rental companies. Rents furniture for both the home and office. Maintains a free design service. Pulls everything together with accessories. Delivery within 48 hours.

Asia Minor Carpets, Inc.

Rugs & carpets
Midtown West

236 5th Avenue, 2nd Floor
near 28th Street
New York, NY 10001
212-447-9066. Fax 212-447-1879
Weekdays 9:30-5:30.

The Edge: Turkish flatweaves from carpets to covered furniture. Large selection of Turkish flatweaves as well as semi-antique and new carpets. A large supply of pillows made from new kilims as well as pillows made from old ones. Also furniture (benches, chairs and ottomans) covered with kilims.

Berdi Abadjian

Rugs & carpets
Midtown East

201 East 57th Street, 2nd Floor
near 3rd Avenue
New York, NY 10022
212-688-2229. Fax 212-688-2384
Weekdays 9-5.

The Edge: Quality antique carpeting. For four generations, specializing in fine-quality antique European, Persian, Turkish and Chinese carpets. No credit cards. Deluxe.

Beshar's

Rugs & carpets
Upper East Side

1513 1st Avenue
near 79th Street
New York, NY 10021
212-288-1998. Fax 212-288-3615
Monday-Wednesday Friday 10-6 Thursday 10-8
Saturday 9-4.

quality	style	service	value
5	4	5	3

The Edge: Quality antique and new Oriental rugs. Offering antique and new Oriental and European rugs since 1898 at prices from $800 to $80,000. Specializes in Aubussons, Chinese, Persian and French needlepoint. Now some antique accessories also. Also rug cleaning and restoring (call 212-292-3301).

Central Carpet

426 Columbus Avenue
near 81st Street
New York, NY 10024
212-362-5485
Monday-Wednesday Friday Saturday 9-6
Thursday 10-7:30 Sunday 11-5.

Rugs & carpets
Upper West Side

4	4	5	3
quality	style	service	value

The Edge: A large selection of carpets. Carpets include Persians, Chinese and Turkish kilims, plus contemporary floor coverings.

Doris Leslie Blau Gallery

724 5th Avenue
between 56th and 57th Streets
New York, NY 10019
212-586-5511
By appointment.

Rugs & carpets
Midtown West

5	5	5	3
quality	style	service	value

The Edge: Collector-quality Oriental carpets. Exquisite antique tapestries and top-of-the-line quality late 19th- to early 20th-century carpets. Best known for her Persian carpets, but also carries Aubussons, Savonneries and needlepoints. When Chris Whittle was amassing, this was one favorite source. No credit cards. Deluxe.

"Really worth visiting, if your budget permits."

Lovelia Enterprises

356 East 41st Street
in Tudor City
New York, NY 10017
212-490-0930. Fax 212-697-8550
By appointment.

Rugs & carpets
Midtown East

The Edge: 15th- to 19th-century reproduction tapestries and rugs. Imports tapestries and miniature rugs, including Aubusson and European Gobelins. Most are reproductions of 15th- to 19th-century designs. Also some tapestries with contemporary patterns. No credit cards.

"Good prices."

Marvin Kagan, Inc.

625 Madison Avenue, 2nd Floor
near 58th Street
New York, NY 10022
212-535-9000. Fax 212-935-7822
Weekdays 9:30-5:30 Saturday 10-5:30.

Rugs & carpets
Midtown East

The Edge: Antique Oriental carpets. Carpets in all sizes and priced from $10,000 to $200,000. Fine antique carpets, including Kerman, Serapi and Tabriz carpets as well as semi-antique Aubussons, Persian and Turkish rugs and tapestries.

Momeni International

36 East 31st Street, 2nd Floor
near Park Avenue
New York, NY 10016
212-532-9577. Fax 212-779-9568
Weekdays 9-5.

Rugs & carpets
Gramercy Pk/Murray Hill

The Edge: Oriental rugs sold wholesale or retail. Decorator discounts available. No credit cards.

Pasargad Carpets

105 Madison Avenue
near 30th Street
New York, NY 10016
212-684-4477. Fax 212-684-4148
Monday-Saturday 9-6 Sunday 11-5.

Rugs & carpets
Gramercy Pk/Murray Hill

The Edge: One-of-a-kind Persian and Oriental carpets from $100 to $100,000. Large selection. Repairs and cleans rugs also. Will buy or trade quality rugs.

Redi-Cut Carpets

208 East 23rd Street
near 2nd Avenue
New York, NY 10010
212-685-3626. Fax 212-685-3826
Weekdays 10-8 Saturday 10-6 Sunday noon-6.

Rugs & carpets
Gramercy Pk/Murray Hill

quality style service value

The Edge: Top-quality remnants. A large selection of home and office carpeting at substantial savings. Installation within two days. Priced from $15 per yard. Discounter.

Rug Warehouse

220 West 80th Street, 2nd Floor
near Broadway
New York, NY 10024
212-787-6665. Fax 212-787-6628
Monday-Wednesday Friday Saturday 10-6
Thursday 10-8 Sunday 11-5.

Rugs & carpets
Upper West Side

quality style service value

The Edge: New and antique rugs. Some handmade but mostly machine-made rugs from China, India, Pakistan and Turkey at prices from $150 to $30,000, with some selected pieces to $100,000. There's an annual three-week sale where rugs are discounted 10% to 15%. Seven-day return policy. Discounter.

Safavieh Carpets

153 Madison Avenue
near 32nd Street
New York, NY 10016
212-683-8399. Fax 212-532-7244
Weekdays 9-6 Saturday 10-6 Sunday 11-5.

Rugs & carpets
Gramercy Pk/Murray Hill

quality style service value

The Edge: Good selection of quality rugs. Features Iranian, Indian, Pakistani, Turkish, Egyptian and Chinese rugs. Prices range from $200 to $100,000. A 30% discount is offered to decorators.

"Beautiful carpets—can bargain."

Vojtech Blau, Inc.

Rugs & carpets
Midtown East

41 East 57th Street
near Madison Avenue
New York, NY 10022
212-249-4525
Weekdays 9-4.

The Edge: Very fine 16th- to 18th-century tapestries and 18th-century Persian rugs. Favors antique Persian rugs but also has fine linens, Aubussons, Savonneries and Turkish and European carpets. Quality antique tapestries in a wide range of sizes and styles. A 20% discount is offered to decorators. No credit cards.

ABC Carpet and Home

Superstores
Flatiron/East Village

888 Broadway
near 19th Street
New York, NY 10003
212-473-3000. Fax 212-645-3809
Monday-Friday 10-8 Saturday 10-7 Sunday 11-6:30.

4	4	4	3
quality	style	service	value

The Edge: Everything for the home. Great styling and products. One-stop shopping for the home from bed and bath accessories to carpeting, linens, antique and reproduction furniture and accessories from Europe, Scandinavia, Asia and the Americas. Country pieces to formal. Excellent taste. Unbelievable selection. Decorators get a 10% discount.

"Lots of style and inventory." "Good selection of remnants." "Service fluctuates, great quality selection, price." "They have great taste and variety, but staggering prices for housewares." "Personal decorators."

Bed, Bath and Beyond

Superstores
Chelsea

620 Avenue of the Americas
between 18th and 19th Streets
New York, NY 10011
212-255-3550
Monday-Saturday 9:30-9 Sunday 10-7.

4	3	3	4
quality	style	service	value

The Edge: A housewares supermarket. One-stop shopping in a store that takes up an entire block, 82,000 square feet. It carries all kitchen needs (cookware, dishes, gadgets, pots, pans), blankets, closetware, drapes, hampers, linens, pillows, picture frames, drapes, rugs and more. Everything imaginable for the bedroom, bathroom and kitchen. OK (not discount) prices.

"Helpful, large selection." "Great selection, generally good price." "Good addition to New York City." "Great place to shop when you send your child to college for the first time—it has everything she'll need."

Crate & Barrel

650 Madison Avenue
near 59th Street
New York, NY 10021
212-308-0011
Weekdays 10-8 Saturday 10-7 Sunday noon-6.

Supersto
Upper

4	5	5	4
quality	style	service	value

The Edge: Attractive fresh-looking furnishings. Large store featuring very attractive furniture and gift items. Good selection and range of basic items. Gift items include Italian ceramics, table linens, glassware, picture frames and more. Reasonable prices, great furniture for first city apartments. In malls across the country and finally now in New York.

"The Madison Avenue shop in New York is terrific."

Gracious Home

1220 3rd Avenue
near 70th Street
New York, NY 10021
212-517-6300. Fax 212-249-1534
Monday-Saturday 9-7 Sunday 10:30-5:30.

Superstores
Upper East Side

4	4	4	3
quality	style	service	value

The Edge: Beloved and shopped by virtually everyone. No store or service seems better known and better appreciated. The shop is large, well organized and fully stocked. You name it, they have it: from nails and screws to appliances, cleaning supplies, curtains, linens, tool rental and a repair department. Service is legendary, but you pay for it.

"Has everything and delivers." "They're very helpful always." "10 for service and value. Expensive but worth it." "Best hardware and home store in New York—they have it all, plus excellent service."

1217 3rd Avenue
between 70th and 71st Streets/10021
212-988-8990
Weekdays 8-7 Saturday 9-7 Sunday 10-6.

Upper East Side

Fanelli Antique Timepieces

790 Madison Avenue, Suite 202
near 67th Street
New York, NY 10028
212-517-2300
Weekdays 11-6 Saturday 11-5.

Timepieces
Upper East Side

4	3	5	3
quality	style	service	value

The Edge: Clocks from the 1880s to the 1920s. Sells and repairs antique clocks. Wonderful rare clocks, including gilded and jeweled clocks. Also quality vintage wristwatches. Favors European and American antique clocks. Also quality repairs.

...sner *Timepieces*

...7 2nd Avenue
...ear 56th Street
New York, NY 10022
212-249-2600
Weekdays 10-6 Saturday 11-4.

Timepieces
Midtown East

quality	style	service	value
4	4	3	3

The Edge: Good selection of quality vintage watches. Buys and sells second-hand and vintage watches and clocks. Featuring Rolex, Patek Philippe and Cartier, among other top designers. Fine watch repairs.

Time Will Tell

962 Madison Avenue
near 75th Street
New York, NY 10021
212-861-2663. Fax 212-288-4069
Monday-Saturday 10-6.

Timepieces
Upper East Side

The Edge: Vintage wristwatches from the 1910s to the 1950s. A large selection of vintage watches. All watches have the original works and are in working order. Features Cartier, Patek Philippe, Rolex, Vacheron & Constantin, plus other top names. Does repairs.

Alpha Puck Designs

139 Fulton Street, Room 210
near Nassau Street
New York, NY 10038
212-267-2561. Fax 212-267-2562
By appointment.

Window treatments
Lower Manhattan

The Edge: Quality, reasonably priced window treatments and upholstery. Custom slipcovers, upholstery, window treatments (Roman shades to drapes). Shop is oriented to designers. Requires 50% cash deposit. Ask for Madeline Boutte. No credit cards.

Country Curtains

Main Street
Stockbridge, MA 01262
800-876-6123. Fax 413-243-1067
Daily 24 hours.

Window treatments
Mail/phone

quality	style	service	value
2	3	4	4

The Edge: Huge selection of inexpensive, ready-made mail-order curtains. Offers three types of catalogs, Country Curtains for casual, Window Ways for blinds and shades and City Curtains containing 100 different styles, the latest looks and nice hardware geared for apartment living. Great for apartment rentals when you don't want to invest in furniture and window treatments. Very responsive, providing good advice on how to hang curtains. Second phone line is 800-785-9215, fax line 413-243- 0211.

"Shop here for function, price and helpful staff."

Drapery Exchange, Inc.
1899 Post Road
Interstate 95 at Exit 11
Darien, CT 06820
203-655-3844
Monday-Saturday 10-5.

Window treatments
Connecticut

quality style service value

The Edge: Second to none for top-of-the-line draperies (including balloon shades) seeking a second life. The store sells—and therefore buys—used draperies in mint condition. All the top fabric houses appear here. The store prices the draperies with half the proceeds going to the consignee. Mainly expensive drapes. Shop will arrange alterations so the treatments will fit your windows. Expensive for used, but top-quality new drapes cost even more. Drapes, even used, can run into the thousands of dollars. No credit cards. No delivery.

Just Shades
21 Spring Street
near Elizabeth Street
New York, NY 10012
212-966-2757. Fax 212-334-6129
Thursday-Tuesday 9:30-4.

Window treatments
SoHo/TriBeCa

quality style service value

The Edge: Hundreds of appealing lamp shades in all shapes and fabrics. They specialize in lamp shades in every conceivable fabric from burlap and parchment to linen and silk. Old shades can be recovered with your own fabric.

"Good for lamp shades—all sizes, styles." "They sell those Stuy town shades!"

Mardi Philips
31 Jane Street
near 8th Avenue
New York, NY 10014-1979
212-924-2604. Fax 212-604-0525
By appointment.

Window treatments
Greenwich Village

quality style service value

The Edge: Elaborate custom window treatments. Specializes in Roman shades and elaborate custom curtain treatments as well as cushions, pillows and slipcovers. Roman shades for a 54- by 72-inch window start at $300, excluding fabric. No credit cards.

Shades From the Midnight Sun
914-779-7237
By appointment only.

Window treatments
Bronxville

The Edge: Custom-made shades. Caters to decorators and individuals. Can match shades to furniture and wallpaper. Shades from $60 to $900 A *New York Times* and *Martha Stewart Living* source.

Sheila's Wallstyles Decorating Center

274 Grand Street
between Eldridge and Forsyth Streets
New York, NY 10002
212-966-1663. Fax 212-226-0412
Sunday-Thursday 9:30-5 Friday 9-2.

Window treatments
Lower East Side/Chinatown

quality style service value

The Edge: Discounts decorator items. Stocks, or is able to order, a wide selection of wallpaper, fabrics, vertical and horizontal blinds and shades. Can make up items into drapes, bedspreads, tablecloths, etc. Discounter.

Sundial-Schwartz

1582 1st Avenue
near 82nd Street
New York, NY 10028
212-289-4969. Fax 212-992-3236
Weekdays 10-4:30 Saturday 10-3. Closed Saturday June-August.

Window treatments
Upper East Side

The Edge: Features mirroring and window treatments. Sundial will install mirrors, remodel and re-silver antique mirrors. Sells custom-design window treatments, blinds, shades, storm windows and draperies. Discounter.

"Reliable."

White Workroom

525 Broadway
near Spring Street
New York, NY 10012
212-941-5910. Fax 212-941-1354
Weekdays 9-6 by appointment.

Window treatments
SoHo/TriBeCa

The Edge: A decorators source for custom draperies. However they will do retail. Pair of side panels with interlining and center-edge trim for a nine-foot window starts at $350, fabric not included. No credit cards. Discounter.

The ratings: **5** excellent   **4** very good   **3** good **2** fair   **1** so-so

Home & home office

Art Station

144 West 27th Street
near 7th Avenue
New York, NY 10001
212-807-8000. Fax 212-807-8495
Weekdays 8-6:30 Saturday 10-3.

Art supplies
Midtown West

The Edge: Everything for the artist. Complete range of supplies for the artist, including drawing
tables, chairs, chalkboards, lamps and framing. Weekly special sale items.

Arthur Brown & Brother, Inc.

2 West 46th Street
near 5th Avenue
New York, NY 10036
212-575-5555. Fax 212-575-5825
Weekdays 9-6:30 Saturday 10-6.

Art supplies
Midtown West

The Edge: Perhaps the city's largest art supply store. Extensive range of materials, including
stationery, art supplies, filofaxes, leather goods and framing materials. Good selection of technical
pens—designed for artists, calligraphers and musicians. Also offers custom framing.

Charrette

215 Lexington Avenue
near 33rd Street
New York, NY 10016
212-683-8822. Fax 212-683-5787
Weekdays 8:30-7 Saturday 10-5 Sunday noon-5. Closed Sunday July and August.

Art supplies
Gramercy Pk/Murray Hill

The Edge: Quality supplies for serious artists, draftsmen, etc. Offers quality supplies for
architects, engineers, draftsmen, graphic designers and artists. Catalog available, with substantial
discounts on all major brands. Discounter.

David Davis Fine Art Materials

65 Paris Street
near Pearl Street
Brooklyn, NY 11201
718-237-1669
Weekdays 9:30-6 Saturday 11-6.

Art supplies
Brooklyn

The Edge: Quality supplies for professional artists. Wide selection of paints, quality brushes,
handmade papers, pastels, drawing books and papers. Davis will make stretchers and easels to any
size.

New York Central Art Supply

Art supplies
Flatiron/East Village

62 3rd Avenue
near 11th Street
New York, NY 10003
212-473-7705. Fax 212-475-2542
Monday-Saturday 8:30-6:30.

The Edge: Incredible selection of papers. In business since 1905. A large selection of imported and domestic papers as well as brushes, canvas, drawing and drafting tools, drawing tables and lamps, easels, paints and stretchers, pens and inks, printmaking supplies. Their toll-free number is 800-950-6111.

Pearl Paint Company

Art supplies
SoHo/TriBeCa

308 Canal Street
near Church Street
New York, NY 10013
212-431-7932. Fax 212-279-8290
Monday-Wednesday Friday Saturday 9-6 Thursday 9-7
Sunday 9-5:30. Closed Saturday July and August.

4	4	5	4
quality	style	service	value

The Edge: Six floors of discounted, fine arts products. Great selection. They say they're the world's largest art supply store. Stocks all major brands of art, graphic, craft and stationery supplies, all discounted 20% to 70%. Prices to $6,000 for printing presses. Binds books as well.

Sam Flax

Art supplies
Chelsea

12 West 20th Street
between 5th and 6th Avenues
New York, NY 10011
212-620-3000. Fax 212-630-0740
Weekdays 8:30-6:30 Saturday 10-6 Sunday noon-5.

3	3	3	3
quality	style	service	value

The Edge: Enormous inventory of quality art supplies. Sells an enormous stock of fine art and drafting supplies, photographic equipment, drafting and drawing tables, storage units, carry cases, pens, picture frames and fine papers. First-rate supplies and unique gifts at full retail price.

Utrecht Art and Drafting Supplies

Art supplies
Flatiron/East Village

111 4th Avenue
between 11th and 12th Streets
New York, NY 10003
212-777-5353
Monday-Saturday 9-6.

The Edge: Huge stock of art and drafting supplies at good prices. One of the largest art supply houses in the country. Manufactures its own line of paint, canvas and related products. Store boasts over 20,000 items carried at discount. Frequent sales reduce prices further. Popular with artists from the student to the professional.

Rafik Film and Video Tape Company

Film services
Flatiron/East Village

814 Broadway, 2nd Floor
between 11th and 12th Streets

New York, NY 10003
212-475-7884
Weekdays 9:30-6:30.

The Edge: Videotape and film supplies. As well as supplies, they duplicate and edit videos, convert films to videos and convert foreign to U.S. format. No delivery. Discounter.

AAA American Flag

Flags
Midtown West

40 West 37th Street
near 6th Avenue
New York, NY 10018
212-279-3524. Fax 212-695-8392
Monday-Thursday 8:30-4 Friday 8:30-3:30.

The Edge: Custom-made flags. Features custom-made corporate logos or family crests plus traditional flags, including assorted sizes of the American flag, state and city flags and flags of more than 150 countries.

Abacrome

Flags
Midtown West

151 West 26th Street
near 7th Avenue
New York, NY 10001
212-989-1190. Fax 212-645-3809
Weekdays 9-5.

The Edge: Custom silk screening. Features custom silk-screened large banners, advertising displays, American and international flags. No credit cards.

Ace Banner and Flag Company

Flags
Midtown West

107 West 27th Street
near 6th Avenue
New York, NY 10001
212-620-9111
Weekdays 7:30-4.

The Edge: Custom display banners. Manufactures all types and sizes of custom display banners. Stocks U.S. and foreign flags. Clients include Carnegie Hall, Cartier, Columbia University, J.P. Morgan and others. Priced from $12 to $2,000.

Solutions

Marketing services
Brooklyn

109 State Street
Brooklyn, NY 11201
718-855-5275
By appointment.

quality style service value

The Edge: Top talent that provides Pizzaaz. A small team of writers and art directors who have created major advertising and marketing campaigns for clients such as Heineken, Jaguar, Yves St. Laurent, *Architectural Digest* and others. Will develop marketing strategies and creative executions for your product or service on a cost-plus basis. (Actual production costs plus creative time billed by the hours, as law firms do.) Very reasonable prices.

"They're quick, clever and fun to work with!"

Amal Printing and Publishing
Printers
Midtown West

630 5th Avenue, concourse level
near 51st Street
New York, NY 10020
212-247-3270. Fax 212-586-6945
Weekdays 9-5:30 or by appointment.

The Edge: Full range of printing services. You don't need to go to them—they'll send a sales rep to you. Personal and business printing, including invitations, business flyers, stationery and cards. All printing done in-house, including binding, letter press and thermography. Offers overnight printing with same-day delivery in Manhattan.

Seeford Organization
Printers
SoHo/TriBeCa

75 Varick Street
between Canal and Watts Streets
New York, NY 10013
212-431-4000. Fax 212-431-4007
Weekdays 7:30-5:30.

The Edge: Quality printing services. Any size, any color, any typeface. No credit cards.

World-Wide Business Centres
Rentals
Midtown East

575 Madison Avenue
between 56th and 57th Streets
New York, NY 10022
212-605-0200
Weekdays 9-5:30 weekends by appointment.

The Edge: Rents office space with full services. Services include conference rooms, desk space, private offices, receptionist, telephone answering, typists and word processing. Operates a full-service travel agency.

Butch Krutchik Designs
Stationery
Mail/phone

212-734-0092
By appointment

The Edge: Creative, handmade, pop-up invitations. Handmade invitations tending to the witty that arrive in a box. Very pricey at $25 per invitation. Takes four weeks to create and engrave. No credit cards. Deluxe.

Dempsey & Carroll
Stationery
Midtown East

110 East 57th Street
between Lexington and Park Avenues

New York, NY 10022
212-486-7526. Fax 212-486-7523
Monday-Saturday 10-6:30.

5 5 5 3
quality style service value

The Edge: Where tradition starts. Elegant engraved stationery in 30 lettering styles, plus party and wedding invitations, Christmas cards, birth announcements, engraved callings cards, business cards, letter and note cards as well as desk accessories. Meets all your needs. Deluxe.

Hudson Jam

111 3rd Avenue
between 13th and 14th Streets
New York, NY 10003
212-473-6666. Fax 212-473-7300
Weekdays 8:30-7 Saturday 10-6.

Stationery
Flatiron/East Village

3 3 3 4
quality style service value

The Edge: Wide range of papers. From business to personal papers, including copies of top brands. If you wonder where those lifelike celebrity cardboard figures come from, come here. They feature over 100 lifelike cardboard individuals, fun and realistic at $30, including Hillary and Bill Clinton, Marilyn Monroe, John Wayne and multiple Disney characters.

621 Avenue of the Americas
near 19th Street/10011
212-255-4593
Weekdays 8:30-8 Saturday 10-6.

Chelsea

1111 2nd Avenue
near 59th Street/10022
212-980-1999
Weekdays 8:30-6 Saturday 10-6.

Midtown East

Hudson Street Papers

357 Bleecker Street
between 10th and Charles Streets
New York, NY 10014
212-229-1064
Monday-Thursday 11-8 Friday noon-9 Saturday 11-9 Sunday noon-6.

Stationery
Greenwich Village

The Edge: European styling in paper and paper-related gifts. A large selection of European-style stationery and paper gift items, plus children's toys. No delivery.

Il Papiro

1021 Lexington Avenue
near 73rd Street
New York, NY 10021
212-288-9330. Fax 212-570-1587
Weekdays 10-6 Saturday 10-5:30. Closed Saturday July and August.

Stationery
Upper East Side

The Edge: A touch of Florence with their wonderful marbleized paper products. Elegant stationery and accessories including picture frames, tissue holders, desk accessories, address books, agendas, photo albums and obelisks.

Jamie Ostrow

876 Madison Avenue
between 71st and 72nd Streets
New York, NY 10021
212-734-8890. Fax 212-472-2430
Monday-Saturday 10-6.

Stationery
Upper East Side

The Edge: Contemporary personalized stationery and invitations. Elegant stationery,
Christmas cards and invitations. Deluxe.

Kate's Paperie

561 Broadway
near Prince Street
New York, NY 10012
212-941-9816. Fax 212-941-9560
Weekdays 10:30-7 Saturday 10-6 Sunday noon-6.

Stationery
SoHo/TriBeCa

5	5	4	3
quality	style	service	value

The Edge: Wonderful papers and accessories. A well-stocked stationery store carrying agendas,
boxes, cards, diaries, frames, holiday ornaments, leather address books, photo albums, stationery,
wrapping papers and more.

"A huge selection of beautiful one-of-a-kind items." "Absolutely the best!"

Mrs. John L. Strong Company

699 Madison Avenue
near 62nd Street
New York, NY 10021
212-838-3775. Fax 212-755-1563
By appointment.

Stationery
Upper East Side

5	5	4	4
quality	style	service	value

The Edge: Well known for beautiful traditional invitations. 100% cotton paper with tissue
paper to match or accent. Hand-lined envelopes with inks and hand-engraved script selected by
you. Beautiful wedding invitations and letter sheets. Engraving takes four to six weeks. Wedding
invitations (classic size and styling) are priced at $860 for 100 invitations. Also sold at Barney's
(on Madison) and Gumps in San Francisco. Deluxe.

"Expensive."

Rebecca Moss

510 Madison Avenue
near 53rd Street
New York, NY 10022
212-832-7671. Fax 212-832-7690
Monday-Saturday 10-6.

Stationery
Midtown East

The Edge: Unique writing instruments. The shop features a good selection of writing papers,
invitations and new and vintage pens. They have a calligraphy computer which can personalize
invitations to look like handwritten calligraphy. Christmas '95 W featured as "wonderful" their
Radiowaves pen by Omas (for $650).

Kroll Office Products
145 East 54th Street
off Lexington Avenue
New York, NY 10022
212-750-5300. Fax 212-838-9878
Weekdays 8:30-6 Saturday 10-6.
Closed Saturday July and August.

Supplies
Midtown East

quality style service value

The Edge: A standard office supply store with an unbelievable range of supplies. Full range of office stationery including multiple styles and price points in calendars, highlighters, pens, paper, office supplies and furniture. Prices are OK. Ask for the corporate discount (10% to 15%) which is given to their large customers.

R&R Packaging Corporation
27 West 20th Street
between 5th and 6th Avenues
New York, NY 10011
212-620-0011. Fax 212-620-0018
Tuesday Thursday 10-6.

Supplies
Chelsea

quality style service value

The Edge: The best of the best wraps and ribbons—wholesale. A wholesale operation which is retail only Tuesday and Thursday. Find all your gift-packaging needs—paper, tissues, bags, boxes, ribbons and more. Simply beautiful gift wrapping. Accepts credit cards for orders $75 and up. Discounter.

Staples the Office Superstore
16 East 34th Street
between 5th and Madison Avenues
New York, NY 10016
212-683-8003
Weekdays 7-7 Saturday 9-6 Sunday 11-5.

Supplies
Gramercy Pk/Murray Hill

quality style service value

The Edge: Large selection that meets most home office needs. From paper to computers, telephones to file folders and of course staples, the store has it all for the home office. Many locations and helpful staff. 15% off.

"Easy to shop, large selection and good prices."

730 3rd Avenue
at 45th Street/10017
212-867-9486. Fax 212-681-7460
Weekdays 7-7 Saturday 9-6 Sunday 11-5.

Midtown East

609 5th Avenue
entrance on 49th Street/10017
212-593-0620
Weekdays 7-7 Saturday 9-6 Sunday 11-5.

Midtown East

57 West 57th Street
at 6th Avenue/10019
212-308-0561
Weekdays 7-8 Saturday 9-6 Sunday 11-5.

Midtown West

1075 Avenue of the Americas
at 41st Street/10018
212-944-6744
Weekdays 7-8 Saturday 9-6 Sunday 11-5.

Midtown West

575 Lexington Avenue
entrance on 51st Street/10022
212-644-2118
Weekdays 7-7 Saturday 9-6 Sunday 11-5.

Midtown East

250 West 34th Street
between 7th and 8th Avenues/10119
212-629-3990
Weekdays 7-7 Saturday 9-6 Sunday 11-5.

Midtown West

State Office Supply Company
150 5th Avenue
near 20th Street
New York, NY 10011
212-243-8025. Fax 212-463-0706
Weekdays 9-5:30 Saturday noon-5.

Supplies
Chelsea

The ratings: **5** excellent 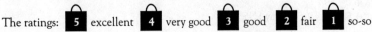 **4** very good **3** good **2** fair **1** so-so

Home renovation

We all know how difficult it is to find trustworthy, competent companies and individuals to do home repairs and renovations. This is doubly true for New York City! So we tapped the private files of friends and business associates for this chapter. The companies and individuals listed below were recommended by a single source. We believe them to be reliable, but we have not had personal experience with their work. Before hiring anyone to do work on your home, ask for and check multiple references, examine the quality of work they have done and monitor closely the progress of the work they do for you. Inclusion in this category is not an endorsement or recommendation by the authors or publisher.

Air Conditioner Power & Cooling

826 42nd Street
Brooklyn, NY 11220
718-784-1300
By appointment.

Air conditioning
Brooklyn

The Edge: Good source to fill your heating and a/c needs. Specialties are installation and repairs.

"Reliable and inexpensive."

Paul Gleicher

2112 Broadway
near 74th Street
New York, NY 10023
212-787-2284
By appointment.

Architects
Upper West Side

The Edge: Architect. Specializes in brownstone restoration and renovation.

"Excellent."

Spitzer and Associates

160 5th Avenue, Suite 611
near 21st Street
New York, NY 10010
212-924-7454
By appointment.

Architects
Gramercy Pk/Murray Hill

The Edge: Architect who is easy to work with.

"Easy to work with. Understands clients' needs. Prices are moderate to high, but quality is excellent."

Renovator - Peter E. Kilroy

Cabinetry/carpenters
Brooklyn

145 Wyckoff Street
Brooklyn, NY 11217
718-802-9105
By appointment.

The Edge: Skilled carpenter. Prefers to work on architectural details, bookcases and kitchens. Does small jobs, including replacing doors.

"Excellent quality at fair prices."

Toledo Interiors

Cabinetry/carpenters
Brooklyn

61 Greenpoint Avenue
Brooklyn, NY 11222
718-349-3610. Fax 718-349-3610
By appointment.

The Edge: Quality custom cabinetry. Eight-year-old custom cabinetry company specializing in cedar closets and one-of-a-kind cabinetry from architectural designs.

Wood-O-Rama, Inc.

Cabinetry/carpenters
Upper West Side

238 West 108th Street
near Broadway
New York, NY 10025
212-749-6483
Monday-Saturday 9-5:30 by appointment.

The Edge: Custom cabinets and wall units.

"Excellent quality and reasonable prices."

Bob Shaw

Electrician
Upper East Side

217 East 88th Street, Suite 4
near 3rd Avenue
New York, NY 10128
212-876-3415
By appointment.

The Edge: Electrician.

"Good quality. Reasonable prices."

Audio Design Associates

Electronics
Westchester

602-610 Mamaroneck Avenue
White Plains, NY 10605
914-946-9595. Fax 914-946-9620
Weekdays 9-5 by appointment.

5	5	5	3
quality	style	service	value

The Edge: High-tech custom electronic systems. Makes and installs audiovisual equipment and home theaters. Integrates electronic systems, connecting pushbutton-controlled drapes, phones and lights with room-to-room audiovisual systems. Touch screen for commands. $800 key pad that resembles a light switch and a volume control can change the station and dim the lights. Charges $125 per hour or $425 per day for labor.

Karp & Centrell

423 Center Avenue
Westwood, NJ 07375
201-666-0777
By appointment.

Electronics
New Jersey

The Edge: Audio and video experts. Designs audio-video home theaters. No credit cards.

"Superior quality. Prices are fair. I recommend them highly."

Agouti Consulting

588 Broadway, Suite 705
near Houston Street
New York, NY 10012
212-941-8514. Fax 212-274-1778
By appointment.

Expediter
SoHo/TriBeCa

The Edge: Expediter. Talk to Jack or Jackie. Able to facilitate getting building permits for construction projects. A specialist in dealing with the city for a Certificate of Occupancy.

"Superior service. Reasonable prices."

Stanley Company, Inc.

63 Third Place
Brooklyn, NY 11231
718-643-3938
By appointment.

Flooring
Brooklyn

The Edge: Flooring contractor and refinisher. Talk to Stephen Clementi. He makes house calls to see what needs to be done.

"I recommend him highly. Reasonable prices."

Jane Gill

290 Riverside Drive, Apt 15B
near 101st Street
New York, NY 10025
212-316-6789
By appointment.

Garden
Upper West Side

The Edge: Horticulturist. Provides landscaping for terrace plantings. Favors using perennials and flowers for accent, but does work with trees and shrubs. Ask to see her portfolio. $100 for consultation credited against future work.

"Superior quality. Pricey but worth it."

C. Deck Contractor
25 Jones Street
New York, NY 10014
212-905-8207. Fax 212-242-0358
By appointment.

General contractors
Greenwich Village

The Edge: General contractor.

"Good quality at reasonable prices."

Goldreich, Page & Throff
45 East 20th Street
near Park Avenue
New York, NY 10003
212-982-1410
By appointment.

General contractors
Flatiron/East Village

The Edge: Consulting engineer and general contractor on building projects.

"He offers excellent-quality workmanship at reasonable prices."

Howard Haimes, Inc.
117 West 17th Street
between 6th and 7th Avenues
New York, NY 10011
212-807-7611. Fax 212-727-3097
By appointment.

General contractors
Chelsea

The Edge: General contractor.

"Superior quality. Reasonable prices. Very professional."

Jack Henry & Company
121A East 89th Street
near Lexington Avenue
New York, NY 10028
212-831-1199
By appointment.

General contractors
Upper East Side

The Edge: General contractor.

"Superior quality. He's pricey, but worth it."

Mid-City Construction

271 Columbia Street
Brooklyn, NY 11231
718-875-3100
By appointment.

General contractors
Brooklyn

The Edge: General contractor. Talk to Pat Valcone.

"Excellent quality."

Quadrant Construction

420 Lexington Avenue, Suite 1927
near 44th Street
New York, NY 10017
212-697-4007
By appointment.

General contractors
Midtown East

The Edge: General contractor. Mostly alterations of commercial and office buildings.

"Excellent quality, but prices are high. Best for office work."

Wm. Crawford Construction

560 Barry Street
Bronx, NY 10474
718-617-5390
By appointment.

General contractors
Bronx

The Edge: General contractor. Very high-end contractor.

"Superior quality, but very pricey."

Jack Corcoran Marble Company

88 West Hills Road
Huntington Station, NY 11746
516-549-8207
By appointment.

Marble & granite
Long Island

The Edge: Marble and granite work. Features custom work for kitchens and bathrooms.

"Excellent quality at reasonable prices. Very professional to deal with."

Amsterdam Corporation

Paint, plaster & tiles
Midtown East

150 East 58th Street
near 3rd Avenue
New York, NY 10022
212-644-1350
By appointment.

The Edge: Tile supplier and consultant. Talk to Barbara Berwick. She knows tiles and offers a wide selection. Prices are moderate.

"Easy to work with. Excellent quality."

Classic Plastering and Tiling

Paint, plaster & tiles
Bronx

2353 Quimby Avenue
Bronx, NY 10472
718-824-4672
Weekdays 9-5.

The Edge: Plastering and tiling contractor.

"Excellent quality at reasonable prices."

Jane Kozlak

Paint, plaster & tiles
Connecticut

58 Laurel Lane
Simsbury, CT 06078
203-658-7218
By appointment.

The Edge: Artist who paints sinks and tiles. This tile designer works on tiles which are provided by you. Then she'll paint to your needs.

"Superior workmanship, but pricey."

Pro-Tech Plumbing and Heating Corp.

150-44 11th Avenue
Whitestone, NY 11357
718-767-9067
By appointment.

Plumbing & heating
Queens

The Edge: Plumbing and heating work.

"Superior quality at reasonable prices. The best!"

John Venekamp
212-875-0441
By appointment.

Project manager
Mail/phone

The Edge: Construction and renovation manager. Represents the owner in managing architect, contractor, co-op board and building departments.

"He makes those impossible projects easy and timely. First-rate." "Provides top-quality service. His prices are reasonable, considering the service."

Al Husted
57 Front Street
Brooklyn, NY 11201
718-625-6464. Fax 718-625-5350
Weekdays 9-5 Saturday 11-5 by appointment.

Stained glass
Brooklyn

The Edge: Stained-glass expert. Repairs and washes stained glass. Sells museum quality pieces and supplies for making and/or repairing stained glass. Works in churches, museums and homes. Maintains a studio where he teaches stained-glass workmanship.

"Superior quality, reasonable prices. Superb stained-glass restoration." "Easy to work with. Makes beautiful pieces."

The ratings: excellent very good good fair so-so

Leisure hours & parties

Ballooms-Balooms
147 Sullivan Street
near Houston Street
New York, NY 10012
212-673-4007
Weekdays 10-6 Saturday noon-6.

Balloons
SoHo/TriBeCa

quality	style	service	value
4	4	4	3

The Edge: Customized imprinted balloons. Provides party balloons and party decorations. Will imprint balloons with names, logos and portraits. Priced at $118 for 50 customized balloons delivered.

A Different Light Bookstore and Cafe
151 West 19th Street
near 7th Avenue
New York, NY 10011
212-989-4850. Fax 212-989-2158
Daily 10-midnight. Cafe closes at 11:30.

Books & magazines
Chelsea

quality	style	service	value
5	5	5	4

The Edge: Gay and lesbian literature. Large selection (15,000 titles) of books and magazines of gay and lesbian literature from poetry to health, psychology, coming out and parenting. Also find U.S. and foreign videos and a cafe and coffee bar. Offers movies on Sundays and readings three to four times weekly. An event calendar at the store.

"Open long hours."

A Photographer's Place
133 Mercer Street
between Prince and Spring Streets
New York, NY 10012
212-431-9358. Fax 212-941-7920
Monday-Saturday 11-8 Sunday noon-6.

Books & magazines
SoHo/TriBeCa

The Edge: For rare books to prints to cameras, this is the place. Thousands of books, many rare, plus prints and a collection of vintage cameras and equipment.

Academy Book Store

10 West 18th Street
near 5th Avenue
New York, NY 10011
212-242-4848. Fax 212-675-9595
Monday-Saturday 9:30-9 Sunday 11-7.

Books & magazines
Chelsea

quality style service value

The Edge: Used-book store. Specializes in out-of-print books. The annex (12 West 18th Street) features CDs, records and tapes.

"Good used art books."

Action Comics

1551 2nd Avenue, 2nd Floor
near 81st Street
New York, NY 10128
212-639-1976. Fax 212-639-1799
Monday-Saturday 11-8 Sunday 11-6.

Books & magazines
Upper East Side

The Edge: Comics from the 1940s to date.

Appelfeld Gallery

1372 York Avenue
near 72nd Street
New York, NY 10021
212-988-7835. Fax 212-876-8915
Weekdays 10-5:30 Saturday by appointment.

Books & magazines
Upper East Side

quality style service value

The Edge: Old-fashioned bookstore filled with rare books. Wonderful source for rare and out-of-print books, first editions and some privately printed books.

"A treasure for the classics and leather books."

Applause Theater & Cinema Books

211 West 71st Street
near Broadway
New York, NY 10023
212-496-7511. Fax 212-761-2856
Monday-Saturday 10-8 Sunday noon-6.

Books & magazines
Upper West Side

quality style service value

The Edge: Specializes in rare and out-of-print books on theater and cinema. A very large selection of these specialty books plus videos. Trade and college bookstores purchase here at a 20% discount.

"A unique and valuable service."

Archiva: The Decorative Arts Book Shop

944 Madison Avenue
near 74th Street
New York, NY 10021
212-439-9194. Fax 212-744-1626
Weekdays 10-6 Saturday 11-5. Summer Sundays noon-5.

Books & magazines
Upper East Side

5	5	5	4
quality	style	service	value

The Edge: Can you find a single source with more on the decorative arts? A wondrous collection of new and out-of-print books on the decorative arts, architectural and garden designs plus some wonderful fashion editions. A full range of U.S. and foreign titles. If you need something, call Joan Gers.

Argosy Book Store

116 East 59th Street
near Lexington Avenue
New York, NY 10022
212-753-4455. Fax 212-593-4784
Weekdays 9-6 Saturday 10:30-5:30.
Closed Saturday May- September.

Books & magazines
Midtown East

4	4	4	4
quality	style	service	value

The Edge: A broad selection of old and rare books. A large, comprehensive bookstore featuring autographs, botanicals, equestrian engravings, first editions, hard-to-find books, maps and prints (including Currier & Ives), and posters. For assistance, contact Judith Lowry.

"Good place to get gifts and autographs." "Great books."

B. Dalton Bookseller

396 Avenue of the Americas
at 8th Street
New York, NY 10011
212-674-8780. Fax 212-475-9082
Monday-Saturday 9:30-11 Sunday noon-8.

Books & magazines
Chelsea

4	4	4	4
quality	style	service	value

The Edge: Wide selection favoring best-sellers. Lots of selection. Favors contemporary books, best-sellers and the like. A good source for remainder books—the ones you meant to buy several years back are likely to be on sale on tables here. A division of Barnes & Noble.

666 5th Avenue
near 52nd Street/10103
212-247-1740. Fax 212-262-9833
Weekdays 8:30-7 Saturday 9:30-6:30.

Midtown West

Barnes & Noble

4 Astor Place
near Broadway
New York, NY 10003
212-420-1322. Fax 212-420-1652
Monday-Saturday 10-midnight Sunday 10-10.

Books & magazines
Flatiron/East Village

4	4	4	4
quality	style	service	value

The Edge: Great selection and comfortable setting encourages browsing. From good reference sections to best-sellers, Barnes & Noble is known for great selections. A wide range of magazines.

Better still are the comfortable lounge chairs and tables to settle in while you make your selection. The cafe in most stores adds civility to book browsing. Discounter.

"A great place—choose your books in comfort."

675 Avenue of the Americas   **Gramercy Pk/Murray Hill**
near 22nd Street/10010
212-727-1227. Fax 212-727-1672
Daily 9-11.

385 5th Avenue   **Gramercy Pk/Murray Hill**
near 36th Street/10016
212-779-7677. Fax 212-696-9525
Weekdays 8-7 weekends 10-6.

109 East 42nd Street   **Midtown East**
between Lexington and Park Avenues/10017
212-818-0973
Weekdays 8-8 Saturday 10-6 Sunday 11-5.

750 3rd Avenue   **Midtown East**
at 47th Street/10017
212-697-2251. Fax 212-697-9273
Weekdays 8-8 Saturday 10-6 Sunday noon-5.

One Penn Plaza   **Midtown West**
near 33rd Street/10119
212-695-1677. Fax 212-695-3396
Weekdays 8-8 weekends 10-7.

901 Avenue of the Americas   **Midtown West**
at 33rd Street/10001
212-268-2505. Fax 212-268-2506
Monday-Saturday 10-8 Sunday 10-6.

600 5th Avenue   **Midtown West**
near 48th Street/10020
212-765-0590. Fax 212-489-2355
Weekdays 8:30-6:45 Saturday 9:45-6 Sunday noon-6.

160 East 54th Street   **Midtown East**
near Lexington Avenue/10022
212-750-8033. Fax 212-750-8038
Weekdays 7-9 Saturday 9-9 Sunday 11-6.

2239 Broadway   **Upper West Side**
near 82nd Street/10024
212-362-8835. Fax 212-362-6908
Sunday-Thursday 9-11 Friday Saturday 9-midnight.

1280 Lexington Avenue
near 86th Street/10028
212-423-9900. Fax 212-369-7859
Monday-Saturday 9-11 Sunday 10-9.

Upper East Side

Barnes & Noble for Kids

120 East 86th Street
near Lexington Avenue
New York, NY 10028
212-427-0686. Fax 212-420-1652
Monday-Saturday 10-midnight Sunday 10-10.

Books & magazines
Upper East Side

5	5	4	4
quality	style	service	value

The Edge: Enormous selection of books for kids. A comfortable setting and a huge range of books for children. The only Barnes & Noble totally devoted to children's books. 20% off.

Barnes & Noble Sales Annex

128 5th Avenue
near 18th Street
New York, NY 10011
212-691-3770. Fax 212-691-6010
Weekdays 9:30-8 Saturday 9:30-6:30 Sunday 11-6.

Books & magazines
Chelsea

The Edge: Great bargains in used and remaindered books. Find two floors of books in 119 categories with prices starting at 69¢ up to hundreds of dollars. Price and selection make this store worth a trip if you're interested in more than just the current best-sellers.

Bauman Rare Books

301 Park Avenue
Waldorf Astoria Hotel at 50th Street
New York, NY 10022
212-759-8300. Fax 212-759-8350
Monday-Saturday 10-7.

Books & magazines
Midtown East

The Edge: A broad selection of rare books. A good selection of early classic literature, history, philosophy and science books. Also autographs and signed materials. Look for rare first editions, often inscribed.

Biography Bookshop

400 Bleecker Street
near 11th Street
New York, NY 10014
212-807-8655
Monday-Thursday noon-8 Friday noon-10 Saturday 11-11 Sunday 11-7.

Books & magazines
Greenwich Village

The Edge: Mostly bios. A large broad selection of biographies, autobiographies and related materials. Some fiction and nonfiction now.

Bookberries

983 Lexington Avenue
near 71st Avenue
New York, NY 10021

Books & magazines
Upper East Side

3	4	4	3
quality	style	service	value

212-794-9400. Fax 212-794-7042
Weekdays 10-7 weekends 10-6.

The Edge: Give thanks for neighborhood bookstores like this one. The side room is chock full of children's books. Clerks are friendly and special orders are accommodated quickly.

Books of Wonder

16 West 18th Street
between 5th and 6th Avenues
New York, NY 10011
212-989-3270
Monday-Saturday 11-7 Sunday 11:30-6.

Books & magazines
Chelsea

quality style service value

The Edge: A very special children's book shop. For children ages 4 to 8. They have an extensive Wizard of Oz section and, along with new titles, they stock rare, out-of-print and vintage childrens' books. Readings every Sunday morning at 11:30am, with a theme day (pet day, mothers day) every second Sunday. A newsletter announces all events.

"Always informed."

Brunner/Mazel Bookshop

19 Union Square West
near 15th Street
New York, NY 10003
212-924-3344
Weekdays 9-6 Saturday 10:30-3:30.

Books & magazines
Flatiron/East Village

The Edge: Features books on the behavioral sciences.

Calvary Bookstore

139 West 57th Street
between 6th and 7th Avenues
New York, NY 10019
212-315-0230
Monday 10-9 Tuesday Thursday Friday 10-6 Wednesday 10-7 Sunday noon-2.

Books & magazines
Midtown West

The Edge: Religious works of all descriptions. Wide range of books on all religions printed in English and in a large range of foreign languages.

Chartwell Booksellers

55 East 52nd Street
between Madison and Park Avenues
New York, NY 10022
212-308-0643. Fax 212-838-7423
Weekdays 9:30-6:30.

Books & magazines
Midtown East

The Edge: An oasis. A very small bookstore featuring best-sellers and very select rare books. Good selection of best-sellers, art, and design books. The rare book collection is eclectic. Helpful staff.

Christian Publications Books & Supply Center

315 West 43rd Street
between 8th and 9th Avenues
New York, NY 10036
212-582-4311. Fax 212-262-1825
Monday-Wednesday 9:30-5:45 Thursday- Friday 9:30- 6:45 Saturday 9:30-4:45.

Books & magazines
Midtown West

The Edge: Largest New York area publisher of Christian books. Also find videos and tapes.

Citybooks

61 Chambers Street
near Broadway
New York, NY 10007
212-669-8245
Weekdays 9-5.

Books & magazines
Lower Manhattan

The Edge: Books about New York. Find the Green Book, which lists all city and state government and agency personnel and telephone numbers by function. Has all the code regulations plus books on the city and New York memorabilia. No credit cards.

Civilized Traveller

2003 Broadway
near 68th Street
New York, NY 10023
212-875-0306
Monday-Saturday 10-9 Sunday noon-7.

Books & magazines
Upper West Side

4 4 4 3
quality style service value

The Edge: Everything for travel. From books to packable rainwear to travel agents, pocket tailors and portable showers.

Two World Financial Center/10281
212-786-3301
Monday-Saturday 10-7 Sunday noon-6.

Lower Manhattan

Coliseum Books, Inc.

1771 Broadway
near 57th Street
New York, NY 10019
212-757-8381. Fax 212-586-5607
Monday 8-10 Tuesday-Thursday 8-11 Friday 8-11:30
Saturday 10-11:30 Sunday noon-8.

Books & magazines
Midtown West

4 4 4 4
quality style service value

The Edge: A very wide selection. Good selection of best-sellers and general-interest books. Crammed full with books.

Complete Traveller Bookstore

199 Madison Avenue
near 35th Street
New York, NY 10016
212-685-9007. Fax 212-481-3253
Weekdays 9-7 Saturday 10-6 Sunday 11-5.

Books & magazines
Gramercy Pk/Murray Hill

5 4 4 4
quality style service value

The Edge: Travel guides about everywhere. A wide selection of new and out-of-print travel guides. Conventional to special-interest guides. Maps plus travel accessories, including money belts, converters and alarm clocks.

"Great inventory." "Great place for travel books."

Doubleday Book Shop

724 5th Avenue
near 57th Street
New York, NY 10022
212-397-0550. Fax 212-307-7681
Monday-Saturday 9-11 Sunday noon-7.

Books & magazines
Midtown East

quality style service value

The Edge: Selection A Barnes & Noble division, featuring general-interest books and best-sellers, of course.

Drama Bookshop

723 7th Avenue
near 48th Street
New York, NY 10019
212-944-0595. Fax 212-921-2013
Monday Tuesday Thursday Friday 9:30-7 Wednesday 9:30-8
Saturday 10:30- 5:30 Sunday noon-5.

Books & magazines
Midtown West

The Edge: Specialty books on the theater and film. Scripts, scores and books on people, practical matters and culture.

Ex Libris

160A East 70th Street
near Lexington Avenue
New York, NY 10021
212-249-2618
By appointment.

Books & magazines
Upper East Side

The Edge: Rare and out-of-print avant-garde art books. Well-stocked shop specializing in rare and out-of-print books on 20th-century avant-garde art. Also graphics, illustrations and posters. No credit cards.

Forbidden Planet

840 Broadway
near 13th Street
New York, NY 10003
212-473-1576. Fax 212-475-6180
Daily 10-8:30.

Books & magazines
Flatiron/East Village

The Edge: Scary masks great for Halloween and parties. Department store for science fiction enthusiasts. Find a vast selection of books, comic books (American and Japanese), T-shirts, toys, etc. Also masks of all sorts and for all tastes.

Glenn Horowitz Booksellers

19 East 76th Street
between 5th and Madison Avenues
New York, NY 10021
212-327-3538
Weekdays 9-5.

Books & magazines
Upper East Side

quality style service value

The Edge: Rare books and manuscripts from the 18th- to the 20th-century. Features first editions. 20th-century American literature is a specialty.

"The East Hampton store is beautiful."

Gotham Book Mart and Gallery

41 West 47th Street
between 5th and 6th Avenues
New York, NY 10036
212-719-4448
Weekdays 9:30-6:30 Saturday 9:30-6.

Books & magazines
Midtown West

quality style service value

The Edge: Seen as an old friend by the reading set. Huge selection, including new books, but also out-of-print rare volumes. Lots of works on 20th-century literature and poetry. Also a large selection of contemporary first editions and magazines. The James Joyce Society meets here. It's also the place for Edward Gorey and modern Irish Literature.

"Fun, rare finds." "All my book friends recommend." "Edward Gorey art."

Gryphon Bookshop

2246 Broadway
near 80th Street
New York, NY 10024
212-362-0706
Daily 10-midnight.

Books & magazines
Upper West Side

quality style service value

The Edge: Large stock of more used, than rare, books. Stocks used and hard-to-find books. First editions of contemporary authors and poetry are a specialty. Will search for out-of-print books.

H.P. Kraus

16 East 46th Street
between 5th and Madison Avenues
New York, NY 10017
212-687-4808. Fax 212-983-4790
Weekdays 9:30-5.

Books & magazines
Midtown East

quality style service value

The Edge: World-famous source for extremely rare early illustrated works. Features five floors of early printed volumes and illustrated works. Sells almost exclusively to libraries and academic institutions. Also extremely rare and early maps.

"Huge selection." "Very lovely maps—great stuff!"

Hacker Art Books

45 West 57th Street, 5th Floor
between 5th and 6th Avenues
New York, NY 10019
212-688-7600
Monday-Saturday 9-6.

Books & magazines
Midtown West

quality style service value

The Edge: Perhaps the largest inventory of scholarly works on art and architecture. Since 1937. Large selection of books from old rare to new books on art and architecture. Also reprints. Bonus books and magazines offered with orders over $200.

Hagstrom Map and Travel Center

57 West 43rd Street
between 5th and 6th Avenues
New York, NY 10036
212-398-1222. Fax 212-398-9856
Weekdays 8:30-5:45.

Books & magazines
Midtown West

quality style service value

The Edge: Nautical charts from Nova Scotia to Trinidad. A wide range of travel and travel-related items, including globes, books, atlases, nautical/aeronautical charts and maps of all 50 states and overseas locations. Maps for all needs—hiking to travel.

Harmer Johnson Books Ltd.

21 East 65th Street, 4th Floor
between 5th and Madison Avenues
New York, NY 10021
212-535-9118. Fax 212-861-9893
Weekdays 10:15-5 Saturday by appointment.

Books & magazines
Upper East Side

The Edge: Scholarly works on ancient art and archeology of Africa, the Pacific and the Americas. Rare, out-of-print and current titles are featured, plus museum catalogs. Offers a search service. No credit cards.

Imperial Fine Books, Inc.

790 Madison Avenue
near 68th Street
New York, NY 10021
212-861-6620. Fax 212-249-0333
Monday-Saturday 10:30-6. Closed Saturday July and August.

Books & magazines
Upper East Side

The Edge: Rare books, including illustrated children's books. Features signed first editions, illustrated volumes and leather-bound sets. Vintage children's books. Offers book binding, cleaning, restoration and search services. Books start at $100.

International Center of Photography

1130 5th Avenue
near 94th Street
New York, NY 10128
212-860-1777. Fax 212-360-6490
Tuesday 11-8 Wednesday-Sunday 11-6.

Books & magazines
Upper East Side

The Edge: A must for photographers. Thousands of books and photo-related accessories (albums, frames, prints and posters).

Irish Book Shop

Books & magazines
SoHo/TriBeCa

580 Broadway
near Prince Street
New York, NY 10012
212-274-1923. Fax 212-431-5413
Weekdays 11-5 Saturday 1-4.

The Edge: Major supplier of Irish-language material in the United States. You'll find current titles to out-of-print, hard-to-find titles. Wide range of subjects. Also find engravings.

J.N. Bartfield Books

Books & magazines
Midtown West

30 West 57th Street, 3rd Floor
between 5th and 6th Avenues
New York, NY 10019
212-245-8890. Fax 212-541-4860
Weekdays 10-5 Saturday 10-2:30. Closed Saturday July and August.

The Edge: Leather-bound books (single volumes and sets). Since 1937. Find illustrated editions of rare and old titles and first editions. A wide range of treasures.

Jewish Museum

Books & magazines
Upper East Side

1109 5th Avenue
near 92nd Street
New York, NY 10128
212-423-3200. Fax 212-423-3292
Monday Wednesday Thursday 11-5:45 Tuesday 11-8 Friday 11-3 Sunday 10-5:45.

The Edge: Judaica. Books and holiday celebratory items. Catalogs from their ever-changing exhibits.

Kinokuniya Bookstore

Books & magazines
Midtown West

10 West 49th Street
near 5th Avenue
New York, NY 10020
212-765-1461. Fax 212-541-9335
Daily 10-7:30.

4	4	4	4
quality	style	service	value

The Edge: City's largest and most complete selection of Japanese books. This New York branch of a Japanese bookstore offers books in Japanese (and some in English). All subjects for those interested in Japan.

Kitchen Arts and Letters

Books & magazines
Upper East Side

1435 Lexington Avenue
between 93rd and 94th Streets
New York, NY 10128
212-876-5550. Fax 212-876-3584
Monday 1-6 Tuesday-Friday 10-6:30 Saturday 11-6. Closed summer weekends.

The Edge: A bookstore dedicated to cooking and dining. More than 9,000 volumes on cooking, food and wine. In addition to cookbooks, a large selection of European books, restaurant guides, wine books, as well as food and cooking memorabilia such as restaurant postcards and vintage ads. An extensive collection of European books.

Librairie de France / Libreria Hispanica

610 5th Avenue
near 49th Street
New York, NY 10020
212-581-8810. Fax 212-265-1094
Monday-Saturday 10-6:15.

Books & magazines
Midtown West

quality style service value

The Edge: French and Spanish books and dictionaries. Full range of French and Spanish books (children, classic, best-sellers), books on tape, language tapes, Michelin travel guides, movies and newspapers. One of the largest foreign-language bookstores in the city.

"Another unique service."

Madison Avenue Bookshop

833 Madison Avenue
between 69th and 70th Streets
New York, NY 10021
212-535-6130. Fax 212-794-5231
Monday-Saturday 10-6.

Books & magazines
Upper East Side

quality style service value

The Edge: Old-world service. All the latest books, including a large selection of coffee table books. Call, charge it to your house account and have it delivered virtually immediately. Ask and get great recommendations from the staff. No credit cards.

Morton, the Interior Design Bookshop

989 3rd Avenue
near 59th Street
New York, NY 10022
212-421-9025
Monday-Saturday 11-7.

Books & magazines
Midtown East

quality style service value

The Edge: The source for design books. Near the D&D (Decorations & Design) building. Sells exclusively books on design, decoration, architecture and gardening. All current titles, including coffee table books.

"Crammed but great resource." "Has everything." For advice/assistance, contact Morton Dossik."

Movie Star News

134 West 18th Street
between 6th and 7th Avenues
New York, NY 10011
212-620-8160. Fax 217-270-634
Weekdays 10-6 Saturday 11-6.

Books & magazines
Chelsea

The Edge: Posters, books, photos and other cinema-related items.

Murder Ink

Books & magazines
Lower Manhattan

1 Whitehall Street
near Bridge Street
New York, NY 10004
212-742-7025
Weekdays 8-6:30 Saturday noon-5.
Closed Saturday July and August.

5	5	5	4
quality	style	service	value

The Edge: Just mysteries and wonderful staff recommendations. Houses one of New York's largest selections of mysteries. Rare and used books from the U.S. and England. Catalog includes staff picks, including children's and young adult mysteries. First editions. Publishers' overstocks at great prices.

"They know mystery books." "Cramped, fun for mystery lovers." "For assistance/advice, contact Jay Pearsall (Broadway location)."

1467 2nd Avenue
near 76th Street/10021
212-517-3222
Monday-Saturday 10-9 Sunday noon-6.

Upper East Side

2486 Broadway
near 92nd Street/10025
212-362-8905
Monday-Wednesday Friday Saturday 10-7:30 Thursday 10-8 Sunday 11-7.

Upper West Side

Mysterious Book Shop

Books & magazines
Midtown West

129 West 56th Street
between 6th and 7th Avenues
New York, NY 10019
212-765-0900. Fax 212-265-5478
Monday-Saturday 11-7.

5	5	5	4
quality	style	service	value

The Edge: A vast selection of mystery titles. Two floors of books. Find paperback books and best-sellers on the first floor and rare, out-of-print and hard-to-find volumes as well as signed first editions of contemporary authors on the second floor.

"Fun to browse—they know the genre." "Great for mystery lovers." "Delightful." "See Otto Penzler for advice or assistance."

NYU Health Sciences Bookstore

Books & magazines
Gramercy Pk/Murray Hill

333 East 29th Street
between 1st and 2nd Avenues
New York, NY 10016
212-532-0756. Fax 212-725-9296
Monday-Thursday 10-7 Friday 10-6 Saturday 11-5.

The Edge: The source for medical and veterinary books.

New York Astrology Center

350 Lexington Avenue, Suite 402
near 40th Street
New York, NY 10016
212-949-7211. Fax 212-949-7274
Weekdays 11-6:30 Saturday 11-5.

Books & magazines
Gramercy Pk/Murray Hill

The Edge: Books and software on astrology and New Age subjects.

New York Bound Bookshop

50 Rockefeller Plaza
near 50th Street
New York, NY 10020
212-245-8503
Weekdays 10-6 Saturday noon-4. Closed Saturday July and August.

Books & magazines
Midtown West

5	4	4	4
quality	style	service	value

The Edge: Anything in print related to New York. A good source for old, rare, out-of-print and current guidebooks, 19th-century newspapers, out-of-print and current city maps, photos and more.

"Engagingly unique."

New York Nautical Instrument & Service Corp.

140 West Broadway
near Thomas Street
New York, NY 10013
212-962-4522. Fax 212-406-8420
Weekdays 9-5 Saturday 9-noon. Closed Saturday June-August.

Books & magazines
SoHo/TriBeCa

The Edge: Vast selection of nautical charts. They claim they have every nautical chart in the world in stock. Also nautical books and other gift items.

Océanie/Afrique Noire

15 West 39th Street, 2nd Floor
near 5th Avenue
New York, NY 10018
212-840-8844. Fax 212-840-3304
Weekdays 10-5 weekends by appointment.

Books & magazines
Midtown West

The Edge: Geographically focused art books. Features rare and out-of-print and current books on Africa, Oceania, Southeast Asia and the Americas. Good source for old and new books on anthropology, contemporary art, history and textiles, as well as auction and museum exhibition catalogs. Will purchase entire libraries as well as single books.

Old Print Shop

150 Lexington Avenue
near 29th Street
New York, NY 10016
212-683-3950. Fax 212-779-8040
Tuesday-Friday 9-5 Saturday 9-4. July and August weekdays 9-5.

Books & magazines
Gramercy Pk/Murray Hill

5	4	4	5
quality	style	service	value

The Edge: 18th- to early 20th-century American prints. A good source for original Anton Schutz, Charles Frederick and Currier & Ives prints, among others. Wonderful scenes of New York City at the turn of the century. Also a large collection of antique maps from all over the world. Some 19th-century French and English engravings. They frame prints well and also stock reproduction and contemporary framing materials.

"Old world in feeling." "Wonderful."

Oscar Wilde Memorial Bookshop

15 Christopher Street
near 6th Avenue
New York, NY 10014
212-255-8097. Fax 212-255-8195
Daily 11:30-8:30.

Books & magazines
Greenwich Village

5	3	3	3
quality	style	service	value

The Edge: First gay bookstore in the city.

"The gay bookstore, good selection."

Pageant Book & Print Shop

114 West Houston Street
near Thomas Street
New York, NY 10012
212-674-5296. Fax 212-674-2609
Monday-Saturday noon-8 Sunday noon-7.

Books & magazines
SoHo/TriBeCa

The Edge: Well stocked with literary collectibles. A special emphasis on American plus early New York maps and 18th- and 19th-century engravings.

Paraclete Book Center

146 East 74th Street
near Lexington Avenue
New York, NY 10021
212-535-4050
Tuesday-Friday 10-6 Saturday 10-5.

Books & magazines
Upper East Side

The Edge: Books for serious Christian scholars.

Perimeter

146 Sullivan Street
near Houston Street
New York, NY 10012
212-529-2275. Fax 212-274-9809
Monday-Saturday noon-7.

Books & magazines
SoHo/TriBeCa

The Edge: Hard-to-find titles on architecture, furniture and design. Design books plus unusual architectural posters, paper models and postcards. Unique collection of books. Their catalog features their 50 top sellers. International focus.

Phyllis Lucas Gallery & Old Print Center

981 2nd Avenue   Books & magazines
near 52nd Street   Midtown East
New York, NY 10022
212-755-1516
Tuesday-Saturday 9-5:30. Closed Saturday July and August.

The Edge: Early American prints. Features early American prints, including engravings,
lithographs and signed limited-edition lithographs. Some reproductions. No credit cards.

"Anything old on paper."

Printed Matter, Inc.

77 Wooster Street   Books & magazines
near Spring Street   SoHo/TriBeCa
New York, NY 10012
212-925-0325. Fax 212-925-0464
Tuesday-Friday 10-6 Saturday 7-11.

The Edge: Exclusively artists books. Features 3,500 titles. Some signed books and some limited
editions. Features contemporary artists primarily.

Rand McNally Map and Travel Store

150 East 52nd Street   Books & magazines
between 3rd and Lexington Avenues   Midtown East
New York, NY 10022
212-758-7488
Weekdays 9-6 weekends noon-5.

The Edge: Vacation-planning guides to just about everywhere. Features vacation-planning
guides, campground directories, games to amuse while traveling and supplies like auto compasses,
highway emergency kits and rechargeable flashlights. Accessories include antique maps and globes
and reproductions. From $45 to $6,500.

Richard B. Arkway, Inc.

59 East 54th Street, Suite 62   Books & magazines
between Park and Madison Avenues   Midtown East
New York, NY 10022
212-751-8135. Fax 212-832-5389
Weekdays 9:30-5.

The Edge: Specialty travel books. Features atlases, books and maps dating from the 16th-
century.

Richard Stoddard - Performing Arts Books

18 East 16th Street, Room 305   Books & magazines
near 5th Avenue   Flatiron/East Village
New York, NY 10003
212-645-9576
Monday Tuesday Thursday-Saturday 11-6.

The Edge: 15,000 Broadway playbills plus rare theatrical materials. Out-of-print materials, plays plus technical titles. Outstanding collection of books covering the theater, original scenic and costume designs. Also books on film, dance, theater and the circus, plus autographs and general theater memorabilia. No delivery.

Rizzoli

454 West Broadway
near Prince Street
New York, NY 10012
212-674-1616
Monday-Thursday 10:30-9
Friday Saturday 10:30-10 Sunday noon-7.

Books & magazines
SoHo/TriBeCa

5	5	4	4
quality	style	service	value

The Edge: First-rate bookstore—big selection, great for browsing. Features best-sellers, coffee table art/design books, music and an international array of magazines. Also CDs.

"Its always a pleasure to spend time at Rizzoli—an oasis of civilization." "A New York institution."

31 West 57th Street
between 5th and 6th Avenues/10019
212-759-2424. Fax 212-826-9754
Monday-Saturday 9-8 Sunday 11-7.

Midtown West

3 World Trade Center/10281
212-385-1400. Fax 212-608-7905
Weekdays 10-7 weekends noon-5.

Lower Manhattan

Science Fiction Shop

168 Thompson Street
near Houston Street
New York, NY 10012
212-473-3010. Fax 212-473-4384
Weekdays noon-7 Saturday 11-7 Sunday noon-6.

Books & magazines
SoHo/TriBeCa

The Edge: Science fiction and horror books. Large selection of books, tapes and periodicals.

Shakespeare & Company Booksellers

716 Broadway
at Washington Place
New York, NY 10003
212-580-7800. Fax 212-979-5711
Sunday-Thursday 10-11 Friday Saturday 10-midnight.

Books & magazines
Flatiron/East Village

5	5	4	4
quality	style	service	value

The Edge: Quality selection—80,000 volumes. Features both a range of general-interest topics and a wide range of special-interest books. Also find greeting cards, literary magazines, maps and foreign magazines.

"Attentive staff."

Spring Street Books

Books & magazines
SoHo/TriBeCa

169 Spring Street
between West Broadway and Thompson Streets
New York, NY 10012
212-529-1330. Fax 212-431-8441
Monday-Thursday 10-11 Friday 10-midnight Saturday 10-1 Sunday 11-10.

The Edge: Small, quality selection. An arty literary oasis in SoHo. Strong on literature and general-interest subjects. Also magazines, foreign periodicals and greeting cards.

St. Marks Comics

Books & magazines
Flatiron/East Village

11 St. Marks Place
between 2nd and 3rd Avenues
New York, NY 10003
212-598-8439. Fax 212-477-1294
Sunday Monday 11-11 Tuesday-Saturday 10-1.

The Edge: New and vintage comics.

Strand Book Store

Books & magazines
Flatiron/East Village

828 Broadway
near 12th Street
New York, NY 10003
212-473-1452. Fax 212-473-2591
Monday-Saturday 9:30-9:30 Sunday 11-9:30.

The Edge: Stocks more than eight million volumes. Very well known. A wide selection of books, including review copies of best-sellers at half price and current fiction and nonfiction. Features a large collection of art books. Their rare book department is extensive. Kiosks are located at Fifth Avenue at 61st and the Tramway Plaza at 2nd Avenue and 60th Street. 25% off.

"Unbelievable selection." "Often find out-of-print books." "Great for used books." "Fun to browse."

95 Fulton Street
near Water Street/10038
212-732-6070
Monday-Saturday 10-9 Sunday 11-8.

Lower Manhattan

Stubbs Books & Prints, Inc.

Books & magazines
Upper East Side

153 East 70th Street
near 3rd Avenue
New York, NY 10021
212-772-3120. Fax 212-794-9071
Weekdays 10-6 Saturday 11-5.

The Edge: Rare and out-of-print books, mostly on architecture and decorative arts, including landscaping. Many practical design books, including decorative suggestions, gardening tips and books on fashion and cooking.

"See Jane Stubbs."

Traveller's Bookstore

75 Rockefeller Plaza
near 52nd Street
New York, NY 10019
212-664-0995. Fax 212-397-3984
Weekdays 9-6 Saturday 11-5.

Books & magazines
Midtown West

quality style service value

The Edge: They have it all when you're on the move.

Union Theological Seminary Bookstore

3041 Broadway
near 121st Street
New York, NY 10027
212-280-1554. Fax 212-280-1416
Monday Wednesday-Friday 9-5 Tuesday 9-7.

Books & magazines
Upper Upper West Side

The Edge: Best for books on all aspects of religion. Located just inside the seminary. Caters to theology students. Also find books on comparative religions, politics, social sciences and more.

Ursus Books & Prints

375 West Broadway
near Broome Street
New York, NY 10012
212-226-7858. Fax 212-737-9306
Weekdays 10-6 Saturday 11-5. Closed Saturday July and August.

Books & magazines
SoHo/TriBeCa

quality style service value

The Edge: Focus on rare art reference books for the sophisticated collector. Two locations—SoHo and the Upper East Side—feature 40,000 volumes with a focus on 19th- and 20th-century art and exhibition catalogs. Materials favored by libraries, universities and serious students. The print department has more than 1,000 17th- to 19th-century prints, many decorative prints, engravings and watercolors. A few out-of-print books on philosophy.

"See Peter Kruas for advice and assistance."

981 Madison Avenue
near 76th Street/10021
212-772-8787. Fax 212-737-9306

Upper East Side

Victor Kamkin, Inc.

925 Broadway
near 21st Street
New York, NY 10010
212-673-0776. Fax 212-673-2473
Weekdays 9:30-5:30 Saturday 10-5.

Books & magazines
Gramercy Pk/Murray Hill

quality style service value

The Edge: Russian bookstore. The shop is filled with Russian titles printed in Cyrillic, with only 20% of the books in English. Includes current titles, children's books, dictionaries, historical works and reference. Also classic painted wooden dolls, records, newspapers and periodicals. No delivery.

"A haven for Russians."

Village Comics

163 Bleecker Street
near Sullivan Street
New York, NY 10012
212-777-2770. Fax 212-475-9727
Monday 11-8 Tuesday Thursday 11-8:30 Wednesday10-9
Friday 9-9 Saturday 10-9 Sunday 11-7.

Books & magazines
SoHo/TriBeCa

The Edge: Knickknacks for the younger set. Comics plus T-shirts, trading cards, videos, limited-edition model kits and more.

940 3rd Avenue
near 57th Street/10022
212-759-6255
Monday Tuesday 12-6 Wednesday 11-7:30 Friday 11:30-7 Saturday 10-9 Sunday 11-7.

Midtown East

Village Comics SciFi Shop

168 Thompson Street
between Bleecker and Houston Streets
New York, NY 10012
212-473-3010. Fax 212-473-4384
Daily noon-7 Saturday 11-7 Sunday noon-6.

Books & magazines
SoHo/TriBeCa

The Edge: Knickknacks with a Science Fiction focus for the younger set. Comics plus T-shirts, trading cards, videos, limited-edition model kits and more relating to science fiction.

Bleecker Bob's Golden Oldie Record Shop

118 West 3rd Street
near MacDougal Street
New York, NY 10012
212-475-9677. Fax 212-477-7902
Sunday-Thursday noon-1am Friday Saturday noon-3am.

CDs, tapes & records
SoHo/TriBeCa

quality style service value

The Edge: Out-of-print and rare pop records. Find new and used popular music from the 1940s to the present. Out-of-print and rare records share space with the latest. They feature jazz, show tunes, modern underground and punk music. No opera and no classical.

Entertainment Warehouse

835 Broadway
near 13th Street
New York, NY 10003
212-475-1844. Fax 212-475-1844
Monday-Saturday 10-10 Sunday noon-8.

CDs, tapes & records
Flatiron/East Village

The Edge: The place to recycle your tapes and CDs. Sells only used CDs and cassettes in good condition, which they shrink-wrap like originals. CDs (mostly rock, pop and classical) are $3 to $13, with boxed sets at $26. You can recycle your CDs and cassettes here.

Golden Disc

239 Bleecker Street
near 6th Avenue
New York, NY 10014
212-255-7899
Monday Tuesday 11:30-8 Wednesday-Saturday 11:30-9.

CDs, tapes & records
Greenwich Village

The Edge: Used CDs and records. The shop specializes in imported and out-of-print discs with a focus on blues, jazz and rock.

Gryphon Record Shop

251 West 72nd Street, 2nd Floor
between Broadway and West End Avenue
New York, NY 10023
212-874-1588
Monday-Saturday 11-7 Sunday noon-6.

CDs, tapes & records
Upper West Side

2	.	2	4
quality	style	service	value

The Edge: Large stock of rare records. Affiliated with Gryphon Bookshop. Features out-of-print and rare LPs. Classical and jazz labels are the specialty.

Jazz Record Center

236 West 26th Street, 8th Floor
between 7th and 8th Avenues
New York, NY 10001
212-675-4480. Fax 212-675-4504
Tuesday-Saturday 10-6. Weekdays 10-6 from Memorial to Labor Day.

CDs, tapes & records
Midtown West

The Edge: Everything you could want related to jazz. A source for rare to modern jazz cassettes, CDs and records. Also printed materials, books, magazines and posters. Huge inventory.

Music Inn

169 West 4th Street
near 6th Avenue
New York, NY 10014
212-243-5715
Tuesday-Saturday 1-7.

CDs, tapes & records
Greenwich Village

The Edge: Ethnic records. Features African, English, Irish and other folk music. Extensive offerings of jazz and blues recordings, even those out of print.

Nostalgia . . . and All That Jazz

217 Thompson Street
near Bleecker Street
New York, NY 10012
212-420-1940
Daily 1:30-9.

CDs, tapes & records
SoHo/TriBeCa

The Edge: Memorable old recordings. Jazz recordings, soundtracks of old movies and recordings of early radio programs, plus a small collection of movie and jazz photographs and posters. No credit cards.

Rebel Rebel

319 Bleecker Street
near 7th Avenue
New York, NY 10014
212-989-0770
Weekdays 12:30-8 weekends 12:30-9.

CDs, tapes & records
Greenwich Village

The Edge: "Now" music—rock, alternative and acid jazz. Find CDs, tapes and records. No delivery.

Record Explosion

142 West 34th Street
near 7th Avenue
New York, NY 10001
212-714-0450
Weekdays 9-8:30 Saturday 9-9 Sunday 10-8.

CDs, tapes & records
Midtown West

The Edge: Broad selection of music. Standard pricing on all types of music from around the world. No delivery.

2 Broadway
near Battery Park/10004
212-509-6444. Fax 212-747-0889
Weekdays 8-7.

Lower Manhattan

507 5th Avenue
near 42nd Street/10017
212-661-6642. Fax 212-747-0889
Monday-Saturday 8-8 Sunday 10-7.

Midtown East

384 5th Avenue
between 35th and 36th Streets/10018
212-736-5624. Fax 212-643-2838
Monday-Wednesday Saturday 9-7 Thursday Friday 9-7:30 Sunday 9-6.

Midtown West

180 Broadway
near John Street/10038
212-693-1510
Weekdays 8-7 Saturday 10-5:30.

Lower Manhattan

Records Revisited

34 West 33rd Street, 2nd Floor
near Broadway
New York, NY 10001
212-695-7155
Weekdays 9-5 Saturday by appointment.

CDs, tapes & records
Midtown West

The Edge: One of the few sources still stocking 78-rpm records. A dying breed, an old-fashioned music store, stocking records. You have to know what you want—it's not a place to browse. No credit cards.

Revolver Records

CDs, tapes & records
Chelsea

45 West 8th Street, 2nd Floor
near 6th Avenue
New York, NY 10011
212-982-6760
Daily 11-10.

The Edge: Discounts soul, jazz and rock CDs. Only CDs, but prices are good. No credit cards.

Sounds

CDs, tapes & records
Flatiron/East Village

16 St. Marks Place
between 2nd and 3rd Avenues
New York, NY 10003
212-677-2727
Monday-Thursday noon-10 Friday Saturday noon-11.

The Edge: Everything—rock, jazz and classical. Good prices on new and used CDs. No credit cards. No delivery.

20 St. Marks Place

Flatiron/East Village

between 2nd and 3rd Avenues/10003
212-677-3444
Monday-Thursday noon-10 Friday Saturday noon-midnight Sunday noon-7.

Tower Records & Video

CDs, tapes & records
Flatiron/East Village

383 Lafayette Street
at 4th Street
New York, NY 10003
212-505-1166. Fax 212-228-5338
Daily 11-11.

| 4 | - | 3 | 4 |
| quality | style | service | value |

The Edge: Beloved for its selection of music and videos by those who can stand the environment. Low, low prices on music and videos. Great selection. No delivery. 20% off.

"Buy all records/tapes there." "Good selection." "I can always find what I want there." "Great selection for the under-30 crowd." "Annoying that bags have to be checked." "It's great for shock value."

692 Broadway

SoHo/TriBeCa

near 4th Street/10012
212-505-1500
Daily 9-midnight.

725 5th Avenue

Midtown East

near 56th Street/10022
212-838-8110
Monday-Saturday 9-9 Sunday 10-7.

2107 Broadway

Upper West Side

near 73rd Street/10023
212-799-2500. Fax 212-799-2559
Daily 9-midnight.

Charlotte's Catering

146 Chambers Street
near West Broadway
New York, NY 10007
212-732-7939
Weekdays 10-6 or by appointment.

Caterers
Lower Manhattan

5	4	4	4
quality	style	service	value

The Edge: Elegant excellent food. Expert full-service catering serves excellent food, provides flowers and waiters. Able to handle all events, including small dinners, dinner dances, business meetings and wedding receptions. Corporate clients include Miramax Films and Lehman Bros. Will deliver takeout for small dinners.

"Very expensive but you can call, order and it's delivered ready for you to serve or reheat—your preference."

Creative Edge Parties

110 Barrow Street
near Washington Street
New York, NY 10014
212-741-3000. Fax 212-741-3888
By appointment.

Caterers
Greenwich Village

5	5	5	5
quality	style	service	value

The Edge: Excellent creative food. Co-owner Robert Spiegel was Glorious Foods' sous-chef. Beautiful food served by well-trained, attractive help. Very beautiful and creative events.

"Excellent."

Feast and Fêtes

20 East 76th Street
between 5th and Madison Avenues
New York, NY 10021
212-737-2224
By appointment.

Caterers
Upper East Side

The Edge: Catering from Restaurant Daniel owner and partner. Jean-Christophe Le Picart joined Daniel Boulard, chef and co-owner of Restaurant Daniel, former chef of Le Cirque, to open Feast and Fêtes catering. How bad can it be?

Flavors Catering and Carry-out

8 West 18th Street
near 5th Avenue
New York, NY 10011
212-647-1234
Weekdays 8:30-6:30.

Caterers
Chelsea

5	5	3	3
quality	style	service	value

The Edge: From Texas- to Tuscany-style food. Specialties include polenta pie, roast vegetables and excellent desserts. Will provide recipes on request. Takeout list includes 25 cold entrees, sandwiches and hot items. Also offers a catering service, which is flexible and designed around your plans. A tasting room upstairs.

"Staff has attitude, but great food; expensive".

Gay Jordan

1065 Lexington Avenue
between 75th and 76th Streets
New York, NY 10021
212-794-2248
By appointment.

Caterers
Upper East Side

4	4	4	4
quality	style	service	value

The Edge: Up there with Glorious Food. Excellent classic French-style food. Parties for a minimum of 8 to 1,500.

"Second best after Glorious Food. "Professional and fair"

Glorious Food

504 East 74th Street
near York Avenue
New York, NY 10021
212-628-2320
By appointment.

Caterers
Upper East Side

5	5	5	5
quality	style	service	value

The Edge: Sets the standard in catering. Impeccable food that's delicious, creative and beautifully presented. Will cater for two to thousands of people at your choice of location. Celebrity clientele. Provides good-looking and well-trained staff who are mostly actors and actresses between engagements. They can accommodate 60 for dinner in their garden terrace setting or on their rooftop. Very expensive.

"Continues to be the best!" "Parties I have been to are great."

Great Performances

287 Spring Street
near Hudson Street
New York, NY 10013
212-727-2424. Fax 212-727-2820
By appointment.

Caterers
SoHo/TriBeCa

4	4	4	4
quality	style	service	value

The Edge: Quality catering from crowds of 12 to hundreds. Professional-quality dining.

"Does a good job consistently."

Neuman & Bogdonoff

406 West 13th Street
near 9th Avenue
New York, NY 10014
212-675-1200. Fax 212-206-7574
Weekdays 6-8:30 Saturday 6-7:30 Sunday 6-6.

Caterers
Greenwich Village

4	4	4	4
quality	style	service	value

The Edge: Very good, not great catering. Owned by the son of the owner of Rosedale Fish Market, which is one of the top fish stores in the city. Closed their takeout shop to focus on catering only. They're flexible, but not surprising—the specialties include fish items (great poached salmon) as well as pasta dishes, salads and basic meats and potatoes. Baked goods feature American classics.

Robbins and Wolfe Catering

521 West Street
near Horatio Street
New York, NY 10014
212-924-6500
By appointment weekdays 9-5.

Caterers
Greenwich Village

5 | 5 | 5 | 5
quality style service value

The Edge: Excellent food served well. Celebrity clientele. Attractive, innovative food.

Taste Caterers

113 Horatio Street
near West Street
New York, NY 10014
212-255-8571
By appointment.

Caterers
Greenwich Village

3 | 4 | 3 | 3
quality style service value

The Edge: Good food. Favors simple California-style cuisine.

Tentation Catering

47 East 19th Street
between Park Avenue South and Broadway
New York, NY 10003
212-353-0070
By appointment weekdays 9-6.

Caterers
Flatiron/East Village

4 | 4 | 3 | 3
quality style service value

The Edge: Consistently very good French food. Dinners for 8 to 2,000. Tastes as exceptional as it looks.

Yura

1645 3rd Avenue
between 92nd and 93rd Streets
New York, NY 10128
212-860-8060. Fax 212-369-0970
Daily 7-8.

Caterers
Upper East Side

3 | 3 | 4 | 4
quality style service value

The Edge: When's she's good, she's great. Catering and takeout featuring "comfort food." Offers chicken salad, tuna salad, fried chicken, meatloaf and macaroni and cheese. Desserts appear to be a first love and include angel-food cake with bittersweet chocolate icing, apple crisp and baked muffins. When available, try the poached plum fruit dessert—it's in a class by itself.

"Food-wise our wedding was a 10, our parents' 50th a 5."

Abrons Arts Center

466 Grand Street
near Pitt Street
New York, NY 10002-4804
212-598-0400
Schedule varies by activity.

Classes & activities
Lower East Side

quality style service value
4 - - 5

The Edge: The Lower East Side's answer to the 92nd Street Y. While a smaller number of programs than the 92nd Street Y, Henry Street Settlement's Abrons Art Center offers an array of classes and workshops in drama, music and the visual arts. Classes are reasonable. A sampling includes: drawing and painting at 10 sessions for $150 or book arts/printmaking (all levels) 10 sessions for $90. Offers private music lessons in just about everything (bassoon, flute, saxophone, clarinet, bass/electric bass, guitar, trumpet, trombone, cello, oboe, vibes, kettle drums, piano, violin, French horn, recorder), including voice. One hour for $16.50 for nonneighborhood students and $15 per hour for neighborhood students. They offer small-group lessons for six students or fewer. Also a summer arts camp program for children ages 6 to 12. The recently redone theater is a jewel and offers a variety of drama, jazz and opera programs.

After School Workshop

122 East 83rd Street
near Lexington Avenue
New York, NY 10028
212-734-7620
Daily 1-6.

Classes & activities
Upper East Side

The Edge: Wonderful educational activities for children. Get help with homework at reading and math workshops, plus classes on computers, arts and crafts, baking, theater training, sports and games. After-school workshops are $140 or $15 per half hour of private tutoring.

Alliance of Resident Theatres

131 Varick Street, Room 904
near Spring Street
New York, NY 10013
212-989-5257
Weekdays 10-6.

Classes & activities
SoHo/TriBeCa

The Edge: Hot seats and news on discounts to Off Broadway. Also called A.R.T. This is an advocacy group for about 250 of New York City's not-for-profit theater groups. Publishes bimonthly *Hot Seats*, which features the Passport to Off Broadway program providing discount coupons (subject to ticket availability) to Off Broadway plays. Discounts range from 10% to 50% and are redeemable at scores of plays currently. No credit cards.

Art Students League

215 West 57th Street
near Broadway
New York, NY 10019
212-247-4510
Weekend classes.

Classes & activities
Midtown West

quality style service value
5 - 5 5

The Edge: Art courses taught by master artists. Courses in various aspects of drawing, including anatomy, are offered on Saturday and Sunday. Half-day (3½ hours) to full-day (7 hours) programs. No credit cards.

Ballet Academy East

1651 3rd Avenue
near 92nd Street
New York, NY 10128
212-410-9140
Daily: children 9-6 adults 6-9.

Classes & activities
Upper East Side

The Edge: Top-notch mother-and-child classes. Classes for children ages 2 and up. Pre-ballet classes for ages 2 to 5 years and classes for all ages to adult. Each class has two teachers and a pianist. Vans run from many private schools. Now offering classes for boys.

Central Park Activities

starting at 59th Street
5th Avenue and Central Park West
New York, NY 10021
212-427-4040
Daily during daylight hours.

Classes & activities
Upper East Side

5 . . 5

quality style service value

The Edge: Manhattan's indispensable playground. Find 90-minute walks and talks led by urban park rangers, on subjects ranging from geology to birdwatching, every Sunday at 2pm, rain or shine. Also find tours Tuesday through Sunday at various times between 10am and 4:30pm. The carousel is open weekdays from 10:30am to 4:30pm and weekends from 10:30am to 5:30pm. The Central Park zoo features wildlife exhibitions and a wonderful children's zoo, open weekdays from 10am to 5pm and weekends and holidays from 10:30am to 5:30pm. The Hechscher Puppet House at the Hechscher Playground presents puppet shows Monday to Friday at 10:30am and noon. Reservations are required. No credit cards.

Children's Acting Academy

1050 5th Avenue
near 87th Street
New York, NY 10028
212-860-7101
Weekdays after 3.

Classes & activities
Upper East Side

The Edge: Acting classes for children. For 23 years, acting classes for 5- to 17-year olds, after school and on Saturdays. Instructors have trained at director Lee Strasberg's Theater Institute and the London Royal Academy.

Children's Museum of the Arts

72 Spring Street
near Broadway
New York, NY 10012
212-941-9198
Tuesday Wednesday Friday-Sunday 11-5 Thursday 11-7.

Classes & activities
SoHo/TriBeCa

The Edge: A museum just for children. For children up to 10 years old. Ever-changing exhibitions. Workshops every hour on the hour in painting, drawing and mask making, among others. Weekend workshops for children over 6 years are included in the admission fee of $5 per child ($4 on weekdays) plus $1 materials fee. No credit cards.

China Institute

125 East 65th Street
near Lexington Avenue
New York, NY 10021
212-744-8181. Fax 212-628-4159
Per class schedule.

Classes & activities
Upper East Side

| 5 | 5 | 5 | 5 |
| quality | style | service | value |

The Edge: A wide range of Chinese courses. A wonderful place to explore your interest in China. Excellent language, poetry and cooking classes. Favorite courses include a one-month, intensive, day-long, five-days-per-week Mandarin course that's given in the summer. Also explore their Mandarin classes for children. Their six-session group cooking class, given in their well-equipped kitchen, is hands-on and costs $300.

"Excellent courses and excellent teachers—seek out Ben Wang."

City Children's Theater of New York

1751 2nd Avenue, Suite 103
between 91st and 92nd Streets
New York, NY 10128
212-289-2900
Per course schedule.

Classes & activities
Upper East Side

The Edge: Trains children ages 5 to 18, in musical theater. Classes emphasize diction, concentration, improvisation, movement and characterization, costumes and set preparation. Performances and stage readings.

Cooper Union

30 Cooper Square
at 3rd Avenue and 7th Street
New York, NY 10003
212-353-4195
Weekend classes.

Classes & activities
Flatiron/East Village

The Edge: Art classes for all. Beginners' drawing class meets on Saturday mornings. A range of classes for more advanced students also.

Diller-Quale

24 East 95th Street
between 5th and Madison Avenues
New York, NY 10128
212-369-1484
Schedule varies.

Classes & activities
Upper East Side

The Edge: Music and art lessons for all ages. Devoted to music, voice and the arts. Provides after-school/after-work programs for all ages. Offers individual and group lessons for all instruments (cello, violin, string and piano), voice and art classes one to three times per week. No credit cards.

German Wine Society
445 Park Avenue
near 56th Street
New York, NY 10022
212-599-6948
As scheduled.

Classes & activities
Midtown East

The Edge: Information center offering travel programs on German wines. Runs occasional social events to encourage the discovery and enjoyment of German wine. Periodic meetings, wine parties and a newsletter. Participates in the annual fall German Wine Academy tour of the German wine region, which includes lectures by experts and visits to the wine-growing region's vineyards and cellars. A wide spectrum of tastings is the hallmark of the tour.

Gotham Writers' Workshop
1841 Broadway, Suite 809
near 60th Street
New York, NY 10023
212-307-9673. Fax 212-307-6325
Evening and weekend classes.

Classes & activities
Upper West Side

The Edge: Comprehensive writers' workshops. Classes on writing fiction, nonfiction, drama, poetry and improvisation. Private instruction and group classes limited to 14 students. The Script Doctor Program provides a professional reading, analysis and fix for $65 per hour.

Ice Studio, Inc.
1034 Lexington Avenue
near 73rd Street
New York, NY 10021
212-535-0304
Call for their current schedule of skating sessions.

Classes & activities
Upper East Side

The Edge: Tiny year-round ice rink located on the second floor of a brownstone. Offers lessons and skate rentals. Lessons are $35 per half hour. No credit cards.

International Wine Center
231 West 29th Street, Suite 210
between 7th and 8th Avenues
New York, NY 10001
212-268-7517
Weekday evenings per schedule. Office open weekdays 9-5.

Classes & activities
Midtown West

The Edge: For the serious wine lover, blind wine tastings over lunch. Tastings and lunches featured for serious amateurs. Priced at $235 for tastings with lunch.

James Beard Foundation
167 West 12th Street
near 7th Avenue
New York, NY 10011
212-675-4984
Per schedule.

Classes & activities
Chelsea

4	4	4	4
quality	style	service	value

The Edge: Special dining events for members and their guests throughout the U.S.
Restaurant news and recommendations, but best of all, features dinners planned around special wines, seasonal specialties and occasions.

Julliard Placement Bureau
60 Lincoln Center Plaza
near 65th Street
New York, NY 10023
212-799-5000. Fax 212-724-0263
Weekdays 9:30-8 Saturday 10-7 Sunday noon-5.

Classes & activities
Upper West Side

The Edge: Professional training by day, amateur education by night. The evening division features lectures on music, applied music and ear and voice training. Over 300 courses are offered each semester, including a survey course on music. Will provide recommendations for piano teachers. Also has a store selling music, books, CDs and tapes.

Learning Annex
116 East 85th Street
near Park Avenue
New York, NY 10028
212-570-6500. Fax 212-570-4004
Primarily evenings and weekends. Office open weekdays 8:30-7:30 Saturday 10-4.

Classes & activities
Upper East Side

The Edge: It's in the neighborhood, if you live uptown, and sometimes it's fun. Has featured speakers on topics of interest, including Joan Rivers on survival and Henry Kissinger on diplomacy.

Lenox Hill Neighborhood House
331 East 70th Street
near 1st Avenue
New York, NY 10021
212-744-5022. Fax 212-744-5150
Weekdays 6:40-9:40 weekends 9-6.

Classes & activities
Upper East Side

The Edge: Toddler and parenting group activities. Activities, including playtime, gym tots and aqua tots for ages 1½ to 3½ years. Also age-appropriate arts and crafts, games, gymnastics and swimming activities, Head Start comprehensive early-childhood programs and teen program for 12- to 18-year olds. Offers weekend computer groups for ages 5 to 18 and gymnastics groups for children ages 3½ to 8. Of course adult programs too. Wonderful pool.

Mannes College of Music
150 West 85th Street
near Amsterdam Avenue
New York, NY 10024
212-580-0210. Fax 212-580-1738
Monday-Saturday 9-4 Sunday 9-6.

Classes & activities
Upper West Side

4	4	3	3
quality	style	service	value

The Edge: Great instruction for the professional or the amateur. Individually designed programs for adults. Instruction for virtually all classical instruments and voice. Special programs for children ages 4 to 18. Small classes, private and semiprivate lessons, orchestral, jazz studies and piano teacher referrals. Classes on weekday afternoons and all day Saturday.

Marymount Manhattan College

221 East 71st Street
near 2nd Avenue
New York, NY 10021
212-517-0564. Fax 212-628-4208
Evenings and weekends.

Classes & activities
Upper East Side

The Edge: Neighborhood school featuring practical courses. Offers over 200 courses covering a wide range of topics, including ancient world, art history, play writing and public relations in the entertainment industry. Focus is on expanding horizons and teaching and reinforcing the fundamentals, such as hands-on computer training, communication skills and writing. They offer certificate programs. For the body—exercise programs featuring low-impact aerobics and swimming in their heated 20- by 60-foot pool. Special tots to teens and over 65 programs.

Metropolitan Museum of Art

1000 5th Avenue
near 82nd Street
New York, NY 10028
212-879-5500. Fax 212-570-3879
Tuesday-Thursday Sunday 9:30-5:15
Friday Saturday 9:30-9.

Classes & activities
Upper East Side

5	5	4	4
quality	style	service	value

The Edge: For the soul—world-class art and instruction. A wonderful permanent art collection and special exhibits. Art and music appreciation courses and concerts, gallery lectures and special childrens' programs. Members' discount.

"A New York treasure." "The courses are exceptional. Don't miss Rosamond Bernier's courses. She's terrific."

National Academy of Design

5 East 89th Street
east of 5th Avenue
New York, NY 10128
212-996-1908. Fax 212-360-6795
Weekdays 9-9 Saturday 9-4.

Classes & activities
Upper East Side

The Edge: Top instruction using live models. Three-hour courses in figure drawing, both clothed and unclothed figures, are conducted on Saturday mornings and afternoons. Will be accepting credit cards soon.

New School

66 West 12th Street
near 5th Avenue
New York, NY 10011
212-229-5630. Fax 212-229-5690
Primarily weekends and evenings.

Classes & activities
Chelsea

5	3	5	3
quality	style	service	value

The Edge: 1,500 courses. If they don't have it, does it exist? Offers courses in business, communications, computers, culinary arts, foreign languages, humanities, music history and appreciation, science, social sciences, theater arts and writing. In addition, special events include workshop at the Met, career planning and cooking, plus their distinguished lecture series and concert programs. Courses for certificate or degree programs.

"The catalog is comprehensive, but not well organized."

New York Academy of Art

111 Franklin Street
near Church Street
New York, NY 10013
212-966-0300. Fax 212-966-3217
Per schedule.

Classes & activities
SoHo/TriBeCa

The Edge: Classic painting well taught. A basic course, Old Master Drawing: Methods and Materials, is offered on 12 Saturdays in three-hour afternoon sessions. Also two uninstructed sketch courses are available for students of all levels who come in and draw the model of the day (models pose for 5- and 20-minute intervals) throughout a three-hour period or for a long pose session in which the model changes the pose only once over the three hours.

New York University School of Continuing Education

7 East 12th Street
near 5th Avenue
New York, NY 10003
212-998-7171. Fax 212-995-3060
Primarily evenings and weekends.

Classes & activities
Flatiron/East Village

4	4	4	4
quality	style	service	value

The Edge: 2,000 courses leading to degrees. Career focus! Courses days, nights and weekends on a wide range of topics, including career (business, real estate) and life enhancement (arts and humanities). Offers more than 2,000 courses for credit and more than 100 certificates, specialized diplomas, undergraduate degrees, and Master's degrees. Free career nights, open houses and other special events.

92nd Street Y

1395 Lexington Avenue
near 92nd Street
New York, NY 10128
212-996-1100. Fax 212-415-5788
Varies by activity, but there's always something going on.

Classes & activities
Upper East Side

5	.	.	5
quality	style	service	value

The Edge: A neighborhood treasure offering everything. You name it, they have it. From culture to sports to children's programs. Lectures from the Who's Who in their field— for example hear Studs Terkel, Charlton Heston, Wendy Wasserstein, Philip Johnson and Caroline Kennedy. Adult programs, including Jewish education, great world of ideas, personal growth, career and finance, language and writing, art, music, dance, 60+ programs, tours and travel, dance, health, fitness and sports. Their health and fitness center has aerobics classes and a full gym and pool. Yearly fitness membership is $884, or $95 monthly. Theater, concerts and a full children's program are also available.

"A true treasure." "Lyrics and Lyricists Program tickets sell out at once."

Parents League

115 East 82nd Street
near Lexington Avenue
New York, NY 10028
212-737-7385
Monday-Thursday 9-4 Friday 9-12.

Classes & activities
Upper East Side

quality style service value

The Edge: Knowledgeable parent-advisors will consult candidly on topics of interest. One of the best city resources for parents. A nonprofit organization which shares information between parents on topics of interest like choosing a school, locating a summer camp, finding a babysitter, selecting after-school activities, summer camps and teen travel. Publishes the *Parents League Calendar and Guide to NY, Parents League Review, Toddler Book* and the *Parents League News.*

Peter Kump's School of Culinary Arts

307 East 92nd Street
near 2nd Avenue
New York, NY 10128
212-410-5152. Fax 212-410-4601
Evening and weekend classes.

Classes & activities
Upper East Side

The Edge: International chefs share their secrets. Names you know teaching bread baking, buffet dishes, cake decoration, spa cuisine, French bistro cooking, Italian, Japanese, Mexican, Vietnamese, wine tasting and more. Evening, Saturday and weekend workshops.

Playspace

2473 Broadway
near 92nd Street
New York, NY 10025
212-769-2300. Fax 212-769-1066
Daily 9-6.

Classes & activities
Upper West Side

The Edge: Indoor playground for children plus a cafe area for parents. 15 play areas, including a bridge with a 20-foot crawling tunnel in the shape of a train and a screened tree house. Party packages are $129 weekdays or $169 weekends for 10 children plus $11.95 for each additional child. Package includes a staff person. For children to 6 years old.

Pratt Institute of Art

295 Lafayette Street
near Houston Street
New York, NY 10012
212-925-8481. Fax 212-941-6397
Per course schedule.

Classes & activities
SoHo/TriBeCa

The Edge: Training by the instructors to the professionals. Basic drawing is offered on Saturday mornings in a 10-week course.

Wines & Spirits

Helmsley Hotel/212 East 42nd Street
between 2nd and 3rd Avenues
718-263-3134
Per course schedule.

Classes & activities
Midtown East

The Edge: Fine wine classes. Harriet Lembeck's 14-week wine courses (10-weeks on wine and 4 on spirits) will be held at the Helmsley in Manhatton this year. 2½ hours per week. $525 per course. Call the phone number above for information.

YWCA

Lexington Avenue and 53rd Street
New York, NY 10022
212-735-9731
Daily 10-9 for classes 6-9 for gym.

Classes & activities
Midtown East

The Edge: In midtown, both a great sports facility and the Crafts Students League. Call for their catalog. The swimming pool is gorgeous and not always crowded. Exercise programs are tailored to busy career people. The Crafts Students League offers programs in crafts and fine arts, teaching basic and master craft techniques in their well-equipped studios. Other programs focus on careers.

Stacks Rare Coins

123 West 57th Street
near 6th Avenue
New York, NY 10019
212-582-2580. Fax 212-245-5018
Weekdays 10-5.

Coins & stamps
Midtown West

The Edge: Ten coin auctions per year. One of the largest rare-coin dealers in the country. Also find rare coins, seals and paper money. For serious collectors. No credit cards. No delivery.

Dorothy Wako

212-686-5569
Weekdays 9:30-5 by appointment

Coordinators
Mail/phone

5	5	3	3
quality	style	service	value

The Edge: Stylistically tops. Flower designs for all events from dinner parties to major society events. Clients have included Dominick Dunne and Julia Roberts. For a Greenwich, Conn. garden wedding, they planted a traditional English garden with the feel of a country cottage. Prices start at $85 and up for a simple dinner party arrangement. No credit cards. Deluxe.

Gourmet Advisory Service, Inc.

315 East 68th Street
near 2nd Avenue
New York, NY 10021
212-535-0005
By appointment.

Coordinators
Upper East Side

5	3	4	4
quality	style	service	value

The Edge: Party designer with strong food skills. Harriet Rose Katz and team can put it all together—food, music (jazz bands, classical quartets and cabaret singers), caterers, florists, invitations and accessories. A pleasure to deal with. You may know them as Liaison, Unlimited. Very expensive. Deluxe.

Perl & Berliner
260 Columbia Avenue
Ft. Lee, NJ 07024
201-224-0034
Weekdays 9-5 for appointments.

Coordinators
New Jersey

The Edge: Creative party skills. Owned by Gail Perl and Carol Berliner. Handled the wedding of Leonard Stern's son Emanuel at the Central Park Zoo and Al Roker's wedding. 25 years' experience. Events for 50 to 1,700. No credit cards.

Philip Baloun Designs
340 West 55th Street
near 9th Avenue
New York, NY 10019
212-307-1675
By appointment.

Coordinators
Midtown West

quality style service value

The Edge: Ability to transform entire spaces into theatrical other worlds. Celebrity clients include the Metropolitan Opera. Views themselves as floral decoration specialists. No credit cards.

Renny - Design for Entertaining
505 Park Avenue
near 59th Street
New York, NY 10022
212-288-7000. Fax 212-593-3549
Monday-Saturday 9-6. Summer Monday-Saturday 9-5.

Coordinators
Midtown East

quality style service value

The Edge: Orchids are a specialty. Romantic arrangements. Also plants and trees. Known for their planning of dramatic party events. Rental of props and the regulars—linens, crystal and dishes. Gorgeous things. Celebrity clients include Brooke Astor, the Newhouses, Agnellis and Safras among others. Renny runs a plant-maintenance and landscaping service. Many of the flowers are grown for him in Bucks County, Penn. Arrangements start at $50.

"Gorgeous, but pricey."

Robert Isabell
410 West 13th Street
near Washington Street
New York, NY 10014
212-645-7767
Weekdays 9-6 for appointments.

Coordinators
Greenwich Village

quality style service value

The Edge: The "Glorious Food" of florists. Periodic sales of items left over from major events. Coordinates flowers, lighting and sound effects. Top of the line with matching attitude.

Did the Steinberg-Tisch wedding, Random House's party in the Winter Garden celebrating the launch of Avedon's autobiography and best known for doing the celebrated Miller (of the Duty Free Shops) daughters' multi-million-dollar weddings. Event planners, no walk-in business. No credit cards. Deluxe.

Chuckles and Friends

Entertainment
Upper West Side

212-496-6228
By appointment.

The Edge: Entertainment for children ages 5 to 10. Chuckles will come to you with entertainment that includes balloons, magic, puppets, music and face paints. Features games, including relay races, for older children. Parents can choose a character (Chuckles, Minnie and Mickey Mouse, Cinderella and Peter Pan) and have the party planned around that character. $165 per hour. No credit cards.

Party Poopers

Entertainment
SoHo/TriBeCa

104 Reade Street
near West Broadway
New York, NY 10013
212-587-9030. Fax 212-587-9030
Weekdays 10-6 for bookings.

The Edge: Parties to go and even better, a private party at their place. Theme parties for younger children, ages 1 to 4, include fairytale land, superhero adventure, medieval party, beauty parlor/fashion show and Mother Goose nursery rhymes. Themes for older children include game show, spookhouse, dance party, secret agent and whodunit. Various facilities available, including a 1,100-square-foot room, a 2,200-square-foot room or both combined. Will provide cake, snacks, drinks and loot bags. An at-home party option is available. No credit cards.

Silly Billy

Entertainment
Mail/phone

212-645-1299. Fax 212-645-8389
By appointment

4	4	4	4
quality	style	service	value

The Edge: Great party entertainment for toddlers to age 11. Provides entertainers for parties, including clowns, balloon sculpture and magic. No credit cards.

Elan Flowers

Florists
SoHo/TriBeCa

108 Wooster Street
near Spring Street
New York, NY 10012
212-343-2426. Fax 212-343-2439
Sunday Monday noon-6 Tuesday-Saturday noon-7.

The Edge: Slightly less expensive for classic European-style bouquets. Features stylish flowers in attractive arrangements in vibrant colors priced from $45, plus delivery. The flowers often have a Victorian style. They source flowers from Holland and France.

Les Fleurs de Maxim's

680 Madison Avenue
near 61st Street
New York, NY 10021
212-752-9889. Fax 212-750-0103
Monday-Saturday 10-6.

Florists
Upper East Side

quality style service value

The Edge: Very attractive flowers. Pierre Cardin is the founder and owner. Does single arrangements to settings for weddings or smaller dinners.

Paul Bott Beautiful Flowers

1305 Madison Avenue
near 92nd Street
New York, NY 10128
212-369-4000. Fax 212-369-4484
Weekdays 9-6 and by appointment.

Florists
Upper East Side

quality style service value

The Edge: Great flowers. Features very creative wonderful flowers nestled in tissues and cellophane. Fresh and dried flowers and plants available. Celebrity clients include William Simon (for his daughter's wedding).

Preston Bailey

88 Lexington Avenue, Studio 16C
between 26th and 27th Streets
New York, NY 10016
212-683-0035
Monday-Saturday 8-5.

Florists
Gramercy Pk/Murray Hill

The Edge: Romantic-style florist—loves to use roses and peonies giving an *Age of Innocence* feeling.

Ronaldo Maia

27 East 67th Street
near Madison Avenue
New York, NY 10021
212-288-1049
Monday-Saturday 9-6.

Florists
Upper East Side

quality style service value

The Edge: Gorgeous Oriental floral styles. Delicate floral styles in wonderful containers.

Simpson & Company and Florist West

852 10th Avenue
near 56th Street
New York, NY 10019
212-772-6670. Fax 212-581-1798
Weekdays 9-6 Saturday 9-1.

Florists
Midtown West

The Edge: Unusual flowers and dried arrangements. Features flowers, plants and freeze-dried flowers, fruits and vegetables in arrangements. Recommended to us but still unknown to our survey panel. Let us know what you think.

Spring Street Garden

186½ Spring Street
near Thompson Street
New York, NY 10012
212-966-2015
Tuesday-Saturday 11:30-7.

Florists
SoHo/TriBeCa

The Edge: Pretty flowers, which appear to be priced about 20% less than at other top florists. Less fussy simple arrangements.

Surroundings

224 West 79th Street
near Broadway
New York, NY 10024
212-580-8982. Fax 212-724-9131
Weekdays 10-7 Saturday 10-6.

Florists
Upper West Side

quality	style	service	value
4	4	5	4

The Edge: Attractive romantic arrangements. Gift baskets also, which can be customized. Imported flowers only. $50 minimum.

VSF

204 West 10th Street
near Bleecker Street
New York, NY 10014
212-206-7236
Monday Tuesday Friday Saturday 10-5
Wednesday Thursday 10-7.

Florists
Greenwich Village

quality	style	service	value
3	5	5	2

The Edge: English garden look. Favors Dutch flowers. Pricey but gorgeous.

"Very snooty."

Venamy Orchids

Route 22 North
Brewster, NY 10509
800-362-3612. Fax 914-278-7646
Monday-Saturday 9-6 Sunday 10-4.

Florists
Westchester

quality	style	service	value
4	4	3	4

The Edge: Hundreds and hundreds of orchids on display. Sells decorative pots and baskets to complement arrangements. Wedding and event orchid displays are a specialty. Delivers to New York City, Fairfield and Westchester and will ship throughout the United States. Provides expert advice and care. Designer/decorator is on the staff. $30 minimum for arrangements. A good-size plant of blooming orchids is priced from $26 to $50+. Wonderful quality. Discounter.

"Reasonable."

Zeze

398 East 52nd Street
near 1st Avenue
New York, NY 10022

Florists
Midtown East

quality	style	service	value
4	4	3	3

212-753-7767. Fax 212-355-5172
Weekdays 8-6.

The Edge: Dramatic arrangements with a touch of whimsy. Wide variety of orchids and flowers. Their large selection of vases is the core ingredient of their dramatic arrangements. $50 minimum, plus delivery ($7 to $15 in Manhattan), $75 minimum outside Manhattan.

Asphalt Green, the Murphy Center

555 East 90th Street
near York Avenue
New York, NY 10128
212-369-8890. Fax 212-369-2630
Weekdays 5:30-10 Saturday-Sunday 8-8.

Gyms
Upper East Side

4	4	3	5
quality	style	service	value

The Edge: A splendid sports facility with a huge array of fitness classes, aquatic activities and sports. Used by schools, groups and individuals of all ages (infant to senior). Fees $35 to $150, depending on the class of membership and age of the member. A wonderful neighborhood attraction.

Atrium Club

115 East 57th Street
near Park Avenue
New York, NY 10022
212-688-9840
Weekdays 6-10 weekends 6-11.

Gyms
Midtown East

4	4	3	4
quality	style	service	value

The Edge: Exercise in a convenient location. Three floors offering aerobics (over 70 classes), cardiovascular equipment and 30- by 40-foot lap pool (often crowded), sun deck and restaurant. Initiation fee is $300, then $113 monthly. Convenient location. Older crowd. No credit cards.

Cardio Fitness Center

200 Park Avenue, 3rd Floor
near 44th Street
New York, NY 10166
212-682-4440
Weekdays 6:30-9:30.

Gyms
Midtown East

5	5	5	3
quality	style	service	value

The Edge: In and out in one hour. Leave your sneakers—they provide the workout clothing. An unassuming, service-oriented, get-it-done (in one hour) club. It's never too crowded. Provides functional blue workout shorts and gray shirts. Best are individually designed programs updated quarterly. CNN is available to keep you amused at all times. If you don't come in, they call to remind you. Good range of equipment, including treadmills, Lifecycles, Stairmasters, Nordic Track and weight equipment. Personal trainers on call to provide advice. $1,600 per year. Very expensive. Deluxe.

"Comfortable—I'm 50, out of shape and love this place."

9 West 57th Street   **Midtown West**
near 5th Avenue/10019
212-753-3980

1221 Avenue of the Americas   **Midtown West**
near 49th Street/10020
212-840-8240

345 Park Avenue   **Midtown East**
near 52nd Street/10022
212-838-4570

885 3rd Avenue   **Midtown East**
near 54th Street/10022
212-888-2120

79 Maiden Lane   **Lower Manhattan**
near Williams Street/10038
212-943-1510

Central Park Challenges

Gyms

5th Avenue
near 60th Street
New York, NY 10021
212-348-4867. Fax 212-348-4479
Various times during the day.
Call for information regarding specific program.

Upper East Side

quality	style	service	value
5	5	.	5

The Edge: Rock climbing in Central Park. Rock-climbing classes in Central Park for anyone over 12 years old. Programs include the Challenge Program, rock climbing for ages 14 and up and Team Building, less physical, trust activities. Sunday classes from 10am to 1pm are $200 for four classes. Classes are limited to groups of 15. The climbing course, geared for beginners to advanced climbers, covers various climbing techniques, balance and safety and uses the park's designed outdoor and indoor walls. No credit cards.

Club La Raquette

Gyms
Midtown West

119 West 56th Street
in the Parker Meridien Hotel near 7th Avenue
New York, NY 10019
212-245-1144
Daily 6-11.

The Edge: Full gym facility at the Parker Meridien Hotel. Offers full gym facilities, aerobics and a pool.

Crunch

Gyms
Flatiron/East Village

54 East 13th Street
between University Place and Broadway
New York, NY 10003
212-475-2018
Weekdays 6:30-10 weekends 8-8.

The Edge: Gym with no membership requirement. Focus is cross training circuit. Full gym with good equipment and a wide range of classes.

404 Lafayette Street
near 4th Street/10003
212-614-0120
Weekdays 24 hours Saturday 5-10 Sunday 7-10.

Flatiron/East Village

162 West 83rd Street
near Amsterdam Avenue/10024
212-875-1902
Weekdays 6-11 weekends 8-8.

Upper West Side

David Barton Gym

552 Avenue of the Americas
between 15th and 16th Streets
New York, NY 10011
212-727-0004
Weekdays 6-midnight Saturday 9-9 Sunday 10-11.

Gyms
Chelsea

The Edge: 10,000-square-foot space with custom-built gym equipment. The focus is on weights and abdominal classes. Fee is $659 per year, with personal training extra. Celebrity clientele.

Downtown Athletic Club

19 West Street
near Battery Place
New York, NY 10004
212-425-7000
Weekdays 6-8:30 weekends 9-5.

Gyms
Lower Manhattan

The Edge: Downtown club. Offers a full-service gym and a great pool. Serves the Wall Street crowd. Also restaurant and rooms. $1,800 per year.

Drag's Gym

50 West 57th Street
between 5th and 6th Avenues
New York, NY 10019
212-757-0724
Weekdays 7-8 Saturday 8-2.

Gyms
Midtown West

The Edge: Pilates methodology. A no-frills gym, featuring small gymnastics classes limited to six people using the Pilates method. Favored by dancers and people with injuries. $18 for group classes, $40 for a private class and $35 for first-time use. Reduce the price by buying multiple sessions. No credit cards.

Equinox Fitness Club

897 Broadway
near 19th Street
New York, NY 10003

Gyms
Flatiron/East Village

| 5 | 5 | 5 | 3 |
| quality | style | service | value |

212-780-9300
Monday-Thursday 5:30-11 Friday 5:30-10 weekends 8:30-9.

The Edge: An attractive 18,000-square-foot spot to sweat. Machines for every interest, including Cybex weight training, Stairmasters, recumbent bikes and more. Cost $825 per year ($82 monthly), plus $295 initiation.

344 Amsterdam Avenue   **Upper West Side**
near 76th Street/10024
212-721-4200
Monday-Thursday 5:30-11 Friday 5:30-10 weekends 8:30-9.

Executive Fitness Center   **Gyms**
3 World Trade Center, 22nd Floor   **Lower Manhattan**
near Vesey Street
New York, NY 10004
212-466-9266
Weekdays 6-9:30 weekends 8-7.

The Edge: Full-service health club. Over 50 pieces of equipment in the gym plus a wonderful pool. Personal trainers. Aerobics.

Lotte Berk Method   **Gyms**
23 East 67th Street   **Upper East Side**
near Madison Avenue
New York, NY 10021

5	5	5	3
quality	style	service	value

212-288-6613. Fax 212-734-0238
Weekdays 7:15-8 Saturday 8:30-2 Sunday 9:30-2.

The Edge: Great workouts! 60-minute sessions for $18 per session in small classes of not more than 10 to 12 women. Wonderful for tightening all those places that need it. No credit cards.

Manhattan Plaza Health Club   **Gyms**
482 West 43rd Street   **Midtown West**
near 10th Avenue
New York, NY 10036
212-563-7001. Fax 212-629-9539
Weekdays 6:30-10 weekends 8:30-7.

The Edge: A gym that has it all but location. Located in the heart of Times Square. Offers aerobics, a climbing wall 20 feet high with 30 available routes, Cybex bikes, Stairmaster and treadmills plus a glass-enclosed swimming pool and sun deck. Fees are $875 per year or $195 initiation plus $67 a month.

New York Athletic Club   **Gyms**
180 Central Park South   **Midtown West**
near 59th Street
New York, NY 10019
212-247-5100. Fax 212-767-7137

The Edge: Great facilities, finally open to women. It finally admitted women! The sponsorship of three members is required, as well as a three- to four-month wait to get in after the interview. Personal trainers, weight equipment and Olympic-size pool are the big attractions. No credit cards.

New York Health and Racquet Club

Gyms

39 Whitehall Street
near Water Street
New York, NY 10004
212-269-9800
Weekdays 6-10 weekends 9-6.

Lower Manhattan

3 3 3 3
quality style service value

The Edge: Convenience and good equipment. Eight locations offering a range of activities, including basketball, racquetball, squash, strength and free weights and equipment, including swimming pools, cardiovascular equipment and spa facilities. Corporate memberships reduce charges. Can be crowded at prime times.

Piers 13 and 14
near the South Street Seaport/10005
212-777-8000
Weekdays 8-7 Saturday 9-5.

Lower Manhattan

132 East 45th Street
near 3rd Avenue/10017
212-986-3100
Weekdays 6-10 weekends 9-6.

Midtown East

110 West 56th Street
near 6th Avenue/10019
212-541-7200
Weekdays 6-10 Saturday 9-9 Sunday 9-6.

Midtown West

1433 York Avenue
near 76th Street/10021
212-737-6666
Weekdays 7-10 weekends 9-9.

Upper East Side

20 East 50th Street
near 5th Avenue/10022
212-593-1500
Weekdays 6-10 Saturday 9-6.

Midtown East

Pumping Iron Gym

Gyms
Upper East Side

403 East 91st Street
between 1st and York Avenues
New York, NY 10128
212-996-5444
Weekdays 6-11:30 weekends 8-8.

The Edge: Weight lifting for beginners to pros. Weight lifting for beginners with a separate aerobics program on two floors, one for weights and the other for cardiovascular equipment.

Personal trainers available. Membership fees are monthly at $72.80 or $624 per year. No credit cards.

Reebok's Sport Club New York

160 Columbus Avenue
near 67th Street
New York, NY 10023
212-362-6800
Monday-Thursday 5-11 Friday 5-10 Saturday Sunday 8- 8.

Gyms
Upper West Side

5 5 5 3
quality style service value

The Edge: One of New York's finest new facilities. 140,000-square-foot gym on the Upper West Side, including large pool with underwater music, a 45-foot climbing wall and two regulation-size basketball courts. Also includes a full salon and spa. $950 initiation fee, then $135 per month.

Sports Training Institute

239 East 49th Street
between 2nd and 3rd Avenues
New York, NY 10017
212-752-7111
Weekdays 5:30-9 Saturday 8:30-2.

Gyms
Midtown East

The Edge: Only one-on-one personal trainers. No frills, just work. Facilities include a stretch room, cardiovascular room and weight room. Initial evaluation $250, then $42.50 to $50 per session with a personal trainer.

Vertical Club

139 West 32nd Street
between 6th and 7th Avenues
New York, NY 10001
212-465-1750
Weekdays 6-10 weekends 9-6.

Gyms
Midtown West

3 3 3 3
quality style service value

The Edge: Where the young chic go to meet and sweat. Offers a good range of equipment and facilities, including a full spa, pool and track at multiple locations. The East 61st Street location is best. Sometimes their promotions offer two years for the price of one year at $1,400. 60 to 80 classes per week.

335 Madison Avenue
near 43rd Street/10017
212-983-5320
Weekdays 6-10 weekends 9-6.

Midtown East

350 West 50th Street
between 8th and 9th Avenues/10019
212-265-9400
Weekdays 6-10 weekends 9-6.

Midtown West

330 East 61st Street
between 1st and 2nd Avenues/10021
212-355-5100
Weekdays 6-10 weekends 9-9.

Upper East Side

World Gym

Gyms
SoHo/TriBeCa

232 Mercer Street
between Bleecker and West 3rd Streets
New York, NY 10012
212-780-7407
Weekdays 5am-midnight weekends 7-9.

The Edge: Offers 140 gym classes per week. Five different levels of aerobics, body boxing and yoga, a full range of cardiovascular equipment and personal trainers. $796 per year.

1926 Broadway
between 64th and 65th Streets/10023
212-874-0942
Daily 24 hours.

Upper West Side

YMCA (West Side)

Gyms
Upper West Side

5 West 63rd Street
between Central Park West and Broadway
New York, NY 10023
212-787-4400
Weekdays 6:30-10 Saturday 8-8 Sunday 9-7.

The Edge: Complete gym facilities plus swimming. Upper West Side health club offering two full-size pools (one for lane swimmers and one for instruction only), 120 classes per week, Universal machines/free weights plus personal trainers for $90 for three one-hour sessions. Membership $684 per year or $57 per month. Also pottery studio and family and children's activities.

Downtown Rifle & Pistol Club

Hunting
Lower Manhattan

24 Murray Street
near Church Street
New York, NY 10007
212-233-5420
Daily 9-9.

The Edge: NY's private pistol club. Membership club. You'll need a license (they'll help) for a pistol. Sells pistols and guns and provides instruction and target practice. Fees $500 the first year, $350 thereafter. No daily passes.

Abigail Kirsch - Pratt Mansion

Locations
Upper East Side

1026 5th Avenue
near 84th Street
New York, NY 10028
212-744-4486
By appointment

quality	style	service	value
4	4	4	4

The Edge: Attractive setting and pretty decor. Catering and party services at the Pratt Mansion, their New York town house, at Tappan Hill, a gray stone mansion that was formerly Mark Twain's home, in Westchester or at their newest location at the New York Botanical Gardens which will have a formal Ballroom (being built now) as well as the more rustic Snuff Mill in the gardens. All settings are divine. They are booking the Botanical Gardens starting April, 1997. The Pratt Mansion holds 150 and Tappan Hill 300. No credit cards.

Other locations:
Tappan Hill   Westchester
81 Highland Avenue
Tarrytown, NY 10591
914-631-3030

New York Botanical Gardens
Southern Boulevard   Bronx
between Mosholu Parkway and Bedord Park Boulevard
Bronx, NY
718-220-0300

American Museum of Natural History

Central Park West
near West 79th Street
New York, NY 10024
212-769-5350. Fax 212-769-5368
By appointment

Locations
Upper West Side

5	5	5	5
quality	style	service	value

The Edge: Theme parties. The museum's party range is wide, from elegant corporate and private functions to theme parties centered around a craft activity. Party bags can be drawn from the gift shops. Sells a wide selection of activity kits, dinosaur books, plush toys, posters, scale models and T-shirts. Multiple areas with space to accommodate thousands.

Americas Society

680 Park Avenue
near 68th Street
New York, NY 10021
212-744-6650
By appointment

Locations
Upper East Side

4	4	3	3
quality	style	service	value

The Edge: Wonderful setting. The main salon, the Simon Bolivar room is decorated with crystal chandeliers and gilt-framed mirrors. Events for 40 to 300. Members only. Expensive. No credit cards.

Boathouse in Central Park

5th Avenue & 72nd Street
in Central Park
New York, NY 10021
212-988-0575
By appointment

Locations
Upper East Side

3	4	3	3
quality	style	service	value

The Edge: Gorgeous classic New York park view, too bad you have to eat there. A very institutional interior and often dreadful food. The adjacent cafe can compete with your privacy (although you can include it in your party). But what makes this place are the Central Park lake and New York skyline views and English garden pavilion setting. Not air-conditioned, so uncomfortable in rain or hot weather. In summer, arrange for the gondola for your quests to take out on the lake. The Pavilion seats 250, and up to 500 if you rent the cafe also.

"Unique location, terrible food."

Burden Mansion

1 East 91st Street
near 5th Avenue
New York, NY 10128
212-722-4745
By appointment

Locations
Upper East Side

quality style service value

The Edge: Majestic and special setting. Part of the Convent of the Sacred Heart. Excellent food, service and style. Can accommodate up to 150. Expensive. No credit cards.

"Beautiful spot, really enjoyed an informal cocktail party there."

Equitable Tower

787 7th Avenue
near 51st Street
New York, NY 10019
212-554-2833
By appointment

Locations
Midtown West

quality style service value

The Edge: Spectacular skyline views in an elegant, but businesslike, setting. Corporate club by day, events by night. Can accommodate 400 people and four parties at the same time. Expensive. Deluxe. No credit cards.

"Great atmosphere." Great place for corporate gatherings." "Costly."

Essex House Hotel Nikko New York

160 Central Park South
near 6th Avenue
New York, NY 10019
212-484-5144. Fax 212-484-4509
Weekdays 9-6.

Locations
Midtown West

quality style service value

The Edge: Elegant ballroom, quality cuisine and service. Less expensive than the St. Regis. Can accommodate 300 quests. Only one function at a time. Deluxe.

"They do a good meeting, but the afternoon desserts needed some help."

Georgian Suite

1-A East 77th Street
between 5th and Madison Avenues
New York, NY 10021
212-734-1468
By appointment.

Locations
Upper East Side

quality style service value

The Edge: Intimate setting. Elegant room in a 5th Avenue apartment building. No credit cards. Deluxe.

Hudson River Club

4 World Financial Center
New York, NY 10281
212-786-1500
Monday-Saturday 11:30-2:30 and 5-10
Sunday 11:30-2:30.

Locations
Lower Manhattan

5	5	5	3
quality	style	service	value

The Edge: Incredible views. Food is good. Views and the interior space are outstanding.

"It's disconcerting to go through an office building after hours for a private function."

Linda Kaye's Birthdaybakers, Party Makers

195 East 76th Street
near 3rd Avenue
New York, NY 10021
212-288-7112. Fax 212-879-6785
By appointment.

Locations
Upper East Side

5	3	4	3
quality	style	service	value

The Edge: Creative children's parties. Party planning for all styles, ages and occasions in their own party room or in your house. Rents tables and chairs for children's parties, designs and makes costumes. Can arrange unique off-premises theme parties all over the city.

Manhattan Penthouse

45 Downing Street
near Bleecker Street
New York, NY 10014
212-627-8838
By appointment

Locations
Greenwich Village

3	3	2	3
quality	style	service	value

The Edge: Good views, moderate prices. Open 7,000-square-foot space, entire top floor with good views on all sides. Features acceptable, but not great, French, American and international cuisine. One party at a time.

Palm House at the Brooklyn Botanical Garden

1000 Washington Avenue
near Eastern Parkway
Brooklyn, NY 11225
718-398-2400. Fax 718-783-1966
By appointment

Locations
Brooklyn

4	5	3	4
quality	style	service	value

The Edge: Beautiful setting in the gardens of the Brooklyn Botanical Garden. The settings capitalize on their celebrated gardens, Victorian greenhouse, and beautiful inside garden pavilions. Food is good. No credit cards.

"Surprisingly costly, so I didn't use it. Functions I've attended have been competent and pretty, although it can be hot."

Plaza Hotel

768 5th Avenue
at 59th Street
New York, NY 10019
212-546-5380. Fax 212-546-5256
Weekdays 9-6 Saturday 9-3 by appointment.

Locations
Midtown West

quality style service value

The Edge: The legendary Plaza. Can accommodate 500 (in the large Baroque Ballroom) to small numbers. 18 functions are possible at a time. A plan to upgrade the hotel amenities, including its food, and restore some of the legendary rooms, including the Palm Court, is underway.

"Great power breakfasts."

Puck Building

295 Lafayette Street
at Houston Street
New York, NY 10012
212-274-8900. Fax 212-226-6835
Weekdays 9:30-5:30 Saturday by appointment.

Locations
SoHo/TriBeCa

quality style service value

The Edge: Attractive space. Very good food and service. The grand ballroom and the building itself are divine. Albeit more architecturally striking than intimate. Events for 50 to 1,000. No credit cards.

"Fun place to visit for others' occasions."

St. Regis

2 East 55th Street
near 5th Avenue
New York, NY 10022
212-753-4500
Monday-Friday 9-5.

Locations
Midtown East

quality style service value

The Edge: A top spot for weddings, priced accordingly. Completely redone. Absolutely gorgeous space, with quality food and attentive service. Accommodates up to 150 for dinner and 600 for cocktails. Very expensive. No credit cards.

Stanhope Hotel

988 5th Avenue
near 81st Street
New York, NY 10028
212-288-5800. Fax 212-517-0088
By appointment.

Locations
Upper East Side

quality style service value

The Edge: A favorite for small, intimate, quality weddings. Perfection for small weddings— good food, service and atmosphere. Two functions are possible at a time with the largest accommodating 120. Moderately expensive.

24 Fifth Avenue Ballroom

24 5th Avenue
near 9th Street
New York, NY 10003
212-254-1300
By appointment.

Locations
Flatiron/East Village

3	3	4	4
quality	style	service	value

The Edge: An elegant art deco glass enclosed cafe ballroom, overlooking Fifth Avenue. The ballroom has a sunken dance floor which accommodates 500, plus space for an outdoor party. They hold only one party at a time, at a cost of $90+ per person. No credit cards.

21 Club

21 West 52nd Street
near 5th Avenue
New York, NY 10019
212-582-7200. Fax 212-581-7138
Monday-Saturday noon-10:30.

Locations
Midtown West

5	5	5	4
quality	style	service	value

The Edge: A New York institution—very masculine and clublike. Food is very good, never great, as long as you keep it simple—grilled meats and wonderful shrimp cocktails in an elegant townhouse setting. Service is legendary. Accommodates 240 quests maximum. Seven functions are possible and are often going at the same time. Very expensive.

"Accommodating staff, great party space." "See Brian Finneray, banquet sales manager."

200 Fifth Club

200 5th Avenue
near 23rd Street
New York, NY 10010
212-675-2080. Fax 212-675-2802
By appointment.

Locations
Gramercy Pk/Murray Hill

3	3	4	3
quality	style	service	value

The Edge: One function at a time and reasonable prices. At the Toy Building, find a baroque-style ballroom, high ceiling and cocktail-hour space that can accommodate 500 people. They provide full-service party planning, customize menus and will hold only one party at a time. Moderate prices.

"Good location and reasonable prices."

Waldorf-Astoria Hotel

301 Park Avenue
between 49th and 50th Streets
New York, NY 10022
212-872-4700
By appointment.

Locations
Midtown East

4	4	3	4
quality	style	service	value

The Edge: Good food, and prices are negotiable. Still a good place to host a big event. Food is good and the hotel is attractive.

Asia Society Bookstore

725 Park Avenue
near 70th Street
New York, NY 10021
212-288-6400. Fax 212-517-8315
Monday-Thursday 10-6:30 Friday 10-8:30
Saturday 11-6 Sunday noon-5.

Museum shops
Upper East Side

quality style service value

The Edge: The selection! A great collection of books and moderately priced Asian crafts.
Find books that cover all aspects of Asia, including art, culture, dictionaries, history, language
tutorials, religion and travel. Books and gifts for children and adults. Gift items include
contemporary baskets, hand-blocked Indian scarves, Javanese shadow puppets, jewelry, note paper,
stoneware and vases.

Cathedral of St. John the Divine

1047 Amsterdam Avenue
near 112th Street
New York, NY 10025
212-222-7200
Daily 9-5.

Museum shops
Upper West Side

quality style service value

The Edge: All gifts related somehow to the Bible, the cathedral or St. John. Hand-
painted/hand-carved reproductions galore of church ornamentation, religious folk art and, at
Christmas, tree ornaments. Wonderful Noah's Ark guests—stuffed and cuddly.

Children's Museum of Manhattan

212 West 83rd Street
between Amsterdam Avenue and Broadway
New York, NY 10024
212-721-1223. Fax 212-721-1127
Monday Wednesday-Friday 1:30-5:30 weekends 10-5.

Museum shops
Upper West Side

The Edge: Just for children, but adults will appreciate the museum too. Wonderful books and
science items for children. Merchandise changes to complement the exhibits.

Metropolitan Museum of Art Gift Shop

1000 5th Avenue
near 82nd Street
New York, NY 10028
212-650-2911. Fax 212-532-7173
Tuesday-Thursday Sunday 9:30-5:15
Friday Saturday 9:30-9.

Museum shops
Upper East Side

quality style service value

The Edge: Lovely inexpensive gifts, particularly jewelry and scarves. A huge gift store
featuring books (serious art books, guide books, cooking and travel guides) and decorative objects
(jewelry, accessories, tableware and art pieces) that are reproductions of works of art from the Met.
Wonderful jewelry, both costume and real. Also children's games and books. Members' discount.

113 Prince Street   **SoHo/TriBeCa**
between Greene and Wooster Streets/10012
212-614-3000. Fax 212-614-3293.
Sunday-Friday 11-7 Sunday 11-8.

in Macy's   **Midtown West**
Broadway at Herald Square
at 34th Street/10001
212-268-7266.
Monday-Saturday 10-8:30 Sunday 11-7.

at Rockefeller Plaza   **Midtown West**
15 West 49th Street
near Rockefeller Center/10020
212-332-1360. Fax 212-332-1390
Weekdays 10-7 weekends 10-6.

The Cloisters   **Upper Upper West Side**
Fort Tryon Park near the Cloisters
at 190th Street
212-650-2277. Fax 212-795-3640
Tuesday-Thursday 9:30-5:15 Friday-Sunday 9:30-5.

Museum of American Folk Art   **Museum shops**
62 West 50th Street   **Midtown West**
near 6th Avenue
New York, NY 10020
212-247-5611
Monday-Saturday 10:30-5:30.

The Edge: The best in handicrafts. Features one-of-a-kind handmade items from the decorative
to the practical, designed by artisans and craftspeople.

Museum of Modern Art, the MOMA Design Store
44 West 53rd Street   **Museum shops**
West of 5th Avenue   **Midtown West**
New York, NY 10019
212-708-9800. Fax 212-833-1100   **5** **5** **5** **5**
Monday-Wednesday 10-6 Thursday Friday 10-8   quality style service value
weekends 10-6.

The Edge: The best for contemporary works. Located across from the museum, the shop
features the best of modern designs, including furniture, jewelry, lighting and small gift items. Sells
authorized versions of furniture by many of the greats, including Breuer, Eames, Frank Lloyd
Wright, Le Corbusier, Mies van der Rohe and Noguchi. Bold area rugs complement the furniture.
At the bookstore find art books, posters, publications and slides of the collection.

Museum of the City of New York Gift Shop
5th Avenue   **Museum shops**
near 103rd Street   **Upper Upper East Side**
New York, NY 10029
212-534-1672. Fax 212-423-0758

Wednesday-Saturday 10-5 Sunday 1-5.

The Edge: Books, guides, maps and novels about the city. For children, tiny inexpensive toys, and for adults, prints, photographs and guides.

National Museum of the American Indian

Old U.S. Custom House/Bowling Green
near Whitehall Street
New York, NY 10004
212-825-6700. Fax 212-825-8180
Tuesday-Saturday 10-4:45.

Museum shops
Lower Manhattan

The Edge: One-of-a-kind Native North and South American crafts. Features traditional Native American crafts, including rugs, baskets, pottery and jewelry (silver and turquoise), as well as books for adults and children.

New York Public Library Shop

5th Avenue
between 40th and 42nd Street
New York, NY 10036
212-930-0678. Fax 212-930-0849
Tuesday Wednesday 11-6 Thursday-Saturday 10-6.

Museum shops
Midtown West

quality	style	service	value
3	4	3	3

The Edge: Patience and Fortitude, the lions that guard the library entrance. Gifts evoking yesteryear are wonderful as house gifts. Find stationery items from note cards to calendars to address books. Styling is classic. For children, find Winnie the Pooh diaries, alphabet books, illustrated children's classic books, games and more.

Pierpont Morgan Library

29 East 36th Street
near Park Avenue
New York, NY 10016
212-685-0008. Fax 212-685-4740
Tuesday-Friday 10:30-5 Saturday 10:30-6 Sunday 2-6.

Museum shops
Gramercy Pk/Murray Hill

The Edge: Books and cards that relate to the library's collection. Includes facsimile editions of manuscripts and scores from the collection. Wonderful gift items, including books, reproductions of drawings and botanical prints and more that relate to the collection.

Seaport Museum Shop

207 Front Street
near South Street
New York, NY 10038
212-748-8663. Fax 212-748-8626
Daily 10-6.

Museum shops
Lower Manhattan

The Edge: Caters to tourists, offering books and toys. Find navigational maps of the New York area waters, maritime books plus the Patrick O'Brian series, tourist T-shirts and children's toys.

Studio Museum in Harlem

144 West 125th Street
near Adam Clayton Powell Boulevard
New York, NY 10027
212-864-0014. Fax 212-666-5753
Wednesday-Friday 10-5 weekends 1-6.

Museum shops
Upper Upper West Side

The Edge: The source for African items. Features handicrafts and art from Africa and black America. An ever-changing assortment of books, carvings, fabrics, pottery, traditional to contemporary jewelry, toys and weavings.

Ukrainian Museum

203 2nd Avenue
near 12th Street
New York, NY 10003
212-228-0110. Fax 212-228-1947
Wednesday-Sunday 1-5.

Museum shops
Flatiron/East Village

The Edge: Ukrainian Easter eggs plus supplies to make Easter eggs. Features contemporary and traditional Ukrainian crafts, including Easter eggs, elaborate embroidered blouses, table linens and more. No credit cards.

United Nations Gift Shop

United Nations Headquarters
1st Avenue and 46th Street
New York, NY 10017
212-963-7700. Fax 212-963-1157
Daily 9-4:30.

Museum shops
Midtown East

quality	style	service	value
4	3	3	4

The Edge: Handicrafts from around the world on the lower level of the U.N. Headquarters. Hundreds of inexpensive items, including hand-carved animals, pin cushions, coin pursues, puzzles and a large selection of jewelry in all price ranges.

Whitney Museum's Store Next Door

943 Madison Avenue
near 75th Street
New York, NY 10021
212-606-0200. Fax 212-472-1963
Tuesday Wednesday Friday Saturday 10-6 Thursday 10-8 Sunday 11-6.

Museum shops
Upper East Side

The Edge: American designs related to the current exhibits. Furniture and accessories for the home and the individual created by top American talent. No delivery.

Little Orchestra Society

220 West 42nd Street
near 7th Avenue
New York, NY 10036
212-704-2100
Scheduled performances.

Music
Midtown West

quality	style	service	value
5	5	3	4

The Edge: Peabody Award–winning Happy Concerts offered for children ages 5 to 12 and Lolli-Pops Concerts for children ages 3 to 5. Happy Concerts are at Avery Fisher Hall in Lincoln Center on Saturdays. The Lolli-Pops Concerts, at Florence Gould Hall at the French Institute / Alliance Française, involve youngsters who conduct the orchestra and play along on toy trumpets and tambourines.

"Wonderful concerts."

Carmine Street Guitar Shop

42 Carmine Street
near Bedford Street
New York, NY 10014
212-691-8400
Monday-Saturday 11-7.

Musical instruments
Greenwich Village

The Edge: Custom made guitars. For amateurs and professionals, the source for both new and used electric and acoustic guitars. Priced from $250 to $1,250. Stocks Gibson, Rickenbacker, Jerry Jones and Washburn as well as custom guitars.

Detrich Pianos

211 West 58th Street
between Broadway and 7th Avenue
New York, NY 10019
212-245-1234. Fax 212-245-5432
Weekdays 10-6 Saturday 10-4.

Musical instruments
Midtown West

5	5	5	5
quality	style	service	value

The Edge: One of the few city places that can refinish and rebuild pianos. Rents, tunes and repairs antique and new pianos. Carries a stock of contemporary music boxes in the shape of pianos made in porcelain, metal and plastic which play classical or pop tunes.

Lapiana Piano Sales

211 West 20th Street
near 7th Avenue
New York, NY 10011
212-243-5762
Monday-Saturday 9-5.

Musical instruments
Chelsea

The Edge: A large range of pianos. Sells most major brands. They rebuild and refinish pianos. Will refer you to teachers and classes. No credit cards.

"Good source for pianos."

Manny's (Musical Instruments)

156 West 48th Street
between 6th and 7th Avenues
New York, NY 10036
212-819-0576
Monday-Saturday 10-6.

Musical instruments
Midtown West

The Edge: **Wide range of musical instruments.** Can refer you to teachers and classes.

Piano Store

158 Ludlow Street
near Stanton Street
New York, NY 10002
212-674-5555. Fax 212-260-4850
Weekdays 10-6 Saturday 10-4.

Musical instruments
Lower East Side/Chinatown

The Edge: **Large stock of antique and used pianos.** Just pianos from the plain to the "grand."

Pro Piano

85 Jane Street
near West 12th Street
New York, NY 10014
212-206-8794. Fax 212-633-1207
Weekdays 8:30-5 Saturday 10-4.

Musical instruments
Greenwich Village

The Edge: **Large selection of pianos to rent.** All major brands of pianos. Priced from $2,000 to $90,000. They'll refer you to teachers and classes.

Harry Hanson

63 Greene Street
near Spring Street
New York, NY 10012
212-431-7682. Fax 212-431-7682
Daily 7-9.

Personal trainers
SoHo/TriBeCa

5	5	5	3
quality	style	service	value

The Edge: **Top trainers. One-on-one focus.** 3,000 square feet of work space. Celebrity clients have included top models like Naomi Cambell and Linda Evangelista and, reportedly, John F. Kennedy Jr. There are 11 trainers on staff who always work one-on-one with you. The focus is on low-impact aerobics. Cost is $45 per hour, or $2,700 for 60 sessions. Body-fat test. Nutritional information. Deluxe.

"Great, but everyone is gorgeous."

Joseph D. Tonti

280 Riverside Drive
near 100th Street
New York, NY 10025
212-662-4679
By appointment.

Personal trainers
Upper West Side

5	5	5	5
quality	style	service	value

The Edge: **Personal trainer.** Body building and training charges on a sliding scale. No credit cards.

"Good quality at reasonable prices."

Larry Tan
225 East 57th Street
near 3rd Avenue
New York, NY 10022
212-753-7280
By appointment.

Personal trainers
Midtown East

quality style service value

The Edge: A kung fu master. Tan has evolved a system of stress reduction through individually designed art forms. Private or group lessons. No credit cards.

" A marvelous teacher."

Plus One Fitness Clinic
200 Liberty Street
near South Street
New York, NY 10005
212-945-2525. Fax 212-945-2797
Weekdays 6-10 Saturday 8-8.

Personal trainers
Lower Manhattan

The Edge: Provides suitable personal trainers. One-on-one training for $65 an hour.

106 Crosby Street
near Prince Street/10012
212-334-1116

SoHo/TriBeCa

301 Park Avenue
at the Waldorf-Astoria, near 49th Street/10022
212-355-3000

Midtown East

Beth Green Studio
212-580-1928
By appointment.

Photographs & video
Mail/phone

quality style service value

The Edge: Recommended photographer. No credit cards.

"Expensive, but worth it."

Lynda Hughes
212-645-8417
By appointment.

Photographs & video
Mail/phone

The Edge: Good photographer. For weddings and special occasions. No credit cards.

Mary Hilliard
212-879-7839
By appointment.

Photographs & video
Mail/phone

The Edge: Excellent photographer. Specializes in shooting weddings, charity galas and opening-night events.

Party Rentals
22 East 72nd Street
between 5th and Madison Avenues
New York, NY 10021
212-594-8510. Fax 212-594-8604
By appointment.

Rentals
Upper East Side

5	5	5	5
quality	style	service	value

The Edge: Used by Glorious Foods. First-rate rentals and excellent service. Exceptional china, linens and crystal available. $300 minimum. No delivery.

Props for Today
330 West 34th Street
between 8th and 9th Avenues
New York, NY 10001
212-244-9600. Fax 212-244-1053
Weekdays 8:30-5.

Rentals
Midtown West

The Edge: A large inventory of party rental items. $100 minimum. Furniture, accessories and table settings for great theme parties. Appointments are recommended for the best service.

Something Different
107-111 Penn Avenue
Patterson, NJ 07503
212-772-0516. Fax 212-742-0317
Weekdays 9-5.

Rentals
New Jersey

5	5	5	.
quality	style	service	value

The Edge: Wonderful party rentals. Quality tablecloths in a good selection of colors and patterns. Ballroom chairs in assorted colors. Attractive service plates (emerald-green glass, cobalt-blue glass, crystal), 30-inch candelabra and whatever else you need. No minimum order required. New Jersey phone number is 201-742-1779.

Claremont Riding Academy
175 West 89th Street
near Amsterdam Avenue
New York, NY 10024
212-724-5100
Weekdays 6:30-10 weekends 6:30-5.

Riding
Upper West Side

4	4	4	4
quality	style	service	value

The Edge: The only riding stable left in Manhattan. In business since 1892. Provides riding in Central Park for experienced riders or group and private classes in the stable. They teach all skill levels and offer equestrian programs.

"Their half-day summer program was terrific for my preteen horse-mad daughter."

Manhattan Sailing School
393 South End Avenue
New York, NY 10280-1003
212-786-3318
In season weekday evenings until sunset, weekends during daylight.

Sailing
Lower Manhattan

The Edge: Sailing lessons in Manhattan harbor. Owns and maintains a fleet of J-24s docked at the North Cove Yacht Harbor in Battery Park City. Offers classes in basic sailing, coastal cruising sailing, racing and bare-boat chartering. Permission to charter sailboats from the school is granted after students reach their skipper's club level. After students learn the fundamentals, there are opportunities to participate in harbor events like competing on teams in the International Yacht Club Challenge. Sailing school gives lessons at $395 for groups of three or four. Courses are given weekends and weekday nights on their J-24.

Barnard Bartending
212-854-4650
By appointment.

Service help
Mail/phone

4	4	4	5
quality	style	service	value

The Edge: Always reliable, and the nicest students show up. This woman's college can provide bartenders, waitresses and just general help. Well trained, as they're required to take a bartending course. Inexpensive, at $13 per hour the fee is $2 per hour less than Columbia Bartending! No credit cards.

Columbia Bartending Agency
212-854-4537
By appointment.

Service help
Mail/phone

4	4	4	4
quality	style	service	value

The Edge: Always reliable, and the nicest students show up. Can provide bartenders, waiters, waitresses and just general help. Well trained as they're required to take a bartending course. Inexpensive at $15 per hour. No credit cards.

Rockefeller Center Ice Skating Rink
600 5th Avenue
near 50th Street
New York, NY 10020
212-332-7654
Weekdays 9-10 Saturday 8:30-midnight Sunday 8:30-10.

Skating
Midtown West

5	5	4	5
quality	style	service	value

The Edge: Skating among the skyscrapers. Everyone's favorite rink, though small. Admission is $6 to $8.50, depending on the time of week and the skater's age; skate rental is $4 and lessons are $23 per half hour. Can arrange birthday parties.

"A wonderful place for evening group parties. Simply magical."

Sky Rink
Skating
Midtown West

450 West 33rd Street, 16th Floor
near 10th Avenue
New York, NY 10001
212-336-6100
Session schedule varies depending on season.

The Edge: One of the largest indoor ice rinks. Admission per session $8 for adults and $6 for children under 12. Lessons $25 per half hour. $3.50 for skate rentals. No credit cards.

Wollman Skating Rink
Skating
Upper East Side

Central Park
East 63rd Street and Park East Drive
New York, NY 10021
212-396-1010
Monday-Thursday 10-6 Friday 10-10 Saturday 11-11 Sunday 11-2.

The Edge: New York's largest rink. Offers outdoor ice skating in the winter, from October through March, and roller skating during the spring and summer. Telephone reservations for lessons only. Individual lessons are $56 per hour or $28 for a half hour; group lessons are $150 for 13 weeks. Admission $6 for adults and $3 for children under 12 years. Rentals are $3 for ice skates and $6 for in-line roller skates. A credit card or $100 cash or a valid passport serves as a refundable deposit for roller skate rentals. No ID is necessary for ice skate rentals. The skate shop sells apparel, skates and T-shirts. A small cafe offering hot chocolate, pizza and the like.

Eastern Tennis Association Metro Region
Tennis
Long Island City

24-16 Queens Plaza South, Room 310
Long Island City, NY 11101
718-937-7676
May-October. Sign up in early April.

The Edge: Inexpensive tennis lessons. Nonprofit organization sponsored by Fox and the New York Tennis Association. Provides six hours of professional group instruction from May through October. Eight to a class, for $54, at participating tennis clubs in Manhattan, the Bronx, Brooklyn, Queens, Staten Island, Long Island and Westchester.

Midtown Tennis Club
Tennis
Midtown West

341 8th Avenue
near 27th Street
New York, NY 10001
212-989-8572
Weekdays 7-10 weekends 8-8.

The Edge: Great courts, midtown location. Eight Har-Tru courts where group and private lessons are available. You must reserve to play, with fees from $35 to $50 an hour or $700 to $1,300 per 20-week session, depending on the hour. Offers an advanced league on Wednesday from 8 to 10:30pm at $45 per hour, Friday-night parties, the "stroke of the week" and adult camp.

New York Racquet & Tennis Club

370 Park Avenue
near 52nd Street
New York, NY 10022
212-753-9700. Fax 212-980-7180
Weekdays 7-11 weekends 10:30-6.

Tennis
Midtown East

The Edge: Where the elite meet to smash. A private club for which a new member must be proposed and seconded by two members. Primarily a social club with racquetball and court tennis. Also fitness facilities. No credit cards. Deluxe.

River Club

447 East 52nd Street
near 1st Avenue
New York, NY 10022
212-751-0100
Daily 24 hours.

Tennis
Midtown East

The Edge: The club where old New York money "hangs." Beautiful private club with excellent facilities. Must be sponsored for membership and it can be difficult to join. A social club (1,000 members) with health facilities, including swimming and tennis. No credit cards. Deluxe.

Sylvia and Danny Kaye Playhouse

695 Park Avenue
69th Street near Hunter College
New York, NY 10021
212-650-3992. Fax 212-650-3635
Evening and weekend performances. Box office open Tuesday-Saturday noon-6 Sunday noon-3 and one hour before each performance.

Theater
Upper East Side

The Edge: Moderately priced entertainment in a jewel of a theater. $20 tickets (range from $10 to $45), members' prices about $15 and student tickets $10. The membership arrangement is simple—just buy tickets to three performances of your choice and you're a member. The playhouse features music, dance and theater, excellent children's productions and performers, including The Paper Bag Players.

TKTS Time Square

Broadway
at 47th Street
New York, NY 10036
Buy matinee tickets 10-2.
Buy matinee and evening tickets 5-8.

Theater
Midtown West

quality	style	service	value
4	.	.	4

The Edge: Discount tickets to much of what's currently on Broadway. What a deal—tickets at 35% to 50% off box office prices.

2 World Trade Center, mezzanine level
Matinee and evening tickets: weekdays 11-5 Saturday 11-3:30.

Lower Manhattan

Theatre Development Fund

Theater,
Midtown West

1501 Broadway, Suite 2110
near 44th Street
New York, NY 10036
212-221-0073
Weekdays 10-6.

The Edge: Reduced-price tickets by mail for students, teachers and retirees. Offers multiple services for theater lovers. Runs TKTS, two discount ticket centers where on the day of the performance (uptown) and for matinees (downtown, the evening before) tickets are sold at 25% to 50% off box office prices. Students, teachers and retired people can receive an application to join TDF by sending them a self-addressed stamped envelope. TDF offers reduced-price tickets to a host of new Broadway and Off Broadway plays. No credit cards.

Davidoff of Geneva

Tobacco
Midtown East

535 Madison Avenue
near 54th Street
New York, NY 10022
212-751-9060. Fax 212-750-1604
Monday-Wednesday Friday 9:30-6 Thursday 10-7:30 Saturday 10-6.

The Edge: Stocks fine tobacco products, pipes and smoking accessories. Hand-rolled cigars from Honduras, humidors in silver and/or mahogany, porcelain tobacco jars, tobacco pouches of lamb nappa and attaché cases with removable cigar humidors.

J.R. Tobacco

Tobacco
Lower Manhattan

219 Broadway
near Vesey Street
New York, NY 10007
212-233-6620
Weekdays 7:45-5:45.

The Edge: Perfume and cigars at 20% to 50% off retail. Huge selection, thousands of cigar brands and all the top fragrances discounted. No price quotes given over the phone, but they say they offer a discount of 20% and more. Call 800-572-4427 for mail order and catalogue.

11 East 45th Street
between 5th and Madison Avenues/10017
212-983-4160. Fax 212-986-9567
Weekdays 7:45-5:45 Saturday 9-3:45.

Midtown East

A Bear's Place

Toys, games & hobbies
Upper East Side

789 Lexington Avenue
near 61st Street
New York, NY 10021
212-826-6465
Weekdays 9-7 Saturday 10-6 Sunday 10-5.

The Edge: Upscale children's furniture and toys. Unique wood and upholstered furniture. Toys include bicycles, trucks and specialty dolls.

Allcraft Tool and Supply Company

Toys, games & hobbies
Midtown West

45 West 46th Street, 3rd Floor
near 6th Avenue
New York, NY 10036
212-840-1860. Fax 212-840-1860
Monday-Wednesday 9:30-5:30 Thursday 10-6 Friday 9:30-5.

The Edge: Everything you'll need to make fine jewelry. Features a complete line of tools and supplies for jewelry making, including silver and metal smithing, wax casting and more. The best source in the city for enameling supplies. Catalog available by calling 718-789-2800.

America's Hobby Center

Toys, games & hobbies
Chelsea

146 West 22nd Street
near 7th Avenue
New York, NY 10011
212-675-8922. Fax 212-633-2754
Weekdays 8:45-5:30 Saturday 9-3:30.

The Edge: The source for model builders. You name the transport, they have the kit and supplies.

Back Pages Antiques

Toys, games & hobbies
SoHo/TriBeCa

125 Greene Street
between Prince and Houston Streets
New York, NY 10012
212-460-5998
Monday-Saturday 9-6 Sunday noon-6.

The Edge: Arcade items, gambling devices and jukeboxes. No credit cards.

Bear Hugs & Baby Dolls

Toys, games & hobbies
Upper East Side

1184 Lexington Avenue
near 81st Street
New York, NY 10028
212-717-1514
Tuesday-Saturday 10-6 Sunday noon-5. Closed Sunday July and August.

The Edge: Bears for all occasions. A great source for Muffy Vander Bear, its accessories and wonderful cuddly animals.

Big City Kite Company

Toys, games & hobbies
Upper East Side

1210 Lexington Avenue
near 81st Street
New York, NY 10028
212-472-2623. Fax 212-472-2998
Monday-Wednesday Friday 11-6:30 Thursday 11-7:30
Saturday 10-6 Sunday noon-5.

3	2	2	3
quality	style	service	value

The Edge: Performance stunt kites. Features kites made in a range of fabrics (from paper to silk), from here and around the world, as well as other flying toys. Also a huge dart selection. Kite repair service available.

Burlington Antique Toys

1082 Madison Avenue
near 82nd Street
New York, NY 10028
212-861-9708
Monday-Saturday 10-6 or by appointment.

Toys, games & hobbies
Upper East Side

3	4	4	3
quality	style	service	value

The Edge: Vast selection of antique and contemporary toy soldiers. While the main focus is toy soldiers, they also sell antique toy cars, airplanes and boats on the lower level of the Burlington Book Shop. They say they have the largest collection of antique and contemporary toy soldiers in the U.S.

Ceramic Supply of New York & New Jersey

534 La Guardia Place
near West 3rd Street
New York, NY 10012
212-475-7236. Fax 212-995-2217
Weekdays 9-6 Saturday 10-5.

Toys, games & hobbies
SoHo/TriBeCa

The Edge: The source for potters. For potters—supplies, equipment and lessons, all in one place.

Compleat Strategist

11 East 33rd Street
between 5th and Madison Avenues
New York, NY 10016
212-685-3880
Monday-Saturday 11-8 Sunday noon-5.

Toys, games & hobbies
Gramercy Pk/Murray Hill

The Edge: Large selection of strategy games. Specializes in military games covering just about every battle and every period in military history. Also chess and backgammon sets, Risk and Monopoly. No delivery.

630 5th Avenue
near 52nd Street/10019
212-265-7449

Midtown West

320 West 57th Street
between 8th and 9th Avenues/10019
212-582-1272

Midtown West

Dollhouse Antics

1343 Madison Avenue
near 94th Street
New York, NY 10128
212-876-2288
Weekdays 11-5:30 Saturday 11-5. Open Sunday in December.

Toys, games & hobbies
Upper East Side

The Edge: Dollhouse registry. For children and collectors, the biggest miniatures store in the city featuring furniture and dollhouses. Everything in miniature; with carpenters on the premises to restore pieces. Large range from top of the line to lower end, with styles from Colonial to Victorian to contemporary. Some pieces are complete with electricity. Gift registry service.

Enchanted Forest

85 Mercer Street
between Spring and Broome Streets
New York, NY 10012
212-925-6677. Fax 212-431-1570
Monday-Saturday 11-7 Sunday noon-6.

Toys, games & hobbies
SoHo/TriBeCa

The Edge: Like coming into a forest. A magical spot for children focusing on animal themes. Features unique lifelike animals, kaleidoscopes, wooden musical instruments and books. What makes it more fun for children is passing through trees, bridges and waterfalls to shop. Their toll-free number is 800-456-4449.

Erica Wilson

717 Madison Avenue
near 63rd Street
New York, NY 10021
212-832-7290
Monday-Wednesday Friday Saturday 10-6 Thursday 10-7.

Toys, games & hobbies
Upper East Side

quality	style	service	value
5	5	4	4

The Edge: The best selection of needlepoint patterns. Known by all for her top-quality (and top-priced) needlework patterns and wools. Also patterns for hand-knit sweaters. Blocking and mounting services.

FAO Schwarz

5th Avenue
between 58th and 59th Streets
New York, NY 10153
212-644-9400. Fax 212-644-2485
Monday-Wednesday Friday Saturday 10-6
Thursday 10-8 Sunday 11-6.

Toys, games & hobbies
Midtown East

quality	style	service	value
5	5	3	2

The Edge: A five-star city attraction. An unbelievable range of toys, including the Barbie Boutique, electric trains, lifesize stuffed animals, battery- operated toys plus all the latest rages. No wonder FAO is the place all out-of-towners and grandparents must visit.

Flosso-Hornmann Magic Company

45 West 34th Street, Room 607
between 5th and 6th Avenues
New York, NY 10001
212-279-6079
Weekdays 10-5 Saturday 10-4.

Toys, games & hobbies
Midtown West

The Edge: You name the trick, this shop has it. The city's oldest magic shop, founded in 1869. You'll find magic acts, books, manuals, historical treatises and equipment.

Game Show
Toys, games & hobbies
474 Avenue of the Americas   **Chelsea**
near 12th Street
New York, NY 10011
212-633-6328. Fax 212-633-6208
Monday-Wednesday Friday Saturday noon-7 Thursday noon-8 Sunday noon-5.

The Edge: Adult toys. An extensive selection of games and puzzles arranged by category from real estate to politics.

1240 Lexington Avenue   **Upper East Side**
between 83rd and 84th Streets/10028
212-472-8011
Monday-Wednesday Friday Saturday 11-6 Thursday 11-7 Sunday noon-5.

Jan's Hobby Shop
Toys, games & hobbies
1557 York Avenue   **Upper East Side**
between 82nd and 83rd Streets
New York, NY 10028
212-861-5075
Monday-Saturday 10-7 Sunday noon-5.

The Edge: Big selection of model kits. Hobby shop features kits for remote-controlled airplanes, cars, ships and tanks. Also makes models and showcases for models.

Jimson's
Toys, games & hobbies
28 East 18th Street   **Flatiron/East Village**
near Broadway
New York, NY 10003
212-477-3386. Fax 212-228-3394
Weekdays 9:30-5:30 Saturday 10-3.

The Edge: Wholesale novelty shop selling gags and tricks

Little Rickie
Toys, games & hobbies
49½ 1st Avenue   **Flatiron/East Village**
near 3rd Street
New York, NY 10003
212-505-6467
Monday-Saturday 11-8 Sunday noon-7.

The Edge: Unique pop culture nostalgia. Find 1950s memorabilia, including Elvis items and classic toys.

Marion & Company
Toys, games & hobbies
147 West 26th Street   **Midtown West**
near 6th Avenue
New York, NY 10001
212-727-8900. Fax 212-727-9223
Weekdays 8-5:30 Saturday 10-4.

The Edge: Gambling equipment and games. Find casino equipment such as tables, chairs, slot machines as well as games such as chess, backgammon, dominoes and cards.

Mary Arnold Toys
962 Lexington Avenue
near 70th Street
New York, NY 10021
212-744-8510. Fax 212-988-8426
Weekdays 9-6 Saturday 10-5.

Toys, games & hobbies
Upper East Side

4	4	5	3
quality	style	service	value

The Edge: An old-fashioned, personable neighborhood toy store with all the latest toys. A neighborhood treasure for more than 60 years. Sells the full range of hot new and classic toys with a good selection of dolls and trucks. You can call and have gifts sent. The staff gives great advice on what's right for all ages. Great wrapping papers.

Myron Toback
25 West 47th Street
between 5th and 6th Avenues
New York, NY 10036
212-398-8300. Fax 212-869-0808
Weekdays 8-4. Closed July 1-14 and December 25-January 1.

Toys, games & hobbies
Midtown West

3	3	3	4
quality	style	service	value

The Edge: Large selections of jewelry tools and materials. Sells bangles and gold, gold-filled and silver chains by the yard, as well as bindings, plate wire, tools and supplies. Make it yourself.

Penny Whistle Toys
448 Columbus Avenue
near 81st Street
New York, NY 10024
212-873-9090. Fax 212-501-8761
Monday-Wednesday Saturday 10-6
Thursday Friday 10-7 Sunday 11-5.

Toys, games & hobbies
Upper West Side

4	4	4	3
quality	style	service	value

The Edge: Upscale store with unique children's toys, especially craft kits. Large selection of good children's gifts, including craft kits, jigsaw puzzles, toy cars, trucks and dolls.

1283 Madison Avenue
near 91st Street/10128
212-369-3868. Fax 212-501-8761
Monday Tuesday 9-6 Wednesday-Friday 9-7 Saturday 10-6 Sunday 11-5.

Upper East Side

Red Caboose
23 West 45th Street
near 5th Avenue
New York, NY 10036
212-575-0155. Fax 212-575-0272
Weekdays 10:45-7 Saturday 10:45-5.

Toys, games & hobbies
Midtown West

The Edge: New and old model railroads. New and antique trains, including vintage Lionel and American Flyer models, and remote-controlled cars and boats. Also construction models. Great selection and range.

Star Magic Space Age Gifts

745 Broadway
near 8th Street
New York, NY 10003
212-228-7770
Monday-Saturday 10-10 Sunday 11-9.

Toys, games & hobbies
Flatiron/East Village

quality style service value
3   3   3   3

The Edge: The stars steal the show here. Features maps of the stars and constellations and telescopes in all sizes. Also books, games and toys—all related to the stars.

"Good place for novelty and cheap, but intriguing, gifts." "Better at the Museum of Natural History."

275 Amsterdam Avenue
near 73rd Street/10023
212-769-2020
Monday-Saturday 10-10 Sunday 11-9.

Upper West Side

1256 Lexington Avenue
near 85th Street/10028
212-988-0300
Monday-Saturday 10-8:30 Sunday 11-6:30.

Upper East Side

Tannen's Magic

24 West 25th Street, 2nd Floor
near 6th Avenue
New York, NY 10010
212-929-4500. Fax 212-929-4565
Weekdays 10-5:30 Saturday 10-4.

Toys, games & hobbies
Gramercy Pk/Murray Hill

The Edge: One of the oldest and largest magic stores in the city. Thousands of tricks. Everything for magic shows. Will provide referrals of magicians for parties.

Tenzing & Pena

956 Madison Avenue
near 75th Street
New York, NY 10021
212-288-8780. Fax 212-288-8601
Monday-Thursday 9:30-5 Friday Saturday 10-6 Sunday noon- 5.

Toys, games & hobbies
Upper East Side

The Edge: Unique games for children. Games, videos, crafts, telescopes and cameras. No delivery.

Toys "R" Us

1293 Broadway
near 34th Street
New York, NY 10001
212-594-8697

Toys, games & hobbies
Midtown West

quality style service value
3   2   2   4

Monday Friday 9-9 Tuesday Wednesday Saturday 9-8
Thursday 9-9:30 Sunday 11-6.

The Edge: Likely to be the lowest prices in town for toys. The country's largest toy chain finally made it to New York. All the latest toys, bikes, wagons, cars and crafts. Don't expect help and, at Christmas, it's every parent on their own. No delivery. Discounter.

2430 Union Square East
between 15th and 16th Streets/10003
212-674-8694

Flatiron/East Village

Village Chess Shop
230 Thompson Street
near West 3rd Street
New York, NY 10012
212-475-8130
Daily noon-midnight.

Toys, games & hobbies
SoHo/TriBeCa

The Edge: Competitive chess games and everything for the chess aficionado. Come to play for about $2 per hour or to buy basic to special chess sets. Find unusual chess sets (in brass, ebony, onyx, pewter and more) as well as backgammon and cribbage sets.

West Side Kids
498 Amsterdam Avenue
near 84th Street
New York, NY 10024
212-496-7282
Monday-Saturday 10-7 Sunday noon-6.

Toys, games & hobbies
Upper West Side

The Edge: Quality books and educational toys for young children. Books and educational toys along with videos, puppet theaters, arts and crafts supplies and the standard toys and party favors. Find inexpensive stocking-stuffer toys at the front of the store.

The ratings: excellent very good good fair so-so

Personal & repair services

Autobahn Service Center
421 East 91st Street
near 1st Avenue
New York, NY 10128
212-289-5800
Weekdays 6:30-6.

Car
Upper East Side

5 5 5 5
quality style service value

The Edge: Honest car repairs. Great for foreign cars. No delivery.

"Best car repairs in Manhattan."

Asian Art Gallery
136 East 57th Street, 7th Floor
near Lexington Avenue
New York, NY 10022
212-688-7243. Fax 212-688-0593
Weekdays 9:30-5 or by appointment.

China, crystal & silver
Midtown East

The Edge: Best for restorations of lacquer and ceramic. Also offers a full range of high-end
antique furniture. Discounts offered to dealers and decorators. No credit cards.

Center Art Studio
250 West 54th Street, Room 901
between Broadway and 8th Avenue
New York, NY 10019
212-247-3550. Fax 212-586-4045
By appointment.

China, crystal & silver
Midtown West

The Edge: Quality repairs of china and glass. If an object is not too small and is in fewer than
50 pieces, it can be reassembled. About half the company's repairs are on ceramics and porcelains.
Color and patterns can be matched. Also works with precious stones. Will pack and crate items for
shipment.

Glass Restorations
1597 York Avenue
between 84th and 85th Streets
New York, NY 10028
212-517-3287
Weekdays 9:30-5.

China, crystal & silver
Upper East Side

The Edge: Excellent repairs on all types of glass. Mr. Jochec, the owner, trained in
Czechoslovakia, has fine craft skills. Minimum two weeks to restore a glass piece. No credit cards.

Hess Restorations

200 Park Avenue South
near 17th Street
New York, NY 10003
212-260-2255
Weekdays 10:30-4 or by appointment.

China, crystal & silver
Flatiron/East Village

quality style service value

The Edge: The restorer recommended by Tiffany's and the Metropolitan Museum of Art.
Restores china, crystal, ivory, lacquer, porcelains, silver, tortoise shell, sculptures and objets d'art.
Replaces blue glass liners for antique silver salt dishes and ice buckets. Accepts shipments of items
to be repaired. Will send an estimate for repair work. No credit cards.

Sano Studio

767 Lexington Avenue
near 60th Street
New York, NY 10021
212-759-6131
Weekdays 10-5.

China, crystal & silver
Upper East Side

The Edge: Repairs antique porcelains. 18 years in the business of restoring ceramic and
porcelain pieces. Minimum repair $50. No delivery.

Vic Rothman for Stained Glass

212-255-2551
By appointment.

China, crystal & silver
Mail/phone

The Edge: Noted expert for stained-glass repair. He has 20+ years of experience. He worked on
St. Paul's Chapel at Columbia University and the Lalique windows at Henri Bendel. Does
residential projects also. No credit cards.

New York Closet Company

1458 3rd Avenue
near 83rd Street
New York, NY 10028
212-439-9500
Monday-Saturday 11-6.

Closet design
Upper East Side

The Edge: Organize your closet with melamine and wire systems. Functional melamine and
wire closet systems tailored to maximize your closet space. Partitions cost $8 to $10 per foot with a
$250 minimum.

Drake Design

140 East 56th Street
between 3rd and Lexington Avenues
New York, NY 10022
212-754-3099
By appointment.

Decorators
Midtown East

5 5 5 5

quality style service value

The Edge: A genius with color and style. Listed in *Vanity Fare* as Generation X's equivalent of Mario Buatta, Mark Hampton, etc. Wonderful style, color sense, cooperative and flexible, so don't be alarmed if he shows up in his Rolls. Charges wholesale plus a design fee. No credit cards.

"Despite our modest (for him) budget, he was patient and clever, making our home a dream. Easy to call for freshening up ideas."

John Barman, Inc.
212-838-9443
By appointment

Decorators
Mail/phone

5	5	5	5
quality	style	service	value

The Edge: For that New York look. Strong designer who listens and gets it done well. Favors classic styling with contemporary elements. Particularly strong at delivering a sophisticated New York look. Wholesale plus a design fee.

"Took my grandmother's Biedermeir furniture and made it look right for my young daughter's first apartment."

Use What You Have
145 East 74th Street
near 3rd Avenue
New York, NY 10021
212-288-8888
Weekdays by appointment.

Decorators
Upper East Side

4	4	4	4
quality	style	service	value

The Edge: Decorating advice on making the most of what you have. Pay per room or on an hourly basis. Advice is given on how to complete and finish a room or revise and move around what you already have to make it look new and better. Reasonably priced. No credit cards.

"Great."

E.C. Electronics
253 West 51st Street
near 8th Avenue
New York, NY 10019
212-586-6156. Fax 212-262-0888
Weekdays 9:30-6 Saturday 10-4.

Electronics, etc.
Midtown West

The Edge: Authorized service center for 15 brands of electronic equipment. Brands include Aiwa, Fuji, Hitachi and Sony.

Pyramid Electronics Ltd.
353 East 76th Street
between 1st and 2nd Avenues
New York, NY 10021
212-628-6500. Fax 212-628-6525
Weekdays 8-5:30 Saturday 9-5.

Electronics, etc.
Upper East Side

The Edge: Repairs VCRs and TVs. No delivery.

Rent-A-Phone

One World Trade Center
near Vessey Street
New York, NY 10048
212-524-9700. Fax 212-488-7886
Weekdays 9-5.

Electronics, etc.
Lower Manhattan

The Edge: Rents cellular phones. Rentals are $5 per day. Usage charges are $1.25 per minute within the five boroughs, $1.75 outside New York and $2 per minute in Canada. No delivery.

Ace Exterminating

460 9th Avenue
between 35th and 36th Streets
New York, NY 10018
212-594-9230. Fax 212-736-2746
Weekdays 8-5.

Exterminator
Midtown West

The Edge: Handles all bug problems. Services homes, offices, stores, museums and hospitals. No credit cards.

Ebel

750 Lexington Avenue
near 59th Street
New York, NY 10022
212-888-3235
Weekdays 9-4:30.

Jewelry & watches
Midtown East

The Edge: Just repairs of Ebel line and "Swiss way." Watch repairs only.

Leon's Jewelry

347 Grand Street
between Essex and Orchard Streets
New York, NY 10002
212-473-4676
Monday-Thursday 9-5 Friday 9-3.

Jewelry & watches
Lower East Side/Chinatown

quality style service value

The Edge: Reliable watch and jewelry repair. Small shop on Grand Street. Sells old watches, wallets and odds-and-ends gold jewelry. Best for simple watch and jewelry repairs, restringing pearls and installing watch batteries and bands. One-man operation in a tiny cluttered shop. No credit cards. No delivery.

Rissin's Jewelry Clinic

4 West 47th Street
near 5th Avenue
New York, NY 10036
212-575-1098
Monday Tuesday and Thursday 9:30-5 for retail customers.

Jewelry & watches
Midtown West

quality style service value

Closed the first two weeks in July and Christmas week

The Edge: Quality repairs from a most reliable source. Joe Rissin, the quintessential New York, talks very fast and is very proud of his work—repairing jewelry from costume to Fabergé. Has worked for the British Museum (Tut exhibit), the Brooklyn Museum, the Guggenheim, and Jewish Museum, among others. Joe is a gemologist and a platinum-trained jeweler. His wife, Toby, specializes in pearl stringing. Known for antique repair, but also repairs eyeglasses, and gives them priority since "they're a necessity." Appraisals for $60 to $65 per hour. Gives estimates. Checks from customers he knows. Be prepared to wait at times. Joe pays attention to your detailed requests, no matter how small. No credit cards.

"I gave him my mother's 55-year-old diamond wedding band to restore. He made it look like it just came new from the original jewelry store. And the price was very reasonable."

Sanko Cultured Pearls
45 West 47th Street
between 6th and 7th Avenues
New York, NY 10036
212-819-0585
Weekdays 9-5. Open weekends at Christmas.

Jewelry & watches
Midtown West

The Edge: Great for pearl restringing. Features a large selection of cultured pearls in various sizes, colors and levels of perfection for sale. And of course pearl restringing. No credit cards.

City Knickerbocker
781 8th Avenue
near 47th Street
New York, NY 10036
212-586-3939. Fax 212-262-2889
Weekdays 8-5.

Light fixtures
Midtown West

quality	style	service	value
4	4	4	4

The Edge: Lamp repair and rewiring. For four generations, since 1906, quality lamp repairs, rewiring, replating and remodeling. No delivery.

Louis Mattia
980 2nd Avenue
near 52nd Street
New York, NY 10022
212-753-2176
Weekdays 9-6.

Light fixtures
Midtown East

quality	style	service	value
4	2	5	5

The Edge: Repairs, cleans, custom-designs and remakes lamps and chandeliers. Repairs, rewires and sells chandeliers, lamps and sconces of every era and style. Favors lighting from the turn of the century. Repairs done downstairs. No credit cards.

Express Car
212-831-8900
By appointment.

Limo rentals
Mail/phone

The Edge: Good car service and reasonable prices.

London Towncars

800-221-4009. Fax 718-786-7625
Daily 24 hours by appointment.

Limo rentals
Mail/phone

quality style service value

The Edge: High-quality reliable service, but you pay for it. Over 100 dark-blue Buick Park Avenues with burgundy leather interiors, plus a cadre of stretch limos. All cars feature phones and uniformed drivers. Used by Citicorp executives CBS celebrities. 24-hour advance notice is suggested but last-minute calls have frequently been met. Deluxe.

"Even in a blizzard when everything else stopped, they got us to the airport."

AAA Locksmiths

44 West 46th Street
near 6th Avenue
New York, NY 10036
212-840-3939. Fax 212-921-5086
Monday-Thursday 8-5:30 Friday 8-5.

Locksmiths
Midtown West

quality style service value

The Edge: Reliable. 50+ years' experience. Clients include Citibank. No credit cards.

"Whenever they've come, they've been great."

Artbag Creations, Inc.

735 Madison Avenue
near 64th Street
New York, NY 10021
212-744-2720. Fax 212-744-2559
Monday-Saturday 9:15-5:45.

Luggage & handbags
Upper East Side

quality style service value

The Edge: Noted for their quality repairs. Can repair and rework fine leather goods. Repairs zippers, restitches and repairs or duplicates handles. Can modify leather items to add compartments or hidden pockets. Will custom-make bags and briefcases. Sell new handbags, belts and buckles, as well.

Carnegie Luggage

1392 Avenue of the Americas
between 56th and 57th Streets
New York, NY 10019
212-586-8210. Fax 212-586-8211
Weekdays 9-5:45 Saturday 9-5.

Luggage & handbags
Midtown West

The Edge: Luggage repairs. Work done immediately or in one to three hours, if it's an emergency.

John R. Gerardo

Luggage & handbags
Midtown West

30 West 31st Street
between Broadway and 5th Avenue
New York, NY 10001
212-695-6955. Fax 212-268-4817
Weekdays 9-5 Saturday 10-2. Closed Saturday July and August.

The Edge: Custom repair work on handbags and luggage. Repairs (does emergency work) including handles, locks, patches and zippers. Also sells a full range of luggage. Same-day delivery available for some items.

Kay Leather Goods Repair Service

Luggage & handbags
Gramercy Pk/Murray Hill

333 5th Avenue
near 33rd Street
New York, NY 10016
212-481-5579
Weekdays 9-5.

The Edge: Repairs and makes quality leather goods. Find attaché cases, belts and handbags. No credit cards. No delivery.

Modern Leather Goods

Luggage & handbags
Midtown West

2 West 32nd Street
between 5th and 6th Avenues
New York, NY 10001
212-947-7770. Fax 212-279-9385
Monday-Friday 8:30-5 Saturday 9-2.

The Edge: Expert leather repairs. Repairs handbags, luggage and the like. Will duplicate your worn-out belts, handbags, or attaché cases. Recommended by the *New York Times* and top leather companies for their moderately priced, excellent work.

Superior Repair Center

Luggage & handbags
Gramercy Pk/Murray Hill

quality style service value

133 Lexington Avenue
near 29th Street
New York, NY 10016
212-889-7211
Monday-Wednesday 10-7 Thursday 10-8 Friday 10-6.

The Edge: Superior leather repair. Widely known. Fixes handbags, luggage and the like. Excellent work at good prices.

"This is where a top Madison Avenue repair shop sent my briefcase!"

Other locations
138 West 72nd Street
near Broadway/10023
212-769-2099
Monday-Thursday 10-7 Friday 10-6 Saturday 10-3.

Upper West Side

International Retinning & Copper Repair
525 West 26th Street
between 10th and 11th Avenues
New York, NY 10001
212-244-4896
Weekdays 9-5.

Metals
Midtown West

The Edge: One of the only places in Manhattan to get metal objects refurbished. Fixes, restores or makes new handles, lids, etc. for virtually all metals (no aluminum or stainless steel). Known for making sheet-metal planter liners for window boxes. Pickup for work costing more than $300. No credit cards.

Thome Silversmiths
49 West 37th Street, Room 605
between 5th and 6th Avenues
New York, NY 10018
212-764-5426
Weekdays 8:30-1 and 2:30-5:30.

Metals
Midtown West

The Edge: Metal restoration. Cleans, repairs, replates silver, silver plate, copper, brass, pewter and gold. Can repair velvet backs of picture frames. No credit cards. No delivery.

A&B Spraying Company
14 Sweetfield Circle
Yonkers, NY 10704
718-652-0132
Weekdays 8:30-8:30.

Miscellaneous
Westchester

The Edge: Custom colors for appliances and furniture. Speciality is painting dental equipment, but uses that technique to color metal furniture and appliances to your specifications. Can match colors to fabrics and wallpapers. Appliances should be done before walls. Charges $150 for a refrigerator. No credit cards.

Antique Furniture Workroom
225 East 24th Street
between 2nd and 3rd Avenues
New York, NY 10010
212-683-0551. Fax 212-693-1561
Weekdays 8-4.

Miscellaneous
Gramercy Pk/Murray Hill

The Edge: Reliable furniture restoration. Along with furniture restoration, gold-leafing and caning. Estimates are given in your home based on the hours required for the work. No credit cards.

Authentic Porcelain Refinishing
51-30 40th Avenue
Woodside, NY 11377
718-726-1481. Fax 212-726-1481

Miscellaneous
Queens

Weekdays 9-6.

The Edge: Porcelain repairs like new. Specializes in bathtub refinishing, sprays wood cabinets and metal furniture. Has color charts or can match colors. Will make house calls with a $225 minimum order. No credit cards.

Authorized Repair Service

Miscellaneous
Midtown West

30 West 57th Street
between 5th and 6th Avenues
New York, NY 10019
212-586-0947. Fax 212-586-1296
Monday Tuesday Thursday Friday 9-5 Wednesday 9-6 Saturday 10-3:30.
Closed Saturdays July and August.

The Edge: A virtual hospital for lighters, pens and shavers. Buys, sells and services antique (from the 1800s) lighters and pens.

Custom Spraying and Reglazing Company

Miscellaneous
Staten Island

52 Rector Street
Staten Island, NY 10314
718-494-3751
Monday-Saturday 9-5.

The Edge: Gives metal furniture a new life! Recently started using electrostatic refinishing process which attracts paints to metal molecularly. $150 job minimum. Custom colors are possible. Family-run business. No credit cards.

Down East Service Center

Miscellaneous
SoHo/TriBeCa

50 Spring Street
near Lafayette Street
New York, NY 10012
212-925-2632
Weekdays 11-6.

The Edge: The source for repairs of camping equipment. Repairs backpacks, hiking boots, hiking equipment, mosquito netting, overnight bags, sleeping equipment, tents.

French-American Reweaving Company

Miscellaneous
Midtown West

119 West 57th Street, Room 1406
between 6th and 7th Avenues
New York, NY 10019
212-765-4670
Weekdays 10:30-5:30 Saturday 11-2.

The Edge: A lifesaver for fabrics. In business for 60 years. Will repair and mend knits and scarves plus a range of fabrics, including silks and leathers. Quality work. Prices depend on the state of the fabric. No credit cards.

Henry Westpfal and Company

Miscellaneous
Midtown West

105 West 30th Street
between 6th and 7th Avenues

New York, NY 10001
212-563-5990. Fax 212-563-5068
Weekdays 9-6.

The Edge: The sharpest edge! Sells scissors (from cuticle cutters to leather-working tools). Also stocks left-handed tools. Sharpens everything.

Saved by the Bell Corporation

11 Riverside Drive
near 73rd Street
New York, NY 10023
212-874-5457
Weekdays 9-7.

Miscellaneous
Upper West Side

quality	style	service	value
5	5	5	5

The Edge: Finally, the part time wife we dream of having. Specialties include corporate relocations, delivery arrangements, party planning, personal shopping and help with organizational problems. Provides personal and professional services on an ad hoc, very flexible basis. No credit cards.

Stone Services, Inc.

Offices in the five boroughs and Westchester
718-293-2055. Fax 718-402-9303
Weekdays 8-6.

Miscellaneous
Mail/phone

The Edge: Spray-paints furniture. Specializes in spray-painting furniture. Offers a variety of finishes, from simple enamels used on household woodwork to costly high-tech paints like Imron, which is very strong, durable and flexible. If object is rusted or dented, Stone Service will reshape and sand it. Also spray-paints furniture, sculptures, wicker, wood, etc.

York End Caning

444 East 84th Street
between 1st and York Avenues
New York, NY 10028
212-288-6843
Weekdays 9-6 Saturday 10-5. Closed Saturday summer and winter.

Miscellaneous
Upper East Side

The Edge: Hand- and machine-caning. Can create a new cane seat to match an old back. Can match the weave and will stain the weave to match the old. No credit cards.

Big John Moving

1602 1st Avenue
near 83rd Street
New York, NY 10028
212-734-3300. Fax 212-978-3837
Office open weekdays 9-5.

Movers
Upper East Side

quality	style	service	value
3	-	5	5

The Edge: Careful movers. Also sells moving supplies, boxes, wraps, paper etc.

"Fair prices, excellent service; careful, nice people."

Brownstone Brothers Moving & Storage

426 East 91st Street
between 1st and York Avenues
New York, NY 10128
212-289-1511
Weekdays 9-6 Saturday 9-1.

Movers
Upper East Side

5	5	5	5
quality	style	service	value

The Edge: Widely used and no complaints. Expensive, but careful movers. Very service oriented.

"Quality movers."

Moishe's Moving Systems

215 Coles Street
Jersey City, NJ 07310
212-439-9191
Call weekdays 9-5. Moves by appointment.

Movers
Mail/phone

3	2	4	4
quality	style	service	value

The Edge: Reliable moving and storage services. In addition, sells boxes and packing materials in all sizes.

Micro-Ovens of New York

970 Woodmansten Place
near Bogart Avenue
Bronx, NY 10462
718-823-7101. Fax 718-823-7101
Weekdays 8:30-5:30 Saturday 9-noon.

Ovens
Bronx

The Edge: Fixes microwaves. Since 1976 an authorized service center for 10 oven makers including Amana, Panasonic and Sharp. Makes house calls all over the metropolitan area. No credit cards.

Margorie Stokes

212-753-0033
By appointment.

Personal shoppers
Mail/phone

The Edge: Personal shopper. Provides access to American designers such as Ciao and David Hayes of California as well as Dior and others. Prices are wholesale plus her 15% commission. Can view clothing at manufacturers but not try it on, so shop retail first. No credit cards. Discounter.

Margot Green

212-772-0892
By appointment.

Personal shoppers
Mail/phone

4	3	5	3
quality	style	service	value

The Edge: Wonderful knits and silks. Specializes in knits and silks from top European and American designers. Spends January through March in Palm Beach. Discounter.

Cohen Carpet Cleaning
212-663-6902
By appointment.

Rugs & carpets
Mail/phone

5 . 5 3
quality style service value

The Edge: Reliable and honest carpet cleaning. One-man operation. Very reliable. Can leave him alone in your house with anything. Very expensive. No credit cards.

Costikyan Ltd.
2813 14th Street
Long Island City, NY 11102
800-247-7847
Weekdays 9-5.

Rugs & carpets
Queens

5 5 5 5
quality style service value

The Edge: Hand-cleaning for priceless Oriental rugs. Quality carpet cleaning. Reasonable prices. No credit cards.

"Recommended—they're trustworthy."

Elite Carpet and Upholstery Cleaning
23 Adams Street
East Rockaway, NY 11518
516-887-5437
Weekdays 9-6.

Rugs & carpets
Queens

The Edge: Carpet and upholstery cleaning for 15 years. $20 per square foot for dry cleaning. Carpet cleaning charges are per room. Pickup and delivery are available at no extra charge. Also fire and flood restoration.

Long Island Carpet Cleaners
301 Norman Avenue
Brooklyn, NY 11222
718-383-7000. Fax 718-389-9152
Weekdays 8-6 Saturday 9-1.

Rugs & carpets
Brooklyn

4 3 4 3
quality style service value

The Edge: Upholstery and carpet cleaning done at your home or office. In business for 76 years. On-site carpet and upholstery cleaning.

Crown Machine Service
2792 Broadway
near 108th Street
New York, NY 10025
212-663-8968
Weekdays 9-6 Saturday 9-4.

Sewing machines
Upper West Side

The Edge: One of New York's largest sewing machine repair shops. Authorized dealer of Elna, Pfaff, Singer, Viking and White machines. Services and rents machines and even makes house calls. Cleaning and oiling starts at $29.95. Weekly rentals start at $25. Add $10 to the bill for house calls.

Park East Sewing Center

Sewing machines
Upper East Side

1358 3rd Avenue
near 77th Street
New York, NY 10021
212-737-1220. Fax 212-734-6368
Monday Thursday 10-7 Tuesday Wednesday Friday 10-6 Saturday 10-5.

The Edge: Repairs and sells sewing machines. Cleaning and oiling start at $35. Free estimates given. An authorized dealer for Bernina, White and New Home.

B. Nelson Shoe Corporation

Shoe repair
Midtown West

1221 Avenue of the Americas
C-2 level, McGraw-Hill Building
New York, NY 10020
212-869-3552
Weekdays 7:30-5:15.

5	-	4	5
quality	style	service	value

The Edge: Excellent shoe repair shop. No delivery.

Evelyn and San

Shoe repair
Upper East Side

400 East 83rd Street
near 1st Avenue
New York, NY 10028
212-628-7618
Weekdays 8-6 Saturday 8-5.

The Edge: Shoe restoration and dying. A good neighborhood source for quality shoe repairs. No credit cards. No delivery.

Jim's Shoe Repair

Shoe repair
Midtown East

50 East 59th Street
between Madison and Park Avenues
New York, NY 10022
212-355-8259
Weekdays 8-5:45 Saturday 9-3:45.
Closed Saturday July and August.

5	4	3	4
quality	style	service	value

The Edge: Excellent shoe repair. Everyone knows and recommends Jim's. Almost always crowded.

Manhattan Shoe Repair

Shoe repair
Gramercy Pk/Murray Hill

6 East 39th Street
near 5th Avenue
New York, NY 10016
212-683-4210
Weekdays 7:30-5:45.

The Edge: Repairs, rebinds and dyes shoes and bags. Quoting the owner: "We've been here for 45 years. We must be doing something right!"

Top Service
845 7th Avenue
near 54th Street
New York, NY 10019
212-765-3190. Fax 212-246-3796
Weekdays 8-6 Saturday 9-1.

Shoe repair
Midtown West

The Edge: Updates old shoes to look stylish. Effective at updating old shoes to look stylish. Possibilities include adding platforms to flat-soled shoes and sneakers; changing buckles, trims, straps; recovers heels. Also dyes shoes to match clothing and cleans fabric shoes. Work for designers and featured in the April 1995 *Martha Stewart Living*. No delivery.

Metro Sofa Service
242 Albany Avenue
Thornwood, NY 10594
914-769-2178. Fax 914-769-3984
By appointment only.

Sofa
Westchester

The Edge: They'll make it right if your sofa can't fit in the elevator. You paid for it, it's too big, but never mind, they'll get it in. Known for assembling and reassembling furniture better than new. Reasonably priced. No credit cards.

Alfonso Sciortino Custom Alterations
57 West 57th Street, Suite 609A
near 6th Avenue
New York, NY 10019
212-888-2846
Daily 10-6.

Tailors
Midtown West

The Edge: Top alterations. One-man operation which offers good tailoring. No credit cards.

Eddie Egras
125 West 72nd Street
near Amsterdam Avenue
New York, NY 10023
212-595-1596
Weekdays 9:30-7 by appointment.

Tailors
Upper West Side

The Edge: Men's tailor. No credit cards.

"Excellent tailor, fair prices."

John's European Boutique
118 East 59th Street, 2nd Floor
near Park Avenue

Tailors
Midtown East

New York, NY 10022
212-752-2239
Weekdays 9-6 Saturday 10-1.

The Edge: Quality tailoring. They do a lot of work for department stores and boutiques. No credit cards.

"Great tailoring at fair prices."

Peppino

Tailors
Upper East Side

780 Lexington Avenue
near 60th Street
New York, NY 10021
212-832-3844
Weekdays 8:30-6:30 Saturday 10-4.

The Edge: Excellent alterations at a fair price. No credit cards.

Forsyth Decorations

Upholsterers
Lower East Side/Chinatown

100 Forsyth Street
between Grand and Broome Streets
New York, NY 10002
212-226-3624. Fax 212-226-6277
Sunday-Thursday 9:30-5 Friday 9-12.

The Edge: Custom fabric work. You provide the fabrics and they'll do custom work from cushions to window treatments to slipcovers. Everything is made to order—there's no store inventory. No credit cards. Discounter.

Pembrooke & Ives

Upholsterers
SoHo/TriBeCa

149 Wooster Street
near Houston Street
New York, NY 10012
212-995-0555
Weekdays 9-6 by appointment.

5	5	5	5
quality	style	service	value

The Edge: Good tailoring and details, often whimsical. A choice upholsterer featuring skirts with box or pencil pleats, shirred skirts and/or buttons. Prices for custom slipcovers start at $500, not including fabric.

Upholstery Unlimited, Inc.

Upholsterers
Midtown West

138 West 25th Street, 11th Floor
between 6th and 7th Avenues
New York, NY 10001
212-924-1230. Fax 212-627-3561
By appointment.

The Edge: Superior-quality upholstery with reasonable prices. Upholstery and drapery specialists. No credit cards.

Pet services & supplies

ASPCA

424 East 92nd Street
near 1st Avenue
New York, NY 10128
212-876-7700
Monday-Saturday 11-7, Sunday noon-5.

Adoption
Upper East Side

3	-	3	5
quality	style	service	value

The Edge: Great source for pets. Wonderful selection of animals needing a home. Adoption of animals is a two-way process. The ASPCA interviews you and all members of your family to ensure the pet you choose suits your lifestyle, meaning that the pet's needs are well met. Some people are turned down. Fee includes medical exam, initial shots and neutering. A Behavior Health Line is available to help you settle the animal into your home. If the animal has health needs, veterinary care is provided. Prices $55 for a dog and $45 for a cat. Also training classes are offered, group lessons at $230 for eight weekly classes ($175 if ASPCA dog). No delivery.

Bide-A-Wee Home Association

410 East 38th Street
near 1st Avenue
New York, NY 10016
212-532-4455. Fax 212-532-6273
Monday-Saturday 10-6 Sunday 10-5.

Adoption
Gramercy Pk/Murray Hill

3	-	3	5
quality	style	service	value

The Edge: Great source for pets. Wonderful selection of animals needing a home. Fee of $55 for dogs and cats under six months ($30 for older animals) includes medical exam, initial shots and neutering. Two forms of ID are required to adopt as well as proof of employment and your current address. Dog training, offered Thursday evenings 7-8, costs $200 for seven sessions. No delivery.

Canine College

40 Marchant Road
Redding, CT 06896
203-938-2124
Daily 24-hour dog boarding. By appointment.

Boarding
Connecticut

5	5	5	4
quality	style	service	value

The Edge: A Relais et Châteaux experience for your pets. These folks have a way with pets. In existence for over 50 years, the place is top-drawer, gorgeous. Boarding, training and grooming services are available. Large private indoor and outdoor runs. Heating and air conditioning make runs comfortable in all weather. Special handling options include individual play time with staff. Training is a one week (plus) formalized program. Manhattan pickup and delivery. No credit cards.

"Our pup came home in better spirits from here than anywhere."

Groomer Direct

1989 Transit Way
Brockport, NY 14420-0915
800-551-5048. Fax 718-637-8244
Weekdays 8-8 Saturday 8:30-5 Sunday 10-4.

Grooming & supplies
Mail/phone

quality style service value

The Edge: All the basics at close to wholesale prices. Discounts all the necessities for your pets. The catalog features crates, leads and collars, toys, treats and grooming supplies. Orders under $50 are subject to a $5 service charge. Discounter.

Karens for People + Pets

1195 Lexington Avenue
near 81st Street
New York, NY 10028
212-472-9440. Fax 212-628-2312
Monday-Saturday 9-6.

Grooming & supplies
Upper East Side

quality style service value

The Edge: Elegance for the family's favorites. Known for the quality of their grooming care (uses hypoallergenic products), the salon sells its products and grooming supplies plus accessories for people and pets.

Pampered Paws

227 East 57th Street
near 2nd Avenue
New York, NY 10022
212-935-7297. Fax 212-935-7386
Monday-Saturday 11-8 Sunday 11-6.

Grooming & supplies
Midtown East

quality style service value

The Edge: The Bergdorf of pet supplies. Luxury items including exotic leather collars and leads, tuxedo and other costume rentals for those special occasions and of course toys, bowls and treats.

Pet Cab

631 West 130th Street
near Broadway
New York, NY 10027
212-491-5313. Fax 212-491-5313
By appointment.

Transportation
Upper Upper West Side

quality style service value

The Edge: If only yellow taxis were as good. Can and will take your pet anywhere. Chauffeurs pets, crated or not, in good health or emergency transportation for injured pets. Can handle dogs, cats, birds or you name it. Has served the ASPCA and the Animal Medical Center, among others. Has stretchers for emergency cases. Can handle aggressive dogs (muzzles are an extra charge). Prices $38 an hour. Minimum charge $22. No credit cards.

Animal Medical Center

510 East 62nd Street
between FDR Drive and York Avenue
New York, NY 10021
212-838-8100
Daily 24 hours per day.

Veterinarians
Upper East Side

5 - 5 4
quality style service value

The Edge: They've seen it all, done it all. The best. The city's most extensive animal hospital.
Staffed and operating 24 hours a day. Specialists are available in everything, 22 subspecialties.
They offer routine veterinary care and emergency treatment. A true city treasure.

"They always make you feel your pet is the one and only."

Manhattan Veterinary Clinic

240 East 80th Street
near 2nd Avenue
New York, NY 10021
212-988-1000. Fax 212-535-8055
Daily 8-6 emergency services from 6-1.

Veterinarians
Upper East Side

The Edge: High-tech, caring hospital. Dr. Marder, director. Full-time working hospital with staff
veterinarians with diagnostic skills (internal medicine) and surgery. Staff surgeon is Dr. Greene.

"My cat fell 12 floors. They performed a miracle—returned a 100% healthy cat, still walking
window sills!"

New York Veterinary Hospital

301 East 55th Street
near 2nd Avenue
New York, NY 10022
212-355-5490. Fax 212-223-3712
Weekdays 8-7 weekends 10-1.

Veterinarians
Midtown East

The Edge: High-tech hospital. Dr. Kessler, senior veterinarian, plus two other resident vets.
Maintains quality hospital facilities. Technicians are on site until midnight. Makes house calls.
Will board animals to 70 pounds. No run, but walks three times daily.

Park East Animal Hospital

52 East 64th Street
near Park Avenue
New York, NY 10021
212-832-8417. Fax 212-355-3620
Appointments: Monday-Thursday 9-8 Friday 9-5:30 Saturday 9-3:30 Sunday 10:30-3.

Veterinarians
Upper East Side

The Edge: 24-hour emergency care and vets who make house calls. Dr. Berman, senior
director at the hospital, plus two other vets. Hospital is open 24 hours a day. Technician or vet is
on site at all times. The veterinarians make house calls when necessary, and offer at-home nursing
care. Facilities are state of the art, with good postoperative recovery equipment. Limited boarding.

University Animal Hospital

354 East 66th Street
near 1st Avenue
New York, NY 10021
212-288-8884. Fax 212-288-9432
Weekdays 8-8 Saturday 9-4 Sunday 9-1 by appointment.

Veterinarians
Upper East Side

The Edge: Vets on call 24 hours per day. Dr. Lawrence Zola is the senior vet here. Two vets are on staff. 24-hour emergency care with doctors on premises or on call 24 hours per day.

Yorkville Animal Hospital

227 East 84th Street
near 2nd Avenue
New York, NY 10028
212-249-8802
Weekdays 9-11:30 and 3:30-5:30.

Veterinarians
Upper East Side

The Edge: Full animal hospital. Performs surgery, dentistry and grooming, all on site. Three vets are on staff. Boards small to medium-size dogs with play time available in their outdoor run. Prices are $22 per day for dogs and $18 per day for cats.

Jim Buck School for Dogs

212-410-2825
By appointment.

Walking
Mail/phone

The Edge: An old-standby dog-walking service. These could be the guys you see mornings with the packs of dogs in toe. Picks up your dog every morning for two hours of training and exercise. Interviews required for pets to ensure they fit into the group. No credit cards.

Urban Animal

212-969-8506. Fax 212-996-9003
Daily by appointment.

Walking
Mail/phone

The Edge: TLC for your beloved pets. Since 1991, these folks have been providing tender, loving care for your pets. Individualized walks (one or two dogs) at a time. Serves over 200 clients. Weekday prices are $12 for half hour walk increasing to $20 for an hour walk. Discounts for more than 10 walks per week. Provides boarding in staff members' homes for dogs and cats—prices are $38 per night for standard dogs increasing to $45 for unneutered male dogs and puppies and include four walks per day. They'll also arrange housesitting, if your pet doesn't like to leave home! Staff is hired based on three references and a trial co-walk test with the owners of Urban Animal. If you need a pet, give them a call as these folks periodically adopt strays and seek good homes for their adoptees. No credit cards.

Sporting goods

Bicycle & Fitness Equipment Store

242-244 East 79th Street
near 3rd Avenue
New York, NY 10021
212-249-9344
Weekdays 9:30-8 weekends 9-7.

Bicycles
Upper East Side

The Edge: Sells and rents all types of bikes and skates (roller and inline). Competitive prices, with last year's models offering the best values. Also standard exercise equipment, including treadmills and aerobic bikes. Good bike repairs. Bike and skate rentals are $6 an hour or $21 a day. No delivery.

Bicycle Habitat

244 Lafayette Street
near Prince Street
New York, NY 10012
212-431-3315. Fax 212-431-3846
Monday-Thursday 10-7 Friday 10-6:30 weekends 10-6.

Bicycles
SoHo/TriBeCa

The Edge: Best bikes and repair classes. This bike store stocks Diamond Back, Mongoose, Trek and UniVega. Bikes priced from $200 to $3,000. You can find cycling accessories and clothing. Good repairs. The store also offers a $150 seven-week repair class which usually meets on Wednesday evenings from 7:30 to 9:30. Bike rentals from $25 per day.

Bicycle Renaissance

430 Columbus Avenue
between 80th and 81st Streets
New York, NY 10024
212-724-2350. Fax 212-875-0612
Weekdays 10-7 Saturday 10-6 Sunday 10-5.

Bicycles
Upper West Side

The Edge: Full-service bike shop. Find top brands of city, racing and touring bikes as well as custom bikes. Also clothing and accessories. Excellent service and repairs. Stocks over 100 parts.

Conrad's Bike Shop

25 Tudor City Place
near 41st Street
New York, NY 10017
212-697-6966. Fax 212-697-6966
Tuesday Thursday-Saturday 10:30-5:30 Wednesday 10:30-7 only in season.

Bicycles
Midtown East

The Edge: For the serious biker—top service, top bikes. Carries only the best frames, bicycles and parts. Mostly European bikes with prices to $1,600. The shop is known for its top service and excellent staff. Also find the clothing and accessories that befit a $1,600 bike!

"The Tiffany's of bike shops!"

Larry & Jeff's Bicycles Plus

Bicycles
Upper East Side

1400 3rd Avenue
near 79th Street
New York, NY 10021
212-794-2929
Daily 10-7.

The Edge: Full-service bike shop. Features every type of bicycle from touring to sports and racing bikes. Brands include Cannondale, Diamond Back, Jamis, GT and Mongoose. Bikes priced from $100. Rentals $25 per day and $7 per hour. All kinds of accessories, clothing and shoes to complement.

Other locations
1690 2nd Avenue
between 87th and 88th Streets/10028
212-722-2201. Fax 212-722-5423

Upper East Side

Toga Bike Shop

Bicycles
Upper West Side

110 West End Avenue
near 64th Street
New York, NY 10023
212-799-9625. Fax 212-799-2834
Monday Tuesday Friday 11-7 Wednesday Thursday 11-8 Saturday 10-6 Sunday 11-6.

The Edge: Among New York's largest and oldest bike shops. Features repairs and equipment. Find touring, sport, city and triathlon bikes, including American Flyer, Colnago Lite Speed, Merlin, Kestrel, Specialized Cannondale, Gary Fisher and Marin. Bikes priced from $259 to $8,000 (custom bikes). Rentals from $35 per day. Discounts from 10% to 20% for prior season's bikes. Free emergency repair and maintenance class open to all on the first and third Tuesdays of the month at 7:15pm. Sells clothing and shoes also.

Blatt Billiards

Billiards
Flatiron/East Village

809 Broadway
near 11th Street
New York, NY 10003
212-674-8855. Fax 212-598-4514
Weekdays 9-6 Saturday 10-4. Closed Saturday July and August.

The Edge: Billiard heaven. Since 1923 nothing appears to have changed. Largest collection of antique, custom and contemporary pool tables and cues. Regulation dart boards and darts.

V. Loria & Sons

Billiards
SoHo/TriBeCa

178 Bowery
near Delancey Street
New York, NY 10012
212-925-0300
Weekdays 10:30-6 Saturday 10:30-4.

The Edge: The place for billiard equipment. Since 1912 the source for indoor games, including billiards, poker, Ping-Pong and gaming tables, pinball machines and bowling equipment. Find new, used, and custom tables. Gear for all these sports and games, including bags, balls, shoes and accessories.

Tents & Trails

21 Park Place
near Broadway
New York, NY 10007
212-227-1760. Fax 212-267-0488
Monday-Wednesday Saturday 9:30-6 Thursday Friday 9:30-7 Sunday noon-6.

Camping
Lower Manhattan

The Edge: Top-of-the-line source for camping supplies to buy or rent. Three floors packed with camping equipment and survival gear for sale or rent. Also clothing in all sizes from children's to adults'. Find hiking boots, down jackets, jeans, backpacks, camping stoves, sleeping bags, tents and ropes. No delivery.

Capezio

1650 Broadway, 2nd Floor
near West 51st Street
New York, NY 10019
212-245-2130. Fax 212-757-7635
Monday-Wednesday Friday 9:30-6:30
Thursday 9:30-7 Saturday 9:30-6.

Dance
Midtown West

quality style service value

The Edge: Selection—everything for the dancer. Full line of dance wear (shoes and clothing), athletic wear and fashion shoes. Traditional and timeless.

Other locations
136 East 61st Street
between Lexington and Park Avenues/10021
212-758-8833
Monday Wednesday Friday 10-6:30 Tuesday Thursday 10-7 Saturday 11-6 Sunday noon-5.

Upper East Side

2121 Broadway, 3rd Floor
near 74th Street/10023
212-799-7774
Monday-Wednesday Friday 10-6 Thursday 11-7 Saturday 10-5.

Upper West Side

Freed of London

922 7th Avenue
near 58th Street
New York, NY 10019
212-489-1055. Fax 212-262-0041
Monday-Saturday 10-6.

Dance
Midtown West

quality style service value

The Edge: The dance establishment's source. Established London supplier of equipment and costumes for the dance community (ballet, gymnastics, tap, jazz and ballroom dancing), plus period shoes. Full range of dance wear, including shoes, leg warmers, leotards, skirts and tutus. Keeps complete line of regulation wear for the Royal Ballet.

"The only place for dance wear."

Repetto

Dance
Upper West Side

30 Lincoln Plaza
62nd Street and Broadway
New York, NY 10023
212-582-3900. Fax 212-582-5545
Monday-Saturday 11-7.

The Edge: French manufacturer of classic dance wear and accessories. Everything for the dance professional as well as exercise clothing for aerobics, gymnastics and jazz. Ballet wear for boys and girls to adults. Catalog costs $3.

DMI Dartmart, Inc.

Darts
Midtown West

160 West 26th Street
near 6th Avenue
New York, NY 10001
212-366-6981. Fax 212-206-6491
Weekdays 10-6:30 Saturday 10-9. Closed Saturday June-August.

The Edge: A good source for darts and all indoor games. Features a wide selection of darts, boards, cabinets and team shirts. Dart sets up to $165 per set. Find indoor games, quality pool tables (at $1,200) and cues, Ping-Pong tables and air-hockey equipment.

Dart Shop Limited

Darts
Flatiron/East Village

30 East 20th Street
between Park Avenue South and Broadway
New York, NY 10003
212-533-8684
Weekdays noon-6 Saturday 11-5.

The Edge: The only dart store in Manhattan devoted solely to darts and darting equipment. Equipment includes tournament quality cabinets, boards, scoreboards for pros and amateurs. Priced from $6.50 to $160. No delivery.

Nautica

Diving
Upper West Side

216 Columbus Avenue
near 70th Street
New York, NY 10023
212-496-0933. Fax 212-721-6735
Monday-Saturday 10-8 Sunday noon-7.

The Edge: Sell only Nautica goods—equipment, clothing and themed items. Find men's clothing, cologne, diving watches plus equipment.

Pan Aqua Diving

Diving
Upper West Side

101 West 75th Street
near Columbus Avenue
New York, NY 10023
212-496-2267. Fax 212-721-2633
Weekdays noon-7 Saturday 10-7 Sunday noon-5.

The Edge: Divers' dreams start here. Top-quality diving gear—air compressors, depth gauges, dive planners, gloves, fins, tanks and wet suits. Find Henderson, Oceanic, O'Neill, ScubaPro, Sea Quest and Tusa equipment. Large price range available. No delivery.

Scuba Network

Diving
Midtown East

124 East 57th Street
between Park and Lexington Avenues
New York, NY 10022
212-750-9160
Monday-Thursday 10:30-7 Friday 10:30-8 Saturday 10:30-6 Sunday noon-5.

The Edge: Tops in equipment. Features top-quality scuba diving equipment plus books and travel guides. No delivery.

Barbara Gee Danskin Center

Exercise
Upper West Side

2487 Broadway
near 82nd Street
New York, NY 10024
212-769-1564
Monday-Saturday 10:30-7:30. After Labor Day Sunday 1-6.

The Edge: 10% off on a full line of exercise wear. Features exercise and dance wear, underwear, lingerie and hosiery. 10% to 20% off for Danskin tights and leotards. Lingerie and underwear is mostly Hanes.

Other locations
2282½ Broadway
at 82nd Street/10024
212-769-2923
Monday-Saturday 10:30-7:30 Sunday 1-6.

Upper West Side

Gym Source

Exercise
Midtown East

40 East 52nd Street
between Park and Madison Avenues
New York, NY 10022
212-688-4222. Fax 212-688-6933
Weekdays 9-6 Saturday 10-5 Closed Saturday July and August.

The Edge: One of the city's best exercise equipment sources. 7,000-square-foot showroom with a huge selection of all major brands of exercise equipment, including treadmills, Lifecycles, stair climbers, weight machines, rowers and more. Will rent equipment with a one-month minimum. The staff will help you design an exercise room for a home or office gym with the equipment that best meets your own goals.

Women's Workout Gear

Exercise
Chelsea

121 7th Avenue
near 17th Street
New York, NY 10011
212-627-1117
Weekdays 11-6:30 Saturday 11-6 Sunday 1:30-5:30.

The Edge: Workout gear for all occasions. Features sports clothing; aerobics and running gear; walking, running and aerobic shoes; bathing suits and goggles; sports bras; weights and exercise mats. Brands include City Lights, Fast Forward, Gilda Marx, Speedo and their own label. No delivery.

Blade Fencing

Fencing
Chelsea

212 West 15th Street
near 7th Avenue
New York, NY 10011
212-620-0114. Fax 212-620-0116
Weekdays 10-7 Saturday 11-3.

The Edge: Meets all fencing needs. Instruction plus all the equipment, clothing and books required to fence in style.

Capitol Fishing Tackle Company

Fishing
Chelsea

3	2	3	3
quality	style	service	value

218 West 23rd Street
near 7th Avenue
New York, NY 10011
212-929-6132. Fax 212-929-0039
Monday-Wednesday Friday 9-6 Thursday 9-7 Saturday 9-5.

The Edge: For the serious saltwater angler. The oldest (since 1897) fishing tackle store in the city. Top-quality equipment includes rods, reels, lures, lines and accessories, with special emphasis on deep-sea saltwater equipment. A good source for inexpensive beginner equipment. A wide range of equipment priced from $2.95 to $800.

"Really fine for saltwater."

Orvis

Fishing
Midtown East

4	3	4	3
quality	style	service	value

355 Madison Avenue
near 45th Street
New York, NY 10017
212-697-3133. Fax 212-697-5826
Weekdays 9-6 Saturday 10-5.

The Edge: Known for their hunting and fishing lines, plus great lessons. Features a complete line of fly-fishing reels, rods, lures and accessories, including bags, fishing vests and jackets, hip boots and waders. Hunting equipment includes guns and equipment for bird hunting. Casual country and safari clothing. Gift items feature fishing and hunting motif items. Best of all are Orvis' trips and fishing lessons.

Foot-Joy Shop

Golf
Midtown East

7 East 52nd Street
between 5th and Madison Avenues
New York, NY 10022
212-753-8522. Fax 212-752-0569
Weekdays 10-5:30 Saturday 10-5.

The Edge: Enormous variety of golf shoes. More than 150 styles, from saddle to wing tip. Some shoes with cleats, some without. Also golf gloves and socks.

New York Golf Center, Inc.

Golf
Midtown West

131 West 35th Street
near Broadway
New York, NY 10001
212-564-2255. Fax 212-244-6941
Daily 10-7. June-August daily 10-8.

The Edge: Large selection favored by golf pros and amateurs. Selection includes Callaway, Honma, Ping, Top-Flite, Titleist and Wilson. Shop features clubs, bags, balls, shoes and accessories. They say they offer a 30% discount.

Richard Metz Golf Studio

Golf
Midtown East

425 Madison Avenue, 3rd Floor
near 49th Street
New York, NY 10017
212-759-6940. Fax 212-888-5417
Weekdays 10-7 Saturday 10-5.

The Edge: Pro shop with practice cages and putting greens. Golfer heaven. Find the latest, top-quality balls, clubs, golf bags, shoes and clothing, plus golfing books and videotapes. Lessons and practice area plus equipment all in one location. Offers instruction at $350 for 10 lessons.

World of Golf

Golf
Midtown East

147 East 47th Street, 2nd Floor
between Lexington and 3rd Avenues
New York, NY 10017
212-755-9398. Fax 212-207-8370
Monday-Saturday 9-7.

The Edge: A New York pro shop. Carries a full range of golf equipment, including clubs, bags, shoes and clothing for the younger set, women and men. A very large selection of all the best names. Also practice aids, books and videos. Discounter.

John Jovino Gun Shop

5 Centre Market Place
near Grand Street
New York, NY 10013
212-925-4881. Fax 212-966-4986
Weekdays 8-6 Saturday 8-3.

Guns
SoHo/TriBeCa

The Edge: New York's gun shop. Since 1911 has featured handguns, rifles, shotguns, and accessories, including ammunition and bulletproof vests. Authorized warranty repair station for virtually all gun manufacturers. Carries most major brands of guns, priced from $100 to $1,000.

Grove Decoys

36 West 44th Street
between 5th and 6th Avenues
New York, NY 10036
212-391-0688
Weekdays 10-5.

Hunting
Midtown West

The Edge: Hundreds of duck decoys. This is the place for devotees of duck decoys.

Hunting World/Angler's World

16 East 53rd Street
between 5th and Madison Avenues
New York, NY 10022
212-755-3400. Fax 212-980-1061
Monday-Saturday 10-6 Sunday 11-5.

Hunting
Midtown East

The Edge: Everything you'll need for a safari or fishing trip. Offers clothing and sporting gear, including a full line of fishing gear. Clothing includes safari jackets, slacks, hats, shooting bags, shoes and clay shooter vests. Luggage with their logo and jewelry.

"More for show than sport."

Goldberg's Marine

12 West 37th Street
between 5th and 6th Avenues
New York, NY 10018
212-594-6065. Fax 212-594-0721
Monday-Saturday 9-6 Sunday 10-5.

Marine
Midtown West

quality style service value

The Edge: New York's source for boaters. Features one of the largest selections in the city of fishing devices and nautical gear. Find the simplest personal equipment (books, clocks, clothing) to sports needs (diving, fishing, waterskiing) to everything for your boat (china to electronics).

"Best prices, and they have it all."

H. Kauffman and Sons

Riding
Gramercy Pk/Murray Hill

419 Park Avenue South
near 29th Street
New York, NY 10016
212-684-6060. Fax 212-213-0389
Monday-Wednesday Friday Saturday 10-6:30 Thursday 10-7 Sunday noon-5.

The Edge: An extremely fine equestrian shop. Known for their riding clothing, saddles, bridles and equipment. They offer quality gifts for horse lovers plus weekend womens sportswear. Riding clothing and boots are excellent quality with good styling. Deluxe.

"Especially good for western riders." "Everything for riding except the horse!"

Miller's Harness Company

Riding
Gramercy Pk/Murray Hill

117 East 24th Street
near Park Avenue
New York, NY 10010
212-673-1400. Fax 212-473-0128
Monday-Wednesday Friday Saturday 10-6 Thursday 10-7.

4	5	5	4
quality	style	service	value

The Edge: Full-line, world-class equestrian store. Features proper riding gear and saddles. Offers all major brands, including Crosby and Hermès. Books, videos and gift items—practical to horsy motif.

"Good selection for English-style riders."

Super Runners Shop

Running
Upper East Side

1337 Lexington Avenue
near 89th Street
New York, NY 10028
212-369-6010. Fax 212-289-7427
Monday-Wednesday Friday 10-7 Thursday 10-9 Saturday 10- 6 Sunday noon- 5.

The Edge: One of the best running stores in the city. Features shoes, running gear and accessories (goggles, sunglasses and watches). Most major brands. No delivery.

Blades West

Skating
Upper West Side

120 West 72nd Street
near Columbus Avenue
New York, NY 10023
212-787-3911
Monday-Saturday 10-8 Sunday 10-6.

The Edge: Meets all blade and board needs. Features a full range of bodyboards, skates, skateboards, snowboards and surfboards for sale or rent plus outfits to match. Maintains a full repair shop on premises.

Peck and Goodie Skates

Skating
Midtown West

919 8th Avenue
near 54th Street
New York, NY 10019
212-246-6123. Fax 212-262-3639
Daily 10-6.

The Edge: Could be the city's finest skate shop. Carries the best equipment from novice to expert figure, hockey and inline skates, equipment and apparel. Hockey skate brands include Bauer, CCM Mega, Riedell and Spteri. Figure skating brands include Don Jackson, Reidell, and Teri. Inline skating brands include K2, Miller, Oxygen, Rollerblade and Viking. Rents inline skates for $15 per day. Offers skate sharpening and repairs.

Bogner

Skiing
Upper East Side

821 Madison Avenue
near 68th Street
New York, NY 10021
212-472-0266. Fax 212-472-0756
Monday-Saturday 10-6.

5	5	5	3
quality	style	service	value

The Edge: High-fashion ski wear. Also some après-ski wear. The "in" colors change each year. Look for golf and tennis wear outside the ski season. Bogner designs only. Very expensive.

"Great-looking clothes and colors."

Scandinavian Ski Shop

Skiing
Midtown West

40 West 57th Street
between 5th and 6th Avenues
New York, NY 10019
212-757-8524. Fax 212-757-8211
Monday-Wednesday Friday 10-7 Thursday 10-8 Saturday 10-6 Sunday 11-5.

The Edge: More practical than glamorous ski equipment and clothing. Best known for its ski equipment and ski wear, but also offers tennis, hiking, skating and swimwear, depending on the season. Three full floors. All top ski lines are featured, including Obermeyer, Emmegi, VdeV, Bogner, LaFont, Postcard and MCM. Children's and adult sizes.

Soccer Sport Supply Company

Soccer
Upper East Side

1745 1st Avenue
between 90th and 91st Streets
New York, NY 10128
212-427-6050. Fax 212-427-8769
Weekdays 10-6 Saturday 10-3.

The Edge: The name says it all. New York's specialist in soccer and rugby equipment. Find shoes, team equipment, and uniforms for basketball, lacrosse, rugby, soccer and softball.

Collector's Stadium

214 Sullivan Street
between West 3rd and Bleecker Streets
New York, NY 10012
212-353-1531. Fax 212-353-1571
Daily 11-7.

Sports-general
SoHo/TriBeCa

The Edge: Anything and everything for collectors. Devoted to sports and comic book memorabilia. Anything the collector would want from autographed baseballs ranging in price from $300 per baseball to over $1,000 for a Michael Jordan autographed ball. Good gift items include Game 1 pieces (clothing actually worn by players at games) and less expensive items such as baseball caps in more than 200 team styles. Items go back to 1890. Old and new comics for kids and adult comic book lovers.

Eastern Mountain Sports

611 Broadway
near Houston Street
New York, NY 10012
212-505-9860
Weekdays 10-9 Saturday 10-6 Sunday noon-6.

Sports-general
SoHo/TriBeCa

5	3	4	4
quality	style	service	value

The Edge: No-frills, well-priced sturdy clothing and equipment. Basic and functional. Climbing, backpacking and camping clothing and equipment. Complete stock of mountaineering, downhill and cross-country skiing equipment.

Other locations
20 West 61st Street
near Broadway/10023
212-397-4860
Weekdays 10-9 Saturday 10-6 Sunday noon-6.

Upper West Side

G&S Sporting Goods

43 Essex Street
near Grand Street
New York, NY 10002
212-777-7590
Sunday-Friday 9-6.

Sports-general
Lower East Side/Chinatown

The Edge: Good prices on the basics—athletic clothing, footwear and equipment. Find sneakers by Converse, Keds, LA Gear, New Balance, Nike and Reebok. Regulation balls for all sports. Also pool cues and accessories, Ping-Pong, badminton, racquetball and sleeping bags. No golf or ski equipment. No delivery. Discounter.

Gerry Cosby and Company

3 Pennsylvania Plaza
at Madison Square Garden
New York, NY 10001
212-563-6464. Fax 212-967-0876

Sports-general
Midtown West

Weekdays 9:30-6:30 Saturday 9:30-6 Sunday noon-5. Open daily starting three hours before Garden sports events.

The Edge: Pro sports apparel. Features a large selection of pro sports jerseys, NFL- and NBA-licensed apparel and souvenirs. Makes protective and sports gear designed for professional use for most sports, including baseball, basketball, football, hockey and lacrosse. Discounter.

Modell's Sporting Goods

200 Broadway
near John Street
New York, NY 10038
212-964-4007. Fax 212-964-1980
Weekdays 8:30-6:30 Saturday 9-4.

Sports-general
Lower Manhattan

The Edge: Large range of moderately priced sporting equipment and clothing. A chain of 50 stores. One of the city's largest sources for gear for almost all sports. Features all major brands with a seasonal focus. No delivery. Discounter.

Paragon Sporting Goods

867 Broadway
near 18th Street
New York, NY 10003
212-255-8036. Fax 212-929-9831
Monday-Saturday 10-8 Sunday 11-6:30.

Sports-general
Flatiron/East Village

5	5	4	3
quality	style	service	value

The Edge: Could be the best, certainly the most comprehensive, sports shop in the city. Over 80,000 square feet on three full floors dedicated to equipment and clothing for the serious sportsman. You name the sport and they have the top-brand equipment and clothing, no matter the season. Also binoculars, down vests and sunglasses. Selection is often unique. Prices are full list.

"New York's finest sports shop."

Spiegel Sporting Goods

105 Nassau Street
near Fulton Street
New York, NY 10038
212-227-8400. Fax 212-267-1552
Weekdays 10-6 Saturday 11-5.

Sports-general
Lower Manhattan

The Edge: Equipment for just about any sport. Since 1916. Known for their special sale prices, which can make items among the lowest priced in the city. When they commit to selling, inexpensively they do just that. No delivery.

Cameo Water Wear

1349 3rd Avenue
near 77th Street
New York, NY 10021
212-570-6606. Fax 212-571-1601
Weekdays 11-8 Saturday 10-6 Sunday noon-5.

Swimming
Upper East Side

4	4	4	3
quality	style	service	value

The Edge: Swimwear always available. Swimwear and coverups available in all seasons and in misses' sizes 6 to 16 to make the most of what you've got. All the leading names and hundreds of suits. No delivery.

Finals

1466 Broadway
between 41st and 42nd Streets
New York, NY 10013
212-302-1308. Fax 212-302-1386
Daily 9-5.

Swimming
SoHo/TriBeCa

The Edge: Swimwear and equipment designed for function. Competition-style bathing suits, goggles and racing caps plus equipment, including kickboards, clocks and the like.

Fila of Madison Avenue

831 Madison Avenue
near 69th Street
New York, NY 10021
212-737-3452. Fax 212-737-3439
Monday-Wednesday Friday Saturday 10-6 Thursday 10-7.

Tennis
Upper East Side

5	4	5	3
quality	style	service	value

The Edge: Fashionable sports garb. From summer to winter, great-looking sportswear. Find tennis workout clothes and swimwear in summer, ski wear in winter.

Mason's Tennis Mart

911 7th Avenue
near 57th Street
New York, NY 10019
212-757-5374
Weekdays 10-7 Saturday 10-6.

Tennis
Midtown West

The Edge: Racquets and clothes for pros. Great selection in top equipment and clothing. Traditional styling favored. Sells bags, balls, ball machines and racquets. Same-day racquet stringing.

Island Sports

1623 York Avenue
near 85th Street
New York, NY 10028
212-744-2000. Fax 212-744-4804
Monday-Wednesday Friday 10-7 Thursday 10-8 Saturday 9:30-6:30 Sunday 10:30-6.

Windsurfing
Upper East Side

The Edge: Equipment for water sports and inline skating. Stocks a large selection of top-name equipment and clothing for most water sports (waterskiing, deep-sea diving) and for roller and inline skating. Offers windsurfing lessons and equipment rental.

Travel & vacation

Capital Reservations
1730 Rhode Island Avenue NW, Suite 506
Washington, DC 20036
800-847-4832. Fax 202-452-0537
Weekdays 9-6 Saturday 9-1.

Discount
Mail/phone

The Edge: Discounts Washington D.C. area hotels. Offers discounts from 30% to 50% on 70 Washington D.C. area one-star to five-star hotels on their list. Hotels include the Willard and the Ritz. Confirmation numbers are given and cancellation is possible until 4pm on the day of arrival.

Central Reservation Services
11420 North Kendall Drive, Suite 108
Miami, FL 33176
800-950-0232. Fax 305-274-1357
Daily 24 hours.

Discount
Mail/phone

The Edge: Discounts on more moderate U.S. hotels and car rentals. Offers good rates at two-star hotels. Discounts from 10% to 40%. Gives conformation numbers..

Cheap Tickets, Inc
800-377-1000
Weekdays 8:30-10 Weekends 10-7.

Discount.
Mail/phone

3	.	3	5
quality	style	service	value

The Edge: The name says it all. Check them out for both domestic and international discount tickets for air, cruises and car rentals. Overnight ticket delivery. Major airlines only.

Discount Hotel Hotline/Hotel Reservation Net
8140 Walnut Hill Lane, Suite 203
Dallas, TX 75231
800-964-6835. Fax 214-361-7299
Daily 24 hours.

Discount
Mail/phone

The Edge: Discounts on hotel rooms in 21 U.S. cities plus London, Paris and Rome. Discounts are 30% to 65% of the posted rate, depending on availability. Cancellation policy depends on the rules of the individual hotels.

Encore Preferred Travel/Encore Marketing
4501 Forbes Boulevard
Lanham, MD 20706
800-638-8976. Fax 301-731-0525
Weekdays 9-7.

Discount
Mail/phone

The Edge: Travel discounts for members. Up to 50% off walk-in rates at major hotel chains in the U.S. and Europe (600 hotels offered). Also discounts on restaurants, car rentals and air travel. $49 annual fee. Upscale resorts offered for a $60 annual fee.

Express Hotel Reservations

800-356-1123   **Discount**
Weekdays 9-6:30.   **Mail/phone**

The Edge: Hotel discounts in New York and Los Angeles exclusively. Emphasis on luxury hotels, but good deals are available on rooms under $100. Expect 10% to 30% off corporate hotel rates. Full price range from moderate to deluxe. Conformation by phone or fax.

Moment's Notice

7301 New Utrecht Avenue   **Discount**
near 73rd Street   **Mail/phone**
Brooklyn, NY 11204
718-234-6295. Fax 718-234-6450
Daily 9-5:30.

The Edge: A clearinghouse for unsold tour and cruise-line tickets. In business for 30 years. A $25 membership fee is required for their discounts. Provides updates on opportunities. Hotline at 212-873-0908.

Quikbook

381 Park Avenue South   **Discount**
near 28th Street   **Mail/phone**
New York, NY 10016
800-789-9887. Fax 212-532-1556
Weekdays 9-5. Fax service daily 24 hours.

The Edge: Discounts hotel rooms in 21 cities. Offers discounted rates of 40% to 70% off regular walk-in rates for hotels in 21 cities in a wide variety of price ranges. Confirmation number by mail or phone. In New York, offers discounts at the Empire (moderate) to the Helmsley and Drake (first class).

Room Exchange

450 7th Avenue   **Discount**
near 35th Street   **Mail/phone**
New York, NY 10018
800-846-7000. Fax 212-760-1013
Weekdays 9-5:30.

The Edge: Discounts on hotel rooms. Offers discounts on 23,000 hotels in the U.S., Bermuda, Canada, Europe, Mexico and the Caribbean. Confirmation numbers provided and the traveler is billed direct. Cancellation possible 48 hours in advance in the U.S. and seven days in advance elsewhere.

San Francisco Reservations/Topaz Hotel Service

22 Second Street, 4th Floor   Discount
San Francisco, CA 94105   Mail/phone
800-677-1550. Fax 415-227-1520
Daily 7-11 Pacific Time.

The Edge: Discounts San Francisco hotels. Offers discounts of 5% to 50% at 225 hotels in the Bay Area, budget to deluxe. Conformation numbers provided. Cancellation policy subject to individual hotel policy.

Travel Bargains

2250 Butler Pike   Discount
Plymouth, PA 19462   Mail/phone
800-872-8385
Weekdays 8-midnight Eastern Time.

The Edge: Discounts domestic and international flights.

White Travel

127 Park Road West   Discount
Hartford, CT 06119   Mail/phone
800-547-4790. Fax 860-236-6177
Weekdays 9-5.

The Edge: Deals on cruises. Wide range of cruises offered at 5% to 65% off the cost of sailing.

The ratings: excellent very good good fair so-so

The Sharpest Edge

The Discounters' Edge

Stores and services that offer discount prices on name brands or special value in other ways.

Clothing & accessories

Bridal, wedding & formal
Cinderella Flower & Feather Company
La Sposa Veils
Ted's Fine Clothing

Buttons, beads & trims
A. Feibush
A.A. Feather Company
Gordon Button Company
M&J Trimming
So-Good

Clothing
Aaron's
Atelier 45
Atelier 86
Bolton's
Burlington Coat Factory
Daffy's Fifth Avenue
Dollar Bill's
Euromoda Ltd.
Fashion Plaza
Fenwick Clothes
Filene's Basement
Fishkin Knitwear
Forman's
Fowad
G&G International
Gilcrest Clothes Company
Giselle Sportswear, Inc.
Gorsart
Harry Rothman's
Irving Baron Clothes
Kenar
Kids "R" Us
Kids Are Magic

Klein's of Monticello
L.S. Men's Clothing
Lea's Designer Fashion
M. Kreinen Sales
Miriam Rigler
Moe Ginsburg
S&W
SYMS
Shulie's
Sue's Discount Better Dresses
Today's Man

Clothing-casual
Eisner Brothers
Labels for Less
Pan Am Sportswear and Menswear
Tobaldi Huomo

Department stores
Century 21

Fabric
A&N Fabrics
Art Max Fabrics
B&J Fabrics
Beckenstein's Men's Fabrics
Felsen Fabrics
Kordol Fabrics
Paron Fabrics
Poli Fabrics
Rosen & Chadick
William N. Ginsburg Company

Furriers
Alixandre
Ben Kahn Salon
Birger Christensen
Christie Bros.
Goldin Feldman
Michael Forrest
Mohl Furs
Trendsetters

Hats
Manny's Millinery Supply Company

Jewelry & watches
Dyckman's
Globemark Enterprises, Inc.
Lawrence W. Ford
Maurice Badler
Paul Seiden Jeweler

Jewelry & watches-costume
Ro Star, Inc.

Jewelry & watches-supply
Jewelry Display of New York
Platt Box Company, Inc.

Leathers
Altman Luggage
Arivel Fashions
Bettinger's Luggage Shop
Fine and Klein

J.S. Suarez
Jobson's Luggage
Leather 99
Leather Outlet
Lexington Luggage
Luggage Plus
Tuscany & Company
Shirts & blouses
Penn Garden Shirts
Shirt Store
Victory, the Shirt Experts
Shoes, socks & stockings
Anbar Shoes
Benedetti Custom Shoes
Broadway Sneakers
Cipriano Shoes
Friedman Hosiery
Lace Up Shoe Shop
Lismore Hosiery
Louis Chock
M. Stever Hosiery Company
Medici Shoes
Richie's Discount Children's Shoes
Sacco Shoes
Schmooz
Shoe City
Sole of Italy
Stapleton Shoe Company
Statesman Shoes
Trevi Shoes
Sweaters
Best of Scotland
Thrift shops
Allan & Suzi
Cancer Care Thrift Shop
Encore
Good-Byes
INA
Irvington Institute Thrift Shop
Memorial Sloan-Kettering Thrift Store
Michael's Resale Dress Shop
Spence-Chapin Thrift Shop
Underwear & lingerie
A.W. Kaufman
Brief Essentials
Chas. Weiss Fashions
Grand Lingerie
Howron Sportswear
Mendel Weiss
Round-the-Clock Pantyhose by Mail
Schachner Fashions

Cosmetics, bath & beauty
Cosmetics, etc.
Cosmetic World and Gift Center
Jay's Perfume Bar
Perfumania
Ricky's
Pharmacies
Love Discount

Food & beverages
Appetizers
Guss Pickles
Homarus, Inc.
Beverages
B&E
Candy, fruit & nuts
Bazzini Importers
Economy Candy Corp.
Sweet Life
Wolsk's Confections
Cheese
Alleva Dairy
Ben's Cheese Shop
East Village Cheese Shop
Murray's Cheese Shop
9th Avenue Cheese Market
Russo & Son Dairy Products
Sal's Gourmet & Cheese Shop
Coffees, teas & spices
Porto Rico Importing Company
Fish & meat
Central Fish Company
Empire Purveyors
Lien Phat Seafood & Meat
Premier Veal
Sea Breeze Fishmarket
Vin Hin Company
General stores
National Wholesale Liquidators
Ralph's Discount City
Indian
Foods of India
Kalustyan Orient Export Trading
Italian
Bianca Pasta
Bruno the King of Ravioli
DiPalo's Fine Food, Inc.
Italian Food Center
Piemonte Ravioli Company
Raffetto's

Oriental
Chinese American Trading Company
Fung Wong Bakery
Han Arum
Kam Kuo Food
Kam Man Food Products
Superstores
Fairway Market
Ninth Avenue International Foods
Sahadi Importing Company, Inc.
Sultan's Delight
Zabar's Appetizers & Caterers
Wines & liquors
Crossroads Wine & Liquor
Garnet Wine & Liquor
Gotham Liquors

Furniture & furnishings

Accessories
Plexi-Craft
Appliances
ABC Trading Company
Bernie's Discount Center
Dembitzer Brothers
Home Sales Enterprises
LVT Price Quote Hotline
Peninsula Buying
Price Watchers
Beds & bedding
Dial-A-Mattress
Chairs & tables
Chairs and Stools, Etc.
China, crystal & silver
Block China Warehouse Store
Ceramica Gift Gallery
Eastern Silver Company
Eastside Gifts & Dinnerware
Fishs Eddy
Jamar
Jean's Silversmiths
Lanac Sales
Michael C. Fina
Nat Schwartz
Williams-Sonoma Outlet
Yellow Door
Contemporary
Foremost Furniture Showrooms
North Carolina Furniture Showrooms
Cookware & cutlery
Broadway Panhandler
Daroma Restaurant Equipment Corp.
E. Rossi

Hung Chong Import
Matas Restaurant Supply
New Cathay Hardware Corporation
Electronics, etc.
Canal Hi-Fi
Computers
Crocodile Computers
47th Street Photo
Foto Electric Supply Company
J&R Music World
Manhattan Electronics Corporation
Micro U.S.A. Computer Depot
Olden Camera
Sound City
Stereo Exchange
Vicmarr Stereo and TV
Wiz
Fabric
Harry Zarin Company
Hyman Hendler and Sons
Intercoastal Textiles
Island Fabric Warehouse
Silk Surplus
Hardware & fixtures
Hastings
Sepco Industries
Light fixtures
Lighting By Gregory
Rosetta Electric Company
Tudor Electrical Supply
Linens
Harris Levy
J. Schachter
Oriental
Oriental Porcelain and Furniture Outlet
Rugs & carpets
Momeni International
Redi-Cut Carpets
Rug Warehouse
Window treatments
Sheila's Wallstyles Decorating Center
Sundial-Schwartz
White Workroom

Home & home office

Art supplies
Charrette
Pearl Paint Company
Utrecht Art and Drafting Supplies
Supplies
R&R Packaging Corporation
Staples the Office Superstore

Leisure hours & parties

Books & magazines
Barnes & Noble
Barnes & Noble Sales Annex
Barnes & Noble for Kids
Strand Book Store
CDs, tapes & records
Tower Records & Video
Classes & activities
Alliance of Resident Theatres
Florists
Venamy Orchids
Theater
TKTS
TKTS Time Square
Theatre Development Fund
Tobacco
J.R. Tobacco
Toys, games & hobbies
Toys "R" Us

Personal & repair services

Upholsterers
Forsyth Decorations
Personal shoppers
Margorie Stokes
Margot Green

Pet services & supplies

Grooming & supplies
Groomer Direct

Sporting Goods

Exercise
Barbara Gee Danskin Center
Golf
New York Golf Center, Inc.
World of Golf
Sports-general
G&S Sporting Goods
Gerry Cosby and Company
Modell's Sporting Goods

Travel & vacation

Discount
Capital Reservations
Central Reservation Services
Cheap Tickets, Inc.
Discount Hotel Hotline / Hotel Reservation Net
Encore Preferred Travel / Encore Marketing
Express Hotel Reservations
Moment's Notice
Quikbook
San Francisco Reservations / Topaz Hotel Service
Travel Bargains

The Deluxe Edge

Stores and services that are deluxe in offering or presentation.

Clothing & accessories

Bridal, wedding & formal
Arnold Scassi
Betsy
Diane Wagner
Sander Witlin
Vera Wang Bridal House Ltd.

Clothing
Alfred Dunhill of London
Bijan
Bonpoint
Burberry Limited
Charivari
Christian Dior
Comme des Garçons
Emanuel Ungaro
Ermenegildo Zegna
Escada Boutique
Exclusive Oilily Store
Gianni Versace
Giorgio Armani
Issey Miyake
Jacadi
La Layette et Plus
Napoleon
Saint Laurent Rive Gauche
St. John Boutique
Valentino
Wicker Garden's Baby/Children
Yohji Yamamoto

Clothing-casual
Lee Anderson

Custom
Alan Flusser at Saks
Alexander Kabbaz
Arthur Gluck
Ascot Chang
Brioni
Cheo Tailors
Chris-Arto Custom Shirt Company
House of Maurizio
Leonard Logsdail
Mandana
One-of-a-Kind
Uma Reddy Ltd.

William Fioravanti

Department stores
Barney's New York
Bergdorf Goodman
Bergdorf Goodman Men's Store
Takashimaya

Furriers
Alixandre
Ben Kahn Salon
Birger Christensen
Christie Bros.
Goldin Feldman
Michael Forrest
Mohl Furs

Hats
Lola Ehrlich Millinery
Vander Linde Designs

Jewelry & watches
A La Vieille Russie
Asprey Limited
Balogh Jewelers
Buccellati
Bulgari
Camilla Dietz Bergeron
Cartier
Christopher Walling
David Webb
Demner
Ellagem
Fred Leighton
H. Stern
Harry Winston
Ilias Lalaounis
Tiffany & Company
Van Cleef & Arpels

Leathers
Bottega Veneta
Ferragamo
Furla
Goldpfeil
Gucci
Hermès
Louis Vuitton
Mark Cross
North Beach Leather
Prada

Shoes, socks & stockings
Fendi
Gelman Custom
Helene Arpels, Inc.
J.M. Weston
Leach-Kale
Manolo Blahnik
Robert Clergerie
Stephane Kelian
Susan Bennis / Warren Edwards

Vanessa Noel
Walter Steiger
Sweaters
Berk of Burlington Arcade London
Cashmere-Cashmere
Missoni
N. Peal
TSE Cashmere
Underwear & lingerie
Montenapoleone

Food & beverages
Appetizers
Caviarteria
Petrossian
Bakery
Sylvia Weinstock Cakes
Superstores
Dean & Deluca

Furniture & furnishings
Accessories
Linda Horn Antiques
Pierre Deux
Antiques
James II Galleries
Art & artifacts
Rosenberg & Stiebel, Inc.
Art deco/art nouveau
Delorenzo
China, crystal & silver
Alice Kwartler
Baccarat, Inc.
Bardith Ltd.
Bernardaud Limoges
Christofle
Daum Boutique
Hoya Crystal Gallery
James Robinson
Lalique
Leo Kaplan Ltd.
Niels Bamberger
Royal Copenhagen Porcelain / Georg Jensen
S.J. Shrubsole
Steuben Glass
Contemporary
Carlyle Custom Convertibles Ltd.
Classic Sofa
English
Eagles Antiques
Florian Papp
Kentshire Galleries
Malcolm Franklin, Inc.

Philip Colleck of London Ltd.
Stair & Company
European
Dalva Brothers
Didier Aaron, Inc.
Frederick P. Victoria and Son, Inc.
French & Company, Inc.
Reymer-Jourdan Antiques
Fireplace
Danny Allessandro Ltd. / Edwin Jackson, Inc.
Garden & wicker
Wicker Garden
Hardware & fixtures
Sherle Wagner International
Light fixtures
Marvin Alexander
Nestle
Linens
Frette
Porthault
Pratesi
Medieval & Renaissance
L'Antiquaire & the Connoisseur
Oriental
Asian House
Chinese Porcelain Company
E&J Frankel Ltd.
J.J. Lally & Company Oriental Art
Ralph M. Chait Galleries
Weisbrod Chinese Art
Quilts & quilting
America Hurrah
Woodard & Greenstein
Rugs & carpets
Berdi Abadjian
Doris Leslie Blau Gallery

Home & home office
Stationery
Butch Krutchik Designs
Dempsey & Carroll
Jamie Ostrow
Mrs. John L. Strong Company

Leisure hours & parties
Coordinators
Dorothy Wako
Gourmet Advisory Service, Inc.
Robert Isabell
Gyms
Cardio Fitness Center
Locations
Equitable Tower

Essex House Hotel Nikko New York
Georgian Suite
Personal trainers
Harry Hanson
Tennis
New York Racquet & Tennis Club
River Club

Personal & repair services
Limo rentals
London Towncars

Sporting Goods
Riding
H. Kauffman and Sons
Skiing
Bogner

The Sharpest Edge *Quality*

🛍 5 🛍 5 🛍 5 🛍 5 🛍 5

Clothing & accessories

Accessories
Julie Artisan's Gallery
Bridal, wedding & formal
Arnold Scassi
Betsy
Kleinfeld and Son
Sander Witlin
Buttons, beads & trims
Tender Buttons
Clothing
Alfred Dunhill of London
Bijan
Burberry Limited
Chanel Boutique
Chocolate Soup
Christian Dior
Davide Cenci
East Side Kids
Emanuel Ungaro
Ermenegildo Zegna
Escada Boutique
Giorgio Armani
Giselle Sportswear, Inc.
Givenchy Boutique
J. Press
Jacadi
Jaeger
La Layette et Plus
Lea's Designer Fashion
Linda Dresner
Magic Windows
Napoleon
Paul Smith
Saint Laurent Rive Gauche
Space Kiddets
St. John Boutique
Valentino
Wicker Garden's Baby/Children
Clothing-casual
Ann Crabtree
Lee Anderson
Peter Elliot
Custom
Ascot Chang
Department stores
Barney's New York
Bergdorf Goodman
Bergdorf Goodman Men's Store
Saks Fifth Avenue
Eyeglasses
Gruen Optika
Fabric
Art Max Fabrics
B&J Fabrics
Paron Fabrics
Poli Fabrics
Furriers
Alixandre
Ben Kahn Salon
Christie Bros.
Goldin Feldman
Hats
Lola Ehrlich Millinery
Worth & Worth
Jewelry & watches
A La Vieille Russie
Asprey Limited
Buccellati
Bulgari
Camilla Dietz Bergeron
Cartier
Christopher Walling
David Webb
Demner
Ellagem
Harry Winston
J. Mavec & Company Ltd.
Mikimoto
Seaman Schepps
Tiffany & Company
Van Cleef & Arpels
Jewelry & watches-costume
Ro Star, Inc.
Leathers
Coach Store
Ferragamo
Ghurka
Goldpfeil
Hermès
Il Bisonte
La Bagagerie
Mark Cross
Tuscany & Company
Maternity
Veronique
Shirts & blouses
Shirt Store
Shoes, socks & stockings
Belgian Shoes
Botticelli
Diego Della Valle

Fendi
Fogal
French Sole
Great Feet
Helene Arpels, Inc.
Manolo Blahnik
Plus 9
Robert Clergerie
Stephane Kelian
Susan Bennis / Warren Edwards
Vanessa Noel
Walter Steiger
Special sizes
Forgotten Woman
Rochester Big & Tall
Sweaters
Berk of Burlington Arcade London
Granny-Made
N. Peal
TSE Cashmere
Thrift shops
Allan & Suzi
Good-Byes
Underwear & lingerie
A.W. Kaufman
Joovay
Montenapoleone
Peress
Samantha Jones
Vintage
Jana Starr Antiques
Jean Hoffman
Western wear
Billy Martin's Western Wear

Cosmetics, bath & beauty
Cosmetics, etc.
Caswell-Massey Company Ltd.
Cosmetics Plus
MAC Cosmetics
Haircuts & hairstylists
Bumble and Bumble
Kenneth's Salon
Orbibe
Salvatore Macri
Thomas Morrisey Salon
Personal care
Lori Klein
Mario Badescu
Miriam Vasicka

Food & beverages
Appetizers
D'Artagnan, Inc.
Guss Pickles
Homarus, Inc.
Murray's Sturgeon Shop
Russ & Daughters
Bakery
Bakery Soutine
Black Hound
Bonte Patisserie
Ecce Panis
Little Pie Company
Patisserie Lanciani
Sylvia Weinstock Cakes
Trois Jean
William Greenberg Jr. Desserts
Beverages
Cork & Bottle
Bread
Columbia Hot Bagels
Ess-A-Bagel
Kossar's Bialystoker Kuchen Bakery
Candy, fruit & nuts
Elk Candy Company and Marzipan
Godiva Chocolatier
La Maison du Chocolat
Neuchâtel Chocolates
Cheese
Ben's Cheese Shop
Ideal Cheese Shop
9th Avenue Cheese Market
Coffees, teas & spices
Angelica's Traditional Herbs and Spices
Aphrodisia
Empire Coffee and Tea
McNulty's Tea and Coffee
Sensuous Bean
Fish & meat
Citarella
Faicco's
Florence Meat Market
H. Oppenheimer Company
Jefferson Market
Lobel's Prime Meats
Gifts
Manhattan Fruitier
Italian
Bruno the King of Ravioli
DiPalo's Fine Food, Inc.
Piemonte Ravioli Company

Oriental
Tan My My
Produce
Likitsakos
Superstores
Agata & Valentina
Balducci's
Dean & Deluca
Gourmet Garage
Grace's Marketplace
Zabar's Appetizers & Caterers
Takeout
E.A.T.
Williams Bar-B-Que
Wines & liquors
Gotham Liquors
Quality House
Warehouse Wines & Spirits

Furniture & furnishings
Accessories
Adrien Linford
Alphabet's
Amy Perlin Antiques
Felissimo
Framed on Madison
H.M. Luther
Mediterranean Shop
Piston's
Primavera Gallery
Rita Ford Music Boxes
Things Japanese
Zona
American
Barton-Sharpe Ltd.
Peter Roberts Antiques
Antiques
Ann Morris Antiques
Arkitektura
Graham Arader
Hyde Park Antiques
James II Galleries
Lee Calicchio Ltd.
Appliances
Home Sales Enterprises
Price Watchers
Art & artifacts
Rosenberg & Stiebel, Inc.
Works Gallery
Art deco/art nouveau
Alice's Antiques
Delorenzo
Macklowe Gallery & Modernism

Auction houses
Christie's
Sotheby's
Children
Art 'n Tapisserie
Bellini
China, crystal & silver
Alice Kwartler
Avventura Glassware Gifts
Baccarat, Inc.
Bardith Ltd.
Bernardaud Limoges
Cardel
Ceramica
Christofle
Eastside Gifts & Dinnerware
Hoffman Gampetro Antiques
Hoya Crystal Gallery
James Robinson
Jean's Silversmiths
Lanac Sales
Leo Kaplan Ltd.
Nathan Horowicz
S.J. Shrubsole
Steuben Glass
Contemporary
Driade/Modern Age
Cookware & cutlery
Bridge Kitchenware
Daroma Restaurant Equipment Corp.
Country
Cobweb
Electronics, etc.
Harvey Electronics
Ken Hansen Imaging
Empire & Biedermeier
Barry Friedman Ltd.
English
Charlotte Moss & Company
Florian Papp
Kentshire Galleries
Lynn Hollyn
Philip Colleck of London Ltd.
European
Dalva Brothers
Didier Aaron, Inc.
Reymer-Jourdan Antiques
Fabric
Hyman Hendler and Sons
Fans
Modern Supply Company
Fireplace
Danny Allessandro Ltd. / Edwin Jackson, Inc.

William H. Jackson
Garden & wicker
Horticultural Society of New York
Wicker Garden
Hardware & fixtures
A.F. Supply Corporation
Country Floors
Hammacher Schlemmer
Kraft Hardware
P.E. Guerin
Waterworks
Light fixtures
Just Bulbs
Let There Be Neon City, Inc.
Marvin Alexander
Nestle
Price Glover
Tudor Electrical Supply
Linens
Ad Hoc Softwares
E. Braun & Company
Frette
Laura Fisher / Antique Quilts & Americana
Leron
Pratesi
Schweitzer Linens
Medieval & Renaissance
L'Antiquaire & the Connoisseur
Oriental
Chinese Porcelain Company
E&J Frankel Ltd.
J.J. Lally & Company Oriental Art
Ralph M. Chait Galleries
Weisbrod Chinese Art
Quilts & quilting
Woodard & Greenstein
Rugs & carpets
Beshar's
Doris Leslie Blau Gallery
Window treatments
Drapery Exchange, Inc.
Mardi Philips

Home & home office

Marketing services
Solutions
Stationery
Dempsey & Carroll
Kate's Paperie
Mrs. John L. Strong Company
Supplies
R&R Packaging Corporation

Home renovation

Electronics, etc.
Audio Design Associates

Leisure hours & parties

Books & magazines
A Different Light Bookstore and Cafe
Appelfeld Gallery
Applause Theater & Cinema Books
Archiva: The Decorative Arts Book Shop
Barnes & Noble for Kids
Books of Wonder
Complete Traveller Bookstore
Glenn Horowitz Booksellers
Gotham Book Mart and Gallery
H.P. Kraus
Hagstrom Map and Travel Center
Librairie de France/Libreria Hispanica
Murder Ink
Mysterious Book Shop
New York Bound Bookshop
Old Print Shop
Oscar Wilde Memorial Bookshop
Rizzoli
Shakespeare & Company Booksellers
Stubbs Books & Prints, Inc.
Ursus Books & Prints
Victor Kamkin, Inc.
Caterers
Charlotte's Catering
Creative Edge Parties
Flavors Catering and Carry-out
Glorious Food
Robbins and Wolfe Catering
Classes & activities
92nd Street Y
Art Students League
Central Park
China Institute
Metropolitan Museum of Art
New School
Coordinators
Dorothy Wako
Gourmet Advisory Service, Inc.
Philip Baloun Designs
Renny - Design for Entertaining
Robert Isabell
Florists
Les Fleurs de Maxim's
Paul Bott Beautiful Flowers
Ronaldo Maia

Gyms
Cardio Fitness Center
Central Park Challenges
Equinox Fitness Club
Lotte Berk Method
Reebok's Sport Club New York
Locations
American Museum of Natural History
Burden Mansion
Essex House Hotel Nikko New York
Hudson River Club
Linda Kaye's Birthdaybakers, Party Makers
St. Regis
Stanhope Hotel
21 Club
Museum shops
Metropolitan Museum of Art Gift Shop
Museum of Modern Art, the MOMA Design
· Store
Music
Little Orchestra Society
Musical instruments
Detrich Pianos
Personal trainers
Harry Hanson
Joseph D. Tonti
Larry Tan
Photographs & video
Beth Green Studio
Rentals
Party Rentals
Something Different
Skating
Rockefeller Center Ice Skating Rink
Toys, games & hobbies
Erica Wilson
FAO Schwarz

Personal & repair services
Car
Autobahn Service Center
China, crystal & silver
Hess Restorations
Decorators

Drake Design
John Barman, Inc.
Jewelry & watches
Rissin's Jewelry Clinic
Limo rentals
London Towncars
Locksmiths
AAA Locksmiths
Miscellaneous
Saved by the Bell Corporation
Movers
Brownstone Brothers Moving & Storage
Rugs & carpets
Cohen Carpet Cleaning
Costikyan Ltd.
Shoe repair
B. Nelson Shoe Corporation
Jim's Shoe Repair
Upholsterers
Pembrooke & Ives

Pet services & supplies
Boarding
Canine College
Veterinarians
Animal Medical Center

Sporting Goods
Dance
Capezio
Freed of London
Skiing
Bogner
Sports-general
Eastern Mountain Sports
Paragon Sporting Goods
Tennis
Fila of Madison Avenue

The Sharpest Edge Quality

4 | 4 | 4 | 4

Clothing & accessories

Accessories
Gallery of Wearable Art
New York Exchange for Women's Work
Bridal, wedding & formal
Nancy Wedding Center Inc
One of a Kind Bride
Paul's Veil and Net
Vera Wang Bridal House Ltd.
Buttons, beads & trims
Bead Store
Gordon Button Company
M&J Trimming
So-Good
Clothing
Aquascutum of London
Atelier 45
Atelier 86
Ben's for Kids
Brooks Brothers
Charivari
Country Road
Dana Buchman
Dollar Bill's
Episode Sportswear
Euromoda Ltd.
Fishkin Knitwear
Forman's
Gianni Versace
Gilcrest Clothes Company
Gorsart
Greenstone & Cie
Klein's of Monticello
L.S. Men's Clothing
M. Kreinen Sales
Miriam Rigler
Moe Ginsburg
Nicole Miller
Paul Stuart
Polo/Ralph Lauren
S&W
SYMS
Saint Laurie Ltd.
Shulie's
Sue's Discount Better Dresses

Tahari
Talbots
Zitomer
Clothing-casual
A/X Armani Exchange
Agnes B.
Banana Republic
Eileen Fisher Boutique
Emporio Armani
Gap
J. Crew
J. McLaughlin
Pan Am Sportswear and Menswear
Wings
Custom
Alan Flusser at Saks
Mandana
Mr. Ned
Department stores
Bloomingdale's
Century 21
Henri Bendel
Lord & Taylor
Macy's
Takashimaya
Fabric
Beckenstein's Men's Fabrics
Saint Remy
Furriers
Michael Forrest
Jewelry & watches
Aaron Faber Gallery
Dyckman's
Fortunoff
Fred Leighton
H. Stern
Ilias Lalaounis
Marina B
Maurice Badler
Reinstein/Ross
Saity Jewelry
Tourneau and Gorevic Collection at Tourneau
Jewelry & watches-costume
Gale Grant Ltd.
Jaded
Jewelry & watches-supply
Jewelry Display of New York
Platt Box Company, Inc.
Leathers
Altman Luggage
Bettinger's Luggage Shop
Bottega Veneta
Crouch & Fitzgerald
Fine and Klein
Furla

Gucci
J.S. Suarez
Jobson's Luggage
Lexington Luggage
Louis Vuitton
North Beach Leather
Prada
Shirts & blouses
Addison on Madison
Victory, the Shirt Experts
Shoes, socks & stockings
Bally of Switzerland
Benedetti Custom Shoes
Broadway Sneakers
Church English Shoes
Cipriano Shoes
Cole-Haan
Eric Shoes
Harry's Shoes
Lace Up Shoe Shop
Lismore Hosiery
Little Eric Shoes
Louis Chock
Maraolo
Medici Shoes
Peter Fox Shoes
Schmooz
To Boot
Tootsi Plohound
Yaska Shoes
Special sizes
Chelsea Atelier
Sweaters
Best of Scotland
Cashmere-Cashmere
Missoni
Thrift shops
Encore
INA
Memorial Sloan-Kettering Thrift Store
Michael's Resale Dress Shop
Spence-Chapin Thrift Shop
Underwear & lingerie
Roberta
Schachner Fashions
Vintage
Andy's Chee-Pee's
Antique Boutique

Cosmetics, bath & beauty
Cosmetics, etc.
Aveda Lifestyle Store

Body Shop
Boyd's Chemist
Floris
Revlon Employee Store
Haircuts & hairstylists
Astor Place Hair Stylists
Julius Caruso Salon
La Coupe

Food & beverages
Appetizers
Aaron Streit, Inc.
Barney Greengrass
Petrossian
Sable's
Schacht Appetizing & Deli
Bakery
De Robertis Pastry
Erotic Baker
Friend of a Farmer
Gertel's
Grossinger's Uptown
Veniero's Pasticceria
Beverages
Milkman
Bread
A. Zito and Son's Bakery
D&G Bakery
H&H Bagels
Orwasher's Bakery
Pick a Bagel
Vesuvio Bakery
Candy, fruit & nuts
Fifth Avenue Chocolatiere
Li-Lac Chocolates
Perugina
Plumbridge
Cheese
Murray's Cheese Shop
Coffees, teas & spices
Oren's Daily Roast
Starbucks Coffee Company
Ten Ren Tea Company
Fish & meat
Akron
Albert's
Central Fish Company
Leonards' Market
Ottomanelli Brothers
Ottomanelli's Meat Market
Pisacane Midtown Corp.
Rosedale Fish & Oyster Market
Salumeria Biellese

Gifts
E.A.T. Gifts
Fraser-Morris
Health food
Healthy Pleasures
Italian
Manganaro's Food and Restaurant
Raffetto's
Produce
Nature's Gifts
Paradise Market
Superstores
Butterfield Market
Fairway Market
Sahadi Importing Company, Inc.
Sultan's Delight
Todaro Brothers
Takeout
Benny's Burritos To Go
Between the Bread
Corrado Kitchen
David's Chicken
El Pollo
International Poultry Company
Lorenzo & Maria's Kitchen
William Poll
Word of Mouth
Wines & liquors
Acker Merrall and Condit
Astor Place Wines & Spirits
Crossroads Wine & Liquor
Morrell & Company
Sherry-Lehmann Wine & Spirits Merchants
67 Wine & Spirits Merchants

Furniture & furnishings
Accessories
Aris Mixon & Company
Bob Pryor Antiques
Gargoyles Ltd. of Philadelphia
Hubert Des Forges
Mabel's
Man-Tiques Ltd.
Portico Home
Serendipity
Slatkin & Company
Urban Archaeology
William Wayne & Company
Antiques
Depression Modern
Portantina

Appliances
Bernie's Discount Center
Bloom and Krup
Art & artifacts
Gallery of Graphic Arts
Art deco/art nouveau
Barry of Chelsea Antiques
Joia Interiors, Inc.
Maison Gerard
Auction houses
Christie's East
Beds & bedding
Dial-A-Mattress
Children
Albee's
China, crystal & silver
Block China Warehouse Store
Fishs Eddy
Guild Antiques
L.S. Collection
La Terrine
Lalique
Malvina L. Solomon
Michael C. Fina
Niels Bamberger
Pottery Barn
S. Wyler, Inc.
Scully & Scully
Simon Pearce
Villeroy & Boch
Waterford/Wedgwood
Williams-Sonoma Outlet
Williams-Sonoma, Inc.
Wolfman Gold & Good Company
Yellow Door
Contemporary
Archetype Gallery
Carlyle Custom Convertibles Ltd.
Knoll
North Carolina Furniture Showrooms
Scott Jordan Furniture
Cookware & cutlery
Broadway Panhandler
Country
Le Fanion
Electronics, etc.
B&H Photo & Electronics
47th Street Photo
J&R Music World
Sharper Image
Software Etc.
Wiz

Empire & Biedermeier
Niall Smith
English
Agostino Antiques Ltd.
Eagles Antiques
Stair & Company
European
Newel Art Galleries, Inc.
Fabric
Harry Zarin Company
Intercoastal Textiles
Silk Surplus
Garden & wicker
Gazebo
Lexington Gardens
New York Botanical Garden's Shop
Treillage Ltd.
Hardware & fixtures
Brookstone Company
Hastings
Ideal Tile of Manhattan
Ideal Tile of Manhattan West
Janovic Plaza
Simon's Hardware
Terra Verde Trading Company
Kitchen
Platypus
Light fixtures
Grand Brass
Lee's Studio
Lightforms
Lighting By Gregory
Rosetta Electric Company
Linens
Harris Levy
Laytner's Linen and Home Center
Porthault
Medieval & Renaissance
Blumka
Oriental
Art Asia
Flying Cranes Antiques Ltd.
Naga Antiques Ltd.
Rugs & carpets
Central Carpet
Redi-Cut Carpets
Rug Warehouse
Safavieh Carpets
Superstores
ABC Carpet and Home
Bed, Bath and Beyond
Crate & Barrel
Gracious Home

Timepieces
Fanelli Antique Timepieces
Fossner Timepieces
Window treatments
Just Shades

Home & home office
Art supplies
Pearl Paint Company
Supplies
Staples the Office Superstore

Leisure hours & parties
Balloons
Ballooms-Balooms
Books & magazines
Argosy Book Store
B. Dalton Bookseller
Barnes & Noble
Civilized Traveller
Hacker Art Books
Kinokuniya Bookstore
Madison Avenue Bookshop
Morton, the Interior Design Bookshop
Strand Book Store
Traveller's Bookstore
CDs, tapes & records
Bleecker Bob's Golden Oldie Record Shop
Tower Records & Video
Caterers
Gay Jordan
Great Performances
Neuman & Bogdonoff
Tentation Catering
Classes & activities
Abrons Arts Center
James Beard Foundation
Mannes College of Music
New York University School of Continuing
  Education
Parents League
Entertainment
Silly Billy
Florists
Surroundings
Venamy Orchids
Zeze
Gyms
Asphalt Green, the Murphy Center
Atrium Club
Locations
Abigail Kirsch
Americas Society

Equitable Tower
Georgian Suite
Palm House at the Brooklyn Botanical Garden
Plaza Hotel
Puck Building
Waldorf-Astoria Hotel
Museum shops
Asia Society Bookstore
Cathedral of St. John the Divine
United Nations Gift Shop
Riding
Claremont Riding Academy
Service help
Barnard Bartending
Columbia Bartending Agency
Theater
TKTS
TKTS Time Square
Toys, games & hobbies
Mary Arnold Toys
Penny Whistle Toys

Personal & repair services
Decorators
Use What You Have
Jewelry & watches
Leon's Jewelry

Light fixtures
City Knickerbocker
Louis Mattia
Luggage & handbags
Artbag Creations, Inc.
Superior Repair Center
Personal shoppers
Margot Green
Rugs & carpets
Long Island Carpet Cleaners

Pet services & supplies
Grooming & supplies
Groomer Direct
Karens for People + Pets
Pampered Paws
Transportation
Pet Cab

Sporting Goods
Fishing
Orvis
Marine
Goldberg's Marine
Riding
Miller's Harness Company
Swimming
Cameo Water Wear

The Sharpest Edge Style

[5] [5] [5] [5] [5]

Clothing & accessories

Accessories
Julie Artisan's Gallery
Bridal, wedding & formal
Betsy
Kleinfeld and Son
Sander Witlin
Buttons, beads & trims
Tender Buttons
Clothing
Bijan
Burberry Limited
Chanel Boutique
Charivari
Chocolate Soup
Dana Buchman
Davide Cenci
East Side Kids
Emanuel Ungaro
Ermenegildo Zegna
Escada Boutique
Gianni Versace
Giorgio Armani
Giselle Sportswear, Inc.
Givenchy Boutique
Jacadi
La Layette et Plus
Lea's Designer Fashion
Linda Dresner
Magic Windows
Matsuda
Napoleon
Saint Laurent Rive Gauche
Space Kiddets
St. John Boutique
Valentino
Clothing-casual
A/X Armani Exchange
Agnes B.
Benetton
Gap
Lee Anderson
Patricia Field
Peter Elliot
Custom

Alan Flusser at Saks
Department stores
Barney's New York
Bergdorf Goodman
Bergdorf Goodman Men's Store
Saks Fifth Avenue
Takashimaya
Fabric
Art Max Fabrics
B&J Fabrics
Poli Fabrics
Furriers
Alixandre
Ben Kahn Salon
Goldin Feldman
Hats
Lola Ehrlich Millinery
Worth & Worth
Jewelry & watches
Buccellati
Bulgari
Camilla Dietz Bergeron
Cartier
Christopher Walling
David Webb
Demner
Ellagem
Fred Leighton
Harry Winston
Tiffany & Company
Van Cleef & Arpels
Jewelry & watches-costume
Gale Grant Ltd.
Leathers
Bottega Veneta
Ferragamo
Furla
Ghurka
Hermès
La Bagagerie
Lederer de Paris, Inc.
Mark Cross
Tuscany & Company
Maternity
Veronique
Shirts & blouses
Victory, the Shirt Experts
Shoes, socks & stockings
Belgian Shoes
Botticelli
Cole-Haan
Diego Della Valle
Fogal
French Sole
Manolo Blahnik
Peter Fox Shoes

Plus 9
Robert Clergerie
Stephane Kelian
To Boot
Vanessa Noel
Walter Steiger
Yaska Shoes
Special sizes
Forgotten Woman
Rochester Big & Tall
Sweaters
Berk of Burlington Arcade London
TSE Cashmere
Thrift shops
Allan & Suzi
Good-Byes
INA
Underwear & lingerie
Joovay
Montenapoleone
Samantha Jones
Vintage
Andy's Chee-Pee's
Jana Starr Antiques
Jean Hoffman

Cosmetics, bath & beauty
Cosmetics, etc.
MAC Cosmetics
Haircuts & hairstylists
Jacques Dessange
Kenneth's Salon
Orbibe
Salvatore Macri
Thomas Morrisey Salon
Personal care
Lori Klein
Miriam Vasicka

Food & beverages
Appetizers
D'Artagnan, Inc.
Bakery
Black Hound
De Robertis Pastry
Sylvia Weinstock Cakes
Trois Jean
Veniero's Pasticceria
Candy, fruit & nuts
Elk Candy Company and Marzipan
Godiva Chocolatier

La Maison du Chocolat
Neuchâtel Chocolates
Coffees, teas & spices
McNulty's Tea and Coffee
Sensuous Bean
Fish & meat
Citarella
H. Oppenheimer Company
Lobel's Prime Meats
Gifts
E.A.T. Gifts
Manhattan Fruitier
Produce
Likitsakos
Superstores
Agata & Valentina
Dean & Deluca

Furniture & furnishings
Accessories
Adrien Linford
Alphabet's
Amy Perlin Antiques
Aris Mixon & Company
Bob Pryor Antiques
Felissimo
Framed on Madison
Gargoyles Ltd. of Philadelphia
H.M. Luther
Hubert Des Forges
John Rosselli International
Linda Horn Antiques
Mediterranean Shop
Piston's
Primavera Gallery
Rita Ford Music Boxes
Slatkin & Company
William Wayne & Company
Zona
American
Barton-Sharpe Ltd.
Peter Roberts Antiques
Antiques
Ann Morris Antiques
Arkitektura
Graham Arader
Hyde Park Antiques
James II Galleries
Portantina
Art & artifacts
Rosenberg & Stiebel, Inc.
Works Gallery

Art deco/art nouveau
Alice's Antiques
Delorenzo
Macklowe Gallery & Modernism
Maison Gerard
Auction houses
Christie's
Sotheby's
Children
Bellini
China, crystal & silver
Alice Kwartler
Avventura Glassware Gifts
Baccarat, Inc.
Bardith Ltd.
Bernardaud Limoges
Ceramica
Christofle
Eastside Gifts & Dinnerware
Guild Antiques
Hoffman Gampetro Antiques
James Robinson
Lanac Sales
Scully & Scully
Steuben Glass
Williams-Sonoma, Inc.
Wolfman Gold & Good Company
Contemporary
Driade/Modern Age
Country
Cobweb
Empire & Biedermeier
Barry Friedman Ltd.
Eileen Lane Antiques
Niall Smith
Victor Antiques Ltd.
English
Charlotte Moss & Company
Florian Papp
Kentshire Galleries
Lynn Hollyn
Philip Colleck of London Ltd.
Stair & Company
European
Dalva Brothers
Didier Aaron, Inc.
John Rosselli Antiques
Newel Art Galleries, Inc.
Reymer-Jourdan Antiques
Fabric
Hyman Hendler and Sons
Fireplace
Danny Allessandro Ltd. / Edwin Jackson, Inc.

Garden & wicker
Lexington Gardens
Treillage Ltd.
Hardware & fixtures
A.F. Supply Corporation
Country Floors
P.E. Guerin
Waterworks
Light fixtures
Marvin Alexander
Nestle
Price Glover
Linens
Ad Hoc Softwares
E. Braun & Company
Frette
Laura Fisher / Antique Quilts & Americana
Laytner's Linen and Home Center
Pratesi
Medieval & Renaissance
L'Antiquaire & the Connoisseur
Oriental
Chinese Porcelain Company
E&J Frankel Ltd.
J.J. Lally & Company Oriental Art
Naga Antiques Ltd.
Ralph M. Chait Galleries
Rugs & carpets
Doris Leslie Blau Gallery
Safavieh Carpets
Superstores
Crate & Barrel
Window treatments
Drapery Exchange, Inc.
Mardi Philips

Home & home office
Marketing services
Solutions
Stationery
Dempsey & Carroll
Kate's Paperie
Mrs. John L. Strong Company

Home renovation
Electronics, etc.
Audio Design Associates

Leisure hours & parties
Books & magazines
A Different Light Bookstore and Cafe
Appelfeld Gallery

Archiva: The Decorative Arts Book Shop
Barnes & Noble for Kids
Glenn Horowitz Booksellers
Gotham Book Mart and Gallery
Murder Ink
Mysterious Book Shop
Rizzoli
Shakespeare & Company Booksellers
Stubbs Books & Prints, Inc.
Ursus Books & Prints
Victor Kamkin, Inc.
Caterers
Creative Edge Parties
Flavors Catering and Carry-out
Glorious Food
Robbins and Wolfe Catering
Classes & activities
Art Students League
China Institute
Metropolitan Museum of Art
Coordinators
Dorothy Wako
Philip Baloun Designs
Renny - Design for Entertaining
Robert Isabell
Florists
Les Fleurs de Maxim's
Paul Bott Beautiful Flowers
Ronaldo Maia
VSF
Gyms
Cardio Fitness Center
Central Park Challenges
Equinox Fitness Club
Lotte Berk Method
Reebok's Sport Club New York
Locations
American Museum of Natural History
Burden Mansion
Equitable Tower
Hudson River Club
Palm House at the Brooklyn Botanical Garden
St. Regis
Stanhope Hotel
21 Club
Museum shops
Metropolitan Museum of Art Gift Shop
Museum of Modern Art, the MOMA Design
  Store
Music
Little Orchestra Society

Musical instruments
Detrich Pianos
Personal trainers
Harry Hanson
Joseph D. Tonti
Larry Tan
Photographs & video
Beth Green Studio
Rentals
Party Rentals
Something Different
Skating
Rockefeller Center Ice Skating Rink
Toys, games & hobbies
Erica Wilson
FAO Schwarz

Personal & repair services
Car
Autobahn Service Center
China, crystal & silver
Hess Restorations
Decorators
Drake Design
John Barman, Inc.
Miscellaneous
Saved by the Bell Corporation
Movers
Brownstone Brothers Moving & Storage
Rugs & carpets
Costikyan Ltd.
Upholsterers
Pembrooke & Ives

Pet services & supplies
Boarding
Canine College
Grooming & supplies
Pampered Paws

Sporting Goods
Dance
Freed of London
Riding
Miller's Harness Company
Skiing
Bogner
Sports-general
Paragon Sporting Goods

The Sharpest Edge Style

Clothing & accessories

Accessories
Gallery of Wearable Art
Bridal, wedding & formal
Arnold Scassi
One of a Kind Bride
Paul's Veil and Net
Vera Wang Bridal House Ltd.
Buttons, beads & trims
Bead Store
Gordon Button Company
M&J Trimming
So-Good
Clothing
Alfred Dunhill of London
Ann Taylor
Atelier 45
Atelier 86
Ben's for Kids
Betsey Johnson
Christian Dior
Country Road
Dollar Bill's
Episode Sportswear
Euromoda Ltd.
Exclusive Oilily Store
Gap Kids and Baby Gap
Gilcrest Clothes Company
Gorsart
Greenstone & Cie
Klein's of Monticello
Limited
M. Kreinen Sales
Miriam Rigler
Nicole Miller
Paul Smith
Paul Stuart
SYMS
Shulie's
Sue's Discount Better Dresses
Tahari
Wicker Garden's Baby/Children
Zitomer
Clothing-casual
Ann Crabtree

Banana Republic
Cockpit
Eileen Fisher Boutique
Emporio Armani
J. Crew
J. McLaughlin
Wings
Custom
Ascot Chang
Mandana
Mr. Ned
Department stores
Bloomingdale's
Century 21
Henri Bendel
Lord & Taylor
Macy's
Eyeglasses
Gruen Optika
Fabric
Beckenstein's Men's Fabrics
Paron Fabrics
Saint Remy
Furriers
Christie Bros.
Jewelry & watches
A La Vieille Russie
Aaron Faber Gallery
Asprey Limited
Fortunoff
Ilias Lalaounis
Maurice Badler
Robert Lee Morris
Saity Jewelry
Seaman Schepps
Tourneau and Gorevic Collection at Tourneau
Jewelry & watches-costume
Jaded
Ro Star, Inc.
Jewelry & watches-supply
Jewelry Display of New York
Leathers
Altman Luggage
Bettinger's Luggage Shop
Crouch & Fitzgerald
Fine and Klein
Goldpfeil
Gucci
Il Bisonte
J.S. Suarez
Jobson's Luggage
Lexington Luggage
Louis Vuitton
North Beach Leather
Prada
Maternity

Motherhood Maternity
Shirts & blouses
Addison on Madison
Shirt Store
Shoes, socks & stockings
Broadway Sneakers
Church English Shoes
Cipriano Shoes
Eric Shoes
Fendi
Great Feet
Harry's Shoes
Helene Arpels, Inc.
Lismore Hosiery
Little Eric Shoes
Louis Chock
Maraolo
Medici Shoes
Nine West
Schmooz
Susan Bennis / Warren Edwards
Tootsi Plohound
Special sizes
Chelsea Atelier
Sweaters
Best of Scotland
Cashmere-Cashmere
Granny-Made
Missoni
N. Peal
Thrift shops
Encore
Memorial Sloan-Kettering Thrift Store
Michael's Resale Dress Shop
Spence-Chapin Thrift Shop
Underwear & lingerie
A.W. Kaufman
Peress
Roberta
Schachner Fashions
Victoria's Secret
Vintage
Alice Underground
Antique Boutique
Reminiscence
Western wear
Billy Martin's Western Wear

Cosmetics, bath & beauty
Cosmetics, etc.
Boyd's Chemist
Cosmetics Plus

Floris
Haircuts & hairstylists
Astor Place Hair Stylists
Bumble and Bumble
Julius Caruso Salon
La Coupe
Personal care
Mario Badescu

Food & beverages
Appetizers
Aaron Streit, Inc.
Murray's Sturgeon Shop
Petrossian
Schacht Appetizing & Deli
Bakery
Bonte Patisserie
Ecce Panis
Erotic Baker
Friend of a Farmer
Little Pie Company
Patisserie Lanciani
Sant Ambroeus Ltd.
Bread
Columbia Hot Bagels
D&G Bakery
H&H Bagels
Pick a Bagel
Vesuvio Bakery
Candy, fruit & nuts
Li-Lac Chocolates
Perugina
Plumbridge
Cheese
Murray's Cheese Shop
9th Avenue Cheese Market
Coffees, teas & spices
.Angelica's Traditional Herbs and Spices
Aphrodisia
Empire Coffee and Tea
Oren's Daily Roast
Starbucks Coffee Company
Ten Ren Tea Company
Fish & meat
Albert's
Faicco's
Florence Meat Market
Jefferson Market
Ottomanelli Brothers
Ottomanelli's Meat Market
Pisacane Midtown Corp.
Salumeria Biellese

Italian
Manganaro's Food and Restaurant
Raffetto's
Produce
Paradise Market
Superstores
Balducci's
Grace's Marketplace
Todaro Brothers
Takeout
E.A.T.
International Poultry Company
Lorenzo & Maria's Kitchen
William Poll
Word of Mouth

Furniture & furnishings

Accessories
Accscentiques
Man-Tiques Ltd.
Portico Home
Serendipity
Urban Archaeology
Antiques
Depression Modern
Lee Calicchio Ltd.
Art & artifacts
Gallery of Graphic Arts
Art deco/art nouveau
Barry of Chelsea Antiques
Joia Interiors, Inc.
Auction houses
Christie's East
Children
Albee's
Art 'n Tapisserie
China, crystal & silver
Fishs Eddy
Hoya Crystal Gallery
L.S. Collection
La Terrine
Lalique
Leo Kaplan Ltd.
Michael C. Fina
Nathan Horowicz
Niels Bamberger
Pottery Barn
S. Wyler, Inc.
S.J. Shrubsole
Simon Pearce
Villeroy & Boch
Waterford/Wedgwood
Williams-Sonoma Outlet

Yellow Door
Contemporary
Archetype Gallery
Carlyle Custom Convertibles Ltd.
Jensen-Lewis
Knoll
North Carolina Furniture Showrooms
Palazzeti
Scott Jordan Furniture
SEE Ltd.
Cookware & cutlery
Bridge Kitchenware
Broadway Panhandler
Country
Le Fanion
Electronics, etc.
Sharper Image
English
Agostino Antiques Ltd.
Eagles Antiques
European
Grange Furniture
Oak-Smith & Jones
Fabric
Intercoastal Textiles
Fireplace
William H. Jackson
Garden & wicker
Gazebo
Horticultural Society of New York
New York Botanical Garden's Shop
Wicker Garden
Hardware & fixtures
Brookstone Company
Hammacher Schlemmer
Hastings
Ideal Tile of Manhattan
Ideal Tile of Manhattan West
Janovic Plaza
Kraft Hardware
Sherle Wagner International
Simon's Hardware
Terra Verde Trading Company
Kitchen
Platypus
Light fixtures
Jerrystyle
Just Bulbs
Lee's Studio
Let There Be Neon City, Inc.
Linens
Leron
Porthault

Schweitzer Linens
Medieval & Renaissance
Blumka
Oriental
Art Asia
Flying Cranes Antiques Ltd.
Weisbrod Chinese Art
Quilts & quilting
Woodard & Greenstein
Rugs & carpets
Beshar's
Central Carpet
Rug Warehouse
Superstores
ABC Carpet and Home
Gracious Home
Timepieces
Fossner Timepieces
Window treatments
Just Shades

Home & home office
Art supplies
Pearl Paint Company
Supplies
R&R Packaging Corporation
Staples the Office Superstore

Leisure hours & parties
Balloons
Ballooms-Balooms
Books & magazines
Argosy Book Store
B. Dalton Bookseller
Barnes & Noble
Bookberries
Books of Wonder
Civilized Traveller
Complete Traveller Bookstore
H.P. Kraus
Hacker Art Books
Hagstrom Map and Travel Center
Kinokuniya Bookstore
Librairie de France/Libreria Hispanica
Madison Avenue Bookshop
Morton, the Interior Design Bookshop
New York Bound Bookshop
Old Print Shop
Strand Book Store
Caterers
Charlotte's Catering

Gay Jordan
Great Performances
Neuman & Bogdonoff
Taste Caterers
Tentation Catering
Classes & activities
James Beard Foundation
Mannes College of Music
New York University School of Continuing
    Education
Parents League
Entertainment
Silly Billy
Florists
Surroundings
Venamy Orchids
Zeze
Gyms
Asphalt Green, the Murphy Center
Atrium Club
Locations
Abigail Kirsch
Americas Society
Boathouse in Central Park
Essex House Hotel Nikko New York
Georgian Suite
Plaza Hotel
Puck Building
Waldorf-Astoria Hotel
Museum shops
Asia Society Bookstore
Cathedral of St. John the Divine
New York Public Library Shop
Riding
Claremont Riding Academy
Service help
Barnard Bartending
Columbia Bartending Agency
Toys, games & hobbies
Burlington Antique Toys
Mary Arnold Toys
Penny Whistle Toys

Personal & repair services
Decorators
Use What You Have
Light fixtures
City Knickerbocker
Luggage & handbags
Artbag Creations, Inc.
Shoe repair
B. Nelson Shoe Corporation

Jim's Shoe Repair

Pet services & supplies
Grooming & supplies
Groomer Direct
Karens for People + Pets

Sporting Goods
Marine
Goldberg's Marine
Swimming
Cameo Water Wear
Tennis
Fila of Madison Avenue

The ratings: excellent very good good fair so-so

The Sharpest Edge
Service

Clothing & accessories

Accessories
Julie Artisan's Gallery
Bridal, wedding & formal
Betsy
Kleinfeld and Son
Sander Witlin
Buttons, beads & trims
Tender Buttons
Clothing
Bijan
Burberry Limited
Chanel Boutique
Charivari
Chocolate Soup
Dana Buchman
Davide Cenci
East Side Kids
Emanuel Ungaro
Ermenegildo Zegna
Escada Boutique
Gianni Versace
Giorgio Armani
Giselle Sportswear, Inc.
Givenchy Boutique
Jacadi
La Layette et Plus
Lea's Designer Fashion
Linda Dresner
Magic Windows
Napoleon
Saint Laurent Rive Gauche
Space Kiddets
St. John Boutique
Valentino
Clothing-casual
A/X Armani Exchange
Agnes B.
Benetton
Gap
Lee Anderson
Patricia Field
Peter Elliot
Custom
Alan Flusser at Saks

Department stores
Barney's New York
Bergdorf Goodman
Bergdorf Goodman Men's Store
Saks Fifth Avenue
Takashimaya
Fabric
Art Max Fabrics
B&J Fabrics
Poli Fabrics
Furriers
Alixandre
Ben Kahn Salon
Goldin Feldman
Hats
Lola Ehrlich Millinery
Worth & Worth
Jewelry & watches
Buccellati
Bulgari
Camilla Dietz Bergeron
Cartier
Christopher Walling
David Webb
Demner
Ellagem
Fred Leighton
Harry Winston
Tiffany & Company
Van Cleef & Arpels
Jewelry & watches-costume
Gale Grant Ltd.
Leathers
Bottega Veneta
Ferragamo
Furla
Ghurka
Hermès
La Bagagerie
Lederer de Paris, Inc.
Mark Cross
Tuscany & Company
Maternity
Veronique
Shirts & blouses
Victory, the Shirt Experts
Shoes, socks & stockings
Belgian Shoes
Botticelli
Cole-Haan
Diego Della Valle
Fogal
French Sole
Manolo Blahnik
Peter Fox Shoes

Plus 9
Robert Clergerie
Stephane Kelian
To Boot
Vanessa Noel
Walter Steiger
Yaska Shoes
Special sizes
Forgotten Woman
Rochester Big & Tall
Sweaters
Berk of Burlington Arcade London
TSE Cashmere
Thrift shops
Allan & Suzi
Good-Byes
INA
Underwear & lingerie
Joovay
Montenapoleone
Samantha Jones
Vintage
Andy's Chee-Pee's
Jana Starr Antiques
Jean Hoffman

Cosmetics, bath & beauty
Cosmetics, etc.
MAC Cosmetics
Haircuts & hairstylists
Jacques Dessange
Kenneth's Salon
Orbibe
Salvatore Macri
Thomas Morrisey Salon
Personal care
Lori Klein
Miriam Vasicka

Food & beverages
Appetizers
D'Artagnan, Inc.
Bakery
Black Hound
De Robertis Pastry
Sylvia Weinstock Cakes
Trois Jean
Veniero's Pasticceria
Candy, fruit & nuts
Elk Candy Company and Marzipan
Godiva Chocolatier
La Maison du Chocolat
Neuchâtel Chocolates

Coffees, teas & spices
McNulty's Tea and Coffee
Sensuous Bean
Fish & meat
Citarella
H. Oppenheimer Company
Lobel's Prime Meats
Gifts
E.A.T. Gifts
Manhattan Fruitier
Produce
Likitsakos
Superstores
Agata & Valentina
Dean & Deluca

Furniture & furnishings
Accessories
Adrien Linford
Alphabet's
Amy Perlin Antiques
Aris Mixon & Company
Bob Pryor Antiques
Felissimo
Framed on Madison
Gargoyles Ltd. of Philadelphia
H.M. Luther
Hubert Des Forges
John Rosselli International
Linda Horn Antiques
Mediterranean Shop
Piston's
Primavera Gallery
Rita Ford Music Boxes
Slatkin & Company
William Wayne & Company
Zona
American
Barton-Sharpe Ltd.
Peter Roberts Antiques
Antiques
Ann Morris Antiques
Arkitektura
Graham Arader
Hyde Park Antiques
James II Galleries
Portantina
Art & artifacts
Rosenberg & Stiebel, Inc.
Works Gallery
Art deco/art nouveau
Alice's Antiques
Delorenzo

Macklowe Gallery & Modernism
Maison Gerard
Auction houses
Christie's
Sotheby's
Children
Bellini
China, crystal & silver
Alice Kwartler
Avventura Glassware Gifts
Baccarat, Inc.
Bardith Ltd.
Bernardaud Limoges
Ceramica
Christofle
Eastside Gifts & Dinnerware
Guild Antiques
Hoffman Gampetro Antiques
James Robinson
Lanac Sales
Scully & Scully
Steuben Glass
Williams-Sonoma, Inc.
Wolfman Gold & Good Company
Contemporary
Driade/Modern Age
Country
Cobweb
Empire & Biedermeier
Barry Friedman Ltd.
Eileen Lane Antiques
Niall Smith
Victor Antiques Ltd.
English
Charlotte Moss & Company
Florian Papp
Kentshire Galleries
Lynn Hollyn
Philip Colleck of London Ltd.
Stair & Company
European
Dalva Brothers
Didier Aaron, Inc.
John Rosselli Antiques
Newel Art Galleries, Inc.
Reymer-Jourdan Antiques
Fabric
Hyman Hendler and Sons
Fireplace
Danny Allessandro Ltd. / Edwin Jackson, Inc.
Garden & wicker
Lexington Gardens

Treillage Ltd.
Hardware & fixtures
A.F. Supply Corporation
Country Floors
P.E. Guerin
Waterworks
Light fixtures
Marvin Alexander
Nestle
Price Glover
Linens
Ad Hoc Softwares
E. Braun & Company
Frette
Laura Fisher / Antique Quilts & Americana
Laytner's Linen and Home Center
Pratesi
Medieval & Renaissance
L'Antiquaire & the Connoisseur
Oriental
Chinese Porcelain Company
E&J Frankel Ltd.
J.J. Lally & Company Oriental Art
Naga Antiques Ltd.
Ralph M. Chait Galleries
Rugs & carpets
Doris Leslie Blau Gallery
Safavieh Carpets
Superstores
Crate & Barrel
Window treatments
Drapery Exchange, Inc.
Mardi Philips

Home & home office
Marketing services
Solutions
Stationery
Dempsey & Carroll
Kate's Paperie
Mrs. John L. Strong Company

Home renovation
Electronics, etc.
Audio Design Associates

Leisure hours & parties
Books & magazines
A Different Light Bookstore and Cafe
Appelfeld Gallery
Archiva: The Decorative Arts Book Shop

Barnes & Noble for Kids
Glenn Horowitz Booksellers
Gotham Book Mart and Gallery
Murder Ink
Mysterious Book Shop
Rizzoli
Shakespeare & Company Booksellers
Stubbs Books & Prints, Inc.
Ursus Books & Prints
Victor Kamkin, Inc.
Caterers
Creative Edge Parties
Flavors Catering and Carry-out
Glorious Food
Robbins and Wolfe Catering
Classes & activities
Art Students League
China Institute
Metropolitan Museum of Art
Coordinators
Dorothy Wako
Philip Baloun Designs
Renny - Design for Entertaining
Robert Isabell
Florists
Les Fleurs de Maxim's
Paul Bott Beautiful Flowers
Ronaldo Maia
VSF
Gyms
Cardio Fitness Center
Central Park Challenges
Equinox Fitness Club
Lotte Berk Method
Reebok's Sport Club New York
Locations
American Museum of Natural History
Burden Mansion
Equitable Tower
Hudson River Club
Palm House at the Brooklyn Botanical Garden
St. Regis
Stanhope Hotel
21 Club
Museum shops
Metropolitan Museum of Art Gift Shop
Museum of Modern Art, the MOMA Design
  Store
Music
Little Orchestra Society

Musical instruments
Detrich Pianos
Personal trainers
Harry Hanson
Joseph D. Tonti
Larry Tan
Photographs & video
Beth Green Studio
Rentals
Party Rentals
Something Different
Skating
Rockefeller Center Ice Skating Rink
Toys, games & hobbies
Erica Wilson
FAO Schwarz

Personal & repair services
Car
Autobahn Service Center
China, crystal & silver
Hess Restorations
Decorators
Drake Design
John Barman, Inc.
Miscellaneous
Saved by the Bell Corporation
Movers
Brownstone Brothers Moving & Storage
Rugs & carpets
Costikyan Ltd.
Upholsterers
Pembrooke & Ives

Pet services & supplies
Boarding
Canine College
Grooming & supplies
Pampered Paws

Sporting Goods
Dance
Freed of London
Riding
Miller's Harness Company
Skiing
Bogner
Sports-general
Paragon Sporting Goods

The Sharpest Edge Service

Clothing & accessories
Clothing
Brooks Brothers
Christian Dior
Gorsart
Jaeger
Miriam Rigler
Paul Stuart
Clothing-casual
Ann Crabtree
Furriers
Christie Bros.
Jewelry & watches
A La Vieille Russie
Asprey Limited
Maurice Badler
Leathers
Coach Store
Crouch & Fitzgerald
Goldpfeil
Gucci
Il Bisonte
Louis Vuitton
Shirts & blouses
Shirt Store
Shoes, socks & stockings
Fendi
Special sizes
Chelsea Atelier
Sweaters
Missoni
Thrift shops
Michael's Resale Dress Shop

Cosmetics, bath & beauty
Haircuts & hairstylists
Brunellier Salon
Julius Caruso Salon
Personal care
Mario Badescu
Pharmacies
Kaufman Pharmacy

Food & beverages
Appetizers
Murray's Sturgeon Shop
Petrossian
Russ & Daughters
Bakery
Bakery Soutine
Cheese
Ideal Cheese Shop
Coffees, teas & spices
Angelica's Traditional Herbs and Spices
Aphrodisia
Starbucks Coffee Company
Fish & meat
Florence Meat Market
Jefferson Market
Rosedale Fish & Oyster Market
Wines & liquors
Quality House

Furniture & furnishings
Accessories
Things Japanese
Appliances
Home Sales Enterprises
Price Watchers
Auction houses
Christie's East
China, crystal & silver
Alice Kwartler
S.J. Shrubsole
Tudor Rose Antiques
Country
Martell Antiques
Electronics, etc.
Ken Hansen Imaging
English
Agostino Antiques Ltd.
European
Grange Furniture
Reymer-Jourdan Antiques
Fabric
Intercoastal Textiles
Fireplace
William H. Jackson
Garden & wicker
Horticultural Society of New York
Treillage Ltd.
Light fixtures
Let There Be Neon City, Inc.
Rugs & carpets
Beshar's

Central Carpet
Timepieces
Fanelli Antique Timepieces

Home & home office
Art supplies
Pearl Paint Company

Leisure hours & parties
Books & magazines
Applause Theater & Cinema Books
B. Dalton Bookseller
Barnes & Noble
Books of Wonder
Classes & activities
New School
Florists
Surroundings
Locations
Essex House Hotel Nikko New York
Service help
Barnard Bartending
Toys, games & hobbies
Mary Arnold Toys

Personal & repair services
Light fixtures
Louis Mattia
Limo rentals
London Towncars
Locksmiths
AAA Locksmiths
Movers
Big John Moving
Personal shoppers
Margot Green
Rugs & carpets
Cohen Carpet Cleaning

Pet services & supplies
Transportation
Pet Cab
Veterinarians
Animal Medical Center

Sporting Goods
Tennis
Fila of Madison Avenue

The ratings: excellent very good good fair so-so

The Sharpest Edge Value

Clothing & accessories

Accessories
Julie Artisan's Gallery
Bridal, wedding & formal
Arnold Scassi
Buttons, beads & trims
Gordon Button Company
So-Good
Clothing
Gap Kids and Baby Gap
L.S. Men's Clothing
M. Kreinen Sales
Moe Ginsburg
Space Kiddets
Clothing-casual
Gap
Pan Am Sportswear and Menswear
Wings
Department stores
Lord & Taylor
Macy's
Fabric
Art Max Fabrics
B&J Fabrics
Poli Fabrics
Furriers
Michael Forrest
Hats
Manny's Millinery Supply Company
Jewelry & watches
Dyckman's
Maurice Badler
Jewelry & watches-costume
Ro Star, Inc.
Jewelry & watches-supply
Platt Box Company, Inc.
Leathers
Bettinger's Luggage Shop
Tuscany & Company
Shoes, socks & stockings
Lismore Hosiery
Plus 9
Special sizes
Rochester Big & Tall
Thrift shops
Cancer Care Thrift Shop

Good-Byes
Irvington Institute Thrift Shop
Memorial Sloan-Kettering Thrift Store
Michael's Resale Dress Shop
Spence-Chapin Thrift Shop
Underwear & lingerie
A.W. Kaufman
Vintage
Alice Underground
Andy's Chee-Pee's

Cosmetics, bath & beauty

Cosmetics, etc.
Cosmetic Show
Revlon Employee Store
Haircuts & hairstylists
Astor Place Hair Stylists
Julius Caruso Salon
Salvatore Macri
Personal care
Lori Klein
Miriam Vasicka

Food & beverages

Appetizers
Aaron Streit, Inc.
Guss Pickles
Homarus, Inc.
Russ & Daughters
Bakery
Bakery Soutine
De Robertis Pastry
Grossinger's Uptown
Patisserie Lanciani
Bread
Ess-A-Bagel
Kossar's Bialystoker Kuchen Bakery
Candy, fruit & nuts
Elk Candy Company and Marzipan
La Maison du Chocolat
Cheese
Ben's Cheese Shop
East Village Cheese Shop
Ideal Cheese Shop
Coffees, teas & spices
McNulty's Tea and Coffee
Sensuous Bean
Fish & meat
Central Fish Company
Faicco's
Florence Meat Market
H. Oppenheimer Company
Ottomanelli's Meat Market
General stores
National Wholesale Liquidators

Italian
DiPalo's Fine Food, Inc.
Piemonte Ravioli Company
Oriental
Tan My My
Produce
Likitsakos
Superstores
Sahadi Importing Company, Inc.
Sultan's Delight
Todaro Brothers
Takeout
El Pollo
Williams Bar-B-Que
Wines & liquors
Garnet Wine & Liquor
Gotham Liquors
Warehouse Wines & Spirits

Furniture & furnishings
Accessories
Man-Tiques Ltd.
Piston's
Things Japanese
American
Barton-Sharpe Ltd.
Antiques
Arkitektura
Appliances
Home Sales Enterprises
Price Watchers
Art & artifacts
Rosenberg & Stiebel, Inc.
Works Gallery
Art deco/art nouveau
Alice's Antiques
Auction houses
Christie's
Christie's East
Sotheby's
China, crystal & silver
Block China Warehouse Store
Eastside Gifts & Dinnerware
Guild Antiques
Lanac Sales
Contemporary
Archetype Gallery
Cookware & cutlery
Daroma Restaurant Equipment Corp.
Country
Cobweb
Electronics, etc.
Ken Hansen Imaging

Empire & Biedermeier
Niall Smith
Fabric
Hyman Hendler and Sons
Fans
Modern Supply Company
Garden & wicker
Deutsch Wicker Furniture
Horticultural Society of New York
Light fixtures
Tudor Electrical Supply
Oriental
Ralph M. Chait Galleries
Rugs & carpets
Safavieh Carpets
Window treatments
Mardi Philips

Home & home office
Marketing services
Solutions
Supplies
R&R Packaging Corporation
Staples the Office Superstore

Leisure hours & parties
Books & magazines
Appelfeld Gallery
Glenn Horowitz Booksellers
Gotham Book Mart and Gallery
Old Print Shop
Strand Book Store
Stubbs Books & Prints, Inc.
Ursus Books & Prints
Caterers
Creative Edge Parties
Glorious Food
Robbins and Wolfe Catering
Classes & activities
92nd Street Y
Abrons Arts Center
Art Students League
Central Park
China Institute
Coordinators
Philip Baloun Designs
Florists
Les Fleurs de Maxim's
Paul Bott Beautiful Flowers
Ronaldo Maia
Gyms
Asphalt Green, the Murphy Center
Central Park Challenges

Locations
American Museum of Natural History
Museum shops
Museum of Modern Art, the MOMA Design
  Store
Musical instruments
Detrich Pianos
Personal trainers
Joseph D. Tonti
Larry Tan
Rentals
Party Rentals
Skating
Rockefeller Center Ice Skating Rink

Personal & repair services
Car
Autobahn Service Center
China, crystal & silver
Hess Restorations
Decorators
Drake Design
John Barman, Inc.
Jewelry & watches
Leon's Jewelry
Rissin's Jewelry Clinic
Light fixtures
Louis Mattia

Locksmiths
AAA Locksmiths
Miscellaneous
Saved by the Bell Corporation
Movers
Big John Moving
Brownstone Brothers Moving & Storage
Rugs & carpets
Costikyan Ltd.
Shoe repair
B. Nelson Shoe Corporation
Upholsterers
Pembrooke & Ives

Pet services & supplies
Adoption
ASPCA
Bide-A-Wee Home Association
Grooming & supplies
Groomer Direct

Sporting Goods
Dance
Freed of London

Travel & vacation
Discount
Cheap Tickets, Inc.

The ratings: **5** excellent **4** very good **3** good **2** fair **1** so-so

The Sharpest Edge Value

Clothing & accessories

Accessories
Gallery of Wearable Art
New York Exchange for Women's Work
Bridal, wedding & formal
Kleinfeld and Son
Nancy Wedding Center Inc
Paul's Veil and Net
Vera Wang Bridal House Ltd.
Buttons, beads & trims
M&J Trimming
Tender Buttons
Clothing
Ann Taylor
Aquascutum of London
Atelier 86
Ben's for Kids
Bolton's
Burberry Limited
Burlington Coat Factory
Christian Dior
Daffy's Fifth Avenue
Dana Buchman
Davide Cenci
Dollar Bill's
East Side Kids
Euromoda Ltd.
Filene's Basement
Fishkin Knitwear
Forman's
Giorgio Armani
Giselle Sportswear, Inc.
Gorsart
Greenstone & Cie
Harry Rothman's
J. Press
Jaeger
Kenar
Kids "R" Us
Klein's of Monticello
Lea's Designer Fashion
Linda Dresner
Magic Windows
Miriam Rigler
S&W

SYMS
Shulie's
St. John Boutique
Sue's Discount Better Dresses
Talbots
Clothing-casual
J. Crew
J. McLaughlin
Lee Anderson
Patricia Field
Peter Elliot
Putumayo
Tobaldi Huomo
Custom
Alan Flusser at Saks
Ascot Chang
Mr. Ned
Department stores
Bergdorf Goodman
Bloomingdale's
Century 21
Saks Fifth Avenue
Takashimaya
Fabric
Beckenstein's Men's Fabrics
Paron Fabrics
Furriers
Alixandre
Christie Bros.
Goldin Feldman
Hats
Worth & Worth
Jewelry & watches
Buccellati
Bulgari
Camilla Dietz Bergeron
Cartier
Christopher Walling
David Webb
Ellagem
Fortunoff
Harry Winston
Seaman Schepps
Tiffany & Company
Van Cleef & Arpels
Jewelry & watches-costume
Gale Grant Ltd.
Ilene Chazanof
Jewelry & watches-supply
Jewelry Display of New York
Leathers
Altman Luggage
Coach Store
Crouch & Fitzgerald
Fine and Klein
Ghurka

Il Bisonte
J.S. Suarez
Jobson's Luggage
Lexington Luggage
Mark Cross
Maternity
Motherhood Maternity
Veronique
Shirts & blouses
Shirt Store
Victory, the Shirt Experts
Shoes, socks & stockings
Cole-Haan
French Sole
Great Feet
Harry's Shoes
Lace Up Shoe Shop
Little Eric Shoes
Louis Chock
Nine West
Peter Fox Shoes
Robert Clergerie
Schmooz
Tootsi Plohound
Vanessa Noel
Walter Steiger
Yaska Shoes
Sweaters
Berk of Burlington Arcade London
Best of Scotland
N. Peal
TSE Cashmere
Thrift shops
Allan & Suzi
Encore
INA
Underwear & lingerie
Chas. Weiss Fashions
Joovay
Mendel Weiss
Peress
Samantha Jones
Schachner Fashions
Victoria's Secret
Vintage
Jana Starr Antiques
Jean Hoffman
Reminiscence

Cosmetics, bath & beauty
Cosmetics, etc.
Aveda Lifestyle Store

Body Shop
Cosmetics Plus
MAC Cosmetics
Haircuts & hairstylists
Bumble and Bumble
La Coupe
Orbibe
Personal care
Mario Badescu

Food & beverages
Appetizers
D'Artagnan, Inc.
Murray's Sturgeon Shop
Sable's
Schacht Appetizing & Deli
Bakery
Black Hound
Bonte Patisserie
Caffè Roma
Cupcake Cafe
Erotic Baker
Friend of a Farmer
Little Pie Company
Royale Pastry Shop
Sant Ambroeus Ltd.
Sylvia Weinstock Cakes
Trois Jean
Veniero's Pasticceria
Beverages
Cork & Bottle
Milkman
Bread
A. Zito and Son's Bakery
D&G Bakery
H&H Bagels
Pick a Bagel
Vesuvio Bakery
Candy, fruit & nuts
Li-Lac Chocolates
Neuchâtel Chocolates
Cheese
Murray's Cheese Shop
9th Avenue Cheese Market
Coffees, teas & spices
Aphrodisia
Empire Coffee and Tea
Ten Ren Tea Company
Fish & meat
Akron
Citarella
Jefferson Market

Leonards' Market
Lobel's Prime Meats
Ottomanelli Brothers
Pisacane Midtown Corp.
Rosedale Fish & Oyster Market
Gifts
Manhattan Fruitier
Health food
Healthy Pleasures
Italian
Bruno the King of Ravioli
Manganaro's Food and Restaurant
Raffetto's
Oriental
Kam Kuo Food
Kam Man Food Products
Superstores
Agata & Valentina
Butterfield Market
Fairway Market
Zabar's Appetizers & Caterers
Takeout
Benny's Burritos To Go
David's Chicken
International Poultry Company
Lorenzo & Maria's Kitchen
Wines & liquors
Astor Place Wines & Spirits
Crossroads Wine & Liquor
Quality House
Sherry-Lehmann Wine & Spirits Merchants
67 Wine & Spirits Merchants

Furniture & furnishings
Accessories
Accscentiques
Amy Perlin Antiques
Aris Mixon & Company
Bob Pryor Antiques
Hubert Des Forges
Portico Home
Primavera Gallery
Rita Ford Music Boxes
Slatkin & Company
American
Peter Roberts Antiques
Antiques
A Repeat Performance
Ann Morris Antiques
Annex Antiques Fair and Flea Market
Depression Modern
James II Galleries
Appliances

ABC Trading Company
Bernie's Discount Center
Art & artifacts
Gallery of Graphic Arts
Art deco/art nouveau
Barry of Chelsea Antiques
Maison Gerard
Oldies, Goldies & Moldies
Auction houses
William Doyle Galleries
Beds & bedding
Dial-A-Mattress
Children
Albee's
Art 'n Tapisserie
China, crystal & silver
Bardith Ltd.
Ceramica
Christofle
Fishs Eddy
Hoffman Gampetro Antiques
Hoya Crystal Gallery
Jamar
James Robinson
Jean's Silversmiths
Michael C. Fina
Nathan Horowicz
Niels Bamberger
Pottery Barn
Simon Pearce
Steuben Glass
Williams-Sonoma Outlet
Williams-Sonoma, Inc.
Wolfman Gold & Good Company
Yellow Door
Contemporary
Knoll
North Carolina Furniture Showrooms
Scott Jordan Furniture
Cookware & cutlery
Bridge Kitchenware
Broadway Panhandler
Country
Martell Antiques
Electronics, etc.
B&H Photo & Electronics
Crocodile Computers
47th Street Photo
Harvey Electronics
J&R Music World
Software Etc.
Stereo Exchange
Wiz

English
Eagles Antiques
Lynn Hollyn
Philip Colleck of London Ltd.
European
Didier Aaron, Inc.
Grange Furniture
Newel Art Galleries, Inc.
Fabric
Harry Zarin Company
Intercoastal Textiles
Silk Surplus
Fireplace
Danny Allessandro Ltd. / Edwin Jackson,
 Inc.
Garden & wicker
Gazebo
New York Botanical Garden's Shop
Wicker Garden
Hardware & fixtures
Country Floors
Hastings
Ideal Tile of Manhattan
Ideal Tile of Manhattan West
Janovic Plaza
Kraft Hardware
P.E. Guerin
Simon's Hardware
Terra Verde Trading Company
Kitchen
Lechter's
Light fixtures
Grand Brass
Let There Be Neon City, Inc.
Lighting By Gregory
Nestle
Price Glover
Linens
Ad Hoc Softwares
E. Braun & Company
Harris Levy
Laura Fisher / Antique Quilts & Americana
Laytner's Linen and Home Center
Leron
Porthault
Schweitzer Linens
Medieval & Renaissance
Blumka
Oriental
Art Asia
E&J Frankel Ltd.
Superstores
Bed, Bath and Beyond

Crate & Barrel
Window treatments
Country Curtains
Drapery Exchange, Inc.
Just Shades

Home & home office
Art supplies
Pearl Paint Company
Stationery
Hudson Jam
Mrs. John L. Strong Company

Leisure hours & parties
Books & magazines
A Different Light Bookstore and Cafe
Applause Theater & Cinema Books
Archiva: The Decorative Arts Book Shop
Argosy Book Store
B. Dalton Bookseller
Barnes & Noble
Barnes & Noble for Kids
Books of Wonder
Complete Traveller Bookstore
H.P. Kraus
Hacker Art Books
Hagstrom Map and Travel Center
Kinokuniya Bookstore
Librairie de France/Libreria Hispanica
Madison Avenue Bookshop
Morton, the Interior Design Bookshop
Murder Ink
Mysterious Book Shop
New York Bound Bookshop
Rizzoli
Shakespeare & Company Booksellers
Victor Kamkin, Inc.
CDs, tapes & records
Gryphon Record Shop
Tower Records & Video
Caterers
Charlotte's Catering
Gay Jordan
Great Performances
Neuman & Bogdonoff
Yura
Classes & activities
James Beard Foundation
Metropolitan Museum of Art
New York University School of
 Continuing Education
Parents League

Coordinators
Gourmet Advisory Service, Inc.
Renny - Design for Entertaining
Entertainment
Silly Billy
Florists
Surroundings
Venamy Orchids
Gyms
Atrium Club
Locations
Abigail Kirsch
Burden Mansion
Essex House Hotel Nikko New York
Palm House at the Brooklyn Botanical Garden
Puck Building
St. Regis
24 Fifth Avenue Ballroom
21 Club
Waldorf-Astoria Hotel
Museum shops
Asia Society Bookstore
Cathedral of St. John the Divine
Metropolitan Museum of Art Gift Shop
United Nations Gift Shop
Music
Little Orchestra Society
Photographs & video
Beth Green Studio
Riding
Claremont Riding Academy
Service help
Barnard Bartending
Columbia Bartending Agency
Theater
TKTS

TKTS Time Square
Toys, games & hobbies
Erica Wilson
Myron Toback
Toys "R" Us

Personal & repair services
Decorators
Use What You Have
Light fixtures
City Knickerbocker
Luggage & handbags
Superior Repair Center
Movers
Moishe's Moving Systems
Personal shoppers
Margot Green
Shoe repair
Jim's Shoe Repair

Pet services & supplies
Boarding
Canine College
Transportation
Pet Cab
Veterinarians
Animal Medical Center

Sporting Goods
Marine
Goldberg's Marine
Riding
Miller's Harness Company
Sports-general
Eastern Mountain Sports

The ratings: **5** excellent **4** very good **3** good **2** fair **1** so-so

Index

—A—

A Bear's Place, 364
A Different Light Bookstore and Cafe, 302
A La Vieille Russie, 66
A Photographer's Place, 302
A Repeat Performance, 206
A&B Spraying Company, 379
A&N Fabrics, 60
A. Feibush, 49
A. Zito and Son's Bakery, 149
A.A. Feather Company, 49
A.F. Supply Corporation, 257
A.T. Harris, 45
A.W. Kaufman, 112
A/X Armani Exchange, 7
AAA American Flag, 289
AAA Locksmiths, 377
Aaron Faber Gallery, 66
Aaron Streit, Inc., 134
Aaron's, 27
Abacrome, 289
ABC Carpet and Home, 282
ABC Trading Company, 209
Abercrombie & Fitch, 7
Abracadabra, 51
Abrons Arts Center, 328
Academy Book Store, 303
Academy Clothes, 116
accessories, 43, 44, 194-196
Accscentiques, 194
Ace Banner and Flag Company, 289
Ace Exterminating, 375
Acker Merrall and Condit, 190
Action Comics, 303
Ad Hoc Softwares, 270
Addison on Madison, 88
adoption, pet, 387
Adorama Camera, 239
Adriana's Caravan, 159
Adrien Linford, 194
AFR (the Furniture Rental People), 278
After School Workshop, 328
Agata & Valentina, 181
Ages Past Antiques, 218
Agnes B., 38
Agostino Antiques Ltd., 247
Agouti Consulting, 297
Air Conditioner Power & Cooling, 295
air conditioning, 295
Akron, 164

Al Husted, 301
Alan Flusser at Saks, 52
Albee's, 217
Albert's, 164
Alcone Warehouse, 121
Aldo Ferrari, Inc., 21
Alexander Kabbaz, 52
Alfonso Sciortino Custom Alterations, 385
Alfred Dunhill of London, 21
Alice Kwartler, 218
Alice Underground, 117
Alice's Antiques, 213
Alixandre, 63
Allan & Suzi, 109
Allan Uniform Rental Service, 51
Allcraft Tool and Supply Company, 365
Alleva Dairy, 156
Alliance of Resident Theatres, 328
Alpha Puck Designs, 284
Alphabet's, 194
Altar Egos, 211
Altman Luggage, 79
AM/PM, 112
Amal Printing and Publishing, 290
America Hurrah, 277
America's Hobby Center, 365
American, furniture, 206
American Museum of Natural History, 348
American Steel Window Service, 257
Americas Society, 348
Amsterdam Corporation, 300
Amy Perlin Antiques, 194
Ananias, 79
Anbar Shoes, 90
Andrea Carrano Boutique, 90
Angelica's Traditional Herbs and Spices, 159
Animal Medical Center, 389
Ann Crabtree, 39
Ann Morris Antiques, 206
Ann Taylor, 27, 96
Annex Antiques Fair and Flea Market, 207
Annie's, 180
Antique Boutique, 117
Antique Cache, 254
Antique Furniture Workroom, 379
antiques, 78, 194, 195, 198, 199, 200, 206-
    209, 213-215, 218, 222, 229, 239, 246-252,
    253, 254, 260, 273-278, 365
Aphrodisia, 159
Appelfeld Gallery, 303
appetizers, 134-137, 185
Applause Theater & Cinema Books, 303
appliances, 209-211, 379

April Cornell, 254
Aquascutum of London, 1
Archetype Gallery, 231
architects, 264, 295
Archiva
  the Decorative Arts Book Shop, 304
Argosy Book Store, 304
Aris Mixon & Company, 195
Arivel Fashions, 79
Arkitektura, 207
Arnold Scassi, 45
art & artifacts, 211-213
Art 'n Tapisserie, 217
Art Asia, 274
art deco/art nouveau, 213-215
Art Max Fabrics, 60
Art Station, 287
Art Students League, 328
art supplies, 287-289
Artbag Creations, Inc., 377
Arthur Brown & Brother, Inc., 287
Arthur Gluck, 52
Ascot Chang, 52
Ashanti, 107
Asia Minor Carpets, Inc., 279
Asia Society Bookstore, 353
Asian Art Gallery, 372
Asian House, 274
ASPCA, 387, 388
Asphalt Green, the Murphy Center, 341
Asprey Limited, 66
Astor Place Hair Stylists, 128
Astor Place Wines & Spirits, 190
Atelier 45, 28
Atelier 86, 28
Atrium Club, 341
auction houses, 215-216
Audio Design Associates, 296
Authentic Porcelain Refinishing, 379
Authorized Repair Service, 380
Autobahn Service Center, 372
Aux Delices Des Bois, 180
Aveda Lifestyle Store, 121
Avventura Glassware Gifts, 218

—B—

B&E, 149
B&H Photo & Electronics, 239
B&J Fabrics, 60
B. Nelson Shoe Corporation, 384
Baccarat, Inc., 219
Back Pages Antiques, 365

Bagelry, 150
Bagels on the Square, 150
Bagutta Boutique, 29
Baked Ideas, 137
bakery, 137-152, 178, 179
Bakery Soutine, 137
Balducci's, 181, 183, 185
Baldwin Fish Market, 164
Baldwin Formals, 45
Ballet Academy East, 329
balloons, 302
Bally of Switzerland, 90
Balogh Jewelers, 67
Banana Republic, 7
Barbara Gee Danskin Center, 395
Barbara Shaum, 80
Bardith Ltd., 219
Barnard Bartending, 361
Barnes & Noble, 304-306, 309
Barnes & Noble for Kids, 306
Barnes & Noble Sales Annex, 306
Barney Greengrass, 134
Barney's New York, 56
Barocca Alimentari, 185
Barry Friedman Ltd., 246
Barry of Chelsea Antiques, 213
Bauman Rare Books, 306
Bazzini Importers, 152
Bead Store, 50
Bear Hugs & Baby Dolls, 365
Beckenstein's Men's Fabrics, 60
Bed, Bath and Beyond, 282
beds & bedding, 216
Belgian Shoes, 90
Bell Bates Company, 173
Bellini, 217
Ben Kahn Salon, 63
Ben's Cheese Shop, 157
Ben's for Kids, 15
Ben's Up and Up, 15
Benedetti Custom Shoes, 91
Benetton, 8
Benny's Burritos To Go, 185
Berdi Abadjian, 279
Bergdorf Goodman, 56, 57
Bergdorf Goodman Men's Store, 57
Berk of Burlington Arcade London, 108
Bernardaud Limoges, 219
Bernie's Discount Center, 209
Beshar's, 279
Best of Scotland, 108
Beth Green Studio, 359
Betsey Johnson, 29

Betsy, 45
Bettinger's Luggage Shop, 80
Between the Bread, 186
beverages, 149
Bianca Pasta, 175
Bicycle & Fitness Equipment Store, 391
Bicycle Habitat, 391
Bicycle Renaissance, 391
bicycles, 391, 392
Big City Kite Company, 365
Big John Moving, 381
Bijan, 21
Bijoux Doux, 138
billiards, 392
Biography Bookshop, 306
Birger Christensen, 63
Black Hound, 138
Blade Fencing, 396
Blades West, 399
Blatt Billiards, 392
Bleecker Bob's Golden Oldie Record Shop, 321
Block China Warehouse Store, 219
Bloom and Krup, 210
Bloomingdale's, 57
Blumka, 273
boarding, 387
Boathouse in Central Park, 348
Bob Pryor Antiques, 195
Bob Shaw, 296
Body Shop, 121
Bogner, 400
Bolton's, 29
Bonpoint, 15
Bonte Patisserie, 138
Bookberries, 306
books & magazines, 302-321, 353
Books of Wonder, 307
Boris Le Beau Jewelers, 67
Bottega Veneta, 80, 84
Botticelli, 91
bread, 141, 149-152, 187
bridal, wedding & formal, 45-49
Bridge Kitchenware, 236
Brief Essentials, 112
Brioni, 53
Broadway Farm, 182
Broadway Panhandler, 237
Broadway Sneakers, 91
Brooks Brothers, 21
Brookstone Company, 258
Brownstone Brothers Moving & Storage, 382

Brunellier Salon, 128
Brunner/Mazel Bookshop, 307
Bruno Magli, 92, 101
Bruno the King of Ravioli, 176
Buccellati, 67
Bulgari, 67, 74
Bumble and Bumble, 128
Burberry Limited, 1
Burden Mansion, 349
Burgundy Wine Company Limited, 191
Burlington Antique Toys, 366
Burlington Coat Factory, 1
Butch Krutchik Designs, 290
Butterfield Market, 182
buttons, beads & trims, 49, 50, 51

—C—

C. Deck Contractor, 298
cabinetry/carpenters, 296
Cafe Lalo, 139
Caffè Roma, 139
Calvary Bookstore, 307
Cameo Water Wear, 402
Camilla Dietz Bergeron, 68
camping, 393
Canard and Company, 186
Cancer Care Thrift Shop, 110
Candle Shop, 195
candy, fruit & nuts, 152-156
Canine College, 387
Capital Reservations, 404
Capitol Fishing Tackle Company, 396
car, 372, 376, 377
Cardel, 220
Cardio Fitness Center, 341
Carlos Colonna, 68
Carlyle Custom Convertibles Ltd., 232
Carmine Street Guitar Shop, 357
Carnegie Luggage, 377
Cartier, 68, 78, 79, 204, 214, 284
casual clothing, 87
Catalano's, 164
caterers, 325-327
Cathedral of St. John the Divine, 353
Caviarteria, 134
CDs, tapes & records, 321, 322, 323, 324
Center Art Studio, 372
Central Carpet, 280
Central Fish Company, 164
Central Park, 329, 342, 360, 362

Central Park Challenges, 342
Central Reservation Services, 404
Century 21, 57
Ceramic Supply of New York & New Jersey, 366
Ceramica, 220
Ceramica Gift Gallery, 220
chairs & tables, 217
Chairs and Stools, Etc., 217
Chanel Boutique, 30
Charivari, 1
Charles P. Rogers Brass Bed Company, 216
Charlotte Moss & Company, 247
Charlotte's Catering, 325
Charrette, 287
Chartwell Booksellers, 307
Chas. Weiss Fashions, 113
cheese, 156-159
Chelsea Atelier, 107
Cheo Tailors, 53
Cheryl Kleinman Cakes, 139
Chess Shop, 371
Chez Laurence, 140
children, 15-20, 93, 98, 101, 217, 218, 272, 306, 307, 328-330, 334, 335, 338, 353, 400
Children's Acting Academy, 329
Children's Museum of Manhattan, 353
Children's Museum of the Arts, 329
China Institute, 330
china, crystal & silver, 218-231, 372-373
Chinese American Trading Company, 178
Chinese Porcelain Company, 274
Chocolate Soup, 15
Chopard, 68
Christian Dior, 2, 27, 94, 112, 114
Christian Publications Books & Supply Center, 308
Christie Bros., 63
Christie's, 215
Christie's East, 215
Christofle, 219, 220
Christopher Walling, 69
Chuckles and Friends, 338
Church English Shoes, 92
Cinderella Flower & Feather Company, 46
Cipriano Shoes, 92
Citarella, 165
City Bakery, 140
City Children's Theater of New York, 330
City Knickerbocker, 376
Citybooks, 308
Citykids, 16
Civilized Traveller, 308

Claremont Riding Academy, 360
classes & activities, 328-336
Classic Plastering and Tiling, 300
Classic Sofa, 232
Claycraft, 254
Clear Plastics, 195
closet design, 373
clothing, 1-43, 45-49, 51-59, 87-89, 107, 108, 112-120
clothing & accessories, 1-120
Club La Raquette, 342
Coach Store, 80
Cobblestones, 264
Cobweb, 238
Cockpit, 9
Coco & Z, 16
Coffee Grinder, 159
coffees, teas & spices, 159-163
Cohen Carpet Cleaning, 383
coins & stamps, 336
Colette Cakes, 140
Coliseum Books, Inc., 308
Collector's Stadium, 401
Columbia Bartending Agency, 361
Columbia Hot Bagels, 136, 150
Comme des Garçons, 2, 111
Commodities, 174
Common Ground, Inc., 196
Compleat Strategist, 366
Complete Traveller Bookstore, 308
Computers, 240, 242
Conrad's Bike Shop, 391
contemporary furniture, 231-236
cookware & cutlery, 236, 237, 238
Cooper Union, 330
coordinators, parties, 336, 337
Cork & Bottle, 149
Corrado Kitchen, 186
Cosmetic Show, 123
Cosmetic World and Gift Center, 123
Cosmetics Plus, 123
cosmetics, bath & beauty, 121-133
cosmetics, etc., 121-128
Costikyan Ltd., 383
costumes, 51, 52
country furniture, 238, 239
Country Curtains, 284
Country Floors, 258
Country Road, 30
Crabtree and Evelyn, 125
Craft Caravan, 196
Crate & Barrel, 283
Creative Edge Parties, 325

Crocodile Computers, 240
Crossroads Wine & Liquor, 191
Crouch & Fitzgerald, 81
Crown Machine Service, 383
Crunch, 342
Cupcake Cafe, 140
custom clothing & shoes 52-56, 88, 91, 94
  (also see tailors)
Custom Shop, 88
Custom Spraying and Reglazing Company,
  380

—D—

D&G Bakery, 150
D'Artagnan, Inc., 134
Daffy's Fifth Avenue, 2
Dalva Brothers, 250
Dana Buchman, 31, 32
dance, 393, 394
Danny Allessandro Ltd. / Edwin Jackson, Inc.,
  253
Daroma Restaurant Equipment Corp., 237
Dart Shop Limited, 394
darts, 394
Daum Boutique, 221
David Barton Gym, 343
David Davis Fine Art Materials, 287
David Webb, 69, 75, 204
David's Chicken, 187
Davide Cenci, 3
Davidoff of Geneva, 364
De Robertis Pastry, 140
Dean & Deluca, 182
decorators, 282, 373, 374
Delorenzo, 214
deluxe 411-413
Dembitzer Brothers, 210
Demner, 69
Dempsey & Carroll, 290
department stores, 56-59
Depression Modern, 207
Detrich Pianos, 357
Deutsch Wicker Furniture, 255
Diane Wagner, 46
Didier Aaron, Inc., 250
Diego Della Valle, 93
Dinosaur Hill, 16
DiPalo's Fine Food, Inc., 176
discount, 407-410
Discount Hotel Hotline/Hotel Reservation
  Net, 404

Distant Origin, 196
diving, 394, 395
DMI Dartmart, Inc., 394
Dollar Bill's, 3
Dollhouse Antics, 366
Doris Leslie Blau Gallery, 280
Dornan, 116
Dorothy Wako, 336
Down East Service Center, 380
Downtown Athletic Club, 343
Downtown Rifle & Pistol Club, 347
Drag's Gym, 343
Dragon Gate Import and Export Company,
  196
Drake Design, 373
Drama Bookshop, 309
Drapery Exchange, Inc., 285
Driade/Modern Age, 233
Dyckman's, 69

—E—

E&J Frankel Ltd., 275
E. Braun & Company, 270
E. Rossi, 237
E.A.T., 187
E.A.T. Gifts, 173
E.C. Electronics, 374
Eagles Antiques, 248
East Side Kids, 93
East Village Cheese Shop, 157
East Village Meat Market, 165
Eastern Mountain Sports, 401
Eastern Silver Company, 221
Eastern Tennis Association Metro Region,
  362
Eastside Gifts & Dinnerware, 221
Ebel, 375
Ecce Panis, 141
Eclectiques, 81
Economy Candy Corp., 152
Eddie Egras, 385
Edith Weber & Company, 70
Eigen Plumbing Supply, 258
Eileen Fisher Boutique, 39
Eileen Lane Antiques, 246
Eileen's Special Cheesecake, 141
Eisenberg and Eisenberg, 22
Eisner Brothers, 9
El Pollo, 187
Elan Flowers, 338
electrician, 296

electronics, etc., 239-245, 296, 297, 374, 375
Elite Carpet and Upholstery Cleaning, 383
Elk Candy Company and Marzipan, 152
Ellagem, 70
Emanuel Ungaro, 31
Empire & Biedermeier, 246, 247
Empire Coffee and Tea, 160
Empire Purveyors, 165
Emporio Armani, 9
Enchanted Forest, 367
Encore, 110
Encore Preferred Travel / Encore Marketing, 404
Enelra, 113
English food 163
English furnishings 198, 200, 201, 203, 206-208, 218, 219, 222, 223, 225, 228, 231, 235, 237, 247-249, 250, 251, 254, 256, 260, 264
entertainment, 321-324, 338
Entertainment Warehouse, 321
Enz's, 3
Episode Sportswear, 31
Equinox Fitness Club, 343
Equitable Tower, 349
Eric Shoes, 93
Erica Wilson, 367
Ermenegildo Zegna, 22, 25
Erotic Baker, 141
Escada Boutique, 32
Essex House Hotel Nikko New York, 349
Euromoda Ltd., 22
European furnishings 200, 206-209, 217, 246-252, 268, 279, 280, 282
Evelyn and San, 384
Ex Libris, 309
Exclusive Oilily Store, 16
Executive Fitness Center, 344
exercise, 336, 341, 395, 396
expediter, 297
Express, 39
Express Car, 376
Express Hotel Reservations, 405
exterminator, 375
eyeglasses, 59

—F—

F. Rozzo & Sons, 165
fabric, 60-62, 252, 253, 386
Faicco's, 166
Fairfax Liquor, 191
Fairway Market, 183

Fanelli Antique Timepieces, 283
fans, 253
FAO Schwarz, 367
Farm & Garden Nursery, 255
Fashion Plaza, 32
Feast and Fêtes, 325
Felissimo, 197
Felsen Fabrics, 61
fencing, 396
Fendi, viii, 82
Fenwick Clothes, 22
Ferragamo, 82
Ferrara's, 141
Fifth Avenue Chocolatiere, 153
Fila of Madison Avenue, 403
Filene's Basement, 4
film services, 288
Finals, 403
Fine & Schapiro, 135
Fine and Klein, 82
fireplace, 253, 254
First Avenue Wines & Spirits, 191
fish & meat, 164-172
Fisher & Levy, 187
fishing, 396
Fishkin Knitwear, 32
Fishs Eddy, 221
flags, 289
Flights of Fancy, 197
flooring, 297
Florence Meat Market, 166
Florian Papp, 248
Floris, 125
florists, 338-340
Flying Cranes Antiques Ltd., 275
Fogal, 94
food & beverages, 134-193
Food Attitude, 142
Foods of India, 175
Forbidden Planet, 309
Foremost Furniture Showrooms, 233
Forgotten Woman, 107
Forman's, 32
Forsyth Decorations, 386
Fortunoff, 70, 197
47th Street Photo, 240
Fossner Timepieces, 284
Foto Electric Supply Company, 240
Fowad, 33
Framed on Madison, 197
Fred Leighton, 70
Frederick P. Victoria and Son, Inc., 250
Freed of London, 393

French & Company, Inc., 250
French Sole, 94
Frette, 271
Friedman Hosiery, 94
Friend of a Farmer, 142
Fung Wong Bakery, 178
Furla, 82
furniture & furnishings, 194-286
furriers, 63, 64

—G—

G&G International, 23
G&S Sporting Goods, 401
Gail Watson Custom Cakes, 142
Gale Grant Ltd., 77
Gallery of Graphic Arts, 211
Gallery of Wearable Art, 43
Game Show, 368
Gampel Supply, 50
Gap, 7, 9-12, 17, 18
garden, 297
garden & wicker, 254-257, 297
Gargoyles Ltd. of Philadelphia, 198
Garnet Wine & Liquor, 191
Garren, 129
Garrett Wade, 258
Gay Jordan, 326
Gazebo, 255
Gelman Custom, 94
Gem Antiques, 222
Gene London's Studio, 46
general contractors, 298, 299
general stores, 172
George N. Antiques, 207
George Paul Jewelers, 71
George Taylor Specialties Company, 259
Georgia Hughes Designs, 65
Georgian Suite, 349
German Wine Society, 331
Gerry Cosby and Company, 401
Gertel's, 142
Ghurka, 83
Gianni Versace, 23
Gifted Ones, 198
gifts, 197, 353-356
Gilberto Designs, 53
Gilcrest Clothes Company, 23
Giordano's Shoes, 95
Giorgio Armani, 4, 9
Giovanni Esposito & Sons Meat Shop, 166
Giraudon Shoes, 95

Giselle Sportswear, Inc., 33
Givenchy Boutique, 33
Glass Restorations, 372
Glendale Bake Shop, 143
Glenn Horowitz Booksellers, 310
Globemark Enterprises, Inc., 71
Glorious Food, 326
Godiva Chocolatier, 153
Goldberg's Marine, 398
Golden Disc, 322
Goldin Feldman, 64
Goldpfeil, 83
Goldreich, Page & Throff, 298
Goldust Memories, 198
golf, 397
Good & Plenty To Go, 188
Good Health, 174
Gordon Button Company, 50
Gordon Novelty Company, 52
Gorsart, 23
Gotham Book Mart and Gallery, 310
Gotham Liquors, 192
Gotham Writers' Workshop, 331
Gourmet Advisory Service, Inc., 336
Gourmet Garage, 183
Grace's Marketplace, 183
Gracious Home, 283
Graham Arader, 207
Grand Brass, 267
Grand Lingerie, 113
Grange Furniture, 250
Great Feet, 95
Great Performances, 326
Greenstone & Cie, 18
Groomer Direct, 388
grooming & supplies, dog, 388
Grossinger's Uptown, 143
Grove Decoys, 398
Gruen Optika, 59
Gryphon Bookshop, 310, 322
Gryphon Record Shop, 322
Gucci, 83
Guild Antiques, 222
guns, 398
Guss Pickles, 135
Gym Source, 395
gyms, 341-397

—H—

H&H Bagels, 151
H. Herzfeld, 54

H. Kauffman and Sons, 399
H. Oppenheimer Company, 166
H. Stern, 71
H.M. Luther, 198
H.P. Kraus, 310
Hacker Art Books, 311
Hagstrom Map and Travel Center, 311
haircuts & hairstylists, 128-131
Hale & Hearty, 188
Hammacher Schlemmer, 259
Hammock World, 198
Han Arum, 178
hardware & fixtures, 257-264
Harmer Johnson Books Ltd., 311
Harriet Love, 40
Harris Levy, 271
Harry Hanson, 358
Harry Rothman's, 24
Harry Wils & Company, 157
Harry Winston, 71, 79
Harry Zarin Company, 252
Harry's Shoes, 95
Harvey Electronics, 241
Hastings, 259
hats, 65, 66
health food, 173-175
Health Nuts, 174
Healthy Pleasures, 174
Helene Arpels, Inc., 96
Henri Bendel, 58, 129
Henry Lehr, 12
Henry Olko, Inc., 218
Henry Westpfal and Company, 380
Herban Kitchen, 174
Hermès, 83, 84, 86, 399
Hess Restorations, 373
Hi Fi Electronics, 241
Hoffman Gampetro Antiques, 222
Hoi Sing Seafood, 166
Hold Everything, 230, 259
Homarus, Inc., 135
home & home office, 287-294
home renovation, 295-301
Home Sales Enterprises, 210
Hors D'oeuvres Unlimited, 135
Horticultural Society of New York, 255
Hoshoni, 199
Hot Stuff Spicy Food, Inc., 160
Houghtaling Mousse Pie Ltd., 143
House of Maurizio, 54
House of Nubian, 4
Howard Haimes, Inc., 298
Howard Kaplan Bath Shop, 260

Howron Sportswear, 113
Hoya Crystal Gallery, 222
Hubert Des Forges, 199
Hudson Jam, 291
Hudson River Club, 350
Hudson Street Papers, 291
Hung Chong Import, 237
Hungarian Viennese Pastry Inc., 143
hunting, 347, 396, 398
Hunting World/Angler's World, 398
Hyde Park Antiques, 208
Hyman Hendler and Sons, 252

—I—

Ice Studio, Inc., 331
Ideal Cheese Shop, 157
Ideal Department Store, 116
Ideal Tile of Manhattan, 260
Ideal Tile of Manhattan West, 260
If Boutique, 34
Il Bisonte, 84
Il Papiro, 291
Ilana Designs, 54
Ilene Chazanof, 77
Ilias Lalaounis, 72
Imperial Fine Books, Inc., 311
INA, 111
Indian, 160, 175, 254, 276, 282, 353
Indian, American, 196, 355
Intercoastal Textiles, 252
International Center of Photography, 311
International Furniture Rentals, 279
International Groceries and Meat Market, 184
International Retinning & Copper Repair, 379
International Wine Center, 331
Irish Book Shop, 312
Irreplaceable Artifacts, 256
Irving Baron Clothes, 24
Irvington Institute Thrift Shop, 111
Island Fabric Warehouse, 253
Island Sports, 403
Issey Miyake, 4
Italian food, 175-178
Italian Food Center, 176

—J—

J&R Music World, 241
J. Crew, 12, 26
J. Mavec & Company Ltd., 72

J. McLaughlin, 13
J. Press, 24
J. Schachter, 271
J.J. Lally & Company Oriental Art, 275
J.M. Weston, 96
J.N. Bartfield Books, 312
J.R. Tobacco, 364
J.S. Suarez, 84
Jacadi, 18
Jack and Company Formal Wear, 46
Jack Corcoran Marble Company, 299
Jack Henry & Company, 298
Jacques Dessange, 129
Jaded, 77
Jaeger, 34, 43
Jamar, 223
James Beard Foundation, 331
James Hepner Antiques, 208
James II Galleries, 208
James Lowe Autographs, 212
James Robinson, 223
Jamie Ostrow, 292
Jan's Hobby Shop, 368
Jana Starr Antiques, 118
Jandreani, 96
Jane Gill, 297
Jane Kozlak, 300
Janovic Plaza, 260
Jazz Record Center, 322
Jean Hoffman, 118
Jean's Silversmiths, 223
Jefferson Market, 167
Jekyll and Hyde Ltd., 24
Jerrystyle, 267
jewelry & watches, 66-79, 375, 376
Jewelry Display of New York, 78
Jewish Museum, 312
Jim Buck School for Dogs, 390
Jim's Shoe Repair, 384
Jimson's, 368
Joan & David, 96
Jobson's Luggage, 84, 86
Joe's Dairy, 158
Joe's Ninth Avenue Meat Market, 167
John Barman, Inc., 374
John Fluevog, 97, 101
John Jovino Gun Shop, 398
John R. Gerardo, 378
John Rosselli Antiques, 251
John Rosselli International, 199
John Venekamp, 301
Joia, 78

Joia Interiors, Inc., 214
Joovay, 113
Jordan Lobster Dock, 167
Joseph, 34
Joseph D. Tonti, 358
Josie Atplace, 72
Julie Artisan's Gallery, 43
Julius Caruso Salon, 129
Julliard Placement Bureau, 332
Just Bulbs, 267
Just Once Ltd., 46
Just Shades, 285

—K—

K&D Liquors, 192
Kadouri & Son, Inc., 154
Kalustyan Orient Export Trading, 175
Kam Kuo Food, 179
Kam Man Food Products, 179
Karens for People + Pets, 388
Karp & Centrell, 297
Katagiri and Company, 179
Kate's Paperie, 292
Kaufman Pharmacy, 132
Kay Leather Goods Repair Service, 378
Ken Hansen Imaging, 241
Kenar, 28, 34
Kenneth Cole, 97
Kentshire Galleries, 248
Kidding Around, 18
Kids, 19
Kids Are Magic, 19
Kinokuniya Bookstore, 312
kitchen, 264-266
Kitchen Arts and Letters, 312
Kitschen, 264
Klein's of Monticello, 4
Kleinfeld and Son, 47
Knoll, 23
Kordol Fabrics, 61
Koreana Art and Antiques, 276
Kossar's Bialystoker Kuchen Bakery, 151
Kraft Hardware, 261
Kraushaar Galleries, Inc., 212
Krishna Gallery of Asian Arts, Inc., 276
Kroll Office Products, 293
Kurowycky Meat Products, 167

—L—

L'Antiquaire & the Connoisseur, 274
L.S. Collection, 223
L.S. Men's Clothing, 24
La Bagagerie, 84
La Boutique Fantasque, 199
La Coupe, 130
La Layette Et Plus, 19
La Lingerie, 114
La Maison du Chocolat, 154
La Sposa Veils, 47
La Terrine, 224
La Valencia, 72
Labels for Less, 40
Lace Up Shoe Shop, 97
Lalique, 204, 214, 219, 224, 231, 373
Lamalle Kitchenware, 238
LaMarca Cheese Shop, 158
Lanac Sales, 224
Lancel, 85
Lapiana Piano Sales, 357
Larry & Jeff's Bicycles Plus, 392
Larry Tan, 359
Laura Ashley, 5
Laura Fisher/Antique Quilts & Americana,
    271
Lauren Bogen Loungerie, 114
Lawrence W. Ford, 72
Laytner's Linen and Home Center, 272
Le Cadet De Gascogne, 251
Le Fanion, 238
Lea's Designer Fashion, 34
Learning Annex, 332
Leather 79-87
Leather Facts, 85
Leather Outlet, 85
leathers, 79-87
Lechter's, 264
Lederer De Paris, Inc., 85
Lee Anderson, 42
Lee Calicchio Ltd., 208
Lee Sam Kitchen & Bath, 266
Lee's Studio, 267
Leekan Designs, Inc., 73
Legacy, 119
Leggiadro, 97
leisure hours & parties, 302-371
Lenox Hill Neighborhood House, 332
Leo Kaplan Ltd., 224
Leon's Jewelry, 375
Leonard Logsdail, 54
Leonards' Market, 168

Leron, 272
Les Fleurs De Maxim's, 339
Les Halles, 168
Let There Be Neon City, Inc., 268
Lexington Gardens, 256
Lexington Luggage, 84, 86
Librairie de France / Libreria Hispanica, 313
Lien Phat Seafood & Meat, 168
light fixtures, 267-270
Lightforms, 268
Lighting By Gregory, 268
Lighting Plus, 268
Likitsakos, 180
Limited, 35
Linda Dresner, 35
Linda Horn Antiques, 200
Linda Kaye's Birthdaybakers, Party Makers,
    350
Linda Morgan Antiques, 78
linens, 19, 202, 270-273
Lismore Hosiery, 98
Little Eric Shoes, 98
Little Folks, 19
Little Orchestra Society, 356
Little Pie Company, 143
Little Rickie, 368
Lobel's Prime Meats, 168
Lobster Place, 169
Locaters, Inc., 225
locations, rental, 347-352
locksmiths, 377
Lola Ehrlich Millinery, 65
London Connection Design, 200
London Towncars, 377
Long Island Carpet Cleaners, 383
Lord & Taylor, 58
Lorenzo & Maria's Kitchen, 188
Lori Klein, 131
Lost City Arts, 212
Lotte Berk Method, 344
Louis Chock, 98
Louis Guy D, 130
Louis Licari Color Group, 130
Louis Mattia, 376
Louis Vuitton, 86
Love Discount, 132
Love Saves the Day, 119
Lovelia Enterprises, 280
luggage & handbags, 377, 378 (also see
    leathers)
Luggage Plus, 86
Lung Fong Chinese Bakery, 179
LVT Price Quote Hotline, 210

Lynda Hughes, 359
Lynn Hollyn, 248

—M—

M&J Trimming, 50
M. Kreinen Sales, 20
M. Rohrs, 160
M. Stever Hosiery Company, 98
Mabel's, 200
MAC Cosmetics, 126
Macklowe Gallery & Modernism, 214
Macy's, 58
Madison Avenue Bookshop, 313
Magic Windows, 20
Maison Gerard, 214
Malcolm Franklin, Inc., 249
Malvina L. Solomon, 225
Mandana, 54
Manfredi, 73
Manganaro's Food and Restaurant, 177
Manhattan Electronics Corporation, 242
Manhattan Fruitier, 173
Manhattan Penthouse, 350
Manhattan Plaza Health Club, 344
Manhattan Sailing School, 361
Manhattan Shoe Repair, 384
Manhattan Veterinary Clinic, 389
Mannes College of Music, 332
Manny's (Musical Instruments), 357
Manny's Millinery Supply Company, 65
Manolo Blahnik, 99
Manrico Cashmere, 109
Maraolo, 99
marble & granite, 299
Marco Polo, 201
Mardi Philips, 285
Margorie Stokes, 382
Margot Green, 382
Marina B, 73
marine, 398
Mario Badescu, 132
Marion & Company, 368
Mark Cross, 84, 86
marketing services, 289
Marnie Carmichael/Noonie's Traditional
    Southern, 144
Marquet Patisserie, 144
Martell Antiques, 239
Marvin Alexander, 269
Marvin Kagan, Inc., 280
Mary Arnold Toys, 369

Mary Hilliard, 360
Marymount Manhattan College, 333
Mason's Tennis Mart, 403
Matas Restaurant Supply, 238
maternity, 87, 88
Matt McGhee, 201
Maurice Badler, 73
Maurice Villency, 234
Max Mara, 35
McNulty's Tea and Coffee, 160
Medici Shoes, 99
medieval & renaissance furniture, 273, 274
Mediterranean Shop, 201
Mendel Weiss, 114
metals, 379
Metro Sofa Service, 385
Metropolitan Museum of Art, 333
Metropolitan Museum of Art Gift Shop, 353
Michael C. Fina, 225
Michael Forrest, 64
Micro U.S.A. Computer Depot, 242
Midtown Tennis Club, 362
Mikimoto, 74
Milkman, 149
Miller's Harness Company, 399
Minardi Minardi Salon, 130
Minna Rosenblatt, 214
Miriam Rigler, 35
Miriam Vasicka, 132
miscellaneous services, 379-381
Missoni, 3, 109
Modern Leather Goods, 378
Modern Supply Company, 253
Moe Ginsburg, 25
Mohl Furs, 64
Moishe's Homemade Kosher Bakery, 144
Moishe's Moving Systems, 382
Momeni International, 281
Moment's Notice, 405
Mondel Chocolates, 155
Montenapoleone, 114
Morrell & Company, 192
Morton, the Interior Design Bookshop, 313
Motherhood Maternity, 87
movers, 381, 382
Movie Star News, 313
Mr. Ned, 55
Mrs. John L. Strong Company, 292
Murder Ink, 314
Murray's Cheese Shop, 158
Murray's Sturgeon Shop, 136
Museum of American Folk Art, 354

Museum of Modern Art, the MOMA Design Store, 354
Museum of the City of New York Gift Shop, 354
museum shops, 353-356
music, 239-246, 321-324, 329, 330, 332, 356-358
Music Inn, 322
musical instruments, 357, 358
Myers of Keswick, 163
Myron Toback, 369
Mysterious Book Shop, 314

—N—

N. Peal, 109
Nader International Foods, 184
Naga Antiques Ltd., 276
Nana, 100
Nancy Wedding Center, Inc., 47
Napoleon, 25
Nat Schwartz, 225
Nathan Horowicz, 225
National Academy of Design, 333
National Museum of the American Indian, 355
National Wholesale Liquidators, 172
Nature Food Centres, 175
Nature's Gifts, 181
Nautica, 394
Nemo Tiles Company, 261
Nestle, 269
Neuchâtel Chocolates, 155
Neuman & Bogdonoff, 326
Nevada Meat Market, 169
New Cathay Hardware Corporation, 238
New Republic Clothiers, 25
New School, 333
New York Academy of Art, 334
New York Astrology Center, 315
New York Athletic Club, 344
New York Botanical Garden's Shop, 256
New York Bound Bookshop, 315
New York Central Art Supply, 288
New York Closet Company, 373
New York Exchange for Women's Work, 44
New York Firefighter's Friend, 44
New York Golf Center, Inc., 397
New York Health and Racquet Club, 345
New York Nautical Instrument & Service Corp., 315
New York Public Library Shop, 355
New York Racquet & Tennis Club, 363

New York University School of Continuing Education, 334
New York Veterinary Hospital, 389
Newel Art Galleries, Inc., 251
Niall Smith, 246
Nicole Miller, 36, 49, 103
Nicolina of New York, 119
Niels Bamberger, 226
Nine West, 100
9th Avenue Cheese Market, 156
Ninth Avenue International Foods, 184
99X, 101
92nd Street Y, 334
North Beach Leather, 87
North Carolina Furniture Showrooms, 234
Nostalgia . . . and All That Jazz, 322
Nuovo Melodrom, 234
NYU Health Sciences Bookstore, 314

—O—

Ocean Sea Food, 169
Oceanie/Afrique Noire, 315
office, 274, 293, 294, 381
Office Furniture Heaven, 274
Old Navy Clothing Company, 13
Old Print Shop, 315
Olden Camera, 242
Oldies, Goldies & Moldies, 215
Omo Norma Kamali, 42
Once Upon a Tart, 145
109, 36
One of a Kind Bride, 48
Only Hearts, 44
Open Pantry, 161
Orbibe, 131
Oren's Daily Roast, 161
oriental furnishings, 197, 237, 238, 274-277, 279, 280, 281, 339
Oriental Porcelain and Furniture Outlet, 276
Orientations Gallery Ltd., 276
Orrefors, 226, 227
Orvis, 396, 397
Orwasher's Bakery, 151
Oscar Wilde Memorial Bookshop, 316
Ottomanelli Brothers, 169, 170
Ottomanelli's Meat Market, 170
ovens, 382

—P—

P.E. Guerin, 261
Pageant Book & Print Shop, 316
paint, plaster & tiles, 300
Palazzeti, 235
Pampered Paws, 388
Pan Am Sportswear and Menswear, 27
Pan Aqua Diving, 395
Pantry & Hearth, 266
Paraclete Book Center, 316
Paradise Market, 181
Paragon Sporting Goods, 402
Parents League, 335
Park Avenue Liquors, 192
Park East Animal Hospital, 389
Park East Kosher Butcher, 170
Park East Sewing Center, 384
Paron Fabrics, 61
Party Poopers, 338
Party Rentals, 360
Pasargad Carpets, 281
Patisserie Claude, 145
Patisserie Lanciani, 145
Patisserie Les Friandises, 145
Patricia Field, 42
Patrician Foods, 177
Paul Bott Beautiful Flowers, 339
Paul Gleicher, 295
Paul Seiden Jeweler, 74
Paul Smith, 25
Paul Stuart, 26
Paul's Veil and Net, 48
Pearl Paint Company, 288
Peck and Goodie Skates, 400
Pembrooke & Ives, 386
Peninsula Buying, 211
Penn Garden Shirts, 89
Penny Whistle Toys, 369
Peppino, 386
Peress, 115
Perfumania, 126
Perimeter, 316
Perl & Berliner, 337
personal & repair services, 372-386
personal care, 131, 132
personal shoppers, 382
personal trainers, 341, 343-346, 358, 359
Perugina, 155
Pet Cab, 388
pet services & supplies, 387-390
Peter Elliot, 13

Peter Fox Shoes, 101
Peter Kump's School of Culinary Arts, 335
Peter Roberts Antiques, 206
Petrossian, 136
pharmacies, 132, 133
Philip Baloun Designs, 337
Philip Colleck of London Ltd., 249
Phone Boutique, 242
photographs & video, services, 359, 360
Phyllis Lucas Gallery & Old Print Center, 317
Piano Store, 358
Pick a Bagel, 152
Piemonte Ravioli Company, 177
Pierpont Morgan Library, 355
Pimlico Way, 256
Pintchik, 262
Pisacane Midtown Corp., 170
Piston's, 202
Platt Box Company, Inc., 79
Platypus, 266
Plaza Hotel, 155, 351
plumbing & heating, 300
Plumbridge, 156
Plus 9, 101
Plus One Fitness Clinic, 359
Poli Fabrics, 61
Polo/Ralph Lauren, 5
Pondicherri, 202
Portantina, 209
Porthault, 272
Portico Home, 202
Porto Rico Importing Company, 161
Poseidon Bakery, 146
Poster America, 212
Pottery Barn, 226, 230
Prada, 35, 87
Pranzo Fine Foods, 189
Pratesi, 273
Pratt Institute of Art, 335
Premier Veal, 170
Prescriptions Limited, 133
Preston Bailey, 339
Price Glover, 269
Price Watchers, 211
Primavera Gallery, 204
Prime Access, 170
Printed Matter, Inc., 317
printers, 290
Pro Piano, 358
produce, 180-183
project managers, 301

Props for Today, 360
Puck Building, 351
Pumping Iron Gym, 345
Putname Rolling Ladder Company, 262
Pyramid Electronics Ltd., 374

—Q—

Quadrant Construction, 299
Quality House, 193
Quarry Tile Marble and Granite, Inc., 262
Quikbook, 405
quilts & quilting, 277, 278

—R—

R&R Packaging Corporation, 293
Raffetto's, 177
Rafik Film and Video Tape Company, 288
Ralph M. Chait Galleries, 277
Ralph's Discount City, 172
Rand McNally Map and Travel Store, 317
Ravioli Store, 178
Rebecca Moss, 292
Rebel Rebel, 323
Red Caboose, 369
Reebok's Sport Club New York, 346
Regal Collection, 277
Reinstein/Ross, 74
Remi To Go, 189
Reminiscence, 119
René, Inc., 203
rentals, 45, 46, 120, 278, 279, 290, 360, 362,
    375, 391, 392
Repetto, 394
Replacement Ltd., 227
Revlon Employee Store, 127
Revolver Records, 324
Richard B. Arkway, Inc., 317
Richard Metz Golf Studio, 397
riding, 360, 399
Rita Ford Music Boxes, 203
Ritter Antik, 247
Ritz Thrift Shop, 64
River Club, 363
Rizzoli, 318
RK Bridal, 48
Ro Star, Inc., 78
Robbins and Wolfe Catering, 327
Robert Clergerie, 93, 102
Robert Isabell, 337
Robert Lee Morris, 74
Roberta, 115

Rochester Big & Tall, 107
Rockefeller Center Ice Skating Rink, 361
Rodier, 43
Ron Ben Israel, 146
Ronaldo Maia, 339
Room Exchange, 405
Rosedale Fish & Oyster Market, 171
Rosen & Chadick, 62
Rosenberg & Stiebel, Inc., 212
Rosenthal Wine Merchant, 193
Rosetta Electric Company, 269
Rosie's Creations, 146
Royal Copenhagen Porcelain/Georg Jensen,
    227
Royale Pastry Shop, 146
Rug Warehouse, 281
rugs & carpets, 202, 279-282, 383
running, 91, 399-402
Russ & Daughters, 136
Russian Arts, 203
Russo & Son Dairy Products, 158

—S—

S&W, 36
S. Wyler, Inc., 227
S.J. Shrubsole, 228
Sable's, 137
Sacco Shoes, 102
Safavieh Carpets, 281
Sahadi Importing Company, Inc., 184
sailing, 361
Saint Laurent Rive Gauche, 36
Saint Laurie Ltd., 6
Saint Remy, 62
Saity Jewelry, 75
Saks Fifth Avenue, 59
Sal's Gourmet & Cheese Shop, 159
Sally Hawkins Gallery, 75
Salumeria Biellese, 171
Salvatore Macri, 131
Sam Flax, 288
Samantha Jones, 115
San Francisco Reservations/Topaz Hotel
    Service, 406
Sander Witlin, 48
Sanko Cultured Pearls, 376
Sano Studio, 373
Sant Ambroeus Ltd., 146
Saved by the Bell Corporation, 381
Scandinavian Ski Shop, 400
Schachner Fashions, 115
Schacht Appetizing & Deli, 137

Schaller & Weber, 171
Schatzie's Prime Meats, 172
Schmooz, 103
Schweitzer Linens, 273
Science Fiction Shop, 318
Scott Jordan Furniture, 235
Scuba Network, 395
Scully & Scully, 228
Sea Breeze Fishmarket, 172
Seaman Schepps, 75
Seaport Museum Shop, 355
Secondhand Rose, 209
SEE Ltd., 235
Seeford Organization, 290
Sensuous Bean, 162
Sepco Industries, 262
Serendipity, 203
service, 336, 337, 361, 381
service help, 361
sewing machines, 383, 384
Shabby Chic, 235
Shades From the Midnight Sun, 285
Sharper Image, 242
Sheila's Wallstyles Decorating Center, 286
Sherle Wagner International, 262
Sheru Enterprises, 48
Shirt Store, 89
shirts & blouses, 88, 89
Shoe City, 103
shoe repair, 384, 385
shoes, socks & stockings, 80, 82, 83, 90-96
Shoofly, 103
Shulie's, 37
Silk Surplus, 253
Silly Billy, 338
Simon Pearce, 228
Simon's Hardware, 263
Simpson & Company and Florist West, 339
67 Wine & Spirits Merchants, 190
skating, 361, 362, 399, 400
skiing, 400
Sky Rink, 362
Slatkin & Company, 204
soccer, 400
Soccer Sport Supply Company, 400
sofa, 232, 385
Software Etc., 243
Solanee, Inc., 229
Solar Antique Tiles, 263
Sole of Italy, 103
Solutions, 289
Something Different, 360

Sotheby's, 215, 216, 275
Sound City, 244
Sounds, 324
Space Kiddets, 20
special sizes, 107
Spectra Research Group, 244
Spiegel Sporting Goods, 402
Spitzer and Associates, 295
sporting goods, 391
Sports Training Institute, 346
Spring Street Books, 319
Spring Street Garden, 340
St. John Boutique, 37
St. Marks Comics, 319
St. Regis, 21, 351
Stacks Rare Coins, 336
stained glass, 301
Stair & Company, 249
Stanhope Hotel, 351
Stanley Company, Inc., 297
Staples the Office Superstore, 293
Stapleton Shoe Company, 103
Star Magic Space Age Gifts, 370
Starbucks Coffee Company, 162
State Office Supply Company, 294
Statesman Shoes, 104
Stephane Kelian, 104
Stephen P. Kahan Ltd., 75
Stereo Exchange, 244
Steuben Glass, 229
Stone Services, Inc., 381
Strand Book Store, 319
Stubbs Books & Prints, Inc., 319
Studio Museum in Harlem, 356
Stupell Ltd., 229
Sue Ekahn/New York, 116
Sue's Discount Better Dresses, 37
Sultan's Delight, 184, 185
Super Runners Shop, 399
Superior Repair Center, 378
superstores, 181-185, 282, 283
supplies, 290-294
Surroundings, 340
Susan Bennis/Warren Edwards, 104
Susan P. Meisel Decorative Arts, 229
Susan Parrish, 278
Swatch, 75, 76
sweaters, 108, 109
Sweet Life, 156
swimming, 402, 403
Sylvia and Danny Kaye Playhouse, 363
Sylvia Weinstock Cakes, 147

SYMS, 5

—T—

Tahari, 28, 37
tailors, 52, 56, 385, 386
Takashimaya, 59, 197
takeout, 139, 147, 171, 185-190, 325, 327
Talbots, 38
Tall Size Shoes, 104
Tan My My, 168, 180
Tannen's Magic, 370
Taste Caterers, 327
Taylor's, 147
Ted's Fine Clothing, 49
Ten Ren Tea Company, 163
Tender Buttons, 50, 51
tennis, 362, 363, 403
Tentation Catering, 327
Tents & Trails, 393
Tenzing & Pena, 370
Terra Verde Trading Company, 263
Terracotta, 204
theater, 303, 329, 330, 334, 363, 364
Theatre Development Fund, 364
Things Japanese, 204
Thomas Morrisey Salon, 129, 131
Thome Silversmiths, 379
thrift shops, 109-112
Tiffany & Company, 76
Tim McKoy Gallery, 205
Time Will Tell, 284
timepieces, 66-77, 283, 284
Tinsel Trading Company, 253
TKTS Time Square, 363
To Boot, 57, 105
tobacco, 364
Tobaldi Huomo, 27
Todaro Brothers, 185
Today's Man, 26
Toga Bike Shop, 392
Toledo Interiors, 296
Tootsi Plohound, 105
Top Service, 385
Tourneau and Gorevic Collection at
     Tourneau, 76
Tower Records & Video, 324
Town Bedding, 216
Toys, 364-371
toys, games & hobbies, 364, 365, 366, 367,
     368, 369, 370, 371
transportation, 388
Trash and Vauderville, 120

travel & vacation, 404
Travel Bargains, 406
Traveller's Bookstore, 320
Treillage Ltd., 257
Trend Clothiers, 26
Trendsetters, 64
Trevi Shoes, 105
Trevor Potts Reproductions, 249
Trois Jean, 147
Trouvaille Francaise, 273
TSE Cashmere, 109
Tudor Electrical Supply, 270
Tudor Rose Antiques, 229
Tuscany & Company, 87
21 Club, 352
24 Fifth Avenue Ballroom, 352
200 Fifth Club, 352

—U—

U.S.E.D., 205
Ukrainian Museum, 356
Uma Reddy Ltd., 55
Umanoff & Parsons, 148
underwear & lingerie, 112-116
uniforms, 116
Union Square Drugs, 133
Union Theological Seminary Bookstore, 320
United Nations Gift Shop, 356
University Animal Hospital, 390
Untitled/Fine Art in Printing, 213
upholsterers, 386
Upholstery Unlimited, Inc., 386
Uplift, Inc., 270
Urban Animal, 390
Urban Archaeology, 205
Urban Outfitters, 13
Ursus Books & Prints, 320
Use What You Have, 374
Utrecht Art and Drafting Supplies, 288

—V—

V. Loria & Sons, 392
Valentino, 38, 55, 63, 89
Vamps, 105
Van Cleef & Arpels, 77, 204
Vander Linde Designs, 65
Vanessa Noel, 106
Venamy Orchids, 340
Veniero's Pasticceria, 148
Vera Wang Bridal House Ltd., 49
Veronique, 88

Vertical Club, 346
Vesuvio Bakery, 152
veterinarians, 389, 390
Vic Rothman for Stained Glass, 373
Vicmarr Stereo and TV, 244
Victor Antiques Ltd., 247
Victor Kamkin, Inc., 320
Victory, the Shirt Experts, 89
Village Chess Shop, 371
Village Comics, 321
Village Comics SciFi Shop, 321
Villeroy & Boch, 230, 231
Vin Hin Company, 172
vintage clothing, 43, 76, 111, 112, 116-120,
   225, 226, 242, 245, 257, 264, 284, 311
Vision of Tibet, 44
Vojtech Blau, Inc., 282
VSF, 340

—W—

W. Weber and Company, 26
walking, dog, 390
Walter Steiger, 106
Warehouse Wines & Spirits, 193
Waterford/Wedgwood, 230
Waterworks, 264
Waves, 245
Weisbrod Chinese Art, 277
Weiss & Mahoney, 14
Weller Fabrics, Inc., 62
West Side Kids, 371
western wear, 120
Whiskey Dust, 120
White Travel, 406
White Workroom, 286
Whitney Museum's Store Next Door, 356
Whittall & Son, 44
Wicker Garden, 20, 257
Wicker Garden's Baby/Children, 20
William Doyle Galleries, 216
William Fioravanti, 55
William Greenberg Jr. Desserts, 148
Zitomer, 6
Zona, 205

William H. Jackson, 254
William Lipton Ltd., 209
William N. Ginsburg Company, 62
William Poll, 189
William Wayne & Company, 205
Willoughby's Camera Store, 245
window treatments, 284-286
windsurfing, 403
wines & liquors, 190-193
Wines & Spirits, 336
Wings, 14
Winslow Furniture, 236
Wiz, 245
Wm. Crawford Construction, 299
Wolfman Gold & Good Company, 231
Wollman Skating Rink, 362
Wolsk's Confections, 156
Women's Workout Gear, 396
Woodard & Greenstein, 278
Word of Mouth, 188, 190
Workbench, 236
Works Gallery, 213
World Gym, 347
World of Golf, 397
Worth & Worth, 66

—Y—

Yaska Shoes, 106
Yellow Door, 231
YMCA (West Side), 347
Yohji Yamamoto, 6
Yonah Schimmel's Knishes Bakery, 137
York End Caning, 381
Yorkville Animal Hospital, 390
Yura, 327
YWCA, 336

—Z—

Zabar's Appetizers & Caterers, 185
Zara, 6, 340

Talk to us

Talk to us

Call 800-445-3557 or mail/fax this form to order
The New York Edge 1997 Savvy Shoppers' Survey

The New York Edge
Order Department
Custom Databanks, Inc.
13925 Esworthy Road
Germantown, MD 20874-3313

800-445-3557. Fax 301-990-4010

Name _____

Address _____Apt_____

City _____ State _____ Zip_____

Daytime telephone (___) _____ _____

Amex ☐   Visa ☐   MasterCard ☐   Diners Club ☐   Carte Blanche ☐

Card Number _____exp _____

Signature of Card Holder _____

	<u>Number</u>	<u>Total</u>
Book @ $14.95*	_____	_____
PC Diskette @ $29.95*	_____	_____
Book + diskette @ $35.95*	_____	_____
Total	_____	_____

* Shipping Included   For PC Check version: Windows ☐   or   DOS ☐

Call us about corporate (volume) sales for books and diskettes